Germany
a country study

Federal Research Division
Library of Congress
Edited by
Eric Solsten
Research Completed
August 1995

On the cover: The Brandenburg Gate in Berlin

Third Edition, First Printing, 1996.

Library of Congress Cataloging-in-Publication Data

Germany : a country study / Federal Research Division,
  Library of Congress ; edited by Eric Solsten.—3rd ed.
        p. cm. — (Area handbook series, ISSN 1057–5294)
  (DA Pam ; 550–173)
        "Supersedes the 1988 edition of East Germany : a coun-
  try study, edited by Stephen R. Burant; and the 1982 edi-
  tion of Federal Republic of Germany : a country study,
  edited by Richard F. Nyrop."—T.p. verso.
        "Research completed August 1995."
        Includes bibliographical references (pp. 545–593) and
  index.
        ISBN 0–8444–0853–0 (hc : alk. paper)
  ——— Copy 3   Z663.275 .G47 1996
        1. Germany. I. Solsten, Eric, 1943– . II. Library of
  Congress. Federal Research Division. III. Series. IV.
  Series: DA Pam ; 550–173.
DD17.G475 1996   96–20927
943—dc20   CIP

Headquarters, Department of the Army
DA Pam 550–173

For sale by the Superintendent of Documents, U.S. Government Printing Office
Washington, D.C. 20402

Foreword

This volume is one in a continuing series of books prepared by the Federal Research Division of the Library of Congress under the Country Studies/Area Handbook Program sponsored by the Department of the Army. The last two pages of this book list the other published studies.

Most books in the series deal with a particular foreign country, describing and analyzing its political, economic, social, and national security systems and institutions, and examining the interrelationships of those systems and the ways they are shaped by historical and cultural factors. Each study is written by a multidisciplinary team of social scientists. The authors seek to provide a basic understanding of the observed society, striving for a dynamic rather than a static portrayal. Particular attention is devoted to the people who make up the society, their origins, dominant beliefs and values, their common interests and the issues on which they are divided, the nature and extent of their involvement with national institutions, and their attitudes toward each other and toward their social system and political order.

The books represent the analysis of the authors and should not be construed as an expression of an official United States government position, policy, or decision. The authors have sought to adhere to accepted standards of scholarly objectivity. Corrections, additions, and suggestions for changes from readers will be welcomed for use in future editions.

> Louis R. Mortimer
> Chief
> Federal Research Division
> Library of Congress
> Washington, DC 20540–4840

Acknowledgments

This edition supersedes *East Germany: A Country Study,* published in 1988, and *Federal Republic of Germany: A Country Study,* published in 1982. The authors wish to acknowledge their use of portions of those volumes in the preparation of this book.

The authors also are grateful to individuals in various United States government agencies who gave their time and special knowledge to provide information and perspective. These individuals include Ralph K. Benesch, who formerly oversaw the Country Studies/Area Handbook Program for the Department of the Army. Frank J. LaScala reviewed portions of the manuscript. Margaret A. Murray of the Office of Management and Budget supplied valuable information.

The authors wish to thank various members of the staff of the Embassy of the Federal Republic of Germany in Washington, D.C., and of the German Information Center in New York. Uwe Petry, consul in the German Consulate General in Los Angeles, provided photographs and other assistance. Monika Dorman of Northern Germany Representation in New York also provided photographs. Often helpful for specific queries were the staffs of the German Historical Institute, the Friedrich Ebert Foundation, and the American Institute for Contemporary German Studies of The Johns Hopkins University, all located in Washington, D.C. Special thanks for many varieties of assistance must also go to William Collins, Douglas Griffin, Hans Köhler, Gisela Peters, and Werner Peters.

Dr. Christa Altenstetter, author of Chapter 4, wishes to acknowledge the financial support of the GSF Research Center for Environment and Health in Munich-Neuherberg during her sabbatical in 1992. She extends particular thanks also to Professor Dr. Wilhelm van Eimeren, director of MEDIS; to the organization's scientific staff—Dr. Jürgen John, Dr. Andreas Mielck, and Dr. Walter Satzinger—for valuable suggestions; and to the MEDIS support staff. Dr. Altenstetter is also grateful to Dr. Bernd Schulte of the Max-Planck-Institut für Ausländisches und Internationales Sozialrecht in Munich for his counsel and to Dorothee Schray, M.A., Staatsinstitut für Schulpädagogik und Bildungsforschung, likewise in Munich, for her library assistance.

Various members of the staff of the Federal Research Division of the Library of Congress assisted in the preparation of the book. Sandra W. Meditz, Federal Research Division coordinator of the handbook series, made helpful suggestions during her review of all parts of the book, as did Andrea M. Savada. Tim Merrill reviewed the sections on geography and telecommunications. Thanks also go to David P. Cabitto, who designed the cover and some of the chapter art and provided graphics support; Marilyn L. Majeska, who managed editing and also edited portions of the manuscript; Laura C. Wells, who helped prepare the Country Profile; Andrea T. Merrill, who managed production; Harriett R. Blood and the firm of Greenhorne and O'Mara, who prepared the topographical map; Thomas D. Hall and the firm of Maryland Mapping and Graphics, who prepared the other maps; Barbara Edgerton and Izella Watson, who did the word processing; and David P. Cabitto, Janie L. Gilchrist, and Izella Watson, who prepared the camera-ready copy.

The following individuals are gratefully acknowledged as well: Vincent Ercolano, who edited most of the chapters; Sheila Ross, who performed the prepublication editorial review; Joan C. Cook, who compiled the index; and Marty Ittner, who created many of the chapter illustrations.

Contents

List of Figures

Preface

Like its predecessors, *East Germany: A Country Study* and *Federal Republic of Germany: A Country Study*, this study attempts to review Germany's history and treat in a concise and objective manner its dominant social, political, economic, and military aspects. Sources of information included books, scholarly journals, foreign and domestic newspapers, official reports of government and international organizations, and numerous periodicals on German and international affairs.

The name *Germany* is used in three senses: first, it refers to the region in Central Europe commonly regarded as constituting Germany, even when there was no central German state, as was the case for most of Germany's history; second, it refers to the unified German state established in 1871 and existing until 1945; and third, since October 3, 1990, it refers to the united Germany, formed by the accession on this date of the German Democratic Republic (GDR, or East Germany) to the Federal Republic of Germany (FRG, or West Germany). The name *Federal Republic of Germany* refers to West Germany from its founding on May 23, 1949, until German unification on October 3, 1990. After this date, it refers to united Germany. For the sake of brevity and variety, the Federal Republic of Germany is often called simply the Federal Republic.

The Federal Republic of Germany consists of sixteen states (*Länder;* sing., *Land*). Five of these *Länder* date from July 1990, when the territory of the German Democratic Republic was once again divided into *Länder.* For this reason, when discussing events since unification, Germans frequently refer to the territory of the former East Germany as the new or eastern *Länder* and call that of the former West Germany the old or western *Länder.* For the sake of convenience and variety, the text often follows this convention to distinguish eastern from western Germany.

Chapter bibliographies appear at the end of the book, and brief comments on some of the more valuable sources recommended for further reading appear at the end of each chapter. A Glossary also is included.

Spellings of place-names used in the book are in most cases those approved by the United States Board on Geographic Names. Exceptions are the use of the conventional English names for a few important cities, rivers, and geographic regions. A list of these names is found in Table A.

Measurements are given in the metric system. A conversion table is provided to assist readers unfamiliar with metric measurements (see table 1, Appendix).

The body of the text reflects information available as of August 1995. Certain other portions of the text, however, have been updated. The Introduction discusses significant events that have occurred since the completion of research, the Country Profile and Glossary include updated information as available, and the Bibliography lists recently published sources thought to be particularly helpful to the reader.

Table A. English Equivalents of Selected German Place-Names

English	German
Baltic Sea	Ostsee
Bavaria	Bayern
Bavarian Forest	Bayerischer Wald
Black Forest	Schwarzwald
Bohemian Forest	Böhmer Wald
Cologne	Köln
Constance, Lake	Bodensee
Danube	Donau
Hanover	Hannover
Hesse	Hessen
Lower Saxony	Niedersachsen
North Sea	Nordsee
Nuremberg	Nürnberg
Mecklenburg-Western Pomerania	Mecklenburg-Vorpommern
Moselle	Mosel
Munich	München
North Rhine-Westphalia	Nordrhein-Westfalen
Rhine	Rhein
Rhineland-Palatinate	Rheinland-Pfalz
Saxony	Sachsen
Saxony-Anhalt	Sachsen-Anhalt
Thuringia	Thüringen

Table B. Selected Abbreviations

ACDA	Arms Control and Disarmament Agency
BDI	Bundesverband der Deutschen Industrie (Federation of German Industry)
CAP.	Common Agricultural Policy
CDU	Christlich Demokratische Union (Christian Democratic Union)
CSCE	Conference on Security and Cooperation in Europe
CSU	Christlich-Soziale Union (Christian Social Union)
DGB	Deutscher Gewerkschaftsbund (Federation of German Trade Unions)
DIHT	Deutscher Industrie- und Handelstag (German Chambers of Industry and Commerce)
EC.	European Community
ECSC	European Coal and Steel Community
EDC	European Defence Community
EEC.	European Economic Community
EFTA.	European Free Trade Association
EMS	European Monetary System
EMU	European Monetary Union
ERM	exchange-rate mechanism
EU.	European Union
FDP.	Freie Demokratische Partei (Free Democratic Party)
FRG.	Federal Republic of Germany
GATT	General Agreement on Tariffs and Trade
GDR	German Democratic Republic
GKV	Gesetzliche Krankenversicherung (statutory health insurance)
KPD	Kommunistische Partei Deutschlands (Communist Party of Germany)
MfS	Ministerium für Stadtssicherheit (Ministry for State Security)
NACC.	North Atlantic Cooperation Council
NATO.	North Atlantic Treaty Organization
NVA	Nationale Volksarmee (National People's Army)
OECD.	Organisation for Economic Co-operation and Development
OEEC.	Organisation for European Economic Co-operation
OSCE	Organization for Security and Cooperation in Europe
PDS.	Partei des Demokratischen Sozialismus (Party of Democratic Socialism)
PfP	Partnership for Peace
RAF.	Rote Armee Fraktion (Red Army Faction)
SED.	Sozialistische Einheitspartei Deutschlands (Socialist Unity Party of Germany)
SPD.	Sozialdemokratische Partei Deutschlands (Social Democratic Party of Germany)
SS	Schutz-Staffel (Guard Detachment)
Stasi	Staatssicherheitsdienst (State Security Service)
WEU	Western European Union

Table C. Chronology of Important Events

Period	Description
ANCIENT PERIOD	
ca. 500 B.C.–A.D. 100	Germanic tribes settle in Germania. Roman army defeated by Suevian tribe at Battle of the Teutoburg Forest in A.D. 9 and pushed west of Rhine River. Romans subsequently reconquer some territory up to Rhine and Danube rivers and construct fortified frontiers.
ca. A.D. 100–600	Migration of Germanic peoples. Collapse of western Roman Empire. Last Roman emperor, Romulus Augustus, deposed in 476 by German armies led by Odovacar. Frankish tribes settle Gaul (France); Lombards settle northern Italy; Anglo-Saxons settle Britain.
MEDIEVAL GERMANY (500–1517)	
Merovingian Dynasty (ca. 500–751)	Merovingian kings rule Frankish tribes. Clovis, Frankish king (486–511), rules over Gaul's mixed Germanic-Roman people. Pepin the Younger, Frankish king (741–68), founds Carolingian Dynasty in 752. Christianization of Germany under leadership of Saint Boniface (ca. 675–754).
Carolingian Dynasty (752–911)	Frankish rule reaches from Spanish marches into central Germany. Charlemagne, Frankish king (768–814), conquers Lombardy in 774. Carolingian Empire established 800; Charlemagne crowned Holy Roman Emperor by pope. Louis I (Louis the Pious) Holy Roman Emperor 814–40. Treaty of Verdun (843) divides Carolingian Empire among three of Charlemagne's grandsons. Germany, France, and Middle Kingdom delineated, and imperial title linked with Middle Kingdom. Louis II (Louis the German) rules east Frankish tribes (843–76). Charles III (Charles the Fat), German king (876–87) and Holy Roman Emperor 881. Arnulf of Carinthia, German king (887–99) and Holy Roman Emperor 896. Barbarian invasions weaken Carolingian rule; German duchies of Franconia, Saxony, Lorraine, Swabia, and Bavaria rise to power. Louis IV, German king (900–911). Conrad I (Conrad of Franconia) elected German king (911–18) following extinction of Carolingian Empire in the east.
Saxon Dynasty (919–1024)	Frankish and Saxon nobles elect Henry I German king (919–36). Subordination of duchies. Otto I (Otto the Great), German king (936–73), gains control of Middle Kingdom, and Holy Roman Empire of the German Nation begins with his coronation as emperor in 962. German empire extends to Elbe River and southeast to Vienna. Otto II, Holy Roman Emperor (973–83). Otto III, Holy Roman Emperor (996–1002). Henry II, Holy Roman Emperor (1014–24).
Salian Dynasty (1024–1125)	Conrad II, Duke of Franconia, founds Salian Dynasty; elected Holy Roman Emperor (1027–39). Henry III, Holy Roman Emperor (1046–56). Henry IV, Holy Roman Emperor (1084–1106),

Table C. Chronology of Important Events

Period	Description
	challenges Pope Gregory VII. Investiture Contest and civil war, 1075–1122; German empire weakens, and German princes begin rise to power. Henry V, Holy Roman Emperor (1111–25). Compromise Concordat of Worms (1122) settles papal-imperial struggle. Lothar III, Saxon noble, elected Holy Roman Emperor (1133–37).
Hohenstaufen Dynasty (1138–1254)	Hohenstaufen kings struggle to restore imperial authority. Conrad III elected German king (1138–52). Frederick I (Frederick Barbarossa), Holy Roman Emperor (1155–90), seeks long and unsuccessfully to establish order and stability in the empire. Beginning of Age of Chivalry, marked by high achievements in literature. Italian expeditions to regain imperial control of Middle Kingdom. Henry VI, Holy Roman Emperor (1191–97). Civil war (1198–1214). Frederick II, Holy Roman Emperor (1220–50), restores imperial administration in Italy and Sicily, but German princes gain concessions. Imperial statute of 1232 establishes secular and ecclesiastical princes as virtually independent rulers within their own territories (principalities). Great Interregnum, 1256–73; anarchy and civil war. German princes gain power and vie for imperial title.
Early Habsburg Dynasty (1273–1519)	Rudolf of Habsburg elected German king (1273–91); acquires Austria and Styria in 1282 and makes Habsburgs strongest German dynasty. Adolf of Nassau elected German king (1292–98). Albert I (Habsburg) elected German king (1298–1308). Henry VII of Luxembourg, Holy Roman Emperor (1312–13), founds dynasty that seriously rivals Habsburgs from its power base in Bohemia. Louis IV (Louis the Bavarian) of House of Wittelsbach, Holy Roman Emperor (1328–47). Charles IV of Luxembourg, Holy Roman Emperor (1355–78), issues Golden Bull of 1356, which grants German princes power to elect emperor and provides basic constitution of Holy Roman Empire. Wenceslas of Bohemia, German king (1378–1400). Rupert of Palatinate, German king (1400–10); Sigismund of Luxembourg, German king (1410–37), Holy Roman Emperor (1433–37), last non-Habsburg emperor until 1742; with this one exception, Habsburgs of Austria provide all emperors from mid-fifteenth century until dissolution of Holy Roman Empire in 1806. Frederick III, Holy Roman Emperor (1452–93). Maximilian I, Holy Roman Emperor (1508–1519).
PROTESTANT REFORMATION AND RELIGIOUS WARS (1517–1648)	Martin Luther posts his ninety-five theses in Wittenberg in 1517 and challenges papal authority. Charles V, Holy Roman Emperor (1519–56). Publication in 1520 of Luther's three revolutionary pamphlets. Luther banned by church and empire in 1521. Charles V's wars against France in 1521–26, 1526–29, 1536–38, and 1542–44. Vienna threatened by Turks in 1529. Diet of Augsburg,

Table C. Chronology of Important Events

Period	Description
	1530; Protestant "Augsburg Confession" presented, and Protestant League of Schmalkalden formed by German princes. War of Schmalkalden (1546–47) between Charles V and Protestant princes. Peace of Augsburg, 1555; Catholicism and Lutheranism formally recognized in Germany, and each prince given right to decide religion to be practiced in his territory. Ferdinand I, Holy Roman Emperor (1558–64). Maximilian II, Holy Roman Emperor (1564–76). Ferdinand II, Holy Roman Emperor (1619–37). Rudolf II, Holy Roman Emperor (1576–1612). Matthias, Holy Roman Emperor (1612–19). Bohemian Revolt, 1618; imperial armies defeat Bohemians at Battle of White Mountain near Prague in 1620. Thirty Years' War (1618–48); Treaty of Prague signed in 1635; continuation of war by France; Treaty of Westphalia, 1648. End of Holy Roman Empire as a major European power.
AGE OF ENLIGHTENED ABSOLUTISM AND FRENCH INVASION (1648–1815)	Frederick William, the Great Elector of Brandenburg-Prussia (1640–88), of Hohenzollern Dynasty, establishes absolute rule. Frederick I, elector of Brandenburg-Prussia (1688–1713), assumes title of king in 1701. Frederick William I, Prussian king (1713–40), creates Prussian civil and military bureaucracy. Frederick II (Frederick the Great), Prussian king (1740–86), reforms his country as enlightened despot. War of the Austrian Succession (1740–48) and Seven Years' War (1756–63) against Austria under Maria Theresa (1740–80) expand Prussian territory. Frederick William II, Prussian king (1786–97). Frederick William III, Prussian king (1797–1840). French invade Rhineland in 1792 and eventually control Germany. Prussia, Austria, and Russia defeat Napoleon at Battle of Leipzig in 1813.
REACTION, REVOLUTION, AND GERMAN UNIFICATION (1815–71)	Congress of Vienna (1814–15) after Napoleon's defeat in War of Liberation (1813–15) establishes German Confederation of thirty-seven states. Prince Clemens von Metternich, Austrian chancellor and foreign minister (1809–48), heads confederation. Reversion to old order of social distinctions under Age of Metternich. Struggle between absolutism and liberalism. Student unions agitate for democratic reform. Carlsbad Decrees (1819) outlaw radical student organizations. Weimar, Bavaria, Baden, and Württemberg enact constitutions, 1818–19. "July Revolution" in France, 1830, sparks revolutionary movements in Germany; Hesse and Saxony enact constitutions. Brunswick, Hanover, and Oldenburg enact constitutions in 1833. Zollverein (Customs Union) created in 1834. March 1848 revolution in Germany. National Assembly at Frankfurt (1848–49) plans constitutional German nation-state. Friedrich Wilhelm IV, Prussian king (1840–58), refuses German crown in 1849; National Assembly dissolved. German Confederation restored in 1851. Prussia agrees to relinquish plans for a Ger-

Table C. Chronology of Important Events

Period	Description
	man union under its leadership in Treaty of Olmütz. Wilhelm I, Prussian king (1858–88); Otto von Bismarck, chancellor (1862–90), unites Germany. Constitutional struggle, 1862–66; Prussian king vies with German liberals in parliament on issue of budget for military expansion; Prussia defeats Austria in Seven Weeks' War (1866); German Confederation dissolved, and Austria excluded from German politics. Austria-Hungary (also known as Austro-Hungarian Empire) created in 1867. North German Confederation formed, headed by Prussia. Franco-Prussian War, 1870–71. Germany united as nation-state—German Empire.
IMPERIAL GERMANY (1871–1918)	Wilhelm I, German emperor (1871–88). Bismarck, chancellor (1871–90). Kulturkampf against Roman Catholic Church begins in 1873. Antisocialist legislation enacted 1878. Dual Alliance (1879) between Germany and Austria-Hungary. Domestic alliance between aristocrats and industrialists in Tariff Agreement of 1879. Comprehensive social legislation program begins in 1881. Triple Alliance (1882) among Germany, Austria-Hungary, and Italy. German colonies established 1884–85 in South-West Africa, Togo, the Cameroons, East Africa, and some Pacific islands. Frederick III, German emperor (March 9–June 15, 1888). Wilhelm II, German emperor (1888–1918). Bismarck's fall, 1890. Leo von Caprivi, chancellor (1890–94). Prince Chlodwig zu Hohenlohe, chancellor 1894–1900. Naval Bill (1898) begins naval race against Britain. Bernhard von Bülow, chancellor (1900–09). Moroccan crisis, 1905, in which Germany intervenes in French and British sphere of influence. Theobald von Bethmann Hollweg, chancellor (1909–17). Moroccan crisis, 1911, in which Germany sends gunboat to port of Agadir. New Naval Bill, 1912. Balkan Wars, 1912–13, a nationalist rebellion against Ottoman rule. Assassination of Austria's Archduke Franz Ferdinand (June 28, 1914) in Sarajevo starts events that culminate in World War I (1914–18); Germany defeated.
WEIMAR REPUBLIC (1918–33)	November Revolution, 1918; Wilhelm II's abdication. Social Democrats proclaim republic. Suppression of left-wing revolt by army in January 1919. Treaty of Versailles, 1919. Social Democrat Friedrich Ebert elected president (1919–25). Right-wing Kapp Putsch attempted, 1920. Communist revolts in central Germany, Hamburg, and Ruhr district, 1921. Astronomical inflation, 1922–23. Occupation of Ruhr by French and Belgian troops, 1923. Hitler's Beer Hall Putsch attempted in Munich, 1923. Gustav Stresemann, chancellor (August–November 1923) and foreign minister (1923–29), formulates policy of rapprochement with West. Dawes Plan on reparations, 1924. French and Belgian troops withdrawn from Ruhr,

Table C. Chronology of Important Events

Period	Description
	1925. Paul von Hindenburg, World War I army commander, elected president (1925–34). Locarno treaties, 1925, and Treaty of Berlin with Soviet Union, 1926. Germany joins League of Nations, 1926. Young Plan on reparations, 1929; Allied troops withdrawn from Rhineland, 1930. Economic depression and cabinet crises, 1929–33. Heinrich Brüning, chancellor 1930–32; government by decree (Article 48 of Weimar Constitution). Franz von Papen, chancellor (May–December 1932); Hitler's National Socialists win Reichstag elections and emerge as Germany's strongest political party, July 1932. Kurt von Schleicher, chancellor (December 1932–January 1933). President Hindenburg appoints Hitler to chancellorship, January 30, 1933.
THIRD REICH (1933–45)	Reichstag fire; Hitler demands presidential emergency decree, February 1933. Enabling Act accords Hitler's cabinet dictatorial powers, March 1933. Germany declared one-party National Socialist state, July 1933. Death of Hindenburg, August 1934; Hitler combines offices of president and chancellor. German rearmament, 1935. Rhineland remilitarized and Berlin-Rome Axis formed, 1936. At secret conference, Hitler announces intention to begin eastward expansion, November 1937. Austrian Anschluss (annexation), March 1938. Czechoslovak Sudetenland annexed, October 1938. Germany occupies Czech-populated provinces of Bohemia and Moravia, March 1939. Poland invaded, September 1939. World War II (1939–45). Germany defeated.
POSTWAR DIVISION (1945–90)	Yalta Conference (February 1945) determines division of Germany into occupation zones. Three zones under United States, British, and French control become Federal Republic of Germany (West Germany) in 1949. Soviet zone becomes German Democratic Republic (East Germany) same year. Konrad Adenauer of Christian Democratic Union elected first chancellor of West Germany (1949–63); Walter Ulbricht of Socialist Unity Party of Germany appointed head of East Germany (1949–71). West German economic boom in 1950s; Stalinization of East Germany in same period. Both states remilitarized in mid-1950s; West Germany becomes member of North Atlantic Treaty Organization (NATO), East Germany joins Warsaw Pact. Treaty of Rome creating European Economic Community (EEC) signed, 1957, with West Germany as member. Berlin Wall built by East Germany (1961). Social Democrat Willy Brandt elected West German chancellor (1969–74); Ulbricht dismissed, and Erich Honecker named East German head (1971–89). Brandt's Ostpolitik results in treaties with Soviet Union, Poland, Czechoslovakia, and Four Power Agreement on Berlin. Basic Treaty between East Germany and West Germany recognizes two Ger-

Table C. Chronology of Important Events

Period	Description
	man states, 1972. Admission of both Germanys to United Nations, 1973. Social Democrat Helmut Schmidt replaces Brandt as West German chancellor (1974–82). Christian Democrat Helmut Kohl becomes West German chancellor (1982–). Helsinki Final Act signed, July 1975. NATO's Dual-Track Decision announced, December 1979. Single European Act signed, December 1985. Growing economic difficulties and internal opposition, coupled with Mikhail Gorbachev's attempts to reform Soviet Union and its empire and his decision not to intervene militarily in East German affairs, lead to collapse of East German regime, late 1989–early 1990.
UNITED GERMANY (1990–)	Rapid path to unification of the two German states according to provisions of Article 23 of Basic Law chosen by popular pressure. First free elections in East Germany end with Christian Democratic victory, March 1990. Economic and currency union established between West Germany and East Germany, July 1, 1990. At meeting with Kohl in Soviet Union, Gorbachev agrees that united Germany may remain in NATO and Soviet troops will leave East Germany in four years, July 1990. Treaty on the Final Settlement with Respect to Germany (the Two-Plus-Four Treaty) establishing Germany's full sovereignty signed, September 1990. Treaty on Good-Neighborliness, Partnership, and Cooperation between West Germany and Soviet Union signed, September 1990. Germany united, October 3, 1990. First all-German Bundestag election held; Christian Democratic victory, December 1990. Maastricht Treaty signed, December 1991. Article 16 of Basic Law amended, restricting right to asylum in Germany, July 1993. European Union established, November 1993. Federal Constitutional Court decides that Bundeswehr may participate in international military operations outside of NATO territory, provided that Bundestag approves, July 1994. Last Russian troops leave Germany, August 1994. Second all-German Bundestag election held; Christian Democratic victory, October 1994.

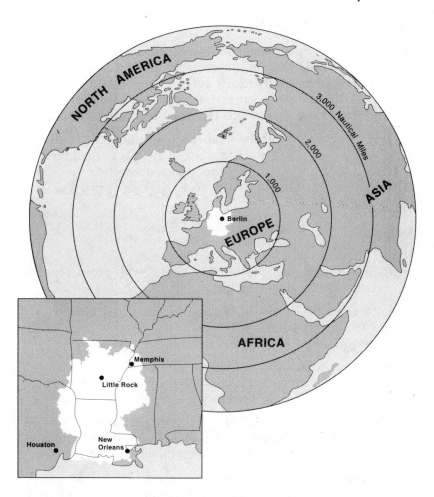

Country

Formal Name: Federal Republic of Germany.

Short Form: Germany or Federal Republic.

Term for Citizen(s): German(s).

Capital: Berlin.

Geography

Size: 356,959 square kilometers.

Topography: Terrain rises from northern coastal lowlands to belt of central uplands, complex and varied in form. To south of uplands, a high plain suddenly rises to Alps in country's extreme south. Most important rivers: Rhine, flowing to north; Elbe, flowing to northwest; and Danube, flowing to southeast.

Climate: Cool, continental climate with abundant rainfall and long overcast season. Lower temperatures with considerable snowfall in east and south. Prone to rapid weather variations from merging of Gulf Stream and extreme northeastern climate conditions.

Society

Population: 81,338,000 (July 1995 estimate) with growth rate of 0.26 percent (July 1995 estimate).

Ethnic Groups: 95.1 percent German, 2.3 percent Turkish, 1.7 percent Italian, 0.4 percent Greek, and 0.4 percent Polish; remainder mainly refugees from former Yugoslavia.

Languages: Standard German, with substantial differences in regional dialects. Three very small linguistic minorities, which speak Sorbian, Danish, or Frisian.

Religion: Protestants, mostly in Evangelical Church in Germany, 30 million; Roman Catholics, 28.2 million; Muslims, 2.5 million; free churches, 195,000; and Jews, 34,000.

Education and Literacy: 99 percent literacy rate in population over age fifteen (1991 estimate). Education compulsory until age eighteen. At age ten, after primary school (*Grundschule*), students attend one of five schools: short-course secondary school (*Hauptschule*); intermediate school (*Realschule*); high school (*Gymnasium*); comprehensive school (*Gesamtschule*); or a school for children with special educational needs (*Sonderschule*). At about age fifteen, students choose among a variety of vocational, technical, and academic schools. Higher education consists of many kinds of technical colleges, advanced vocational schools, and universities.

Health and Welfare: About 90 percent of population covered by comprehensive compulsory insurance for sickness, accidents, disability, long-term care, and retirement. Most of remainder enrolled in voluntary insurance programs; the very poor are covered by state-financed welfare programs. Quality of medical care generally excellent. Comfortable pensions paid according to life-time earnings and indexed to meet cost-of-living increases. Wide variety of other social welfare benefits managed by both government and private agencies available to those in need. Life expectancy 76.6 years for total population (73.5 years for males and 79.9 years for females) (1995 estimates). Infant mortality rate 6.3 deaths per 1,000 live births (1995 estimate). Total fertility rate 1.5 children born per woman (1995 estimate).

Economy

Gross Domestic Product (GDP): In 1994 US$1,840 billion, or about US$27,800 per capita. Real growth rate 2.4 percent, inflation rate 3.0 percent, and unemployment rate 8.2 percent.

Agriculture: 3 percent of labor force and 1 percent of GDP in 1992. Main crops wheat, potatoes, sugar beets, and barley.

Industry: 38 percent of labor force and 38 percent of GDP in 1992. Products highly specialized goods, including machine products of all varieties, chemicals, electrical products, construction, food and beverages, lignite, textiles, and petroleum and gas refining.

Services: 59 percent of labor force and 61 percent of GDP in 1992.

Exports: US$428 billion in 1994, mainly highly specialized industrial products, including motor vehicles, machines, electronic goods, and chemicals.

Imports: US$376 billion in 1994, including food, petroleum products, manufactured goods, electrical products, automobiles, and apparel.

Foreign Trade by Region: Imports in 1994: European Union (EU) 47.6 percent, European Free Trade Association (EFTA) 14.0 percent, developing countries 11.5 percent, former European communist bloc countries 8.1 percent, United States and Canada 7.7 percent, Japan 5.6 percent, other dynamic Asian economies 3.7 percent, and Organization of the Petroleum Exporting Countries (OPEC) 2.0 percent. Exports in 1994: EU 48.9 percent, EFTA 15.1 percent, developing countries 11.5 percent, United States and Canada 8.5 percent, former European communist bloc countries 7.1, Japan 2.6 percent, other dynamic Asian economies 3.5 percent, and OPEC 2.6 percent.

Balance of Payments: In 1994 trade balance US$52 billion; current account showed deficit of US$20 billion; capital account balance US$24 billion.

Fiscal Year: Calendar year.

Currency and Exchange Rate: Deutsche mark (DM). In April 1996, exchange rate US$1 = DM1.51.

Transportation and Telecommunications

Roads: 226,000 kilometers in 1992, of which 11,000 kilometers four lanes or more.

Railroads: 40,000 kilometers in 1994, of which 16,000 kilometers electrified.

Airports: 660 total. Twelve civilian airports provide passenger and cargo service within country and to rest of world.

Ports: Several dozen large, well-equipped ocean and inland ports.

Inland Waterways: 6,900 kilometers of navigable inland waterways, including extensive system of canals. Inland waterways account for about 20 percent of freight shipping.

Telecommunications: Highly developed, modern tele-communications service linking all parts of the country and connecting with systems abroad.

Government and Politics

Government: Basic Law of 1949, as amended, functions as constitution. Federalist system whereby federal government shares authority with sixteen state (*Land*; pl., *Länder*) governments. Dual executive consists of chancellor, who is head of government, and president, who is head of state. Two federal legislative bodies form national parliament: Bundesrat (Federal Council or upper house), consisting of sixty-nine members appointed by *Land* governments in proportion to population; and Bundestag (Federal Diet or lower house), main legislative body, consisting of 672 popularly elected members. Chancellor is elected by Bundestag and functions as prime minister in cabinet.

Politics: Since 1982 a conservative coalition in power consisting of Christian Democratic Union (Christlich Demokratische Union—CDU); its sister party, Christian Social Union (Christlich-Soziale Union—CSU), based in Bavaria; and Free Democratic Party (Freie Demokratische Partei—FDP). Opposition consists of Social Democratic Party of Germany (Sozialdemokratische Partei Deutschlands—SPD), Alliance 90/The Greens (Bündnis 90/Die Grünen), Party of Democratic Socialism (Partei des Demokratischen Sozia-lismus—PDS), based mainly in territory of former German Democratic Republic, and a number of very small parties. Federal elections for Bundestag usually held every four years; *Land* and local elections scattered throughout term of federal officeholders. All citizens eighteen and older eligible to vote; high voter turnout.

Judicial System: Independent judiciary using civil law system. Highest court is Federal Constitutional Court.

International Affairs: Member of European Union (EU), North Atlantic Treaty Organization (NATO), Organisation for Economic Co-operation and Development (OECD), Organization for Security and Cooperation in Europe (OSCE), United Nations (UN) and its specialized agencies, and Western European Union (WEU).

National Security

Armed Forces: In October 1995, Federal Armed Forces (Bundeswehr) consisted of army, navy, and air force, totaling 335,800, including 137,300 conscripts. Army personnel amounted to 234,000, including 112,800 conscripts; navy 28,500, including 4,500 Naval Air Arm personnel and 5,800 conscripts; and air force 73,300, including 18,700 conscripts. Reserves totaled 356,200 (337,100 in army, 12,600 in navy, and 6,500 in air force.). Enlisted personnel have reserve obligation to age forty-five; officers and noncommissioned officers, to age sixty.

Military Budget: In 1996, US$32.2 billion.

Internal Security Forces: Federal Border Force of 24,000 (early 1995) under Ministry of Interior. Trained and equipped as light infantry, but duty does not include military activities. Each *Land* maintains units of Readiness Police similarly trained. Readiness Police can be moved across *Land* lines if needed for emergency duty, such as during civil disturbances.

Figure 1. Administrative Divisions of Germany, 1995

Introduction

GERMANY WAS UNITED on October 3, 1990. Unification brought together a people separated for more than four decades by the division of Europe into two hostile blocs in the aftermath of World War II. The line that divided the continent ran through a defeated and occupied Germany. By late 1949, two states had emerged in divided Germany: the Federal Republic of Germany (FRG, or West Germany), a member of the Western bloc under the leadership of the United States; and the German Democratic Republic (GDR, or East Germany), part of the Eastern bloc led by the Soviet Union. Although the two German states were composed of a people speaking one language and sharing the same traditions, they came to have the political systems of their respective blocs. West Germany developed into a democratic capitalist state like its Western neighbors; East Germany had imposed on it the Soviet Union's communist dictatorship and command economy.

Although the leaders of each state were committed to the eventual unification of Germany and often invoked its necessity, with the passage of time the likely realization of unification receded into the distant future. Relations between the two states worsened during the 1950s as several million East Germans, unwilling to live in an increasingly Stalinized society, fled to the West. August 1961 saw the sealing of the common German border with the construction of the Berlin Wall. In the early 1970s, however, diplomatic relations between the two states were regularized by the Basic Treaty, signed in 1972. During the remainder of the decade and during the 1980s, relations improved, and contacts between the citizens of the two states increased greatly. In 1987 Erich Honecker became the first East German leader to make a state visit to West Germany.

As of the late 1980s, however, no well-informed observer foresaw German unification as being likely in the near future. In fact, its prospect seemed so remote that some politicians advocated abandoning unification as a long-term goal. Those who remained committed to Germany's ultimate unification frankly admitted that decades would probably pass before it happened.

The events leading to unification in October 1990 were unexpected, and they occurred at a frantic pace. In the eleven months between the opening of the Berlin Wall in November 1989 and unification, the forty-year-old East German dictatorship collapsed, Western political and economic systems were introduced in the East, new treaties altered long-standing diplomatic relationships between Germany and neighboring states, and two radically different societies began to grow together.

The rapid collapse of the East German regime surprised everyone. East Germany appeared to be the most economically successful of all Eastern-bloc countries. Its citizens enjoyed a modest yet decent standard of living and cradle-to-grave security provided by a government-run welfare system. They traveled to other East European countries for their summer vacations, watched West German television, and hoped for better living conditions and more freedom in the future. Most East Germans acquiesced in the communist regime's restrictions, having fashioned areas of personal freedom in their private lives. A small opposition movement operated within the shelter of the Protestant church, the country's sole relatively independent social institution. When opposition figures became too troublesome, the regime dealt with them by depriving them of their livelihood, sending them to prison, or expelling them to West Germany.

The regime's elderly, hard-line leadership opposed the reforms of Soviet leader Mikhail Gorbachev, who sought to make socialism more efficient by introducing capitalist incentives and reducing central control. Encouraged by this liberalization and the application of Gorbachev's reforms in neighboring Poland and Hungary, the regime's opponents became bolder during the summer and fall of 1989 and mounted mass demonstrations that doubled and doubled again in size from week to week.

Soviet officials advised the Honecker regime not to expect outside support. Without foreign military assistance for the first time, the GDR leadership decided against the use of force to quell the burgeoning demonstrations. Honecker was ousted in mid-October, and more realistic leaders sought to save the regime by making concessions. In November travel abroad became possible, and East Germans swarmed into West Germany, many intending to remain there. Reforms could no longer satisfy East Germans, however, who wanted the freedoms and living standard of West Germany.

West German chancellor Helmut Kohl (1982–) seized the political initiative in late November with his Ten-Point Plan for unification. Yet, even he thought several years and an intervening stage, such as a confederational structure, would be necessary before unification of the two Germanys could occur. By early 1990, however, the need to stop the massive flow of East Germans westward made speedy unification imperative. In addition, revolutionary change in other Eastern-bloc counties made solutions that a short time earlier had appeared out of the question suddenly seem feasible. The Treaty on Monetary, Economic, and Social Union between the two German states was signed in May and went into effect in July. The two Germanys signed the Unification Treaty in August. The Treaty on the Final Settlement with Respect to Germany, the so-called Two-Plus-Four Treaty, was signed in September by the two Germanys and the four victors of World War II—Britain, France, the Soviet Union, and the United States. The treaty restored full sovereignty to Germany and ended the Cold War era.

When unification occurred on October 3, 1990, it was a happy, yet subdued occasion. The many problems of joining such diverse societies were already apparent. The vaunted East German economy was coming to be seen as a Potemkin's village, with many of its most prestigious firms uncompetitive in a market economy. East German environmental problems were also proving much more serious than anyone had foreseen; remedies would cost astronomical sums. West Germans had discovered also that their long-lost eastern cousins differed from them in many ways and that relations between them were often rife with misunderstandings. A complete melding of the two societies would take years, perhaps even a generation or two. The legal unification arranged by the treaties of 1990 was only the beginning of a long process toward a truly united Germany.

In its long history, Germany has rarely been united. For most of the two millennia that central Europe has been inhabited by German-speaking peoples, the area called Germany was divided into hundreds of states, many quite small, including duchies, principalities, free cities, and ecclesiastical states. Not even the Romans united Germany under one government; they managed to occupy only its southern and western portions. At the beginning of the ninth century, Charlemagne established an empire, but within a generation its existence was more symbolic than real.

Medieval Germany was marked by division. As France and England began their centuries-long evolution into united nation-states, Germany was racked by a ceaseless series of wars among local rulers. The Habsburg Dynasty's long monopoly of the crown of the Holy Roman Empire provided only the semblance of German unity. Within the empire, German princes warred against one another as before. The Protestant Reformation deprived Germany of even its religious unity, leaving its population Roman Catholic, Lutheran, and Calvinist. These religious divisions gave military strife an added ferocity in the Thirty Years' War (1618–48), during which Germany was ravaged to a degree not seen again until World War II.

The Peace of Westphalia of 1648 left Germany divided into hundreds of states. During the next two centuries, the two largest of these states—Prussia and Austria—jockeyed for dominance. The smaller states sought to retain their independence by allying themselves with one, then the other, depending on local conditions. From the mid-1790s until Prussia, Austria, and Russia defeated Napoleon at the Battle of Leipzig in 1813 and drove him out of Germany, much of the country was occupied by French troops. Napoleon's officials abolished numerous small states, and, as a result, in 1815, after the Congress of Vienna, Germany consisted of about forty states.

During the next half-century, pressures for German unification grew. Scholars, bureaucrats, students, journalists, and businessmen agitated for a united Germany that would bring with it uniform laws and a single currency and that would replace the benighted absolutism of petty German states with democracy. The revolutions of 1848 seemed at first likely to realize this dream of unity and freedom, but the monarch who was offered the crown of a united Germany, King Friedrich Wilhelm IV of Prussia, rejected it. The king, like the other rulers of Germany's kingdoms, opposed German unity because he saw it as a threat to his power.

Despite the opposition of conservative forces, German unification came just over two decades later, in 1871, when Germany was unified and transformed into an empire under Emperor Wilhelm I, king of Prussia. Unification was not brought about by revolutionary or liberal forces, but by a conservative Prussian aristocrat, Otto von Bismarck. Sensing the power of nationalism, Bismarck sought to use it for his own aims, the preservation of a feudal social order and the triumph of his country, Prussia, in the long contest with Austria for preeminence in Germany. By a series of masterful diplomatic maneuvers and three brief and dazzlingly successful military campaigns, Bismarck achieved a united Germany without Austria. He brought together the so-called "small Germany," consisting of Prussia and the remaining German states, some of which had been subdued by Prussian armies before they became part of a Germany ruled by a Prussian emperor.

Although united Germany had a parliament, the Reichstag, elected through universal male suffrage, supreme power rested with the emperor and his ministers, who were not responsible to the Reichstag. Although the Reichstag could contest the government's decisions, in the end the emperor could largely govern as he saw fit. Supporting the emperor were the nobility, large rural landowners, business and financial elites, the civil service, the Protestant clergy, and the military. The military, which had made unification possible, enjoyed tremendous prestige. Led by an aristocratic officer corps sworn to feudal values and opposed to parliamentary democracy and the rights of a free citizenry, the military embodied the spirit of the German Empire.

Opposition to this authoritarian regime with its feudal structures was found mainly in the Roman Catholic Center Party, the Socialist Party, and in a variety of liberal and regional political groups opposed to Prussia's hegemony over Germany. In the long term, Bismarck and his successors were not able to subjugate this opposition. By 1912 the Socialists had come to have the largest number of representatives in the Reichstag. They and the Center Party made governing increasingly difficult for the empire's conservative leadership.

Despite the presence of these opposition groups, however, a truly representative parliamentary democracy did not exist. As a result, Germans had little opportunity to learn the art of practical politics. With few exceptions, this had also been the case throughout German history. Although Germany's states were usually well managed by an efficient and honest civil service, they were authoritarian. Government was seen as the business of the rulers; the ruled were to be obedient and silent.

Because they were inexperienced in democratic government, Germans in the nineteenth century were often viewed as political children, incapable of governing themselves. In addition, seeing the excesses of the French Revolution, many thoughtful Germans came to the conclusion that democracy was not suitable for Germany. The success of democratic political institutions in Britain and the United States did not convince these skeptics; they feared that the passions of the ignorant masses could too easily be inflamed. Even many German liberals found the idea that ordinary citizens ought to determine how public business should be conducted too radical a notion. Instead, they recommended that parliaments consisting of the educated and the prosperous should serve as advisory bodies to noble rulers.

Germany's defeat in World War I in 1918 meant the end of the German Empire. The emperor was forced to abdicate, and a republic—the Weimar Republic—was established with a constitution that provided for a parliamentary democracy in which the government was ultimately responsible to the people. The new republic's first president and prime minister were convinced democrats, and Germany seemed ready at last to join the community of democratic nations.

The Weimar Republic ultimately disappointed those who had hoped it would introduce democracy to Germany. By mid-1933 it had been destroyed by Adolf Hitler, its declared enemy since his first days in the public arena. Hitler was a political genius who sensed and exploited the worries and resentments of many Germans, knew when to act, and possessed a sure instinct for power. His greatest weapon in his quest for political power, however, was the disdain many Germans felt for the new republic.

Many Germans held the Weimar Republic responsible for Germany's defeat. At the war's end, no foreign troops stood on German soil, and military victory still seemed likely. Instead of victory, however, in the view of many, the republic's Socialist politicians arranged a humiliating peace. Many Germans were also affronted by the spectacle of parliamentary politics. The republic's numerous small parties made forming stable and coherent coalition governments very difficult. Frequent elections failed to yield effective governments. Government policies also often failed to solve pressing social and economic problems.

These shortcomings undermined the legitimacy of the Weimar Republic. The upper classes, the judiciary, the police, the civil service, educators, the military, and much of the middle class gave the republic only halfhearted support at best. Many members of these groups despised the republic and wanted it replaced with an authoritarian system of government. The early years of the Weimar Republic saw frequent attempts to destroy it by force, mostly from the right, but also from the left.

A modest economic recovery from 1924 to 1929 gave the Weimar Republic a brief respite. The severe social stress engendered by the Great Depression, however, swelled the vote received by extreme antidemocratic parties in the election of 1930 and the two elections of 1932. The government ruled by emergency decree. In January 1933, leading conservative politicians formed a new government with Hitler as chancellor. They intended to harness him and his party, now the country's largest, to realize their own aim of replacing the republic with an authoritarian government. Within a few months, however, Hitler had outmaneuvered them and established a totalitarian regime. Only in 1945 did a military alliance of dozens of nations succeed in deposing him, and only after his regime and the nation it ruled had committed crimes of unparalleled enormity.

In the aftermath of World War II, Germany came to consist of two states. One, East Germany, never attained real legitimacy in the eyes of its citizens and had to use force to prevent them from fleeing to the West. The other, West Germany, was resoundingly successful. Within two decades of defeat, it had become one of the world's richest nations, with a prosperity that extended to all segments of the population. The economy performed so successfully that eventually several million foreigners came to West Germany to work as well. West German and foreign workers alike were protected from need arising from sickness, accidents, and old age by an extensive, mostly nongovernment welfare system.

Along with this material success, a vigorous democracy developed. To avoid the Weimar Republic's weak coalition governments, the West German constitution, the Basic Law, permitted only those parties with at least 5 percent of the vote to sit in the Bundestag, the lower house of its parliament. This provision meant that stable parliamentary governments could be formed fairly easily, and efficient government became possible. In contrast to the Weimar Republic, the Basic Law banned political parties opposed to democracy.

From the first national election in 1949, West German politics has been dominated by two large catchall parties (*Volksparteien*; sing., *Volkspartei*), whose support came from voters formerly allied to many smaller parties. The moderate Christian Democratic Union (Christlich Demokratische Union—CDU), allied with its small sister party active in Bavaria, the Christian Social Union (Christlich-Soziale Union—CSU), won the votes of a broad range of Roman Catholic and Protestant voters. For the first time in German history, members of the two religions worked together to attain their political goals. The CDU/CSU also had left and right wings, which had to cooperate if the alliance were to win elections and exercise power. After much debate, the CDU/CSU's various wings formulated the concept of a social market economy—free-market capitalism combined with an extensive social net. The CDU/CSU alliance has successfully held together its diverse membership and, with the exception of the 1969–82 period, has headed all the Federal Republic's governments since 1949, when CDU leader Konrad Adenauer became the country's first chancellor.

The Federal Republic's other large popular party is the Social Democratic Party of Germany (Sozialdemokratische Partei Deutschlands—SPD), which receives much of the working-class vote. In the early years of the Federal Republic, the SPD was feared by many voters because of its socialist aims. With time, however, the party moderated its positions; for example, it accepted West German rearmament in the mid-1950s and came to support the social market economy. It also won the trust of suspicious voters by participating in many local and state (*Land*; pl., *Länder*) governments. After joining with the CDU/CSU to form a coalition government at the national level from 1966 to 1969, the SPD and the small, liberal Free Democratic Party (Freie Demokratische Partei—FDP) formed a coalition government with SDP leader Willy Brandt as chancellor. The SPD-FDP coalition lasted until 1982. In that year, the FDP and the CDU/CSU formed a new coalition government with Helmut Kohl as chancellor, a coalition still in power in mid-1996.

Many observers maintain that German democracy is in a transition stage. The SPD has lost its most steady source of support as an increasingly advanced economy has reduced the size of the blue-collar working class. An increasingly secular and sophisticated society has also cut into the CDU/CSU stable pool of confessional voters. Thus, since the 1980s, the large catchall parties have been confronted with an increasingly volatile electorate. Both parties have experienced declining memberships. As these parties have worked to woo a more diverse electorate, they have moderated their stances to such a degree that many voters have difficulty telling them apart.

Despite CDU losses in the October 1994 national elections, the CDU/CSU-FDP coalition survived, but with a majority of only ten seats. The SPD's share of the vote rose in these elections, but not enough to take power at the national level. The SPD has been more successful in elections at the *Land* level in recent years and has often controlled the Bundesrat, parliament's upper house. However, it lost its sole control of North Rhine-Westphalia in the elections of May 1995 and did even worse in October 1995 *Land* elections in Berlin. SPD leader Rudolf Sharping was deposed a month later and replaced by Oskar Lafontaine, who had led the party to defeat in the 1990 national elections. Lafontaine's resurrection did not appear to solve the party's long-standing leadership problem because it lost badly in the *Land* elections of March 1996 in Schleswig-Holstein, Rhineland-Palatinate, and Baden-Württemberg.

As the two large parties face diminishing pools of secure votes, growing numbers of young and educated voters have come to support the ecological party, Alliance 90/The Greens (Bündnis 90/Die Grünen), which, after having elected its first representatives to the Bundestag in 1983, in 1994 became the body's third-largest party, displacing the FDP. As of mid-1996, the Greens had a skilled leader, Joschka Fischer, who has transformed the party from a group of apolitical idealists into a highly pragmatic, but still principled, political force that examines nearly every facet of German life from a fresh standpoint. Some observers hold that the party represents the future of German politics.

The party displaced by the Greens, the FDP, has been a partner in all coalition governments at the national level since 1969. Pledged to classic European liberal political values, the FDP has distinguished itself by its advocacy of the legal rights of the individual. In recent years, however, the party has struggled for its survival because of leadership problems and because its close embrace of the CDU/CSU has caused it to lose its political identity in the eyes of many voters. By late 1995, the party seemed on the verge of political extinction; it suffered a steep drop in its vote in the national election of October 1994 and a long string of losses in elections at the *Land* level. In March 1996, however, the FDP increased its vote and won seats in all three *Land* elections held during the month. Although the

FDP was represented in only four *Land* parliaments as of mid-1996, these election results allow the party to retain its role as a coalition-maker in governments at the national level.

In addition to the Greens, another new party that has altered German politics is the Party of Democratic Socialism (Partei des Demokratischen Sozialismus—PDS). Able to win votes only in eastern Germany, the PDS has the support of voters who regret the extent to which or the way in which East Germany was swallowed up by the Federal Republic. Although the PDS is the successor to East Germany's communist Socialist Unity Party of Germany (Sozialistische Einheitspartei Deutschlands—SED), it does not recommend that the East German regime be restored. Rather, it demands that eastern German interests be given greater respect by western Germans, who are often seen as arrogant and overbearing by eastern Germans. The PDS has thirty seats in the Bundestag and is represented in the parliaments of the eastern *Länder,* but is not a partner in any coalition. Because the PDS owes its success to the sometimes legitimate anger of easterners at how they have fared in a united Germany, observers believe that the influence of the PDS will wane as these *Länder* become more integrated into united Germany.

In addition to the above parties, several small right-wing parties are politically active. None have representatives in the Bundestag. The Republikaner, which at about 25,000 members is the largest of these parties, has representatives in the Baden-Württemberg parliament after winning 11 percent of the vote in 1992 and 9 percent of the vote in elections there in March 1996. The campaigns of these right-wing parties are based mainly on a fervid nationalism and a dislike of Germany's foreign residents. They stop short of clearly espousing Hitlerian doctrines, however, because doing so would mean their being banned and their leaders possibly being imprisoned.

In addition to parties of the extreme right, authorities estimate that a few thousand violent right-wing extremists are active within Germany. Most are disaffected young males with few job prospects. Although comparatively few in number in a country of 80 million, they have received international attention when they have attacked or killed foreign workers living in Germany or vandalized Jewish cemeteries or synagogues. The world's alarm at such occurrences is easily understandable, given Germany's history in the first half of the twentieth century. Yet few observers believe that these extreme right-wing elements pose a threat to German democracy or have any chance of gaining political influence, let alone coming to power.

Germans of the late twentieth century differ greatly from those of its first half. The extreme nationalism of the interwar period finds little support in the Germany of the 1990s, for example. Unlike Germany's failure to achieve victory in World War I, which to many Germans of the interwar period appeared to have been caused by the treachery of Socialist politicians rather than by military defeat, Germany's unconditional surrender in 1945 was obviously unavoidable given the military situation at the war's end. Moreover, because Hitler clearly started the war, Germany is judged, to some extent at least, to have deserved its terrible consequences. Thus, in contrast to Germans of the interwar period, few postwar Germans have demanded revenge for Germany's sufferings or advocated the seizure of lost territory. This absence of an aggressive nationalism can be seen in the foreign policy of the Federal Republic. Unlike the diplomacy of the empire and the Hitler regime, this foreign policy has always had as its first principle multilateralism, a principle realized through Germany's active membership in a great variety of international organizations.

Germans have also become convinced democrats. They understand and appreciate the workings of parliamentary democracy with its loyal opposition, concessions, and the peaceful passing of power from one government to another; they know the importance of an independent judiciary in protecting individual rights; and they value a free and powerful press. Under a democratic system of government, West Germans have experienced the most successful period of German history, and, whatever the system's failings, they are unwilling to reject it for panaceas of earlier eras. Eastern Germans are now learning Western democratic values after decades of political repression. Having experienced a multitude of political and economic disasters under totalitarian regimes of the right and the left, Germans have matured and become political adults no longer susceptible to the utopian promises of demagogues.

Germany does face some serious challenges in the second half of the 1990s and in the new century. The most immediate challenge is to fully integrate eastern Germany and its inhabitants into the advanced social market economy and society of western Germany.

As of mid-1996, much had already been done to foster the formation of a strong eastern economy and to bring its components up to global standards. In the 1990–95 period, more than US$650 billion had been transferred from western Germany to eastern Germany. This enormous financial infusion has markedly improved eastern living standards, and specialists believe that by the late 1990s, the east's infrastructure will be the most advanced in Europe. Unemployment in eastern Germany has consistently remained at about 15 percent, however, about one-third above the national level, despite eastern growth rates about three times higher than those in western Germany. Many of the older jobless are not likely to find employment comparable to what they had under the communist system. Yet, many eastern Germans have fared well in the new economy and have adapted well to its demands.

Achieving complete social unification is expected to take a generation or two. Decades of life in diverse societies have created two peoples with different attitudes. Easterners are generally less ambitious and concerned with their careers than their western counterparts. Their more relaxed work ethic sometimes raises the ire of western Germans. Many easterners also take offense at what has seemed to them arrogant or patronizing attitudes of westerners. The "implosion" of East Germany in 1990 prevented a slower, more nuanced introduction of Western institutions and habits of thought to the east that would have resulted in fewer bruised feelings. Polls of recent years have found a growing convergence of beliefs and opinions between the two peoples, however, a trend almost certain to continue.

The most serious problem confronting Germany in the long term is one faced by all advanced, high-wage industrial countries—how to meet the challenges posed by an increasingly globalized economy in which highly skilled workers of lesser developed countries are available at one-tenth the wages of wealthy countries. For Germany these countries are not located only in Asia, but next door in the former Eastern bloc. By the 1990s, German wages were among the world's highest, some 50 percent higher than those of the United States, for example. Germany's extensive social safety net is a principal reason for its high wage cost, yet no political party can expect to significantly cut into social programs and retain the favor of voters.

In addition to high wages, the German economy faces structural problems because the areas in which it has long been strongest—the chemical industry and machine production, for example—are not areas in which most future economic growth will occur. Having been so successful in their traditional fields of expertise, German businessmen are somewhat conservative, not given to risky entrepreneurship, and have not invested in new areas such as computers and biotechnology. Economists see little reason to believe that Germany can overtake the leaders in these fields, most notably the United States and Japan.

Germany also faces serious demographic problems. Population growth in recent decades has been slow; in many years, the number of Germans has actually declined because the birth rate has been so low. Given this long-standing trend, specialists wonder how Germans will continue to maintain their generous pension system, an unfunded system that operates on the pay-as-you-go principle, according to which retirees are supported by today's workers. If present trends continue, by 2030 the ratio of retirees to workers will be one to one.

An obvious solution to this problem is to import workers. However, because Germans do not regard their country as a nation of immigrants, importing workers is not currently seen as a politically acceptable solution. As of the mid-1990s, Germany had about 7 million foreign residents, including 2 million Muslims, and more foreign workers are not wanted. Germany has not yet successfully integrated the foreigners already on its soil: archaic immigration laws make it difficult to became a German citizen, and xenophobic attitudes of many Germans often make foreign residents, even those born and raised in the country and speaking perfect German, feel unwanted. In time, demographic realities may cause Germans to view more favorably the permanent presence of a substantial non-German population and lead them to adopt more liberal notions of citizenship.

Unification and the ending of the Cold War have meant that Germany must adjust itself to a new international environment. The disastrous failures of German foreign policy in the first half of the twentieth century have caused Germans to approach this challenge warily. Until the demise of the Soviet Union, Germans could enjoy the certainties of the Cold War, both they and their neighbors secure in the knowledge that the superpowers would contain any possible German aggression.

Throughout the postwar era, West Germany was a model citizen of the community of nations, content to be the most devoted participant in the movement toward Europe's economic and social unification. West German politicians shared the fears of their foreign neighbors of a resurgent, aggressive Germany and sought to ensure their country's containment by embedding it in international organizations. In the mid-1950s, for example, West Germany rearmed, but as a member of the North Atlantic Treaty Organization (NATO—see Glossary).

Since the end of the Cold War, however, united Germany has occupied an exposed position in Central Europe, with settled, secure neighbors in the west and unpredictable and insecure neighbors to the east. Because of this exposure, German policy makers wish to extend the European Union (EU—see Glossary) and NATO eastward, at a minimum bringing Poland, the Czech Republic, and Hungary into both organizations. In the German view, these countries could serve as a buffer between Germany and uncertain developments in Russia and other members of the former Soviet Union. At the same time as this so-called widening of West European institutions is being undertaken, Germany is working for their deepening by pressing for increased European unity. As of mid-1996, Helmut Kohl remained the continent's most important advocate of realizing a common European currency through the European Monetary Union (EMU—see Glossary) by the turn of the century. However unrealistic this timetable may prove to be, in the postwar era Germany has steadfastly worked to realize German writer Thomas Mann's ideal of a Europeanized Germany and rejected his nightmare of a Germanized Europe.

June 19, 1996   Eric Solsten

Chapter 1. Historical Setting: Early History to 1945

Martin Luther, 1483–1546, the main figure of the Protestant Reformation

PEOPLE HAVE DWELLED for thousands of years in the territory now occupied by the Federal Republic of Germany. The first significant written account of this area's inhabitants is *Germania*, written about A.D. 98 by the Roman historian Tacitus. The Germanic tribes he describes are believed to have come from Scandinavia to Germany about 100 B.C., perhaps induced to migrate by overpopulation. The Germanic tribes living to the west of the Rhine River and south of the Main River were soon subdued by the Romans and incorporated into the Roman Empire. Tribes living to the east and north of these rivers remained free but had more or less friendly relations with the Romans for several centuries. Beginning in the fourth century A.D., new westward migrations of eastern peoples caused the Germanic tribes to move into the Roman Empire, which by the late fifth century ceased to exist.

One of the largest Germanic tribes, the Franks, came to control the territory that was to become France and much of what is now western Germany and Italy. In A.D. 800 their ruler, Charlemagne, was crowned in Rome by the pope as emperor of all of this territory. Because of its vastness, Charlemagne's empire split into three kingdoms within two generations, the inhabitants of the West Frankish Kingdom speaking an early form of French and those in the East Frankish Kingdom speaking an early form of German. The tribes of the eastern kingdom—Franconians, Saxons, Bavarians, Swabians, and several others—were ruled by descendants of Charlemagne until 911, when they elected a Franconian, Conrad I, to be their king. Some historians regard Conrad's election as the beginning of what can properly be considered German history.

German kings soon added the Middle Kingdom to their realm and adjudged themselves rulers of what would later be called the Holy Roman Empire. In 962 Otto I became the first of the German kings crowned emperor in Rome. By the middle of the next century, the German lands ruled by the emperors were the richest and most politically powerful part of Europe. German princes stopped the westward advances of the Magyar tribe, and Germans began moving eastward to begin a long process of colonization. During the next few centuries, however, the great expense of the wars to maintain the empire against its enemies, chiefly other German princes and the wealthy and powerful papacy and its allies, depleted Germany's wealth and slowed its development. Unlike France or England, where a central royal power was slowly established over regional princes, Germany remained divided into a multitude of smaller entities often warring with one another or in combinations against the emperors. None of the local princes, or any of the emperors, were strong enough to control Germany for a sustained period.

Germany's so-called particularism, that is, the existence within it of many states of various sizes and kinds, such as principalities, electorates, ecclesiastical territories, and free cities, became characteristic by the early Middle Ages and persisted until 1871, when the country was finally united. This disunity was exacerbated by the Protestant Reformation of the sixteenth century, which ended Germany's religious unity by converting many Germans to Lutheranism and Calvinism. For several centuries, adherents to these two varieties of Protestantism viewed each other with as much hostility and suspicion as they did Roman Catholics. For their part, Catholics frequently resorted to force to defend themselves against Protestants or to convert them. As a result, Germans were divided not only by territory but also by religion.

The terrible destruction of the Thirty Years' War of 1618–48, a war partially religious in nature, reduced German particularism, as did the reforms enacted during the age of enlightened absolutism (1648–1789) and later the growth of nationalism and industrialism in the nineteenth century. In 1815 the Congress of Vienna stipulated that the several hundred states existing in Germany before the French Revolution be replaced with thirty-eight states, some of them quite small. In subsequent decades, the two largest of these states, Austria and Prussia, vied for primacy in a Germany that was gradually unifying under a variety of social and economic pressures. The politician responsible for German unification was Otto von Bismarck, whose brilliant diplomacy and ruthless practice of statecraft secured Prussian hegemony in a united Germany in 1871. The new state, proclaimed the German Empire, did not include Austria and its extensive empire of many non-German territories and peoples.

Imperial Germany prospered. Its economy grew rapidly, and by the turn of the century it rivaled Britain's in size. Although the empire's constitution did not provide for a political system in which the government was responsible to parliament, political parties were founded that represented the main social groups. Roman Catholic and socialist parties contended with conservative and progressive parties and with a conservative monarchy to determine how Germany should be governed.

After Bismarck's dismissal in 1890 by the young emperor Wilhelm II, Germany stepped up its competition with other European states for colonies and for what it considered its proper place among the great states. An aggressive program of military expansion instilled fear of Germany in its neighbors. Several decades of military and colonial competition and a number of diplomatic crises made for a tense international atmosphere by 1914. In the early summer of that year, Germany's rulers acted on the belief that their country's survival depended on a successful war against Russia and France. German strategists felt that a war against these countries had to be waged by 1916 if it were to be won because after that year Russian and French military reforms would be complete, making German victory doubtful. This logic led Germany to get drawn into a war between its ally Austria-Hungary and Russia. Within weeks, a complicated system of alliances escalated that regional conflict into World War I, which ended with Germany's defeat in November 1918.

The Weimar Republic, established at war's end, was the first attempt to institute parliamentary democracy in Germany. The republic never enjoyed the wholehearted support of many Germans, however, and from the start it was under savage attack from elements of the left and, more important, from the right. Moreover, it was burdened during its fifteen-year existence with serious economic problems. During the second half of the 1920s, when foreign loans fed German prosperity, parliamentary politics functioned better, yet many of the established elites remained hostile to it. With the onset of the Great Depression, parliamentary politics became impossible, and the government ruled by decree. Economic crisis favored extremist politicians, and Adolf Hitler's National Socialist German Workers' Party became the strongest party after the summer elections of 1932. In January 1933, the republic's elected president, Paul von Hindenburg, the World War I army commander, named a government headed by Hitler.

Within a few months, Hitler accomplished the "legal revolution" that removed his opponents. By 1935 his regime had transformed Germany into a totalitarian state. Hitler achieved notable economic and diplomatic successes during the first five years of his rule. However, in September 1939 he made a fatal gamble by invading Poland and starting World War II. The eventual defeat of Hitler's Third Reich in 1945 occurred only after the loss of tens of millions of lives, many from military causes, many from sickness and starvation, and many from what has come to be called the Holocaust.

Early History

The Germanic tribes, which probably originated from a mixture of peoples along the Baltic Sea coast, inhabited the northern part of the European continent by about 500 B.C. By 100 B.C., they had advanced into the central and southern areas of present-day Germany. At that time, there were three major tribal groups: the eastern Germanic peoples lived along the Oder and Vistula rivers; the northern Germanic peoples inhabited the southern part of present-day Scandinavia; and the western Germanic peoples inhabited the extreme south of Jutland and the area between the North Sea and the Elbe, Rhine, and Main rivers. The Rhine provided a temporary boundary between Germanic and Roman territory after the defeat of the Suevian tribe by Julius Caesar about 70 B.C. The threatening presence of warlike tribes beyond the Rhine prompted the Romans to pursue a campaign of expansion into Germanic territory. However, the defeat of the provincial governor Varus by Arminius at the Battle of the Teutoburg Forest in A.D. 9 halted Roman expansion; Arminius had learned the enemy's strategies during his military training in the Roman armies. This battle brought about the liberation of the greater part of Germany from Roman domination. The Rhine River was once again the boundary line until the Romans reoccupied territory on its eastern bank and built the Limes, a fortification 300 kilometers long, in the first century A.D.

The second through the sixth centuries was a period of change and destruction in which eastern and western Germanic tribes left their native lands and settled in newly acquired territories. This period of Germanic history, which later supplied material for heroic epics, included the downfall of the Roman Empire and resulted in a considerable expansion of habitable area for the Germanic peoples. However, with the exception of those kingdoms established by Franks and Anglo-Saxons, Germanic kingdoms founded in such other parts of Europe as Italy and Spain were of relatively short duration because they were assimilated by the native populations.

The conquest of Roman Gaul by Frankish tribes in the late fifth century became a milestone of European history; it was the Franks who were to become the founders of a civilized German state.

Medieval Germany

The Merovingian Dynasty, ca. 500–751

In Gaul a fusion of Roman and Germanic societies occurred. Clovis, a Salian Frank belonging to a family supposedly descended from a mythical hero named Merovech, became the absolute ruler of a Germanic kingdom of mixed Roman-Germanic population in 486. He consolidated his rule with victories over the Gallo-Romans and all the Frankish tribes, and his successors made other Germanic tribes subjects of the Merovingian Dynasty. The remaining 250 years of the dynasty, however, were marked by internecine struggles and a gradual decline. During the period of Merovingian rule, the Franks reluctantly began to adopt Christianity following the baptism of Clovis, an event that inaugurated the alliance between the Frankish kingdom and the Roman Catholic Church. The most notable of the missionaries responsible for Christianizing the tribes living in Germany was Saint Boniface (ca. 675–754), an English missionary who is considered the founder of German Christianity.

The Carolingian Dynasty, 752–911

Charlemagne inherited the Frankish crown in 768. During his reign (768–814), he subdued Bavaria, conquered Lombardy and Saxony, and established his authority in central Italy. By the end of the eighth century, his kingdom, later to become known as the First Reich (empire in German), included present-day France, the Netherlands, Belgium, and Luxembourg, as well as a narrow strip of northern Spain, much of Germany and Austria, and much of the northern half of Italy. Charlemagne, founder of an empire that was Roman, Christian, and Germanic, was crowned emperor in Rome by the pope in 800.

The Carolingian Empire was based on an alliance between the emperor, who was a temporal ruler supported by a military retinue, and the pope of the Roman Catholic Church, who granted spiritual sanction to the imperial mission. Charlemagne and his son Louis I (r. 814–40) established centralized authority, appointed imperial counts as administrators, and developed a hierarchical feudal structure headed by the emperor. Reliant on personal leadership rather than the Roman concept of legalistic government, Charlemagne's empire lasted less than a century.

A period of warfare followed the death of Louis. The Treaty of Verdun (843) restored peace and divided the empire among three sons, geographically and politically delineating the approximate future territories of Germany, France, and the area between them, known as the Middle Kingdom (see fig. 2). The eastern Carolingian kings ruled the East Frankish Kingdom, what is now Germany and Austria; the western Carolingian kings ruled the West Frankish Kingdom, what became France. The imperial title, however, came to depend increasingly on rule over the Middle Kingdom. By this time, in addition to a geographical and political delineation, a cultural and linguistic split had occurred. The eastern Frankish tribes still spoke Germanic dialects; the language of the western Frankish tribes, under the influence of Gallo-Latin, had developed into Old French. Because of these linguistic differences, the Treaty of Verdun had to be written in two languages.

Not only had Charlemagne's empire been divided into three kingdoms, but the East Frankish Kingdom was being weakened by the rise of regional duchies, the so-called stem duchies of Franconia, Saxony, Bavaria, Swabia, and Lorraine, which acquired the trappings of petty kingdoms. The fragmentation in the east marked the beginning of German particularism, in which territorial rulers promoted their own interests and autonomy without regard to the kingdom as a whole. The duchies were strengthened when the Carolingian line died out in 911; subsequent kings would have no direct blood link to the throne with which to legitimate their claims to power against the territorial dukes.

The Saxon Dynasty, 919–1024

Because the dukes of the East Frankish Kingdom had wearied of being ruled by a foreign king, they elected a German to serve as their king once the Carolingian line expired. The election of Conrad I (r. 911–18), Duke of Franconia, as the first German king has been marked by some historians as the beginning of German history. Conrad's successor, Henry I (r. 919–36), Duke of Saxony, was powerful enough to designate his son Otto I (r. 936–73) as his successor. Otto was so able a ruler that he came to be known as Otto the Great. He overpowered other territorial dukes who rebelled against his rule and reversed the particularist trend for a time. But he failed to establish the principle of hereditary succession, and the German dukes continued to elect one of their number as king. But through military successes and alliances with the church, which had extensive properties and military forces of its own, Otto expanded the crown lands, thus laying the foundation of monarchical power. Henry, Otto, and the later Saxon kings also encouraged eastward expansion and colonization, thereby extending German rule to parts of the Slavic territories of Poland and Bohemia. The Magyars' westward expansion was halted by Otto in 955 at the Battle of Lechfeld in southern Germany.

In 962 Otto, who had also gained control of the Middle Kingdom, was formally crowned king of the Romans. The possessor of this title would, in time, be known as the Holy Roman Emperor. The coronation came to be seen as the founding of the Holy Roman Empire, an institution that lasted until 1806 and profoundly influenced the course of German history. The coronation of Otto was a moment of glory for the German monarchy, but its long-term consequences were not beneficial because as German kings sought to exercise the offices of the empire they became involved in Italian affairs, often to such an extent that they neglected the governing of Germany. Because German kings were so often in Italy, the German nobility became stronger. In addition, the presence of German kings in Italy as emperors soon caused them to come into conflict with the papacy, which did not hesitate to seek allies in Italy or Germany to limit imperial power. A last problem was that the succession to the German throne was often uncertain or was hotly contested because it was not inheritable, but could only be attained through election by the German dukes. This circumstance made the formation of an orderly or stable central government nearly impossible. In the opinion of some historians, Otto's triumph in Rome in 962 ultimately was disastrous for Germany because it delayed German unification by centuries.

The Salian Dynasty, 1024–1125

After the death of the last Saxon king in 1024, the crown passed to the Salians, a Frankish tribe. The four Salian kings—Conrad II, Henry III, Henry IV, and Henry V—who ruled Germany as kings from 1024 to 1125, established their monarchy

9

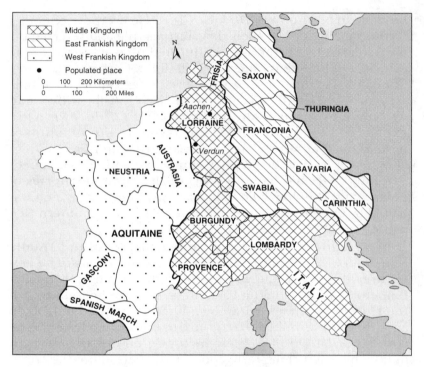

Source: Based on information from Geoffrey Barraclough, *The Origins of Modern Germany*, Oxford, 1949, 12.

Figure 2. The Carolingian Empire Divided by the Treaty of Verdun, A.D. 843

as a major European power. Their main accomplishment was the development of a permanent administrative system based on a class of public officials answerable to the crown.

A principal reason for the success of the early Salians was their alliance with the church, a policy begun by Otto I, which gave them the material support they needed to subdue rebellious dukes. In time, however, the church came to regret this close relationship. The relationship broke down in 1075 during what came to be known as the Investiture Contest, a struggle in which the reformist pope, Gregory VII, demanded that Henry IV (r. 1056–1106) renounce his rights over the German church. The pope also attacked the concept of monarchy by divine right and gained the support of significant elements of the German nobility interested in limiting imperial absolutism. More important, the pope forbade church officials under pain of excommunication to support Henry as they had so freely done in the past. In the end, Henry journeyed to Canossa in northern Italy in 1077 to do penance and to receive absolution from the pope. However, he resumed the practice of lay investiture (appointment of religious officials by civil authorities) and arranged the election of an antipope.

The German monarch's struggle with the papacy resulted in a war that ravaged German lands from 1077 until the Concordat of Worms in 1122. This agreement stipulated that the pope was to appoint high church officials but gave the German king the right to veto the papal choices. Imperial control of Italy was lost for a time, and the imperial crown became dependent on the political support of competing aristocratic factions. Feudalism also became more widespread as freemen sought protection by swearing allegiance to a lord. These powerful local rulers, having thereby acquired extensive territories and large military retinues, took over administration within their territories and organized it around an increasing number of castles. The most powerful of these local rulers came to be called princes rather than dukes.

According to the laws of the German feudal system, the king had no claims on the vassals of the other princes, only on those living within his family's territory. Lacking the support of the formerly independent vassals and weakened by the increasing hostility of the church, the monarchy lost its preeminence. Thus, the Investiture Contest strengthened local power in Germany in contrast to what was happening in France and England, where the growth of a centralized royal power was under way.

The Investiture Contest had an additional effect. The long struggle between emperor and pope hurt Germany's intellectual life—in this period largely confined to monasteries—and Germany no longer led or even kept pace with developments occurring in France and Italy. For instance, no universities were founded in Germany until the fourteenth century.

The Hohenstaufen Dynasty, 1138–1254

Following the death of Henry V (r. 1106–25), the last of the Salian kings, the dukes refused to elect his nephew because they feared that he might restore royal power. Instead, they elected a noble connected to the Saxon noble family Welf (often written as Guelf). This choice inflamed the Hohenstaufen family of Swabia, which also had a claim to the throne. Although a Hohenstaufen became king in 1138, the dynastic feud with the Welfs continued. The feud became international in nature when the Welfs sided with the papacy and its allies, most notably the cities of northern Italy, against the imperial ambitions of the Hohenstaufen Dynasty.

The second of the Hohenstaufen rulers, Frederick I (r. 1152–90), also known as Frederick Barbarossa because of his red beard, struggled throughout his reign to restore the power and prestige of the German monarchy, but he had little success. Because the German dukes had grown stronger both during and after the Investiture Contest and because royal access to the resources of the church in Germany was much reduced, Frederick was forced to go to Italy to find the finances needed to restore the king's power in Germany. He was soon crowned emperor in Italy, but decades of warfare on the peninsula yielded scant results. The papacy and the prosperous city-states of northern Italy were traditional enemies, but the fear of imperial domination caused them to join ranks to fight Frederick. Under the skilled leadership of Pope Alexander III, the alliance suffered many defeats but ultimately was able to deny the emperor a complete victory in Italy. Frederick returned to Germany old and embittered. He had vanquished one notable opponent and member of the Welf family, Saxony's Henry the Lion, but his hopes of restoring the power and prestige of his family and the monarchy seemed unlikely to be met by the end of his life.

During Frederick's long stays in Italy, the German princes became stronger and began a successful colonization of Slavic lands. Offers of reduced taxes and manorial duties enticed many Germans to settle in the east as the area's original inhabitants were killed or driven away. Because of this colonization, the empire increased in size and came to include Pomerania, Silesia, Bohemia, and Moravia. A quickening economic life in Germany increased the number of towns and gave them greater importance. It was also during this period that castles and courts replaced monasteries as centers of culture. Growing out of this courtly culture, German medieval literature reached its peak in lyrical love poetry, the *Minnesang*, and in narrative epic poems such as *Tristan*, *Parzival*, and the *Nibelungenlied*.

Frederick died in 1190 while on a crusade and was succeeded by his son, Henry VI (r. 1190–97). Elected king even before his father's death, Henry went to Rome to be crowned emperor. A death in his wife's family gave him possession of Sicily, a source of vast wealth. Henry failed to make royal and imperial succession hereditary, but in 1196 he succeeded in gaining a pledge that his infant son Frederick would receive the German crown. Faced with difficulties in Italy and confident that he would realize his wishes in Germany at a later date, Henry returned to the south, where it appeared he might unify the peninsula under the Hohenstaufen name. After a series of military victories, however, he died of natural causes in Sicily in 1197.

Because the election of the three-year-old Frederick to be German king appeared likely to make orderly rule difficult, the boy's uncle, Philip, was chosen to serve in his place. Other factions elected a Welf candidate, Otto IV, as counterking, and a long civil war began. Philip was murdered by Otto IV in 1208. Otto IV in turn was killed by the French at the Battle of Bouvines in 1214. Frederick returned to Germany in 1212 from Sicily, where he had grown up, and became king in 1215. As Frederick II (r. 1215–50), he spent little time in Germany because his main concerns lay in Italy. Frederick made significant concessions to the German nobles, such as those put forth in an imperial statute of 1232, which made princes virtually independent rulers within their territories. The clergy also became more powerful. Although Frederick was one of the most energetic, imaginative, and capable rulers of the Middle Ages, he did nothing to draw the disparate forces in Germany together. His legacy was thus that local rulers had more authority after his reign than before it.

By the time of Frederick's death in 1250, there was little centralized power in Germany. The Great Interregnum (1256–73), a period of anarchy in which there was no emperor and German princes vied for individual advantage, followed the death of Frederick's son Conrad IV in 1254. In this short period, the German nobility managed to strip many powers away from the already diminished monarchy. Rather than establish sovereign states, however, many nobles tended to look after their families. Their many heirs created more and smaller estates. A largely free class of officials also formed, many of whom eventually acquired hereditary rights to administrative and legal offices. These trends compounded political fragmentation within Germany.

Despite the political chaos of the Hohenstaufen period, the population grew from an estimated 8 million in 1200 to about 14 million in 1300, and the number of towns increased tenfold. The most heavily urbanized areas of Germany were located in the south and the west. Towns often developed a degree of independence, but many were subordinate to local rulers or the emperor. Colonization of the east also continued in the thirteenth century, most notably through the efforts of the Knights of the Teutonic Order, a society of soldier-monks. German merchants also began trading extensively on the Baltic.

The Empire under the Early Habsburgs

The Great Interregnum ended in 1273 with the election of Rudolf of Habsburg as king-emperor. After the interregnum period, Germany's emperors came from three powerful dynastic houses: Luxemburg (in Bohemia), Wittelsbach (in Bavaria), and Habsburg (in Austria). These families alternated on the imperial throne until the crown returned in the mid-fifteenth century to the Habsburgs, who retained it with only one short break until the dissolution of the Holy Roman Empire in 1806.

The Golden Bull of 1356, an edict promulgated by Emperor Charles IV (r. 1355–78) of the Luxemburg family, provided the basic constitution of the empire up to its dissolution. It formalized the practice of having seven electors—the archbishops of the cities of Trier, Cologne, and Mainz, and the rulers of the Palatinate, Saxony, Brandenburg, and Bohemia—choose the emperor, and it represented a further political consolidation of the principalities. The Golden Bull ended the long-standing attempt of various emperors to unite Germany under a hereditary monarchy. Henceforth, the emperor shared power with other great nobles like himself and was regarded as merely the first among equals. Without the cooperation of the other princes, he could not rule.

The princes were not absolute rulers either. They had made so many concessions to other secular and ecclesiastical powers in their struggle against the emperor that many smaller principalities, ecclesiastical states, and towns had retained a degree of independence. Some of the smaller noble holdings were so poor that they had to resort to outright extortion of travelers and merchants to sustain themselves, with the result that journeying through Germany could be perilous in the late Middle Ages. All of Germany was under the nominal control of the emperor, but because his power was so weak or uncertain, local authorities had to maintain order—yet another indication of Germany's political fragmentation.

Despite the lack of a strong central authority, Germany prospered during the fourteenth and fifteenth centuries. Its population increased from about 14 million in 1300 to about 16 million in 1500, even though the Black Death killed as much as one-third of the population in the mid-fourteenth century.

Located in the center of Europe, Germany was active in international trade. Rivers flowing to the north and the east and the Alpine passes made Germany a natural conduit conveying goods from the Mediterranean to northern Europe. Germany became a noted manufacturing center. Trade and manufacturing led to the growth of towns, and in 1500 an estimated 10 percent of the population lived in urban areas. Many towns became wealthy and were governed by a sophisticated and self-confident merchant oligarchy. Dozens of towns in northern Germany joined together to form the Hanseatic League, a trading federation that managed shipping and trade on the Baltic and in many inland areas, even into Bohemia and Hungary. The Hanseatic League had commercial offices in such widely dispersed towns as London, Bergen (in present-day Norway), and Novgorod (in present-day Russia). The league was at one time so powerful that it successfully waged war against the king of Denmark. In southern Germany, towns banded together on occasion to protect their interests against encroachments by either imperial or local powers. Although these urban confederations were not always strong enough to defeat their opponents, they sometimes succeeded in helping their members to avoid complete subjugation. In what was eventually to become Switzerland, one confederation of towns had sufficient military might to win virtual independence from the Holy Roman Empire in 1499.

The Knights of the Teutonic Order continued their settlement of the east until their dissolution early in the sixteenth century, in spite of a serious defeat at the hands of the Poles at the Battle of Tannenberg in 1410. The lands that came under the control of this monastic military, whose members were pledged to chastity and to the conquest and conversion of heathens, included territory that one day would become eastern Prussia and would be inhabited by Germans until 1945. German settlement in areas south of the territories controlled by the Knights of the Teutonic Order also continued, but generally at the behest of eastern rulers who valued the skills of German peasant-farmers. These new settlers were part of a long process of peaceful German immigration to the east that lasted for centuries, with Germans moving into all of eastern Europe and even deep into Russia.

Intellectual growth accompanied German expansion. Several universities were founded, and Germany came into increased contact with the humanists active elsewhere in Europe. The invention of movable type in the middle of the fifteenth century in Germany also contributed to a more lively intellectual climate. Religious ferment was common, most notably the heretical movement engendered by the teachings of Jan Hus (ca. 1372–1415) in Bohemia. Hus eventually was executed, but the dissatisfaction he felt toward the established church was shared by many others throughout German-speaking lands, as could be seen in the frequent occurrences of popular, mystical religious revivalism after his death.

The Protestant Reformation

On the eve of the Protestant Reformation, the institutions of the Holy Roman Empire were widely thought to be in need of improvement. The Habsburg emperors Frederick III (r. 1440–93) and his son Maximilian I (r. 1493–1519) both cooperated with individual local rulers to enact changes. However, the imperial and local parties had different aims, the former wishing to strengthen the empire, the latter aiming to secure greater independence by formalizing their rights and ensuring regular procedures for the conduct of public business. In 1489 the procedures of the imperial diet, the Reichstag, in which representatives of all states within the empire met, were reorganized. One of the reforms allowed participation in the diet by representatives of the towns. In 1495 Maximilian declared an empirewide peace and made arrangements to reduce the lawlessness and violence that often marked relations among local rulers.

Maximilian's reforms were not enough to cure the ills of the empire, and relations between it and the princes and ecclesiastical states often were tense. Disputes frequently involved complicated constellations of powers with occasional interference from abroad, most notably France. Charles V (r. 1519–56) was elected emperor in 1519 only after he paid large bribes to the seven electors and agreed to many restrictions on his powers, restrictions he often later ignored (see fig. 3).

A changing economy also made for discontent among those unable to profit from new conditions. Some of the empire's inhabitants had become quite rich, most notably the Fugger family of Augsburg, whose members had replaced the bankers of northern Italy as Europe's leading financiers. The Fuggers

had come to manage the financial affairs of the Habsburg Dynasty, which, in combination with increased trade between south and north, made Germany Europe's financial center for a few decades. However, other groups in Germany were experiencing hardship. A burgeoning rural population found it difficult to get enough to eat, and many peasants went to the towns to seek a living. Municipal officials responded by seeking to bar rural newcomers. Within towns that were not prospering, relations between the classes became more tense as social mobility was reduced by a declining economy.

Martin Luther

On the eve of All Saints' Day in 1517, Martin Luther, a professor of theology at Wittenberg University in Saxony, posted ninety-five theses on a church door. Luther's primary concern was the sale of indulgences—papal grants of reduced punishment in the afterlife, including releases from purgatory. First written in Latin, the theses were soon translated into German and widely distributed. Summoned by church authorities to explain his writings, Luther became embroiled in further controversy and in 1520 wrote his three most famous tracts, in which he attacked the papacy and exposed church corruption, acknowledged the validity of only two of the seven sacraments, and argued for the supremacy of faith over good works. In 1521 Luther was summoned to appear before Emperor Charles V at the Diet of Worms. Refusing to recant his writings, he was banned under the Edict of Worms. Secreted away by the ruler of Saxony, Frederick the Wise, Luther retreated to the castle of Wartburg, where he worked on a translation of the New Testament and wrote numerous religious tracts.

Luther's disagreements with the doctrines of the Roman Catholic Church set off a chain of events that within a few decades destroyed Germany's religious unity. Although one of the most influential figures in German history, Luther was only one of many who were critical of the Roman Catholic Church. However, because of the power of his ideas and the enormous influence of his writings, it is he who is regarded as the initiator of the Protestant Reformation. Luther quickly acquired a large following among those disgusted by rampant church corruption and unfulfilled by mechanistic religious services. Many warmed to his contention that religion must be simplified into a close relationship of human beings with God without the extensive mediation of the Roman Catholic Church and its accretion of tradition.

Luther magnified the inherent potency of his ideas by articulating them in a language that was without rival in clarity and force. He strove to make the Scriptures accessible to ordinary worshipers by translating them into vernacular German. This he did with such genius that the German dialect he used became the written language of all of Germany. Without Luther's translation of the Bible, Germany might have come to use a number of mutually incomprehensible languages, as was the case in the northwestern part of the Holy Roman Empire, where local dialects evolved into what is now modern Dutch. Luther also wrote hymns that are still sung in Christian religious services all over the world.

A less exalted reason for the wide distribution of Luther's doctrines was the development of printing with movable type. The Reformation created a demand for all kinds of religious writings. The readership was so great that the number of books printed in Germany increased from about 150 in 1518 to nearly 1,000 six years later.

Luther's ideas soon coalesced into a body of doctrines called Lutheranism. Powerful supporters such as princes and free cities accepted Lutheranism for many reasons, some because they sincerely supported reform, others out of narrow self-interest. In some areas, a jurisdiction would adopt Lutheranism because a large neighboring state had done so. In other areas, rulers accepted it because they sought to retain control over their subjects who had embraced it earlier. Nearly all the imperial cities became Lutheran, despite the fact that the emperor, to whom they were subordinate, was hostile to the movement. Historians have found no single convincing explanation of why one area became Lutheran and another did not, because so many social, economic, and religious factors were involved.

Given the revolutionary nature of Lutheranism and the economic and political tensions of the period, it is not surprising that the Reformation soon became marked by violence and extremism. The Knights' War of 1522–23, in which members of the lower nobility rebelled against the authorities in southwestern Germany, was quickly crushed. Some of the rampaging knights were ardent supporters of Luther. The Peasants' War of 1524–25 was more serious, involving as many as 300,000 peasants in southwestern and central Germany. Influenced somewhat by the new religious ideas but responding mostly to changing economic conditions, the peasants' rebellion spread quickly, but without coordination. It also received support from some dissatisfied city dwellers and from some noblemen of arms who led its ragged armies. Although the peasants' rebellion was the largest uprising in German history, it was quickly suppressed, with about 100,000 casualties. In the 1530s, the Anabaptists, a radical Christian sect, seized several towns, their objective being to construct a just society. They were likewise brutally suppressed by the authorities.

Luther opposed the peasants' cause and wrote an impassioned tract demanding their quick suppression. However radical his religious views, Luther was a social and political conservative. He believed that the end of the world was imminent and regarded practical affairs as having little importance compared with the effort to win eternal salvation. Therefore, he counseled obedience to worldly authorities if they allowed freedom of worship. Lutheranism thus became a means of upholding the worldly status quo and the leaders who adopted the new faith. In contrast to England, where Protestantism retained a significant radical social element, German Protestantism became an integral part of the state. Some historians maintain that this integration of state and church has deprived Germany of a deeply rooted tradition of political dissent as found in Britain and the United States.

Resistance to Lutheranism

Although Lutheranism had powerful supporters, its survival was by no means certain. Its main opponent was the Habsburg emperor Charles V, who had inherited Spain, the Netherlands, southern Italy, Sicily, and the Austrian lands as patrimony and who hoped to restore the unity of the German Empire by keeping it Roman Catholic. Charles had been out of Germany between 1521 and 1530, and when he returned he found that the new religion had won too many adherents to be easily uprooted. In addition, he could not devote himself singlemindedly to combating it but also had to struggle with powerful external enemies. One was Francis I (r. 1515–47) of France, who attacked the empire from the west, having resolved to destroy the power of the Habsburgs. Another threat was posed by the Turks, who were attacking the empire from the east. Even the papacy at times conspired against its coreligionist because it feared Charles was becoming too powerful.

Within Germany, forces were also arrayed against Charles. In 1531 Protestant leaders created the League of Schmalkalden to oppose him. By 1545 northeastern and northwestern Germany and large parts of southern Germany had become Protestant. Despite the significant victory over the Protestants at the Battle of Mühlberg in 1547, Charles still was not powerful enough to impose his will on the German princes.

The Peace of Augsburg

By the early 1550s, it was apparent that a negotiated settlement was necessary. In 1555 the Peace of Augsburg was signed. The settlement, which represented a victory for the princes, granted recognition to both Lutheranism and Roman Catholicism in Germany, and each ruler gained the right to decide the religion to be practiced within his state. Subjects not of this faith could move to another state with their property, and disputes between the religions were to be settled in court.

The Protestant Reformation strengthened the long-standing trend toward particularism in Germany. German leaders, whether Protestant or Catholic, became yet more powerful at the expense of the central governing institution, the empire. Protestant leaders gained by receiving lands that formerly belonged to the Roman Catholic Church, although not to as great an extent as, for example, would occur in England. Each prince also became the head of the established church within his territory. Catholic leaders benefited because the Roman Catholic Church, in order to help them withstand Protestantism, gave them greater access to church resources within their territories. Germany was also less united than before because Germans were no longer of one faith, a situation officially recognized by the Peace of Augsburg. The agreement did not bring sectarian peace, however, because the religious question in Germany had not yet been settled fully.

The Thirty Years' War, 1618–48

Germany enjoyed a time of relative quiet between the Peace of Augsburg, signed in 1555, and the outbreak of the Thirty Years' War in 1618. The empire functioned in a more regular way than previously, and its federal nature was more evident than in the past. The Reichstag met frequently to deal with public matters, and the emperors Ferdinand I (r. 1556–64) and Maximilian II (r. 1564–76) were cautious rulers concerned mostly with strengthening their family's hold on Austria and adjacent areas. Rudolf II (r. 1576–1612) was an indolent and capricious ruler who generally followed his advisers' counsel. As a result, some German states were able to expand their territories by annexing smaller neighbors in the absence of an engaged and attentive emperor. Local rivalries engendered tensions that often were based on religious affiliation.

The Counter-Reformation and Religious Tensions

The Peace of Augsburg brought peace but did not settle the religious disagreements in Germany. For one thing, its signatories did not recognize Calvinism, a relatively stringent form of Protestantism that was gaining prominence around the time the Augsburg treaty was signed, in what has been called the Second Reformation. Adherents to both Calvinism and Lutheranism worked to spread their influence and gain converts in the face of the Counter-Reformation, the attempt of the Roman Catholic Church to regroup and reverse the spread of Protestantism. Followers of all three religions were at times successful, but only at the expense of the others.

Fear of religious subversion caused rulers to monitor the conduct of their subjects more closely. Attempting to help the modern reader understand the intensity and pervasiveness of this fear, Mary Fulbrook, a noted British historian of Germany, has likened it to the anxiety prevailing in the first years of the Cold War. An example of the social paranoia engendered by the religious tensions of the period is Protestant Germany's refusal until 1700 to accept the Gregorian calendar introduced by the papacy in 1582 because the reform entailed a one-time loss of the days between October 5 and 14. Many Protestants suspected that Roman Catholics were attempting somehow to steal this time for themselves.

By the first decades of the seventeenth century, religious controversy had become so obstructive that at times the Reichstag could not conduct business. In 1608, for example, Calvinists walked out of the body, preventing the levying of a tax to fight a war against the Turks. In the same year, the Evangelical Union was established by a few states and cities of the empire to defend the Protestant cause. In 1609 a number of Roman Catholic states countered by forming the Catholic League. Although both bodies were less concerned with a sectarian war than with the specific aims of their member states, their formation was an indication of how easily disputes could acquire a religious aspect.

Military Campaigns

The Thirty Years' War resulted from a local rebellion, but the admixture of religion transformed it into a European conflict that lasted for more than a generation and devastated Germany. In 1618 Bohemian nobles opposed the decision of Emperor Matthias (r. 1608–19) to designate his Catholic cousin Ferdinand king of Bohemia. Instead, the nobles elected Frederick of the Palatinate, a German Calvinist, to be their king. In 1620, in an attempt to wrest control from the nobles, imperial armies and the Catholic League under General Johann von Tilly defeated the Protestant Bohemians at the Battle of White Mountain near Prague. The Protestant princes, alarmed by the strength of the Catholic League and the possibility of Roman Catholic supremacy in Europe, decided to renew their struggle against Emperor Matthias. They were aided by France, which, although Roman Catholic, was opposed to the increasing power of the Habsburgs, the dynastic family to which Matthias and Ferdinand belonged. Despite French aid, by the late 1620s imperial armies of Emperor Ferdinand II (r. 1619–37) and the Catholic League, under the supreme command of General Albrecht von Wallenstein, had defeated the Protestants and secured a foothold in northern Germany.

In his time of triumph, Ferdinand overreached himself by publishing in 1629 the Edict of Restitution, which required that all properties of the Roman Catholic Church taken since 1552 be returned to their original owners. The edict renewed Protestant resistance. Catholic powers also began to oppose Ferdinand because they feared he was becoming too powerful. Invading armies from Sweden, secretly supported by Catholic France, marched deep into Germany, winning numerous victories. The Catholic general Tilly and Sweden's Protestant king, Gustavus Adolphus, were killed in separate battles. Wallenstein was assassinated on Emperor Ferdinand's orders because he feared his general was becoming too powerful. After the triumph of the Spanish army over Swedish forces at the Battle of Nördlingen in 1634, a truce was arranged between the emperor and some of the German princes under the Treaty of Prague. France then invaded Germany, not for religious reasons but because the House of Bourbon, the dynastic family of several French and Spanish monarchs, wished to ensure that the House of Habsburg did not become too powerful. This invasion is illustrative of the French axiom that Germany must always remain divided into small, easily manipulated states. (Indeed, preventing a united Germany remained an objective of French foreign policy even late in the twentieth century.) Because of French participation, the war continued until the Peace of Westphalia was signed in 1648.

The Peace of Westphalia

The Peace of Westphalia largely settled German affairs for the next century and a half. It ended religious conflicts between the states and included official recognition of Calvinism. Its signatories altered the boundaries of the empire by recognizing that Switzerland and the Netherlands had become sovereign states outside the empire. Portions of Alsace and Lorraine went to France. Sweden received some territory in northern Germany, which in the long run it could not retain. Brandenburg became stronger, as did Saxony and Bavaria. In addition, states within the empire acquired greater independence with the right to have their own foreign policies and form alliances, even with states outside the empire. As a result of these changes, the Holy Roman Empire lost much of what remained of its power and would never again be a significant actor on the international stage. The Habsburgs would continue to be crowned emperors, but their strength would derive from their own holdings, not from leadership of the empire. Germany was less united in 1648 than in 1618, and German particularism had been strengthened once again.

The Thirty Years' War had a devastating effect on the German people. Historians have usually estimated that between one-fourth and one-third of the population perished from direct military causes or from illness and starvation related to the war. Some regions were affected much more than others. For example, an estimated three-quarters of Württemberg's population died between 1634 and 1639. Overall losses were serious enough that historians believe that it took a century after the Thirty Years' War for Germany's population to reach the level of 1618.

Germany's economy was also severely disrupted by the ravages of the Thirty Years' War. The war exacerbated the economic decline that had begun in the second half of the sixteenth century as the European economy shifted westward to the Atlantic states—Spain, France, England, and the Low

Countries. The shift in trade meant that Germany was no longer located at the center of European commerce but on its fringes. The thriving economies of many German towns in the late Middle Ages and first half of the sixteenth century gradually dried up, and Germany as a whole entered a long period of economic stagnation that ended only in the second half of the nineteenth century.

The Age of Enlightened Absolutism, 1648–1789

Although the Holy Roman Empire no longer had a significant role in European politics after the Thirty Years' War, it remained important in Germany, providing a framework for the many German states' and cities' conduct of their public affairs. The Reichstag, which remained in session at Regensburg from 1663 until the empire's dissolution in 1806, provided a forum for the settlement of disputes. On occasion, votes were taken to remove incompetent or tyrannical rulers of member states. The empire's most important service was that it provided a measure of security to Germany's many small states and free cities, without which some would have been swallowed up by larger neighbors. Because of its weakened condition, the empire could no longer dominate Germany, even when headed by ambitious and capable men such as Charles VI (r. 1711–40). During the 1720s, he attempted unsuccessfully to breathe new life into the empire. Later emperors returned to the traditional Habsburg practice of using the imperial throne to benefit their own dynastic holdings.

For nearly a century after the Peace of Westphalia, the main danger to German states came from abroad. France was the chief threat, seizing parts of southwestern Germany in the late 1600s, among them the city of Strasbourg in 1681. French troops also fought on German soil during the War of the Spanish Succession (1701–14). In addition to these military actions, France formed alliances with some German states, most significantly with Bavaria, which sought support against neighboring Austria. The Ottoman Empire also posed a threat. In 1683 its forces besieged Vienna. The Germans ultimately were successful against the Ottoman Empire, and after the Treaty of Passarowitz of 1718, the Turks were no longer a danger.

Austria and Prussia

The most important German power after the Peace of Westphalia was Austria, followed by a few other states with much smaller populations, most notably Brandenburg, Saxony, and Bavaria. Austria retained its preeminence until the second half of the nineteenth century, but in the eighteenth century Brandenburg had become a serious rival, annexing valuable Austrian territory. The rivalry came to form the so-called dualism of the empire, that is, the presence in it of two powerful states, neither of which was strong enough to dominate the empire and for that reason sought the support of smaller states. The smaller states worked to derive their own advantages from German dualism, none being willing to cede sovereignty to either Austria or Prussia.

In 1648 Brandenburg was a small state in northern Germany. It had been ruled by the Hohenzollern Dynasty since the late fifteenth century and consisted of the core region and its capital, Berlin; eastern Pomerania; an area around Magdeburg; the former holdings of the Knights of the Teutonic Order in eastern Prussia; and some smaller holdings in western Germany. Brandenburg became known as Prussia in 1701 when its ruler crowned himself King Frederick I of Prussia. Prussia acquired the rest of Pomerania after defeating Sweden in the Great Northern War (1700–21). Prussia's increase in size and influence may be attributed to a succession of capable leaders, all of whom enjoyed long reigns. The first was Frederick William (r. 1640–88), known as the Great Elector. He increased his family's power by granting favors to the nobility, weakening the independence of the towns, and maintaining a professional standing army. His son Frederick I (r. 1688–1713) established Prussia as a kingdom. Frederick further strengthened the army, but not nearly as much as his son Frederick William I (r. 1713–40), who also modernized the kingdom's bureaucracy. Frederick II (r. 1740–86), known to posterity as Frederick the Great, continued along the same lines as his father but showed much greater imagination and ruthlessness, transforming his small kingdom into one of the great powers of Europe.

In 1740 Frederick seized Silesia, a wealthy province that belonged to the Habsburgs and had a population of about 1 million inhabitants. Maria Theresa (r. 1740–80), the new Habsburg empress, was unable to regain possession of Silesia, which remained under Prussian control at the end of the War of the Austrian Succession (1740–48). Frederick retained Silesia even after facing a coalition of France, Austria, and Russia during the Seven Years' War (1756–63). Frederick expanded Prussian territory still further in 1772, when, with his erstwhile enemies Russia and Austria, he took part in the First Partition of Poland. This last seizure was highly beneficial to Frederick because it linked eastern Prussia with much of his kingdom's western holdings.

Although Prussia and Austria were rivals, they had some important characteristics in common. Neither state was populated by a single people, but by numerous peoples speaking different languages and belonging to different religions. Neither state was located entirely within the empire. Both had sizable territories to the east of the empire, and it was there that they hoped mainly to expand. Both states were governed by enlightened monarchs, who, having only to cajole the nobility with occasional concessions, saw government as for the people but not by the people. Hence, both states were governed by the most efficient methods known to the eighteenth century, and both were fairly tolerant according to the standards of the time. Prussia accepted many Protestants expelled from other states, most notably the Huguenots who fled France after the Edict of Nantes in 1685. Austria became one of the first states to allow Jews to settle where they liked within its boundaries and to practice the professions of their choice.

The Smaller States

By the eighteenth century, none of the other states of the empire were strong enough to have territorial ambitions to match those of Prussia and Austria. Some of the larger states, such as Saxony, Bavaria, and Württemberg, also maintained standing armies, but their smaller size compelled them to seek allies, some from outside the empire. With the exception of the free cities and ecclesiastical states, smaller states, like Austria and Prussia, were governed by a hereditary monarch who ruled either with the consent or help of the nobility and with the help of an increasingly well-trained bureaucracy. Only a few states, such as Württemberg, could boast of an active democracy of the kind evolving in Britain and France. Except in a few free cities, such as Frankfurt am Main and Hamburg, which were active in international trade, Germany's commercial class was neither strong nor self-confident. Farmers in western Germany were largely free; those in the east were often serfs. However, whether in the east or the west, most who worked the land lived at the subsistence level.

*Frederick the Great, king of
Prussia, 1740–86
Courtesy German
Information Center, New York*

Despite its lack of popular democracy, Germany was generally well governed. The state bureaucracies gained in power
and expertise, and efficiency and probity were esteemed. During the eighteenth century, the principles of the Enlightenment came to be widely disseminated and applied. Although
there were no political challenges to enlightened absolutism,
as was the case in France, all phenomena, including religion,
were subject to critical, reasoned examination to determine
their rationality. In this more tolerant environment, differing
religious views could still create social friction, but ways were
found for the empire's three main religions—Roman Catholicism, Lutheranism, and Calvinism—to coexist in most states.
The expulsion of about 20,000 Protestants from the ecclesiastical state of Salzburg during 1731–32 was viewed by the educated public at the time as a harking back to less enlightened
days.

Several new universities were founded, some soon considered among Europe's best. An increasingly literate public made
possible a jump in the number of journals and newspapers. At
the end of the seventeenth century, most books printed in Germany were in Latin. By the end of the next century, all but 5
percent were in German. The eighteenth century also saw a
refinement of the German language and a flowering of German literature with the appearance of such figures as Gotthold

Lessing, Johann Wolfgang von Goethe, and Friedrich Schiller. German music also reached great heights with the Bach family, George Frederick Handel, Joseph Haydn, and Wolfgang Amadeus Mozart.

The French Revolution and Germany

The French Revolution, which erupted in 1789 with the storming of the Bastille in Paris, at first gained the enthusiastic approval of some German intellectuals, who welcomed the proclamation of a constitution and a bill of rights. Within a few years, most of this support had dissipated, replaced by fear of a newly aggressive French nationalism and horror at the execution of the revolution's opponents. In 1792 French troops invaded Germany and were at first pushed back by imperial forces. But at the Battle of Valmy in late 1792, the French army, a revolutionary citizens' army fighting on its own soil, defeated the professional imperial army. By 1794 France had secured control of the Rhineland, which it was to occupy for twenty years.

During the Rhineland occupation, France followed its traditional policy of keeping Austria and Prussia apart and manipulating the smaller German states. In observance of the Treaty of Basel of 1795, Prussian and German forces north of the Main River ceased efforts against the French. Austria endured repeated defeats at the hands of the French, most notably at the Battle of Austerlitz in 1805. At this battle, Russians fought alongside Austrians against the French, who were aided by forces from several south German states, including Bavaria, Baden, and Württemberg.

Prussia reentered the war against France in 1806, but its forces were badly beaten at the Battle of Jena that same year. Prussia was abandoned by its ally Russia and lost territory as a result of the Treaty of Tilsit in 1807. These national humiliations motivated the Prussians to undertake a serious program of social and military reform. The most noted of the reformers—Karl vom Stein, Karl August von Hardenberg, Wilhelm von Humboldt, and Gerhard von Scharnhorst, along with many others—improved the country's laws, education, administration, and military organization. Scharnhorst, responsible for military reforms, emphasized the importance to the army of moral incentives, personal courage, and individual responsibility. He also introduced the principle of competition and abandoned the privileges accorded to nobility within the officer corps. A revitalized Prussia joined with Austria and Russia to defeat Napoleon at the Battle of Leipzig in late 1813 and drove him out of Germany. Prussian forces under General Gebhard von Blücher were essential to the final victory over Napoleon at the Battle of Waterloo in 1815.

Despite Napoleon's defeat, some of the changes he had brought to Germany during the French occupation were retained. Public administration was improved, feudalism was weakened, the power of the trade guilds was reduced, and the Napoleonic Code replaced traditional legal codes in many areas. The new legal code was popular and remained in effect in the Rhineland until 1900. As a result of these reforms, some areas of Germany were better prepared for the coming of industrialization in the nineteenth century.

French occupation authorities also allowed many smaller states, ecclesiastical entities, and free cities to be incorporated into their larger neighbors. Approximately 300 states had existed within the Holy Roman Empire in 1789; only about forty remained by 1814. The empire ceased to exist in 1806 when Francis II of Austria gave up his imperial title. In its place, Napoleon had created the Confederation of the Rhine, made up of the states of western and southern Germany, under French direction. Austria and Prussia were not members. The confederation was to provide Napoleon with troops for his military campaigns. After his defeat, the confederation was dissolved.

The German Confederation, 1815–66

The Congress of Vienna (1814–15), convened after Napoleon's defeat, sought to restore order to a Europe disrupted by revolutionary and imperial France. Its members' objective was a constellation of states and a balance of power that would ensure peace and stability after a quarter-century of revolution and war. In addition to the delegates of many small states, the congress included representatives of five large European states: Austria, Prussia, Russia, Britain, and France. After months of deliberations, the congress established an international political order that was to endure for nearly 100 years and that brought Europe a measure of peace.

The congress made no effort to restore the Holy Roman Empire and its 300-odd states. Instead, it accepted the disappearance of many small states that had occurred since 1789 and created the German Confederation. The confederation consisted of thirty-eight sovereign states and four free cities and included the five large kingdoms of Austria, Prussia, Saxony, Bavaria, and Württemberg (see fig. 4). The confederation met at a diet in Frankfurt, with an Austrian always serving as president.

Prince Clemens von Metternich, who directed Austria's foreign policy from 1809 until 1848, was the dominant political figure within the confederation. He waged a decades-long campaign to prevent the spread of revolution in Europe by seeking to restore much of the political and social order that had existed before the French Revolution. Metternich's Carlsbad Decrees of 1819 established a pervasive system of press censorship and regulation of the universities that dampened German intellectual life and hindered the publication of writings advocating the principles of liberalism. In the 1820s, he engineered the formation of the Holy Alliance of the monarchs of Austria, Prussia, and Russia to quash political, social, and economic developments within Central and Eastern Europe thought to threaten political stability.

Economic and Political Trends Toward Unification

It was not possible for Metternich and his allies to suppress completely the desire for liberal reforms, including the establishment of constitutional parliamentary government, economic freedom, and civil liberties. Some of these reforms had already been under discussion during the eighteenth-century Enlightenment, and awareness of their desirability had spread during the Napoleonic era. In addition, the economic reforms introduced into the Rhineland by France had taken hold. The business class that formed after 1815 pressed for abolition of restrictive trade practices favored by traditional handicraft guilds. Businessmen also sought a common currency and system of measurements for Germany, as well as a reduction of the numerous tolls that made road and river travel expensive and slow.

During the 1820s, significant progress was made in reducing customs duties among German states. At Prussian instigation, the Zollverein (Customs Union) began to form, and by the mid-1830s it included all the most important German states except Austria. Prussia saw to it that its chief rival within Germany was excluded from the union. Vienna, for its part, did not realize at this early point the political and economic significance of intra-German trade.

Many of Germany's liberal intelligentsia—lower government officials, men of letters, professors, and lawyers—who pushed for representative government and greater political freedom were also interested in some form of German unity. They argued that liberal political reforms could only be enacted in a larger political entity. Germany's small, traditional states offered little scope for political reform.

Among those groups desiring reform, there was, ironically, little unity. Many businessmen were interested only in reforms that would facilitate commerce, and they gave little thought to politics. Political liberals were split into a number of camps. Some wished for a greater degree of political representation, but, given a widespread fear of what the masses might do if they had access to power, these liberals were content to have aristocrats as leaders. Others desired a democratic constitution, but with a hereditary king as ruler. A minority of liberals were ardent democrats who desired to establish a republic with parliamentary democracy and universal suffrage.

The ideal of a united Germany had been awakened within liberal groups by the writings of scholars and literary figures such as Johann Gottfried Herder (1744–1803) and by the achievements of French nationalism after the revolution. France's easy victories over Germany's small states made the union of a people with a common language and historical memory desirable for practical reasons alone. Others were impressed by the political and commercial accomplishments of Britain, which made those of the small German states seem insignificant. Some writers warmed to romantic evocations of Germany's glory during the Middle Ages.

Many members of Germany's aristocratic ruling class were opposed to national unity because they feared it would mean the disappearance of their small states into a large Germany. Metternich opposed a united Germany because the Habsburg Empire did not embrace a single people speaking one language, but many peoples speaking different languages. The empire would not easily fit into a united Germany. He desired instead the continued existence of the loosely organized German Confederation with its forty-odd members, none equal to Austria in strength. Prussia's kings and its conservative elite sometimes objected to Austria's primacy in the confederation, but they had little desire for German unification, which they regarded as a potential threat to Prussia's existence.

Germany's lower classes—farmers, artisans, and factory workers—were not included in the discussions about political and economic reform. Germany's farmers had been freed to some degree from many obligations and dues owed to the landowning aristocracy, but they were often desperately poor, earning barely enough to survive. Farmers west of the Elbe River usually had properties too small to yield any kind of prosperity. Farmers east of the Elbe often were landless laborers hired to work on large estates. Artisans, that is, skilled workers in handicrafts and trades belonging to the traditional guilds, saw their economic position worsen as a result of the industrialization that had begun to appear in Germany after 1815. The guilds attempted to stop factory construction and unrestricted commerce, but strong economic trends ran counter to their wishes. Factory workers, in contrast, were doing well compared with these other groups and were generally content with their lot when the economy as a whole prospered.

The Revolutions of 1848

Europe endured hard times during much of the 1840s. A series of bad harvests culminating in the potato blight of 1845–46 brought widespread misery and some starvation. An economic depression added to the hardship, spreading discontent among the poor and the middle class alike. A popular uprising in Paris in February 1848 turned into a revolution, forcing the French king Louis Philippe to flee to Britain.

The success of the revolution sparked revolts elsewhere in Europe. Numerous German cities were shaken by uprisings in which crowds consisting mainly of the urban poor, but also of students and members of the liberal middle class, stormed their rulers' palaces and demanded fundamental reform. Berlin and Vienna were especially hard hit by what came to be called the revolutions of 1848. The rulers of both cities, like rulers elsewhere, quickly acceded to the demands of their rebellious subjects and promised constitutions and representative government. Conservative governments fell, and Metternich fled to Britain. Liberals called for a national convention to draft a constitution for all of Germany. The National Assembly, consisting of about 800 delegates from throughout Germany, met in a church in Frankfurt, the Paulskirche, from May 1848 to March 1849 for this purpose.

The Restoration

Within just a few months, liberal hopes for a reformed Germany were disappointed. Conservative forces saw that the liberal movement was divided into a number of camps having sharply different aims. Furthermore, the liberals had little support left among the lower classes, who had supported them in the first weeks of the revolution by constructing barricades and massing before their rulers' palaces. Few liberals desired popular democracy or were willing to enact radical economic reforms that would help farmers and artisans. As a result of this timidity, the masses deserted the liberals. Thus, conservatives were able to win sizable elements of these groups to their side by promising to address their concerns. Factory workers had largely withheld support from the liberal cause because they earned relatively good wages compared with farmers and artisans.

Once the conservatives regrouped and launched their successful counterattack across Germany, many of the reforms promised in March 1848 were forgotten. The National Assembly published the constitution it had drafted during months of hard debate. It proposed the unification of Germany as a federation with a hereditary emperor and a parliament with delegates elected directly. The constitution resolved the dispute between supporters of "Little Germany," that is, a united Germany that would exclude Austria and the Habsburg Empire, and those supporting "Large Germany," which would include both. The constitution advocated the latter.

The Prussian king, Friedrich Wilhelm IV (r. 1840–58), was elected united Germany's first emperor. He refused the crown, stating that he could be elected only by other kings. At that point, the assembly disbanded. A few subsequent rebellions by democratic liberals drew some popular support in 1849, but they were easily crushed and their leaders executed or imprisoned. Some of these ardent democrats fled to the United States. Among them was Carl Schurz, who later fought at the Battle of Gettysburg as a Union officer, served one term as a United States senator from Missouri, and was appointed secretary of the interior by United States president Rutherford B. Hayes.

The German Confederation was reestablished, and conservatives held the reins of power even more tightly than before. The failure of the 1848 revolutions also meant that Germany was not united as many had hoped. However, some of the liberals' more practical proposals came to fruition later in the 1850s and 1860s when it was realized that they were essential to economic efficiency. Many commercial restrictions were abolished. The guilds, with their desire to turn back the clock and restore preindustrial conditions, were defeated, and impediments to the free use of capital were reduced. The "hungry forties" gave way to the prosperity of the 1850s as the German economy modernized and laid the foundations for spectacular growth later in the century.

Bismarck and Unification

Liberal hopes for German unification were not met during the politically turbulent 1848–49 period. A Prussian plan for a smaller union was dropped in late 1850 after Austria threatened Prussia with war. Despite this setback, desire for some kind of German unity, either with or without Austria, grew during the 1850s and 1860s. It was no longer a notion cherished by a few, but had proponents in all social classes. An indication of this wider range of support was the change of mind about German nationalism experienced by an obscure Prussian diplomat, Otto von Bismarck. He had been an adamant opponent of German nationalism in the late 1840s. During the 1850s, however, Bismarck had concluded that Prussia would have to harness German nationalism for its own purposes if it were to thrive. He believed too that Prussia's well-being depended on wresting primacy in Germany from its traditional enemy, Austria.

In 1862 King Wilhelm I of Prussia (r. 1858–88) chose Bismarck to serve as his minister president. Descended from the Junker, Prussia's aristocratic landowning class, Bismarck hated parliamentary democracy and championed the dominance of the monarchy and aristocracy. However, gifted at judging political forces and sizing up a situation, Bismarck contended that conservatives would have to come to terms with other social groups if they were to continue to direct Prussian affairs. The king had summoned Bismarck to direct Prussia's government in the face of the Prussian parliament's refusal to pass a budget because it disagreed with army reforms desired by the king and his military advisers. Although he could not secure parliament's consent to the government's budget, Bismarck was a tactician skilled and ruthless enough to govern without parliament's consent from 1862 to 1866.

Otto von Bismarck, 1815–98, united Germany under a Prussian emperor.
Courtesy German Information Center, New York

As an ardent and aggressive Prussian nationalist, Bismarck had long been an opponent of Austria because both states sought primacy within the same area—Germany. Austria had been weakened by reverses abroad, including the loss of territory in Italy, and by the 1860s, because of clumsy diplomacy, had no foreign allies outside Germany. Bismarck used a diplomatic dispute to provoke Austria to declare war on Prussia in 1866. Against expectations, Prussia quickly won the Seven Weeks' War (also known as the Austro-Prussian War) against Austria and its south German allies. Bismarck imposed a lenient peace on Austria because he recognized that Prussia might later need the Austrians as allies. But he dealt harshly with the other German states that had resisted Prussia and expanded Prussian territory by annexing Hanover, Schleswig-Holstein, some smaller states, and the city of Frankfurt. The German Confederation was replaced by the North German Confederation and was furnished with both a constitution and a parliament. Austria was excluded from Germany. South German states outside the confederation—Baden, Württemberg, and Bavaria—were tied to Prussia by military alliances.

Bismarck's military and political successes were remarkable, but the first had been achieved at considerable risk, and the second were by no means complete. Luck had played a part in the decisive victory at the Battle of Königgrätz (Hradec Králóve in the present-day Czech Republic); otherwise, the war might have lasted much longer than it did. None of the larger German states had supported either Prussia's war or the formation of the North German Confederation led by Prussia. The states that formed what is often called the Third Germany, that is, Germany exclusive of Austria and Prussia, did not desire to come under the control of either of those states. None of them wished to be pulled into a war that showed little likelihood of benefiting any of them. In the Seven Weeks' War, the support they gave Austria had been lukewarm.

In 1870 Bismarck engineered another war, this time against France. The conflict would become known to history as the Franco-Prussian War. Nationalistic fervor was ignited by the promised annexation of Lorraine and Alsace, which had belonged to the Holy Roman Empire and had been seized by France in the seventeenth century. With this goal in sight, the south German states eagerly joined in the war against the country that had come to be seen as Germany's traditional enemy. Bismarck's major war aim—the voluntary entry of the south German states into a constitutional German nation-state— occurred during the patriotic frenzy generated by stunning military victories against French forces in the fall of 1870. Months before a peace treaty was signed with France in May 1871, a united Germany was established as the German Empire, and the Prussian king, Wilhelm I, was crowned its emperor in the Hall of Mirrors at Versailles.

Imperial Germany

The German Empire—often called the Second Reich to distinguish it from the First Reich, established by Charlemagne in 800—was based on two compromises. The first was between the king of Prussia and the rulers of the other German states, who agreed to accept him as the kaiser (emperor) of a united Germany, provided they could continue to rule their states largely as they had in the past. The second was the agreement among many segments of German society to accept a unified Germany based on a constitution that combined a powerful authoritarian monarchy with a weak representative body, the Reichstag, elected by universal male suffrage. No one was completely satisfied with the bargain. The kaiser had to contend with a parliament elected by the people in a secret vote. The people were represented in a parliament having limited control over the kaiser.

As had been the tradition in Prussia, the kaiser controlled foreign policy and the army through his handpicked ministers, who formed the government and prepared legislation. The government was headed by a chancellor, also selected by the kaiser, who served in this post at the kaiser's pleasure and could be dismissed by him at any time. The Bundesrat (Federal Council) represented Germany's princes. About one-third of its seats were held by Prussians. Conceived as an upper house to the Reichstag, the Bundesrat, like the Reichstag, was required to vote on legislation drawn up by the government before it became law. The Reichstag had no power to draft legislation. In addition, the government's actions were not subject to the Reichstag's approval, and the government was not drawn from the Reichstag, as is ordinarily the case in parliamentary democracies.

The government needed the approval of the Bundesrat and the Reichstag to enact legislative proposals, and the kaiser and his chancellor had many means of securing this approval. Conservative in nature, the Bundesrat was usually docile and needed little wooing. Compliant in the early years of the empire, the Reichstag, by contrast, became less so with time. The easiest means of controlling the Reichstag was to threaten it with new elections in the hope of getting a legislative body more attuned to the intentions of the government. During elections the government campaigned for the parties it favored, sometimes cynically conjuring up fears of national catastrophe if particular parties won many seats. The government also bargained with parties, granting them what they sought in exchange for votes. A last means of taming the Reichstag was to spread rumors of a possible coup d'état by the army and the repeal of the constitution and universal suffrage. This technique was used repeatedly in imperial Germany and could even frighten the conservative Bundesrat. However little many of the Reichstag members might like the empire's political order, the prospect of naked despotism pleased them even less.

Although the Reichstag did not wield real power, elections to it were hotly contested, and Bismarck and later chancellors and governments were concerned with their outcome. As more-democratic parties came to dominate in the Reichstag, governing became more difficult for the kaiser and his officials. During the later decades of the reign of Wilhelm II (r. 1888–1918), the empire's governing system experienced such difficulties that some conservatives advocated scrapping it, and democrats argued for a new, truly parliamentary system. A fear of these drastic choices and their possible effects caused Germany to muddle through with the existing system until the disaster of World War I culminated in that system's abolition.

Political Parties

Six major political parties were active in imperial Germany: the Conservative Party, the Free Conservative Party, the National Liberal Party, the Progressive Party, the Center Party, and the Social Democratic Party of Germany (Sozial-demokratische Partei Deutschlands—SPD). Only the SPD survived both the empire and the Weimar Republic (1918–33) and came to play a vital role in the Federal Republic. Even though the German Empire lacked a genuinely democratic system, the six main parties accurately reflected the interests and hopes of most of its people.

The most right-wing of the six parties was the Conservative Party, which represented Prussian nationalism, aristocracy, and landed property. Many of its members remained opposed to German unification because they feared Prussia's gradual absorption by the empire. The Conservatives also detested the Reichstag because it was elected by universal suffrage. The Free Conservative Party represented industrialists and large commercial interests. The views of this party most closely matched those of Bismarck. Its members supported unification because they saw it as unavoidable. The National Liberal Party was composed of liberals who had accepted Germany's lack of full democracy because they valued national unity more. They continued to favor a laissez-faire economic policy and secularization. In time, National Liberals became some of the strongest supporters of the acquisition of colonies and a substantial naval buildup, both key issues in the 1880s and 1890s.

Unlike the members of the National Liberal Party, members of the Progressive Party remained faithful to all the principles of European liberalism and championed the extension of parliament's powers. This party was in the forefront of those opposed to the authoritarian rule of Bismarck and his successors. The Center Party was Germany's Roman Catholic party and had strong support in southern Germany, the Rhineland, and in parts of Prussia with significant Polish populations. It was conservative regarding monarchical authority but progressive in matters of social reform. Bismarck's brutal campaign against the Roman Catholic Church in the 1870s—the Kulturkampf (cultural struggle), an attempt to reduce the church's power over education and its role in many other areas of German society—turned the Center Party against him. By the late 1870s, Bismarck had to concede victory to the party, which had become stronger through its resistance to the government's persecution. The party remained important during the Weimar Republic and was the forerunner of the Federal Republic's moderate conservative parties, the Christian Democratic Union (Christlich Demokratische Union—CDU) and the Christian Social Union (Christlich-Soziale Union—CSU).

The Marxist SPD was founded in Gotha in 1875, a fusion of Ferdinand Lassalle's General German Workers' Association (formed in 1863), which advocated state socialism, and the Social Democratic Labor Party (formed in 1869), headed by August Bebel and Wilhelm Liebknecht, which aspired to establish a classless communist society. The SPD advocated a mixture of revolution and quiet work within the parliamentary system. The clearest statement of this impossible combination was the Erfurt Program of 1891. The former method frightened nearly all Germans to the party's right, while the latter would build the SPD into the largest party in the Reichstag after the elections of 1912.

Once Bismarck gave up his campaign against Germany's Roman Catholics, whom he had seen for a time as a Vatican-controlled threat to the stability of the empire, he attacked the SPD with a series of antisocialist laws beginning in 1878. A positive aspect of Bismarck's campaign to contain the SPD was a number of laws passed in the 1880s establishing national health insurance and old-age pensions. Bismarck's hope was that if workers were protected by the government, they would come to support it and see no need for revolution. Bismarck's antisocialist campaign, which continued until his dismissal in 1890 by Wilhelm II, severely restricted the activities of the SPD. Ironically, the laws may have inadvertently benefited the SPD by forcing it to work within legal channels. As a result of its sustained activity within the political system, the SPD became a cautious, pragmatic party, which, despite its fiery Marxist rhetoric, won increasing numbers of seats in the Reichstag and achieved some improvements in working and living conditions for Germany's working class.

The Economy and Population Growth

Germany experienced an economic boom immediately after

unification. For the first time, the country was a single economic entity, and old impediments to internal trade were lifted. The federal chancellery published a new commercial code and established a uniform currency. The indemnity that France had to pay Germany after losing the 1870–71 war provided capital for railroad construction and building projects. A speculative boom resulted, characterized by large-scale formation of joint-stock companies and unscrupulous investment practices. This period of intense financial speculation and construction, called by Germans the Gründerzeit (founders' time), ended with the stock market crash of 1873.

Despite the crash and several subsequent periods of economic depression, Germany's economy grew rapidly. By 1900 it rivaled the more-established British economy as the world's largest. German coal production, about one-third of Britain's in 1880, increased sixfold by 1913, almost equaling British yields that year. German steel production increased more than tenfold in the same period, surpassing British production by far.

Industrialization began later in Germany than in Britain, and the German economy was not a significant part of the world economy until late in the nineteenth century. Germany's industrialization started with the building of railroads in the 1840s and 1850s and the subsequent development of coal mining and iron and steel production, activities that made up what is called the First Industrial Revolution. In Germany, the Second Industrial Revolution, that is, the growth of chemical and electrical industries, followed the enormous expansion of coal and steel production so closely that the country can be said to have experienced the two revolutions almost simultaneously. Germany took an early lead in the chemical and electrical industries. Its chemists became renowned for their discoveries, and by 1914 the country was producing half the world's electrical equipment. As a result of these developments, Germany became the continent's industrial giant.

Germany's population also expanded rapidly, growing from 41.0 million in 1871 to 49.7 million in 1891 and 65.3 million in 1911. The expanding and industrializing economy changed the way this rapidly expanding population earned its livelihood. In 1871 about 49 percent of the workforce was engaged in agriculture; by 1907 only 35 percent was. In the same period, industry's share of the rapidly growing workforce rose from 31 percent to 40 percent. Urban birth rates were often the country's highest, but there was much migration from rural areas to urban areas, where most industry was located. Berlin, by far the country's largest city and a major industrial center, grew from almost 1 million inhabitants in 1875 to 2 million in 1910. Many smaller cities, especially those in areas with much industry—such as the Ruhr region, the upper Rhine Valley, the Neckar Valley, and Saxony—tripled or quadrupled in size during this period.

The Tariff Agreement of 1879 and Its Social Consequences

The crash of 1873 and the subsequent depression began the gradual dissolution of Bismarck's alliance with the National Liberals that had begun after his triumphs of 1866. In the late 1870s, Bismarck began negotiations with the economically protectionist Conservative Party and Center Party toward the formation of a new government coalition. Conservative electoral gains and National Liberal losses in 1879 brought a conservative coalition to power. Bismarck then abandoned his former allies in the National Liberal Party and put in place a system of tariffs that benefited the landed gentry of eastern Prussia—threatened by imports of cheaper grains from Russia and the United States—and industrialists who were afraid to compete with cheaper foreign manufactured goods and who believed they needed more time to establish themselves.

Bismarck's alliance with the Prussian landowning class and powerful industrialists and the parties representing their interests had profound social effects. From that point on, conservative groups had the upper hand in German society. The German middle class began to imitate its conservative social superiors rather than attempt to impose its own liberal, middle-class values on Germany. The prestige of the military became so great that many middle-class males sought to enhance their social standing by becoming officers in the reserves. The middle classes also became more susceptible to the nationalistic clamor for colonies and "a place in the sun" that was to become ever more virulent in the next few decades.

Bismarck's Foreign Policy

Bismarck sincerely regarded the new German Empire as "satiated," that is, having no desire to expand further and hence posing no threat to its neighbors. The chancellor held that the country had to adjust to its new circumstances and that this would take decades. For this reason, he sought to convince the other European states of Germany's desire to live in peace, hoping thereby to secure Germany against attack. He aimed to arrange this security through a system of alliances. Believing that France would remain Germany's enemy because of the annexation of Alsace-Lorraine, an action he had opposed because of the enmity it would cause, he turned to other states.

Bismarck arranged an alliance with Austria-Hungary in 1879 and one with Italy in 1882. His triumph, however, was a secret alliance he formed by means of the Reinsurance Treaty with Russia in 1887, although its terms violated the spirit of the treaty with Austria-Hungary. However much these agreements contributed to German security, Bismarck's plunge into the European scramble for overseas colonies ultimately weakened it by awakening British fears about Germany's long-term geopolitical aims. Subsequent feelers he put out with a view to establishing an understanding with Britain were rebuffed. In 1890 Bismarck was dismissed by young Kaiser Wilhelm over a dispute about antisocialist legislation.

Foreign Policy in the Wilhelmine Era

Foreign policy in the Wilhelmine Era (1890–1914) turned away from Bismarck's cautious diplomacy of the 1871–90 period. It was also marked by a shrill aggressiveness. Brusque, clumsy diplomacy was backed by increased armaments production, most notably the creation of a large fleet of battleships capable of challenging the British navy. This new bellicosity alarmed the rest of Europe, and by about 1907 German policy makers had succeeded in creating Bismarck's nightmare: a Germany "encircled" by an alliance of hostile neighbors—in this case Russia, France, and Britain—in an alliance called the Triple Entente.

The first brick to fall out of Bismarck's carefully crafted edifice was Germany's Reinsurance Treaty with Russia. Harmed by Prussian trade policies, Russia did not renew the treaty and instead turned to France for economic assistance and military security. The two countries formally allied in early 1893. Britain joined them in 1907, even though France and Britain had nearly gone to war over a colonial dispute in 1898. Britain's main reason for abandoning its usual posture as an aloof observer of developments on the continent was Germany's plan to build a fleet of sixty battleships of the formidable Dreadnought class.

The German naval expansion program had many domestic supporters. The kaiser deeply admired the navy of his grandmother, Queen Victoria of Britain, and wanted one as large for himself. Powerful lobbying groups in Germany desired a large navy to give Germany a worldwide role and to protect a growing German colonial empire in Africa and the Pacific. Industry wanted large government contracts. Some political parties promoted naval expansion and an aggressive foreign policy to win votes from a nervous electorate they kept worked up with jingoistic rhetoric.

The chief figure in promoting the naval buildup was Admiral Alfred von Tirpitz, who is considered the founder of the modern German navy. Tirpitz was an effective spokesman for the program and had the ear of the kaiser and his advisers. In 1898, after the Reichstag passed the first Naval Bill, Anglo-German relations deteriorated. The Supplementary Naval Act of 1900 further strained relations with Britain, as did a proposed Berlin-Baghdad railroad through the Ottoman Empire, a project that threatened British as well as Russian interests in the Balkans. Two crises over Morocco, in 1905 and 1911, drove France and Britain closer together and made for a tense international atmosphere. The great powers remained neutral during the Balkan Wars (1912–13), a nationalist rebellion against Ottoman rule, but European tensions were increased still further, and the expectation that there would eventually be war on the continent became more certain.

The assassination of Archduke Franz Ferdinand in Sarajevo on June 28, 1914, set off a series of diplomatic and military decisions that would end peace in Europe. The kaiser gave a so-called blank check to his ally, Austria-Hungary, saying that Germany would support any Habsburg measure taken against Serbia, which had backed the assassination. Austria-Hungary's ultimatum to Serbia in late July was so harsh that war became inevitable. Within days, a set of interlocking alliances had Europe's great powers embroiled in what would become World War I.

World War I

Germany's leadership had hoped for a limited war between Austria-Hungary and Serbia. But because Russian forces had been mobilized in support of Serbia, the German leadership made the decision to support its ally. The Schlieffen Plan, based on the assumption that Germany would face a two-front war because of a French-Russian alliance, required a rapid invasion through neutral Belgium to ensure the quick defeat of France. Once the western front was secure, the bulk of German forces could attack and defeat Russia, which would not yet be completely ready for war because it would mobilize its gigantic forces slowly.

Despite initial successes, Germany's strategy failed, and its troops became tied down in trench warfare in France. For the next four years, there would be little progress in the west, where advances were usually measured in meters rather than in kilometers. Under the command of Paul von Hindenburg and Erich Ludendorff, the army scored a number of significant victories against Russia. But it was only in early 1918 that Russia was defeated. Even after this victory in the east, however, Germany remained mired in a long war for which it had not prepared.

Germany's war aims were annexationist in nature and foresaw an enlarged Germany, with Belgium and Poland as vassal states and with colonies in Africa. In its first years, there was widespread support for the war. Even the SPD supported it, considering it a defensive effort and voting in favor of war credits. By 1916, however, opposition to the war had mounted within the general population, which had to endure many hardships, including food shortages. A growing number of Reichstag deputies came to demand a peace without annexations. Frustrated in its quest for peace, in April 1917 a segment of the SPD broke with the party and formed the Independent Social Democratic Party of Germany. In July the Reichstag passed a resolution calling for a peace without annexations. In its wake, Chancellor Theobald von Bethmann Hollweg was forced to resign, and Hindenburg and Ludendorff came to exercise a control over Germany until late 1918 that amounted to a virtual military dictatorship.

Military leaders refused a moderate peace because they were convinced until very late in the war that victory ultimately would be theirs. Another reason for their insistence on a settlement that fulfilled expansionist aims was that the government had not financed the war with higher taxes but with bonds. Taxes had been seen as unnecessary because it was expected that the government would redeem these bonds after the war with payments from Germany's vanquished enemies. Thus, only an expansionist victory would keep the state solvent and save millions of German bondholders from financial ruin.

After the Bolshevik Revolution of November 1917, Russia and Germany began peace negotiations. In March 1918, the two countries signed the Treaty of Brest-Litovsk. The defeat of Russia enabled Germany to transfer troops from the eastern to the western front. Two large offensives in the west were met by an Allied counteroffensive that began in July. German troops were pressed back, and it became evident to many officers that Germany could not win the war. In September Ludendorff recommended that Germany sue for peace. In October extensive reforms democratized the Reichstag and gave Germany a constitutional monarchy. A coalition of progressive forces was formed, headed by SPD politician Friedrich Ebert. The military allowed the birth of a democratic parliament because it did not want to be held responsible for the inevitable armistice that would end the war on terms highly unfavorable to Germany. Instead, the civilian government that signed the truce was to take the blame for the nation's defeat.

The political reforms of October were overshadowed by a popular uprising that began on November 3 when sailors in Kiel mutinied. They refused to go out on what they considered a suicide mission against British naval forces. The revolt grew quickly and within a week appeared to be burgeoning into a revolution that could well overthrow the established social order. On November 9, the kaiser was forced to abdicate, and the SPD proclaimed a republic. A provisional government headed by Ebert promised elections for a national assembly to draft a new constitution. In an attempt to control the popular uprising, Ebert agreed to back the army if it would suppress the revolt. On November 11, the government signed the armistice that ended the war. Germany's loses included about 1.6 million dead and more than 4 million wounded.

Signed in June 1919, the Treaty of Versailles limited Germany to an army of 100,000 soldiers. The treaty also stipulated that the Rhineland be demilitarized and occupied by the western Allies for fifteen years and that Germany surrender Alsace-Lorraine, northern Schleswig-Holstein, a portion of western Prussia that became known as the Polish Corridor because it gave Poland access to the Baltic, and all overseas colonies. Also, an Allied Reparations Commission was established and charged with setting the amount of war-damage payments that would be demanded of Germany. The treaty also included the "war guilt clause," ascribing responsibility for World War I to Germany and Austria-Hungary.

The Weimar Republic, 1918–33

The Weimar Constitution

The Weimar Republic, proclaimed on November 9, 1918, was born in the throes of military defeat and social revolution. In January 1919, a National Assembly was elected to draft a constitution. The government, composed of members from the assembly, came to be called the Weimar coalition and included the SPD; the German Democratic Party (Deutsche Demokratische Partei—DDP), a descendant of the Progressive Party of the prewar period; and the Center Party. The percentage of the vote gained by this coalition of parties in favor of the republic (76.2 percent, with 38 percent for the SPD alone) suggested broad popular support for the republic. The antirepublican, conservative German National People's Party (Deutschnationale Volkspartei—DNVP) and the German People's Party (Deutsche Volkspartei—DVP) received a combined total of 10.3 percent of the vote. The Independent Social Democratic Party of Germany, which had split from the SPD during the war, won 8 percent of the vote. In February the assembly elected Friedrich Ebert as the republic's first president.

In mid-1919 the assembly ratified the constitution of the new Weimar Republic, so named because its constitution was drafted in the small city where the poets Goethe and Schiller had lived. The constitution established a federal republic consisting of nineteen states (*Länder*, sing., *Land*) (see fig. 5). The republic's government was a mixed strong president and parliamentary system, with the president seen by many as a sort of substitute kaiser. The president was elected by popular direct ballot to a seven-year term and could be reelected. He appointed the chancellor and, pursuant to the chancellor's nominations, also appointed the cabinet ministers. However, the cabinet had to reflect the party composition of the Reichstag and was also responsible to this body. Election to the Reichstag was by secret ballot and popular vote. Suffrage was universal. Thus, Germany had a truly democratic parliamentary system. However, the president had the right to dismiss the cabinet, dissolve the Reichstag, and veto legislation. The legislative powers of the Reichstag were further weakened by the provision for presidential recourse to popular plebiscite. Article 48, the so-called emergency clause, accorded the president the right to allow the cabinet to govern without the consent of

parliament whenever it was deemed essential to maintaining public order.

Problems of Parliamentary Politics

The Weimar Republic was beset with serious problems from the outset that led many Germans either to withhold support from the new parliamentary democracy or to seek actively to destroy it. The extreme left and much of the right provided the republic's most vitriolic opponents. Its supporters included the bulk of the left, represented by the SPD, and the moderate right, made up of the Center Party and the DDP. However, at key times these supporters failed to behave responsibly because of political inexperience, narrow self-interest, or unrealistic party programs.

The most serious obstacle the new republic faced was the refusal of many Germans to accept its legitimacy. The extreme left regarded it as an instrument of the propertied to prevent revolution, recalling Ebert's agreement with the military in November 1918 that resulted in the army's bloody suppression of the left-wing revolts of late 1918 and early 1919. In the face of this SPD-military alliance, elements of the left considered the SPD as great a barrier to their goals as the conservatives. Represented by the Communist Party of Germany (Kommunistische Partei Deutschlands—KPD), the extreme left felt such an enduring hostility to the Weimar Republic that at times it cooperated with the extreme right in efforts to destroy the republic.

The right posed a graver threat to the Weimar Republic than did the extreme left because it enjoyed the support of most of Germany's establishment: the military, the financial elites, the state bureaucracy, the educational system, and much of the press. Unlike political parties in well-established democracies, the right-wing parties in the Reichstag could not be considered a loyal opposition because their ultimate aim was to abolish the new system of government. The right opposed democracy and desired to establish a conservative authoritarian regime. The right styled those who were party to the armistice and to the Treaty of Versailles as "November criminals" because of Germany's loss of territory and sovereignty and the burden of enormous war reparations. The increasing acceptance by many of the "stab in the back" legend, which attributed Germany's defeat in World War I to the treachery of the SPD and others on the left rather than to the military might of the Allies, intensified the hatred many rightists felt toward the republic. Like some on the extreme left, many on the right used violence, either petty and random or large-scale and concerted, to attain their ends. Throughout the short life of the Weimar Republic, various political groups maintained gangs of youths organized into paramilitary forces.

In addition to venomous political opposition, the republic had to contend with a weak economy plagued by high rates of inflation and unemployment. Inflation was fueled partly by the enormous wartime debts the imperial government had contracted rather than raise taxes to finance the war. Even more inflationary were the enormous war reparations demanded by the Allies, which made economic recovery seem impossible to many objective expert observers. Inflation ruined many middle-class Germans, who saw their savings and pensions wiped out. Unemployment also remained epidemic throughout the 1920s, hurting millions of wage earners and their families. Their economic misery made these groups susceptible to the claims of extremist political parties.

The pervasive social and political discontent growing out of Germans' grievances, justified or not, soon had consequences. A right-wing coup d'état in March 1920, the Kapp Putsch— named for its leader, Wolfgang Kapp—failed only because of a general strike.The military had refused to intervene, although it did brutally suppress some Communist-inspired uprisings shortly thereafter. The establishment's tacit support of unlawful right-wing actions such as the Kapp Putsch and violent repression of the left endured to the end of the Weimar Republic. This support could also be seen in the sentences meted out by the courts to perpetrators of political violence. Right-wing terrorists usually received mild or negligible sentences, while those on the left were dealt with severely, even though left-wing violence was but a fraction of that committed by the right.

Dissatisfaction with the republic was also evident in the June 1920 elections, in which the Weimar coalition lost its majority. A combined total vote of 28.9 percent for the DNVP, a descendant of the prewar Conservatives, and the DVP, composed mainly of National Liberals, reflected German middle-class disillusionment with democracy. Both parties wished to abolish the Weimar constitution. SPD strength fell to 21.7 percent, as some workers defected to the extreme left. The Independent Social Democratic Party of Germany, formed during the war, effectively ceased to exist as some members joined the KPD, formed in December 1918, and the remainder reunited with the SPD.

The Weimar coalition never regained its majority. Because no party ever gained as much as 50 percent of the vote, unstable coalition governments became the rule in the 1920s, and by the end of the decade more than a dozen governments had been formed, none capable of unified action on major problems. The SPD and the Center Party often could agree on questions of foreign policy, such as compliance with the provisions of the Treaty of Versailles, but split on domestic issues. Conversely, the Center Party agreed with parties to its right on domestic issues but split with them on foreign policy. Thus, minority governments were formed that often showed little internal coherence during their brief lives.

The year 1923 was one of crisis for the republic. In January French and Belgian troops occupied the highly industrialized Ruhr area because of German defaults on reparations payments. The Weimar government responded by calling upon the Ruhr population to stop all industrial activity. The government also began printing money at such a rate that it soon became virtually worthless; by the fall of 1923, wheelbarrows were needed to carry enough currency for simple purchases as inflation reached rates beyond comprehension. In 1914 US$1 had equaled 4 marks. By mid-1920, US$1 was worth 40 marks, by early 1922 about 200 marks, a year later 18,000 marks, and by November 1923 4.2 trillion marks. In addition, the country was racked by strikes, paramilitary street violence, and rumors of planned uprisings by both the left and the right. In August, in the midst of this chaos, President Ebert asked Gustav Stresemann, head of the DVP, to form a new government to resolve the crisis.

The Stresemann Era

Stresemann was a *Vernunftrepublikaner,* that is, someone who supported the Weimar Republic because it seemed the best course of action rather than from a firm commitment to parliamentary democracy. During the war, Stresemann had supported imperial aims and desired extensive annexation of foreign territory. After the war, he remained a monarchist and founded the DVP to oppose the republic. In early 1920, he wished for the success of the Kapp Putsch. However, shocked by the assassinations of several prominent politicians, he had gradually come to believe that the effective functioning of the

Weimar Republic was the best safeguard against violent regimes of either the left or the right. He also became convinced that Germany's economic problems and differences with other countries could best be resolved through negotiated agreements.

Chancellor only from August to November 1923, Stresemann headed the "great coalition," an alliance that included the SPD, the Center Party, the DDP, and the DVP. In this brief period, he ended passive resistance in the Ruhr area and introduced measures to bring the currency situation under control. Because of the failure of several coup attempts—including one by Adolf Hitler in Munich—and a general quieting of the atmosphere after these problems had been solved, the Weimar Republic was granted a period of relative tranquillity that lasted until the end of the decade. Overriding issues were by no means settled, but, for a few years, the republic functioned more like an established democracy.

After his resignation from the chancellorship because of opposition from the right and left, Stresemann served as German foreign minister until his death in 1929. A brilliant negotiator and a shrewd diplomat, Stresemann arranged a rapprochement with the Allies. Reparations payments were made easier by the Reichstag's acceptance in mid-1924 of the Dawes Plan, which had been devised by an American banker, Charles G. Dawes, to effect significant reductions in payments until 1929. That year, only months before his death, Stresemann negotiated a further reduction as part of the Young Plan, also named for an American banker, Owen D. Young. The Dawes Plan had also provided for the withdrawal of French and Belgian troops from the Ruhr district, which was completed in 1925. In addition, beginning in the mid-1920s, loans from the United States stimulated the German economy, instigating a period of growth that lasted until 1930.

The Locarno treaties, signed in 1925 by Germany and the Allies, were the centerpiece of Stresemann's attempt at rapprochement with the West. A prerequisite to Germany's admission to the League of Nations in 1926, the treaties formalized German acceptance of the demilitarization of the Rhineland and guaranteed the western frontier as defined by the Treaty of Versailles. Both Britain and Germany preferred to leave the question of the eastern frontier open. In 1926 the German and Soviet governments signed the Treaty of Berlin, which pledged

Germany and the Soviet Union to neutrality in the event of an attack on either country by foreign powers.

The Locarno treaties, the Treaty of Berlin, and Germany's membership in the League of Nations were successes that earned Stresemann world renown. Within Germany, however, these achievements were condemned by many on the right who charged that these agreements implied German recognition of the validity of the Treaty of Versailles. To them, Stresemann's diplomacy, as able as Bismarck's in the opinion of some historians, was tantamount to treachery because Germany was honor bound to take by force that which the rightists felt was owed it. Because of these opinions and continued dissatisfaction on the right with the political system established by the Weimar Constitution, the Center Party and the parties to its right became more right-wing during the latter 1920s, as did even Stresemann's own party, the DVP.

Hitler and the Rise of National Socialism

Adolf Hitler was born in the Austrian border town of Braunau am Inn in 1889. When he was seventeen, he was refused admission to the Vienna Art Academy, having been found insufficiently talented. He remained in Vienna, however, where he led a bohemian existence, acquiring an ideology based on belief in a German master race that was threatened by an international Jewish conspiracy responsible for many of the world's problems. Hitler remained in Vienna until 1913, when he moved to Munich. After serving with bravery in the German army during World War I, he joined the right-wing Bavarian German Workers' Party in 1919. The following year, the party changed its name to the National Socialist German Workers' Party (National-Sozialistische Deutsche Arbeiterpartei—NSDAP). Its members were known as Nazis, a term derived from the German pronunciation of "National." In 1921 Hitler assumed leadership of the NSDAP.

As leader of the NSDAP, Hitler reorganized the party and encouraged the assimilation of other radical right-wing groups. Gangs of unemployed demobilized soldiers were gathered under the command of a former army officer, Ernst Röhm, to form the Storm Troops (Sturmabteilung—SA), Hitler's private army. Under Hitler's leadership, the NSDAP joined with others on the right in denouncing the Weimar Republic and the "November criminals" who had signed the Treaty of Versailles. The postwar economic slump won the party a following among unemployed ex-soldiers, the lower middle class, and small farmers; in 1923 membership totaled about 55,000. General Ludendorff supported the former corporal in the Beer Hall Putsch of November 1923 in Munich, an attempt to overthrow the Bavarian government. The putsch failed, and Hitler received a light sentence of five years, of which he served less than one. Incarcerated in relative comfort, he wrote *Mein Kampf* (My Struggle), in which he set out his long-term political aims.

After the failure of the putsch, Hitler turned to "legal revolution" as the means to power and chose two parallel paths to take the Nazis to that goal. First, the NSDAP would employ propaganda to create a national mass party capable of coming to power through electoral successes. Second, the party would develop a bureaucratic structure and prepare itself to assume roles in government. Beginning in the mid-1920s, Nazi groups sprang up in other parts of Germany. In 1927 the NSDAP organized the first Nuremberg party congress, a mass political rally. By 1928 party membership exceeded 100,000; the Nazis, however, polled only 2.6 percent of the vote in the Reichstag elections in May.

A mere splinter party in 1928, the NSDAP became better known the following year when it formed an alliance with the DNVP to launch a plebiscite against the Young Plan on the issue of reparations. The DNVP's leader, Alfred Hugenberg, owner of a large newspaper chain, considered Hitler's spellbinding oratory a useful means of attracting votes. The DNVP-NSDAP union brought the NSDAP within the framework of a socially influential coalition of the antirepublican right. As a result, Hitler's party acquired respectability and access to wealthy contributors.

Had it not been for the economic collapse that began with the Wall Street stock market crash of October 1929, Hitler probably would not have come to power. The Great Depression hit Germany hard because the German economy's well-being depended on short-term loans from the United States. Once these loans were recalled, Germany was devastated. Unemployment went from 8.5 percent in 1929 to 14 percent in 1930, to 21.9 percent in 1931, and, at its peak, to 29.9 percent in 1932. Compounding the effects of the Depression were the drastic economic measures taken by Center Party politician Heinrich Brüning, who served as chancellor from March 1930 until the end of May 1932. Brüning's budget cuts were designed to cause so much misery that the Allies would excuse Germany from making any further reparations payments. In this at least, Brüning succeeded. United States president Herbert Hoover declared a "reparations moratorium" in 1932. In the meantime, the Depression deepened, and social discontent intensified to the point that Germany seemed on the verge of civil war.

In times of desperation, voters are ready for extreme solutions, and the NSDAP exploited the situation. Skilled Nazi propagandist Joseph Goebbels launched an intensive media campaign that ceaselessly expounded a few simple notions until even the dullest voter knew Hitler's basic program. The party's program was broad and general enough to appeal to many unemployed people, farmers, white-collar workers, members of the middle class who had been hurt by the Depression or had lost status since the end of World War I, and young people eager to dedicate themselves to nationalist ideals. If voters were not drawn to some aspects of the party platform, they might agree with others. Like other right-wing groups, the party blamed the Treaty of Versailles and reparations for the developing crisis. Nazi propaganda attacked the Weimar political system, the "November criminals," Marxists, internationalists, and Jews. Besides promising a solution to the economic crisis, the NSDAP offered the German people a sense of national pride and the promise of restored order.

Three elections—in September 1930, in July 1932, and in November 1932—were held between the onset of the Depression and Hitler's appointment as chancellor in January 1933. The vote shares of the SPD and the Center Party fluctuated somewhat yet remained much as they had been in 1928, when the SPD held a large plurality of 153 seats in the Reichstag and the Center Party held sixty-one, third after the DNVP's seventy-three seats. The shares of the parties of the extreme left and extreme right, the KPD and the NSDAP, respectively, increased dramatically in this period, KPD holdings almost doubling from fifty-four in 1928 to 100 in November 1932. The NSDAP's success was even greater. Beginning with twelve seats in 1928, the Nazis increased their delegation seats nearly tenfold, to 107 seats in 1930. They doubled their holdings to 230 in the summer of 1932. This made the NSDAP the largest party in the Reichstag, far surpassing the SPD with its 133 seats. The gains of the NSDAP came at the expense of the other right-wing parties.

Chancellor Brüning was unable to secure parliamentary majorities for his austerity policy, so he ruled by decree, a right given him by President Hindenburg. Head of the German army during World War I, Hindenburg had been elected president in 1925. Ruling without parliament was a major step in moving away from parliamentary democracy and had the approval of many on the right. Many historians see this development as part of a strategic plan formulated at the time by elements of the conservative establishment to abolish the republic and replace it with an authoritarian regime.

By late May 1932, Hindenburg had found Brüning insufficiently pliable and named a more conservative politician, Franz von Papen, as his successor. After the mid-1932 elections that made the NSDAP Germany's largest party, Papen sought to harness Hitler for the purposes of traditional conservatives by offering him the post of vice chancellor in a new cabinet. Hitler refused this offer, demanding the chancellorship instead.

General Kurt von Schleicher, a master intriguer and a leader of the conservative campaign to abolish the republic, convinced Hindenburg to dismiss Papen. Schleicher formed a new government in December but lost Hindenburg's support within a month. On January 30, 1933, Papen again put together a cabinet, this time with Hitler as chancellor. Papen and other conservatives thought they could tame Hitler by tying him down with the responsibilities of government and transferring to themselves his tremendous popularity with a large portion of the electorate. But they proved no match for his ruthlessness and his genius at knowing how—and when—to seize power. Within two months, Hitler had dictatorial control over Germany.

The Third Reich, 1933–45

The Consolidation of Power

Hitler rapidly transformed the Weimar Republic into a dictatorship. The National Socialists accomplished their "revolution" within months, using a combination of legal procedure, persuasion, and terror. Because the parties forming the cabinet did not have a parliamentary majority, Hindenburg called for the dissolution of the Reichstag and set March 5, 1933, as the date for new elections. A week before election day, the Reichstag building was destroyed by fire. The Nazis blamed the fire on the Communists, and on February 28 the president, invoking Article 48 of the constitution, signed a decree that granted the Nazis the right to quash the political opposition. Authorized by the decree, the SA arrested or intimidated Socialists and Communists.

The election of March 5 was the last held in Germany until after World War II. Although opposition parties were severely harassed, the NSDAP won only 43.9 percent of the vote. Nonetheless, with the help of political allies, Hitler presented the Reichstag with the proposal for an Enabling Act that, if passed by a two-thirds majority, would allow him to govern without parliament for four years. On March 23, the proposal was passed with the support of the Center Party and others. All Communists and some Social Democrats were prevented from voting.

Hitler used the Enabling Act to implement *Gleichschaltung* (synchronization), that is, the policy of subordinating all institutions and organizations to Nazi control. First, left-wing political parties were banned; then, in July 1933, Germany was declared a one-party state. The civil service and judiciary were purged of "non-Aryans" (Jews) and leftists. Local and state governments were reorganized and staffed with Nazis. Trade unions were dissolved and replaced with Nazi organizations. Even the NSDAP was purged of its social-revolutionary wing, the SA. The enormous and unruly SA was brought under control by a massacre of its leadership at the end of June 1934 in the "night of the long knives." Other opponents were also killed during this purge, among them Schleicher. After Hindenburg's death in early August 1934, Hitler combined the offices of the president and the chancellor. With the SA tamed, Hitler assured the army that he regarded it as Germany's military force, and the soldiers swore an oath of personal allegiance to Hitler, pledging unconditional obedience. Heinrich Himmler's Guard Detachment (Schutz-Staffel—SS) replaced the SA as Hitler's private army.

Once the regime was established, terror was the principal means used to maintain its control of Germany. Police arrests, which had focused originally on Communists and Socialists, were extended to other groups, most particularly to Jews. This systematic use of terror was highly effective in silencing resistance. Some enemies of the regime fled abroad. However, all but a tiny minority of those opposed to Hitler resigned themselves to suppressing their opinions in public and hoping for the regime's eventual demise.

Like its secular institutions, Germany's churches were subjected to Nazi pressure. They resisted incorporation into the regime and retained a substantial degree of independence. This situation was tolerated by the regime, provided that the churches did not interfere with its efforts to control public life. When the churches were outraged by such Nazi practices as euthanasia, they protested. The regime responded by more carefully concealing such medical procedures. Otherwise, with the exception of a few brave isolated clergymen, the churches rarely spoke out against the regime. The regime's chief victims—Jews, Communists, Socialists, labor leaders, and writers—generally had not been close to the churches, and their persecution was witnessed in silence.

Joseph Goebbels, the minister of propaganda, contributed to the regime's consolidation with the establishment of the Reich Cultural Chamber, which extended *Gleichschaltung* to the educational system, the radio, and the cultural institutions. However, an elaborate system of censorship was not considered necessary to control the press. Non-Nazi party newspapers had already been suppressed. The editors of the remaining newspapers soon were able to figure out what was deemed suitable for public consumption. Goebbels also took an interest in Germany's substantial film industry, pressuring it to make pleasant, amusing films that would distract the German public in its leisure hours.

The regime soon achieved its desired consolidation. Many Germans supported it, some out of opportunism, some because they liked certain aspects of it such as full employment, which was quickly achieved. The regime also brought social order, something many Germans welcomed after fifteen years of political and economic chaos. Many were won over by Hitler's diplomatic successes, which began soon after he came to power and continued through the 1930s and which seemed to restore Germany to what they saw as its rightful place in the international community.

Foreign Policy

Once his regime was consolidated, Hitler took little interest in domestic policy, his sole concern being that Germany become sufficiently strong to realize his long-term geopolitical goal of creating a German empire that would dominate western Europe and extend deep into Russia. In a first step toward this goal, he made a de facto revision to the Treaty of Versailles by ceasing to heed its restrictions on German rearmament. Soon after becoming chancellor, Hitler ordered that rearmament, secretly under way since the early 1920s, be stepped up. Later in 1933, he withdrew Germany from the League of Nations to reduce possible foreign control over Germany. In 1935 he announced that Germany had begun rearmament, would greatly increase the size of its army, and had established an air force. Italy, France, and Britain protested these actions but did nothing further, and Hitler soon signed an agreement with Britain permitting Germany to maintain a navy one-third the size of the British fleet. In 1936 Hitler remilitarized the Rhineland, in violation of various treaties. There was no foreign opposition.

In 1936 Germany began closer relations with fascist Italy, a pariah state because of its invasion of Ethiopia the year before. The two antidemocratic states joined together to assist General Francisco Franco in overthrowing Spain's republican government during the Spanish Civil War (1936–39). In November 1936, Germany and Italy formed the Berlin-Rome Axis. That same year, Germany, Italy, and Japan signed the Anti-Comintern Pact, the three signatories pledging to defend each other against the Soviet Union and international communism.

It was also in 1936 that Hitler informed the regime's top officials that Germany must be ready for war by 1940. In response, the Four-Year Plan was established. Developed under the direction of Hermann Goering, it set forth production quotas and market guidelines. Efforts to regiment the economy were not without conflict. Some of the economic elite desired that Germany be integrated into the world's economy. Others advocated autarchy, that is, firmly basing the German economy in Central Europe and securing its raw materials through barter agreements.

In the end, no clear decision on the management of the German economy was made. Large weapons contracts with industrial firms soon had the economy running at top speed, and full employment was reached by 1937. Wages did not increase much for ordinary workers, but job security after years of economic depression was much appreciated. The rearmament program was not placed on a sound financial footing, however. Taxes were not increased to pay for it because the regime feared that this would dissatisfy workers. Instead, the regime tapped the country's foreign reserves, which were largely exhausted by 1939. The regime also shunned a rigorous organization of rearmament because it feared the social tensions this might engender. The production of consumer goods was not curtailed either, again based on the belief that the morale of the population had to remain high if Germany were to become strong. In addition, because Hitler expected that the wars waged in pursuit of his foreign policy goals would be short, he judged great supplies of weapons to be unnecessary. Thus, when war began in September 1939 with the invasion of Poland, Germany had a broad and impressive range of weapons, but not much in the way of replacements. As in World War I, the regime expected that the defeated would pay for Germany's expansion.

Through 1937 Hitler's foreign policy had the approval of traditional conservatives. However, because many of them were skeptical about his long-range goals, Hitler replaced a number of high military officers and diplomats with more pliable subordinates. In March 1938, the German army was permitted to occupy Austria by that country's browbeaten political leadership. The annexation (Anschluss) of Austria was welcomed by most Austrians, who wished to become part of a greater Germany, something forbidden by the Treaty of Versailles. In September 1938, British prime minister Neville Chamberlain consented to Hitler's desire to take possession of the Sudetenland, an area in Czechoslovakia bordering Germany that was inhabited by about 3 million Germans. In March 1939, Germany occupied the Czech-populated western provinces of Bohemia and Moravia, and Slovakia was made a German puppet state.

Immediately after the German occupation of Bohemia and Moravia, Britain and France finally became convinced of Hitler's expansionist objectives and announced their intention to defend the sovereignty of Poland. Because Hitler had concluded that he could not hope for British neutrality in the coming war, he formed a formal military alliance with Italy—the Pact of Steel. In August he signed a nonaggression pact with the Soviet Union, thus apparently freeing Germany from repeating the two-front war it had fought in World War I.

The Outbreak of World War II

On September 1, 1939, German troops invaded Poland. Britain and France declared war on Germany two days later. By the end of the month, Hitler's armies had overrun western Poland. Soviet armies occupied eastern Poland, and the two countries subsequently formally divided Poland between them. In April 1940, German forces conquered Denmark and Norway, and in May they struck at the Netherlands, Belgium, Luxembourg, and France. French and British troops offered ineffective resistance against the lightning-like strikes, or blitzkrieg, of German tanks and airplanes. A large part of the French army surrendered, and some 300,000 British and French soldiers were trapped at Dunkirk on the coast of northern France. However, because Hitler, for a combination of political and military reasons, had halted the advance of his armored divisions, the British were able to rescue the men at Dunkirk. France, however, surrendered in June.

For Hitler the war in the west was a sideshow, a prelude to the building of an empire in eastern Europe and the Soviet Union. Hitler had hoped that Britain would stay out of the war. In his vision of the near future, he foresaw the two countries sharing the world between them—Britain would keep its overseas empire, and Germany would construct a new one to its east. When approached with the suggestion of a separate peace, British prime minister Winston Churchill rejected the offer and rallied his people to fight on. The Third Reich experienced its first military defeat in the Battle of Britain, in which the Royal Air Force, during the summer and fall of 1940, prevented the German air force from gaining the air superiority necessary for an invasion of Britain. Consequently, Hitler postponed the invasion.

Hitler concluded by June 1941 that Britain's continuing resistance was not a serious impediment to his main geopolitical goal of creating an empire extending east from Germany deep into the Soviet Union. On June 22, 1941, negating their 1939 nonaggression pact, Germany invaded the Soviet Union. Eagerness to realize his long-held dream caused Hitler to gamble everything on a quick military campaign. He had anticipated victory within three months, but effective Soviet resistance and the early onset of winter stopped German advances. A counteroffensive, launched in early 1942, drove the Germans back from Moscow. In the summer of 1942, Hitler shifted the attack to the south of the Soviet Union and began a large offensive to secure the Caucasian oil fields. By September 1942, the Axis controlled an area extending from northern Norway to North Africa and from France to Stalingrad.

Japan's attack on the United States naval base at Pearl Harbor on December 7, 1941, brought the United States into the war. In support of Germany's fellow Axis power, Hitler immediately declared war on the United States. But with the United States involvement, a coalition now existed that, with its vast human and material resources, was almost certain to defeat the Third Reich. To ensure that the alliance not break apart as had happened in 1918 when Russia signed a truce with Germany, the Allies swore to fight Germany until an unconditional surrender was secured. Another reason the Allies wanted the complete military defeat of Germany was that they wished to preclude any possibility of German politicians claiming that "a stab in the back" had caused Germany's undoing, as they had done after World War I.

The military turning point of the war in Europe came with the Soviet victory at Stalingrad in the winter of 1942–43; some 300,000 of Germany's finest troops were either killed or captured. By May 1943, Allied armies had driven the Axis forces out of Africa and had landed in Italy. Also of great importance, by 1943 the United States and British navies had succeeded in substantially reducing the German submarine threat to shipping. This cleared the way for the movement of arms and troops to Britain in preparation for a cross-channel invasion of France.

Total Mobilization, Resistance, and the Holocaust

Once it became clear that the war would not be a short one, Germany's industry was reorganized for a total mobilization. Between February 1942 and July 1944, armaments production increased threefold despite intense Allied bombing raids. Much of the labor for this increase came from the employment of some 7 million foreigners, taken from their homelands and forced to work under terrible conditions. Also contributing to the Nazi war effort was the systematic requisitioning of raw materials and food from occupied territories. As a result, Germans remained fairly well fed for most of the war, in contrast to the hunger endured during World War I.

Despite their comparative physical well-being until late in the war, it gradually became clear to many Germans that the regime's series of military triumphs had come to an end. Even the most intense, mendacious propaganda could not conceal that Germany's forces were being beaten back. Sharing this growing awareness that defeat was likely, a group of military officers decided to assassinate Hitler. Although elements of the military had long opposed him, no one had acted to this point.

View of Berlin, 1945
Courtesy German Information Center, New York

During 1943 and 1944, the conspirators, who included many high-ranking officers and numerous prominent civilians, worked out elaborate plans for seizing power after the dictator's death. On June 20, 1944, the conspirators ignited a bomb that would probably have killed Hitler except for a stroke of bad luck—the misplacement of the device under a conference room table. The regime struck back and after months of reprisals had killed several thousand people, among them one field marshal and twenty-two generals. Several earlier attempts on Hitler's life had also failed. Because of these failures, it would be up to the Allies to remove Hitler and his regime from power.

Anti-Semitism was one of the Third Reich's most faithfully executed policies. Hitler saw the Jews' existence as inimical to the well-being of the German race. In his youth in Vienna, he had come to believe in a social Darwinist, life-or-death struggle of the races, with that between the German race and the Jews being the most savage. Because of his adherence to these racist notions, he dreamed of creating a German empire completely free of Jews, believing that if the Jewish "bacillus" were permitted to remain within the Teutonic empire, the empire would become corrupted and fail.

Upon taking power, the Nazis began immediately to rid Germany of its Jewish citizens. In the Aryan Paragraph of 1933, the regime decreed that Jews could not hold civil service positions. The Nuremberg Laws of 1935 deprived Jews of the right to citizenship and restricted relationships between "Aryans" (racially pure Germans) and Jews. After the Kristallnacht (Crystal Night) of November 9, 1938, an organized act of violence perpetrated by Nazis against Jews in all parts of Germany, the persecution of Jews entered a new phase. Random acts of violence, by then commonplace, were replaced by the systematic isolation of the Jewish population in Germany, which had numbered about 600,000 in the early 1930s.

Until 1941 there had been plans to "cleanse" Germany of Jews by gathering them together and expelling them from the Reich. One plan had as its goal the transfer of Germany's Jews to Madagascar. A contingent of Jews had even been moved to southern France in preparation. However, wartime conditions and the presence of millions of Jews in Poland, the Soviet Union, and other occupied areas in Eastern Europe gradually led to the adoption of another plan: the systematic extermination of all Jews who came under German control. Techniques that had been developed for the regime's euthanasia program came to be used against Jews. Discussions in January 1942 at the Wannsee Conference on the outskirts of Berlin led to the improved organization and coordination of the program of genocide.

Killing came to be done in an efficient, factorylike fashion in large extermination camps run by Himmler's Special Duty Section (Sonderdienst—SD). The tempo of the mass murder of Jewish men, women, and children was accelerated toward the end of the war. Hitler's preoccupation with the "final solution" was so great that the transport of Jews was at times given preference over the transport of war matériel. Authorities generally agree that about 6 million European Jews died in the Holocaust. A large number (about 4.5 million) of those killed came from Poland and the Soviet Union; about 125,000 German Jews were murdered.

Defeat

In June 1944, American, British, and Canadian forces invaded France, driving the Germans back and liberating Paris by August. A German counteroffensive in the Ardennes began in late December was beaten back after heavy fighting in what became known as the Battle of the Bulge. Soviet troops, meanwhile, advanced from the east. Western forces reached the Rhine River in March 1945; simultaneously, Soviet armies overran most of Czechoslovakia and pressed on toward Berlin. Although faced with certain defeat, Hitler insisted that every German city, every village, and "every square meter" be defended or left behind as "scorched earth." The Western Allies and the Soviet forces made their first contact, in Saxony, on April 27. Three days later, Hitler committed suicide in a Berlin bunker. Berlin fell to the Soviet forces on May 2; on May 7, the Third Reich surrendered unconditionally. It is estimated that about 55 million people died in the European theater during World War II. About 8 million of these dead were German.

*   *   *

A good introduction to German history is Mary Fulbrook's *A Concise History of Germany*, which not only presents the most important events but also examines various interpretations of them. The book closes with a bibliography of recent scholarship. Geoffrey Barraclough's *The Origins of Modern Germany* is a classic study of the German Middle Ages. *Early Modern Germany, 1477–1806* by Michael Hughes is a good introduction to this period. C.V. Wedgwood's classic, *The Thirty Years' War*, is engrossing reading and is widely available. A more recent treatment of the war is found in *The Thirty Years' War*, a well-integrated collection of articles about the conflict by noted specialists edited by Geoffrey Parker.

James J. Sheehan's subtle and learned *German History, 1770–1866* is the standard work in English on the period. Theodore S. Hamerow's *Restoration, Revolution, Reaction*, concise and beautifully written, deals with the main political, economic, and social trends between 1815 and 1871. Gordon A. Craig's *Germany, 1866–1945*, a survey of these years by the English-speaking world's dean of German studies, can be found in many libraries. Volker Rolf Berghahn's *Imperial Germany, 1871–1914* provides a sophisticated analysis of Germany between unification and the outbreak of World War I. James Joll's brief *The Origins of the First World War* examines interpretations of why this war occurred. *The German Dictatorship* by Karl Dietrich Bracher is an excellent treatment of the ideological sources of national socialism and provides an analytical history of Hitler's regime. Donald Cameron Watt's magisterial *How War Came* examines the diplomatic maneuvering leading up to World War II. Gerhard L. Weinberg's *A World at Arms* is an authoritative and comprehensive survey of the war. (For further information and complete citations, see Bibliography.)

Chapter 2. Historical Setting: 1945 to 1990

Half-timbered houses of the seventeenth century in Frankfurt am Main

GERMANY WAS UNITED ON OCTOBER 3, 1990. This event came after forty-five years of division that had begun with the partition of Germany into four occupation zones following its defeat in 1945 by the Four Powers—the United States, Britain, France, and the Soviet Union. Once a powerful nation, Germany lay vanquished at the end of World War II. The war's human cost had been staggering. Millions of Germans had died or had suffered terribly during the conflict, both in combat and on the home front. Intensive Allied bombing raids, invasions, and subsequent social upheaval had forced millions of Germans from their homes. Not since the ravages of the Thirty Years' War had Germans experienced such misery. Beyond the physical destruction, Germans had been confronted with the moral devastation of defeat.

Germans refer to the immediate aftermath of the war as the *Stunde Null* (Zero Hour), the point in time when Germany ceased to exist as a state and the rebuilding of the country would begin. At first, Germany was administered by the Four Powers, each with its own occupation zone. In time, Germans themselves began to play a role in the governing of these zones. Political parties were formed, and, within months of the war's end, the first elections were held. Although most people were concerned with mere physical survival, much was accomplished in rebuilding cities, fashioning a new economy, and integrating the millions of refugees from the eastern areas of Germany that had been lost after the war.

Overshadowing these events within Germany, however, was the gradual emergence of the Cold War during the second half of the 1940s. By the decade's end, the two superpowers—the United States and the Soviet Union—had faced off in an increasingly ideological confrontation. The Iron Curtain between them cut Germany in two. Although the Allies' original plans envisioned that Germany would remain a single state, Western and Eastern concepts of political, social, and economic organization gradually led the three Western zones to join together, becoming separate from the Soviet zone and ultimately leading to the formation in 1949 of two German states. The three Western occupation zones became the Federal Republic of Germany (FRG, or West Germany), and the Soviet zone became the German Democratic Republic (GDR, or East Germany).

During the next four decades, the two states led separate existences. West Germany joined the Western community of nations, while East Germany became the westernmost part of the Soviet empire. The two German states, with a common language and history, were separated by the mutual suspicion and hostility of the superpowers. In the mid-1950s, both German states rearmed. The FRG's armed forces, the Bundeswehr, became a vital part of the North Atlantic Treaty Organization (NATO). The GDR's National People's Army (Nationale Volksarmee—NVA) became a key component of the Warsaw Pact. The construction of the Berlin Wall in 1961 by the GDR further divided the two states.

In West Germany, by the early 1950s a system of parliamentary democracy with free and contending political parties was firmly established. The Christian Democratic Union (Christlich Demokratische Union—CDU), along with its sister party, the Christian Social Union (Christlich-Soziale Union—CSU), led the coalitions that governed West Germany at the national level for two decades until late 1969. In that year, the Social Democratic Party of Germany (Sozialdemokratische Partei Deutschlands—SPD) formed the first of a series of coalition governments with the Free Democratic Party (Freie Demokratische Partei—FDP) that governed the country until 1982. Late that year, the SPD was ousted from power when the CDU/CSU and the FDP formed a new coalition government. These parties ruled for the rest of the 1980s. As successful, however, as West Germany's adoption of democratic politics had been after 1945, the country's economic recovery was so strong that it was commonly referred to as the "economic miracle " (*Wirtschaftswunder*). By the 1960s, West Germany was among the world's wealthiest countries, and by the 1990s, Germany's economy and central bank played the leading role in Europe's economy.

East Germany was not so fortunate. A socialist dictatorship was put in place and carefully watched by its Soviet masters. As in the Soviet Union, political opposition was suppressed, the press censored, and the economy owned and controlled by the state. East Germany's economy performed modestly when compared with that of West Germany, but of all the socialist economies it was the most successful. Unlike West Germany, East Germany was not freely supported by its citizens. Indeed, force was needed to keep East Germans from fleeing to the West. Although some consolidation of the GDR was assured by the construction of the Berlin Wall, the GDR remained an artificial entity maintained by Soviet military power. Once this support was withdrawn, the GDR collapsed.

During the four decades of division, relations between the two German states were reserved and sometimes hostile. Despite their common language and history, the citizens of the two states had limited direct contact with one another. At times, during the 1960s, for example, contact was reduced to a minimum. During the 1970s, however, the two peoples began to mix more freely as their governments negotiated treaties that made relations between the two states more open. During the 1980s, although relations continued to improve and contacts between the two peoples became more frequent, persons attempting to flee from East Germany still died along its mined borders, GDR officials continued to harass and arrest dissidents, and the Socialist Unity Party of Germany (Sozialistische Einheitspartei Deutschlands—SED) rigidly controlled political life.

A key reason for the collapse of the GDR was the poor performance of its state-owned and centrally directed economy. The efforts of Soviet president Mikhail Gorbachev, beginning in the mid-1980s, to liberalize the Soviet Union and reform its economy were met with hostility by the GDR's top leadership. Word of these measures nevertheless reached East German grassroots opposition groups. Encouraged by the waves of reform in the Soviet Union and in neighboring socialist states, opposition in the East German population grew and became more and more vocal, despite increased state repression. By the second half of 1989, the East German opposition consisted of a number of groups with a variety of aims and was strong enough to stage large demonstrations.

The massive flow of East Germans to the West through neighboring socialist countries in the summer and fall of 1989, particularly through Hungary, was telling evidence that the GDR did not have the support of its citizens. Public opposition to the regime became ever more open and demanding. In late 1989, confronted with crushing economic problems, unable to control the borders of neighboring states, and told by the Soviet leadership not to expect outside help in quelling domestic protest, the GDR leadership resigned in the face of massive and constantly growing public demonstrations. After elections in the spring of 1990, the critics of the SED regime took over the government. On October 3, 1990, the GDR ceased to exist, and its territory and people were joined to the FRG. The division of Germany that had lasted decades was ended.

Postwar Occupation and Division

On May 8, 1945, the unconditional surrender of the German armed forces (Wehrmacht) was signed by Field Marshal Wilhelm Keitel in Berlin, ending World War II for Germany. The German people were suddenly confronted by a situation never before experienced in their history: the entire German territory was occupied by foreign armies, cities and infrastructure were largely reduced to rubble, the country was flooded with millions of refugees from the east, and large portions of the population were suffering from hunger and the loss of their homes. The nation-state founded by Otto von Bismarck in 1871 lay in ruins.

The Establishment of Occupation Zones

The total breakdown of civil administration throughout the country required immediate measures to ensure the rebuilding of civil authority. After deposing Admiral Karl Dönitz, Hitler's successor as head of state, and his government, the Allies issued a unilateral declaration on June 5, 1945, that proclaimed their supreme authority over German territory, short of annexation. The Allies would govern Germany through four occupation zones, one for each of the Four Powers—the United States, Britain, France, and the Soviet Union.

The establishment of zones of occupation had been decided at a series of conferences. At the conference in Casablanca, held in January 1943, British prime minister Winston Churchill's proposal to invade the Balkans and East-Central Europe via Greece was rejected. This decision opened the road for Soviet occupation of eastern Germany. At the Tehran Conference in late 1943, the western border of postwar Poland and the division of Germany were among the topics discussed. As a result of the conference, a commission began to work out detailed plans for the occupation and administration of Germany after the war. At the Yalta Conference in February 1945, participants decided that in addition to United States, British, and Soviet occupation zones in Germany, the French were also to have an occupation zone, carved out of the United States and British zones.

The relative harmony that had prevailed among the United States, Britain, and the Soviet Union began to show strains at the Potsdam Conference, held from July 17 to August 2, 1945. In most instances, Soviet leader Joseph Stalin was successful in getting the settlements he desired. One of his most far-reaching victories was securing the conference's approval of his decision to compensate Poland for the loss of territory in the east to the Soviet Union by awarding it administrative control over parts of Germany. Pending the negotiation of a peace treaty with Germany, Poland was to administer the German provinces of Pomerania, Silesia, and the southern portion of East Prussia. The forcible "transfer" to the west of Germans living in these provinces was likewise approved.

The movement westward of Germans living east of a line formed by the Oder and western Neisse rivers resulted in the death or disappearance of approximately 2 million Germans, while an estimated 12 million Germans lost their homes. The presence of these millions of refugees in what remained German territory in the west was a severe hardship for the local populations and the occupation authorities.

The conferees at Potsdam also decided that each occupying power was to receive reparations in the form of goods and industrial equipment in compensation for its losses during the war. Because most German industry lay outside its zone, it was agreed that the Soviet Union was to take industrial plants from the other zones and in exchange supply them with agricultural products. The Allies, remembering the political costs of financial reparations after World War I, had decided that reparations consisting of payments in kind were less likely to imperil the peace after World War II.

The final document of the Potsdam Conference, the Potsdam Accord, also included provisions for demilitarizing and denazifying Germany and for restructuring German political life on democratic principles. German economic unity was to be preserved.

The boundaries of the four occupation zones established at Yalta generally followed the borders of the former German federal states (*Länder*, sing., *Land*). Only Prussia constituted an exception: it was dissolved altogether, and its territory was absorbed by the remaining German *Länder* in northern and northwestern Germany. Prussia's former capital, Berlin, differed from the rest of Germany in that it was occupied by all four Allies—and thus had so-called Four Power status. The occupation zone of the United States consisted of the *Land* of Hesse, the northern half of the present-day *Land* of Baden-Württemberg, Bavaria, and the southern part of Greater Berlin. The British zone consisted of the *Länder* of Schleswig-Holstein, Lower Saxony, North Rhine-Westphalia, and the western sector of Greater Berlin. The French were apportioned the *Länder* of Rhineland-Palatinate, the Saarland—which later received a special status—the southern half of Baden-Württemberg, and the northern sector of Greater Berlin. The Soviet Union controlled the *Länder* of Mecklenburg, Brandenburg, Saxony, Saxony-Anhalt, Thuringia, and the eastern sector of Greater Berlin, which constituted almost half the total area of the city.

The zones were governed by the Allied Control Council (ACC), consisting of the four supreme commanders of the Allied Forces. The ACC's decisions were to be unanimous. If agreement could not be reached, the commanders would forego unified actions, and each would confine his attention to his own zone, where he had supreme authority. Indeed, the ACC had no executive authority of its own, but rather had to rely on the cooperation of each military governor to implement its decisions in his occupation zone. Given the immense problems involved in establishing a provisional administration, unanimity was often lacking, and occupation policies soon varied.

The French, for instance, vetoed the establishment of a central German administration, a decision that furthered the country's eventual division. Because they had not participated in the Potsdam Conference, the French did not feel bound to the conference's decision that the country would remain an economic unit. Instead, the French sought to extract as much as they could from Germany and even annexed the Saar area for a time.

The Soviet occupiers likewise sought to recover as much as possible from Germany as compensation for the losses their country had sustained during the war. Unlike the French, however, they sought to influence Germany as a whole and hoped to hold an expanded area of influence. In their own zone, the Soviet authorities quickly moved toward establishing a socialist society like their own.

The United States had the greatest interest in denazification and in the establishment of a liberal democratic system. Early plans, such as the Morgenthau Plan to keep Germans poor by basing their economy on agriculture, were dropped as the Soviet Union came to be seen as a threat and Germany as a potential ally.

Britain had the least ambitious plans for its zone. However, British authorities soon realized that unless Germany became economically self-sufficient, British taxpayers would bear the expense of feeding its population. To facilitate German economic self-sufficiency, United States and British occupation policies soon merged, and by the beginning of 1947 their zones had been joined into one economic area—the Bizone.

The Nuremberg Trials and Denazification

The Allies agreed that Germany should never again have the opportunity to destroy European peace as it had in the two world wars. A principal aim of the Allies was to prevent the resurgence of a powerful and aggressive Germany. As a first step toward demilitarizing, denazifying, and democratizing Germany, the Allies established an international military tribunal in August 1945 to jointly try individuals considered responsible for the outbreak of the war and for crimes committed by the Hitler regime (see The Third Reich, 1933–45, ch. 1). Nuremberg, the city where the most elaborate political rallies of the Hitler regime had been staged, was chosen as the location for the trials, which began in November 1945.

On trial were twenty-two men seen as principally responsible for the National Socialist regime, its administration, and the direction of the German armed forces, the Wehrmacht. Among the defendants accused of conspiracy, crimes against peace, crimes against humanity, and war crimes were Hermann Goering, Wilhelm Keitel, Joachim von Ribbentrop, Rudolf Hess, and Albert Speer. Although many Germans considered the accusation of conspiracy to be on questionable legal grounds, the accusers were successful in unveiling the background of developments that had led to the outbreak of World War II, as well as the extent of the atrocities committed in the name of the Hitler regime. Twelve of the accused were sentenced to death, seven received prison sentences, and three were acquitted.

The trials received wide publicity in Germany and throughout the world. Although many Germans maintained that it would have been better if the defendants had faced a German tribunal rather than one imposed by the war's foreign victors, they agreed that the trials made public much information about the mass murders and other crimes that otherwise might not have come to light. The German people and the rest of the world reacted with horror and dismay to the revelations. The trials of these more prominent figures of the Hitler regime were followed by the trials of thousands of lesser offenders.

The Allies did not seek merely to punish the leadership of the National Socialist regime, but to purge all elements of national socialism from public life. One phase of the denazification process dealt with lower-level personnel connected with the Nazi regime. Their pasts were reviewed to determine if the parts they had played in the regime were sufficiently grievous to warrant their exclusion from roles in a new Germany's politics or government. Germans with experience in government and not involved in the Nazi regime were needed to cooperate with occupation authorities in the administration of the zones.

The process of denazification was carried out diversely in the various zones. The most elaborate procedures were instituted in the United States zone, where investigated individuals were required to complete highly detailed questionnaires concerning their personal histories and to appear at hearings before panels of German adjudicators. In the British and French zones, denazification was pursued with less vigor because the authorities thought it more important to reestablish a functioning bureaucracy in their sectors.

Denazification was most rigorous in the Soviet sector. Civil servants, teachers, and legal officials with significant Nazi pasts were thoroughly purged. Denazification was also used as an instrument for seizing the resources of the so-called "class enemy": former Nazis who owned factories or estates were denounced and their property confiscated. After participating in the social transformation, some former Nazis were pardoned and even gained high positions within the new communist ruling class.

The denazification process mandated that simpler cases involving lesser offenders be tried before more complicated cases involving officials higher up in the Nazi regime. With time, however, prosecution became less severe, and the United States came to be more concerned with the Cold War. When denazification ended in March 1948, the more serious cases had not yet been tried. As a result, numerous former Nazi functionaries escaped justice, much to the regret of many Germans.

Political Parties and Democratization

The reintroduction of democratic political parties in Germany was one of the primary concerns of the Allies during the final phase of the war. The Soviet authorities were the first to reestablish political parties in their zone. They ordered the formation of political parties on June 10, 1945, well before such a directive was issued in the Western zones. In addition to seeking to control their own zone, they hoped to influence the emerging political constellations in the Western zones by the early mobilization of a strong leftist movement.

On June 11, the Communist Party of Germany (Kommunistische Partei Deutschlands—KPD) was reestablished in the Soviet zone under a German leadership that, for the most part, had lived for years in Moscow. Wilhelm Pieck was its chairman. Shortly thereafter, the Social Democratic Party of Germany (Sozialdemokratische Partei Deutschlands—SPD) was also reconstituted, under the leadership of Otto Grotewohl. When it became obvious that the SPD would emerge as the most popular leftist party in the Soviet zone, the Soviet authorities forced the merger of the KPD and the SPD in April 1946 and subsequently, from this merger, the formation of the Socialist Unity Party of Germany (Sozialistische Einheitspartei Deutschlands—SED). The Communists clearly had the upper hand in SED leadership. Vigorous resistance to the merger of the two leftist parties came from Social Democrats in the Western zones, led by Kurt Schumacher, a veteran Social Democratic politician and member of the Reichstag during the Weimar Republic and a political prisoner during the Third Reich. As a result of this principled opposition to Communist control, the rebuilding of the SPD in the Western zones took a separate course.

The SED sought to retain the image of a political force open to the masses, and it governed through the active participation of its members. It also competed with other parties in regional elections. After the *Land* elections of October 1946 in which the SED failed to obtain an absolute majority, the party resorted to different tactics in order to secure its grip on the electorate. SED leaders created an Anti-Fascist Bloc consisting of all political parties that was to guarantee the introduction of an antifascist and democratic order in the Soviet zone. From the very beginning, the SED could veto any proposal from any other bloc party not in accordance with its ideals for a socialist society. As a result, the two other political parties authorized in the Soviet zone were purged of their leadership, and their party programs were realigned in support of SED goals. The two other parties were the Christian Democratic Union (Christlich Demokratische Union—CDU), which represented middle-class interests, and the Liberal Democratic Party of Germany (Liberal-Demokratische Partei Deutschlands—LDPD), which represented the liberal political tradition that dated back to the late 1840s.

Two additional bloc parties were established in 1948 in the Soviet zone to represent groups still without a specific political party. The Democratic Peasants' Party of Germany (Demokratische Bauernpartei Deutschlands—DBD) was formed to prepare farmers for the planned land reform, which would involve extensive nationalizations. The second party, the National Democratic Party of Germany (National-Demokratische Partei Deutschlands—NDPD), was to work at reintegrating into a socialist society approximately 2 million people of right-wing views. The group included veterans and a relatively large number of former members of the National Socialist German Workers' Party (National-Sozialistiche Deutsche Arbeiterpartei—NSDAP), Adolf Hitler's party.

The Social Democratic Party that operated in the Western zones was, in contrast to the Eastern SPD, markedly anticommunist (see Social Democratic Party of Germany, ch. 7). This attitude reflected a continuation of its bitter hostility to the Communists during the Weimar Republic. The reestablished party, headed by Kurt Schumacher and, after his death, by Erich Ollenhauer, could look back on a distinguished history of creating better living conditions for the working class within the context of parliamentary democracy. Although anticommunist, the SPD's leadership still regarded the party as Marxist and remained committed to working for a socialist economy. As such, the SPD envisioned a neutral socialist Germany located between the capitalist economies of the West and the Soviet dictatorship of the East. The SPD was able to build on its extensive working-class membership, which predated Hitler's seizure of power in 1933.

For the conservative forces, the political beginning after 1945 appeared more difficult because of past fragmentation on regional and denominational lines. The persecution and suppression suffered during the Third Reich by conservative Catholics and Protestants alike gave rise to a unified Christian conservative party, which would represent all who opposed communism and socialism and who held traditional Christian middle-class values. At first, several regional political organizations formed in Berlin, Cologne, and Frankfurt am Main. On December 16, 1945, it was agreed that their collective designation should be called the Christian Democratic Union (Christlich Demokratische Union—CDU) (see Christian Democratic Union/Christian Social Union, ch. 7).

During the initial phase of development, members of the Christian labor unions strongly influenced the program of the conservative movement. Although they did not dispute the concept of private ownership of property, they advocated state control for many principal industries. During the 1950s, a market-oriented policy that was combined with a strong social component came to dominate the party.

The Bavarian Christian conservative organization, the Christian Social Union (Christlich-Soziale Union—CSU), founded in October 1946, remained a separate party organization and kept its name even after the foundation of the FRG. It followed a more pronounced conservative ideological party line than the CDU.

Even more difficult than the political unification of Christian conservatives was the consolidation of the liberal movement in postwar Germany. Traditionally, the liberals had been divided into a conservative national liberal wing and a more leftist-oriented liberal movement. There was also a reservoir of voters who understood themselves to be truly liberal in that they did not commit themselves to any ideology. Common to all of the party groupings, however, was the rejection of a planned economy. A number of independent liberal party groups existed for a time in southwestern Germany and in Hesse, Hamburg, and Berlin. In November 1948, most of them united in the Free Democratic Party (Freie Demokratische Partei—FDP), whose main figure, Theodor Heuss, became the first federal president of the FRG (see table 2, Appendix; Free Democratic Party, ch. 7).

The Creation of the Bizone

By early 1946, the Western Allies—the United States and Britain in particular—had become convinced that Soviet expansionism had to be contained. The Soviet Union's seizure of Polish territory and the drawing of the Oder-Neisse border (which gave formerly German territory to Poland), its antidemocratic actions in other countries occupied by Soviet forces, and its policies toward areas such as Greece and Turkey persuaded Western leaders that the Soviet Union was aiming for communist domination of Europe. Churchill's use of the expression "Iron Curtain" to describe the Soviet cordoning off of a sphere of influence in Europe illustrated a basic change in attitude toward Soviet intentions on the part of Western leaders. As a result of this change, Germany came to be seen more as a potential ally than as a defeated enemy.

The change in attitude led United States officials to take a more active role in Germany. A notable early example of this policy change was a speech given in Stuttgart in September 1946 by the United States secretary of state, James F. Byrnes, proposing the transfer of administrative functions from the existing military governments to a single civilian German administration. Byrnes stated that the United States had not defeated the Nazi dictatorship to keep Germans suppressed but instead wanted them to become a free, self-governing, and prosperous people. The speech was the first significant indication that Germany was not to remain an outcast but was, according to Byrnes, to have "an honorable place among the free and peace-loving nations of the world."

Neither the Soviet Union nor France desired a revitalized Germany, but after intensive negotiations, a unified economic zone, the Bizone, consisting of the United States and British zones, was proclaimed on January 1, 1947. After a difficult beginning, the Bizone proved itself a success, and its population of 40 million began to benefit from an improving economy. Only in the spring of 1949, after a period of sustained economic growth, did the French occupation zone join the Bizone, creating the Trizone.

In mid-1947 the European Recovery Program, or Marshall Plan as it is more widely known, was announced. The plan's aim was to stimulate the economies on the continent through the infusion of large-scale credits for the promotion of trade between Europe and the United States. The United States stipulated only that Europe's economy was to be united and that Europeans were to participate actively in the administration of the program. The Soviet Union suspected that the proposal was a means to prevent it from harvesting the fruits of the victory over fascism. Deeming the proposal a direct affront to its communist ideology by "American economic imperialism," the Soviet Union promptly rejected participation in the program, as did the East European states, obviously acting on Soviet orders.

To fulfill the precondition of economic cooperation in Europe, sixteen Western countries joined the Organisation for European Economic Co-operation (OEEC—see Glossary) in early 1948. In April 1948, the United States Congress approved the Foreign Assistance Act, which arranged the provision of aid. Shortly thereafter, industrial products, consumer goods, credits, and outright monetary gifts started to flow into the impoverished economies of Western Europe. Cities, industries, and infrastructure destroyed during the war were rapidly rebuilt, and the economies of the war-torn countries began to recover. In the Western zones, aid from the Marshall Plan laid the foundations for the West German "economic miracle" of the 1950s.

A functioning currency system was also needed for a growing economy. The war economy of the National Socialist government had created an oversupply of currency not matched by a supply of goods. To combat the resulting black-market economy, especially noticeable in large cities, and to aid economic recovery in western Germany, a central bank was founded and a currency reform was proclaimed on June 19, 1948. The reform introduced the deutsche mark. In exchange for sixty reichsmarks, each citizen received DM40 (for value of the deutsche mark—see Glossary). Additionally, controls over prices and basic supplies were lifted by authorities, thus abruptly wiping out the black market.

The swift action of the Western powers took the Soviet authorities by surprise, and they quickly implemented a separate currency reform for their zone and all of Berlin. The Western powers, however, had already ordered the distribution of deutsche marks in their sectors of the city. This measure, which for the Soviet Union represented the culmination of the Western policy to undermine Soviet efforts to build a socialist society in its zone, produced a sudden dramatic reaction, the Soviet blockade of Berlin.

On June 24, 1948, Soviet troops blocked all road and rail connections to West Berlin. Within a few days, shipping on the Spree and Havel rivers was halted; electric power, which had been supplied to West Berlin by plants in the Soviet zone, was cut off; and supplies of fresh food from the surrounding coun-

tryside were suddenly unavailable. The Four Power status of
Berlin, agreed upon by the Allied victors, had not included any
provisions regarding traffic by land to and from Berlin through
the Soviet zone. It had, however, established three air corridors
from the Western zones to the city.

The three Western powers acted swiftly: an airlift of unprecedented dimensions was organized to supply the 2.5 million
inhabitants of the Western sectors of Berlin with what they
needed to survive. The United States military governor in Germany, General Lucius D. Clay, successfully coordinated the airlift, which deployed 230 United States and 150 British
airplanes. Up to 10,000 tons of supplies were flown in daily,
including coal and other heating fuels for the winter. Altogether, about 275,000 flights succeeded in keeping West Berliners alive for nearly a year.

The Soviet Union had not expected such Western resolve.
Failing in its attempt to starve the Western Allies out of Berlin,
it lifted the blockade on May 12, 1949. The Western Allies, led
by the United States, had stood their ground without provoking armed conflict. Although the blockade had ended, its
effects on Berlin were lasting. By June 16, 1948, realizing that it
would not achieve its goal of a socialist Germany, the Soviet
Union withdrew from the ACC, prompting the Western Allies
to create a separate administration for their sectors. At the end
of 1948, two municipal administrations existed, and Berlin had
become a divided city. A more significant effect was perhaps
that, in Western eyes, Berlin was no longer seen as the capital
of Hitler's Germany but rather as a symbol of freedom and the
struggle to preserve Western civic values.

The Birth of the Federal Republic of Germany

Participants at the Potsdam Conference had agreed that the
foreign ministers of the four victorious powers should meet to
implement and monitor the conference's decisions about postwar Europe. During their fifth meeting, held in London in late
1947, prospects for concluding a peace treaty with Germany
were examined. Following lengthy discussions on the question
of reparations, the conference ended without any concrete
decisions.

The tense atmosphere during the talks and the uncoopera-
tive attitude of the Soviet participants convinced the Western
Allies of the necessity of a common political order for the three
Western zones. At the request of France, the Western Allies

were joined by Belgium, the Netherlands, and Luxembourg at the subsequent Six Power Conference in London, which met in two sessions in the spring of 1948.

The recommendations of this conference were contained in the so-called Frankfurt Documents, which the military governors of the Western zones issued to German political leaders, the minister presidents of the Western *Länder* on July 1, 1948. The documents called for convening a national convention to draft a constitution for a German state formed from the Western occupation zones. The documents also contained the announcement of an Occupation Statute, which was to define the position of the occupation powers vis-à-vis the new state.

The minister presidents initially objected to the creation of a separate political entity in the west because they feared such an entity would cement the division of Germany. Gradually, however, it became apparent that the division of the country was already a fact. To emphasize the provisional nature of the document they were to draft, the minister presidents rejected the designation "constitution" and agreed on the term "Basic Law" (Grundgesetz). Final approval of the Basic Law, whose articles were to be worked out by a parliamentary council, was to be given by a vote of the *Land* diets, and not by referendum, as suggested in the Frankfurt Documents. Once the Allies had accepted these and other modifications, a constitutional convention was called to draft the Basic Law.

The convention met in August 1948 in Bavaria at Herrenchiemsee. After completing its work, the Parliamentary Council, consisting of sixty-five delegates from the respective *Land* diets and chaired by leading CDU politician Konrad Adenauer, met in Bonn in the fall of 1948 to work out the final details of the document. After months of debate, the final text of the Basic Law was approved by a vote of fifty-three to twelve on May 8, 1949. The new law was ratified by all *Land* diets, with the exception of the Bavarian parliament, which objected to the emphasis on a strong central authority for the new state. After approval by the Western military governors, the Basic Law was promulgated on May 23, 1949. A new state, the Federal Republic of Germany (FRG, or West Germany), had come into existence (see fig. 6).

The members of the Parliamentary Council that fashioned the articles of the Basic Law were fully aware of the constitutional deficiencies that had brought down the Weimar Republic. They sought, therefore, to approve a law that would make it

Figure 6. Germany, 1949–90

impossible to circumvent democratic procedures, as had occurred in the past. The powers of the lower house, the Bundestag, and the federal chancellor were enhanced considerably at the expense of the federal president, who was reduced to a figurehead (see Government Institutions, ch. 7). Prime consideration was given to the basic rights and the dignity of the individual. The significance of the *Länder* was enhanced by their direct influence on legislation through representation in the upper house, the Bundesrat. The Basic Law also safe-guarded parliamentary government by protecting the federal chancellor from being forced from power through a simple vote of no-confidence. Instead, a constructive vote of no-confidence was required, that is, the vote's sponsors were required to name a replacement able to win the necessary parliamentary support. The Basic Law also supported the principle of a free market, as well as a strong social security system. In summary, the new Basic Law showed striking similarities to the constitution of the United States. To underscore its provisional character, Article 146 of the Basic Law stated that the document was to be replaced as soon as all German people were free to determine their own future.

According to the Basic Law, the Federal Constitutional Court could ban a political party that aimed at obstructing or abolishing the system of democracy. The activities of a number of openly antidemocratic parties during the Weimar Republic had inspired the authors of the Basic Law to include this strong provision. In 1952 the Socialist Reich Party (Sozialistische Reichspartei—SRP), a successor to the NSDAP, became the first party to be banned. The SRP had maintained that the Third Reich still existed legally, and it had denied the legitimacy of the FRG as a state. A few years later, the KPD was also suspended. Although the KPD was at first represented in all *Land* parliaments, it gradually lost support. After 1951 the leadership of the KPD began to pursue an openly revolutionary course and advocated the overthrow of the government. After five years of deliberations, the Federal Constitutional Court declared the KPD unconstitutional.

The Birth of the German Democratic Republic

As with the birth of the FRG, the formation of a separate nation-state in the Soviet zone also took only a few years. In late 1947, the SED convened the "German People's Congress for Unity and a Just Peace" in Berlin. To demonstrate the SED's claim of responsibility for the political future of all Germans, representatives from the Western zones were invited. The congress demanded the negotiation of a peace treaty for the whole of Germany and the establishment of a German central government. An SED-controlled organization was founded to win support for the realization of these demands in all occupation zones.

The Second People's Congress, held in March 1948, proposed a referendum on German unity, rejected the Marshall Plan, and recognized the Oder-Neisse border, which separated the Soviet zone from territory that was administered by Poland but that had once been part of Germany. Thereafter, few Western politicians had any doubts about the goals of the SED-sponsored congress. The congress elected a People's Council and created a constitutional committee to draft a constitution for a "German Democratic Republic," which was to apply to all of postwar Germany. The constitutional committee submitted the new constitution to the People's Council, and it was approved on March 19, 1949.

The Third People's Congress, its membership chosen by the SED, met in May 1949, just after the ending of the Berlin blockade. Apparently reacting to current events in the Western zones, where the Basic Law establishing the West German government in Bonn had just been approved, the congress approved the draft constitution of the German Democratic Republic (GDR, or East Germany).

A new People's Council, elected during the Third People's Congress, was convened for the first time on October 7, 1949, and the constitution of the GDR went into effect the same day. The Soviet military administration was dissolved, and its administrative functions were transferred to East German authorities. The People's Council was renamed and began its work as the Volkskammer (People's Chamber), the parliament of the GDR. A second parliamentary chamber, the Länderkammer (Provincial Chamber), consisting of thirty-four deputies, was constituted by the five *Land* diets on October 11, 1949. Wilhelm Pieck became the first president of the GDR on the same day, and the newly formed cabinet, under the leadership of Otto Grotewohl, was installed on October 12, 1949.

According to the first constitution of the GDR, its citizens enjoyed certain basic rights, even the right to strike. In reality, however, there was little freedom. According to the constitution, both the Council of State (Staatsrat) and the Council of Ministers (Ministerrat) were elected by and responsible to the Volkskammer. All parties and mass organizations represented in this body were united in the National Front, under the ideological leadership of the SED. The Volkskammer was a mere forum for speeches and mock debates. In reality, all policy matters were decided by the Politburo of the SED, on which most important functionaries of the Council of State and the Council of Ministers had a seat.

The party structure of the SED had been reorganized in the image of the Communist Party of the Soviet Union even before the foundation of the GDR, and the system of *nomenklatura* (see Glossary), with its strict system of ideological education and selection of candidates for all functions in party and state, was introduced. Within a few months, East Germany became a model for all other satellites of the Soviet Union.

West Germany and the Community of Nations

At the end of World War II, Germany was a defeated nation occupied by foreign powers. It had lost its national sovereignty, and the world saw it as a pariah, guilty of crimes without parallel in history. In addition to rebuilding their shattered country in a physical sense, most leading German politicians saw their main goals in the coming decades as restoring their country's reputation, regaining its sovereignty, and becoming once again a member in good standing in the community of nations.

The figure who dominated West Germany's politics in its first two decades was Konrad Adenauer, a politician totally committed to restoring his country to an honored place among nations. He saw little likelihood that the Soviet occupation of East Germany would soon end; hence, he sought to build a strong West Germany firmly attached to the Western community of parliamentary democracies. As president of the Parliamentary Council, Adenauer had played a leading role in the process of finalizing and passing the Basic Law in 1949.

Even before he participated in fashioning the country's constitution, Adenauer had had a long and eventful political career. Born in 1876 in Cologne, he studied law and economics and became active in local politics. As a member of the Catholic-based Center Party, he became the mayor of his home town in 1917. The National Socialists deposed him in 1933, and, after the attempt on Hitler's life on July 20, 1944, he was arrested and imprisoned for four months. After the war, the United States reinstalled him as mayor of Cologne. The British military authorities, however, fired him from this position because of alleged incompetence. In March 1946, Adenauer became chairman of the CDU in the British occupation zone and, after having shown extraordinary leadership in the deliberations on the Basic Law, became the first chancellor of the newly formed state (see table 3, Appendix).

One of Adenauer's main goals was regaining his country's sovereignty. Although the Basic Law gave full legislative, executive, and judicial powers to the new FRG and its *Länder*, certain powers were reserved for the occupying authorities. The Occupation Statute, drawn up in April 1949 by the foreign ministers of the Four Powers, gave the occupation authorities the right to supervise the new state's foreign policy, trade, and civil aviation, as well as the right, under special circumstances, to assume complete control over their own occupation zones.

By means of another statute, the Ruhr Statute, likewise concluded in April 1949, the administration of the resources and industrial potential of the Ruhr area was also kept under foreign control. In the past, the area had been a key element in the building of Germany's military machine. France, in particular, sought safeguards against future threats to its national security by arranging the creation of the International Authority for the Ruhr, which, under the direction of France, Belgium, the Netherlands, and Luxembourg, controlled the distribution of the area's resources.

Although the Ruhr Statute was designed to prevent Germany from ever again becoming a threat to its neighbors, it later served as the first instrument of economic cooperation for the region. In conformity with the Petersberg Agreement of November 1949 with the Western Allies, the FRG became a member of the International Authority for the Ruhr and was granted the right to establish consular relations with foreign countries. Furthermore, the dismantling of German industrial plants in the Ruhr area was largely stopped, and Germany was allowed to again build merchant ships. The winning of these important concessions was Adenauer's first major success as chancellor.

In the spring of 1950, French foreign minister Robert Schuman recommended the creation of the European Coal and Steel Community (ECSC) to revive European economic cooperation and prevent future conflict between France and Germany. According to Schuman's plan, countries willing to place their coal and steel industries under an independent authority could join.

Once again, Adenauer seized the opportunity to further integrate West Germany into Western Europe. Against the SPD's strong opposition, the FRG entered into negotiations with France, Belgium, the Netherlands, Luxembourg, and Italy on the formation of the ECSC. Negotiations were successfully concluded in June 1952. The ECSC superseded the International Authority for the Ruhr and laid the foundations of the future European Community (EC—see Glossary; see European Union, ch. 8). Adenauer's conciliatory but resolute foreign policy also secured the admission in 1951 of the FRG into the Council of Europe, a body established in May 1949 to promote European ideals and principles.

Another important step for the FRG on its path toward reentry into the community of nations was Adenauer's unwavering position on restitution to the victims of Nazi crimes. Of particular significance was the normalization of relations with Israel and with the Jewish people in general. Although the terrible atrocities that had occurred during the war could not be undone, material restitution could at least improve the lot of the survivors. In 1952 a reparations agreement with Israel was arranged that called for the payment of DM3 billion to the Jewish state over the next twelve years. Additional agreements with Jewish organizations provided for restitution to Jewish victims throughout the world. Through such actions, the FRG sought to meet its obligations as the legal successor to the German Reich, a position it had accepted since the FRG's founding.

Rearmament and the European Defense Community

The outbreak of the Korean War in 1950 convinced Western leaders of the growing threat of international communism. The United States began to encourage the Europeans—the FRG in particular—to contribute to their own defense. For Germany, five years after having lost the most devastating of all wars, this meant forming an army, a step unthinkable for many Germans. Germany's rearmament was also anathema to some of its neighbors, especially France. As the Korean War continued, however, opposition to rearmament lessened within the FRG, and China's entry in the war caused France to revise its negative position toward German rearmament.

To contain a newly armed Germany, French officials proposed the creation of the European Defense Community (EDC) under the aegis of the North Atlantic Treaty Organization (NATO). Adenauer quickly agreed to join the EDC because he saw membership as likely to increase his country's sovereignty. The treaties establishing the EDC were signed in May 1952 in Bonn by the Western Allies and the FRG. Although the Bundestag ratified the treaties, the EDC was ultimately blocked by France's parliament, the National Assembly, because it opposed putting French troops under foreign command. The French veto meant that a new formula was needed to allay French fears of a strong Germany.

The negotiations surrounding the planned rearmament of the FRG and the creation of the EDC provoked a Soviet countermeasure. After a second East German proposal for talks on a possible unification of the two Germanys failed because of the FRG's demands for free elections in the GDR, the Soviet Union put forth a new proposal to the Western Allies in March 1952. The Soviet Union would agree to German unification if the Oder-Neisse border were recognized as final and if a unified Germany were to remain neutral. If the proposal were accepted, Allied troops would leave Germany within one year, and the country would obtain its full sovereignty.

Although the offer was directed to the Western Allies, its content was aimed directly at the West German public and aroused lively discussion about the country's future. Adenauer was convinced, however, that even if the Soviet proposal were serious, an acceptance of the plan would mean Germany's exclusion from the community of Western democracies and an uncertain future. Together with the Western Allies, which did not wish to act without his consent, Adenauer continued to demand free elections supervised by the United Nations (UN) in all of Germany as a precondition for negotiations. The Soviet Union declined and abandoned its proposal. Adenauer was harshly criticized by the opposition for not having seized this opportunity for unification. As his impressive victory in the Bundestag elections of 1953 clearly demonstrated, however, Adenauer had acted according to the wishes of the overwhelming majority of West Germans (see table 4, Appendix).

Adenauer's decision to turn down the Soviet proposal was convincing evidence that the FRG intended to remain firmly anchored in the Western defense community. After plans for the EDC had failed because of the French veto, negotiations were successfully concluded on the Treaties of Paris in May 1954, which ended the Occupation Statute and made the FRG a member of the Western European Union (WEU—see Glossary) and of NATO (see The North Atlantic Treaty Organization; Western European Union, ch. 8). On May 5, 1955, the FRG declared its sovereignty as a country and, as a new member of NATO, undertook to contribute to the organization's defense effort by building up its own armed forces, the Bundeswehr (see Creation of the Bundeswehr, ch. 9).

The FRG contributed to NATO's defense effort by building up the Bundeswehr, an undertaking that met with considerable opposition within the population. For many, the memories of the war were still too vivid. To avoid separating the army from the country's civilian and political life, as was the case during the Weimar Republic, laws were passed that guaranteed civilian control over the armed forces and gave the individual soldier a new status. Members of the conscription army were to be "citizens in uniform" and were encouraged to take an active part in democratic politics. Although West Germans generally remained less than enthusiastic about their new army, the majority accepted the responsibility of sharing the burden of defense with the United States and the other members of NATO.

By 1955 the Soviet Union had abandoned efforts to secure a neutralized Germany, having become convinced of the FRG's firm position within the Western Alliance. Following the Four Power Conference in Geneva in July 1955, Chancellor Adenauer accepted an invitation to visit Moscow, seeking to open new lines of communication with the East without compromising the FRG's firm commitment to the West. In Moscow in September, he arranged for the release of 10,000 German war prisoners. In addition, without having recognized the division of Germany or the Oder-Neisse line as permanent, West German negotiators also established diplomatic relations with the Soviet Union.

The Soviet Union had recognized the GDR as a state in 1954, and the two countries maintained diplomatic relations with one another. The FRG had not, however, recognized the GDR. And to dissuade other countries from recognizing East Germany, Adenauer's foreign policy adviser, Walter Hallstein, proposed that the FRG break diplomatic relations with any country that recognized the GDR. The proposal was based on the FRG's claim, as a democratic state, to be the only legitimate representative of the German people. The Hallstein Doctrine was adopted as a principle of West German foreign policy in September 1955 and remained in effect until the late 1960s.

Another important development in the FRG's relations with its neighbors was that the Saarland rejoined the FRG in 1957. After World War II, France had attempted to separate this region economically and politically from the rest of Germany. In 1947 the Saarland received its own constitution and was virtually autonomous. During negotiations leading to the Treaties of Paris, the FRG and France agreed, in the Saar Statute, that the Saarland should become a territory under the control of the Council of Europe. However, in the referendum of October 1955, which was supposed to confirm the Saar Statute, Saarland voters rejected the statute by a two-thirds majority, an indication that they wished their region to become part of the FRG. On January 1, 1957, the Saarland became a West German *Land.*

In addition to his success in building a close and firm relationship with the United States, another of Adenauer's great foreign policy achievements was reconciliation with France, with which Germany had been locked in rivalry and conflict for centuries. In spite of remaining disagreements on the areas of European integration and NATO, a basis for the development of more normal relations between their two countries was forged upon a good personal understanding between Adenauer and French president Charles de Gaulle, who had assumed the French presidency in 1958.

The German-French Friendship Treaty (Élysée Treaty), which went into effect in January 1963, called for regular consultations between the two governments, semiannual meetings of the chiefs of state, and a youth exchange program. The treaty was seen by many as a positive step in the history of a difficult relationship between the two countries. Of greater importance to the majority of West Germans, however, was the country's relationship with the United States and its secure place within the Western defense community.

Social Market Economy

Germany's economic growth during the first decades after the war at times overshadowed its marked success at joining the international community. In 1945 the country's economy was shattered. A good part of what survived was later dismantled and carried off by the victorious Allies. Within Germany there was much argument about how to rebuild the economy and what its nature should be. Socialist politicians argued for a central distribution system, extensive state controls, and the nationalization of banks and industry. Their main opponent was Ludwig Erhard, a liberal economist appointed to head the office of economic affairs in the Bizone, who later became minister for economics and ultimately FRG chancellor (1963–66), succeeding Adenauer.

Erhard's concept of a socially responsive market economy based on free trade and private enterprise, aided by the infusion of capital through the Marshall Plan, proved to be the ideal basis for the strong recovery of the West German economy, culminating in the economic miracle (*Wirtschaftswunder*) of the 1950s (see The Social Market Economy, ch. 5). In some areas, for instance in housing and in agriculture, prevailing circumstances required the introduction of price controls and subsidies. Controls to prevent the formation of cartels and to foster monetary stability also remained the state's responsibility. The state likewise furthered the accumulation of private capital and protected ordinary citizens by establishing a generous system of social services that included statutory health, unemployment, and pension insurance programs.

West Germany's economy functioned very well for several decades, and the country became one of the world's wealthiest (see The Economic Miracle and Beyond, ch. 5). Thanks to the strong social welfare component and the system of codetermination, which gave workers in factories some say about their management, West German industry enjoyed a long period of labor peace. The export-oriented economy received another boost with the creation of the European Economic Community (EEC—see Glossary) by the Treaty of Rome in March 1957. West Germany was one of the EEC's founding members.

Ludwig Erhard and the Grand Coalition

Konrad Adenauer assumed the chancellorship of the newly founded FRG in 1949, at the age of seventy-three. From the beginning, his primary foreign policy goals had been the achievement of German reunification through a policy of strength, the building of strong relations with the United States, and reconciliation with France.

Until the elections of 1961, Adenauer had enjoyed the support of a healthy CDU/CSU majority in the Bundestag. Various domestic issues and very likely also the Berlin crisis, however, reduced the CDU/CSU's strength in the Bundestag and forced the formation of a coalition government with the FDP. The work of this government was impeded by differences of opinion from the outset. Following the resignation of FDP cabinet members in protest over a controversy surrounding the arrest of Rudolf Augstein, editor of the newsmagazine *Der Spiegel*, for allegedly having reported classified material concerning NATO exercises, the working climate of the coalition deteriorated.

Forced to accept the resignation of his powerful minister of defense, Franz Josef Strauss, who had had Augstein arrested, and facing an erosion of support within the CDU, Adenauer resigned on October 15, 1963.

Ludwig Erhard succeeded Adenauer as chancellor. Under Erhard's leadership, the CDU/CSU-FDP coalition remained in power until 1966. Erhard's more liberal economic policy toward the East European states that maintained diplomatic relations with East Germany made maintaining the Hallstein Doctrine difficult. In addition, his position of favoring close coordination of German foreign policy with the United States was resisted by the "Gaullists," even those in his own party, who favored a continuation of Adenauer's close relations with France.

The CDU/CSU did well in the elections of 1965, but relations with the FDP had deteriorated. A recession and a budget crisis caused the FDP to drop out of the coalition. Erhard ruled with a minority government for a short time, but after the opposition's significant gains in several *Land* elections, his party formed a new coalition government with the SPD. Erhard resigned as chancellor in November 1966, less successful in that position than he had been as the "father of the economic miracle."

When the CDU/CSU entered into a coalition with the SPD in December 1966, West Germany was experiencing unprecedented economic troubles. High unemployment, a relatively high budget deficit, and an unexpected rise in support for right-wing groups, such as the National Democratic Party of Germany (Nationaldemokratische Partei Deutschlands— NPD), brought West Germany's largest parties together to form what was called the Grand Coalition. Kurt Georg Kiesinger (CDU), who had served as minister president of Baden-Württemberg, was appointed chancellor; Willy Brandt (SPD), the governing mayor of Berlin, became vice chancellor and minister of foreign affairs; and Karl Schiller (SPD) was appointed minister for economics. Considered by many as "unnatural" because the coalition partners came from opposite ends of the political spectrum, the coalition was seen as a temporary solution needed to gain the cooperation of the trade unions and stabilize the economy.

The Ulbricht Era, 1949–71

Soviet dictator Stalin died in March 1953. In large portions

*Konrad Adenauer, federal
chancellor, 1949–63
Ludwig Erhard, federal
chancellor, 1963–66
Kurt Georg Kiesinger, federal
chancellor, 1966–69
Courtesy German
Information Center, New York*

of the East German population, particularly among workers suffering under the high production quotas set by the SED, Stalin's death gave rise to hopes for an improvement in living conditions and for an easing of political terror. In an attempt to stave off increasing unrest among the population as living standards were worsening and production quotas were being raised, the East German leadership, headed by General Secretary Walter Ulbricht, announced new economic policies that would end price hikes and increase the availability of consumer goods. Ulbricht refused, however, to lower production goals for industry and construction, which had been increased by 10 percent on May 28, 1953.

On the new parade grounds at East Berlin's Stalin Allee, a symbol of communist pride, enraged workers assembled in protest on June 16. The following day, demonstrations were held in most industrial cities of the GDR. Demands were made for comprehensive economic reforms and political changes, including Ulbricht's resignation and free elections. Overwhelmed by such widespread opposition to their policies, the East German authorities were unable to quell the protests. Soviet military units stationed in East Germany were called in and, with the help of East German police units, suppressed the unrest within two days. Order was restored at a cost of an estimated several dozen deaths and 1,000 arrests. Ulbricht, the figure largely responsible for the causes of the demonstrations, had triumphed, but the uprising demonstrated the frailty of the East German regime and signaled the East German population's "will to freedom."

Born in Leipzig in 1893, Ulbricht had served on the Western Front in World War I and had joined the KPD in 1919. He advanced quickly in the party hierarchy, becoming Reichstag deputy in 1928. After Hitler's seizure of power, Ulbricht went into exile. From 1937 to 1945, he worked for the party in Moscow. After the war, he returned to Berlin to build up the KPD under the protection of the Soviet Union. By 1950 he was chairman of the SED and through a variety of positions ruled the East German state with an iron fist for the next two decades by successfully eliminating every potential competitor within the SED leadership.

Consolidation of the New State

The most important instrument employed by East German authorities to guarantee their absolute rule was the State Security Service (Staatssicherheitsdienst, commonly referred to as the Stasi). Founded in early 1950 as the secret service branch of the Ministry for State Security (Ministerium für Staatssicherheit—MfS), the Stasi came to exercise almost complete control over the population of the GDR. During the first five years of its existence, Stasi personnel were trained by Soviet instructors. In addition to its surveillance of the East German population—which was carried out with sinister thoroughness up until the final days of the GDR—the Stasi conducted extensive espionage activities in the West, particularly in the FRG.

Aside from its approximately 100,000 full-time employees, the Stasi could also rely on the assistance of nearly 2 million civilian spies, or so-called informal employees (*Informelle Mitarbeiter*—IM), who reported regularly from domestic listening posts or from abroad. Experts agree that before its dissolution in 1990, the Stasi had developed the most perfect spying system ever devised to watch over its own citizens. It had truly realized the idea of the "glass-citizen," whose every activity was known to and controlled by the state. In Stasi headquarters in East Berlin, detailed information on individual citizens was collected in huge archives, which survived, largely intact, the downfall of the East German state.

An equally important role in building a permanent power base for the SED was played by mass organizations. One of the most important was the Free German Youth (Freie Deutsche Jugend—FDJ), founded in March 1946, in which young people between the ages of fourteen and twenty-five were to be indoctrinated as members of a new socialist society. Together with its suborganization for youngsters from six to fourteen years of age, the Young Pioneers—later called the Pioneer Organization "Ernst Thälmann," in memory of the chief of the KPD during the Weimar Republic, who was killed in a concentration camp—the FDJ soon became an effective instrument for influencing the coming generations. An important part of its influence was that membership in the FDJ soon determined access to institutions of higher learning, recreation and sports facilities, and ultimately career opportunities.

Another important mass organization was the Free German Trade Union Federation (Freier Deutscher Gewerkschaftsbund—FDGB), which attempted to motivate the workforce to achieve production goals and also provided members with opportunities for inexpensive vacations at FDGB-owned seashore resorts. Similarly, the interests of women were served by the Democratic Women's Federation of Germany.

By the end of 1947, all facets of society were organized in associations and groupings under the control of the SED. The GDR authorities also sought to deprive potential enemies within the state of the traditions and institutions upon which the state and society had been founded. A primary target for complete transformation was the court system. Judges and attorneys soon came to be used as mere instruments to carry out Marxist-Leninist goals. The legality of actions was determined by the political leadership.

The SED also declared the traditional administrative division of East Germany into five *Länder* an obstacle to "efficient" governance. The five *Länder*, all grown out of long historical traditions, were abolished and fourteen administrative districts established. This measure gave the central government in East Berlin much greater control over the activities in these districts, which were now much smaller, and, equally important, allowed it to break with another aspect of Germany's despised bourgeois history.

Planned Economy

In the GDR, as in the other new "people's republics," the authorities' goal of abolishing private property and every trace of capitalism was to be implemented in several steps. By taking possession of all resources, as well as of the means of production and distribution, the socialist state hoped to be able to compete successfully with the capitalist West and finally demonstrate the superiority of the socialist system.

Patterned on the Soviet model, the East German economy was transformed into a state-controlled, centrally planned production and distribution system by 1948. Beginning in 1945, large tracts of real estate and factories were taken over by the state under reform programs for agriculture and industry. After the foundation of the GDR, these reforms were pursued with vigor. In 1949 the new state became a member of the Council for Mutual Economic Assistance (Comecon), which included all other Soviet satellite states and had been created in order to coordinate economic planning in socialist states worldwide.

The concept of multiyear plans was introduced with the First Five-Year Plan of 1951. It was intended to make up war losses and also make possible reparations payments to the Soviet

Union. For this purpose, heavy industry was built up on a large scale. Production goals could not be reached, however, because of a chronic shortage of raw materials. The manufacture of consumer products was neglected completely.

The Second Five-Year Plan, started in 1956, aimed to complete the nationalization of all industrial concerns and the collectivization of agricultural enterprises. By the early 1960s, *Kombinate* (collective farms) accounted for about 90 percent of all farm production. Private farmers who resisted collectivization were arrested.

When production began to decline in the early 1960s, the SED introduced the so-called New Economic System of decentralized planning, which delegated some production decisions previously the prerogative of the central planning authorities to the Association of Publicly Owned Enterprises (Vereinigung Volkseigener Betriebe—VVB). The VVB was to foster specialized production within individual branches of industry, including the previously neglected production of consumer goods. Production declined even further, however, and it became increasingly evident to many East Germans that their "planned economy" had lost the economic battle with the capitalist West.

The Warsaw Pact and the National People's Army

The Warsaw Pact, which included the Soviet Union and all its satellite states in Eastern Europe, was created on May 14, 1955, just days after the FRG joined NATO. Like NATO, its Western counterpart, the Warsaw Pact guaranteed mutual military assistance to its members in the event of an attack and coordination of all member forces in a unified command. The existence of this command, which was situated in Moscow, allowed the Soviet Union to station troops on its allies' territories. Each member state was also obligated to establish its own armed forces. In the GDR, the People's Police (Volkspolizei, or Vopo) had created paramilitary units in 1952. The Soviet Union had unofficially helped form East German naval and air force units beginning in 1950.

On March 1, 1956, the National People's Army (Nationale Volksarmee—NVA) was officially created by transferring the existing paramilitary units of the People's Police to the NVA. The new army was officially under the leadership of the SED and under the direction of the newly created Ministry for National Defense. Initially, the NVA was to be staffed by volunteers only, but in 1962, when recruitment presented increasing difficulties for the SED and its support organizations, conscription was introduced. Before the construction of the Berlin Wall, conscription had been seen as impossible to enforce.

As early as the 1950s, the NVA became the most effective and best-equipped fighting force in the Warsaw Pact aside from the Soviet army. By the early 1980s, the NVA had an active strength of 167,000, of which approximately 60,000 were professional soldiers; there were approximately 3 million reservists. Most weapons were of Soviet origin.

The Berlin Wall

Besides its increasing economic difficulties, by the end of the 1950s the GDR encountered another problem that began to threaten its existence: large numbers of people were leaving East Germany for the West. Nearly half of those who fled the GDR were under twenty-five years of age. Although crossing the border between the two German states had become dangerous after new security measures were introduced in the early 1950s and severe penalties for the crime of "flight from the republic" (*Republikflucht*) were introduced by GDR authorities in 1957, a relatively safe escape route remained via West Berlin, which could be reached from East Berlin using the city's public transportation network. Once in West Berlin, refugees were registered and then transported to the FRG by air.

Alarmed by the continuous population drain, the East German Politburo ordered the erection of a wall along the border between West Berlin and East Berlin. On Sunday morning, August 13, 1961, workers began building a three-meter-high concrete wall along the border of the Soviet sector of the city. Within a few hours, public transportation lines were cut, and West Berlin was sealed off from East Germany. Chancellor Adenauer and West Berlin's governing mayor, Willy Brandt, sought to calm the outraged West Berliners. The Western Allies did not react with force because they were unwilling to endanger world peace. Up to that date, nearly 3.5 million had left the GDR for West Germany. After the building of the wall, the stream of refugees decreased to a mere trickle.

Despite the construction of the Berlin Wall, many East Germans still tried to escape. Several hundred of those attempting to leave the GDR were killed; others were captured, perhaps after being wounded by automatic guns or mines along the border, and sentenced to long prison terms. With the sealing off of East Berlin, the East German regime had solved the refugee situation.

The "Socialist State of the German Nation"

The building of the Wall effectively halted large-scale emigration from the GDR. Although the SED failed to gain the active support of the majority of the population, young people, especially, began to tolerate the regime, at least passively. In the absence of any alternatives, they fulfilled their routine duties in youth organizations, schools, and workplaces. By the mid-1960s, the regime could afford to lessen internal pressures on its citizens, who, encouraged by increased production of consumer goods, had largely given up their open resentment against the SED and had turned their attention to improving their standard of living.

Ulbricht's state visit to Egypt in 1965 ended the GDR's political isolation. A previously unknown pride in East German achievements and a feeling of distinct GDR identity began to develop, first among ruling party functionaries and then gradually among segments of the population. In 1967 the GDR leadership, encouraged by these developments, attempted to gain official recognition of its autonomy from the FRG. When the FRG refused to grant recognition, the GDR government proclaimed a separate GDR citizenship and introduced a visa requirement for West Germans traveling to West Berlin and to the GDR. With these measures, the GDR began to practice a policy of new assertiveness and ideological delimitation (*Abgrenzung*) in response to the FRG's policy of recognizing only one German citizenship.

Membership in the UN was a primary foreign policy goal of the GDR in the late 1960s. A veto by the Western powers in the UN Security Council blocked the GDR's bid, however. The GDR did gain admission to the International Olympic Committee, which permitted East German athletes to participate in the Olympic games as a separate team. For the GDR, however, the ultimate breakthrough in the area of foreign policy—a treaty with the FRG—came only after international political tensions began to ease under the new spirit of détente.

Following the conclusion of the Treaty of Moscow between the FRG and the Soviet Union in January 1970, a new era of communication began between the two German states that culminated in the signing of the Basic Treaty in December 1972. The next year, both states became members of the UN, and most countries came to recognize the GDR. Permanent diplomatic representations, in lieu of embassies, were established, respectively, by the FRG in East Berlin and by the GDR in Bonn, demonstrating the new climate of mutual respect and cooperation between the two German states.

In this new setting, there was no longer room for Walter Ulbricht, who had maintained a policy of confrontation with the West for many years. The Soviet Union, which had demonstrated considerably more flexibility than the GDR leadership during its negotiations with the FRG, was also irritated by the failure of Ulbricht's economic program and by his attempts to demonstrate ideological independence by adhering to conservative Marxist principles. In 1971 the Soviet authorities ordered that Ulbricht be relieved of power. His replacement was Erich Honecker, who, as secretary of the Central Committee of the SED for security matters, had been directly responsible for the building of the Berlin Wall.

The Social Democratic-Free Democratic Coalition, 1969–82

In the West German Bundestag elections of September 1969, the CDU/CSU remained the largest political group, holding eighteen more seats than the SPD. With the help of the FDP, which had earlier supported the candidacy of the SPD minister of justice Gustav Heinemann for the federal presidency, Willy Brandt was able to form an SPD-FDP coalition government, with himself as federal chancellor. The SPD-FDP coalition lasted until late 1982 and was noted for its accomplishments in the area of foreign policy. The formation of this new coalition forced the CDU/CSU into opposition for the first time in the history of West Germany.

Willy Brandt

Willy Brandt became the first democratically elected Social Democrat to hold the chancellorship. Born in Lübeck in 1913, Brandt first joined the SPD in 1930 and later joined a smaller leftist grouping, the Socialist Workers Party (Sozialistiche Arbeiterpartei—SAP). After Hitler came to power, Brandt emigrated to Norway, where he became a citizen and worked as a journalist. After Germany occupied Norway in 1940, he fled to Sweden. Brandt returned to Germany after the war as a news correspondent and later as a Norwegian diplomat in Berlin.

After he had again assumed German citizenship, Brandt rejoined the SPD in 1947. He became mayor of Berlin in 1957 and was the SPD candidate for the chancellorship in 1961. In the late 1950s, Brandt was a principal architect of the SPD's rejection of its Marxist past and adoption of the Bad Godesburg Program, in which the party accepted the free-market principle. The triumph of the CDU/CSU in the 1957 national elections and widespread and increasing prosperity made such a step necessary if the SPD were to win the electorate's favor. In 1964 Brandt became the chairman of the SPD. From 1966 to 1969, he served as minister for foreign affairs and vice chancellor in the Grand Coalition.

When Brandt became chancellor in 1969, he proposed a new policy toward the communist states of Eastern Europe; this policy later became known as Ostpolitik (policy toward the East). In recognition of his efforts toward détente in Europe, he received the Nobel Prize for Peace in 1971. In the early 1970s, Brandt also engineered a package of treaties that normalized the FRG's relations with the Soviet Union and with Poland, the GDR, and other Soviet-bloc nations. He successfully withstood a vote of no-confidence in the Bundestag in April 1972 and won the Bundestag elections in November 1972 with an impressive relative majority of nearly 45 percent. Brandt resigned in May 1974, shocked by the discovery that one of his personal assistants, Günter Guillaume, was a spy for the GDR.

In domestic policy, Brandt and his FDP coalition partners initiated legal reforms, including the passage of more liberal laws regarding divorce and abortion, the latter reform generating intense public discussion. Education reforms calling for new types of schools and for overhauling administration of the universities were only partially carried out. Brandt and his coalition partners were more successful in realizing their foreign policy goals than in achieving their domestic aims.

Ostpolitik

West Germany's relations with the East European states had virtually stagnated since the establishment of the Hallstein Doctrine in the mid-1950s. In 1970, in an attempt to lessen tensions in Europe, Brandt and his FDP minister for foreign affairs, Walter Scheel, agreed to negotiate with the communist bloc. For the first time since 1948, the top politicians of the FRG and the GDR held talks, with Brandt and the East German prime minister, Willi Stoph, meeting in Erfurt in East Germany and Kassel in West Germany. Although the talks produced no concrete results because Brandt refused to recognize the GDR as a sovereign state, communication lines were reopened.

After coordinating policy goals with the United States, the FRG also entered negotiations with the Soviet Union on a treaty normalizing relations, in which both countries renounced the use of force. The FRG agreed to make no territorial claims, and it recognized de facto the Oder-Neisse border and the border between the FRG and the GDR. FRG negotiators, however, insisted that such agreements did not alter the West German position on future reunification of the country and that the responsibilities of the Four Powers in Germany remained unchanged by the treaty. They also linked the signing of the treaty to a Soviet promise to open talks on normalizing the Berlin situation. After the Soviet Union had agreed to these conditions, the Treaty of Moscow was signed in August 1970. The agreement opened the road to negotiations with other countries of the Soviet bloc.

In December 1970, after ten months of complicated negotiations, the FRG and Poland signed the Treaty of Warsaw. The treaty contained essentially the same points as the Treaty of Moscow on the question of Poland's western border, the renunciation of territorial claims by the FRG, and the ongoing responsibilities of the Four Powers. In return, Poland agreed to allow ethnic Germans still in Poland to emigrate to the FRG. During the subsequent debates on the ratification of the two treaties, the CDU/CSU and part of the FDP made their consent contingent on the formulation of a strong statement by the Bundestag underscoring Germany's right to reunification in self-determination and of the Allies' responsibilities for Germany and Berlin.

Concurrent with the negotiations on the treaties of Moscow and Warsaw, the Four Powers undertook to end disagreement about the status of Berlin in talks that ultimately led to the Four Power Agreement (also known as the Quadripartite Agreement) of September 1971. The talks, which began in March 1970, got off to a difficult start because the Western Allies and the Soviet Union were deeply divided over their basic interpretation of the "status of Berlin." After they "agreed to disagree" on this point, progress was finally made, and all sides concurred that the status quo of Berlin should not be changed unilaterally.

*Willy Brandt, federal
chancellor, 1969–74
Courtesy German
Information Center, New York*

*Helmut Schmidt, federal
chancellor, 1974–82
Courtesy German
Information Center, New York*

The Soviet Union made two very important concessions: traffic to and from West Berlin would be unimpeded in the future, and the existing ties of West Berlin to the FRG were given de facto recognition. Soviet officials, however, insisted that West Berlin was not to be considered a territory belonging to the FRG and therefore was not to be governed by it. Furthermore, the Soviet Union made the conclusion of the agreement among the Four Powers contingent on the signing of the Treaty of Moscow between the FRG and the Soviet Union, which was still under negotiation. They thereby established the same linkage that the FRG had demanded, but in reverse.

The Four Power Agreement charged the governments of West Berlin and the GDR with negotiating an accord that would regulate access to and from West Berlin from the FRG and secure the right of West Berliners to visit East Berlin and the GDR. The Transit Agreement of May 1972 arranged these matters and also secured the rights of GDR citizens to visit the FRG, but only in cases of family emergency.

Following the negotiations on traffic between the FRG and the GDR, both sides recognized the feasibility of arriving at a more comprehensive treaty between the two German states. Talks began in August 1972 and culminated in December 1972 with the signing of the Basic Treaty. In the treaty, both states committed themselves to developing normal relations on the basis of equality, guaranteeing their mutual territorial integrity as well as the border between them, and recognizing each other's independence and sovereignty. They also agreed to the exchange of "permanent missions" in Bonn and East Berlin to further relations.

After the bitterly contested approval of the Basic Treaty by the SPD-FDP-controlled Bundestag in May 1973, a political decision that the CDU/CSU had warned against for decades became a reality: West Germany's de facto recognition of East Germany as a separate state. To many conservatives, the Basic Treaty represented the failure of the Hallstein Doctrine and a final blow to the possibility of Germany's reunification. Bavaria filed a suit in the Federal Constitutional Court in Karlsruhe to prevent the treaty's implementation, but the court held the treaty to be compatible with the provisions of the Basic Law. As a result of the treaty, the FRG and the GDR became members of the UN in June 1973.

Among the states to the east, Czechoslovakia remained the only neighbor with which West Germany had not yet normalized diplomatic relations. Negotiations with this country proved to be considerably more difficult than those with the Soviet Union or Poland. The main obstacle was a difference in interpreting the Munich Agreement of September 1938. On the one hand, the FRG maintained that the accord itself had to be considered legally valid but that the occupation of Czechoslovakia in March 1939 had voided its provisions. Czechoslovakia, on the other hand, insisted that the accord be considered void from the very beginning. Both sides finally agreed that the accord was to be considered void, but that all legal proceedings in the occupied territory between 1938 and 1945 were to be upheld. Once this basic understanding had been reached, the treaty with Czechoslovakia, known as the Treaty of Prague, similar in content to the Treaty of Warsaw, was signed in December 1973, and diplomatic relations were established. Shortly thereafter, West Germany exchanged ambassadors with Hungary and Bulgaria.

Helmut Schmidt

Following Brandt's resignation in May 1974, the SPD-FDP coalition partners unanimously agreed that Minister of Finance Helmut Schmidt should head the new government. At fifty-five, Schmidt became the youngest chancellor of the FRG. Born in Hamburg in 1918, he served as an officer in World War II. After the war, he joined the SPD and served in Hamburg's municipal government, where he acquired a national reputation as a top-notch manager because of his competence in dealing with a severe flood in 1962. He was the SPD faction leader in the Bundestag and minister of defense in the first SPD-FDP cabinet. Schmidt gradually became recognized at home and abroad as a pragmatic politician and an expert in economic and defense matters. His first cabinet included the FDP's Hans-Dietrich Genscher as minister of foreign affairs. Genscher replaced Walter Scheel, who had been elected federal president in 1974.

Schmidt was confronted with a number of serious problems. The economic turbulence caused by the oil crisis of 1973 had affected the FRG, and a ban on the use of automobiles on Sundays had been introduced to preserve scarce fuel reserves. Perhaps as a result of the crisis, Germans began to recognize limitations to economic growth and simultaneously to become aware of ecological dangers to the environment inherent in their lifestyle. As a result, environmental movements sprang up throughout the FRG.

Worries about the environment and about long-term economic growth became widespread in the next few years, and the almost limitless optimism of the postwar period began to give way to a mood of uncertainty about the future. Unemployment was also on the rise, and labor unions, traditionally reliable allies of the SPD, began to depart from their position of solidarity with the SPD-FDP government. In this increasingly difficult economic and political environment, Schmidt tried to steer a steady course, one often too conservative for his party and from which necessary support was at times lacking.

The Student Movement and Terrorism

In addition to troubling economic and environmental problems for which no easy solutions were available, West Germany and its politicians had to contend with two new sources of social unrest: the student movement of the late 1960s and early

1970s, and left-wing terrorism, which originated in the late 1960s, but which had its greatest impact in the 1970s.

Inspired by the student movement in the United States and by the international movement opposing the war in Vietnam, as well as by rising opposition to the traditional administration of German universities, students organized protest movements at a number of German universities in the late 1960s. Sit-ins, disruption of lectures, and attacks against buildings housing major publishing companies, such as the Axel Springer Group, were staged by a minority of student groups, primarily those with Marxist ties. Protesters claimed that an "extra-parliamentary opposition" was needed to ensure representation of the people in a state that was governed largely by two major parties. The student protest movement had little support among the population, however, and was finally absorbed by the established parties.

Terrorism was also a concern during this period (see Dissidence and Terrorist Activity, ch. 9). A few radical student elements sought to realize their aims through political terrorism. Small groups launched violent attacks against "symbols of capitalism." They fire-bombed department stores in several cities, broke into police stations, robbed banks, and attacked United States military installations.

One terrorist group, notorious for its brutality, became known as the Baader-Meinhof Gang, named after its leaders, Andreas Baader and Ulrike Meinhof. Calling themselves the Red Army Faction (Rote Armee Fraktion—RAF), their aim was to assassinate the "levers of the imperialist power structure," thereby provoking the state to abandon lawful methods of fighting terrorism. The arrest and imprisonment in 1972 of the main RAF leaders led to an intensification of terrorist acts by the group, which culminated in 1977 in the kidnapping of Hanns-Martin Schleyer, the president of the Federation of German Employers' Associations (Bundesvereinigung der Deutschen Arbeitgeberverbände—BDA) and in the hijacking six weeks later of a Lufthansa passenger airplane to Mogadishu, Somalia.

The aim of both these terrorist actions was the release of Baader and the other RAF prisoners. In a spectacular rescue action, the Lufthansa airplane was stormed by a special unit of the West German Federal Border Force, ending a five-day odyssey through the Middle East. Failing in their coup, Baader and three other RAF leaders committed suicide in their prison cells, and Schleyer was subsequently murdered by his kidnappers. The police had been successful in discovering hideouts, strategy papers, and caches of weapons, however, which led to the severe weakening of the organization of the RAF.

Nevertheless, supported by various international terrorist groups, including the GDR's Stasi, the RAF maintained a small network committed to assassinating prominent public figures. In 1989 they were responsible for the murder of Alfred Herrhausen, a top executive of the Deutsche Bank in Frankfurt, and in 1991 for the murder of Detlev Karsten Rohwedder, president of the Treuhandanstalt, the agency that managed the privatization of property in the former GDR (see Unification and Its Aftermath, ch. 5).

The Greens

In the aftermath of the oil crisis of 1973, regional political groups concerned with environmental issues began to put up candidates in communal and regional elections. In 1980 a number of ecological groups, alternative action movements, and various women's rights organizations banded together on the national level to form the political party that came to be called the Greens (Die Grünen).

Although the political views of the various groups in the new party were widely diverse, all agreed that the continuous expansion of the economy was detrimental to the environment and that disarmament was imperative if mankind were to survive. The Greens' support for radical peace movements and their demand that the FRG withdraw from NATO prevented many West Germans from taking the Greens seriously as a political force. In the Bundestag elections of 1980, they could muster only 1.5 percent of the vote, not enough to win any parliamentary seats. In the 1983 elections, however, they broke the 5 percent barrier and won twenty-seven seats in the Bundestag.

Differing ideological orientations within the Greens soon began to undermine the party's effectiveness in the political process. Two different factions emerged: the dogmatic fundamentalists (Fundis), who were unwilling to make any compromises on policy in order to win political allies; and the realists (Realos), who were ready to enter into a coalition with the SPD on the communal and *Land* level in order to put environmentalist ideas into practice.

Another cause of disagreement within the party organization of the Greens was the principle of rotation of seats in the

Bundestag and in *Land* diets. This policy required deputies to give up their seats after only half a term so that other Green candidates would have an opportunity to participate in the political process. As a result, experienced representatives who understood the workings of parliament were forced to relinquish their seats and were relegated to subordinate work in the party. Such unrealistic policies persuaded numerous talented Green politicians to withdraw from active politics, or to leave the party altogether. In 1984 a party leadership consisting only of women was elected, giving the Greens an image of practicing reverse discrimination.

Although the Realos among the Greens subsequently participated in *Land* governments as cabinet members, the party remained on the periphery of politics during the remainder of the 1980s (see The Greens, ch. 7). Nevertheless, the Greens positively influenced the views of the traditional political parties concerning the ecology and the preservation of natural resources.

The Christian Democratic/Christian Socialist-Free Democratic Coalition, 1983–

The SPD-FDP coalition formed in 1969 became increasingly strained in the early 1980s, leading to concerns among the FDP leadership about its stability. The SPD had become deeply divided because many of its members found Chancellor Schmidt's policies too conservative. Particularly troublesome was his position on NATO's Dual-Track Decision, which required the stationing of new missiles in West Germany if Soviet missiles were not withdrawn. FDP chairman Genscher feared that Schmidt would lose the backing of the SPD as its left wing became more influential. As a result of these fears, Genscher began to urge a change in the political constellation governing West Germany and the formation of a coalition with the CDU/CSU.

The SPD-FDP coalition broke apart in September 1982 when the FDP minister of economics, Otto Lambsdorff, advocated cutting social welfare expenditures. Schmidt countered by threatening to fire Lambsdorff. The threat prompted the resignation of all FDP cabinet members. Schmidt presided over a minority government for a few days until the FDP, together with the CDU/CSU, raised a constructive vote of no-confidence against the government. Schmidt lost the vote, and Helmut Kohl, head of the CDU, formed a new coalition government composed of the CDU, its sister party the CSU, and the FDP. Kohl himself became chancellor on October 1, 1982.

Born in 1930 in Ludwigshafen in the heavily Roman Catholic and conservative Rhineland-Palatinate, Kohl was a founding member and leader of the CDU youth organization in his hometown. He served as minister president of the Rhineland-Palatinate from 1969 to 1976, and in the 1976 national elections he ran unsuccessfully against SPD candidate Chancellor Schmidt for the office of chancellor.

In the 1980 national elections, Franz Josef Strauss was the CDU/CSU candidate for chancellor. Strauss, Bavaria's minister president and head of the CSU, was one of Germany's most influential and colorful politicians. He believed the CDU/CSU could come to power in Bonn without the help of the FDP. After Strauss lost the elections and Schmidt remained chancellor, however, Kohl began to steer toward an eventual coalition with the FDP because he did not think that conservatives could win an absolute majority at the national level.

New elections for the Bundestag were held in 1983, several months after Kohl had assumed the chancellorship. The results gave Kohl's government a clear majority and confirmed him as chancellor. Throughout his career, Kohl demonstrated a strong determination, extraordinary political skills, and a keen sense for the political will of the German people. His key role in the German reunification process has deservedly earned him a position of distinction in German history.

In the first half of the 1980s, West German politics were dominated by the heated discussion of NATO's Dual-Track Decision. The peace movement mounted numerous demonstrations to protest the possible stationing of United States missiles in West Germany should the Soviet Union not remove its newly stationed SS–20 missiles from Eastern Europe.

In the mid-1970s, the Soviet Union had decided to modernize its intermediate-range missile arsenal by the introduction and stationing of the advanced ground-based SS–20 systems. With a range of approximately 5,000 kilometers, the SS–20 was capable of delivering a 150-kiloton nuclear warhead within a target radius of 400 meters—a capability that could not be matched by any NATO weapon. It was clear that the missile's target area was Central Europe. Chancellor Schmidt had been among the first to warn of the danger posed by this new Soviet weapon system. The United States reacted quickly by developing two new weapon systems—the Pershing II intermediate-range rocket and the cruise missile. Although the Pershing II possessed a considerably shorter range and a much smaller warhead than the SS–20, it was capable of hitting its potential target with almost absolute accuracy.

At the NATO conference of foreign and defense ministers held in December 1979, officials decided to deploy 108 Pershing II rockets and 464 cruise missiles in Europe by the end of 1983. They also agreed to enter negotiations as soon as possible with the Soviet Union on the stationing of medium-range missiles in Europe. If Soviet missiles were withdrawn from Central Europe, United States missiles would not be positioned in West Germany. The United States-Soviet Union talks began in Geneva in November 1981 and continued for two years, but without achieving results.

NATO's Dual-Track Decision met with mounting opposition from the West German and European peace movement, and numerous rallies were held in the early 1980s. In the fall of 1983, protest demonstrations throughout the FRG were aimed at influencing the imminent decision of the Bundestag on deployment. Demonstrators feared that if missiles were stationed on German soil, the German population would be wiped out in the event of a possible nuclear exchange, while the Soviet Union would remain unaffected. With time, however, the peace movement became increasingly divided, and after 1983 it began to have less influence on public opinion. Most West Germans saw the Soviet Union as responsible for the escalation of the arms race by their deployment of the SS–20 and, in addition, mistrusted the Soviet Union's apparently keen interest in the peace movement in Western Europe.

Chancellor Kohl and his new government were determined to stand by West Germany's commitment to its NATO partners. After a lengthy debate in the Bundestag, the CDU/CSU-FDP majority coalition voted for deployment, with the SPD and the Greens opposing. Stationing of the missiles began immediately, and the Soviet Union withdrew from the Geneva negotiations. By the mid-1980s, as international tensions began to ease, public attention turned to new prospects for détente between West and East.

The Honecker Era, 1971–89

Ulbricht's successor in East Germany was Erich Honecker.

Born in 1913 in the Saarland, Honecker joined the Communist Party of Germany (Kommunistische Partei Deutschlands— KPD) in 1929. As a full-time functionary of the party, he continued his work in the underground movement after Hitler came to power in 1933 and until arrested by the Nazis in 1935. Imprisoned until the end of World War II, Honecker resumed his career in 1945 as a leading KPD functionary, becoming Ulbricht's assistant on the latter's return to Germany from the Soviet Union in 1945. From 1946 to 1955, Honecker served as chairman of the youth organization, the Free German Youth (Freie Deutsche Jugend—FDJ). He became a member of the SED Politburo in 1958. As secretary for security matters of the SED Central Committee, Honecker was directly responsible for the building of the Berlin Wall in 1961. When Ulbricht was removed from power in 1971, Honecker succeeded him in his party functions and became chief of the SED. Honecker was head of state of the GDR from 1976 until his resignation in 1989. After his fall from power, Honecker found refuge in the Embassy of Chile in Moscow until his extradition to Berlin in 1992, where he was brought to trial. He was released from custody in 1993 for health reasons and went to Chile, where he died in 1994. Although less rigid than Ulbricht, as evidenced by his willingness to sign agreements with the West that opened the GDR somewhat and made the lives of its citizens easier, Honecker remained a convinced communist until his death.

The Conference on Security and Cooperation in Europe

Keen to gain international recognition of its sphere of interest and believing that such recognition would solidify its grip on its East European satellite states, the Soviet Union, beginning in the early 1970s, sponsored an initiative calling for the convening of a Conference on Security and Cooperation in Europe (CSCE—see Glossary). For the West, such meetings meant the possibility of tying the Soviet Union and its satellites to an international security system, thereby lessening tensions, furthering economic cooperation, and obtaining humanitarian improvements for the people of Eastern Europe. The first of the series of conferences opened in July 1973 in Helsinki and was attended by the foreign ministers of the thirty-five member states. At the conference's final meeting in 1975, the heads of state of all member countries were in attendance for the signing of the Final Act, or the Helsinki Accords.

As subsequent CSCE conferences showed, Soviet officials had totally underestimated the effect of the provisions for the exchange of information, which allowed for the unscrambled reception of Western media broadcasts within the geographic area of the Warsaw Pact countries. East Germans benefited especially from access to West German radio and television programs, which furnished previously unobtainable news about world events. Television viewers in the East also became aware of an obviously far superior standard of living in the West and developed a new awareness of the deficiencies of the communist regime, an awareness that fifteen years later led to the events that brought down that regime.

The New East German Constitution and the Question of Identity

Although the GDR had finally achieved its goal of international recognition with the signing of the Basic Treaty in December 1972, renewed concerns about the stability and identity of the GDR as a second German state drove the SED Politburo toward a policy of reaffirming the socialist nature of the state. As early as 1971, Honecker had launched a campaign to foster a socialist identity among East Germans and to counter West German emphasis on the historical unity of the German nation. In 1974 the GDR constitution was even amended to increase a sense of separate development. All references in the document to the "German nation" and to German national heritage were deleted.

The SED had long revised German history to make it conform to socialist purposes. Symbols of Prussian heritage in Berlin, such as the equestrian statue of Prussian king Frederick the Great, had been removed. And in 1950, Ulbricht had ordered the 500-year-old palace of the Hohenzollern Dynasty demolished because it was a symbol of "feudal repression."

Just as the SED was striving to develop a separate GDR consciousness and loyalty, however, the new access to Western media, arranged by the CSCE process and formalized in the Helsinki Accords of 1975, was engendering a growing enthusiasm among East Germans for West Germany's Ostpolitik. Honecker sought to counter this development by devising a new formula: "citizenship, GDR; nationality, German." After the SED's Ninth Party Congress in May 1976, Honecker went one step further: figures of Prussian history, such as the reformers Karl vom Stein, Karl August von Hardenberg, Gerhard von Scharnhorst, and the founder of Berlin University,Wilhelm von Humboldt, were rehabilitated and claimed as historical ancestors of the GDR. Frederick the Great and Otto von Bismarck were also restored to prominence. Even Martin Luther was judged a worthy historical figure who needed to be understood within the context of his times.

These concessions did not alter the regime's harsh policy toward dissidents, however. Primary targets were artists and writers who advocated reforms and democratization, including Wolf Biermann, a poet-singer popular among East German youth who was expelled from the GDR in 1976. A wave of persecution of other dissident intellectuals followed. Some were imprisoned; others were deported to West Germany. Nonetheless, political statements by East German intellectuals, some going so far as to advocate reunification, continued to appear anonymously in the West German press.

Relations Between the Two Germanys

Although Honecker pursued a tough policy against internal dissidents and carefully guarded the GDR's unique identity as the state in which the old Marxist dream of socialism had become a reality, he was keenly aware of the necessity for communication and reasonable working relations with the FRG. His dream of being received at the White House as a guest of state by United States president Ronald Reagan was never realized, but Honecker opened more lines of communication to Western politicians than had his predecessors.

As a consequence of the Helsinki Accords, the reception of Western news media broadcasts was tacitly allowed in the GDR. In the early 1980s, it also became possible for citizens of the GDR who were not yet pensioners to visit relatives in the West in cases involving urgent family matters. Under a new regulation, refugees who had gone to the West before 1981 and had therefore automatically lost their GDR citizenship could now enter the GDR with their West German passport. These measures benefited East Germans and, together with access to Western television, helped to create a new relaxed atmosphere in the GDR.

On the economic side, the GDR fully utilized the advantages of the Interzone Trading Agreement, which allowed special consideration for the export of goods from the GDR to the FRG and other EC member states, as well as the import of vital industrial products from the West. Diplomatic relations with the EC were established in 1988, a reversal of the former policy that saw the organization as a threat to the GDR's sovereignty. The annual Leipzig Industrial Fair also provided a convenient forum for meeting Western politicians and industrialists.

The severe shortage of Western currency in the GDR, one of the key concerns of the SED leadership, was alleviated by agreements with the FRG that tripled the bulk contributions to the East German postal administration by the FRG. Similar agreements, financially advantageous to the GDR, improved the highway links to West Berlin. More significant, however, was the granting of bank credits amounting to DM2 billion to the GDR during 1983 and 1984. The CSU leader and minister president of Bavaria, Franz Josef Strauss, was the principal negotiator of these credit agreements.

At first, the credits appeared to yield positive results along the inner-German border, where mines and automatic guns, which had so long posed a deadly threat to East Germans attempting to flee to the FRG, were dismantled. Later, however, it became clear that these devices had been replaced by nearly impenetrable electronic warning systems and with trained dogs at certain sectors along the border. The order to shoot at refugees was not rescinded but remained in effect almost until the end of the GDR regime. Also remaining in effect were strict controls for West German citizens at GDR border crossings and on transit routes to and from West Berlin, although there were no further reports of people being abused at border checkpoints.

However much relations improved between the two states in some areas, the stance of the SED leadership toward the FRG's NATO membership remained hostile. Harsh attacks in the East German press labeling the FRG as an "American missile launcher" became more frequent during the debates on the stationing of Pershing II and cruise missiles. On occasion, high-level official visits were canceled to signal the GDR's opposition to Western military policies. The FRG responded in kind. For example, Federal President Karl Carstens (1979–84) did not attend as planned the East German celebrations on the occasion of the 500th anniversary of the birth of Martin Luther in 1983.

In October 1987, when the two superpowers were striving for détente and disarmament and the relations between the two Germanys were cordial, Honecker visited Bonn as the GDR head of state. The visit, postponed several times, was in

Federal Chancellor Helmut Kohl (1982–   ), right, at a meeting
in Bonn in 1987 with Erich Honecker, leader of East Germany,
1971–89
Courtesy German Information Center, New York

response to Chancellor Schmidt's visit to East Germany in 1981. Honecker was in the West German capital for an "official working meeting." He signed agreements for cooperation in the areas of science and technology, as well as environmental protection. Honecker's statement that the border dividing the two Germanys would one day be seen as a line "connecting" the two states, similar to the border between the GDR and Poland, attracted thoughtful public attention in the West. Honecker was cordially received by members of the government, in the words of Federal President Richard von Weizsäcker (1984–94), as a "German among Germans." However, at various stages of the visit—which subsequently took him to several federal states, including his native Saarland—large numbers of demonstrators chanted, "The wall must go."

The East German media coverage of the visit provided the opportunity for Chancellor Kohl to speak to "all the people in Germany" and to call for the breaking down of barriers "in accordance with the wishes of the German people." Although the visit yielded no immediate concrete results and Honecker's hopes of increased political recognition for the GDR were not realized, a dialogue had begun that could make the division of Germany more bearable for the people involved. As of late 1987, however, there was still little hope of overcoming the division itself.

The Peace Movement and Internal Resistance

The GDR leadership welcomed protests against weapons and war as long as they occurred in the FRG. However, when a small group of East German pacifists advocating the conversion of "swords into plowshares" demonstrated in 1981 against the presence of Soviet missiles on GDR soil, as well as against the destruction of the environment by the dumping of industrial waste and the use of nuclear power generally, they were arrested, prosecuted, and in some cases expelled from the GDR. Church organizations in the GDR—considered subversive by their mere existence—and individual pastors who protected and defended demonstrators at risk to their own safety became targets of increased surveillance by the Stasi, as did individual churchgoers, who by 1988 were frequently arrested and interrogated.

The mounting nervousness of the GDR leadership became evident in June 1987 when large crowds of East Berlin youth gathered on their side of the Wall, along with young people from all over the GDR, to hear two rock concerts being held in West Berlin near the Reichstag building. When the crowd broke into frenzied cries for freedom and unification, police cleared the area, arresting and forcibly removing Western news reporters filming the incident.

In the local elections of May 17, 1989, the "united list" led by the SED received 98.9 percent of the vote, obviously the result of massive manipulation, which enraged large segments of the population who had previously remained silent. In the next months, persistent public complaints against the prevailing living conditions and lack of basic freedoms, voiced by church groups and by opposition groups, inspired the population to take to the streets in large numbers. The largest of the new opposition groups was the New Forum, founded in September 1989 by Bärbel Bohley, Jens Reich, and others.

During the fall of 1989, mass demonstrations of several hundred thousand people were taking place, first in what soon became traditional Monday demonstrations in Leipzig and later in Berlin and other large cities. For the first time, GDR rulers realized that they were losing control: the demonstrations were too massive to be quelled by intimidation or even mass arrests; and shooting at the demonstrators was out of the question because of the sheer size of the crowds and the absence of Soviet support for draconian measures.

Beginning in the summer of 1989, the regime was threatened by another development. Among the thousands of GDR citizens that traveled by car on "vacation" to the socialist "brother country" Hungary, some 600 were successful in crossing illegally into Austria, where they were enthusiastically welcomed before traveling on to the FRG. Others wanting to escape the GDR took refuge in the embassies of the FRG in Budapest, Prague, and Warsaw. On September 11, Hungary legalized travel over the border to Austria for GDR citizens heading for the FRG, enabling 15,000 to take this route within a few days. Eventually, the GDR leadership was forced to allow special trains to carry thousands of GDR refugees who had received permission to emigrate to the West after taking sanctuary in the FRG's embassies in Prague and Warsaw. As the trains traveled through the GDR, many more refugees tried to climb aboard, so the government refused to further allow such transports.

The Last Days of East Germany

In January 1988, Honecker paid a state visit to France. By all indications, the long stretch of international isolation appeared to have been successfully overcome. The GDR finally seemed to be taking its long-sought place among the international community of nations. In the minds of the GDR's old-guard communists, the long-awaited international political recognition was seen as a favorable omen that seemed to coincide symbolically with the fortieth anniversary of the East German state.

In spite of Honecker's declaration as late as January 1989 that "The Wall will still stand in fifty and also in a hundred years," the effects of *glasnost* and *perestroika* had begun to be evident in the Soviet Union and throughout Eastern Europe.

Although the GDR leadership tried to deny the reality of these developments, for most East Germans the reforms of Soviet leader Gorbachev were symbols of a new era that would inevitably also reach the GDR. The GDR leadership's frantic attempts to block the news coming out of the Soviet Union by preventing the distribution of Russian newsmagazines only strengthened growing protest within the population.

In Berlin, on October 7, the GDR leadership celebrated the fortieth anniversary of the foundation of the East German state. In his address, Honecker sharply condemned the FRG for interfering in the GDR's internal affairs and for encouraging protesters. Still convinced of his mission to secure the survival of the GDR as a state, he proclaimed: "Socialism will be halted in its course neither by ox, nor ass." The prophetic retort by Gorbachev, honored guest at the celebrations, as quoted to the international press, more accurately reflected imminent realities: "He who comes too late will suffer the consequences of history."

The consequences of not having held in check the earlier large demonstrations against the regime's inflexibility came two days later when 70,000 protesters shouting "We are the people" demonstrated in Leipzig. When the police took no action during these historic hours of October 9, 1989, it became clear to everyone that the days of the GDR were numbered. After the crowds in Leipzig reached over 100,000 protesters on October 16, the Central Committee of the SED—previously kept in the background by Honecker and his comrades in the party leadership—took control. Honecker resigned from his offices as head of state and party leader on October 18.

Egon Krenz, longtime member of the Politburo and FDJ chairman, became Honecker's successor as general secretary of the SED. On October 24, Krenz also assumed the chairmanship of the Council of State. On his orders, all police actions against demonstrators were discontinued. On November 4, the largest demonstration in GDR history took place, with over 1 million people in East Berlin demanding democracy and free elections. Confronted with this wave of popular opposition, the GDR government, under Prime Minister Willi Stoph, resigned on November 7. The Politburo followed suit on November 8. Finally, on the evening of November 9, Politburo member Günter Schabowski announced the opening of the border crossings into the FRG.

East Germans fleeing to West Germany in 1989
Courtesy German Information Center, New York

Opening of the Berlin Wall and Unification

November 9, 1989, will be remembered as one of the great
moments of German history. On that day, the dreadful Berlin
Wall, which for twenty-eight years had been the symbol of German division, cutting through the heart of the old capital city,
was unexpectedly opened by GDR border police. In joyful dis-
belief, Germans from both sides climbed up on the Wall, which
had been called "the ugliest edifice in the world." They
embraced each other and sang and danced in the streets. Some
began chiseling away chips of the Wall as if to have a personal
hand in tearing it down, or at least to carry away a piece of German history. East Germans immediately began pouring into
West Germany. Within a few days, over 1 million persons per
day had seized the chance to see their western neighbor first-
hand.

On November 13, Hans Modrow was elected minister president of the GDR. After Chancellor Kohl had presented his Ten-Point Plan for the step-by-step unification of Germany to the Bundestag on November 28, the Volkskammer struck the leadership role of the SED from the constitution of the GDR on December 1 (see Unification, ch. 8). The SED Politburo resigned on December 3, and Krenz stepped down as chairman of the Council of State on December 6. One day later, the Round Table talks started among the SED, the GDR's other political parties, and the opposition. On December 22, the Brandenburg Gate in Berlin was opened for pedestrian traffic.

During January 1990, negotiations at the Round Table continued. Free elections to the Volkskammer were scheduled for March 18. The conservative opposition, under CDU leadership, waged a joint campaign under the banner of the Alliance for Germany, consisting of the CDU, the German Social Union (Deutsche Soziale Union—DSU), a sister party of the CSU, and the Democratic Awakening (Demokratischer Aufbruch—DA). The elections on March 18 produced a clear majority for the Alliance for Germany. On April 12, a CDU politician, Lothar de Maizière, was elected the new minister president.

The unusually poor showing of the SPD in these final East German elections may be explained by the party's reluctance to support German unification and also by the fact that the public was aware of the close contacts that the SPD leadership had maintained with the SED over the years. The success of the conservative parties was repeated in the communal elections on May 6, which were seen as a correction to the manipulated vote of the previous year.

As a precondition for German unity, the Two-Plus-Four Talks among the two German governments and the four victorious powers of World War II began on May 5. Held in four sessions, the last of which was on September 12, the talks culminated in the signing of the Treaty on the Final Settlement with Respect to Germany (the Two-Plus-Four Treaty). These talks settled questions relating to the eastern border of Germany, the strength of Germany's military forces, and the schedule of Allied troop withdrawal from German soil.

During a visit to Moscow in early February, Chancellor Kohl had received assurances from Gorbachev that the Soviet Union would respect the wishes of both Germanys to unite. Kohl realized that in order to seize this historic opportunity for Germany, swift action and final determination were crucial. In a cordial meeting between Gorbachev and Chancellor Kohl on July 16, unified Germany's membership in NATO and its full sovereignty were conceded by the Soviet president.

The first concrete step toward unification was the monetary, economic, and social union of West Germany and East Germany on July 1, as had been agreed in May in a treaty between the two German states. The monetary union introduced the deutsche mark into East Germany. Although there had been concern about the GDR's precarious financial situation, the full extent of the disastrous consequences of forty years of communist rule only came to light in the summer of 1990. It was soon clear that the first massive aid package for the East German economy, comprising DM115 billion, was just the beginning of a long and expensive rebuilding of a country reduced to shambles by the SED.

Divided by futile discussions about the speed of unification, the new government coalition in East Berlin had begun to fall apart during July 1990, when its SPD members resigned. Persuaded by the mounting economic and social problems that unification was necessary, the Volkskammer finally agreed on October 3, 1990, as the date of German unification.

On the occasion of the first free elections in the GDR, Chancellor Kohl took the opportunity to publicly express his gratitude to the United States, which had been Germany's most reliable ally during the process of unification. Once the first prerequisite for future unification had been established, namely, the willingness of Gorbachev to consider negotiations on unification in light of the dramatic events of the fall of 1989, the consent of the other victorious powers had to be secured.

Statements voicing concerns and even fears of a reemergence of an aggressive unified Germany suddenly appeared in the international press and media, as well as in unofficial remarks made by political figures throughout Europe. Even the FRG's major NATO partners in Europe—Britain and France—had become rather comfortable with the prevailing situation, that is, being allied with an economically potent, but politically weak, semisovereign West Germany.

Although lip service in support of future unification of Germany was common in the postwar era, no one dreamed of its eventual realization. When the historic constellation allowing unification appeared, swift and decisive action on the part of Chancellor Kohl and the unwavering, strong support given by the United States government for the early completion of the unification process were key elements in surmounting the last hurdles during the final phase of the Two-Plus-Four Talks.

The unification treaty, consisting of more than 1,000 pages, was approved by a large majority in the Bundestag and the Volkskammer on September 20, 1990. After this last procedural step, nothing stood in the way of formal unification. At midnight on October 3, the German Democratic Republic joined the Federal Republic of Germany. Unification celebrations were held all over Germany, especially in Berlin, where leading political figures from West and East joined the joyful crowds who filled the streets between the Reichstag building and Alexanderplatz to watch a fireworks display. Germans celebrated unity without a hint of nationalistic pathos, but with dignity and in an atmosphere reminiscent of a country fair. Yet the world realized that an historic epoch had come to a peaceful end.

*   *   *

A good starting point for readers seeking to learn more about the founding, consolidation, and final reunification of the two German states is *Germany from Partition to Reunification* by Henry Ashby Turner, Jr. Another concise and expert account is Peter Pulzer's *German Politics, 1945–1995*. Longer accounts by noted historians are Volker Rolf Berghahn's *Modern Germany*, which starts with events at the turn of the century and ends in the mid-1980s, and Mary Fulbrook's *The Divided Nation*, which begins with the aftermath of World War I and ends with unification. Fulbrook's *The Two Germanies, 1945–1990* is a concise survey of the many ways historians have interpreted recent German history.

Dennis L. Bark and David R. Gress's detailed two-volume *A History of West Germany* is widely available. David Childs's *The GDR: Moscow's German Ally* is a highly readable history of the German Democratic Republic. Mary Fulbrook's *Anatomy of a Dictatorship* examines the nature of the East German state and how it failed.

A useful documentation of the postwar years and the question of reunification can be found in *The German Question*, edited by Walther Hubatsch, with Wolfgang Heidelmeyer et al. Timothy Garton Ash's *In Europe's Name* is a searching analysis of Ostpolitik, from Adenauer to Kohl. Konrad H. Jarausch provides a concise account of the events of 1989 and 1990 in his scholarly *The Rush to German Unity*. Stephen F. Szabo's *The Diplomacy of German Unification* is a good brief account of the international aspects of unification. A more detailed treatment of this subject is *Germany Unified and Europe Transformed* by Philip Zelikow and Condoleezza Rice. (For further information and complete citations, see Bibliography.)

Chapter 3. The Society and Its Environment

Cologne Cathedral, begun in 1248, was completed only in 1880.

THE OPENING OF THE BERLIN WALL on November 9, 1989, was one of the most dramatic events of the post-World War II period. In the ensuing months, much more than just the graffiti-covered concrete panels of that infamous structure came crashing down during carnival-like celebrations. After four decades, the division of an entire continent, a nation, and a society came to an abrupt end.

A powerful force setting the revolutionary change in motion was a substantial movement of people from the German Democratic Republic (GDR, or East Germany) westward. Throughout its forty-year history, the GDR had resorted to extreme measures to control its borders and halt the exodus of productive workers. The most extreme of these measures was the erection in 1961 of the Berlin Wall to check the sustained movement of East Germans to the Federal Republic of Germany (FRG, or West Germany), whose booming economy had created millions of new jobs. Nearly three decades later, for a period of several years beginning in the summer of 1989, the appeal of West Germany, even with its economy mired in recession, prompted another wave of migration of more than 700,000 East Germans, most between the ages of eighteen and thirty.

The FRG's absorption of the GDR in 1990 enlarged its area by about 30 percent and increased its population about 20 percent. Integrating this new territory has proven to be a Herculean task. Prior to unification, West Germans enjoyed one of the highest standards of living in the world and a per capita income exceeding that of the United States. East Germans were prosperous by the standards of the communist world but had a living standard considerably below that of Western Europe. As the costs of unification have accumulated, the time when easterners will attain the standard of living of westerners has receded further into the future.

In the early 1990s, the five new eastern states (*Länder*, sing., *Land*) experienced substantial depopulation as a result of a plummeting birth rate and the internal migration of eastern Germans to the west. All social groups in the east were affected by the hasty merger, but the position of women was even more negatively affected. In particular, the rapid privatization of the socialist command economy led to much unemployment among women and the dismantling of an extensive child-care system. The east's elderly, who generally had incomes and savings much below their counterparts in the western *Länder*, also suffered hardship.

Unification inevitably revealed a series of unpleasant surprises about the closed economy and society of what had been East Germany. One of the most distressing was the deplorable state of the environment. Among the world's most environmentally conscious peoples, West Germans were shocked by the levels of ecological damage in the east. Environmental degradation, most noticeably badly polluted air and water, was perhaps a more important cause of the inequalities in living standards between east and west than smaller living quarters and lower wages. Surveying the dilapidated infrastructure and housing stock, observers dubbed the newly incorporated territory "Germany's Appalachia."

By mid-1995 it appeared that the physical and administrative mergers of the two German states would be far easier to accomplish than the social aspect of the union. In the postwar period, the two Germanys had assiduously developed two mutually exclusive models of society. Thus, the major challenge lay in harmonizing and integrating these societies, which were only gradually emerging from the long shadows cast by four decades of separate development in antagonistic systems.

Physical Setting

Roughly the size of Montana and situated even farther north, unified Germany has an area of 356,959 square kilometers. Extending 853 kilometers from its northern border with Denmark to the Alps in the south, it is the sixth largest country in Europe. At its widest, Germany measures approximately 650 kilometers from the Belgian-German border in the west to the Polish frontier in the east.

The territory of the former East Germany (divided into five new *Länder* in 1990) accounts for almost one-third of united Germany's territory and one-fifth of its population. After a close vote, in 1993 the Bundestag, the lower house of Germany's parliament, voted to transfer the capital from Bonn in the west to Berlin, a city-state in the east surrounded by the *Land* of Brandenburg. The relocation process is expected to be concluded by about the year 2000, following the transfer of the Bundestag, the Bundesrat, the Chancellory, and ten of the eighteen federal ministries.

Topography

With its irregular, elongated shape, Germany provides an excellent example of a recurring sequence of landforms found the world over. A plain dotted with lakes, moors, marshes, and heaths retreats from the sea and reaches inland, where it becomes a landscape of hills crisscrossed by streams, rivers, and valleys. These hills lead upward, gradually forming high plateaus and woodlands and eventually climaxing in spectacular mountain ranges.

As of the mid-1990s, about 37 percent of the country's area was arable; 17 percent consisted of meadows and pastures; 30 percent was forests and woodlands; and 16 percent was devoted to other uses. Geographers often divide Germany into four distinct topographic regions: the North German Lowland; the Central German Uplands; Southern Germany; and the Alpine Foreland and the Alps (see fig. 7).

North German Lowland

The North German Lowland is a part of the Great European Plain that sweeps across Europe from the Pyrenees in France to the Ural Mountains in Russia. All of the *Länder* of Schleswig-Holstein, Hamburg, Bremen, Mecklenburg-Western Pomerania, Brandenburg, Berlin, most of Lower Saxony and Saxony-Anhalt, and parts of Saxony and North Rhine-Westphalia are located in this region.

Hills in the lowland only rarely reach 200 meters in height, and most of the region is well under 100 meters above sea level. The lowlands slope almost imperceptibly toward the sea. The North Sea portion of the coastline is devoid of cliffs and has wide expanses of sand, marsh, and mud flats (*Watten*). The mud flats between the Elbe estuary and the Netherlands border are believed to have been above sea level during Roman history and to have been inundated when the shoreline sank during the thirteenth century. In the western area, the former line of inshore sand dunes became the East Frisian Islands. The mud flats between the islands and the shore are exposed at very low tides and are crossed by innumerable channels varying in size from those cut by small creeks to those serving as the estuaries of the Elbe and Weser rivers. The mud and sand are constantly shifting, and all harbor and shipping channels require continuing maintenance.

The offshore islands have maximum elevations of fewer than thirty-five meters and have been subject to eroding forces that have washed away whole sections during severe storms. Shorelines most subject to eroding tides were stabilized during the late nineteenth and early twentieth centuries.

Although the East Frisian Islands are strung along the coast in a nearly straight line, the North Frisian Islands are irregularly shaped and are haphazardly positioned. They were also once a part of the mainland, and a large portion of the mud flats between the islands and the coast is exposed during low tides.

The Baltic Sea coast of Schleswig-Holstein differs markedly from its North Sea coast. It is indented by a number of small, deep fjords with steep banks, which were carved by rivers when the land was covered with glacial ice. Farther to the east, the Baltic shore is flat and sandy. Rügen, Germany's largest island, lies just offshore of Stralsund.

Wherever the region's terrain is rolling and drainage is satisfactory, the land is highly productive. This is especially true of the areas that contain a very fertile siltlike loess soil, better than most German soils. Such areas, called *Börden* (sing., *Börde*), are located along the southern edge of the North German Lowland beginning west of the Rhine near the Ruhr Valley and extending eastward and into the Leipzig Basin. The Magdeburg *Börde* is the best known of these areas. Other *Börden* are located near Frankfurt am Main, northern Baden-Württemberg, and in an area to the north of Ulm and Munich. Because the areas with loess soil also have a moderate continental climate with a long growing season, they are considered Germany's breadbasket.

Central German Uplands

The Central German Uplands are Germany's portion of the Central European Uplands; they extend from the Massif Central in France to Poland and the Czech Republic. Germany's uplands are generally moderate in height and seldom reach elevations above 1,100 meters. The region encompasses all of the Saarland, Hesse, and Thuringia; the north of Rhineland-Palatinate; substantial southern portions of North Rhine-Westphalia, Lower Saxony, and Saxony-Anhalt; and western parts of Saxony.

In the west, the Central German Uplands begin with the Rheinish Uplands, a massive rectangular block of slate and shale with a gently rolling plateau of about 400 meters in elevation and peaks of about 800 to 900 meters. The Rheinish

Uplands are divided by two deep and dramatic river valleys—the Moselle and the Rhine. The high hilly area to the south of the Moselle is the Hunsrück; the one to its north is the Eifel. The Rhine separates these areas from their extensions to the east, the Taunus, and, to the north, the Westerwald. To the north and east of the Westerwald are further distinct areas of the Rheinish Uplands, most notably the small range of hills known as the Siebengebirge, across the Rhine from Bonn, and the larger hilly regions—the Siegerland, Bergishes Land, Sauerland, and the Rothaargebirge. The higher elevations of the Rheinish Uplands are heavily forested; lower-lying areas are well suited for the growing of grain, fruit, and early potatoes.

Because of the low elevations of its valleys (200 to 350 meters), the Uplands of Hesse provide an easily traveled passageway through the Central German Uplands. Although not as dramatic as the Rhine Valley, for hundreds of years this passageway—the so-called Hessian Corridor—has been an important route between the south and the north, with Frankfurt am Main at one end and Hanover at the other, and Kassel on the Weser River in its center. The headwaters of the Weser have created a number of narrow but fertile valleys. The highlands of the Uplands of Hesse are volcanic in origin. The most notable of these volcanic highlands are the Rhön (950 meters) and the Vogelsburg (774 meters).

To the north of the Uplands of Hesse lie two low ranges, the Teutoburger Wald and the Wiehengebirge, which are the northernmost fringes of the Central German Uplands. It is at the Porta Westfalica near Minden that the Weser River breaks through the latter range to reach the North German Lowland.

One of the highest points in the Central German Uplands is at Brocken (1,142 meters) in the Harz Mountains. This range is situated about forty kilometers to the northeast of Göttingen and forms the northwestern boundary of the Leipzig Basin, an extension of the North German Lowland. The Harz are still largely forested at lower levels; barren moors cover higher elevations. An important center for tourism in the 1990s, the range was once an important source for many minerals.

The Thüringer Wald, located in southwestern Thuringia, is a narrow range about 100 kilometers long, with its highest point just under 1,000 meters. Running in a northwesterly direction, it links the Central German Uplands with the Bohemian Massif of the Czech Republic and forms the southwestern boundary of the Leipzig Basin. The basin's southeastern boundary is formed by the Erzgebirge range, which extends to the north-east at a right angle to the Thüringer Wald. Part of the Bohemian Massif, the Erzgebirge range reaches 1,214 meters at its highest point.

The southeasternmost portion of the Central German Uplands consists of the Bohemian Forest and the much smaller Bavarian Forest. Both ranges belong to the Bohemian Massif. The Bohemian Forest, with heights up to 1,450 meters, forms a natural boundary between Germany and the Czech Republic.

Southern Germany

Between the Central German Uplands and the Alpine Foreland and the Alps lies the geographical region of Southern Germany, which includes most of Baden-Württemberg, much of northern Bavaria, and portions of Hesse and Rhineland-Palatinate. The Main River runs through the northern portion of this region. The Upper Rhine River Valley, nearly 300 kilometers long and about fifty kilometers wide, serves as its western boundary. The Rhine's wide river valley here is in sharp contrast to its high narrow valley in the Rheinish Uplands. The southern boundaries of the region of Southern Germany are formed by extensions of the Jura Mountains of France and Switzerland. These ranges are separate from those of the Central German Uplands. One of these Jura ranges forms the Black Forest, whose highest peak is the Feldberg at 1,493 meters, and, continuing north, the less elevated Odenwald and Spessart hills. Another Jura range forms the Swabian Alb (see Glossary) and its continuation, the Franconian Alb. Up to 1,000 meters in height and approximately forty kilometers wide, the two albs form a long arc—400 kilometers long—from the southern end of the Black Forest to near Bayreuth and the hills of the Frankenwald region, which is part of the Central German Uplands. The Hardt Mountains in Rhineland-Palatinate, located to the west of the Rhine, are also an offshoot of the Jura Mountains.

The landscape of the Southern Germany region is often that of scarp and vale, with the eroded sandstone and limestone scarps facing to the northwest. The lowland terraces of the Rhine, Main, and Neckar river valleys, with their dry and warm climate, are suitable for agriculture and are highly productive. The loess and loam soils of the Rhine-Main Plain are cultivated extensively, and orchards and vineyards flourish. The Rhine-Main Plain is densely populated, and Frankfurt am

Main, at its center, serves both as Germany's financial capital and as a major European transportation hub.

Alpine Foreland and the Alps

The Alpine Foreland makes up most of Bavaria and a good part of Baden-Württemberg. The foreland is roughly triangular in shape, about 400 kilometers long from west to east with a maximum width of about 150 kilometers north to south, and is bounded by Lake Constance and the Alps to the south, the Swabian and Franconian albs to the north, and the Bavarian Forest to the east. Elevation within the foreland rises gently from about 400 meters near the Danube, which flows along its north, to about 750 meters at the beginning of the Alpine foothills. With the exception of Munich and the small cities of Augsburg, Ingolstadt, and Ulm, the foreland is primarily rural. Soils are generally poor, with the exception of some areas with loess soil, and much of the region is pasture or is sown to hardy crops.

Germany's portion of the Alps accounts for a very small part of the country's area and consists only of a narrow fringe of mountains that runs along the country's border with Switzerland and Austria from Lake Constance in the west to Salzburg, Austria, in the east. The western section of the German Alps are the Algäuer Alps, located between Lake Constance and the Lech River. The Bavarian Alps, the central section, lie between the Lech and Inn rivers and contain Germany's highest peak, the Zugspitze (2,963 meters). The Salzburg Alps, which begin at the Inn River and encircle Berchtesgaden, make up the easternmost section of Germany's Alps.

Drainage

The greater part of the country drains into the North Sea via the Rhine, Ems, Weser, and Elbe rivers, which flow in a north-northwest direction. In the east, the Oder River and its tributary, the Neisse River, flow northward into the Baltic Sea and mark the border with Poland. With the exception of the Lahn River, which flows southward before joining the Rhine, most of the tributaries of these rivers flow in a west-to-east or east-to-west direction. In an exception to the south-north pattern of major rivers, the Danube River rises in the Black Forest and flows in a southeasterly direction, traversing Bavaria before crossing into Austria at Passau on the long journey to the Black

Sea. The Iller, Lech, Isar, and Inn rivers flow from the south into the Danube and drain the Alpine Foreland.

The Rhine, Germany's longest and most important river, originates in Switzerland, from where it flows into Lake Constance (actually a river basin). At the lake's west end, it begins a long course (800 kilometers) to the Netherlands, at first marking the boundary between Germany and Switzerland and later that between Germany and France. Of the Rhine's three most important tributaries, the Moselle River drains parts of the Rheinish Uplands, the Main drains areas between the Central German Uplands and the Franconian Alb, and the Neckar River drains the area between the Black Forest and the Swabian Alb. Because these rivers keep the Rhine high during the winter and because melting snow in the Alps keeps it high during the spring and summer, the river generally has a high steady flow, which accounts for its being the busiest waterway in Europe.

Climate

Although located mostly at latitudes north of the United States-Canadian border and thus closer to the Arctic Circle than to the equator, Germany's climate is moderate and is generally without sustained periods of cold or heat. Northwestern and coastal Germany have a maritime climate caused by warm westerly winds from the North Sea; the climate is characterized by warm summers and mild cloudy winters. Farther inland, the climate is continental, marked by greater diurnal and seasonal variations in temperature, with warmer summers and colder winters.

In addition to the maritime and continental climates that predominate over most of the country, the Alpine regions in the extreme south and, to a lesser degree, some areas of the Central German Uplands have a so-called mountain climate. This climate is characterized by lower temperatures because of higher altitudes and greater precipitation caused by air becoming moisture-laden as it lifts over higher terrain.

The major air masses contributing to the maritime weather are the Icelandic low-pressure system and the Azores high-pressure system. The Icelandic lows rotate in a counterclockwise direction and tend to move to the east and southeast as they approach Europe. The Azores highs move eastward and rotate in a clockwise direction. Both of these air masses furnish West-

Bamberg in northern Bavaria
One of Heidelberg's town gates
Courtesy Germany Information Center, New York

ern Europe with moisture-laden clouds propelled by westerly winds.

The northern lowlands frequently experience a situation (more often during the winter months) when they are between these air masses and are simultaneously influenced by both. At such times, winds come from the west and are usually strong. When only one of the systems is dominant, it is more often the Icelandic low. In spite of their nearly polar origin, Icelandic lows are warmed by the Gulf Stream, and areas on the country's North Sea coast have midwinter temperatures averaging more than 1.6° C. This temperature is more than three degrees above the average for the latitude, which is shared by central Labrador and some bitterly cold regions in Siberia.

When continental weather systems originating to the east are responsible for the weather, conditions are markedly different. In the winter months, these systems have high-pressure air masses that bring bright, clear, cold weather. The local people describe these air masses as Siberian highs and usually expect them to last for about two weeks. An occasional condition called *föhn*, or warm wind, arises when the center of a low-pressure system deviates to the south of its usual path and crosses the central part of the country. In this atmospheric condition, warm tropical air is drawn across the Alps and loses moisture on the southern slopes of the mountains. The air warms significantly as it compresses during its descent from the northern slopes. In the springtime, these winds dissipate the cloud cover and melt the snows. Many people respond to the rapid weather changes caused by the *föhn* with headaches, irritability, and circulatory problems.

The yearly mean temperature for the country is about 9° C. Other than for variations caused by shelter and elevation, the annual mean temperature is fairly constant throughout the country. Temperature extremes between night and day and summer and winter are considerably less in the north than in the south.

During January, the coldest month, the average temperature is approximately 1.6°C in the north and about −2°C in the south. In July, the warmest month, the situation reverses, and it is cooler in the north than in the south. The northern coastal region has July temperatures averaging between 16°C and 18°C; at some locations in the south, the average is 19.4°C or slightly higher.

Annual precipitation varies from 2,000 millimeters a year in the southern mountains to a low of 400 millimeters in the vicinity of Mainz. Over most of the country, it averages between 600 millimeters and 800 millimeters per annum.

The Environment

Unification abruptly transformed the Federal Republic from a country with a solid, even excellent, environmental record to one facing a whole range of ecological disasters—the result of the GDR's decades-long abuse of its natural habitat. The estimated costs of restoring the environment in the new *Länder* grew as information became available about how much damage it had sustained. Expert estimates of from DM130 billion to DM220 billion (for value of the deutsche mark—see Glossary) in the spring of 1990 had increased to a possible DM400 billion two years later.

The two Germanys differed greatly in their approaches toward protecting the environment. Beginning in the late 1960s, ecological concerns had become increasingly common in West Germany, as was repeatedly demonstrated in opinion polls. A 1990 poll, for example, found that more than 70 percent of those West Germans questioned held that environmental protection should be the highest priority for the government and the economy.

In East Germany, environmental activism was minimal. For decades the GDR had followed standard Soviet practices in regard to industrial and urban development, scrimping on or avoiding entirely key infrastructure investments such as water-treatment facilities and air-pollution abatement. The comprehensive and intelligent Socialist Environmental Management Act of 1968 was poorly implemented and, more important, largely ignored after the late 1970s when East German authorities decided that Western economic growth could only be matched by sacrificing the environment. This policy was followed throughout the 1980s.

West German environmental legislation initially lagged behind that of East Germany. For the first decades after World War II, West Germans were concerned with reconstructing their country and its economy. Early efforts to deal with the environment met with little interest. The attainment of widespread prosperity and the coming to maturity of a new generation with so-called postmaterialist values led to an interest in protecting the environment. The late 1960s and the early 1970s saw the passage of several dozen laws relating to the environment, the most important of which were the Waste Disposal Law and the Emission Protection Law, both passed in 1972. In 1974 the Federal Environmental Agency was established. The new legislation established the principles of Germany's environmental policies, still in effect in the mid-1990s: preventing pollution by monitoring new products and projects; requiring the polluter, rather than society at large, to pay damages; and relying on cooperation among government, industry, and society to protect the environment.

The oil crisis of 1973–74 and the ensuing worldwide recession led to a tapering off of environmental activism on the part of the West German government and the political parties. However, numerous citizens' groups formed and pressed for increased environmental protection (see Citizens' Initiative Associations, ch. 7). The accident at the Three Mile Island nuclear power plant in the United States in 1979 also spurred the growth of such groups. Elements of the environmental movement formed a political party, the Greens (Die Grünen) in 1980, which in 1983 won seats in the Bundestag (see The Greens, ch. 7). Of greatest importance were domestic ecological problems such as pollution in the Baltic Sea and the Rhine and Main rivers and damage to the country's forests from acid rain.

During the early 1980s, concerns about the environment became widespread in the general population, and all political parties were forced to address them. These concerns were raised still higher by a series of ecological disasters in 1986: the accident at the nuclear plant at Chernobyl in the Soviet Union and serious spills of dangerous chemicals into the Rhine at Basel in Switzerland. Immediately after the Chernobyl disaster, Chancellor Helmut Kohl created the Ministry of the Environment, Nature Conservation, and Reactor Safety.

Stricter environmental controls led to marked improvements in air quality. Between 1966 and 1988, sulfur dioxide emissions in West Germany fell by one-third. Dust levels, which stood at 3.2 million tons in 1980, fell to 550,000 tons by the late 1980s. The quality of river water also improved. The Rhine and Main rivers, nearly "biologically dead" in the 1960s, supported several species of fish by the early 1990s. The Ruhr River, located in the heart of the country's largest manufacturing region, became the cleanest "industrial" river in West Germany after the construction of a series of dams and the reforestation of slag heaps and wastelands.

At unification, the ecological situation in the new *Länder* was quite different. Because 95 percent of industrial wastewater had been discharged without treatment and 32 percent of households were not connected to sewerage systems, more than 40 percent of the rivers of the new *Länder* and 24 percent of their lakes were totally unfit as sources of drinking water; only 3 percent of their rivers and 1 percent of their lakes were considered ecologically healthy. Some rivers had pollution levels 200 times higher than that permitted by European Community (EC—see Glossary) environmental standards. The widespread use of brown coal had resulted in record emissions of sulfur dioxide, which rose by one-fifth between 1980 and 1988. Moreover, decades of brown coal strip mining had left some eastern areas resembling a lunar landscape. Other areas had been contaminated by the mining and processing of uranium, primarily to service the Soviet nuclear sector.

Although East German per capita waste production had been much lower than that of West Germany, the East German government had negotiated away this advantage and jeopardized ecological security in the bargain. In the 1980s, the GDR had earned hard currency by importing and carelessly disposing of millions of tons of West Germany's trash, exacerbating soil degradation and groundwater contamination. Some 60 percent of industrial waste had been deposited without controls. Of about 11,000 landfill sites, more than 10,000 were uncontrolled. With more than 28,000 potentially hazardous sites, the cleanup effort required in the east appears comparable in scope to the Superfund campaign in the United States.

The Cold War had also damaged East Germany's environment and to a lesser extent that of West Germany. For nearly five decades, millions of troops from the East and the West had made intensive use of the territory of the two Germanys as military bases and training sites. Cleanup costs were estimated in the hundreds of millions of dollars. In recognition of this situation, the United States Department of Defense allocated funds to repair environmental damage in the Federal Republic. In contrast, Soviet and later Russian forces, although they reportedly occupied as much as 2.5 percent of East German territory, were paid to leave the country and did so without compensating Germany for the extreme environmental damage they had caused.

With unification in 1990, the new *Länder* became subject to the environmental laws of the Federal Republic and the EC, although both sets of laws were to be applied gradually. Standards in some areas, such as emissions control, would not come into effect until after 2000. The ecological situation in the new *Länder* soon changed for the better, although much of the improvement stemmed less from the imposition of new standards than from the closing, for economic reasons, of outmoded plants that had caused much pollution. Projects such as constructing new air, water, and soil treatment plants and modernizing old ones, reducing the amounts of brown coal consumed, and cleaning up dump sites will gradually undo decades of ecological damage. Some environmental policies in the new *Länder,* like those in the old *Länder,* are preventive in nature. Because of the irresponsible practices of the former GDR, however, a great number are also restorative.

Serious environmental problems continue to confront Germany. Despite the efforts begun in the early 1970s, the "death of the forest" (*Waldsterben*) caused by acid rain continues. In 1992 about 68 percent of the country's trees had suffered significant ecological damage. Forests in northwestern Germany had suffered the least damage from acid rain, those in the south and east the most. Chemical emissions from automobiles are a serious cause of this problem. Only since 1993, however, have new vehicles been required to have catalytic converters. Germany's farmers also cause much pollution through intensive use of fertilizers. Because they are a powerful interest group, it has been difficult to pass legislation to regulate their farming methods.

Nuclear power presents a special dilemma for Germany. In western Germany, support for that power source, which in the mid-1990s supplied about 35 percent of the country's energy requirement, has fluctuated depending upon international events and crises. As of the mid-1990s, however, there appeared little chance that any more nuclear plants would be constructed in the near future.

Upon unification, the Federal Republic inherited East Germany's two nuclear power plants, which had been built to Soviet specifications. Decommissioning these plants would increase reliance on polluting coal-fired power plants. Despite this prospect, the likelihood of a Chernobyl-like disaster prompted the shutdown of these unsafe nuclear power plants. As of 1995, new, more ecologically friendly power plants are being built in the new *Länder* to replace nuclear power and brown coal-fired plants.

Population

The population of Germany manifests trends characteristic of most advanced industrial countries: lower marriage rates, delayed marriage and child-bearing, low fertility rates, small household size, high divorce rates, and extended life expectancy. The population of indigenous Germans has been in decline since 1972 in the west and since 1969 in the east because the number of births has not kept pace with the number of deaths. In 1990 only five of the sixteen *Länder* registered growth in population because of natural increase.

Household size decreased from 3.0 persons in 1950 to 2.3 in 1990. Marriage rates have slackened, while divorce rates have risen or remained stable at high rates. In the late 1980s, almost one-third of all marriages ended in divorce. Infant mortality has steadily declined, and life expectancy has risen, albeit more slowly in eastern Germany. As in the United States, a greater proportion of the population is moving into advanced age. In 1871 only 4.6 percent of the population was sixty-five years of age or older. By 1939 that proportion had risen to 7.8 percent, and by 1992 it had risen to about 15 percent. By 2000 it is estimated that one-quarter of the population will be sixty or older.

Since the 1950s, the population of Germany has become more diverse. Millions of foreigners have migrated to Germany, seeking employment, citizenship, or asylum. In contrast to the native population, foreigners in Germany tend to have more children and larger households. In 1988 their average household size was 3.5 persons. Depending upon their origins and social status, foreigners in Germany have been integrated into society in widely varying degrees.

Historical Background

Since the first unification of Germany in 1871 to form the German Empire, the population and territorial expanse of Germany have fluctuated considerably, chiefly as a result of gains and losses in war. At the time of its founding, the empire was home to some 41 million people, most of whom lived in villages or small towns (see table 5, Appendix). As industrialization and urbanization accelerated over the next forty years, the population increased significantly to 64.6 million, according to

149

the 1910 census. About two-thirds of this population lived in towns with more than 2,000 inhabitants, and the number of large cities had grown from eight in 1871 to eighty-four in 1910. Stimulating population growth were improvements in sanitary and working conditions and in medicine. Another significant source of growth was an influx of immigrants from Eastern Europe, who came to Germany to work on farms and in mines and factories. This wave of immigrants, the first of several groups that would swell Germany's population in the succeeding decades, helped compensate for the millions of Germans who left their country in search of a better life, many of whom went to the United States.

At the outbreak of World War I in 1914, the population of Germany had reached about 68 million. A major demographic catastrophe, the war claimed 2.8 million lives and caused a steep decline in the birth rate. In addition, the 1919 Treaty of Versailles awarded territories containing approximately 7 million German inhabitants to the victors and to newly independent or reconstituted countries in Eastern Europe.

In the 1930s, during the regime of Adolf Hitler, a period of expansion added both territory and population to the Third Reich. Following the annexation of Austria in 1938 and the Sudetenland (part of Czechoslovakia) in 1939, German territory and population encompassed 586,126 square kilometers and 79.7 million people, according to the 1939 census. The census found that women still outnumbered men (40.4 million to 38.7 million), despite a leveling trend in the interwar period.

The carnage of World War II surpassed that of World War I. German war losses alone were estimated at 7 million, about half of whom died in battle. Ruined, defeated, and divided into zones of occupation, a much smaller Germany emerged in 1945 with a population about the same as in 1910. In the immediate postwar period, however, more than 12 million persons— expelled Germans and displaced persons—immigrated to Germany or used the country as a transit point en route to other destinations, adding to the population.

By 1950 the newly established Federal Republic of Germany had a population of about 50 million, more than 9 million of whom were "expellees." The German Democratic Republic had about 4 million newcomers and 14 million natives (see table 6, Appendix). Most of the expellees came from East Prussia, Pomerania, Silesia, and the Sudetenland, all one-time German territories held by other countries at the end of World War II. The majority of the settlers in West Germany remained, found work in the rapidly recovering economy, and in time were successfully integrated into the society. Between 1950 and 1989, West Germany's population grew from 50 million to 62.1 million. Resettled Germans and refugees from former eastern territories and their families constituted approximately 20 percent of the country's population. From its earliest years, West Germany had become either a temporary or a final destination for millions of migrants. Yet despite this influx, the country did not develop an identity as a country of immigration as did, for example, the United States or Canada.

The situation in East Germany was much different. From its founding in 1949, the GDR struggled to stabilize its population and thwart emigration. In the course of its forty-year history, almost one-quarter of East Germany's population fled the state to settle in West Germany. In the 1950s alone, more than 2 million people moved west, a migration that triggered the regime's radical solution in August 1961—the construction of the Berlin Wall (see The Berlin Wall, ch. 2). During most of its existence, the only segment of East Germany's population permitted to leave for West Germany were retirees, whose resettlement there was unofficially encouraged to reduce the GDR's pension payments. As a result, the number of persons sixty years of age and older in the GDR fell from 22.1 percent in 1970 to 18.3 percent in 1985 and made the East German population younger than that of West Germany.

Deprived of a regular supply of workers by the construction of the Berlin Wall, the Federal Republic in the 1960s absorbed yet another wave of migrants. Laborers were recruited through agreements with seven countries: Italy, Spain, Greece, Turkey, Portugal, Tunisia, and Morocco. Between 1955 and 1973, the number of foreign workers, called guest workers (*Gastarbeiter*) to emphasize the intended temporary nature of their contracts, grew from about 100,000 to about 2.5 million. Originally brought in for three-year shifts, most workers—mainly single men—remained and made a valuable contribution to the booming West German economy. In the early 1970s, however, a recession brought on by the international energy crisis slowed the West German economy; the importing of workers officially came to an end in 1973 (see Immigration, this ch.).

In the 1980s and early 1990s, the fourth and most controversial wave of immigrants to West Germany were asylum-seekers and political refugees—ethnic Germans from Poland, Yugoslavia, Czechoslovakia, and territories belonging to the former Soviet Union and also East Germans who moved west as the GDR collapsed. Many Germans were angered by the financial and social costs these immigrants required because they believed many asylum-seekers were drawn to Germany more by the desire for a better standard of living than by the need to escape political oppression. Many ethnic Germans hardly seemed German: some did not even speak German.

Fertility

Despite the Berlin Wall and the fortified boundary that divided them, the two Germanys had many similar demographic developments in the postwar period. In the late 1950s and especially in the 1960s, both Germanys experienced a "baby boom," stimulated by increased economic prosperity and a heightened sense of security. During the second half of the 1960s, East Germany's population grew slightly, an unusual occurrence. In West Germany, the absolute peak in births, 1.3 million, was reached in 1965. In that year, births outnumbered deaths by 417,504.

After the baby boom, both countries experienced periods of zero population growth when the annual number of births failed to compensate for the annual number of deaths. As of 1993, with the exclusion of foreigners' births, deaths have outnumbered births every year since 1976 in the old *Länder*. Since 1986 the same has been true for the new *Länder*. When the West German total fertility rate reached its historic peacetime low of fewer than 1.3 children per woman of child-bearing age in 1985, popular newsmagazines caused a sensation with cover stories that warned of the eventual disappearance of the Germans. In the former GDR, a pronatalist policy temporarily had modest success in boosting the birth rate in the mid-1970s, but the population declined there for two reasons: emigration and low fertility. This was especially noticeable after the fall of the Berlin Wall in November 1989 when emigration soared. Low fertility also continued to be a problem. Between 1989 and 1991, eastern Germany's total fertility rate fell by 38 percent. In 1991 the rate was 0.98, well below West Germany's lowest level.

Although its population was just one-fifth that of West Germany, until 1986 East Germany officially topped in absolute terms West Germany in both the number of births outside marriage and the number of abortions. This situation was accounted for in part by a chronic lack of birth control choices in the former Soviet bloc and the practice of using abortion as a regular means of curbing unwanted pregnancies. In 1988 one-third of all births in the GDR were to unwed mothers, whereas in the FRG only one-tenth were. The trend of out-of-wedlock births in the east continued to increase after unification. By 1992 nearly 42 percent of the babies born in the new *Länder* were to single mothers, compared with 12 percent in the old *Länder*.

Until mid-1993, when a more restrictive West German law came into effect, the eastern section of Germany recognized the right of abortion on demand. The highest rate was reached in 1972, when one-third of pregnancies were aborted. By 1989 the rate had declined, but the probability of an abortion was still one in every four pregnancies. In the old *Länder*, legal abortions were restricted to special circumstances based on such factors as the physical or mental health of the mother or fetus. In 1989 West Germany officially registered 75,297 abortions, compared with about 74,000 for East Germany. Social, cultural, and economic factors accounted for the differences in frequency of abortion and extramarital birth rates.

Following unification, a trend termed demographic paralysis was observed in the former East Germany when the number of births fell by 50 percent between 1990 and 1993. From 1988 to mid-1993, the crude birth rate fell from 12.9 per 1,000 to 5.3 per 1,000, an abrupt and precipitous decline unmatched in an industrial society in peacetime. Especially hard hit by skyrocketing unemployment and adrift in an alien market economy, record numbers of women in the new *Länder* stopped having children. Some reports indicated that by the summer of 1993 as many as two-thirds of working women in the east had lost their jobs since unification. In that same year, the marriage rate fell by half.

Age-Gender Distribution

In the early 1990s, an age-gender distribution pyramid of unified Germany's population displayed at its apex the legacy of heavy war casualties: a preponderance of elderly women too great to be explained by women's greater longevity. Official statistics show that in 1990 there were approximately 2.7 million more females than males (41.2 million versus 38.5 million) in Germany. In the same year, so many wives had outlived their husbands, either because of war deaths or because of the lower

153

life expectancy of males, that the 4.9 million elderly widows in the country accounted for approximately 6 percent of the total population. Population specialists have forecast the transformation of the pyramid into a mushroom, as the effect of slackening birth rates pushes the population bulge higher up the age categories. In 1990 about 50 percent of the population was under thirty-seven years of age (see fig. 8).

The progressive aging of Germany's population has been rapid. In 1970 those aged seventeen or younger made up 27.2 percent of the population, those aged eighteen to sixty-five accounted for 59.1 percent, and those aged sixty-five and older were 13.7 percent. By 1990 these shares had changed to 19.2 percent, 65.8 percent, and 15 percent, respectively. The implications of this trend for social welfare and security are a cause of concern. In the early 1990s, one pensioner was financed by three employees. If present trends continue, forecasts indicate that by 2030 as much as 28 percent of Germany's population will be elderly, and there will be a 1:1 ratio between pensioners and workers.

Mortality

In the postwar period, the former GDR developed a comprehensive health care system that made steady advances in reducing infant mortality and extending life expectancy for both men and women. Early in the postwar period, life expectancy in some categories was actually longer for East Germans than for West Germans, and infant mortality was lower until 1980. However, starting in the mid-1970s, West Germany began to register longer life expectancies in every age-group, and after 1980 the infant mortality rate dropped below that of East Germany. In 1988 infant mortality in West Germany was 7.6 per 1,000 live births and 8.1 per 1,000 in East Germany.

The better health and longevity of West Germans probably stemmed from an increased interest in quality of life issues, personal health, and the environment. East Germans, in contrast, suffered the ill effects of the Soviet model of a traditional rust-belt industrial economy, with minimal concern for workers' safety and health and wanton disregard of the need to protect the environment. Improving environmental conditions and a more health-conscious way of living should gradually reduce remaining health differences among Germans. In mid-1995 unified Germany had an estimated mortality rate of about eleven per 1,000, and life expectancy was estimated at 76.6

years (73.5 years for males and 79.9 years for females). The major causes of death were the same as those of other advanced countries (see Current Health Care Issues and Outlook for the Future, ch. 4).

Population Distribution and Urbanization

Following unification, the Federal Republic encompassed 356,958 square kilometers and was one of the largest countries in Europe. With about 81.3 million people in mid-1995, it ranked second behind Russia in population among the countries of Europe. Unification actually reduced the Federal Republic's population density, however, because East Germany, which had a large rural area, was more sparsely populated. With an average of 228 persons per square kilometer in late 1993, unified Germany ranked third in population density among European countries. It ranked behind the Netherlands and Belgium, which had 363 and 329 persons per square kilometer, respectively.

Germany's population density varies greatly. The most densely populated *Länder* are Berlin, Hamburg, and Bremen, with densities of 3,898, 2,236, and 1,697 persons per square kilometer, respectively, at the end of 1992 (see table 7, Appendix). The least densely populated are two new *Länder*, Mecklenburg-Western Pomerania and Brandenburg, both mostly rural in character. They had population densities of eighty and eighty-six persons per square kilometer, respectively, at the end of 1992. Other *Länder* are closer to the national average: the largest *Land*, Bavaria, with 167 persons per square kilometer, is mostly rural, but its capital is the large city of Munich; Rhineland-Palatinate, with 196 persons per square kilometer, is also mostly rural but has numerous heavily populated areas along the Rhine; and Saxony, with 252 persons per square kilometer, also has a number of heavily populated areas.

The *Land* with the most population, one-fifth of the nation's total, is North Rhine-Westphalia. With a population density of 519 persons per square kilometer at the end of 1992, it is the most heavily settled of all *Länder*, with the exception of the three city *Länder* of Bremen, Hamburg, and Berlin. North Rhine-Westphalia's density is caused by its many cities; several dozen of these cities have populations above 100,000, including five with populations above 500,000. Many of these cities are located so close together that they form one of Europe's

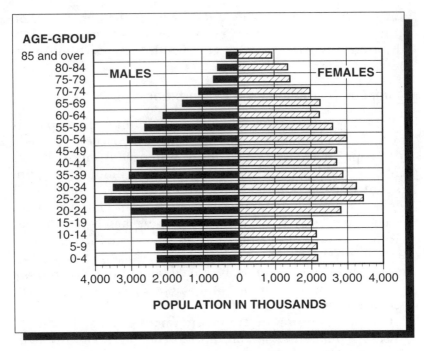

AGE-GROUP

POPULATION IN THOUSANDS

Source: Based on information from Federal Republic of Germany, Statistisches
Bundesamt, *Statistisches Jahrbuch 1994 für die Bundesrepublik Deutschland*,
Wiesbaden, 1994, 66.

Figure 8. Population by Age and Gender, 1992

largest urban agglomerations, the Ruhrstadt (Ruhr City), with
a population of about 5 million.

The Federal Republic has few very large cities and many
medium-sized ones, a reflection of the centuries when the
name *Germany* designated a geographical area consisting of
many small and medium-sized states, each with its own capital
(see table 8, Appendix). Berlin, by far the largest city, with a
population of 3.5 million at the end of 1993, is certain to grow
in population as more of the government moves there in the
second half of the 1990s and as businesses relocate their headquarters to the new capital. Some estimates predict that
Greater Berlin will have a population of 8 million by early in
the twenty-first century.

Berlin already dwarfs the only other cities having more than
1 million inhabitants: Hamburg with 1.7 million and Munich
with 1.3 million. Ten cities have populations between 500,000
and 1 million, seventeen between 250,000 and 500,000, and

fifty-four between 100,000 and 250,000. In the early 1990s, about one-third of the population lived in cities with 100,000 residents or more, one-third in cities and towns with populations between 50,000 and 100,000, and one-third in villages and small towns.

Other densely populated areas are located in the southwest. They are Greater Stuttgart; the Rhine-Main area with its center of Frankfurt am Main; and the Rhine-Neckar region with its center in Mannheim. The greater Nuremberg and Hanover regions are also significant population centers. The new *Länder* are thinly settled except for Berlin and the regions of Dresden-Leipzig and Chemnitz-Zwickau.

Urban areas in the east are more densely populated than those in the west because the GDR saw little of the suburbanization seen in West Germany. As a result, there is a greater contrast between urban and rural areas in the new *Länder* than in the west. West Germany's suburbanization, however, is not nearly as extensive as that experienced by the United States after the end of World War II. Compared with cities in the United States, German cities are fairly compact, and their inhabitants can quickly reach small villages and farmlands.

Germany's population growth has been slow since the late 1960s. Many regions have shown little or no growth, or have even declined in population. The greatest growth has been in the south, where the populations of Baden-Württemberg and Bavaria each increased by well over 1 million between 1970 and 1993. (Each had also grown by over 1 million in the 1960s.) North Rhine-Westphalia, which had grown by 1 million in the 1960s, added another 750,000 to its population between 1970 and 1993, a small increase, given a total population of nearly 18 million at the end of 1993. Bremen, Hamburg, and the Saarland experienced some population loss between 1970 and 1993. With the exception of united Berlin, all the new *Länder* lost population between the fall of the Berlin Wall and the end of 1993. In general, this development reflected long-term trends in East Germany, although the rate of decline has been higher since unification.

Immigration

Immigration has been a primary force shaping demographic developments in the two Germanys in the postwar period (see Historical Background, this ch.). After the erection of the Berlin Wall in 1961, the immigration flow, first into West Germany

157

and later into united Germany, consisted mainly of workers from southern Europe. In addition, the immigrants included several other groups: a small but steady stream of East German immigrants (*Übersiedler*) during the 1980s that exploded in size in 1990 (389,000) but by 1993 had fallen by more than half (172,000) and was somewhat offset by movement from west to east (119,000); several million ethnic Germans (*Aussiedler*) from East European countries, especially the former Soviet Union; and several million persons seeking asylum from political oppression, most of whom were from East European countries.

Foreign Residents

As of early 1994, approximately 6.8 million registered foreigners resided in Germany. Turks made up the largest group (1.9 million), followed by immigrants from the former Yugoslavia (930,000), Italians (565,000), Greeks (350,000), Poles (260,000), and Austrians (185,000). About 25 percent of these foreign residents, most of whom were born in Germany, are under the age of eighteen. Because of the higher birth rate of foreigners, one of every ten births in Germany is to a foreigner. However, because recruiting of *Gastarbeiter* stopped in 1973 at the onset of a worldwide recession, most foreign workers are middle-aged and have lived in Germany for several decades.

The foreign population is not distributed evenly. More than two-thirds live in the *Länder* of North Rhine-Westphalia, Baden-Württemberg, and Bavaria, where in 1990 they made up 9, 10, and 7 percent of the population, respectively. Foreigners live mainly in urban areas; in 1989 approximately 23 percent of foreign residents lived in Hamburg and Berlin. Foreigners often live in particular areas of large cities. (For example, Kreuzberg in Berlin and Kalk in Cologne both have large Turkish communities.) There are few foreigners in the new *Länder*. Of the roughly 190,000 foreigners living in the former GDR in 1989 because of work contracts, many have since been repatriated to Vietnam, Mozambique, Cuba, and other developing countries that were friendly to the GDR regime.

Foreigners began arriving in West Germany in large numbers in the 1960s after the construction of the Berlin Wall ended migration from East Germany. Recruited mainly from a number of countries in southern Europe, *Gastarbeiter* were not expected to stay beyond the terms of their work permits. However, many opted to remain in West Germany and subsequently

brought their families there to live. As a result, and owing to higher birth rates, the foreign population in Germany has increased substantially (see table 9, Appendix). By offering financial incentives, West German authorities hoped to encourage some *Gastarbeiter* to return to their native countries, but relatively few took advantage of these provisions. A tightening of entry restrictions also caused many to remain in Germany rather than risk not being readmitted after spending time in their home country.

Although no longer recruited abroad, Germany's foreign residents remain vital to the economy, parts of which would shut down if they were to depart. They also contribute to the country's welfare and social insurance programs by paying twice as much in taxes and insurance premiums as they receive in benefits. In the long term, their presence may be seen as vital because they have a positive birth rate. The birth rate among native Germans is so low that some studies have estimated that Germany will require approximately 200,000 immigrants a year to maintain its population into the next century and support its array of social welfare benefits.

Most Germans do not see their country as a land of immigration like the United States or Canada, and no demographic or social issue has generated greater controversy than the presence of foreigners in the Federal Republic. In an opinion poll taken in 1982, two-thirds of West Germans said that there were too many foreigners in Germany, and one-half thought that foreigners should be sent back to their countries of origin. In 1992 another poll found that the "foreigner problem" ranked as the most serious issue for western Germans and was third in importance for eastern Germans.

According to the foreigners law that went into effect in mid-1993, foreigners living in Germany for fifteen years may become German citizens if they have no criminal record and renounce their original citizenship. Young foreigners who have resided eight years in Germany may become citizens if they have attended German schools for six years and apply for citizenship between the ages of sixteen and twenty-three. Usually, however, German citizenship depends not on where one is born (*ius solis*) but on the nationality of the father or, since 1974, on the mother (*ius sanguinis*). Thus, to many, German citizenship depends on being born German and cannot rightfully be acquired through a legal process. This notion makes it practically impossible for naturalized citizens or their children to be considered German. Some reformers advocate eliminating the concept of German blood in the 1913 law regulating citizenship, but the issue is an emotional one, and such a change has little popular support.

Ethnic Germans

Ethnic Germans have immigrated to Germany since the end of World War II. At first, these immigrants were Germans who had resided in areas that had formerly been German territory. Later, the offspring of German settlers who in previous centuries had settled in areas of Eastern Europe and Russia came to be regarded as ethnic Germans and as such had the right to German citizenship according to Article 116 of the Basic Law. Because they became citizens immediately upon arrival in Germany, ethnic Germans received much financial and social assistance to ease their integration into society. Housing, vocational training, and many other types of assistance, even language training—because many did not know the language of their forebears—were liberally provided.

With the gradual opening of the Soviet empire in the 1980s, the numbers of ethnic Germans coming to West Germany swelled. In the mid-1980s, about 40,000 came each year. In 1987 the number doubled and in 1988 doubled again. In 1990 nearly 400,000 ethnic Germans came to the Federal Republic. In the 1991–93 period, about 400,000 ethnic Germans settled in Germany. Since January 1993, immigration of ethnic Germans has been limited to 220,000 per year.

Because this influx could no longer be managed, especially because of the vast expense of unification, restrictions on the right of ethnic Germans to return to Germany became effective in January 1991. Under the new restrictions, once in Germany ethnic Germans are assigned to certain areas. If they leave these areas, they lose many of their benefits and are treated as if they were foreigners. The government has also established programs to encourage the estimated several million ethnic Germans who still live in the former Soviet Union and Eastern Europe to remain there. Although ethnic Germans are entitled to German citizenship by virtue of their bloodlines, to many Germans they do not seem German, and their social integration has frequently been difficult.

Asylum-Seekers

To atone for the crimes of the Third Reich, Article 16/2 of West Germany's Basic Law offers liberal asylum rights to those suffering political persecution. Until the 1980s, relatively few refugees took advantage of this provision. But in the second half of the decade, a new class of "jet-age refugees" began to make its way to Europe and especially to West Germany, which accepted more than any other West European country. In the mid-1980s, many refugees came from Iran and Lebanon. By 1991 most refugees originated in regions of war-torn former Yugoslavia, Romania, or Turkey. From 1986 to 1989, about 380,000 refugees sought asylum inWest Germany. By comparison, in the 1990–92 period, nearly 900,000 people sought refuge in a united Germany.

Although only about 5 percent of requests for asylum are approved, slow processing and appeals mean that many refugees remain in Germany for years. Because financial aid is also provided for the refugees' living expenses, their presence has become a burden on federal and local government. The resulting social tensions made imperative an amendment to the constitutional provision regarding asylum. After heated debate, in 1993 the Bundestag passed legislation that amended the Basic Law and tightened restrictions on granting asylum. One important change is that asylum-seekers are no longer to be admitted into Germany if they have applied from a third country. In addition, more funds are to be allotted to processing applications, so that asylum-seekers remain in Germany for shorter periods.

Ethnic Minorities

In the early 1990s, there were between 50,000 and 60,000 Gypsies in Germany. They were divided into two groups: the Sinti, who have lived for hundreds of years in Germany and who have largely adopted conventional modes of living and employment; and the Roma, many of whom fled Romania following the 1989 revolution that toppled the Nicolae Ceausescu regime. The lifestyle and work habits of the mobile Roma clash with those of most Germans. As a result, in 1992 the German government signed an agreement with Romania providing for the repatriation of thousands of Roma in exchange for cash payments to be used for housing and job training.

Several other minority groups, officially recognized and their languages protected, also live in Germany. For more than 1,000 years, the Sorbs, a Slavic nationality, have lived as an ethnic minority in Brandenburg and Saxony. As of 1993, there were about 120,000 Sorbs in Germany. In addition, about 60,000 Danish speakers live in Schleswig-Holstein, a reminder of the area's Danish past; and about 12,000 speakers of the Frisian language live on the Frisian Islands and on the northwestern coast.

Germany once had a prosperous and largely assimilated Jewish population of about 600,000. In the 1930s and 1940s, most German Jews were exiled, were imprisoned, or perished in Nazi death camps (see Total Mobilization, Resistance, and the Holocaust, ch. 1). By the early 1990s, Germany's Jewish community was only about 40,000. Its numbers were growing, however, as the result of the immigration of some Israelis and Russian Jews. One of the most eloquent spokespersons for the rights of minorities and a tireless advocate for greater tolerance is the community's leader, Ignaz Bubnis.

Turkish restaurant in Berlin
Courtesy German Information
Center, New York
Italian grocery store in Cologne
Courtesy Eric Solsten

Women in Society

For centuries, a woman's role in German society was summed up and circumscribed by the three "K" words: *Kinder* (children), *Kirche* (church), and *Küche* (kitchen). Throughout the twentieth century, however, women have gradually won victories in their quest for equal rights. In 1919 they received the right to vote. Profound changes also were wrought by World War II. During the war, women assumed positions traditionally held by men. After the war, the so-called *Trümmerfrauen* (women of the rubble) tended the wounded, buried the dead, salvaged belongings, and began the arduous task of rebuilding war-torn Germany by simply clearing away the rubble.

In West Germany, the Basic Law of 1949 declared that men and women were equal, but it was not until 1957 that the civil code was amended to conform with this statement. Even in the early 1950s, women could be dismissed from the civil service when they married. After World War II, despite the severe shortage of young men that made marriage impossible for many women, traditional marriage once again became society's ideal. Employment and social welfare programs remained predicated on the male breadwinner model. West Germany turned to millions of migrants or immigrants—including large numbers of GDR refugees—to satisfy its booming economy's labor requirements. Women became homemakers and mothers again and largely withdrew from employment outside the home.

In the east, however, women remained in the workforce. The Soviet-style system mandated women's participation in the economy, and the government implemented this key objective by opening up educational and vocational opportunities to women. As early as 1950, marriage and family laws also had been rewritten to accommodate working mothers. Abortion was legalized and funded by the state in the first trimester of pregnancy. An extensive system of social supports, such as a highly developed day-care network for children, was also put in place to permit women to be both mothers and workers. Emancipated "from above" for economic and ideological reasons, women in the east entered institutes of higher learning and the labor force in record numbers while still maintaining the household. East Germany had to rely on women because of its declining population; the situation was made more critical by the fact that most of those fleeing to West Germany were men.

Because of these developments, about 90 percent of East German women worked outside the home. They made up about half the membership in the two most important mass organizations of the former GDR—the Free German Trade Union Federation (Freier Deutscher Gewerkschaftsbund—FDGB) and the Free German Youth (Freie Deutsche Jugend—FDJ). In 1988 slightly more than one-third of the membership of the ruling Socialist Unity Party of Germany (Sozialistische Einheitspartei Deutschlands—SED) consisted of women. In contrast, only about 4.4 percent of West German women were members of a political party.

After several decades of conforming to traditional social patterns, West German women began to demand changes. Following patterns in Europe and the United States, emancipation in the Federal Republic originated "from below," with women themselves. In the 1970s, the women's movement gathered momentum, having emerged as an outgrowth of student protests in the late 1960s (see Citizens' Initiative Associations, ch. 7). Rallying around the causes of equal rights (including the right to abortion, which was somewhat restricted in West Germany), the movement succeeded in having legislation passed in 1977 that granted a woman equal rights in marriage. A woman could work outside the home and file for divorce without her husband's permission. Divorce was permitted when the marriage partners could no longer be reconciled.

Women also made gains in education in both Germanys. By the mid-1960s, East German women accounted for about half of all secondary school graduates who had prepared to study at institutes of higher learning in the GDR; by the 1975–76 academic year, they were in the majority (53 percent). To assist women in completing their studies, an extensive support system, including supplementary payments and child care, was provided. Expanded educational opportunities for West German women were slower in coming and never equaled the levels reached in the east. Only in the early 1980s did West German women qualify for admission to universities in the same numbers as men. Although fewer than that number pursued college and university studies, between 1970 and 1989 the percentage of female students increased from 31 percent to 41 percent. Two factors were believed to be responsible for the discrepancy between eastern and western rates of attendance at institutes of higher learning: West German women had a stronger orientation toward traditional familial relations; and they had dimmer prospects for admission to particular academic departments and for professional employment after graduation.

Despite significant gains, discrimination remains in united Germany. Income inequalities persist: a woman's wages and salaries range between 65 percent and 78 percent of a man's for many positions. In most fields, women do not hold key positions. Generally, the higher the position, the more powerful is male dominance. For example, women are heavily represented in the traditional care-giving fields of health and education, but even in such fields there is a wide disparity between the number of females working in hospitals (75 percent of total staff) and schools (more than 50 percent) and the number of female physicians (4 percent) and principals (20 percent in the west and 32 percent in the east). In the late 1980s, only 5 percent of university professors in West Germany were women.

Although substantial barriers to equality of the sexes in Germany remain as a result of a persistently patriarchal family structure and work environment, women have managed to gain isolated high-profile victories. A separate national office for women's affairs was created in West Germany in 1980, and similar agencies have been established in most *Länder* in united Germany. Since the mid-1980s, offices responsible for working toward women's equality have been active, first in West Germany and after unification in the new *Länder*. The Equality Offices (*Gleichstellungstellen*) have as one of their tasks ensuring that women occupy a more equitable share of positions in the public sector.

Some women have succeeded in reaching positions of power. One of the most successful women in politics in the 1990s is Rita Süssmuth, president of the Bundestag. In the field of industry, Birgit Breuel assumed the leadership, following the assassination of Detlev Rohwedder in April 1991, of the Treuhandanstalt (Trust Agency), the powerful agency charged with privatizing the former East German economy. Other influential and prominent German women in the mid-1990s are Marion von Dönhoff, coeditor of *Die Zeit*, and Elizabeth Noelle-Neumann, director of the Allensbach Public Opinion Institute. Yet despite this progress, a 1991 article in an influential weekly magazine made it clear how far women must go to achieve equality. The magazine's list of the 100 most powerful people in Germany included only four women.

Almost all segments of eastern German society encountered tremendous difficulty in the unification process, but women suffered the most. Some reports indicated that two-thirds of working women in the new *Länder* were unemployed, and many more were turned into part-time workers as a result of privatization, downsizing of firms, and elimination of support services such as day-care and after-school centers. To improve their prospects for employment, some women in eastern Germany reportedly were resorting to sterilization, one of the factors contributing to the steep decline in births from twelve per 1,000 in 1989 to 5.3 per 1,000 in 1993.

Among the issues that demonstrated differences between women of the old and new *Länder,* one of the most contentious was abortion. In 1991 there were about 125,000 registered abortions performed in Germany, about 50,000 of which were in the east. Although the number of registered abortions in both parts of Germany had been declining in recent years, the actual number of abortions was estimated at about 250,000. For a time following unification, the restrictive western and permissive eastern legislation on abortion continued in force. In June 1992, however, the Bundestag voted to ease abortion restrictions and to permit the procedure during the first twelve weeks of pregnancy with compulsory counseling. Resorting to what had been a successful policy in the early 1970s, those opposed to the new law, including Chancellor Helmut Kohl, appealed to the Federal Constitutional Court in Karlsruhe to nullify the new law. Just before it was scheduled to take effect, the law was blocked when the court issued an injunction. Subsequently, a new restrictive law came to apply in all of Germany (see Political Developments since Unification, ch. 7).

Marriage and Family

Like most other advanced countries in the postwar era, Germany recorded fewer marriages, more divorces, and smaller families. In 1960 there were 690,000 marriages, compared with 516,000 in 1990. The total for 1993 amounted to only 442,000, but most of this decline was caused by a drop of than more 50 percent in the number of marriages in the new *Länder* between 1990 and 1993. Until 1990 the decline in marriages in East Germany had been appreciably greater than in West Germany (from 215,000 in 1950 to 137,000 in 1989, compared with 536,000 and 399,000 in the same years in West Germany), but not nearly as steep in the 1990–93 period. Just as the dramatic social changes brought to the new *Länder* by unification affected birth rates there, so they also affected marriages rates.

Another difference in marriage practices between the two Germanys had been that easterners marrying for the first time did so at an earlier age than westerners. Easterners did so, it is believed, because of their desire to have children and hence qualify for low-cost child care and housing benefits. Following unification this difference remained. In 1992 the average age at first marriage was 29.0 for men and 26.5 for women in the old *Länder,* compared with 27.1 for men and 25.1 for women in the new *Länder.* Since the mid-1970s, the average age at which people marry has slowly risen for both genders in both parts of Germany.

As the number of marriages declined, the frequency of divorce increased in both states. Between 1960 and 1990, the number of divorces in West Germany more than doubled, increasing from 49,000 to 123,000 and yielding a divorce rate of about 30 percent. Divorce was always more common in East Germany than it was in West Germany. The number of divorces roughly doubled between 1960 and 1988, going from 25,000 to 49,000. In 1986 there was a record divorce rate of 46 percent. Although home to only 20 percent of the total population, the new *Länder* accounted for 29 percent of all divorces in 1990. After unification, however, the incidence of divorce decreased greatly in the east, perhaps in response to the overall uncertainty and insecurity of future prospects for single mothers in unified Germany. In 1992 the number of divorces in the new *Länder* amounted to only 10,000. In 1993, however, this number rose to 18,000, an increase of 78 percent.

Despite the increasing likelihood of divorce, in 1990 about 89 percent of all families consisted of married couples, and about 70 percent of those of marriage age were married. In both east and west, however, the failure of these families to produce the necessary number of children for population replacement was striking. Of the 15 million married couples in the former West Germany, about 57 percent had children. Forty-seven percent of couples with children had one child, 38 percent had two children, and 13 percent had three or more children. In 1950 the average number of persons in German households was 3.0. By 1990 this figure had declined to 2.3. In 1991 four-person households accounted for 13 percent of the total number of households, three-person households for 16 percent, two-person households for 31 percent, and single-person households for 35 percent. In the early 1990s, only foreign families were regularly having two or more children, with the Turkish subgroup being the largest in terms of family size.

Like West Germany, East Germany had provided legislative protection for the family and married couples, together with generous maternity leave and pay provisions. In the east, however, it was assumed that the mother would rejoin the workforce soon after maternity leave, and an elaborate child-care system was put in place. Virtually all women could obtain excellent care for their children if they wished. In the west, many mothers gave up their careers or interrupted them for long periods following the birth of a child because child care was generally unavailable. As a result, in 1990 women of child-bearing age in the east had more children (1.67) than women in the west (1.42). Supported by the state, eastern women had long been accustomed to balancing child-rearing and a profession. After unification, however, the new *Länder* experienced a precipitous decline in births because of high unemployment, especially among women (see Fertility, this ch.).

By the mid-1990s, the newest trend in household formation was what became known as nonmarital living partnerships. Between 1972 and 1990, the number of such households increased sevenfold, to 963,000, or 2.7 percent of all households. Almost 90 percent of these were childless households. Most young people were opting to live together before deciding to marry. This factor pushed the average age at marriage higher.

Another sign of the movement away from the traditional concept of family and of the manifestation of sexual freedom was the rising number of out-of-wedlock births. In the late 1980s, about one in ten West German and three in ten East German births were to unmarried women.

In the postwar period, it became clear that marriage had lost its former position as the only legitimate locus for sexual activity. In the early 1990s, polls indicated that 60 percent of German sixteen-year-olds were sexually active, compared with 15 percent in the 1950s.

In the past, when regional differences were acute, convention held that marriages between a Prussian and a Bavarian, between a Catholic and a Protestant, and definitely between a Christian and a Jew were "mixed" marriages. In modern Germany, only unions between Germans and foreigners are considered mixed. Of 516,000 marriages in 1990, about 6 percent were between Germans and foreigners. Most often German women married Americans, Italians, Turks, and Yugoslavs, and German men married Yugoslavs, Poles, Filipinos, and Austrians. In 1974 legislation was passed conferring automatic citizenship on children born of these unions.

Housing

There is a wide range of housing stock in Germany, from mansions and country estates for the wealthy, to tents and welfare hotels for the needy and homeless. Most Germans live in self-contained apartments or in single-family houses. Single-story and two-story townhouse-like dwellings characterize the tidy neighborhoods of small towns and medium-sized cities, and high-rise apartment buildings are common in larger cities. In many communities, merchants, tradespeople, and shopkeepers continue to live above their stores, and clustered farmhouses still form the nucleus of many villages.

After World War II, West Germany faced a severe housing shortage. Not only had the war destroyed much of the housing, but the millions of refugees from the east had to find new accommodations. According to one estimate, there were 10 million dwellings for 17 million households. The housing shortage often forced several families to share a single dwelling. In the 1950s and 1960s, a tremendous surge in construction, supported heavily by the government, resulted in the construction of as many as 700,000 dwellings in a single year. Gradually, the housing crisis eased. The problems that persisted generally involved a shortage of affordable housing in urban areas. Housing conditions in East Germany also improved greatly. However, much of the housing was badly designed and poorly constructed, and even at the state's demise in 1990, the overall housing supply was inadequate.

Unification revealed significant differences in the quality, variety, and size of dwellings in the two Germanys. In West Germany, about 70 percent of the housing stock had been built after 1948, with 95 percent of the dwellings having their own bathrooms and 75 percent having central heating. In East Germany, 55 percent of the housing stock had been built before 1948, with only 75 percent of the dwellings having bathrooms and only 47 percent having central heating. In addition, much of the housing in East Germany was in poor condition because the authorities had maintained rents at such low levels that funds were not available for essential repairs.

In 1992 united Germany had approximately 34.5 million dwellings with 149 million rooms, for a total of 2.8 billion square meters of living space. Dwellings in the west were larger than those in the east. In 1992 dwellings in the old *Länder* had an average floor space of 82.7 square meters for an average of 35.1 square meters per person, compared with 64.5 square meters and an average of 29.0 square meters per person in the new *Länder.*

The federal government has responded with special measures to rectify housing problems in the new *Länder,* launching an ambitious program to upgrade and expand housing. By 1993 about 1.1 million units had been modernized. Specialists have estimated that bringing housing in the east up to western standards will require the construction of 140,000 new dwellings a year until 2005.

Unification also revealed significant differences with respect to home ownership. In the early 1990s, approximately 40 percent of residents owned their dwellings in the old *Länder,* compared with 25 percent in the new *Länder.*

Prior to unification, a housing shortage had developed in West Germany because of increased immigration and the rising number of single householders. The arrival of several million refugees, ethnic Germans, and eastern Germans coincided with a steep drop in the availability of inexpensive housing. Despite the construction of as many as 400,000 new dwellings each year, as of 1993 the need for housing outpaced the supply. A housing shortage exists because the country's 35 million households exceed the number of dwellings by about 500,000.

The housing shortage and a lack of available land for building in densely populated areas have driven up real estate prices. In 1992 a single-family free-standing house with 125 square meters of floor space cost DM300,000 in Dresden, DM450,000 in Hamburg, DM590,000 in Frankfurt am Main, DM800,000 in Berlin, and DM910,000 in Munich. In western Germany, the average price of building land was DM129 per square meter, compared with DM32 per square meter in the east.

Because decent housing is seen as a basic right in Germany, the government provides financial aid to households devoting too great a share of their income to housing costs. The aid can subsidize their rents or help pay mortgages. In the early 1990s, some 3 million households received this type of aid. Despite these programs, however, homelessness remains a problem. In the early 1990s, some specialists estimated the number of homeless at between 800,000 and 1 million, while others believed it to be as low as 150,000. The homeless receive aid from government and charitable organizations, which provide an array of social services and shelters (see Provisions of the Social Welfare System, ch. 4).

Religion

Roman Catholicism, one of Germany's two principal religions, traces its origins there to the eighth-century missionary work of Saint Boniface (see Medieval Germany, ch. 1). In the next centuries, Roman Catholicism made more converts and spread eastward. In the twelfth and thirteenth centuries, the Knights of the Teutonic Order spread German and Roman Catholic influence by force of arms along the southern Baltic Coast and into Russia. In 1517, however, Martin Luther challenged papal authority and what he saw as the commercialization of his faith. In the process, Luther changed the course of European and world history and established the second major faith in Germany—Protestantism (see The Protestant Reformation, ch. 1).

Religious differences played a decisive role in the Thirty Years' War (see The Thirty Years' War, 1618–48, ch. 1). An enduring legacy of the Protestant Reformation and this conflict was the division of Germany into fairly distinct regions of religious practice. Roman Catholicism remained the preeminent faith in the southern and western German states, while Protestantism became firmly established in the northeastern and central regions. Pockets of Roman Catholicism existed in Oldenburg in the north and in areas of Hesse. Protestant congregations could be found in north Baden and northeastern Bavaria.

The unification of Germany in 1871 under Prussian leadership led to the strengthening of Protestantism (see Bismarck and Unification, ch. 1). Otto von Bismarck sought to weaken Roman Catholic influence through an anti-Roman Catholic campaign, the Kulturkampf, in the early 1870s. The Jesuit order was prohibited in Germany, and its members were expelled from the country. In Prussia the "Falk laws," named for Adalbert Falk, Bismarck's minister of culture, mandated German citizenship and attendance at German universities for clergymen, state inspection of schools, and state confirmation of parish and episcopal appointments. Although relations between the Roman Catholic Church and the state were subsequently improved through negotiations with the Vatican, the Kulturkampf engendered in Roman Catholics a deep distrust of the empire and enmity toward Prussia.

Prior to World War II, about two-thirds of the German population was Protestant and the remainder Roman Catholic. Bavaria was a Roman Catholic stronghold. Roman Catholics were also well represented in the populations of Baden-Württemberg, the Saarland, and in much of the Rhineland. Elsewhere in Germany, especially in the north and northeast, Protestants were in the majority.

During the Hitler regime, except for individual acts of resistance, the established churches were unable or unwilling to mount a serious challenge to the supremacy of the state (see The Third Reich, 1933–45, ch. 1). A Nazi, Ludwig Müller, was installed as the Lutheran bishop in Berlin. Although raised a Roman Catholic, Hitler respected only the power and organization of the Roman Catholic Church, not its tenets. In July 1933, shortly after coming to power, the Nazis scored their first diplomatic success by concluding a concordat with the Vatican, regulating church-state relations. In return for keeping the right to maintain denominational schools nationwide, the Vatican assured the Nazis that Roman Catholic clergy would refrain from political activity, that the government would have a say in the choice of bishops, and that changes in diocesan boundaries would be subject to government approval. However, the Nazis soon violated the concordat's terms, and by the late 1930s almost all denominational schools had been abolished.

Toward the end of 1933, an opposition group under the leadership of Lutheran pastors Martin Niemöller and Dietrich Bonhoeffer formed the "Confessing Church." The members of this church opposed the takeover of the Lutheran Church by the Nazis. Many of its members were eventually arrested, and some were executed—among them, Bonhoeffer—by the end of World War II.

Postwar Christianity

The postwar division of Germany left roughly equal numbers of Roman Catholics and Protestants in West Germany. East Germany had five times as many Protestants as Roman Catholics. There the authorities waged a persistent and largely successful campaign to minimize the influence and authority of the Protestant and Roman Catholic churches.

In the Federal Republic, freedom of religion is guaranteed by Article 4 of the Basic Law, and the churches enjoy a special legal status as corporate bodies. In theory, there is constitutional separation of church and state, but church financing complicates this separation. To support churches and their work, most Germans in the old *Länder* pay a voluntary church tax, amounting to an 8 or 9 percent surcharge on income tax paid. Living in a society known for consensus and conformity, few West Germans formally withdrew from the established churches before the 1980s and hence continued to pay the tax.

Beginning in the 1980s, negative attitudes toward the tax and the churches become more common, and people began leaving the churches in significant numbers. Between 1980 and 1992, about 1.0 million Roman Catholics and 1.2 million Protestants gave up their church memberships. A faltering economy and increased taxes caused many to withdraw for financial reasons. In a 1992 poll, approximately 42 percent of those queried stated that the church tax was "much too high"; 64 percent favored abolishing the tax and supporting the churches through voluntary contributions. Fourteen percent of those Roman Catholics and Protestants polled stated that they were likely to withdraw or definitely would withdraw from their church.

In a society increasingly materialist and secular, the spiritual and moral positions of the churches became irrelevant to many. Among the younger generation seeking autonomy and self-fulfillment, allegiance was no longer simply surrendered without question to institutions of authority. Attendance at services dropped off significantly, and the institution of the church quietly disappeared from the lives of many Germans.

In East Germany, although the constitution theoretically provided for freedom of religion, the Marxist-Leninist state placed formidable obstacles before those seeking to exercise that basic right. Enormous pressure was exerted on citizens to renounce religion. East Germans who practiced their religion were denied educational and professional opportunities, for example. Consequently, at unification the majority of East Germans were either not baptized or had left their church.

In the 1990s, polls in the new *Länder* revealed that more than 70 percent of East Germans did not believe in God. Young people were even less religious. Some polls found that only 16 percent of East German schoolchildren believed in God. An entire generation had been raised without the religious rituals that traditionally had marked life's milestones. Secular rituals had been substituted. For example, the *Jugendweihe* (youth dedication) gradually supplanted the Christian practice of confirmation.

After unification in 1990, there were nominally 30.2 million Protestants and 26.7 million Roman Catholics in united Germany. Roman Catholics and Protestants combined amounted to about 76 percent of the German population and 71 percent of the country's total population.

Although less extreme than in the past, attitudes toward religion continue to polarize German society. In the 1990s, especially in the western *Länder*, attitudinal differences separate many younger Germans with humanistic values (concern for the environment, the rights of women and minorities, and peace and disarmament issues) from an older generation who hold traditional religious values. Many others of the postwar generations have accepted the values of popular culture and consumerism and have left the churches because they no longer seem significant. Millions of Germans of all ages, however, continue to profess a religion for a variety of reasons, among them strong religious beliefs, social pressure to conform, preservation of educational and employment opportunities, support for essential church social-welfare activities, and (in the western *Länder*) the enduring appeal of Christian rituals surrounding baptism, marriage, and burial.

As of 1995, it was difficult to determine to what extent Germans in the new *Länder* would return to religion. In the early 1990s, popular magazines featured stories about the "heathenization" of Germany. Although such a provocative characterization of trends seems exaggerated, the incorporation of the former East Germany did dilute religious influence in united Germany. Conversely, however, the opening of eastern Germany gave missionaries from the old *Länder* and from around the world the chance to rekindle religious fervor. In the old *Länder*, the churches have continued their vitally important work of operating an extensive network of hospitals, nursing homes, and other social institutions. The need for such services and facilities is greatest in the five new *Länder*, and the churches quickly stepped in to help.

Roman Catholicism

With about 28.2 million members, the Roman Catholic Church in unified Germany is organized into five archdioceses, eighteen dioceses, three diocesan offices, and one apostolic administration. Two of the archdioceses are based in Bavaria (Munich/Freising and Bamberg) and two in North Rhine-Westphalia (Cologne and Paderborn). More than 57 percent of all German Roman Catholics live in these two *Länder*. Another 28 percent live in the three *Länder* of Baden-Württemberg, Hesse, and Rhineland-Palatinate. Only about 900 of the church's 13,000 parishes and other pastoral centers are located in the new *Länder*. The number of Roman Catholics in East Germany declined from 2 million shortly after the war to 800,000 by 1992. Serving these Roman Catholics are two dioceses, one in Brandenburg (Berlin) and the other in Saxony (Dresden).

Between 1970 and 1989, the number of Roman Catholics attending Sunday mass in West Germany declined from 37 percent to 23 percent. Between 1970 and 1990, the number of annual baptisms fell from about 370,000 to around 300,000. Approximately 470,000 Roman Catholics officially left the church between 1985 and 1990. In the same period, about 25,000 returned to the church, and another 25,000 converted to other religions.

Despite the diminishing numbers of Roman Catholics, the church tax enables the Roman Catholic Church to remain strong financially. In 1992 the church's share of tax revenues amounted to approximately DM8.5 billion. An additional DM8 billion was received in the form of government subsidies, service payments, property, and contributions. Much of this support is returned to society through an extensive network of church-operated kindergartens, senior citizen centers, and hospitals. The main Roman Catholic charitable organization is the Deutscher Caritasverband, which had about 400,000 employees in 1992.

As the FRG has become an increasingly secular society, the centuries-old traditional authority of the Roman Catholic Church in matters of morality has declined, especially among German youth. Many German Roman Catholics routinely ignore the church and in particular the pope's positions on such key issues as birth control, premarital sex, divorce, and abortion. For years the number of ordinations in Germany has declined. To address this issue, most German Catholics favor permitting priests to marry, and many support the ordination of women.

Periodically, independent reformist clergymen challenge the church hierarchy and doctrine. Often they do so with the support of many German Catholics. In the 1970s, Hans Küng, a theologian at Tübingen University, used his position and charisma to criticize the idea of papal infallibility and other dogmas. In the early 1990s, major differences of opinion between the laity and church authorities were revealed by a clash between a reform-minded priest and the archbishop in Paderborn, the most conservative German diocese. For beliefs deemed contrary to Vatican policies and dogma, Father Eugen Drewermann was defrocked by Archbishop Johannes Degenhardt. In the tradition of Luther, Drewermann continued to express his unorthodox views outside the church—at universities and in the media, including talk shows. A 1992 survey indicated that among all Germans, Drewermann was more popular than Pope John Paul II.

Protestantism

In the mid-1990s, most of the country's roughly 30 million Protestants were organized into twenty-four member churches of the Evangelical Church in Germany (Evangelische Kirche in Deutschland—EKD), headquartered in Hanover. Later in the decade, the church's headquarters is scheduled to relocate to Berlin. The mainline Protestant churches belong to one of three groups: Lutheran (ten); Reformed, or Calvinist (two); and United, or Lutheran-Calvinist (twelve). The largest number of congregations is in Saxony, Berlin, Brandenburg, Lower Saxony, Bavaria, Thuringia, and Baden-Württemberg. Protestant clergy are permitted to marry, and women are actively engaged in the ministry. One of the most prominent women in the EKD and in Germany in the mid-1990s was Maria Jepsen, bishop of Hamburg.

In the early 1990s, about 5 percent of German Protestants attended weekly services. Annual baptisms declined from about 346,000 in 1970 to around 257,000 in 1990. Of the 257,000 baptisms in 1990, only about 12 percent took place in the former East Germany. Out of 219,000 confirmations in 1990, about 10 percent involved East German youth. Like their Roman Catholic counterparts, Protestant churches are well supported by taxes and contributions. The EKD also runs numerous hospitals and other social institutions and is a vitally important member of the country's system of social welfare. The main Protestant charitable organization is the Diakonisches Werk; it has about 350,000 employees.

In East Germany, Protestant churches became a focal point of opposition during the 1980s. This was possible because of an agreement with the authorities in 1978 that granted the churches a degree of independence. Opposition groups, composed of believers and nonbelievers alike, subsequently were able to meet at the churches, where they discussed peace issues and how East Germany could be reformed. In 1989 these churches, in particular those in Leipzig, became staging points for the massive demonstrations that led to the collapse of the communist regime (see The Peace Movement and Internal Resistance, ch. 2).

Free Churches

The free churches in Germany include about a dozen affiliated but independent churches and congregations that emerged from Protestant renewal movements, primarily in the nineteenth century. Some free churches practice baptism, and others accept a simple public declaration of faith. Prominent among the former are Baptists and Methodists, who set up religious communities in Germany in 1834 and 1849, respectively. Methodism was brought to Germany by immigrants returning from the United States. Since 1854 a third group, the Free Evangelical Congregations, has practiced baptism of believers, without making it a precondition for membership in the congregation.

Although the various free churches follow different practices, they differ from the two main religions in Germany in that they are independent of the state. The free churches, seeing themselves as "free churches in a free country," seek no special treatment from the state and are funded almost exclusively by members' voluntary contributions.

The emergence of these independent churches was accompanied by their persecution and denunciation as sects. For this reason, overcoming prejudice has been a long and arduous process. After World War II, the free churches were cofounders of the Study Group of Christian Churches in West Germany and West Berlin. They used this organization as a forum for fraternal interaction with other churches.

The tenets of the free churches stress the importance of the New Testament, freely expressed belief in Jesus Christ and a life of service devoted to him, personal piety, and the sanctity of human life. Conscientious objection to military service is a part of the teachings of some free churches. Many free churches emphasize the autonomy of the local parish and prefer to be called a community rather than a church.

Since 1926 the original members of the Free Churches in Germany have cooperated with one another through the Meeting of Evangelical Free Churches. These churches are the Association of Evangelical Free Church Congregations, the Association of Free Evangelical Congregations, and the Evangelical Methodist Church. Five additional churches have guest membership status: the Christian Study Group Mülheim/Ruhr, the Sacred Army in Germany, the European-Festland Fraternal Uniate, the Church of the Nazarene, and the Association of German Mennonite Communities. These eight free churches have a combined membership of approximately 195,000, organized in about 1,500 parishes or communities. Almost all these churches are legal corporate bodies.

In recent years, the free churches' interaction and cooperation with the established Protestant churches have intensified. A few such activities include missionary work, Bible groups, and humanitarian efforts such as "Bread for the World."

Orthodox Churches

Eastern Orthodox Christianity in Germany derives mainly from the hundreds of thousands of Serbs who came to the country in the 1960s and 1970s as *Gastarbeiter*. The breakup of the former Yugoslavia in the early 1990s caused thousands more Serbs to come to Germany. Many of the Slavs from other East European countries also belong to the Eastern Orthodox Church. Germany's large Greek population belongs mostly to the Greek Orthodox Church.

Judaism

When Hitler came to power in 1933, approximately 600,000 Jews lived in Germany, some of whom were among the most prominent members of society. Over the next twelve years, most fled or were murdered, along with millions of East European Jews, Slavs, and other nationalities. As of January 1992, seventy-six Jewish congregations and *Land* associations had about 34,000 members, with the largest communities located in Berlin and Frankfurt am Main. In the late 1980s and early 1990s, several thousand Soviet Jews of German ancestry took advantage of liberalized Soviet emigration policies and German naturalization laws and resettled in the Federal Republic. However, since unification in 1990 and the outbreak of radical right-wing violence, some in the Jewish community, remembering similar events in the 1930s, have left. Although most hate-crimes and violence have been aimed at foreign workers and asylum-seekers, there have been scattered incidents of attacks on Jewish synagogues and memorials.

Islam

Following the influx of foreign laborers in the 1960s and early 1970s, Islam established a religious presence in Germany, making it the religion with the country's third largest membership. As of 1994, approximately 2 million Muslims resided in Germany. Most of the Muslims are either Turkish, Kurdish, Iranian, or Palestinian. Additional Muslims have entered the country as refugees, fleeing the ethnic and religious conflict in the former Yugoslavia.

Social Structure and Social Mobility

Despite continuing although lessening differences in living standards between the old and new *Länder*, in the mid-1990s German social structure consists mainly of a large, prosperous central stratum containing about 60 percent of the population. This stratum includes mid-level civil servants, most salaried employees, skilled blue-collar workers, and a shrinking pool of farmers. A smaller wealthier group consisting of an upper-middle class and an upper class offsets the poverty experienced by a poor lower class. Hence in terms of social indicators such as education, average income, and property ownership, Germany ranks among the world's leading countries. In terms of income, for example, in 1991 the average German family had a net monthly income of DM4,905, second highest among members of the EC.

Social Structure

Most of the workforce is employed in the services sector. West Germany completed the transition from an industrial economy to one dominated by the services sector in the 1970s, and by the late 1980s this sector employed two-thirds of the workforce. In contrast, when the Berlin Wall fell, East Germany still had not made this transition. Because more of the work-

Turks praying at a mosque in Berlin
A hospital operated by the Evangelical Church
Courtesy German Information Center, New York

force was engaged in industry and agriculture than in the services sector, its socioeconomic structure resembled that of West Germany in 1965.

Rainer Geissler, a German sociologist, has examined his country's social structure in light of the economic changes that have taken place in the postwar era. Because of the growth of the services sector and the doubling of state employees since 1950, he has discarded earlier divisions of German society into an elite class, middle class, and worker class, with a small services class consisting of employees of all levels. He has replaced this division with a more nuanced model that better reflects these postwar changes. As the economy of the new *Länder* is incorporated into the western economy, its much simpler social structure (elite, self-employed, salaried employees, and workers) will come to resemble that of the old *Länder.*

According to Geissler, at the end of the 1980s West Germany's largest group (28 percent of the population) was an educated salaried middle class, employed either in the services sector or in the manufacturing sector as educated, white-collar employees. Some members of this group earned very high salaries; others earned skilled blue-collar wages. This professional class has expanded at the expense of the old middle class, which amounted to only 7 percent of the population at the end of the 1980s. A less educated segment of the services sector, or white-collar employee sector, amounted to 9 percent of the population. Geissler divided the working class into three groups: an elite of the best-trained and best-paid workers (12 percent); skilled workers (18 percent), about 5 percent of whom are foreigners; and unskilled workers (15 percent), about 25 percent of whom are foreigners. A portion of this last group live below the poverty line. Farmers and their families make up 6 percent of the population. At the top of his model of the social structure, Geissler posits an elite of less than 1 percent.

The Elite

During the centuries when Germany was a collection of medium-and small-sized states, wealth and power were concentrated in the hands of the nobility, landed gentry, and wealthy merchants in the cities. With the collapse of the German Empire in 1918, the nobility and landed gentry suffered a major setback, but they still retained much power and influence. During the interwar years, however, much political power devolved to representatives of other classes. A vivid illustration of the transfer of power was former army corporal Adolf Hitler's assumption of the German presidency following the death of General Paul von Hindenburg in 1934.

The old propertied and monied elites suffered an additional loss of power after World War II. In the new worker-dominated GDR, they saw their property confiscated and their power evaporate. West German society was transformed by the rapidly expanding social market economy and the migration of millions of displaced persons from the east, many of whom were well educated and capable. Some of the old elite and their offspring retained positions of influence (most notably in the military and the diplomatic corps), but to an extent greater than ever before, the elite class became open to society as a whole.

According to Geissler, Germany's elite numbers just a few thousand, less than 1 percent of the population, but its influence far outweighs its numbers. The elite consists of persons occupying key positions in such social sectors as business, politics, labor unions, the civil service, the media, and the churches. Membership in the elite is based on performance and is rarely inherited. For this reason, Germany's elite is pluralist in nature because members of lower social strata can enter it by rising to the top of a social sector. The openness of elite positions varies. Sons of workers routinely come to hold high positions in labor unions or in the SPD, but rarely in banking or the diplomatic corps. A vital criterion for advancement is a university degree, most notably a law degree, because about one-third of Germany's elite consists of lawyers.

Entry into East Germany's elite was determined almost exclusively by ideological considerations. Small and entrenched, the East German elite has been characterized as monopolistic, in contrast to that of the West German elite, where numerous groups shared or competed for power. Most of the GDR elite has lost power since the fall of the Berlin Wall. As a result, a new elite similar to the pluralistic elite of the old *Länder* is forming in the new *Länder.*

The Self-Employed

The self-employed provide a service on their own or are the owners of firms that provide a service or a product. In West Germany in 1989, the self-employed constituted 8.8 percent of the workforce, compared with 16.0 percent in 1950; their decline was even steeper in East Germany, from 20.4 to 2.2 percent over the same period. The self-employed are a heterogeneous group, encompassing shipping magnates and seamstresses and artists and gas station owners. As a result, the earnings of the group's members vary considerably—some members are wealthy, most rank in the upper middle or middle class in terms of income and social prestige, and some (about 7 percent of this group) are poor. Excluding farmers, annual household income of the self-employed in the old *Länder* in 1991 amounted to about DM150,000, almost triple the average household income.

As property owners and food producers, farmers are a small but significant part of the self-employed. In both Germanys, the number of farmers fell dramatically in the postwar era: in the west, from 5 million (or 10 percent of the population) in 1950 to 864,000 (or 1.4 percent) in 1989; in the east, from 740,000 in 1951 to only 3,000 in the early 1990s.

A typical agricultural enterprise in the old *Länder* is a small- or medium-sized farm worked by the owner, assisted by one or two family members. Some farmers are wealthy, while others only earn a bare subsistence. Farmers' average household income is lower than that of most other self-employed but is about 25 percent higher than the national average.

Salaried Employees

The number of salaried employees grew greatly in the postwar era in West Germany, from 16 percent of the workforce in 1950, to 33 percent in 1974, and to 42 percent in 1989. Salaried employees work in three main areas: commercial, technical, and administrative. In 1989, 68 percent of salaried employees worked in the services sector and 32 percent in industry.

Geissler divides salaried employees (including civil servants) into two groups: a lower group that performs simple routine tasks (hairdressers, salesclerks, bus drivers, and low-level civil servants such as letter carriers) and that in 1989 accounted for 9 percent of West Germany's population; and an upper group with advanced education and responsibility, often unsupervised, that performs complex tasks (accountants, teachers, lawyers, and engineers) and that accounted for 28 percent of the population. The jobs of the upper group often involve much stress, and half its members have complained of it, compared with less than one-fourth of skilled workers.

In 1988 the households of salaried employees in West Germany earned on the whole 36 percent more than workers' households. Studies have found that despite their modest social prestige and income, only 13 percent of the lower group of salaried employees regard themselves as workers. Salaried employees as a whole see themselves as belonging to the middle class. According to various studies cited by Geissler, the social animosity that prevailed between salaried employees and workers in the first half of the twentieth century has evolved into a more subtle sense of belonging to different groups. This feeling of distinctness is most strongly felt by salaried employees far removed from the workbench, for example, those in banking.

Generally speaking, salaried employees tend to believe that they must look out for themselves on an individual basis, rather than collectively, as is more common among workers. The higher salaried employees rise in their profession, the more likely this is to be the case. In consequence, a smaller portion of salaried employees are members of labor unions than are workers.

Civil Servants

Civil servants (*Beamten*) have a long tradition in Germany. Their number more than doubled between 1950 and 1989, from 790,000 to 1.8 million in West Germany, where they accounted for 6.6 percent of the workforce. Because teachers and professors are civil servants in Germany, much of this increase came from the expansion of education in the postwar era. Only about one-third of those working for the state are regarded as civil servants. The remainder are either hourly or salaried employees without the special status and rights of civil servants. In 1989 civil servants and government employees accounted for 16.6 percent of the workforce.

Civil servants have complete job security, generous pensions, and higher net incomes than salaried employees. In return for these advantages, civil servants are to serve the state loyally and carry out their duties in a nonpartisan way. This does not, however, prevent civil servants from being active in politics and even being elected to public office.

Workers

Although West Germany became primarily a services-sector economy in the 1970s, blue-collar workers remain a vitally important segment of the workforce, even though they are outnumbered by salaried employees. At the end of the 1980s,

185

workers accounted for two-fifths of the workforce in West Germany, a drop from three-fifths in 1900 and slightly more than one-half in 1960. The social market economy and powerful trade unions greatly improved workers' working conditions, job security, and living standards in the postwar era. Between 1970 and 1989, for example, their average net earnings increased 41 percent in real terms, more than any other group except for the self-employed (not including farmers) and pensioners. In the 1980s, about 43 percent of skilled workers and 29 percent of unskilled or partially trained workers lived in their own houses or apartments; automobile ownership and lengthy vacations (often abroad) had become the rule.

As a result of these changes, German workers no longer live separately from the rest of society as was the case in the nineteenth century and for much of the twentieth century. The gradual, so-called deproletarianization has caused some sociologists to maintain that it is no longer accurate to speak of German workers as a separate social group. Geissler is aware of the much-improved living standards of the workers and the gradual disappearance of a proletarian lifestyle, but he maintains that workers still constitute a distinct group because their earnings are lower than average, their work is physically demanding and closely supervised, and their children's opportunities for social advancement are not as good as those of most other groups. In addition, most workers still regard themselves as members of the working class, although a growing percentage see themselves as middle class.

According to Geissler, the working class is composed of three distinct subgroups: elite, skilled, and unskilled or partially trained workers. In the mid-1980s, about 12 percent of the population lived in the households of the worker elite, 19 percent in those of skilled workers, and 16 percent in those of the unskilled.

The worker elite, which is composed of supervisors and highly trained personnel, enjoys better pay than the other groups. Its work is less physically demanding and resembles that of salaried employees. Only one-third of the sons of the worker elite remain workers, and about one-half of the group see themselves as members of the middle class.

Skilled workers have completed a set course of vocational training. This group has expanded in recent decades and in the early 1990s outnumbered the unskilled, which even as late as 1970 accounted for 57 percent of workers.

Unskilled workers perform the poorest paid and dirtiest tasks. Foreigners account for about 25 percent of this group and German women for about 38 percent. A portion of this group lives below the poverty line. In addition to their other burdens, the unskilled are most likely to become unemployed and involved in criminal activity.

The Poor

As a large, urbanized, industrial country with a diverse population, Germany has a portion of its population living in poverty. The European Union (EU—see Glossary) classifies as poor those households that have less than half the average net income. According to this definition, in 1992 approximately 7.5 percent of the population in the old *Länder* and 14.8 percent in the new *Länder* were poor. The number of poor has been growing since 1970, when the number of those receiving social assistance reached its lowest point of 750,000. In the early 1990s, one study estimated that in 1992 there were 4.6 million recipients of various kinds of social assistance, nearly 700,000 of whom lived in the new *Länder.* Households with three or more children and single parents were the most likely recipients of social assistance.

Social Mobility

Upward social mobility, or the ability or chance of offspring to improve their social position relative to that of their parents, expanded in both Germanys during the postwar era. The growth of the services sector was the primary cause of this expansion. The large, well-trained workforce required by this sector was supplied by a greatly expanded education system. As a result, many Germans received a better education than had their parents.

The postwar era saw the formation of a large, newly educated middle class, which grew at the expense of the small traditional middle class, many of whose members were merchants and the owners of small firms. Joining this older middle class was difficult because membership required capital, property, and other kinds of assets. For this reason, it was a relatively closed class, and its members were usually the offspring of existing members. By contrast, joining the new professional middle class depended on academic training, something readily available in postwar West Germany, where education was inexpensive and financial aid was easily obtainable.

One study measuring social mobility in the postwar decades used a six-level model to track Germans born between 1930 and 1949. It found that 20 percent had moved up to the next higher level, 10 percent had moved up two levels, and 2 percent had moved up three levels. Some downward mobility was recorded as well. For example, 1 percent had dropped three levels.

Opportunities for upward social mobility varied, however, according to one's place in society. Blue-collar workers, for example, did not show as much social mobility as other classes, although their mobility increased somewhat in the late postwar decades. A commonly used index to measure social mobility is the percentage of sons remaining within the social stratum or milieu of their fathers. West German studies have shown that in 1970 only 5 percent of blue-collar workers' sons managed to move up into better paying, higher status professions in the services sector. By 1979 the percentage had more than doubled to 11 percent. The percentage of sons of lower-level salaried and public-sector employees moving into elevated professional positions had increased from 12 to 22 percent in the same period.

Another study examined the likelihood of different groups securing a position in the two top levels of the services sector. The first and upper level accounts for about 10 percent of total employment and consists of positions in medicine, law, higher education, upper levels of administration, and the like. The second and lower level accounts for about 15 percent of employment and consists of positions in teaching, mid-level management, retailing, computers, and the like. The study found that about two-thirds of those employed in the top level and nearly three-fifths of those in the second level are the offspring of persons employed in these levels. Only about 20 percent of the sons of workers are employed in these levels. Access to the top level is very restricted, with 4 percent of the sons of skilled workers and 2 percent of the sons of unskilled workers employed there. Almost no farmers' sons move into the top levels.

Geissler has found three occupational categories particularly conducive to upward mobility: the self-employed, the nonmanual service providers, and the worker elite. Self-recruitment in the three categories is relatively low. Geissler holds that this indicates that the offspring of those so employed are finding higher status positions. In contrast to these groups, 93 percent of farmers are the sons of farmers; farmers' offspring who leave the farm usually become either skilled or unskilled workers.

As of the first half of the 1990s, social mobility trends in the new *Länder* had not yet stabilized. Both upward and downward mobility are greater than in the old *Länder.* The widespread disqualification of the GDR elite meant downward mobility for many. The rapid transformation of the social structure through the replacement of a command socialist economy with a social market economy is also causing much social mobility, especially between generations. Children often do not work in the same sector as their parents. A new social class of entrepreneurs is being formed as the new *Länder* become integrated into the western economy.

The Search for a New National Identity

In the aftermath of unification, Germans are searching for a new identity. There appear to be at least two distinct German identities, and obstacles to their speedy fusion seem formidable.

In the postwar period, West Germany became an upwardly mobile, success-oriented society. By 1990 a broad and prosperous middle-class and upper-middle-class society had developed. Although they still worked hard to earn the vacation and working conditions among the best in the world, West Germans sought to create a "leisure society." There was a movement, for example, advocating the adoption of a four-day workweek. Work was intrinsically less important to West Germans than to East Germans; instead, they prized personal fulfillment, recreation, health, and the natural environment.

Through a remarkable transformation, West Germans had rehabilitated themselves, had become internationally oriented, and had assumed a leading role within the larger European community. Members of the older generation, especially those "blessed by a late birth" (too young to be Nazis), were self-assured and proud of the Federal Republic's political, economic, and social achievements. Starting in the 1960s, the younger generation discovered new freedoms and exercised them. In the 1970s and 1980s, youth- and student-led protests were mounted against nuclear weapons and nuclear power plants and in favor of peace, disarmament, and environmental protection.

By the early 1990s, most of the 1960s generation had been assimilated into the German establishment, but its experiences in challenging authority and winning concessions produced evolutionary changes in German society, economy, and culture. This generation's influence could be seen in the huge candlelight vigils staged by people of all ages to protest right-wing violence and xenophobia.

On the other side of the fortified border, East German society was decidedly working class, with comparatively minor class distinctions. Where there were significant income differentials, the extra money was of little consequence in an economy marked by shortages of most consumer goods. The state apparatus provided security in the form of guaranteed employment, free education and health care, and subsidized low rent. Homelessness was unknown in the GDR. Other social ills such as violent crime, drug abuse, and prostitution also were much less prevalent than in the west.

In terms of their attitude toward state authority and the family, easterners manifested values characteristic of westerners in the late 1950s and 1960s. On the factory floor or the collective farm, conditions were often primitive and the workweek long (forty-three or more hours). The workforce, too, was reminiscent of an earlier Germany, with greater numbers employed in smokestack industries or in fields and mines, and far fewer in the services or information sector. One of many revelations after unification was the information illiteracy of easterners.

With few external options or diversions, East Germans identified with home and family more than their counterparts in the west. Deprived of the means and liberty to travel outside communist Eastern Europe, they formed what some sociologists called a "niche society," retreating into an inner circle to find a degree of privacy.

For three generations, East Germans had been indoctrinated in the thought processes of two forms of totalitarianism in succession: nazism and communism. With the collapse of communism, Germans living in the new *Länder* had few values and beliefs, aside from personal ones, with which to identify. Embittered by the seemingly imperialistic imposition of all things West German, some easterners developed "an identity of defiance" (*Trotzidentität*).

In the initial stage of union, Germans focused on the profound differences that had evolved in the two states since the end of World War II. In the Federal Republic, one of the world's wealthiest countries, quality-of-life issues played key roles in defining one's place and identity in society. Home ownership, travel experiences, and leisure activities of all kinds were translated into powerful status symbols.

In stark contrast, the state owned practically all property in East Germany. Expectations of improving individual or family lifestyles were modest. Overall, the eastern *Länder* were decades behind the west in most categories measuring standard of living. Coming from a society grown accustomed to measuring itself and others by the yardstick of material prosperity, it was not surprising that West Germans felt more in common with their neighbors to the west, in whose countries they frequently traveled.

In some respects, the former GDR stood in relation to the FRG as a colony to an imperial power, and it was not long before westerners and easterners began acting out the roles of "know-it-alls" (westerners) and "whimpering easterners." Within several years of the opening of the Berlin Wall, the former East Germany was transformed from a full-employment society to one having more than 1 million unemployed and hundreds of thousands of part-time workers.

Forced resocialization has weighed heavily on eastern Germans' self-esteem. The cleft between east and west is sufficiently deep and wide to make easterners appear to be foreigners in their own land, or at best second-class citizens. By August 1992, the situation had deteriorated to the point where a headline on the cover of *Der Spiegel*, the influential weekly magazine, summed it up in three words: "Germans Against Germans."

In modern European history, the merging of two fundamentally different social, political, and economic systems such as those that evolved in the two Germanys has no precedent. Fortunately for the newly united country, most Germans still rely on the traditional traits of diligence, orderliness, discipline, and thrift, and these shared values ultimately should resolve the problems associated with the merger of two states and societies at vastly different levels of development and achievement.

*   *   *

As of mid-1995, no postunification survey of German geography in English had been published. The standard text remains Roy E.H. Mellor's *The Two Germanies*. Alun Jones's *The New Germany*, published in 1994, deals with key social and economic developments since unification. *Developments in German Politics,* edited by Gordon Smith, William E. Paterson, Peter H. Merkl, and Stephen Padgett, includes chapters dealing with aspects of German society, including ones on women, the environment, and immigration policies. Each chapter has been written by a noted specialist and includes suggestions for further reading. *German Politics and Society,* a quarterly journal published by the Center for German and European Studies of the University of California at Berkeley, contains a variety of scholarly articles dealing with German society. A more journalistic approach is John Ardagh's widely available and highly informative *Germany and the Germans.*

Three articles especially illuminating on demographic developments are "Germany's Population: Turbulent Past, Uncertain Future" by Gerhard Heilig, Thomas Büttner, and Wolfgang Lutz; "Bericht 1990 zur demographischen Lage: Trends in beiden Teilen Deutschlands und Ausländer in der Bundesrepublik Deutschland" by Charlotte Höhn, Ulrich Mammey, and Hartmut Wendt; and "Demographic Shocks after Communism: Eastern Germany, 1989–93" by Nicholas Eberstadt.

A comprehensive survey of German social structure is Rainer Geissler's *Die Sozialstruktur Deutschlands.* The German government's annual statistical survey, *Statistisches Jahrbuch für die Bundesrepublik Deutschland,* provides much statistical information about many aspects of German society. *Facts about Germany,* edited by Arno Kappler and Adriane Grevel, periodically updated and available from German embassies, contains brief surveys of several areas covered in this chapter. (For further information and complete citations, see Bibliography.)

Chapter 4. Social Welfare, Health Care, and Education

Ludwig van Beethoven, 1770–1827, received his early music training in Bonn.

THE DEVELOPMENT OF SOCIAL POLICY in Germany has followed a unique historical path. During a long process of growth and social experimentation, Germany combined a vigorous and highly competitive capitalist economy with a social welfare system that, with some exceptions, has provided its citizens cradle-to-grave security. The system's benefits are so extensive that by the 1990s annual total spending by the state, employers, and private households on health care, pensions, and other aspects of what Germans call the social safety net amounted to roughly DM1 trillion (for value of the deutsche mark—see Glossary) and accounted for about one-third of the country's gross national product (GNP—see Glossary). Unlike many of the world's advanced countries, however, Germany does not provide its citizens with health care, pensions, and other social welfare benefits through a centralized state-run system. Rather, it provides these benefits via a complex network of national agencies and a large number of independent regional and local entities—some public, some quasi-public, and many private and voluntary. Many of these structures date from the nineteenth century, and some from much earlier.

The legislation that established the basis of this system dates from the 1880s and was passed by imperial Germany's parliament, the Reichstag, with the dual purpose of helping German workers meet life's vicissitudes and thereby making them less susceptible to socialism. This legislation set the main principles that have guided the development of social policy in Germany to the present day: membership in insurance programs is mandated by law; the administration of these programs is delegated to nonstate bodies with representatives of the insured and employers; entitlement to benefits is linked to past contributions rather than need; benefits and contributions are related to earnings; and financing is secured through wage taxes levied on the employer and the employee and, depending on the program, sometimes through additional state financing.

These insurance programs were developed from the bottom up. They first covered elements of the working class and then extended coverage to ever broader segments of the population and incorporated additional risks. Over time, these programs came to provide a wide net of entitlements to those individuals having a steady work history.

By international standards, the German welfare system is comprehensive and generous. However, not everyone benefits equally. In the mid-1990s, the so-called safety net was deficient for the lower-income strata and the unemployed. It was also inadequate for persons needing what Germans term "social aid," that is, assistance in times of hardship. In 1994, for example, 4.6 million persons needed social aid, a 100 percent increase since the 1980s. Germans who had been citizens of the former German Democratic Republic (GDR, or East Germany), which became part of the Federal Republic of Germany (FRG, or West Germany) in 1990, tend to be overrepresented in each of these groups.

Women are more at a disadvantage than any other social group. This fact stems from the bias of German social insurance programs in favor of a male breadwinner model; most women receive social and health protection by virtue of their dependent status as spouse. Hence, despite the existence of a comprehensive interlocking social net, women face inequalities in accruing benefits in their own right because of periods spent rearing children or caring for an elderly parent. Divorced women also fare poorly because of the welfare system's provisions, as do widows, whose pensions are low.

In addition to these problems or shortcomings, Germany's social welfare and health programs have had to contend with the unification of the former West Germany and East Germany in 1990. West Germany's approach to social insurance, health insurance, unemployment insurance (which did not exist in the former GDR), accident insurance, and social aid and assistance has been applied to East Germany. This fact has meant that the complex and heterogeneous organizational and financial arrangements present in the former West Germany to deliver health and social services have had to be built up in the former East Germany, in many cases entirely from scratch.

The need for this extension of social welfare programs follows logically from the former East Germany's transition to a free-market economy in which employment, health care, and social insurance benefits have always been highly contingent upon each other. In the absence of an East German democratic tradition and attitudes supportive of the new institutions and, as well, of adequate private organizational resources and skilled manpower, Germany's attempt to integrate two entirely different systems of social protection, education, and health care purely by means of law, administrative provisions, and financial resources is bound to produce problems for years to come.

In the mid-1990s, representatives of Germany's political parties, businesses, unions, and voluntary social services agencies continued to wage a vigorous debate over social policy. At issue is the role to be played by state and/or nongovernmental voluntary charitable agencies, churches, and other social service providers and how to find a politically acceptable mix of public and private institutions. Ever since the nineteenth century, especially during periods of economic and social crisis, there has been a recurrent demand to shift from insurance-based programs to a universal flat-rate and tax-financed program in order to secure a minimum income for all. However, there has never been sufficient political support for eliminating insurance-based programs. In the postwar period, business groups and the Christian Democratic Union (Christlich Demokratische Union—CDU), with the exception of the left wing within the CDU, tended to support the continued segmentation of the labor force into separate insurance-based programs for various occupational groups. In contrast, the labor unions and the Social Democratic Party of Germany (Sozialdemokratische Partei Deutschlands—SPD) tended to support unitary programs for the entire labor force.

The great costs of unification have raised the possibility of ending the steady expansion of social welfare programs that had been going on for more than a century. The current conservative governing coalition has proposed reductions in benefits to finance unification. Other factors such as the increasingly competitive global economy and structural changes in the labor market have also raised questions about the continued affordability of German social policy. As a result, the government is increasingly listening to employers who insist that their share of employee benefit payments be reduced in order that German business remain competitive in a global economy.

The integration of the two entirely different education systems that emerged after the 1945 division of the country has also raised many controversial issues. No consensus has emerged on whether Germany should adopt the unified school system found in the former East Germany or the heterogeneous three-tiered system of the former West Germany. Nor is there consensus on whether to increase the number of school years by one year for students in eastern Germany or to reduce the thirteen years of schooling in western Germany to twelve years. A greater uniformity within the country's education system is also needed because the plethora of school tracks and the diversity of curricula and qualifying examinations might indeed endanger the mobility of students and teachers within Germany and within Europe in general.

Social Insurance and Welfare Programs

Historical Development

After Germany was united in 1871 under the direction of Otto von Bismarck, the nation developed a common government structure and social policy. But the fact that united Germany had been formed out of four kingdoms, five grand duchies, twelve duchies, twelve principalities, and three free cities was a crucial factor in the way social welfare was administrated. Although after unification social welfare policy was increasingly formulated on the national level, the social insurance programs implementing national policy were aimed at different social strata and were administered in highly decentralized ways.

The new social welfare system that developed after unification in 1871 used existing decentralized structures to provide an ever increasing range of benefits. Because of this, most social welfare programs in Germany are not administered by state bureaucracies. Instead, except for the period when Germany was ruled by the regime of Adolf Hitler (1933–45) and when the former East Germany (1949–90) established a state-run social welfare program, the organizations implementing social policy have been private voluntary entities, some of which date from the Middle Ages. Thus, Germany has implemented a national social policy through an extensive decentralized and pluralistic network of voluntary agencies.

Germans see their economy as a social market economy, that is, one that combines a capitalist mode of production with the belief that society should protect all its members from economic and social need. Such protection is provided by a system of social insurance to which people contribute according to their incomes with the understanding that they may someday need its assistance. The belief that society is responsible for the well-being of its members is called solidarity, or *Solidarität*, and is a key concept of German social policy.

Germans have combined the notion of solidarity with federal and decentralized arrangements of power sharing, or *Subsidarität*, another concept that lies at the heart of German political culture and is characteristic of all German-speaking countries. Fundamentally, *Subsidarität* means building social organizations and society from the bottom up rather than from the top down. As a result of this concept, Germans rely on grassroots social entities whenever possible to provide social services and make use of higher-level institutions only when lower-level ones are found to be inadequate.

Solidarität and *Subsidarität* have affected the development of a national social policy, but most of all they have shaped its implementation. For example, Germany's social insurance programs are quasi-public self-governing bodies subject in most cases to labor and management control, but they are largely independent of the public sector, which retains only supervisory powers. The primary providers of most social assistance services are private-sector voluntary organizations, most of which are church related. Government offices at the regional and local levels generally determine and handle cash benefits and allowances established at the national level.

Some of the most important voluntary social service agencies and church-related groups predate the unification of Germany in 1871; others date from the last decades of the nineteenth century. The first German chapter of the International Red Cross was founded in 1863. Out of it grew the German Red Cross, one of the country's key voluntary agencies. The Innere Mission, which later became the Diakonisches Werk of the Evangelical Church in Germany, was founded in 1848. The Roman Catholic charity Deutscher Caritasverband, the largest of the voluntary welfare associations, dates from 1897. The German Non-Denominational Welfare Association, as it became known after 1932, was founded in 1920 to represent all nonchurch-related hospitals. The Workers' Welfare Organization was founded in 1919 from numerous Social Democratic women's groups working for the well-being of children.

Despite the radically different political regimes in power in Germany since 1871, German social policy has shown a remarkable degree of continuity in organizational arrangements and financing. Change has been largely of an incremental nature, and new programs have conformed to previously existing principles and patterns.

The beginning of the national German social welfare system occurred in the 1880s while Bismarck was in power. A primary motivation for social legislation was the government's desire to erode support for socialism among workers and to establish the superiority of the Prussian state over the churches. The government hoped that provision of economic security in case of major risks and loss of income would promote political integration and political stability. Three laws laid the foundations of the German social welfare system: the Health Insurance of Workers Law of 1883, which provided protection against the temporary loss of income as a result of illness; the Accident Insurance Law of 1884, which aided workers injured on the job; and the Old Age and Invalidity Insurance Law of 1889. Initially, these three laws covered only the top segments of the blue-collar working class.

The second phase of the German social welfare system spanned the period from 1890, the year of Bismarck's resignation, to 1918. During this period, improvements were made in the initial programs. The National Insurance Code of 1911 integrated the three separate insurance programs into a unified social security system, and compulsory coverage and benefits were extended to white-collar workers. Survivors' pensions for widows were also introduced in 1911. (The many amendments to the National Insurance Code of 1911 were later integrated into the Social Insurance Code of 1988.) In 1916 survivors' benefits were increased, and the retirement age for workers was reduced from seventy to sixty-five. Because its cooperation was needed to maintain production during World War I, the working class acquired more political influence and won greater social protection and representation during this period. Efforts were also made to develop mechanisms for settling labor disputes and organizing voluntary employee committees, issues taken up by new labor legislation and decrees. Most efforts were completed by the mid-1920s.

The Weimar Republic (1918–33) saw a further expansion of social welfare programs. In 1920 war victims' benefits were added to the social welfare system. In 1922 the Youth Welfare Act was passed, which today continues to serve as the basic vehicle for all youth-related programs. Unemployment relief was consolidated in 1923 into a regular assistance program, financed by employees and employers. The same year, the 1913 agreement between doctors and sickness funds about who could treat sickness-funds patients was integrated into the

National Insurance Code. Also in 1923, a national law on miners created a single agency for the administration of social insurance programs for miners; before the law went into effect, 110 separate associations had administered the program. In 1924 a modern public assistance program replaced the poor relief legislation of 1870, and in 1925 the accident insurance program was reformed, allowing occupational diseases to become insurable risks. In 1927 a national unemployment insurance program was also established. These gains in social insurance and assistance programs were threatened by the Great Depression of the early 1930s, however. Reduced wages meant smaller contributions to social insurance and assistance programs, all of which were soon on the brink of bankruptcy.

The Hitler regime introduced major changes in individual programs and program administration. In 1934 the regime dismantled the self-governance structure of all social insurance programs and appointed directors who reported to the central authorities. The regime made many improvements in social insurance programs and benefits, but these changes were conceived to serve the regime rather than the population. In 1938 artisans came to be covered under compulsory social insurance, and in 1941 public health insurance coverage was extended to pensioners. In 1942 all wage-earners regardless of occupation were covered by accident insurance, health care became unlimited, and maternity leave was extended to twelve fully paid weeks with job protection.

Two separate German states evolved after World War II, each with its own social welfare programs. In the GDR, the state became even stronger than it had been under Hitler. The communist-directed Socialist Unity Party of Germany (Sozialistische Einheitspartei Deutschlands—SED) had a near monopoly of control over all social and political institutions, including those that administered social welfare programs.

Initially, the GDR retained separate social insurance plans, but by 1956 the plans had been unified into two compulsory, centrally controlled, and hierarchically organized systems that provided universal flat-rate benefits. Special programs also served the so-called technical and scientific intelligentsia, civil servants, police, and members of the National People's Army (Nationale Volksarmee—NVA) and other security organizations. All programs were heavily state subsidized, unlike those in West Germany. Because the right to work was guaranteed, unemployment insurance did not exist.

West Germany moved away from Hitler's central state direction and returned to decentralized administration and control. Social insurance and social protection programs under labor and management control, which were characteristic of the Weimar period, were restored. The return to separate earnings-related and means-tested benefits for different groups meant that social insurance, social compensation, and public assistance (or social aid) were not integrated into one overall administration, as some Germans wished and as the Allied Control Council had intended in 1946 when it drafted a unified national insurance system. In the mid-1970s, legislators attempted to consolidate the goals, the protection, and the entitlements as much as possible. But they failed to develop a coherently organized and uniform system that would have eliminated disparities in individual entitlements. Indeed, by the mid-1990s the disparities in welfare benefits entitlements in unified Germany had become more significant than ever before.

Provisions of the Social Welfare System

The German social welfare tradition divides entitlement programs into three types. The first and most common type consists of contributory social insurance programs that protect those who pay into them from loss of income and unplanned expenditures because of illness, accident, old age or disability, and unemployment. The second type consists of noncontributory social compensation programs that provide tax-financed social welfare (such as health care, pensions, and other benefits) to those—civil servants, for example—who perform a public service to society. Tax-financed social compensation is also provided to those who have suffered from income loss or disability as a result of military or other public service, and allowances are provided to their dependents in the case of death. Since 1976 victims of violent crimes have also been eligible for social compensation. In addition, social compensation can consist of payments to all members of society and includes tax-funded child, housing, and educational allowances. The third type of social welfare programs provides social aid, or assistance, to persons in need who are not eligible for assistance from the other two kinds of social entitlement programs or who need additional aid because they are still in need—for example, if their pensions are too small to provide them with decent housing. Aid can consist of general income maintenance payments (including payments for food, housing, clothing, and furniture) and assistance for those with special needs, such as the disabled, and individuals without health insurance (0.3 percent of the total German population).

In order to better measure the extent of social welfare expenditures, since 1960 the Germans have used the concept of a social budget to lump together all forms of social spending, whether by the government, by the country's large social insurance programs, or by other sources. The steady expansion of social welfare programs and the increased costs of such items as pensions and medical care caused West Germany's social budget to increase tenfold between 1960 and 1990, from DM68.9 billion in 1960 to DM703.1 billion in 1990. The West German economy expanded greatly in this period so that the social budget's share of GNP increased from about one-fifth in 1960 to about one-third by 1990. Roughly two-fifths of the 1990 social budget went to pension payments and one-third to health care. By 1992 the social budget had grown to about DM900 billion, a sharp increase caused by the unification of the two Germanys. Unification meant an increased population and many special needs of the five new states (*Länder*, sing., *Land*) in eastern Germany.

In 1990 the public sector (federal, *Land*, and local governments) paid for about 38 percent of the social budget, employers for 32 percent, and private households for about 29 percent. The remainder was financed by social insurance and private organizations.

The cost of the social budget for an average wage earner is difficult to assess. By the mid-1990s, however, a typical wage earner was estimated to pay about one-fifth of his or her income in direct taxes (only part of which went to the social budget) and another one-fifth for the compulsory social insurance programs. In addition, there were many indirect taxes, which accounted for about two-fifths of all tax revenue. The most important of the indirect taxes is the value-added tax (VAT—see Glossary), set in 1993 at 15 percent for most goods and at 7 percent for basic commodities each time it is assessed. Given Germany's demographic trends, the cost of the social budget is certain to increase in the coming decades.

Social Insurance

The social insurance program was established in 1889 and provides retirement pay. Although the central government has always formulated social insurance policy, the implementation of the program is decentralized. In unified Germany, control over the blue-collar insurance programs remains in the hands of twenty-three *Land*-based insurance agencies and four federal insurance agencies. In the old *Länder* in western Germany, eighteen *Land*-based insurance agencies serve people in geographical districts that conform to those established in the nineteenth century, not to the geographical entities created after 1945. With the assistance of staff from the West German insurance agencies, five *Land*-based and self-governing insurance agencies were established in the new *Länder.*

Four federal insurance agencies serve four groups in unified Germany: federal railroad workers, merchant marine seamen, miners, and white-collar workers. Civil servants and their dependents are covered by a separate retirement program financed by outlays from federal, *Land,* and local governments. Other retirement programs provide retirement income for registered craftsmen, agricultural workers, and self-employed professionals.

Because of population trends that indicate a worsening worker/retiree ratio and the likelihood of solvency problems in the next century, the pension reform of 1992 increased the usual retirement age from sixty-three to sixty-five, beginning in 2001. Whatever the legal retirement age, many Germans retire early for health reasons on disability pensions.

The amount of retirement pay is determined by the length and level of the insured person's contributions. Contributions in 1995 were scheduled to amount to 18.6 percent of an employee's annual gross income up to a maximum of DM93,600 in the old *Länder* and DM76,800 in the new *Länder,* with the employee and employer each paying half. In the early 1990s, the average retirement pension amounted to about DM1,600 per month for retired persons over the age of sixty. This meant that Germany had the fourth-highest pensions in Europe, surpassed only by Luxemburg, France, and Denmark. In 1957 legislation was passed that required pensions to be indexed, that is, raised according to average wage increases.

Unemployment Insurance

Unemployment insurance was introduced in 1927, relatively late in comparison with the pioneering programs of the nineteenth century. It replaced the welfare program for the unemployed that had been created in 1919. With the exception of

The exterior and a living room of an apartment house for pensioners
in Reutlingen, Baden-Württemberg
Courtesy German Information Center, New York

civil servants, all employed individuals and trainees, irrespective of salary or wage levels, are covered by the program. Contributions in 1995 to unemployment insurance were scheduled to amount to 6.5 percent of an employee's gross pay up to DM96,600 in the old *Länder* and DM76,800 in the new *Länder*, with the employee and employer each paying half. In return, the employee receives unemployment pay of 68 percent of net earnings for a married worker and 63 percent for a nonmarried worker, provided that the unemployed person has worked for 360 insurable days in the last three years before being laid off. Unemployment pay can be paid from the first day of unemployment for seventy-eight to 832 weekdays, depending on the length of insured employment and the age of the unemployed. In the early 1990s, unemployment pay averaged DM1,300 per month. Once unemployment pay runs out, the employee is eligible for unemployment aid, which averaged DM975 a month in the early 1990s. Because the unemployed frequently do not receive enough benefits to maintain their basic living standard, local social welfare entities often provide additional assistance. During unemployment, entitlements to benefits of other social insurance and health insurance programs remain in place.

The unemployment insurance program is administered through a three-tiered administration: a federal labor agency, regional labor agencies in the *Länder*, and local labor offices. Unlike the labor-management partnership in the administration of the other insurance programs, this program is controlled by tripartite boards composed of representatives of labor, management, and governments at the federal, *Land*, and local level. Because East Germany did not have an unemployment insurance program, the adoption of such a program in the new *Länder* has entailed numerous administrative problems. In addition, unemployment there is higher than in the old *Länder* (in 1994 about 15 percent, compared with 10 percent in the old *Länder*).

Accident Insurance

Enacted in 1884, the accident insurance program initially covered only accidents in the workplace. In 1925 occupational diseases also came to be covered. In the post-1945 era, cash and in-kind benefits such as rehabilitation and vocational training were expanded and improved. Travel to and from work is also now covered. If an accident leads to total disability, the injured person receives a pension amounting to 66 percent of the latest year's earnings. Survivor pensions can amount to a maximum of 80 percent of earnings. Disability pensions and survivors' benefits were indexed in 1957, that is, adjusted according to wage increases. In addition to covering members of the labor force, the plan also covers students and children; their coverage is paid for out of general tax revenues. Employers pay premiums for their employees; premiums amount to 1.44 percent of an employee's gross earnings. The self-employed are also able to enroll in the program.

Social Assistance

Social assistance is provided to persons who, for any of a number of reasons, are unable to provide themselves with a decent standard of living. In 1991 some 4.2 million persons received various forms of social assistance. In the same year, the most important reasons that people needed social assistance were unemployment (34 percent; social assistance is paid once unemployment pay runs out), pensions or incomes too small to allow their recipients a decent standard of living (11 and 7 percent, respectively), refusal of divorced fathers to pay child support (11 percent), and sickness (6 percent). Half of all recipients of social assistance are single elderly women. Foreigners residing in Germany also receive social assistance at a higher than average rate because they are more likely to be unemployed or earn low incomes.

Unlike the benefits provided by social insurance programs, social assistance is funded by taxes and is not determined by previous contributions. Social assistance is means tested, and recipients generally must have exhausted their savings. The incomes of a recipient's close relatives (parents and children) may also be considered when assessing the provision of social assistance. In the mid-1990s, social assistance for the head of household amounted to about DM500 a month in the old *Länder*; 80 percent of this amount was allocated for the spouse, and 50 to 90 percent of this amount was allocated for the children, depending on their ages. In addition to these benefits, social assistance can cover housing costs, medical care, clothing, winter heating, and many other expenses.

Other Social Benefits

In addition to social assistance, Germany's social welfare system provides many other tax-funded benefits. The most widely paid benefit is that of the child allowance. It is paid to parents of all income levels to lessen the burden of raising children. Benefits are generally paid until the child reaches the age of sixteen and thereafter up to the age of twenty-seven if the child is receiving an education. In the mid-1990s, DM70 a month was paid for the first child, DM130 for the second, DM220 for the third, and DM240 for the fourth and subsequent children. Upper-income parents receive smaller amounts. Child benefits are tax exempt. Taxpayers also have an annual income tax exemption of DM4,104 for each dependent child.

Since 1986 payments for child rearing have also been made to parents who are either unemployed or working only up to nineteen hours per week. In 1994 these payments amounted to DM600 a month per child for the first six months of the child's life; after this age, household income was considered. Payments continue until the child's second birthday. Beginning in 1994, a single parent with a net annual income of more than DM75,000 and a couple with a net annual income of more than DM100,000 were no longer eligible to receive this benefit.

A single parent raising a child and receiving inadequate financial support from the other parent is eligible to receive maintenance payments up to a child's twelfth birthday for a maximum period of seventy-two months. In 1994 in the old *Länder*, these payments could amount to as much as DM291 a month for children up to age six and DM353 a month for children between the ages of six and twelve.

Families and single individuals can also receive payments to help them with housing expenses if their incomes are insufficient to afford decent shelter. Unlike housing aid provided through social assistance, aid of this nature does not require that recipients exhaust their savings or lack close relatives to assist them.

The disabled are also served by a broad range of medical and vocational programs designed to provide them with humane living conditions. Statutory social insurance programs are responsible for meeting the various needs of their members who become disabled. In addition, government agencies at the federal, *Land,* and local levels seek to provide employment and help with special housing and transportation provisions. Employment of the disabled is furthered by federal legislation that requires firms employing more than fifteen persons to reserve 6 percent of positions for the disabled or to make annual compensatory payments. In 1994 Germany had nearly 600 sheltered workplaces able to provide special employment for about 140,000 disabled persons unable to find employment in the general economy.

Since 1995 German residents have been obliged to join a new social insurance program that arranges for its members' future need for long-term nursing care. Those with public health insurance will continue with that insurance; those with private health insurance are obliged to secure a new insurance policy to arrange long-term nursing care. The new insurance program will initially cover the expenses of long-term nursing provided at home; monthly benefits, in some special cases, will go up to DM3,750 but usually will be set at much lower levels depending on the kind of nursing care provided and the condition of the insured person's health. Some benefits will be provided in kind, such as visits by health care professionals to the home. Some benefits will be cash payments to friends or relatives who provide nonprofessional nursing care. Beginning in mid-1996, long-term institutional care will also be covered.

Until this program was instituted, the lack of long-term nursing care was seen as the single most important shortcoming in the country's system of social welfare. One effect of this shortcoming was that patients who should have been receiving nursing care at home or in a nursing institution remained instead in hospitals, a more expensive form of treatment. As of late 1994, officials had set an initial contribution of 1 percent of incomes up to DM68,400 a year in the old *Länder* and DM53,100 in the new *Länder*, with the employee and the employer each paying half. Part of the costs of long-term nursing care may in the future be covered by abolishing a public holiday that always falls on a workday. To cover the cost of long-term institutional nursing care, the contribution rate will increase to 1.7 percent in mid-1996. The great expense of this benefit may require the abolition of a second public holiday.

The administration of the nursing care insurance program is unique. It overlaps somewhat that of the sickness funds but will also include many federal, *Land*, and local agencies. In fact, the program will involve more implementors than all other social insurance programs combined. Implementation problems arise primarily from different entitlements and services provided through social assistance, or social aid, and by nursing care insurance. Problems also stem from differing evaluations by sickness-funds medical experts about who needs care and how much and what kind of nursing care is needed throughout Germany.

Current Social Welfare Issues and Outlook for the Future

As of mid-1995, the policy and institutional features that characterized the development of German social policy over the last century continued to provide the overall umbrella of social policy in Germany. This has meant the continuation of separate programs for different groups in the labor force; decentralized and mostly nongovernment, self-administering bodies and private grassroots voluntary social welfare agencies; an emphasis on earnings-related individualized cash benefits determined by past contributions rather than by need; and a continued reliance on social insurance programs. For most people living in Germany, these programs have worked well and in the postwar period have provided a continuous expansion of coverage and improved benefits.

Behind these achievements, however, are hidden inequities and inequalities. During the last forty years, the system favored the improvement of benefits for those with a continuous work record. For the most part, these were male workers and women who had never left the workforce. They received earnings-related insurance benefits while other population groups tended to receive means-tested benefits or a combination of the two.

The number of individuals receiving means-tested social assistance, however, was increasing in the former FRG even prior to unification. And in 1995, in a united Germany, the recipients of social assistance included a growing number of impoverished elderly women, female-headed single households, and families with several children. For example, a 1992 study found that households with a sick or disabled person needing constant home care, households with a newborn child, and non-German households had an increased likelihood of receiving social assistance benefits.

Women are more heavily represented among the disadvantaged than men. Their lower wages on average mean smaller benefits because of smaller contributions into insurance programs. In addition, the time women spend caring for children and other relatives generally means that women have shorter work histories, which affects their pension levels. German welfare regulations also place divorced and separated women at a disadvantage.

The new *Länder* present a challenge to Germany's social welfare system. From the perspective of individuals, unification brought a number of social and institutional innovations and

improvements in living conditions, along with a few new entitlements—for example, disability pay, retirement for men
under the age of sixty-five, and pensions for widows and widow-
ers. However, the abolition of familiar social service centers,
child-care facilities, and nursing homes, coupled with inexperienced staff in administrative agencies, has increased social and
psychological stress for many in the east. Women of child-bearing age living in the new *Länder* have been particularly affected
because before unification they had better prenatal and postnatal care, the right to abortion, and a fairly widespread network of day-care centers at work or in their communities.

The lack of private voluntary organizations in the new
Länder has made the administration of social programs there
difficult. Western German voluntary and church-related agencies have provided and still do provide much assistance. They
have also assisted in setting up local and district government
offices and have trained new manpower to decide on entitlements, calculate benefits, and interpret new laws. But a serious
shortage of social workers and facilities to train or retrain them
remains.

The difference between the two Germanys in terms of benefits received and resources available for different social strata
will continue for some time. The resulting dissatisfaction and
social decline can be considered time bombs that might bring
future political, social, and psychological instability.

National Health Insurance and Medical Care

Germany's health care system provides its residents with
nearly universal access to comprehensive high-quality medical
care and a choice of physicians. Over 90 percent of the population receives health care through the country's statutory health
care insurance program. Membership in this program is compulsory for all those earning less than a periodically revised
income ceiling. Nearly all of the remainder of the population
receives health care via private for-profit insurance companies.
Everyone uses the same health care facilities.

Although the federal government has an important role in
specifying national health care policies and although the
Länder control the hospital sector, the country's health care system is not government run. Instead, it is administered by
national and regional self-governing associations of payers and
providers. These associations play key roles in specifying the
details of national health policy and negotiate with one

another about financing and providing health care. In addition, instead of being paid for by taxes, the system is financed mostly by health care insurance premiums, both compulsory and voluntary.

In early 1993, the Health Care Structural Reform Act (Gesundheitsstrukturgesetz—GSG) came into effect, marking the end of a more than a century-long period in which benefits and services under statutory public health insurance had been extended to ever larger segments of the population. Rising health expenditures may prompt policy makers to impose further restrictions on providers and consumers of health care. These high expenditures have been caused by a rapidly aging population (retirees' costs rose by 962 percent between 1972 and 1992), the intensive and costly use of advanced-technology medical procedures, and other economic and budgetary pressures. As of mid-1995, the drafting of new reform proposals was under way.

For residents of the former GDR, the era of free care ended in 1991. The political decision to adopt the FRG's health care system required the reorganization of nearly all components of health care in the new *Länder.* As of mid-1995, the reorganization of the health care system in the former GDR still was far from completion.

Development of the Health Care System

Nearly everyone residing in Germany is guaranteed access to high-quality comprehensive health care. Statutory health insurance (Gesetzliche Krankenversicherung—GKV) has provided an organizational framework for the delivery of public health care and has shaped the roles of payers, insurance or sickness funds, and providers, physicians, and hospitals since the Health Insurance Act was adopted in 1883. In 1885 the GKV provided medical protection for 26 percent of the lower-paid segments of the labor force, or 10 percent of the population. As with social insurance, health insurance coverage was gradually extended by including ever more occupational groups in the plan and by steadily raising the income ceiling. Those earning less than the ceiling were required to participate in the insurance program. In 1995 the income ceiling was an annual income of about DM70,00 in the old *Länder* and DM57,600 in the new *Länder.*

In 1901 transport and office workers came to be covered by public health insurance, followed in 1911 by agricultural and forestry workers and domestic servants, and in 1914 by civil servants. Coverage was extended to the unemployed in 1918, to seamen in 1927, and to all dependents in 1930. In 1941 legislation was passed that allowed workers whose incomes had risen above the income ceiling for compulsory membership to continue their insurance on a voluntary basis. The same year, coverage was extended to all retired Germans. Salespeople came under the plan in 1966, self-employed agricultural workers in 1972, and students and the disabled in 1975.

The 1883 health insurance law did not address the relationship between sickness funds and doctors. The funds had full authority to determine which doctors became participating doctors and to set the rules and conditions under which they did so. These rules and conditions were laid down in individual contracts. Doctors, who had grown increasingly dissatisfied with these contracts and their limited access to the practice of medicine with the sickness funds, mobilized and founded a professional association (Hartmannbund) in 1900 and even went on strike several times. In 1913 doctors and sickness funds established a system of collective bargaining to determine the distribution of licenses and doctors' remuneration. This approach is still practiced, although the system has undergone many modifications since 1913.

The formation of two German states in the second half of the 1940s resulted in two different German health systems. In East Germany, a centralized state-run system was put in place, and physicians became state employees. In West Germany, the prewar system was reestablished. It was supervised by the government but was not government run. According to the Basic Law of 1949, Germany's constitution, the federal government has exclusive authority in public health insurance matters and sets broad policy in relation to the GKV. The government's authority applies in particular to benefits, eligibility, compulsory membership, covered risks (physical, emotional, mental, curative, and preventive), income maintenance during temporary illness, employer-employee contributions to the GKV, and other central issues. However, except for the funding of some benefits and the planning and financing of hospitals, the responsibility for administering and providing health care has been delegated to nonstate entities, including national and regional associations of health care providers, *Land* hospital associations, nonprofit insurance funds, private insurance companies, and voluntary organizations.

Portability of coverage, eligibility, and benefits are independent of any regional and/or local reinterpretations by either insurers, politicians, administrators, or health care providers. Universal coverage is honored by any medical office or hospital. Check-ins at doctors' offices, hospitals, and specialized facilities are simple, and individuals receive immediate medical attention. No one in need of care can be turned away without running a risk of violating the code of medical ethics or *Land* hospital laws.

The health care system has achieved a high degree of equity and justice, despite its fragmented federal organization: no single group is in a position to dictate the terms of service delivery, reimbursement, remuneration, quality of care, or any other important concerns. The right to health care is regarded as sacrosanct. Universality of coverage, comprehensive benefits, the principle of the healthy paying for the sick, and a redistributive element in the financing of health care have been endorsed by all political parties and are secured in the Basic Law.

By the mid-1990s, health care benefits provided through the GKV were extensive and included ambulatory care (care provided by office-based physicians), choice of office-based physicians, hospital care, full pay to mothers (from six weeks before to eight weeks after childbirth), extensive home help, health checkups, sick leave to care for relatives, rehabilitation and physical therapy, medical appliances (such as artificial limbs), drugs, and stays of up to one month in health spas every few years. Persons who are unable to work because of illness receive full pay for six weeks, then 80 percent of their income for up to seventy-eight weeks. In an attempt to contain costs, beginning in the 1980s some of these benefits required copayments by the insured. Although these fees were generally very low, some copayments were substantial. For example, insured patients paid half the cost of dentures, although most other dental care was paid by health insurance.

The system has managed these achievements relatively economically. In 1992 about 8.1 percent of the gross domestic product (GDP—see Glossary) went into medical care, or US$1,232 per capita, compared with 12.1 percent of GDP and US$2,354 per capita in the United States. Even so, Germany devoted about one-third of its overall social budget to health care, an amount surpassed only by retirement payments.

The German health care community has made a serious and sustained effort to control the growth of health costs since the mid-1970s. The steep rise in health expenditures in the first half of the 1970s prompted the passage of the Health Insurance Cost Containment Act of 1977. The law established an advisory board, the Concerted Action in Health Care, to suggest nonbinding guidelines for health care costs. Chaired by the federal minister for health, its sixty members represent the most important interest groups having a stake in health care. The board has contributed to slowing the growth of health care costs, but further legislation has been necessary.

Modest copayments for medications, dental treatment, hospitalization, and other items were introduced in 1982 for members of sickness funds. These payments were further increased by the Health Care Reform Act of 1989 (Gesundheitsreformgesetz—GRG) and again by the Health Care Structural Reform Act (Gesundheitsstrukturgesetz—GSG) of 1993. The GSG also introduced new regulatory instruments to monitor more closely access to medical practice, to reorganize sickness-funds governance, and to control medication costs and prospective hospital payments. In addition, it proposed measures to overcome the separation between ambulatory medical care and hospital care that prevailed in the former FRG.

Health Insurance

Some 92 percent of Germany's residents receive health care through statutory health insurance, that is, the GKV. As of late 1992, the GKV relied on about 1,200 nonprofit sickness funds that collect premiums from their members and pay health care providers according to negotiated agreements. Those not insured through these funds, mostly civil servants and the self-employed, have private for-profit insurance. An estimated 0.3 percent of the population has no health insurance of any kind. They are generally the rich who do not need it and the very poor, who receive health care through social assistance.

Sickness funds are divided into two categories: primary funds and substitute funds. Workers earning less than the periodically revised income ceiling are required to belong to the primary funds; those earning more than this ceiling may be members on a voluntary basis. Some primary-fund members have a choice of funds. Others do not and become members of a particular fund because of their occupation or place of residence. According to figures from the Ministry of Labor and

Social Affairs for late 1992, of the six types of primary funds, local sickness funds, then about 270 in number, are the most important. Organized geographically, they supply about 46 percent of the insured workforce with health insurance. About 800 company-based funds, located in firms with more than 450 employees, cover about 11 percent of workers. Some 180 occupational funds organized by craft cover another 2.5 percent. There are three other kinds of primary funds (about two dozen in all); they supply insurance for self-employed farmers, sailors, and miners and cover about 4 percent of the workforce. There are also two kinds of substitute funds; they provide health insurance to white-collar and blue-collar workers earning more than the income ceiling. Substitute funds are organized on a national basis, and membership is voluntary. Such funds cover about 34 percent of insured workers.

Employers and employees each pay half of a member's premiums, which in the first half of the 1990s averaged between 12 and 13 percent of a worker's gross earnings up to the income ceiling. Premiums are set according to earnings rather than risk and are not affected by a member's marital status, family size, or health; they are the same for all members of a particular fund with the same earnings. In a household with two wage earners, each pays the full premium assessed by his or her sickness fund. The unemployed remain members of their sickness fund. Their contributions are paid by federal and local government offices, with one-third coming from local social assistance offices. The contributions of retirees are paid by the pensioners themselves and by their pension funds. Thus, the public health insurance program redistributes from higher to lower income groups, from the healthy to the sick, from the young to the old, from the employed to the unemployed, and from those without children to those with children.

Because some funds have poorer overall health profiles than others as a result of the occupations of their members, the number of dependents and pensioners among its members, or other factors, premiums can range from as low as about 6.5 percent to as much as 16.0 percent of a member's gross earnings. To counter this inequity, a national reserve fund makes payments to funds with high numbers of pensioners. The GSG of 1993 mandates an equalization of contribution rates across all sickness funds by authorizing payments to funds burdened with health risks associated with age and gender.

About 11 percent of Germans pay for private health insurance provided by about forty for-profit insurance carriers. A good portion of those choosing private insurance are civil servants who want insurance to cover the roughly 50 percent of their medical bills not covered by the government. Some sickness-fund members buy additional private insurance to secure such extras as a private room or a choice of physicians while in a hospital. Otherwise, the medical care provided to the publicly and privately insured is identical, and the same medical facilities are used. Self-employed persons earning above the income ceiling must have private insurance. Members of a sickness fund who leave it for a private insurance carrier will generally not be allowed to return to public insurance.

Although private insurance companies pay health care providers about twice the amount paid by the primary sickness funds, private insurance is often cheaper than statutory health insurance, especially for policyholders without dependents. As is the case for members of sickness funds, employees who have private insurance have half their premiums paid by their employers. German private health insurance is unusual in that whatever the insured person's age, his or her premium will remain that set for his or her age cohort when the policy initially was taken. Premiums rise only according to increases in overall health care costs. Policyholders generally stay with their original policy because if they change companies, they will pay the higher rates of an older age cohort.

Health Care Providers

Germany's principal health care providers are its physicians, dentists, and three types of hospitals (public, private nonprofit, and private for-profit). The health industry also includes large pharmaceutical companies and the manufacturers of various kinds of medical supplies. Public health departments, which are operated by the *Länder*, are not an important part of German health care. The public health clinics in the new *Länder* are being phased out during the integration of the two medical systems.

Germany's supply of physicians is high. Students who meet academic requirements have a constitutionally guaranteed right to study medicine. This fact, plus an excellent and inexpensive university system, has resulted in the country's educating physicians at a much higher per capita rate than the United States. Between 1970 and 1990, the number of physicians in the former West Germany more than doubled, and in 1991 the country had 3.2 physicians per 1,000 population, a higher ratio than most other members of the Organisation for Economic Co-operation and Development (OECD—see Glossary). (In 1990 the United States rate was 2.3 per 1,000.) With 11.5 physician visits per person per year in 1988, West Germans and Italians went to a doctor more frequently than other Europeans. (In 1989 the United States rate was 5.3 visits per person per year.) Even so, expenditures to physicians per capita amounted to less than half (US$193) of those in the United States (US$414).

German physicians have good incomes (dentists earn even more), although their average earnings have declined from six to three times the average wage since efforts at cost containment began in the 1970s. The high number of physicians could reduce physicians' earnings still further. In addition, many young physicians face unemployment. The GSG of 1993, for example, mandates a reduction in the number of office-based physicians who treat GKV patients (generally about 90 percent of physicians join the association that allows them this practice). The law also has the long-term goal of limiting the number of specialists in geographic areas where they are overrepresented.

German health care makes a sharp distinction between physicians who provide office-based or ambulatory care and physicians who work in hospitals. Office-based physicians are fee-for-service entrepreneurs whose incomes depend on the amount and kinds of medical care they provide. In contrast, hospital physicians are salaried employees of the hospitals in which they work. Very few hospital physicians are permitted to bill their patients. Until recent health reform legislation, the two types of physicians did not work together. Once an ambulatory-care physician decided that a patient should enter a hospital (only in emergencies could a patient go directly to a hospital), the patient's care was entirely taken over by a hospital-based physician. When a patient left the hospital, by law he or she again came under the care of an office-based physician. Since the late 1970s, hospital-based physicians have outnumbered ambulatory-care physicians. In 1990 there were about 96,000 of the former and 75,000 of the latter in the old *Länder*.

The GRG aimed at encouraging a better integration of office and hospital care, but little progress was made. The GSG of 1993 intended to lessen the traditional division by, among

University clinic in Münster,
North Rhine-Westphalia
Courtesy German Information
Center, New York

other reforms, making it possible for hospital-based physicians to see their patients after their release from the hospital. It is expected that lessening the separation of the types of medical care will reduce overall health care costs, but as of mid-1995 no marked successes in achieving this goal had been noticed. Additionally, new budgeting rules that go into effect in 1996 may cause outpatient surgery, still unusual in Germany, to become more common by making it more profitable for hospitals.

The ownership of hospitals (there were a total of about 3,100 hospitals in the early 1990s) is the outcome of historical development and regional traditions rather than conscious policy and has resulted in three types of hospitals: public, nonprofit, and private for-profit. Each type accounts for about one-third of the hospitals. Public-sector hospitals are mostly owned by the *Länder,* municipalities, and counties and provide about 50 percent of all hospital beds. Nonprofit hospitals, typically run by Catholic or Protestant organizations, provide about 35 percent of the beds, and for-profit hospitals account for 15 percent.

Germany has too many hospital resources. In 1988 the ratio of 10.9 patient beds per 1,000 population in the former West Germany was higher than the OECD average. The number of admissions as a percentage of the total German population was

21.5 percent, significantly above the OECD average of 16.1 percent. The average length of stay of 16.6 days was below the OECD average but quite high by United States standards. Germany's inpatient occupancy rate was 86.5 percent, also fairly high by international standards.

Between 1972 and 1986, the federal government and the *Länder* were jointly responsible for hospital policy making, but in 1986 the *Land* governments once again assumed sole responsibility. *Länder* own and partially finance medical school hospitals and accredited teaching hospitals. They enforce accreditation and licensing of health facilities and of health professionals working in social services. The *Länder* are responsible for policy development and implementation of social and nursing services, social assistance, youth services, and social work. Most important, the *Länder* remain responsible for the effective and efficient allocation and distribution of hospital resources.

Remuneration of Health Care Providers

Each year the national associations of sickness funds negotiate agreements with the national associations of sickness-funds physicians. The same bargaining procedures apply to dental care. The associations work with guidelines suggested by the Advisory Council for the Concerted Action in Health Care and establish umbrella agreements on guidelines for the delivery of medical care and fee schedules tied to the relative value scales of about 2,000 medical procedures. At the national level, the Federal Committee of Sickness Funds Physicians and Sickness Funds is a key player, although it is little known outside the circle of health care practitioners and experts. It sets spending limits on the practice of medicine in physicians' offices, determines the inclusion of new medical procedures and preventive services, adjusts the remuneration of physicians, and formulates guidelines on the distribution and joint use of sophisticated medical technology and equipment by ambulatory-care or office-based physicians and hospital physicians.

At the regional level, regional associations of sickness funds and regional associations of sickness-funds physicians negotiate specific contracts, including overall health budgets, reimbursement contracts for all physicians in a region, procedures for monitoring physicians, and reference standards for prescription drugs.

A key instrument for containing GKV health care costs is the global budget, introduced in the mid-1980s, which sets limits on total health care expenditures. The GSG of 1993 retained cost containment methods until 1996, when it is hoped that structural reforms will no longer make it necessary. By means of the global budget, regional increases in total medical expenditures are linked to overall wage increases of sickness-funds members. The sickness funds transfer monies amounting to the negotiated budget to the regional associations of sickness-funds physicians; the associations pay their members on the basis of points earned from services performed in a billing period. The value of the services is determined by the negotiated fee-for-service schedule, which assigns points to each service according to the relative value scale. No exchange of money occurs between sickness-fund patient and physician. Privately insured patients pay their physicians themselves and are reimbursed by their insurance companies.

The monetary value of a point is determined by dividing the total value of points billed by all sickness-funds physicians into the region's total negotiated health budget. A greater than expected number of services billed will mean that a point has less value, and a physician will earn less for a particular service than in a previous year. To prevent physicians from attempting to earn more by billing more services, committees of doctors and sickness funds closely scrutinize physician practices. Excess billing practices are easily detected by means of statistical profiles of diagnostic and therapeutic practices that identify departures of individual doctors from the group average (a form of community rating). Physicians found guilty of improper conduct are penalized. The same procedures apply to dentists.

Land hospital associations and *Land* associations of sickness funds negotiate the general standards for hospital care and procedures and criteria by which to monitor the appropriate and efficient delivery of medical care. Each hospital negotiates a contract on hospital care and the prices for hospital services with the regional sickness-funds association. Until 1993 hospitals' operating costs (of which salaries made up as much as 75 percent) were covered by per diem rates paid by public and private insurance. Hospital investments and equipment are financed by *Land* general revenues.

The GSG of 1993 developed a more sophisticated reimbursement method for hospitals than the simple per diem rate in an attempt to achieve greater hospital efficiency and thereby reduce costs. The law requires that four sets of costs be negotiated for each hospital: payments to diagnosis-related groups for the full treatment of a case, with the possibility of an extra payment if a patient is hospitalized for an unusual length of time; special payments for surgery and treatments before and after surgery; departmental allowances that reimburse the hospital for all nursing and medical procedures per patient per day; and finally a basic allowance for all nonmedical procedures and covered accommodations, food, television, and similar expenses. The law also introduced new aggregate spending targets and spending caps on hospitals for the period 1993 to 1995. Moreover, the law imposes more stringent capital spending controls on hospital construction and expensive medical equipment.

Current Health Care Issues and Outlook for the Future

German health care has long overemphasized curative medicine and neglected preventive medicine and health promotion. In 1994 the Advisory Council for the Concerted Action in Health Care recognized this imbalance and recommended improving prenatal and postnatal care, providing more vaccinations for young children, and better educating the public about the dangers of alcohol consumption and smoking both during pregnancy and at other times. The council also found that schoolchildren need more sports, dental care, and sex education, and that they should be taught better dietary habits. Adolescents require better information about the dangers of drug abuse, sexually transmitted diseases, and obesity. All adults should exercise more and make better use of available cancer and dental screening. The council further recommended that fewer prescription drugs be taken (the cost for prescription drugs for the elderly is almost one-third higher than the cost of physician visits). Improving the control of blood pressure, counseling diabetics, eliminating occupational hazards, and promoting self-help groups are other goals.

The council also found that many older Germans have bad dietary habits. Although eating habits have improved in recent decades, the German diet is rich in fats, carbohydrates, and sugar and is deficient in fruits and vegetables. In addition, the consumption of tobacco and alcohol is high, although it decreased between 1980 and 1990 among both men and women. Because of these factors, specialists estimate that 30 to

40 percent of the population has health problems related to diet.

Cardiovascular diseases are the cause of about half of all deaths, followed by cancer, which accounts for about one-quarter of deaths (see table 10, Appendix). Modern medicine has largely eradicated traditional threats to health such as tuberculosis, diphtheria, and pneumonia. Marked improvements are also seen in other areas, such as infant and maternal mortality rates. In 1970 infant mortality rates (defined as deaths under one year of age per 1,000 live births) were 18.5 in the former East Germany and 23.4 in the former West Germany, compared with an estimated 6.3 in united Germany by 1995. Maternal deaths fell from 140 per 100,000 live births in the mid-1950s to fewer than ten per 100,000 by 1989 in the former West Germany. A similar improvement was measured in the former East Germany.

A new health problem is acquired immune deficiency syndrome (AIDS). By late 1994, a total of 11,854 AIDS cases had been reported in Germany.

Another institutional challenge is extending the old *Länder* health care system based on statutory health insurance to the new *Länder*. Achieving this goal has meant a complete overhaul of the GDR's state-run and highly centralized system; the introduction of insurance funds, private insurance, and voluntary organizations; and the training of physicians to become fee-for-service entrepreneurs, rather than salaried state employees as they were under the old system. The Treaty on Monetary, Economic, and Social Union of May 18, 1990, also set the goal of bringing hospitals in the former GDR up to the standards of those in the West. An ambitious program to invest about US$1 billion per year beginning in 1995 will be aimed at this last goal, with about 40 percent of funds coming from the federal government, another 40 percent from the new *Länder,* and 20 percent from public and private insurance carriers. It is expected that realization of the full integration of the two health systems will take many years, however.

Education

Germany has one of the world's best and most extensive school and university systems. Although shortcomings exist, on the whole the country's varied and multifaceted education system addresses well the needs of a population with widely differing characteristics and abilities. Some young people are best

served by a traditional classroom-based education that pre-
pares them for study at a wide choice of institutions of higher
learning. Others profit more from vocational training and education consisting of on-the-job training combined with classroom instruction. At the end of this kind of education,
graduates enter the workforce with a useful skill or profession.
Other students may choose one of many combinations of elements of these two paths, or decide later in life to embark on
one of them by means of adult education and night school.
Because education in Germany costs little compared with that
in the United States, for example, and because educational
support of various kinds is widely available, Germans are likely
to receive education and training suited to their abilities and
desires.

But however well Germans have arranged their system of
education, problems remain. The integration of two entirely
different education systems within the country's highly federalized system had not been completed as of mid-1995. In addition, the country's vaunted system of higher education is beset
by severe overcrowding despite its great expansion since the
1960s. Moreover, many who begin study at the university level
are not adequately prepared to meet its demands. Many others
who successfully complete their courses of study can find no
suitable employment once they graduate. Solving these problems will engage the country's educators and public into the
next century.

Historical Background

The origins of the German education system date back to
church schools in the Middle Ages. The first university was
founded in 1386 in Heidelberg; others were subsequently
established in Cologne, Leipzig, Freiburg, and a number of
other cities. These universities, which trained only a small intellectual elite of a few thousand, focused on the classics and religion. In the sixteenth century, the Reformation led to the
founding of universities along sectarian lines. It was also in this
century that cities promulgated the first regulations regarding
elementary schools. By the eighteenth century, elementary
schools had increasingly been separated from churches and
had come under the direction of state authorities. Prussia, for
example, made school attendance for all children between the
ages of five and fourteen compulsory in 1763. A number of uni-

versities dedicated to science also came into being in the eighteenth century.

The defeat of Prussia by France led to a reform of education by the Berlin scholar Wilhelm von Humboldt (1767–1835). His reforms in secondary schools have shaped the German education system to the present day. He required university-level training for high school teachers and modernized the structure and curriculum of the *Gymnasium*, the preparatory school. He also proposed an orientation phase after the *Gymnasium* and a qualifying examination known as the *Abitur* for university admission. In 1810 Humboldt founded the university in Berlin that now bears his name. Humboldt also introduced the three principles that guided German universities until the 1960s: academic freedom, the unity of teaching and research, and self-government by the professors. Also of much influence in education, both within Germany and abroad, was Friedrich Froebel's development of the kindergarten in 1837.

For much of the nineteenth century, Germany had two distinctive educational tracks: the *Gymnasium*, which provided a classical education for elites; and the *Volksschule*, which was attended for eight years by about 90 percent of children. The two schools were administered and supervised separately. Later in the century, two additional types of school emerged: the *Realgymnasium*, which substituted modern languages for the classics, and the *Oberrealschule*, which emphasized mathematics and science. Most children, however, could not attend the schools that prepared students for the professions or university entrance because of the schools' high standards and long duration. Hence, around the turn of the century, the *Mittelschule*, or middle school, was introduced to meet parental demand for expanded educational and economic opportunities. Children entered the *Mittelschule* after three years of elementary school, and they attended that school for six years.

In the nineteenth century, new universities were established in a number of major German cities, including Munich, Hamburg, and Frankfurt am Main. The older universities had been located mainly in smaller cities, such as Heidelberg. Many of the new universities were technical universities, and Germany soon attained a leadership in science that it lost only with World War II. Universities were state supported but largely independent in matters of curriculum and administration. A university degree brought much social status and was the prerequisite for entering the professions and the higher levels of the civil service.

A serious problem of German education before World War I was the rigid differentiation between primary education, received by all, and secondary education, received mainly by the children of the more prosperous classes. This division meant that most children of the poor had no access to secondary schooling and subsequent study at the university level. After the war, the Weimar constitution outlined a democratic vision of education that would address the problem: supervision by the state, with broad legislative powers over education; uniform teacher training; a minimum of eight years of primary school attendance; continuing education until the age of eighteen years; and free education and teaching materials. Many of these reform proposals never came to fruition, however.

During the Hitler era (1933–45), the national government reversed the tradition of provincial and local control of education and sought centralized control as part of the regime's aim to impose its political and racist ideology on society. Despite an agreement with the Vatican that theoretically guaranteed the independence of Roman Catholic schools, during the 1930s the regime considerably reduced church control of the parochial school system. Universities also lost their independence. By 1936 approximately 14 percent of all professors had been dismissed because of their political views or ethnic background. The introduction of two years of military service and six months of required labor led to a rapid decline in university enrollment. By 1939 all but six universities had closed.

After the defeat of the Hitler regime in 1945, the rebuilding of the education system in the occupied zones was influenced by the political interests and educational philosophy of the occupying powers: the United States, Britain, and France in what became West Germany; and the Soviet Union in East Germany. As a result, two different education systems developed. Their political, ideological, and cultural objectives and their core curricula reflected the socioeconomic and political-ideological environments that prevailed in the two parts of Germany from 1945 to 1989.

The Western Allies had differing views on education, but the insistence of the United States on the "reeducation" of German youth, meaning an education in and for democracy, proved the most persuasive. Thus, the West German education system was shaped by the democratic values of federalism, individualism,

Lunchtime in a Grundschule *in North Rhine-Westphalia*
Playground at a Grundschule *in Berlin*
Courtesy German Information Center, New York

227

and the provision of a range of educational choices and opportunities by a variety of public and private institutions. Students began to express themselves more freely than before and to exercise a greater degree of influence on education. In West Germany, religious institutions regained their footing and reputation. By contrast, the East German education system was centralized. The communist-controlled Socialist Unity Party of Germany (Sozialistische Einheitspartei Deutschlands—SED) retained a monopoly over education and subjected it to rigid control.

Both Germanys faced the task of "denazifying" teachers and reeducating students, but they moved in different directions. The authorities in the East sought teachers who had opposed fascism and who were committed to a Marxist-Leninist ideology. In the West, authorities dismissed several thousand teachers and replaced them with educators holding democratic values. The ensuing Western reform program included reconstructing facilities and reinvigorating the system. In 1953 reforms were introduced that aimed at standardizing education throughout the *Länder.* In the 1960s, reforms were undertaken that introduced apprentice shops and new instruction techniques for vocational training.

The 1970s saw further major educational reform, detailed in the document *Structural Plans for the Educational System.* The plan was approved in 1970 by the Council of Education, which was established in 1957 to serve as an advisory committee for the entire education system, and by each *Land* minister of education and cultural affairs. The main components of the reform program were the reorganization of the upper level of the *Gymnasium,* the recruitment of more students into colleges and universities, and the establishment of the comprehensive school (*Gesamtschule*). The *Gesamtschule* brings together the three kinds of secondary schools—the *Hauptschule,* the *Realschule,* and the *Gymnasium*—in an attempt to diminish what some perceived as the elitist bias of the traditional secondary education system. The program also proposed expanding adult education and vocational training programs.

The reform program achieved some but not all of its goals. The university entrance examination was made easier, and the number of students attending institutions of higher education rose from just over 200,000 in 1960 to about 1.9 million in the 1992–93 academic year (see table 11, Appendix). Between 1959 and 1979, twenty new universities were built, and university academic staff increased from 19,000 to 78,000. However, some Germans opposed the lowering of university entrance standards, and some also resisted the introduction of the *Gesamtschule*. In addition, the worldwide recession brought on by the oil crisis of 1973 caused serious financial problems for the government at all levels and made reforms difficult to realize.

Despite the different educational policies implemented by the two Germanys between 1945 and 1990, both systems regarded education as a constitutional right and a public responsibility, emphasized the importance of a broad general education (*Allgemeinbildung*), taught vocational education through the so-called dual system that combined classroom instruction with on-the-job training, required students to pass the *Abitur* examination before beginning university studies, and were committed to Humboldt's concept of university students' becoming educated by doing research. Despite these similarities, the systems differed in many important details, and the structural divergence was considerable.

Educational Policy Making and Administration

The Basic Law of 1949 reaffirmed the nineteenth-century tradition under which the *Länder* were responsible for education. Article 30 clearly established the autonomy of the *Länder* in most educational and cultural matters, including the financing of education, the maintenance of schools, teacher training, the setting of teachers' qualifications and educational standards, and the development of standardized curricula. In higher, or tertiary, education, the *Länder* share responsibility with the federal government. The federal government, for example, oversees vocational education and training, a very important component of Germany's system of education. The federal government also controls the financing of stipends and educational allowances and the promotion of research and support of young scientists through fellowships. In addition, the federal government also has passed framework laws on general principles of higher education. However, the federal government has no power to reform higher education institutions; this power remains a prerogative of the *Länder.*

Most teachers and university-level professors are civil servants with life tenure and high standing in society. They receive generous fringe benefits and relatively lucrative compensation, while making no contributions to social security programs. In Bavaria, for example, the average starting salary for an elemen-

tary or secondary school teacher in the early 1990s was about
US$40,000. A senior teacher in a *Gymnasium* earned about
US$53,000.

Postsecondary education is a shared responsibility implemented through "cooperative federalism" and joint policy
areas. The federal government and the sixteen old *Länder*
cooperate extensively with regard to the establishment, expansion, and modernization of institutions of higher education,
including their financing.

To counterbalance decentralized authority and provide leadership in education, the development of educational policy
and implementation is influenced by a number of nationwide
joint permanent advisory bodies. These include the Planning
Committee for the Construction of Institutions of Higher
Learning and the Scientific Council. Planning for education
and the promotion of research by the federal government and
the *Länder* have become more important since unification and
are implemented by the Federal and *Land* Commission on
Educational Planning and the Promotion of Research.

Educational Finances

Education is the second largest item of public spending after
social security and welfare and in the 1990–91 academic year
amounted to 4 percent of GNP. Education is not paid for by
local property taxes but rather out of general revenues. Since
1949 the federal government, the *Länder*, and the local governments, including in some cases intercommunal single or multi-
purpose districts (*Zweckverbände*), have shared in financing
education. For elementary, primary, and secondary education,
the *Länder* and the local governments are the major funding
sources. The *Länder* are responsible for teachers' salaries, curriculum development, and the setting of standards and qualifications. Local governments are responsible for the
maintenance and operation of school facilities. The *Länder*
remain the main source of funding for higher education, but
the federal government also plays a role. In 1991 the *Länder*
paid about 74 percent of total education costs (68 percent in
1970); local governments contributed 16 percent (24 percent
in 1970); and the federal government contributed 10 percent
(8 percent in 1970).

The Education System

The Basic Law of 1949 grants every German citizen the right

to self-fulfillment. In theory, citizens are able to choose the type of education they want and are given access to their preferred occupation or profession. The goal of educational policy is therefore to provide each citizen with opportunities to grow personally, professionally, and as a citizen in accordance with his or her abilities and preferences. The *Länder* are to provide equal educational opportunities and quality education for all through a variety of educational institutions.

Education is free and in most types of school is coeducational. Almost all elementary and secondary schools and about 95 percent of higher education institutions are public. College, graduate, and postgraduate students pay a nominal fee ranging from DM35 to DM60 a semester, which includes extensive rights to health care and other social benefits. When churches or private organizations run kindergartens, they do so independently, and the public sector is not involved.

According to the terms of the Düsseldorf Treaty of 1955, the first major attempt to unify or coordinate the school systems of the *Länder*, school attendance is mandatory for a minimum of nine years (or in some *Länder* ten years), beginning at age six. A student who starts vocational training as an apprentice must attend a part-time vocational school until the age of eighteen.

Elementary and Primary Education

The first level of education is called elementary education and consists of kindergarten for children ages three to five (see fig. 9). Attendance is voluntary. In the first half of the 1990s, about 80 percent of children were in kindergarten. Beginning in 1996, all children will be guaranteed a place in kindergarten. Because the former GDR had maintained an extensive kindergarten system, the new *Länder* had enough kindergarten places to meet this requirement. In contrast, in the early 1990s the old *Länder* had only enough places to accommodate about 75 percent of children in the relevant age-group.

The second level of education is called primary education and consists of the *Grundschule* (basic school). Children between the ages of six and ten attend the *Grundschule* from grades one through four. Children are evaluated in the fourth grade and tracked according to their academic records, teacher evaluations, and parent-teacher discussions. The three tracks lead to different secondary schools and play a significant role in determining a child's subsequent educational options.

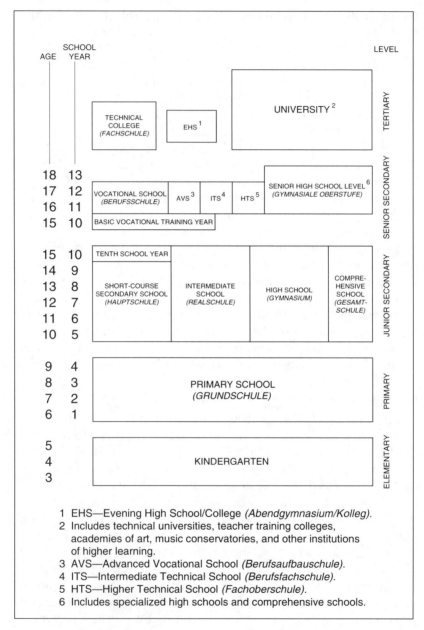

SCHOOL
AGE YEAR · LEVEL

	TECHNICAL COLLEGE *(FACHSCHULE)*	EHS [1]	UNIVERSITY [2]	TERTIARY

18 13
17 12 · VOCATIONAL SCHOOL *(BERUFSSCHULE)* · AVS [3] · ITS [4] · HTS [5] · SENIOR HIGH SCHOOL LEVEL [6] *(GYMNASIALE OBERSTUFE)*
16 11
15 10 · BASIC VOCATIONAL TRAINING YEAR

SENIOR SECONDARY

15 10 · TENTH SCHOOL YEAR
14 9
13 8 · SHORT-COURSE SECONDARY SCHOOL *(HAUPTSCHULE)* · INTERMEDIATE SCHOOL *(REALSCHULE)* · HIGH SCHOOL *(GYMNASIUM)* · COMPRE-HENSIVE SCHOOL *(GESAMT-SCHULE)*
12 7
11 6
10 5

JUNIOR SECONDARY

9 4
8 3 · PRIMARY SCHOOL *(GRUNDSCHULE)* · PRIMARY
7 2
6 1

5
4 · KINDERGARTEN · ELEMENTARY
3

1 EHS—Evening High School/College *(Abendgymnasium/Kolleg)*.
2 Includes technical universities, teacher training colleges, academies of art, music conservatories, and other institutions of higher learning.
3 AVS—Advanced Vocational School *(Berufsaufbauschule)*.
4 ITS—Intermediate Technical School *(Berufsfachschule)*.
5 HTS—Higher Technical School *(Fachoberschule)*.
6 Includes specialized high schools and comprehensive schools.

Source: Based on information from Arno Kappler and Adriane Grevel, eds., *Facts about Germany*, Frankfurt am Main, 1994, 407.

Figure 9. Structure of the Education System, 1994

Junior Secondary Education

Secondary education, the third level of education, is divided into two levels: junior secondary education (also called intermediate secondary education) and senior secondary education. Upon completion of the *Grundschule*, students between the ages of ten and sixteen attend one of the following types of secondary schools: the *Hauptschule*, the *Realschule*, the *Gymnasium*, the *Gesamtschule*, or the *Sonderschule* (for children with special educational needs). Students who complete this level of education receive an intermediate school certificate. Adults who attend two years of classes in evening schools can also earn these intermediate school certificates, which permit further study.

Junior secondary education starts with two years (grades five and six) of orientation courses during which students explore a variety of educational career paths open to them. The courses are designed to provide more time for the student and parents to decide upon appropriate subsequent education.

The *Hauptschule*, often called a short-course secondary school in English, lasts five or six years and consists of grades five to nine or five to ten depending on the *Land*. Some *Länder* require a compulsory tenth year or offer a two-year orientation program. About one-third of students completing primary school continue in the *Hauptschule*. The curriculum stresses preparation for a vocation as well as mathematics, history, geography, German, and one foreign language. After receiving their diploma, graduates either become apprentices in shops or factories while taking compulsory part-time courses or attend some form of full-time vocational school until the age of eighteen.

Another one-third of primary school graduates attend the *Realschule*, sometimes called the intermediate school. These schools include grades five through ten. Students seeking access to middle levels of government, industry, and business attend the *Realschule*. The curriculum is the same as that of the *Hauptschule*, but students take an additional foreign language, shorthand, wordprocessing, and bookkeeping, and they learn some computer skills. Graduation from the *Realschule* enables students to enter a *Fachoberschule* (a higher technical school) or a *Fachgymnasium* (a specialized high school or grammar school) for the next stage of secondary education. A special program makes it possible for a few students to transfer into the *Gymnasium*, but this is exceptional.

The *Gymnasium,* sometimes called high school or grammar school in English, begins upon completion of the *Grundschule* or the orientation grades and includes grades five through thirteen. The number of students attending the *Gymnasium* has increased dramatically in recent decades; by the mid-1990s, about one-third of all primary school graduates completed a course of study at the *Gymnasium,* which gives them the right to study at the university level. In the 1990s, the *Gymnasium* continued to be the primary educational route into the universities, although other routes have been created.

The *Gesamtschule* originated in the late 1960s to provide a broader range of educational opportunities for students than the traditional *Gymnasium.* The *Gesamtschule* has an all-inclusive curriculum for students ages ten to eighteen and a good deal of freedom to choose coursework. Some schools of this type have been established as all-day schools, unlike the *Gymnasium,* which is a part-day school with extensive homework assignments. The popularity of the *Gesamtschule* has been mixed. It has been resisted in more conservative areas, especially in Bavaria, where only one such school had been established by the beginning of the 1990s. A few more were established in Bavaria in the next few years; their presence is marginal when compared with the *Gymnasium,* of which there were 395 in 1994. Even North Rhine-Westphalia, Germany's most populous *Land* and an outspoken supporter of the *Gesamtschule,* had only 181, compared with 623 of the traditional *Gymasium.*

Senior Secondary Education

The variety of educational programs, tracks, and opportunities available to students increases at the senior secondary level. The largest single student group attends the senior level of the *Gymnasium,* the *Gymnasiale Oberstufe.* This level includes the traditional academically oriented *Gymnasium,* the vocational *Gymnasium,* the occupation-specific *Fachgymnasium,* and the *Gesamtschule.* Graduation from these schools requires passing the *Abitur,* the qualifying examination for studying at the university level. Until the late 1970s, nearly everyone who passed the *Abitur* had access to an institution of higher education. However, in the 1980s the *numerus clausus,* a restrictive quota system that had been introduced for the study of medicine in the late 1960s, began to be used for other popular fields of study. Strict selection criteria limiting access to higher education had become necessary because the demand for places at universities had become much greater than the supply.

Vocational Education and Training

The German education system has been praised for its ability to provide quality general education combined with excellent specific training for a profession or a skilled occupation. In 1992 about 65 percent of the country's workforce had been trained through vocational education. In the same year, 2.3 million young people were enrolled in vocational or trade schools.

Building upon the junior secondary program, the *Berufsschulen* are two- and three-year vocational schools that prepare young people for a profession. In the 1992–93 academic year, there were 1.8 million enrolled in these schools. About 264,000 individuals attended *Berufsfachschulen,* also called intermediate technical schools (ITS). These schools usually offer full-time vocation-specific programs. They are attended by students who want to train for a specialty or those already in the workforce who want to earn the equivalent of an intermediate school certificate from a *Realschule.* Full-time programs take between twelve and eighteen months, and part-time programs take between three and three-and-one-half years. Other types of schools designed to prepare students for different kinds of vocational careers are the higher technical school (HTS), the *Fachoberschule,* attended by about 75,000 persons in 1992–93, and the advanced vocational school (AVS), the *Berufsaufbauschule,* attended by about 6,500 persons in the same year. Students can choose to attend one of these three kinds of schools after graduating with an intermediate school certificate from a *Realschule* or an equivalent school.

The method of teaching used in vocational schools is called the dual system because it combines classroom study with a work-related apprenticeship system. The length of schooling/ training depends on prior vocational experience and may entail one year of full-time instruction or up to three years of part-time training.

Students can earn the *Fachhochschulreife* after successfully completing vocational education and passing a qualifying entrance examination. The *Fachhochschulreife* entitles a student to enter a *Fachhochschule,* or a training college, and to continue postsecondary occupational or professional training in engineering or technical fields. Such programs last from six months to three years (full-time instruction) or six to eight years (part-time instruction). Some students with many years of practical experience or those with special skills may also attend a *Fachhochschule.*

Vocational education and training is a joint government-industry program. The federal government and the *Länder* share in the financing of vocational education in public vocational schools, with the federal government bearing a slightly higher share (58 percent in 1991) than the *Länder.* On-the-job vocational training, whose cost is entirely borne by companies and businesses, is more costly to provide than vocational education. In the early 1990s, companies and businesses annually spent 2 percent of their payrolls on training.

Tertiary or Higher Education

In the 1992–93 academic year, higher education was available at 314 institutions of higher learning, with about 1.9 million students enrolled. Institutions of higher learning included eighty-one universities and technical universities, seven comprehensive universities (*Gesamthochschulen*), eight teacher-training colleges, seventeen theological seminaries, 126 profession-specific technical colleges, thirty training facilities in public administration (*Verwaltungsfachhochschulen*), and forty-five academies for art, music, and literature. Nearly 80 percent, or 250, of these institutions were located in the old *Länder,* and sixty-four were in the new *Länder.* Baden-Württemberg and North Rhine-Westphalia had the largest share of these institutions, sixty-one and forty-nine, respectively. In 1990 about 69.7 percent of students at tertiary-level institutions went to universities and engineering schools, and another 21.7 percent attended vocational training colleges (*Fachhochschulen*).

German university students can complete their first degree in about five years, but on average university studies last seven years. Advanced degrees require further study. Because tuition at institutions of higher education amounts to no more than a nominal fee except at the handful of private universities, study at the university level means only meeting living expenses. An extensive federal and *Land* program provides interest-free loans to students coming from lower-income households. Half of the loan must be paid within five years of graduation. Students graduating in the top third of their class or within a shorter time than usual have portions of their loans forgiven. Loans are also available to students receiving technical and

A sixth-grade class at the Geschwister Scholl Gymnasium in Pulheim,
North Rhine-Westphalia
Courtesy William Collins

vocational training. In the early 1990s, about half of all students were obliged to work while attending university.

Unlike the United States, Germany does not have a group of elite universities; none enjoys a reputation for greater overall excellence than is enjoyed by the others. Instead, particular departments of some universities are commonly seen as very good in their field. For example, the University of Cologne has a noted economics faculty. Also in contrast to the United States, German universities do not offer much in the way of campus life, and collegiate athletics are nearly nonexistent. Universities generally consist of small clusters of buildings dispersed throughout the city in which they are located. Students do not live on university property, although some are housed in student dormitories operated by churches or other nonprofit organizations.

Education in the New *Länder*

The Soviet-supported SED centralized and politicized education far more than had been the case during the Hitler era. About 70 percent of teachers and all school counselors, superintendents, members of the teachers' union, and school administrators were SED members, often performing both professional and party functions. In theory, parents were part of the educational process, but in practice they were expected to support party educational policy. Teacher-student ratios were low—1:5 compared with 1:18 in West Germany.

Under the new system, public education was expanded by establishing preschools and kindergartens. Because most women returned to work after six months of maternity leave, these new schools were widely attended. Lowered standards of admission and scholarships expanded access to higher education for working-class children and diminished its elitist bias. The state emphasized education in "socialist values" and Marxism-Leninism at all levels of the system, following the Soviet model. Students were required to spend one day per week working in a factory, in an office, or on a farm in order to reinforce the importance of labor.

In terms of organization, all types of schools were replaced by a uniform ten-grade polytechnic school, which emphasized technical education. Upon graduation from this school, about 85 percent of students entered a two-year vocational education school. The remaining students attended special classes to prepare for university studies, some going to an extension of secondary school for two years, others attending vocational school for three years. The GDR had six universities, nine technical universities, and several dozen specialized institutions of higher education. In the 1950s and 1960s, the children of workers were favored for university study. In later decades, the children of the intelligentsia (state officials, professionals, and academicians) again formed a greater part of the student population. However, in addition to passing the qualifying examination, students had to demonstrate political loyalty and commitment to Marxist-Leninist ideology. Throughout their schooling, children were constantly exposed to party ideology and values.

The system had a strong vocational element that focused on providing a bridge to adult work. The system was particularly successful in some respects; literacy was practically universal by 1989, and the proportion of unskilled workers and trainees in the workforce fell from 70 percent in 1955 to 13 percent in 1989. The system was best suited to the teaching of mathematics, the natural sciences, and other technical and nonideological subjects. It was less effective in teaching the social sciences, current affairs, and information technology. Language teaching emphasized Russian, which was compulsory. Few learned other European languages such as English or French.

The revolutionary events of November 1989 led to an abrupt transformation of the institutional, political, and philosophical foundations of education in the GDR. In heated debates, grassroots groups of parents, teachers, and citizens discussed the future of education and vocational training in the new *Länder.* By May 1990, the GDR educational leadership had been dismissed, and steps had been taken to reduce the bloated educational bureaucracy. Evaluation commissions reassessed the quality of research and academic institutions and their staff, and many social science departments suspended activity until they were evaluated. Departments of Marxism-Leninism were closed outright, and most institutions modeled on the Soviet system were dismantled.

In May 1990, the ministers of education of the *Länder* agreed that the new *Länder* should develop their own educational strategies. The unification treaty of August 31, 1990, specified that this should be done by June 30, 1991, when the new *Länder* were expected to have passed new laws on education. A major change effected by those laws is the replacement of the general polytechnic school with the range of educational models prevailing in West Germany. The five new *Länder,* with the exception of Brandenburg, introduced the four-year *Grundschule.* Brandenburg established a six-year *Grundschule,* like that found in Berlin. Secondary schooling also resembles that of the old *Länder* in that the *Gymnasium* is common to all; however, other schools at the junior secondary level differ somewhat in their names and organization. Education at the senior secondary level resembles closely that of the old *Länder.*

Higher education has also seen changes. To improve geographic access to higher education, regions previously without institutions of higher learning have received a number of such institutions. In other regions, institutions of higher learning have been abolished, some of which have been replaced by *Fachhochschulen,* nonexistent in the former GDR. University staffs have also been cut, sometimes by as much as 50 percent. Within two or three years of unification, about 25 percent of university faculty were arrivals from the old *Länder*. By late 1994, institutions of higher learning in the new *Länder* had benefited from annual payments from western Germany of about DM3 billion.

Although the old structure has been replaced, observers agree that the values and preferences internalized by parents, students, and teachers who came to maturity in the GDR can be expected to survive for many years. Because it lasted decades longer than nazism, the Marxist-Leninist influence on education in the new *Länder* will probably take far longer to overcome.

Current Education Issues and Outlook for the Future

Germany's system of education faces a number of challenges, among them a surplus of teachers in a period of declining birth rates. A chief problem is reconciling the tradition of *Land* responsibility for education, which has resulted in a variety of school types, programs, and standards, with the need for a uniform national system. This is the central problem concerning whether or how to integrate the education systems of the new *Länder* with those of the old *Länder*. Such an integration will entail deciding whether to increase the number of years of schooling by one year for eastern Germans or to reduce the thirteen years of schooling for western Germans to twelve. It will also mean deciding on whether to introduce a postsecondary vocational qualifying examination (*Fachabitur*) in the new *Länder* to mirror the one that has existed in the former FRG since the 1970s. Other unresolved issues relate to such questions as educational standards, qualifications, and the mutual recognition of qualifying examinations and diplomas. The diversity resulting from a reluctance to impose the same standard norms and diplomas in all *Länder*, in contrast to France and many other European countries, is so extreme that some observers think it may hinder the mobility of students and teachers within Germany and the larger Europe.

Unification has also thrown into sharp focus the ongoing debate about the weaknesses of the university system in the former FRG. Many West German universities are overcrowded, understaffed, underequipped, and underfinanced. Frequently criticized are the length and structure of degree courses, the excessive length of studies, the high number of long-term students, and the disturbingly high number of dropouts who leave higher education without graduating. Some of these problems

German university students
Students outside Bonn's Friedrich Wilhelm University
Courtesy German Information Center, New York

241

result from Germany's success in expanding access to secondary education. About 34 percent of all students graduated with the *Abitur* in 1990, compared with only 11 percent in 1970.

Critics charge that many students who fail to complete their university studies may not have been well educated. A 1994 study cast serious doubt on the assumption that passing the *Abitur* is adequate preparation for study at a university. It found that almost one-third of those who had passed the examination failed to complete their coursework at institutions of higher education and that the number of dropouts had quadrupled from 14,000 in the mid-1970s to 60,000 two decades later. The study also found that on average, dropouts left the university after three years, or six semesters, that women had a higher dropout rate than men, and that the highest dropout rate was in liberal arts, formerly the core of university studies.

Students cited a lack of correlation between curriculum content and career goals as one reason for breaking off their studies. One out of three students also reported feeling unprepared for higher education. Other reasons listed were the limited opportunities in the labor market, overcrowding, anonymity (impersonality), a lack of mentors, and the poor quality of teaching. Financial reasons also were mentioned more often than they had been in the mid-1970s.

As remedies, some advocate establishing a better balance between pure and applied research and teaching, making a distinction between first-degree courses offering training for a profession and research-oriented postgraduate courses, and substituting well-defined curricula for the existing uncoordinated requirements. Delegating a larger share of teaching to a new breed of middle-rank lecturers has also been recommended.

*　　　*　　　*

The best and most comprehensive historical and comparative account of German social policy, although published in 1988, is a nearly book-length chapter by Jens Alber in *Growth to Limits* (Vol. 2), edited by Peter Flora. Peter J. Katzenstein also provides a good introduction to German social policy in *Policy and Politics in West Germany*. Stephan Leibfried is the author of valuable articles on various aspects of German social policy, as is Arnold J. Heidenheimer. Alfred J. Kahn and Sheila B. Kamerman have written on family and child care policies.

Analyses in English of recent developments regarding specific programs after unification are regrettably rare. An exception is "Social Policy: One State, Two-Tier Welfare" by Steen Mangen. A new British periodical, *Journal of European Social Policy*, publishes research findings in English and is beginning to fill the gap in this area. Examples of the journal's articles include Winifried Schmähl's article on the 1992 reform of public pensions; Wolfgang Voges and Götz Rohwer's very useful article on social assistance; Kirsten Scheiwe's report on poverty risks of mothers in Belgium, Germany, and Britain; and Rudolph Bauer's analysis of voluntary welfare associations in Germany and the United States.

The literature on the German health care system in English is extensive. Written for readers in the United States and dating from 1993, Richard A. Knox's *Germany: One Nation with Health Care for All* is an excellent discussion of the system's components. A more recent publication is Ullrich K. Hoffmeyer's long article "The Health Care System in Germany." It includes a discussion of the Health Care Structural Reform Act of 1993. Other useful sources are John K. Iglehart's articles in the *New England Journal of Medicine*, Deborah A. Stone's article "German Unification: East Meets West in the Doctor's Office," and "Global Budgeting in Germany: Lessons for the United States" by Klaus-Dirk Henke, Margaret A. Murray, and Claudia Ade.

There is no recent one-volume comprehensive survey of the German education system. Christoph Führ's *Schools and Institutions of Higher Education in the Federal Republic of Germany*, dating from 1989, is still quite useful, however, as is his more recent book, *On the Education System in the Five New Laender of the Federal Republic of Germany*. Also valuable is Peter J. Katzenstein's discussion of university reform in his book *Policy and Politics in West Germany*. Val D. Rust and Diane Rust examine the difficulties of integrating the two German education systems in *The Unification of German Education*.

The Press and Information Office of the Federal Republic of Germany publishes brief accounts in English and German on a variety of topics, including social programs. These can be obtained through the German Information Center in New York. (For further information and complete citations, see Bibliography.)

Chapter 5. The Domestic Economy

The Frankfurt am Main skyline. In the foreground is the Paulskirche, meeting place of the 1848–49 National Assembly.

THE GERMAN ECONOMY is replete with contradictions. It is modern but old-fashioned. It is immensely powerful but suffers from serious structural weaknesses. It is subject to national laws and rules but is so closely tied into the European Union (EU— see Glossary) that it is no longer truly independent. It has a central bank that controls European monetary policy and has a deepening impact on the global economy but that also insists on making its decisions mainly on the basis of domestic considerations. Finally, although Germany must compete against highly efficient economies outside its own continent, it continues to carry the expense and burden of traditional industries that drain resources that could be better used elsewhere.

The German economy as it is known today is an outgrowth of the 1990 merger between the dominant economy of the Federal Republic of Germany (FRG, or West Germany) and that of the German Democratic Republic (GDR, or East Germany). This merger will one day produce a massive economic entity that will constitute the fulcrum of Europe as a production center, as well as a transportation and communications center. But each partner brings different elements to the mix, and the merger has proved difficult and costly. The merger will dominate Germany's economic policy and reality until well into the next century.

The record of the West German economy during the four decades before unification shows a signal achievement. The first decade, that of the 1950s, had been that of the "economic miracle." The second decade, that of the 1960s, had seen consolidation and the first signs of trouble. The 1970s had brought the oil shocks, the generous social programs, the rising deficits, and finally a loss of control. In the 1980s, new policies at home and a more stable environment abroad had combined to put West Germany back on the path of growth.

The East German economy had been a powerhouse in Eastern Europe, where Moscow had relied on it to produce machine tools, chemicals, and electronics. But it had grown increasingly inefficient, and its currency had become worthless outside its own borders. East Germans had felt frustrated at their lack of true material well-being, as well as their lack of freedom. They joined their economy enthusiastically with that of West Germany in 1990. The merger gave them a rude shock, however, in part because of the simultaneous collapse of East Germany's markets in the Soviet empire and in part because of the inefficiencies that the communist system had left behind.

The united German economy is a dominant force in world markets because of the strong export orientation that has been part of the German tradition for centuries. Although the burdens of unification have cut into West Germany's traditional export surplus, German industry continues to produce some of the best machine tools, automobiles, trucks, chemicals, and engineering products in the world. Its management culture, which mingles competition and cooperation, stresses quality and durability above all other virtues. Because many German companies are small or medium-sized, they are able to concentrate on a few production lines that compete effectively even if they are expensive.

The German culture of cooperation also extends to the relations between the private sector and the government. The social market economy, in which all elements of the system cooperate, stresses the importance of having all parties to the social contract work together. Workers play a role in management. Managers mingle with workers. The bureaucracy attempts to create an environment in which all parties serve a common purpose. Although the rules intended to prevent the recurrence of the German cartel system of the last century are strictly enforced by the Bundeskartellamt (Federal Cartel Office), certain practices that would be forbidden under United States antitrust laws are widely tolerated in Germany.

The dominant force in the German economy is the banking system. The central bank, the Bundesbank, is deeply committed to maintaining the value of the nation's currency, the deutsche mark, even at some potential cost to economic growth. It fears inflation above all other ills and is determined to prevent the recurrence of Germany's ruinous Great Inflation of the early 1920s. Private banks also play an important role. German industrial and service companies rely much more on bank finance than on equity capital. The banks provide the money and in turn sit on the supervisory boards of most of Germany's corporations. From that vantage point, they stress the traditional banking virtues of slow but steady and nonrisky growth. Their influence and thinking permeate the economy.

German agriculture is not as strong as German industry. It is a relatively small part of the gross domestic product (GDP—see Glossary) and is heavily subsidized by the EU's Common Agricultural Policy (CAP—see Glossary) and by the German government itself. The accession of East Germany to a united Germany expanded the relative size of the agricultural sector and somewhat improved its efficiency, but Germany is not an agricultural producer like Spain or Italy.

West Germany developed a system of high wages and high social benefits that has been carried over into united Germany. The extent and the generosity of its social programs now leave Germany at a competitive disadvantage with respect to the states of Eastern Europe and Asia. German labor costs are above those of most other states, not because of the wages themselves—which are high by global standards but not out of line with German labor productivity—but because of social costs, which impose burdens equal to the wages themselves. Thus, German companies and German workers must decide either to abandon some of the social programs that are at the core of the revered social market economy or to risk losing out in the increasingly intense global competition of the 1990s and beyond. The Germans have not solved this problem, but they are beginning to address it more seriously than before.

Patterns of Development

History

Medieval Germany, lying on the open Central European Plain, was divided into hundreds of contending kingdoms, principalities, dukedoms, bishoprics, and free cities. Economic survival in that environment, like political or even physical survival, did not mean expanding across unlimited terrain, as in the United States. It meant a constant struggle that required collaboration with some, competition with others, and an intimate understanding among government, commerce, and production. A desire to save was also born in the German experience of political, military, and economic uncertainty.

Even under these difficult conditions, Germany had already developed a strong economy during the Middle Ages. It was based on guild and craft production, but with elements of merchant capitalism and mercantilism. The trade conducted by its cities ranged far and wide throughout Europe in all directions, and Germany as a whole often had trade surpluses with neighboring states. One reason for these exports was the sheer necessity for the small states to sell abroad in order to buy the many things they could not produce at home.

The German guilds of the Middle Ages established the German tradition of creating products known for quality and durability. A craftsman was not permitted to pursue a trade until he could demonstrate the ability to make high-quality products. Out of that same tradition came an equally strong passion for education and vocational training, for no craftsman was recognized until he had thoroughly learned a trade, passed a test, and been certified.

The Industrial Revolution reached Germany long after it had flowered in Britain, and the governments of the German states supported local industry because they did not want to be left behind. Many enterprises were government initiated, government financed, government managed, or government subsidized. As industry grew and prospered in the nineteenth century, Prussia and other German states consciously supported all economic development and especially transportation and industry.

The north German states were for the most part richer in natural resources than the southern states. They had vast agricultural tracts from Schleswig-Holstein in the west through Prussia in the east. They also had coal and iron in the Ruhr Valley. Through the practice of primogeniture, widely followed in northern Germany, large estates and fortunes grew. So did close relations between their owners and local as well as national governments.

The south German states were relatively poor in natural resources except for their people, and those Germans therefore engaged more often in small economic enterprises. They also had no primogeniture rule but subdivided the land among several offspring, leading those offspring to remain in their native towns but not fully able to support themselves from their small parcels of land. The south German states, therefore, fostered cottage industries, crafts, and a more independent and self-reliant spirit less closely linked to the government.

German banks played central roles in financing German industry. They also shaped industrywide producer cooperatives, known as cartels. Different banks formed cartels in different industries. Cartel contracts were accepted as legal and binding by German courts although they were held to be illegal in Britain and the United States.

The first German cartel was a salt cartel, the Neckar Salt Union of 1828, formed in Württemberg and Baden. The process of cartelization began slowly, but the cartel movement took hold after 1873 in the economic depression that followed the postunification speculative bubble. It began in heavy industry and spread throughout other industries. By 1900 there were 275 cartels in operation; by 1908, over 500. By some estimates, different cartel arrangements may have numbered in the thousands at different times, but many German companies stayed outside the cartels because they did not welcome the restrictions that membership imposed.

The government played a powerful role in the industrialization of the German Empire founded by Otto von Bismarck in 1871 (see Bismarck and Unification, ch. 1). It supported not only heavy industry but also crafts and trades because it wanted to maintain prosperity in all parts of the empire. Even where the national government did not act, the highly autonomous regional and local governments supported their own industries. Each state tried to be as self-sufficient as possible.

Despite the several ups and downs of prosperity and depression that marked the first decades of the German Empire, the ultimate wealth of the empire proved immense. German aristocrats, landowners, bankers, and producers created what might be termed the first German economic miracle, the turn-of-the-century surge in German industry and commerce during which bankers, industrialists, mercantilists, the military, and the monarchy joined forces.

The German Empire also established, under Bismarck's direction, the social compact under which the German laboring classes supported the national ambitions of the newly united German state in exchange for a system of social welfare that would make them, if not full participants in the system, at least its beneficiaries and pensioners. Bismarck was not a socialist, but he believed that it was necessary to accept portions of the socialist platform to sustain prosperity and social cohesion.

From the prosperity of the empire during the Wilhelmine era (1890–1914), Germany plunged into World War I, a war it was to lose and one that spawned many of the economic crises that would destroy the successor Weimar Republic (see The Weimar Republic, 1918–33, ch. 1). Even the British economist John Maynard Keynes denounced the 1919 Treaty of Versailles as ruinous to German and global prosperity. The war and the treaty were followed by the Great Inflation of the early 1920s that wreaked havoc on Germany's social structure and political stability. During that inflation, the value of the nation's currency, the Reichsmark, collapsed from 8.9 per US$1 in 1918 to

4.2 trillion per US$1 by November 1923. Then, after a brief period of prosperity during the mid-1920s, came the Great Depression, which destroyed what remained of the German middle class and paved the way for the dictatorship of Adolf Hitler. During the Hitler era (1933–45), the economy developed a hothouse prosperity, supported with high government subsidies to those sectors that Hitler favored because they gave Germany military power and economic autarchy, that is, economic independence from the global economy. Finally, the entire enterprise collapsed in the *Stunde Null* (Zero Hour), when Germany lay in ruins at the end of World War II in May 1945 and when every German knew that he or she had to begin life all over again.

The first several years after World War II were years of bitter penury for the Germans. Their land, their homes, and their property lay in ruin. Millions were forced to flee with nothing but the clothes on their backs. Tens of millions did not have enough to eat or to wear. Inflation raged. Parker pens, nylon stockings, and Camel cigarettes represented the accepted, if not the legal, tender of the time. Occupation projections showed that the average German would be able to purchase a plate every five years, a pair of shoes every twelve years, and a suit every fifty years.

As Germany's postwar economic and political leaders shaped their plans for the future German economy, they saw in ruin a new beginning, an opportunity to position Germany on a new and totally different path. The economy was to be an instrument for prosperity, but it was also to safeguard democracy and to help maintain a stable society. The new German leaders wanted social peace as well as economic prosperity. They wanted an economic system that would give all an equal opportunity in order to avoid creating underprivileged social groups whose bitter frustration would erupt into revolution and—in turn—repression.

The man who took full advantage of Germany's postwar opportunity was Ludwig Erhard, who was determined to shape a new and different kind of German economy. He was given his chance by United States officials, who found him working in Nuremberg and who saw that many of his ideas coincided with their own.

Erhard's first step was currency reform: the abolition of the Reichsmark and the creation of a new currency, the deutsche mark. He carried out that reform on June 20, 1948, installing the new currency with the concurrence of the Western Allies but also taking advantage of the opportunity to abolish most Nazi and occupation rules and regulations in order to establish the genesis of a free economy. The currency reform, whose purpose was to provide a respected store of value and a widely accepted legal tender, succeeded brilliantly. It established the foundations of the West German economy and of the West German state.

The Social Market Economy

The Germans proudly label their economy a "*soziale Marktwirtschaft,*" or "social market economy," to show that the system as it has developed after World War II has both a material and a social—or human—dimension. They stress the importance of the term "market" because after the Nazi experience they wanted an economy free of state intervention and domination. The only state role in the new West German economy was to protect the competitive environment from monopolistic or oligopolistic tendencies—including its own. The term "social" is stressed because West Germans wanted an economy that would not only help the wealthy but also care for the workers and others who might not prove able to cope with the strenuous competitive demands of a market economy. The term "social" was chosen rather than "socialist" to distinguish their system from those in which the state claimed the right to direct the economy or to intervene in it.

Beyond these principles of the social market economy, but linked to it, comes a more traditional German concept, that of *Ordnung,* which can be directly translated to mean order but which really means an economy, society, and polity that are structured but not dictatorial. The founders of the social market economy insisted that *Denken in Ordnungen*—to think in terms of systems of order—was essential. They also spoke of *Ordo-Liberalismus* because the essence of the concept is that this must be a freely chosen order, not a command order.

Over time, the term "social" in the social market economy began to take on a life of its own. It moved the West German economy toward an extensive social welfare system that has become one of the most expensive in the world. Moreover, the West German federal government and the states (*Länder,* sing., *Land*) began to compensate for irregularities in economic cycles and for shifts in world production by beginning to shelter and support some sectors and industries. In an even greater departure from the Erhard tradition, the government became an instrument for the preservation of existing industries rather than a force for renewal. In the 1970s, the state assumed an ever more important role in the economy. During the 1980s, Chancellor Helmut Kohl tried to reduce that state role, and he succeeded in part, but German unification again compelled the German government to assume a stronger role in the economy. Thus, the contradiction between the terms "social" and "market" has remained an element for debate in Germany.

Given the internal contradiction in its philosophy, the German economy is both conservative and dynamic. It is conservative in the sense that it draws on the part of the German tradition that envisages some state role in the economy and a cautious attitude toward investment and risk-taking. It is dynamic in the sense that it is directed toward growth—even if that growth may be slow and steady rather than spectacular. It tries to combine the virtues of a market system with the virtues of a social welfare system.

The Economic Miracle and Beyond

The economic reforms and the new West German system received powerful support from a number of sources: investment funds under the European Recovery Program, more commonly known as the Marshall Plan; the stimulus to German industry provided by the diversion of other Western resources for Korean War production; and the German readiness to work hard for low wages until productivity had risen. But the essential component of success was the revival of confidence brought on by Erhard's reforms and by the new currency.

The West German boom that began in 1950 was truly memorable. The growth rate of industrial production was 25.0 percent in 1950 and 18.1 percent in 1951. Growth continued at a high rate for most of the 1950s, despite occasional slowdowns. By 1960 industrial production had risen to two-and-one-half times the level of 1950 and far beyond any that the Nazis had reached during the 1930s in all of Germany. GDP rose by two-thirds during the same decade. The number of persons employed rose from 13.8 million in 1950 to 19.8 million in 1960, and the unemployment rate fell from 10.3 percent to 1.2 percent.

Labor also benefited in due course from the boom. Although wage demands and pay increases had been modest at first, wages and salaries rose over 80 percent between 1949 and

1955, catching up with growth. West German social programs were given a considerable boost in 1957, just before a national election, when the government decided to initiate a number of social programs and to expand others.

In 1957 West Germany gained a new central bank, the Deutsche Bundesbank, generally called simply the Bundesbank, which succeeded the Bank Deutscher Länder and was given much more authority over monetary policy. That year also saw the establishment of the Bundeskartellamt (Federal Cartel Office), designed to prevent the return of German monopolies and cartels. Six years later, in 1963, the Bundestag, the lower house of Germany's parliament, at Erhard's urging established the Council of Economic Experts to provide objective evaluations on which to base German economic policy.

The West German economy did not grow as fast or as consistently in the 1960s as it had during the 1950s, in part because such a torrid pace could not be sustained, in part because the supply of fresh labor from East Germany was cut off by the Berlin Wall, built in 1961, and in part because the Bundesbank became disturbed about potential overheating and moved several times to slow the pace of growth. Erhard, who had succeeded Konrad Adenauer as chancellor, was voted out of office in December 1966, largely—although not entirely—because of the economic problems of the Federal Republic. He was replaced by the Grand Coalition consisting of the Christian Democratic Union (Christlich Demokratische Union—CDU), its sister party the Christian Social Union (Christlich-Soziale Union—CSU), and the Social Democratic Party of Germany (Sozialdemokratische Partei Deutschlands—SPD) under Chancellor Kurt Georg Kiesinger of the CDU.

Under the pressure of the slowdown, the new West German Grand Coalition government abandoned Erhard's broad laissez-faire orientation. The new minister for economics, Karl Schiller, argued strongly for legislation that would give the federal government and his ministry greater authority to guide economic policy. In 1967 the Bundestag passed the Law for Promoting Stability and Growth, known as the Magna Carta of medium-term economic management. That law, which remains in effect although never again applied as energetically as in Schiller's time, provided for coordination of federal, *Land*, and local budget plans in order to give fiscal policy a stronger impact. The law also set a number of optimistic targets for the four basic standards by which West German economic success was henceforth to be measured: currency stability, economic growth, employment levels, and trade balance. Those standards became popularly known as the *magisches Viereck*, the "magic rectangle" or the "magic polygon."

Schiller followed a different concept from Erhard's. He was one of the rare German Keynesians, and he brought to his new tasks the unshakable conviction that government had both the obligation and the capacity to shape economic trends and to smooth out and even eliminate the business cycle. Schiller's chosen formula was *Globalsteuerung*, or global guidance, a process by which government would not intervene in the details of the economy but would establish broad guidelines that would foster uninterrupted noninflationary growth.

Schiller's success in the Grand Coalition helped to give the SPD an electoral victory in 1969 and a chance to form a new coalition government with the Free Democratic Party (Freie Demokratische Partei—FDP) under Willy Brandt. The SPD-FDP coalition expanded the West German social security system, substantially increasing the size and cost of the social budget. Social program costs grew by over 10 percent a year during much of the 1970s, introducing into the budget an unalterable obligation that reduced fiscal flexibility (although Schiller and other Keynesians believed that it would have an anticyclical effect). This came back to haunt Schiller as well as every German government since then. Schiller himself had to resign in 1972 when the West German and global economies were in a downturn and when all his ideas did not seem able to revive West German prosperity. Willy Brandt himself resigned two years later.

Helmut Schmidt, Brandt's successor, was intensely interested in economics but also faced great problems, including the dramatic upsurge in oil prices of 1973–74. West Germany's GDP in 1975 fell by 1.4 percent (in constant prices), the first time since the founding of the FRG that it had fallen so sharply. The West German trade balance also fell as global demand declined and as the terms of trade deteriorated because of the rise in petroleum prices.

By 1976 the worst was over. West German growth resumed, and the inflation rate began to decline (see table 12, Appendix). Although neither reached the favorable levels that had come to be taken for granted during the 1950s and early 1960s, they were accepted as tolerable after the turbulence of the previous years. Schmidt began to be known as a *Macher* (achiever), and the government won reelection in 1976. Schmidt's success led him and his party to claim that they had built *Modell Deutschland* (the German model).

But the economy again turned down and, despite efforts to stimulate growth by government deficits, failed to revive quickly. It was only by mid-1978 that Schmidt and the Bundesbank were able to bring the economy into balance. After that, the economy continued expanding through 1979 and much of 1980, helping Schmidt win reelection in 1980. But the upturn proved to be uneven and unrewarding, as the problems of the mid-1970s rapidly returned. By early 1981, Schmidt faced the worst possible situation: growth fell and unemployment rose, but inflation did not abate.

By the fall of 1982, Schmidt's coalition government collapsed as the FDP withdrew to join a coalition led by Helmut Kohl, the leader of the CDU/CSU. He began to direct what was termed *die Wende* (the turning or the reversal). The government proceeded to implement new policies to reduce the government role in the economy and within a year won a popular vote in support of the new course.

Within its broad policy, the new government had several main objectives: to reduce the federal deficit by cutting expenditures as well as taxes, to reduce government restrictions and regulations, and to improve the flexibility and performance of the labor market. The government also carried through a series of privatization measures, selling almost DM10 billion (for value of the deutsche mark—see Glossary) in shares of such diverse state-owned institutions as VEBA, VIAG, Volkswagen, Lufthansa, and Salzgitter. Through all these steps, the state role in the West German economy declined from 52 percent to 46 percent of GDP between 1982 and 1990, according to Bundesbank statistics.

Although the policies of *die Wende* changed the mood of the West German economy and reinstalled a measure of confidence, progress came unevenly and haltingly. During most of the 1980s, the figures on growth and inflation improved but slowly, and the figures on unemployment barely moved at all. There was little job growth until the end of the decade. When the statistics did change, however, even modestly, it was at least in the right direction.

Nonetheless, it also remained true that West German growth did not again reach the levels that it had attained in the early years of the Federal Republic. There had been a decline in the growth rate since the 1950s, an upturn in unemployment since the 1960s, and a gradual increase in inflation except during or after a severe downturn.

Global economic statistics also showed a decline in West German output and vitality. They showed that the West German share of total world production had grown from 6.6 percent in 1965 to 7.9 percent by 1975. Twelve years later, in 1987, however, it had fallen to 7.4 percent, largely because of the more rapid growth of Japan and other Asian states. Even adding the estimated GDP of the former East Germany at its peak before unification would not have brought the all-German share above 8.2 percent by 1989 and would leave all of Germany with barely a greater share of world production than West Germany alone had reached fifteen years earlier.

It was only in the late 1980s that West Germany's economy finally began to grow more rapidly. The growth rate for West German GDP rose to 3.7 percent in 1988 and 3.6 percent in 1989, the highest levels of the decade. The unemployment rate also fell to 7.6 percent in 1989, despite an influx of workers from abroad. Thus, the results of the late 1980s appeared to vindicate the West German supply-side revolution. Tax rate reductions had led to greater vitality and revenues. Although the cumulative public-sector deficit had gone above the DM1 trillion level, the public sector was growing more slowly than before.

The year 1989 was the last year of the West German economy as a separate and separable institution. From 1990 the positive and negative distortions generated by German unification set in, and the West German economy began to reorient itself toward economic and political union with what had been East Germany. The economy turned gradually and massively from its primarily West European and global orientation toward an increasingly intense concentration on the requirements and the opportunities of unification.

Unification and Its Aftermath

The East German and West German economies at the time of unification looked very similar. They both concentrated on industrial production, especially machine tools, chemicals, automobiles, and precision manufactures. Both had a well-trained labor force and an important export component, although their exports went largely in opposite directions. But the East German economy was highly centralized and guided by a detailed and purportedly precise planning system, with virtually no private property and with no room for decision or initiative.

On July 1, 1990, the economies of the two Germanys became one. It was the first time in history that a capitalist and a socialist economy had suddenly become one, and there were no precise guidelines on how it could be done. Instead, there were a number of problems, of which the most severe were the comparatively poor productivity of the former East German economy and its links to the collapsing socialist economies of the Soviet Union and Eastern Europe.

Even before economic unification, the West German government had decided that one of its first tasks was to privatize the East German economy. For this reason, it had taken over in June the Treuhandanstalt (Trust Agency, commonly known as Treuhand), which had been established by the GDR to take over East German firms and to turn them over to new management through privatization. The agency assumed the assets and liabilities of about 8,000 East German enterprises in order to sell them to German and other bidders. By the time the Treuhand was disbanded at the end of 1994, it had privatized some 14,000 enterprises.

As economic unification proceeded, issues that had been recognized but inadequately understood in advance began to surface. There was massive confusion about property rights. As wave after wave of Nazi, Soviet, and later GDR expropriations had taken place between 1933 and 1989, there was often little knowledge of the actual ownership of property. More than 2 million claims on properties in the territory of the former GDR were filed by the December 31, 1992, deadline. As more claimants emerged, with many winning cases in the courts, potential investors were often scared off.

Another problem was that East German production costs had been very high. The conversion rates of East German marks to deutsche marks often kept those costs high, as did the early wage negotiations, which resulted in wages far above the productivity level. Western German firms found it easier and cheaper to serve their new eastern German markets by expanding production in western facilities.

A third problem was that the inadequate infrastructure also became a problem for many potential investors. Telephone service was improved only very slowly. Many investors also complained about energy shortages, as many East German power stations were shut down for safety and other reasons. Roads and railroads had to be virtually rebuilt because they had been so badly maintained.

In addition to these practical problems, there was also a deep policy dilemma that underlay the entire process of unification. From the beginning, there had been a pernicious link between the earlier and later phases of the East German transition to a free-market economy. Policies calculated to make the initial adjustment as painless as possible hampered long-run growth and prosperity. Real economic efficiency could only be achieved by permitting and even forcing considerable immediate dislocations, whereas temporary compromises might lead to permanent structural burdens. However, excessive disruptions could jeopardize the economic and political stability required for a smooth unification process and might also cause streams of East Germans to move west. The government was never able to solve this dilemma. When it was forced to choose, it usually selected the more expensive and slower course to encourage persons to stay in the east.

Despite these problems, the process of unification moved ahead, albeit slowly. The Treuhand, staffed almost entirely by Germans from the west, became the virtual government of eastern Germany. In the course of privatization, the agency decided which companies would live and which would die, which communities would thrive and which would shrivel, and which eastern *Länder* would be prosperous and which would not. It also decided who might or might not buy eastern firms or services.

Whether correct or not, reports persisted throughout the first years of unification that foreign enterprises were being screened more carefully and more skeptically than German firms even as they were being invited to invest. Less than 5 percent of all investment in eastern Germany was non-German, and most of that was from companies with subsidiaries in western Germany who were expanding them to the east. The Japanese did not invest, although they had earlier expressed some interest, and the offices Treuhand established in New York and Tokyo found few investors.

As might have been expected, the economy of eastern Germany went into a deep and precipitous slump immediately after unification. Within a year after unification, the number of unemployed rose above 3 million. Industrial production in eastern Germany fell to less than half the previous rate, and the total regional product fell precipitously through 1991. One estimate was that in 1991 the entire production of eastern Germany amounted to less than 8 percent of that of western Germany.

Because the process of unification was managed by persons from western Germany, new eastern firms were usually subsidiaries of western firms, and they followed the western ownership and management patterns. Bank participation became customary, especially because the large Frankfurt banks assumed the assets of the former East German State Bank, and most eastern firms thus owed money to those Frankfurt banks. The banks installed their representatives on the boards of the new firms and assumed some supervisory functions—either directly or through control by western firms with bank representation. The Treuhand had close contacts with western German banks. Many of its employees came from those banks and planned to return to their jobs at the banks.

Because of these circumstances, private investment and economic growth came to eastern Germany at a relatively slow rate. Little new equity capital flowed in. Investment during the early years of unification was only 1 percent of the all-German GDP, when much more was needed to jump-start the economy of eastern Germany. Much of the investment was for the purchase of eastern German companies, not yet for their rehabilitation. Many western German firms bought eastern firms on a standby basis, making sure they could produce in the east when the time came and paying enough wages to satisfy the Treuhand but not starting production. Many others, including Daimler-Benz, did not even meet the commitments that they had made when they had purchased the eastern German firms from the Treuhand. Thus, western German private investment was not strong enough to boost the eastern German economy.

As private funds lagged, and in part because those funds lagged, federal budget investments and expenditures began flowing into eastern Germany at a consistently high rate. Government funds were used essentially for two purposes: infrastructure investment projects (roads, bridges, railroads, and so on), and income maintenance (unemployment compensation, social security, and other social costs). The infrastructure projects sustained employment levels, and the income maintenance programs sustained income. But neither had an early growth payoff.

Although the precise level of German official expenditures in eastern Germany has been difficult to estimate because funds appropriated in one year might have been spent in another, it is beyond dispute that the federal government expended well over DM350 billion in eastern Germany during the first three years after economic, or monetary, unification. After 1992 this requirement has continued at an annual level of around DM150 billion, so that the sum of private and public funds put into eastern Germany during the half-decade between monetary unification in 1990 and the end of 1995 would probably amount to at least DM750 billion and perhaps as much as DM850 billion. Between one-fifth and one-fourth of those funds were private, and the remainder were government funds. This constituted an infusion of outside money of about DM50,000 for every resident of eastern Germany, a far greater level of assistance than contemplated for any other area that had been behind the Iron Curtain and a token of German determination to bring eastern Germany to western levels as quickly as possible.

As eastern Germany went into a deep recession during the first phase of unification, the western German economy went into a small boom. Western German GDP grew at a rate of 4.6 percent for 1990, reflecting the new demand from eastern Germany. The highest growth rate came during the second half of 1990, but growth continued at only a slightly slower pace into early 1991. Prices, however, remained relatively stable because the cost of living grew at only 2.8 percent despite some high wage settlements in some industries. Employment rose during the year, from 28.0 million to 28.7 million, and the unemployment rate sank to 7.2 percent. Notably, the number of registered unemployed in western Germany only declined by about 300,000, showing that at least half of the new jobs in western Germany had been taken by persons who had moved to or were commuting from eastern Germany.

The dramatic improvement in the western German figures resulted from the opening in eastern Germany of a large new market of 16 million persons and the simultaneous availability of many new workers from eastern Germany. Many easterners did not want the shoddy goods produced at home, preferring western consumer products and food. Moreover, many easterners were coming to the west to work. By the end of 1990, as many as 250,000 were commuting to work in the west, and that

An advanced model of a plant-protection tractor in use in Saxony
Courtesy German Information Center, New York

number was estimated to have grown to 350,000 or even 400,000 by the middle of 1991.

This meant that western Germany not only had a vast new market but also a growth of over 1 percent in its workforce, as sharp an increase as since the days of the economic miracle. It also increased its capital base because eastern German deposits were placed in western German banks that had come east and because those deposits moved back to the central German financial market at Frankfurt.

The Bundesbank became worried about three elements of the sudden boom: the sudden financial shifts between east and west, which led to a jump in money supply; government deficits resulting from large expenditures in eastern Germany; and the potentially inflationary effects of a rapid growth rate in the west. The bank warned that interest rates would have to remain high to keep price increases under control. The bank raised short-term interest rates sharply through 1991 and 1992, with the average rate of short-term interest climbing from 7.1 percent in 1989 to 8.5 percent in 1990, to 9.2 percent in 1991, and to 9.5 percent in 1992. The Bundesbank permitted rates to begin falling only in 1993—to 7.3 percent—when it believed that the inflationary pressures had been contained by the recessionary effects of the credit squeeze.

As the Bundesbank's policies began to take hold, growth slowed in western Germany, from 4.2 percent in the first quarter of 1991 to 0.8 percent in the last quarter of 1992. For all of 1992, the western German growth rate was 1.5 percent, a decline from the 3.7 percent rate of 1991 and even more from the 4.6 percent rate of 1990. The eastern German growth rate was 6.1 percent during 1992, well below the 7 percent to 10 percent growth rate originally anticipated for the region. The number of employed in western Germany fell for the first time in ten years, by 89,000 persons.

Despite the slowdown, during 1992 the German economy reached a milestone of sorts. With the addition of eastern German production, Germany's GDP rose for the first time above DM3 trillion. Of that total, the new *Länder* contributed a gross regional product of DM231 billion, or 7.7 percent. However, the total of German unemployed also reached a record number, 4 million. Two-thirds of that number were unemployed in western Germany; the other one-third were unemployed in eastern Germany. Eastern Germany contributed more to unemployment than to production.

The 1992 depression continued into 1993, so that the economy actually registered a negative growth rate of –1.2 percent. By 1994, however, after the Bundesbank had been lowering short-term interest rates for over a year, German growth resumed at an annual rate of about 2.4 percent, but unemployment declined only very slowly despite the uptrend in GDP growth. It was expected that stronger growth would begin reducing the numbers of unemployed by 1995 and that Germany would return to its postwar path toward prosperity. But the absorption of eastern Germany, and the methods by which it had been accomplished, had exacted a high price throughout all of Germany.

Structural and Technological Questions

Although Germany is one of the world's most powerful economies, there have been growing doubts within Germany about the state of its economy. The principal doubts have been about the ability of the German economy to modernize quickly enough to keep up in an increasingly competitive global environment. There is also a fundamental debate about the direction that the economy must take if it is to remain successful and prosperous. That debate includes a seminal discussion about Germany's place in the global division of labor, an issue of immense importance to an exporting nation such as Germany.

Those who have led the debate, and those who have insisted most firmly that Germany's economy must change, are those who have seen the world economy changing in directions that would increasingly relegate Germany to a second rank. They have seen the coming of a world in which the work performed by traditional German production sectors—whether coal, steel, chemicals, agriculture, electronics, or machinery—can be done better and more cheaply elsewhere. They believe firmly that Germany has to deemphasize some of those sectors and abandon others in order to move with the greatest speed and the most powerful possible commitment into new areas that will lead the growth of the world economy.

Five German institutes charged with analyzing economic issues have played a central role in the debate, issuing a series of reports and recommendations throughout the 1980s and 1990s in which they warned that the German economy had to change—and change quickly. They complained ever more insistently about what they described as the inadequate response of federal, *Land,* and local governments to the needs of the evolving global economy.

Those who opposed the arguments of the institutes fell into several categories. Some remained committed to traditional economic sectors, which they believed could still perform competitively, especially if enough effort was made to modernize and rationalize them or to find particular specialties. Others supported traditional sectors, not for economic but for social and political reasons. Still others believed that the issues had to be raised and understood but that action could and perhaps should be postponed.

The basic complaint about modernization has been that the German economy has not remained at the forefront of global development and progress and is not moving decisively into the ranks of the most advanced industrial societies, such as the United States, Japan, and the smaller Asian economies. The institutes have pointed out that new technologies—such as computer hardware and software—could not only improve traditional production but also could become new industries in themselves.

As part of their assertion that Germany was not modernizing quickly enough, the institutes have also expressed concern that the country has not given adequate priority to research and development and that German capital has not been venturesome enough. They have argued that funds have not gone sufficiently into the kinds of research or into the start-up ventures that have helped keep the United States at the forefront of international inventiveness even as that country's traditional industries have declined.

This does not mean that German industry does not invest in research and development. EU statistics have consistently shown that Germany has been either first or second in European research and development expenditures, with only France coming close enough to be a real competitor. But those same and related statistics also have shown that the German lead has been shrinking and that Germany does not have the lead in computer-oriented research and development. In particular, they have shown that Germany has not been doing well at the global level, lagging behind the United States and even further behind Japan in the pace at which it has been increasing its research expenditures. In advanced-technology areas, Germany has been trailing badly. The total German private and public research effort has consistently amounted to about 2.8 percent of GDP, but that is about the same percentage as the United States and Japan and is clearly not enough to allow the smaller German economy to keep up. A German patent office study showed that by 1989 West Germany had fallen behind in three of four major areas of domestic patent grants compared with Japan and the United States.

German technological progress has been uneven. The country has certainly remained competitive in biotechnology and general medical research. The same could be said about its competitive position in smaller robotic machine tools and in many areas of electronic and even specialized computer research. But this does not compensate fully for the lag in cellular communications, microtechnology, and computers.

The German government has been slow to assist firms in technological development. There has been strong German financial and scientific participation in a variety of European programs, such as Esprit, Eureka, Jessi, Race, or Brite—programs that are designed to internationalize research at the European level to enable the smaller European states to compete against the United States and Japan. These European efforts are significant, but their results as of the mid-1990s have not allayed the concerns of many Germans about falling behind.

The institutes have also addressed another problem, the German lag in establishing new ventures. This shortcoming goes to the core of the total functioning of the German system, including the conservatism of banking and financial practices. Germany has not found a way to create an environment in which small entrepreneurs in new fields arise in large numbers.

With unification as Germany's principal economic priority, the debate about structural reform has taken second place, and the government is giving it less priority than it received in the 1980s. But it remains an issue and will continue to be so as other parts of the world economy—including Eastern Europe—become more competitive.

The Role of Government and Other Institutions

The Federal Government Role

The German federal government plays a crucial role in the German economy, sometimes directly and sometimes indirectly through the effects of other policies on the economy. Unlike the Japanese government, there is no single ministry that attempts to direct industrial government and competitiveness, but government policy can have wide-ranging effects because of the many offices that play a role.

The three principal figures responsible for economic policy are the chancellor, the minister for economics, and the minister of finance. The three positions have rarely been held simultaneously by members of a single party and are usually divided among two or sometimes three parties. Economic policy therefore has to reflect the interests of at least two political parties, with all that this means in terms of compromise and conciliation. The coalition negotiations to form a new government after a national election are never more delicate or more difficult than when they touch on economic policies.

The main parties have different economic philosophies and pursue generally different objectives. The CDU and the CSU are conservative, business-oriented parties, but with a long tradition of support for social welfare programs. The FDP is liberal in the British sense, very much in favor of the free market and a minimum of government regulation. The SPD believes in combining political freedom with large social programs and government involvement in the economy. It is impossible for any of the three parties to be in a government with the others without yielding something, and government policy has therefore usually contained a mixture of sometimes contradictory objectives that then must be resolved by compromises within the cabinet.

The Chancellor

The way the chancellor and his office, the Chancellory, deal with the economy depends very much on the incumbent's interests and personal style. For example, under Helmut Schmidt (1974–82), who was very interested in economic matters, the Chancellory shaped, directed, and coordinated the economic policy of the entire government economic apparatus. It also kept close contact with the business and financial community, including the Bundesbank, and became deeply involved in long-range planning. Helmut Kohl (1982–), however, has operated very differently, using the Chancellory for limited day-to-day coordination but not attempting to use it to manage the economic policy of the government. He has used the political, not the bureaucratic, structure to make policy, working through the CDU/CSU and the FDP or through personal contacts. Although Kohl was definitely in charge of *die Wende* and other government policies, he has not usually presented himself as either the originator or the executor of economic and financial policy. He has chosen to control events from behind the scenes, reducing the government's visibility as well as its role.

The Minister of Finance and the Minister for Economy

In the cabinet, roles are more fixed, although they might change in accordance with personalities and political parties. The *primus inter pares* over the last several decades has been the minister of finance. He is responsible for the federal budget, which has become ever more important as the government's share of national income has grown and as governments increasingly use the budget to set priorities and guide national economic activity. The minister of finance also accompanies the chancellor to the annual financial summits and is the main German spokesperson in the meetings of the Group of Seven

(G–7—see Glossary), the world's principal economic powers. He is thus in a position to manage not only domestic but also international financial policy for Germany and to coordinate the two.

The minister for economics, once the government's chief economic policy maker (especially when the minister was Ludwig Erhard), has gradually lost power as many of the important functions have been transferred to other ministries—including new ministries concerned with environment and research. Since the 1970s, the minister for economics has functioned more like a United States secretary of commerce, remaining a principal channel for contact with industry, labor, and semi-public associations. But several of the ministers have complained in bitter frustration that they were not able to carry out the policies they wanted.

The Bundeskartellamt

The Bundeskartellamt (Federal Cartel Office) is the institution specifically instructed and empowered to prevent a return to the monopolies and cartels that periodically controlled much of the German economy between the 1870s and 1940s. The policies of the office, like the office itself, have been controversial, with some Germans wanting it to have greater power and others believing that it is already abusing its existing authority.

The Bundeskartellamt was established in 1957. Many, including Erhard, believed that it had not been given enough authority to restrict cartels and other monopolistic practices. The Western Allies had insisted that the fledgling Federal Republic have such a law, but West German business associations used their influence to undercut the authority of the Bundeskartellamt to the point where it has sometimes been described as a "Swiss cheese with countless holes." Some of the holes in the Swiss cheese were closed in 1973, when the Bundestag passed a merger law (*Fusionsgesetz*) intended to block monopolies in advance so that the Bundeskartellamt would not always have to act after the fact.

In retrospect, the laws and the office have performed a central and useful function, but they have not been able to prevent a gradual shift toward ever larger companies in Germany. The number of mergers in West Germany increased rapidly during the late 1980s, rising to over 1,000 per year. And the Bundeskartellamt has not been effective in curtailing the countless informal contacts and discussions that have characterized the German system (like other European systems) and that would be suspect and perhaps illegal in the United States.

Because the Bundeskartellamt tends to use nonconfrontational tactics, the office has often been denounced as ineffective. Critics contend that the office has actually blocked very few mergers or other forms of cooperation. They also assert that hidden monopolistic or oligopolistic practices have been creeping back into the German economy. But others argue that the very existence of the Bundeskartellamt has enhanced competition and that the office's predilection for solving problems through nonjudicial processes fits properly into the German system and is therefore effective in that system.

Despite its title, the Bundeskartellamt does not have the final authority over German mergers and acquisitions. That authority is reserved for the political level, the Ministry for Economics, which on more than one occasion has overruled the Bundeskartellamt. After the Bundeskartellamt had raised a number of searching questions about the legality and propriety of Daimler-Benz's 1989 acquisition of Messerschmidt-Bölkow-Blohm (MBB), and after it had even disapproved the acquisition, the minister for economics approved the merger on condition that Daimler-Benz and MBB sell off majority control in a small marine and technology division. The government justified the step by recalling that it had specifically sought the merger to support MBB—which was engaged in military production and could not be permitted to collapse—with Daimler-Benz's financial resources.

The Bundeskartellamt has faced a particularly difficult task in the integration of the East German and West German economies. Many eastern German firms could not survive unless they could merge with large western German firms. The process may, however, create new enterprises whose size and combination of resources could open the way for monopolistic or oligopolistic temptations. Powerful economic and political pressures for such mergers exist, especially to help revitalize eastern Germany, but they also raise serious questions about their potentially negative impact on competition. Under those circumstances, the Bundeskartellamt has acted with considerable circumspection, blocking some mergers but approving most of them.

The Bundeskartellamt faces an even greater problem in the growing Europeanization of German business under the aegis of deeper EU integration. It became clear by the early 1990s that the EU's European Commission in Brussels was prepared to permit greater cooperation between European firms in order to compete more effectively against the worldwide reach of the giant corporations of the United States and Japan. Such cooperation went against German cartel laws. To solve the problem, the Bundeskartellamt announced in early 1993 that it would permit greater degrees of cooperation between small- and medium-sized German firms if that cooperation actually led to greater intra-European competition.

Land and Local Governments

Because Germany has a federal system, state (*Land*; pl., *Länder*) and local governments also have important functions. This reflects the German tradition, which before Hitler combined a mix of national, *Land*, and local structures with carefully defined and deliberately circumscribed powers. *Land* and even local authorities are involved in many economic functions, such as social services, development and energy policy, education (including vocational training), public housing, environmental protection, and industrial policy. They also share certain tax revenues that are centrally collected but distributed among the central, *Land*, and local authorities in accordance with carefully negotiated ratios that were changed after unification slightly to the advantage of the new eastern *Länder.*

The *Länder* do not always act and think alike. Different old *Länder* have followed different economic policies since the early years of the Federal Republic. On the one hand, the minister presidents, or heads, of two *Länder*, Bavaria and Baden-Württemberg, have stressed industrial development policies that have departed radically from those of others, putting their *Länder* into the forefront of German technological development. On the other hand, the *Länder* of North Rhine-Westphalia and the Saarland for a long time concentrated their resources on subsidizing coal and steel production, entering the competition for new industries much later than other *Länder.* The possibility for creating separate *Land* policies has also encouraged some new *Länder* to try their own development policies. They have invited potential investors from other countries to visit them, and they have engaged in export promotion.

Government Subsidies

The *Länder* are not alone in subsidizing or supporting certain industries: the federal government does it to a massive and increasingly significant degree. Despite Germany's commitment to a social market economy, exceptions to market principles existed in West Germany and are proliferating in united Germany. German economic institutes and experts have repeatedly warned that authorities at various levels have supported many economic activities that should long ago have been discontinued or compelled to become competitive. Federal and *Land* authorities have ignored the complaints of the economists but have usually promised to reduce or eliminate subsidies as soon as feasible.

Before unification, the West German government and various *Länder* supported a number of industries and services, such as coal, steel, aerospace, shipbuilding, and agriculture, with the federal government supporting activities across the board and the *Länder* supporting locally important and influential industries. Between 1970 and 1989, the total volume of subsidies, including those paid through the European Community (EC—see Glossary), rose from DM12 billion to over DM45 billion. The level of subsidies rose almost uninterruptedly, even after Kohl assumed office and his government had committed itself to reducing them. Although some categories of subsidies—for example, those for agriculture—were not fully under West German but rather under EC control, even the portion specifically designated for German farmers also rose by 250 percent during the 1980s. Overall, the federal government provided about one-third of total West German subsidies. The other two-thirds came from the *Länder* and the localities. During the late 1980s and early 1990s, the total has generally averaged around 6 percent of West German GDP, although it has risen because of unification.

Despite the concern expressed about West German subsidies, a 1990 Organisation for Economic Co-operation and Development (OECD—see Glossary) survey of Germany concluded that German subsidies were not unusually high by the standards of the EC. The OECD described them as being around the average for OECD countries. Separate International Monetary Fund (IMF—see Glossary) and Ministry of Finance studies reached a similar conclusion, indicating that West Germany was actually somewhat below the average among EC members in the level of subsidies.

Although such conclusions might have offered some comfort as a matter of general policy, it remains true that some German industries—especially in the traditional coal and steel complex—are dependent on subsidies to such an extent that they would have to be closed if they no longer benefited from government support of one kind or another. But subsidies are also often paid even to some of the largest and most profitable German concerns, such as Daimler-Benz, Siemens, Bayer, and Volkswagen, for special production or research lines. Those companies have usually stated that the subsidies cover only a minute part of their expenditures.

After unification, the combined subsidies of western and eastern budgets rose even higher, and the new all-German government has found itself compelled to provide even more subsidies in order not to permit an excessive level of structural unemployment in the former East Germany. Official East German statistics suggested that the level of subsidies in the GDR budget was 30 percent, but in reality the level may have been much higher because of the generally low level of productivity in the GDR. Although no total figures for German subsidies have been available in the confusion and diversity of programs since unification, the government has already promised to keep a number of unprofitable East German ventures (such as the steel complex around Eisenhüttenstadt and the shipbuilding docks around Rostock) in production until they become competitive—which will not be for decades, if at all.

Government Expenditures and the National Debt

Beyond subsidies, German politicians, businessmen, and economists have consistently had difficulty calculating the most suitable role for the state in the German economy. Many economists believed that the role of the state had become too large in West Germany during the 1970s because of government ownership of large companies, because of subsidies, and because of the high social welfare programs established by the SPD-led governments. The right level after unification is even more difficult to define and to agree upon, because eastern Germany will need much more infrastructure construction and many more social programs than western Germany for many years to come.

As a share of national income, German government expenditures at all levels were 15 percent before World War I, 25 percent during the interwar period, 35 percent around 1960, 48 percent in 1975, and about 50 percent by 1980–81. The government's share of spending, although worrisome to the West Germans, still remained lower than that of several other European states, such as Sweden, the Netherlands, France, and Belgium. West Germany and Britain were the only major European states to reduce government spending as a share of GDP during the 1980s. But their government share still remained higher than that of two principal competitors, the United States, at about 37 percent, and Japan, at about 33 percent. The German share has risen well over 50 percent again during the early 1990s because of the costs of unification, and there is little if any prospect that it will decline again until the end of the decade.

Despite the declining deficits of the 1980s, the cumulative public-sector debt of various levels of German government has grown during virtually the entire existence of the Federal Republic. During the 1960s, the total debt doubled. During the 1970s, it doubled every five years. The growth rate in debt began to slow after the first years of the 1980s, but it began to rise rapidly during the 1990s as a result of unification. By the end of 1989, the West German government said that the total public-sector debt in Germany was DM1,020 billion, or 45 percent of what was then West German GDP. By the early 1990s, however, that figure had risen by several 100 billion deutsche marks and was estimated to be almost DM1.5 trillion, or 50 percent of united German GDP. It rose to over DM1.6 trillion by the end of 1993 and is expected to rise to over 60 percent of GDP by the mid-1990s and then to begin to decline slowly after that. Interest payments on the public debt have become the second largest single line item in the German budget, absorbing 14 percent of the budget.

The Associations

All participants in the German national economy organize themselves into various associations. They do so either voluntarily or, in some associations, as a legal requirement. The associations are commonly known in German as the *Verbände*. Over 1,200 are represented in Bonn. Each plays a chosen or assigned role, and together they help contribute to a broad framework of cooperation mingled with competition.

All the *Verbände* operate as lobbies in Germany itself, working with the parliament, the Bundestag, and the bureaucracy, and they also lobby appropriate EU offices in Brussels. But they are far more than lobbies. They act as sector and regional coordinators. Some not only exercise a voice toward the government but also represent a forum where industrialists or others can meet and talk about business affairs. Some serve as planning institutions, collecting and disseminating information on anticipated sales, production capacities, and investment goals. Others negotiate and settle conflicts between different firms or industries. They help to administer the German economic mechanism as a whole.

Among the main associations are the Federation of German Industry (Bundesverband der Deutschen Industrie—BDI) and the German Chambers of Industry and Commerce (Deutscher Industrie- und Handelstag—DIHT). The BDI is the central organization representing the interests and policies of German industry. Because of its role in organizing and representing German industry, the BDI has immense influence. Any German government, even one with an SPD majority, will consult with it before making any policy or introducing any legislation that could affect German industry or the German economy as a whole. So will key members of the Bundestag. The BDI has no individual members, but only other associations of one or another industry, so that it is in effect an association of associations.

The DIHT is the umbrella organization of the German Chambers of Commerce. It represents all business interests, but especially small business, on a regional as well as a sectoral basis. Membership is obligatory for German firms, and membership is on an individual or a company basis rather than on an association basis as in the BDI.

Some of the powers of the chambers of commerce in Germany would be exercised by government authorities in almost any other country. The chambers participate in vocational training programs, issue licenses and work permits, set store hours, solve disputes between members, issue certificates of origin, run stock exchanges, and so on. They are legally entitled to make their views known in a variety of governmental forums from the local to the national level, and they thus have direct as well as indirect influence over many elements of the economy. Their functions are central to the operation of the German system, as they have been throughout much of German history.

The chambers constitute an important link not only in the formal but also in the informal coordinating mechanisms that operate throughout the economy. Whereas the BDI might be more visible in national policy matters and might influence national government decisions more directly, the chambers and the DIHT have a more pervasive presence at the local and regional level than at the national level. They shape and often author most of the regulations that determine how commerce and industry can act, helping to establish the day-to-day rules under which production and trade take place.

Another important interest organization is the Federation of German Employers' Associations (Bundesvereinigung der Deutschen Arbeitgeberverbände—BDA). It coordinates the collective bargaining strategy of German employers, administers the strike fund, gives legal advice, and deals with matters relating to social policy. Eight member federations organize enterprises in industry, handicrafts, commerce, banking, agriculture, transportation, insurance, and publishing.

A broad division of labor exists among the separate German employers' associations. The BDI, for which the closest United States parallel is the National Association of Manufacturers, mainly addresses matters of broad economic policy. It is, however, much more influential than any parallel United States organization. It helps shape Germany's policies in the EU and is a voice for an open trading system. The DIHT might be compared to the United States Chamber of Commerce. It represents regional interests as well as the interests of small- and medium-sized enterprises. It exercises a great deal more influence and even authority locally. The BDA concentrates on labor and social legislation and also acts as the representative of employers with the trade unions.

German farmers are organized into the German Farmers' Association (Deutscher Bauernverband—DBV). This organization has over 1 million members. It has exercised a powerful influence on German and European agricultural policies, helping to keep production and consumption prices above world levels. The proportional influence of the DBV has grown since German unification because agriculture represented a more important share of eastern German than western German production (see Agriculture, this ch.).

The Culture of German Management

German management, as it has evolved over the centuries and has established itself since World War II, has a distinct style and culture. Like so many things German, it goes back to the medieval guild and merchant tradition, but it also has a sense of the future and of the long term.

The German style of competition is rigorous but not ruinous. Although companies might compete for the same general market, as Daimler-Benz and BMW do, they generally seek market share rather than market domination. Many compete for a specific niche. German companies despise price competition. Instead, they engage in what German managers describe as *Leistungswettbewerb*, competition on the basis of excellence in their products and services. They compete on a price basis only when it is necessary, as in the sale of bulk materials like chemicals or steel.

The German manager concentrates intensely on two objectives: product quality and product service. He wants his company to be the best, and he wants it to have the best products. The manager and his entire team are strongly product oriented, confident that a good product will sell itself. But the manager also places a high premium on customer satisfaction, and Germans are ready to style a product to suit a customer's wishes. The watchwords for most German managers and companies are quality, responsiveness, dedication, and follow-up.

Product orientation usually also means production orientation. Most German managers, even at senior levels, know their production lines. They follow production methods closely and know their shop floors intimately. They cannot understand managers in the United States who want only to see financial statements and "the bottom line" rather than inspect a plant's production processes. A German manager believes deeply that a good-quality production line and a good-quality product will do more for the bottom line than anything else. Relations between German managers and workers are often close, because they believe that they are working together to create a good product.

If there is a third objective beyond quality and service, it is cooperation—or at least coordination—with government. German industry works closely with government. German management is sensitive to government standards, government policies, and government regulations. Virtually all German products are subject to norms—the German Industrial Norms (Deutsche Industrie Normen—DIN)—established through consultation between industry and government but with strong inputs from the management associations, chambers of commerce, and trade unions. As a result of these practices, the concept of private initiative operating within a public framework lies firmly imbedded in the consciousness of German managers.

The German management style is not litigious. Neither the government, the trade unions, nor the business community encourages litigation if there is no clear sign of genuine and deliberate injury. Firms do not maintain large legal staffs. Disagreements are often talked out, sometimes over a conference table, sometimes over a beer, and sometimes in a gathering called by a chamber of commerce or an industrial association. Differences are usually settled quietly, often privately. Frequent litigation is regarded as reflecting more on the accuser than on the accused. Because of these attitudes, Germany has comparatively few lawyers. With one-third the population and one-third the GDP of the United States, Germany has about one-twentieth the number of lawyers.

German managers are drawn largely from the ranks of engineers and technicians, from those who manufacture, design, or service, although more nonengineers have risen to the top in recent years. They are better paid than other Europeans (except the Swiss), but on average receive about two-thirds of the income that their American counterparts expect.

Because managers usually remain in one firm throughout their careers, rising slowly through the ranks, they do not need a visible bottom-line result quickly. Managers do not need to be concerned about how their careers might be affected by a company's or a division's progress, or lack of progress, for each year and certainly not for each quarter.

German taxation also induces management toward long-term planning. German tax legislation and accounting practices permit German firms to allocate considerable sums to reserves. German capital gains tax rules exempt capital gains income if the assets are held for more than six months or, in the case of real estate, for more than two years.

Because management has not been regarded in Germany as a separate science, it was rare until the 1980s to find courses in management techniques such as those taught at schools of management in the United States. Germans believed that management as a separate discipline bred selfishness, disloyalty, bureaucratic maneuvering, short-term thinking, and a dangerous tendency to neglect quality production. Instead, courses at German universities concentrated more on business administration, or *Betriebswirtschaft*, producing a *Betriebswirt* degree. Despite this, two West German schools for business administra-

*A robot in use at a Daimler-Benz plant in Stuttgart
Turbine manufacture at the Kraftwerk-Union plant in Berlin
Courtesy German Information Center, New York*

tion, the Hochschule für Unternehmensführung and the European Business School, were established during the 1980s, but they teach in ways that reinforce rather than overturn traditional German ways of management.

Out of this compendium of business practices arises what might be termed a German management style, with the following characteristics: collegial, consensual, product- and quality-oriented, export-conscious, and loyal to one company and committed to its long-term prospects. One could legitimately conclude from this that the German system could stifle change because it is not as innovative, aggressive, or results-oriented as the United States management style. That, however, would not be correct, for change can and does take place. It occurs gradually, not always obviously, under the mottoes of stability and permanence, with the least dislocation possible, and often under competitive pressures from abroad. German managers themselves occasionally speculate that change might come too slowly, but they are not certain whether or how to alter the system and its incentive structures.

Labor and Codetermination

Labor

German labor has as much of a culture as German management. The abilities and the attitudes of the labor force have contributed at least as much to the success of the German system as those of management, and perhaps even more so. Many workers, especially in small- or medium-sized firms, regard themselves as serious professionals with a stake in their company and are usually treated as such. They live in comfortable circumstances, not as the factory workers of old. They usually travel abroad, often own foreign property, and otherwise lead lives that had formerly been reserved for the middle class.

German workers have consistently had the highest level of education of any group of workers in Europe, with much of that education acquired after they finish formal secondary school training. Worker training usually lasts two to three years and may last longer for highly specialized vocations (see The Education System, ch. 4). About 2.5 million Germans, or almost half of the fifteen- to nineteen-year-old age-group of both genders, annually receive vocational training within a range of about 400 designated occupational specialties, often on the basis of contracts with preselected employers.

Of the many fields to choose from in German vocational training, most apprentices select from about twenty specializations. Young men prefer training in manufacturing, crafts, carpentry, electronics, or painting. Young women prefer training in sales, industrial purchasing, officework or banking, or medical assistance. Even while they are in training, the students might receive up to DM1,200 in salary per month, although most receive less than that, down to DM255.

After finishing vocational training, students can go to technical colleges located all over Germany, or to public health or nursing colleges, and they can move on to advanced specialization courses in programs for continuing education. Those systems exist separately from academic colleges and universities but can be as demanding.

The programs are expensive for industry as well as for government. One estimate was that West German industry before unification spent about DM35 billion annually to support the program. The philosophy governing the expenditure of time and money was articulated by the head of personnel at Volkswagen, who said: "Training costs money; not to train costs a great deal more money."

The high level of training of German workers produces a "quality time" labor productivity formula. The German worker spends fewer hours per year at work than any competitor, averaging an annual 1,708 hours compared with 1,763 in France, 1,778 in Britain, 1,912 in the United States, and 2,166 in Japan. Yet Germany has the highest share of world trade in goods with a high skill content: 20 percent, as against 17 percent for Japan, 15 percent for the United States, and 7 percent for France.

Many of western Germany's labor traditions have moved smoothly to eastern Germany since unification. Vocational training already existed in the GDR, and labor in East Germany was not as inefficient as management or as the often antiquated production machinery. Therefore, although there have been problems of adjustment, especially for older workers in the east who were not accustomed to the pace of a modern production site, on the whole the eastern labor force has adapted well.

Many of the generalizations that can be made about German labor cannot be applied equally to the foreign workers who constitute about one-tenth of the country's labor force. The 2 million foreigners employed in Germany often work in very large companies, on assembly lines, in mining and chemical operations with little prospect for advancement, or in some service sectors at menial tasks under difficult conditions. Approximately 25 percent of foreigners work in steel and iron foundries, another 25 percent in hotels and restaurants (often as cleaning staff), and another 15 percent on automobile assembly lines. Certain industries, such as steel production, textiles, or mining, could not function without them.

Among the principal reasons for the decline in Germany's economic growth have been the high costs associated with production. German labor costs per hour in the manufacturing industry have achieved the dubious honor of being the highest in the world—largely because of high social costs. As the Bundesbank's tight money policies have consistently made the deutsche mark ever stronger, German labor costs have grown even higher against those in other countries. In part because of the rise in the value of the deutsche mark, total German wage costs were estimated by 1992 to be about 50 percent higher than in the average West European state, the United States, or Japan, and many times higher than those prevailing in most Asian states, in Eastern Europe, or in the developing world. The Bundesbank estimated that those costs had risen by almost 10 percent between the beginning of 1991 and the beginning of 1993. Chancellor Kohl himself complained that German workers could not afford to continue to have "the shortest working week, the lowest number of working years, and above all, which is the worst, the shortest machine operating time . . . in all the European Community." But, although a number of German wage settlements in 1993 and 1994 raised wages by less than the anticipated inflation rate, there are no signs that German labor is prepared to lower its income to meet international competition. The average German worker believes that quality production and efficiency justify his or her high income.

Codetermination

Codetermination (*Mitbestimmung*), under which German workers or their representatives sit on the governing boards or the factory councils of most German firms, is a classic example of how the German system reconciles apparent opposites and points them to a common purpose and in a common direction. Codetermination did not come about in West Germany in a single step. It evolved and expanded through five different West German laws, beginning in 1951 and continuing in 1952,

1954, 1972, and 1976. The first three laws were passed by CDU-led coalition governments, the last two by SPD-led governments. All the codetermination statutes were applied to eastern Germany after unification. Through the combination of those laws, 85 percent of all German employees are included in some form of codetermination.

Codetermination takes place through two structures, the *Aufsichtsrat* (supervisory board) in a large enterprise and/or the *Betriebsrat* (factory council) in most companies. Over two-thirds of all German firms have a *Betriebsrat.* Only about one-fourth have an *Aufsichtsrat.* Many large firms have both. If a firm is large enough to have both, the workers are twice represented. Depending on the size of the firm, the *Aufsichtsrat* must have between one-third and one-half worker membership. The *Betriebsrat* is composed entirely of employee representatives.

The result of forty years of codetermination is the kind of bargain typical of the way the German economy is managed. Management can largely direct the functioning of the company. It makes investment, financial, operational, and market decisions, but it makes those decisions through a mechanism in which labor can have a voice. Labor can make certain that the conditions under which the workers operate are socially acceptable. It can also make certain that the workers benefit from the company's well-being. But labor in turn has a stake in ensuring that the demands and actions of the workers do not jeopardize the firm itself.

In addition to their participation in company management, German workers are also represented in trade unions. The principal organization is the Federation of German Trade Unions (Deutscher Gewerkschaftsbund—DGB), an umbrella organization that joins seventeen trade unions along industry lines that match those of the BDA (see Labor Unions, ch. 7). Trade union membership is not obligatory in Germany. Less than one-half of all West German workers belonged to the trade unions in 1989, but German unification has led to a rise in trade union membership in absolute and percentage terms because the East German workers were accustomed to union membership.

Agriculture, Forestry, and Fishing

Agriculture

Agriculture is a small sector of the German economy (see

table 13, Appendix). It has declined in importance all during the twentieth century and by 1989 amounted to only 1.6 percent of West German GDP. Although agriculture's share of East German GDP was twice as high as in the west, even after the two economies are completely united, agriculture's share of GDP is expected to amount to only about 2 percent. However, despite the sector's small size, it remains politically important.

The number of farms had decreased steadily in West Germany, from 1.6 million in 1950 to 630,000 in 1990. In East Germany, where farms were collectivized under the socialist regime, there had been about 5,100 agricultural production collectives with an average of 4,100 hectares under cultivation. Since unification, about three-quarters of the collectives have remained as cooperatives, partnerships, or joint-stock companies. The others were returned to their original owners—if those owners could be found—or were privately sold, becoming about 14,000 private farms. In western Germany and in the newly privatized farms in eastern Germany, family farms predominate. For the 630,000 farms, there are 750,000 full-time employees. There are also, however, many more part-time employees, and most farms do not represent their owners' full-time occupation.

Although the number of farms has declined, production has actually increased through more efficient production methods. By the early 1990s, a single farmer could produce enough food for seventy-five persons, far more than was the case in the 1950s or 1960s.

Agricultural products vary from region to region. In the flat terrain of northern Germany and especially in the eastern portions, cereals and sugar beets are grown. Elsewhere, with the terrain more hilly and even mountainous, farmers produce vegetables, milk, pork, or beef (see table 14; table 15, Appendix). Almost all large cities are surrounded by fruit orchards and vegetable farms. Most river valleys in southern and western Germany, especially along the Rhine and the Main, have vineyards. Beer is produced mainly, but not exclusively, in Bavaria.

Since the 1960s, German agricultural policy has not been made in Germany but in the EC. All agricultural laws and regulations are written in Brussels, often after difficult negotiations between food-producing and food-consuming states. The main objective of those negotiations is to obtain high incomes for the farmers while keeping market prices low enough to avoid consumer protests. To make up the difference, the EC adopted the Common Agricultural Policy (CAP—see Glossary) subsidy program and the export subsidy program, both of which benefit German farmers as well as other EU farmers. In return, the German farmers have complied with European directives on the quality and quantity of production.

Forestry

Germany also has significant lumber production. Almost one-third of Germany's total land area, especially in the south, is forested. German forests produce nearly 40 million cubic meters of timber every year, satisfying two-thirds of domestic demand. However, Germany has to import most of its hardwood.

There has been growing concern for decades about environmental damage to Germany's forests. By the 1970s, trees were losing their needles or leaves and were growing less full than in the past (see The Environment, ch. 3). A number of laws and regulations have attempted to stem this phenomenon, which the Germans call *Waldsterben* (death of the forest). The Forest Preservation and Forestry Promotion Act was passed in West Germany in 1975 to prevent destructive and wasteful timber policies. It now applies to all of Germany. Under the act, forest owners must return cut areas to their original condition, converting forests into timber farms in which the cut trees are replaced by seedlings. This policy works better for pine than for other timber. However, despite legislation and the great attention paid to the forests, no lasting solution has yet been found. As a result of the decades of ecological damage, many German forests, including the highland Black Forest in the southwest, are badly depleted.

Fishing

The German fishing industry also suffers from depletion, because its principal fishing grounds have become overfished by the many modern fishing fleets that enter North European waters. German vessels have long fished the North Sea, the Baltic Sea, and the Atlantic Ocean off the British Isles and around Greenland, all areas where many competing fishing fleets also operate. The German ocean-fishing fleet has shrunk. Germany attempted through the EC to establish rules that would prevent overfishing, but those rules have proved difficult to enforce.

Industry

Manufacturing

The German economy is essentially a processing economy. This was true of both West Germany and East Germany before unification. It will remain true in the future, although the detailed shares of GDP remain to be determined by unification and may not be clearly evident until the mid- or late 1990s.

Before unification, 40 percent of the German workforce was involved in manufacturing, with the main industries being machine tools, automotive manufacturing, electrical engineering, iron, steel, chemicals, and optics. Although the industrial sector in the former East Germany is still evolving, manufacturing in that part of Germany is expected to concentrate in the same industries over time. Thus, the future German economy will retain a powerful industrial component that will likely total well above 30 percent of German GDP.

Almost all areas of western Germany have some industry. The main industrial areas are the Ruhr district in North Rhine-Westphalia, the traditional center of German coal, steel, and heavy industry; the concentration of industry around several large cities, such as Hanover, Munich, Frankfurt am Main, and Stuttgart; the chemical production areas that stretch mainly along the Rhine River in Baden-Württemberg and farther north; and the automotive manufacturing centers, increasingly concentrated in southern Germany in Bavaria and Baden-Württemberg.

In eastern Germany, the main industrial manufacturing areas are in Saxony, Saxony-Anhalt, and Thuringia, principally concentrated in the Leipzig, Dresden, Halle, and Chemnitz regions. Before World War II, Saxony was the technology center of Central Europe. The Elbe River, like the Rhine, attracted chemical and other industry along its shores. It is uncertain which eastern German industries will survive, but the firms in the southern part of the region appear to have better chances than those farther north. Even before unification, more industry was concentrated in the south than in the north. The districts in northern East Germany had industrial employment below 25 percent, those around Berlin had industrial employment between 25 and 35 percent, and those south of Berlin had over 35 percent employment in industry. No such clear geographical delineation for sector employment existed in West Germany.

The glory of German industry is not in the big firms that are well known around the world, such as Daimler-Benz, Volkswagen, Siemens, or Bayer (see table 16, Appendix). It is in the small- and medium-sized firms that constitute what the Germans call the *Mittelstand*. Although that term has political and social as well as management connotations, it has been widely accepted to mean companies that employ fewer than 500 workers. Such firms constitute 98 percent of all German companies, hire 80 percent of all employees, are responsible for a significant share of exports, and provide one of the firmest foundations of the middle class.

The government has supported and furthered the *Mittelstand*, in part for political reasons, but also because it makes a crucial contribution to the economy. The government has established special provisions that permit those firms to cooperate if they do not thereby hinder competition. It makes available special funds to promote research and development by *Mittelstand* companies. After unification, the government used investment and tax incentives to encourage *Mittelstand* companies to invest in eastern Germany.

The single most successful German industry is mechanical engineering, with a total turnover in 1991 of DM240 billion. Unlike many industries in Germany and elsewhere, it is dominated by small rather than large companies. It includes over 4,000 firms throughout Germany. Only 3 percent of the companies have more than 1,000 employees. German mechanical engineering has a range of more than 17,000 products. Almost two-thirds of the products are exported.

The best-known industry and the second-largest, with a turnover of DM217 billion in 1991, is automotive manufacturing. Such companies as Daimler-Benz, Volkswagen, and Bayerische Motorenwerke (BMW) are known throughout the world. Almost half of all German-produced automobiles are exported, mainly to other EU members and to North America.

Electrical engineering ranks third in importance among German industries, with a turnover of DM207 billion in 1991. The biggest single firm is Siemens, although Bosch also ranks among Germany's largest companies. Products range from giant electric generating turbines exported all over the world to smaller electric engines and some consumer goods.

The chemical industry, with a total output of DM166 billion in 1991, is based principally on three large corporations that have been leaders in the field for 100 years—Hoechst, Bayer, and BASF. There are also many medium-sized companies. About one-half of the industry's products are exported.

Other important industries are the traditional German industries of steel and coal mining, both heavily subsidized and still large employers. Precision engineering remains a strong area. Aerospace is a small but growing industry, also heavily subsidized, and German companies often join with companies from other EU countries—such as Airbus and military aircraft production (see fig. 10).

One reason to believe that the eastern and western portions of the united Germany will again knit together into one large manufacturing economy is that such an economy has been part of the German tradition for centuries and that both Germanys have specialized in the same general industrial sectors. Some analysts contend that the eastern economy will even have a competitive edge later in the 1990s because of the vast sums being invested in modernizing its industrial plant.

Energy and Natural Resources

Like most modern states, Germany relies principally on fossil fuels as sources of energy. About 40 percent of German energy consumption comes from petroleum, largely for trucks and automobiles. About 30 percent comes from domestic coal deposits, half from lignite, or brown coal, in the east and the other half from anthracite located in the west. Natural gas provides about 17 percent of energy consumed, and nuclear energy about 10 percent. Other sources of energy, such as hydroelectric, solar, or wind-powered electric power plants, are relatively insignificant. Most production is in private hands.

Electrical power comes almost equally from three sources: the largest (31 percent) is generated by lignite, the next largest (28 percent) from nuclear reactors, and the third largest (26 percent) from anthracite. Natural gas provides about 7 percent. Those proportions will undoubtedly shift over time because of the high pollution levels generated by the relatively inefficient lignite, especially in the new *Länder*, where it accounts for over 90 percent of electricity production (see table 17, Appendix). The public's aversion to nuclear power that developed in Germany in the 1980s will likewise cause this source of power to become less important. Natural gas will become more significant.

The necessary reduction of brown coal consumption is unfortunate for the nation's economy because it and anthracite are Germany's only significant natural resources. As of 1993, Germany was the world's largest producer of brown coal, mining nearly twice as much as the next greatest producer, Russia. Anthracite mining is also significant, and Germany was the world's ninth greatest producer of this substance in 1993.

Germany has over twenty nuclear reactors, most of them small and having production levels below 2,000 megawatts per reactor. It has virtually no domestic uranium deposits and must import enriched uranium for its reactors. Most of the reactors in operation in the early 1990s were built during the 1970s and early 1980s. Reliance on nuclear power has become controversial, however. Because of the controversy, no new nuclear reactor has entered service since 1988. A number of older reactors dating to the 1960s have ceased operations. A major international energy crisis would be needed to renew impetus in Germany's nuclear energy program because the country is densely populated, and most of its inhabitants do not want a reactor near their houses or offices.

Germany must import almost all the oil and gas that it uses. In 1993 the three largest suppliers of crude petroleum were Norway (18.4 percent of the total), the Commonwealth of Independent States (CIS—see Glossary) (17.4 percent), and Britain (12.4 percent) (see table 18, Appendix). Germany has its own modest oil deposits, estimated in 1990 at 50 million tons, in the North German Plain. It has a share of North Sea gas reserves and production, with reserves estimated in 1990 at 9.9 billion cubic meters. But these are not adequate long-term sources. Thus, Germany will increase its imports of oil and gas, most likely from Russia. East Germany relied heavily on Soviet gas before unification, and united Germany will want to purchase petrochemicals from Russia to enable Russia to pay for the German manufactures that Russia is purchasing.

Like all modern economies, Germany has become increasingly cost conscious and conservation conscious about energy consumption. Whereas GDP in West Germany rose by about 50 percent from 1973 to the early 1990s, energy consumption rose by only 7 percent.

The Financial System

The Bundesbank

The single most important economic institution in Germany outside the federal government is the central bank, the

Figure 10. Economic Activity, 1995

Deutsche Bundesbank (commonly called the Bundesbank). It has the dominant voice in German monetary policy. Through that voice, it establishes and maintains a firm policy in favor of solid currency value within Germany and increasingly within the EU and even the world at large.

If a central bank's reputation is its most precious asset, the Bundesbank is among the world's most highly endowed institutions. Its contribution to the economic and political stability of

West Germany and Western Europe in the postwar years was almost legendary and was given due respect even by those who disagreed with some or many of its policies.

Although the Bundesbank often appears to be the principal maker of German economic policy, its exact powers are carefully set forth and circumscribed in the 1957 law establishing the bank. The law assigned to the bank the responsibility for "the preservation of the value of German currency," a mandate that was so important that it was clearly intended to override the bank's other principal task, "to support the general economic policy of the federal government." Even the latter task was carefully limited by the specific provision that the bank "shall be independent of instructions from the federal government."

The government does have a role, if it wishes to exercise it. Government representatives can and at times do attend the meetings of the bank's governing board, the Central Bank Council (see Glossary), although the government cannot block the bank's actions but is authorized only to delay them for no longer than two weeks. There are also informal contacts between the government and the bank, and it is not unusual for senior officials at the Chancellory or the Ministry of Finance to know in advance what the council might be expected to decide at its next meeting.

The bank has more authority in the realm of monetary policy than any other major European central bank. It is most closely based, at least in its structure although not in its formal mandate, on the United States Federal Reserve Bank. It exercises more functions than the Federal Reserve, however, in part because it carries out some exchange responsibilities that are assigned to the United States Department of the Treasury. The Bundesbank issues money and makes monetary policy by controlling short-term interest rates such as the discount rate for loans to other banks and the Lombard rate (see Glossary) for short-term funding for business.

As of mid-1995, the president of the Bundesbank was Hans Tietmeyer, who made his mark in the economics and finance ministries as a career official and then as a state secretary. Kohl appointed him Bundesbank president in 1993. The Bundesbank's Central Bank Council has seventeen members, with the majority of nine being the presidents of regional or *Land* central banks. The representatives of these banks can, therefore, outnumber the eight members of the Central Bank Council who work out of the bank's executive office in Frankfurt am Main, the Direktorium (Directorate—see Glossary), giving the bank a strong orientation toward developments in the country as a whole, while public and foreign attention usually concentrates on the Directorate. *Land* central bank presidents are nominated by *Land* governments. They do not serve at any government's pleasure, including that of the *Land* that nominated them. The members of the council who are in the Directorate are appointed by the president upon the nomination of the chancellor, but even these members are not subject to government direction.

The single most important fact about the Bundesbank, however, is its powerful and consistent anti-inflationary philosophy. That philosophy, grounded in its absolute determination to avoid the social upheaval caused by the Great Inflation of the early 1920s, is central to the bank's thinking on every occasion and has given it enormous influence. Although a number of economists, especially some in the United States, have long argued that the Bundesbank's policies are excessively restrictive and potentially deflationary, the bank is popular with most German voters and with much of German business. The voters do not wish to see their savings eroded by inflation. Businessmen are inclined to believe that a lower inflation rate will permit them to hold down their costs and remain highly competitive over the long run although others might receive some temporary advantage from devaluation. Germans believe that a country with a stable currency will be able to have lower capital and labor costs because lower inflation expectations make lower interest rates and stable wages acceptable.

German demographic realities have added further reasons for anti-inflationary policies. As the population ages and as more Germans live on pensions or on fixed investment incomes, the importance of price stability has become a powerful consideration for a growing sector of the electorate. That sector of the electorate fully supports the Bundesbank's anti-inflationary policies.

Banking and Its Role in the Economy

The German economy is a bank economy, with the main role in finance and credit being played by commercial and savings banks while other forms of credit are secondary. Banks provide most of the country's investment capital because of the high German savings rate and because most Germans prefer to

A petroleum refinery in Ludwigshafen, Rhineland-Palatinate
Courtesy German Information Center, New York
A nuclear power plant outside Munich
Courtesy Inter Nationes, Bonn

put those savings into banks rather than into stocks or bonds. As with many other German economic phenomena, this bank role is not new. Banks have played a central role in German financial and economic history since the Middle Ages.

German banks function as universal banks, able to offer a full range of banking, saving, foreign exchange, and investment services to their depositors and clients. They hold funds or other assets, broker securities, underwrite equity issues, give advice on asset placement, manage accounts, and so on. About one-quarter of German banks are commercial. Most of the remainder are savings banks, mainly owned locally or regionally and operating under public statutes, or cooperatives that perform such specialized services as agricultural, crafts, or mortgage lending.

The three best known and most important German universal banks—the Deutsche Bank, the Dresdner Bank, and the Commerzbank—are omnipresent throughout unified Germany and have immense influence. These banks opened hundreds of new offices in the east during unification and sent large staffs of bankers to manage offices and to train permanent personnel there. In effect, they were the principal agents for control of Germany's economic unification.

But the "big three," as they are often known, are not the only large banks in Germany. A number of other banks, including regional banks, are even more important than the big three within their areas of operations. The DG Bank, which operates out of Frankfurt am Main, has a higher nominal capital stock than that of the Commerzbank. The Westdeutsche Landesbank, headquartered in Düsseldorf and owned in part by the *Land* of North Rhine-Westphalia, has a higher nominal capital stock value than that of the Deutsche Bank. The value of the combined nominal stock of the three major banks in Bavaria is even higher, and those banks have helped finance the economic boom in southern Germany. Other major banks exist in other *Länder,* often owned in part by the *Länder* themselves with additional capital coming from state-wide savings associations or other local institutions. An important element in the German savings system is the Postbank, the postal savings bank, with 27,000 employees. Almost one in three Germans has an account in the Postbank, using it for savings and for personal financial transactions such as paying monthly bills in preference to bank accounts. The Postbank has 24 million savings accounts and hopes to branch into other areas of financial services.

The most important and most controversial aspect of German banking is the role that banks play as shareholders and policy makers in the country's industrial firms. It has been estimated that banks directly or indirectly hold more than 25 percent of the voting capital in one-quarter of Germany's largest corporations and hold about 28 percent of all seats on the supervisory boards. The banks are empowered to vote not only their own shares but also, by proxy, shares that they hold for their clients. Although there are indications that the banks' ownership proportion of major firms has been reduced over time as other sources of investment funds have become more available, the combined influence and presence of the banks is considerable. They are even said to pool information on the basis of which they steer investments throughout the economy.

According to a Commerzbank listing of ownership of 10,000 large West German companies, the Deutsche Bank owns shares in seventy-seven different firms, the Dresdner Bank in fifty-five, and the Commerzbank in forty-eight. Other smaller banks are also widely invested. The Commerzbank listing did not show the bond or loan holdings of the banks or the votes they exercised in proxy, but it did show that in pure ownership terms alone the banks have a strong voice in a significant number of major German companies. The positions that the banks hold could afford wide opportunities to influence industrial decision making, although they are not the kinds of true monopoly positions that earlier German cartel arrangements offered.

A mid-1980s study by the government agency that examines potential monopolies, the Monopolkommission, looking only at major companies, concluded that the three major banks could vote well over three-quarters of the shares of many major German corporations and that all banks together had even greater voting authority. The power of the banks also is evident in the seats they hold on the boards of the country's most important corporations, with bank presidents or representatives sitting on the boards of every major German firm.

The banks do not appear to want to seize industrial power or make production decisions. They would be hard put to exercise monopoly power, and their actions on individual boards are clearly subject to enough scrutiny—at least by other board members—that improper actions would become widely known. German business is prepared to accept the power and influence of the banks and to see it perpetuated. Nonetheless, the direction of bank influence probably adds a conservative element to German economic decision making because banks traditionally prefer to avoid risk-taking in favor of slow but steady dividends and debt repayment. They also could be accused of becoming new masters of German cartel-like structures, with banks directing separate firms toward similar policies even if the firms themselves are not colluding.

The role of the banks in the economy has raised questions. Some political figures, including FDP leader Otto Lambsdorff, have charged that the banks have accumulated excessive power. Newspapers and magazines, including business journals, periodically make the same charge. But there are no indications that the system is changing or will change in response to those criticisms. One could even argue that it is more pervasive than ever, as banks now also play roles in managing former East German firms that were privatized with western bank funds.

Nonbank Financing

Ever since the collapse of the Berlin stock exchange after Hitler's seizure of power in 1933, Germany has lacked a major international market for bonds and equities. Nothing in Germany rivals those of New York or Tokyo, and even the London market does more overall trading than Frankfurt. London even trades almost one-third of all German shares. There are now ten regional exchanges in Germany, but no single exchange is very large.

To help promote nonbank financing and a greater German interest in equities, the German government has launched a drive for what it terms Finanzplatz Deutschland, making stock and bond trading easier in Germany and subordinating the roles of the smaller exchanges to the Frankfurt exchange as the major site for German nonbank finance. Proposals include a futures market, improved electronic links among regional markets, some computerized trading, longer opening hours, freedom for firms to issue commercial paper, and the elimination of a small but annoying German turnover tax on securities transactions. They also include tighter national supervision to prevent misuse of the exchanges and of new methods of finance. Finally, there are tight restrictions on insider training, and a supervisory organization that will correspond to the

Securities and Exchange Commission in the United States is being created.

The smaller regional exchanges have objected that some of the steps proposed under the Finanzplatz Deutschland proposal violate the federal principle on which postwar West Germany had been founded, and they have been supported by the *Land* governments that do not want Frankfurt to have too much power. Therefore, not all parts of the government plan have been carried out as soon as its proponents wished. Nonetheless, an important step has been taken in the merger of the Frankfurt stock exchange and the German futures and options exchanges, the Deutsche Terminbörse (DTB).

Despite such measures to encourage equity placements, most German firms still do not seek equity financing, and even if they do, they often work through banks to obtain it. West Germany had 370,000 limited liability companies or closed corporations (*Gesellschaften mit beschränkter Haftung*—GmbH) as against 2,300 corporations (*Aktiengesellschaften*—AG). Of those, only 619 had their shares quoted on the markets at the end of 1990, and the number thereafter grew only slowly. There has been no upsurge toward new equity finance as a result of unification, with many East German firms being taken over by West German firms and with banks supplying the needed financing as well as sitting on new boards. Although there are some signs that German firms appear to be turning increasingly to exchanges for funds, and the volume of such placements increased over the late 1980s and early 1990s, many firms still feel more comfortable with their established banking links.

A step that may lead to a greater financial role for Frankfurt in Germany itself as well as in Europe has been the EU's 1994 decision to place the new European central bank in Frankfurt when that bank is established. This would reinforce Frankfurt's place as the center of the European Monetary Union (EMU— see Glossary) and also as the center of German finance (see Germany and the European Monetary Union, ch. 6). Berlin's emergence as a center for trade and services with Eastern Europe might over time boost Berlin's prospects as an alternative center of German finance.

Other Services

Transportation

Germany has one of the world's largest and most sophisticated transportation systems. This reflects the intensely mobile nature of the German population, who are among the world's most active drivers, tourists, and travelers. It also reflects Germany's location in the center of Europe and the many far-reaching industrial and commercial relationships developed over centuries. Because of the density of the network, many towns, but especially such major cities as Berlin, Frankfurt am Main, Munich, and Hamburg, function as transportation and communications centers, lying either at the intersections of major east-west and north-south routes or on transshipment points of ship, barge, road, and railroad traffic. With Europe again uniting from the Atlantic to the Urals, Germany's position as a transportation and communications hub for the continent will become ever more important.

To cope with the additional demands caused by German and European unification, the German government has designated seventeen major transport routes to be either completed or rebuilt as soon as possible during the last decade of the twentieth century and the first decade of the twenty-first century. The first transport plan for newly united Germany was adopted in 1993 and will cost DM453 billion by the year 2012. More than half of the investment will be dedicated to rail and waterway travel, not road travel (see fig. 11).

Trucks have been the most important instrument for freight transport throughout Germany for decades. They carried 203 billion ton-kilometers of freight in 1992, with railroads second (83 billion ton-kilometers) and inland shipping (55 billion ton-kilometers) third. But the railroad system is also perceived as very important, and it will be extensively modernized. The Deutsche Bahn railroad company, formed in January 1994 from the East German and West German railroad systems and to be gradually privatized, has a network of over 40,000 kilometers at standard 1.435 meter gauge, of which 16,000 kilometers are electrified. Perhaps 8,000 kilometers of German railroad tracks will be eliminated through rationalization. To speed traffic, new high-speed railroad tracks have been designed to permit special trains to move at up to 250 kilometers per hour between such principal cities as Hamburg and Munich, with more tracks to follow. The purpose of these new trains is to relieve some of the pressure on airports by making surface transportation fast and attractive for distances of fewer than 500 kilometers.

A Lufthansa Boeing 737–300 at Berlin-Tegel Airport
Courtesy German Information Center, New York
The Rhine-Main-Danube Canal, which completes the link between the
North Sea and the Black Sea
Courtesy Inter Nationes, Bonn

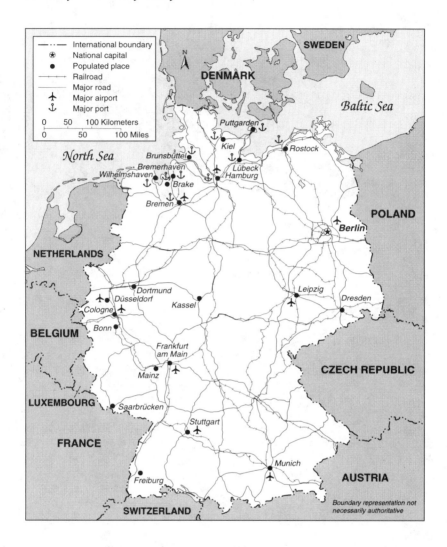

Figure 11. Transportation System, 1995

Germany has one of the densest road networks in the world and the largest after the United States. There were a total of 226,000 kilometers of roads in 1992, including more than 11,000 kilometers of four-or-more-lane superhighways. Nonetheless, especially in crowded areas and for the long routes toward southern Europe, many trucks are carried piggyback on trains to increase speed and to reduce pollution. The former East German system required several years of rebuilding after

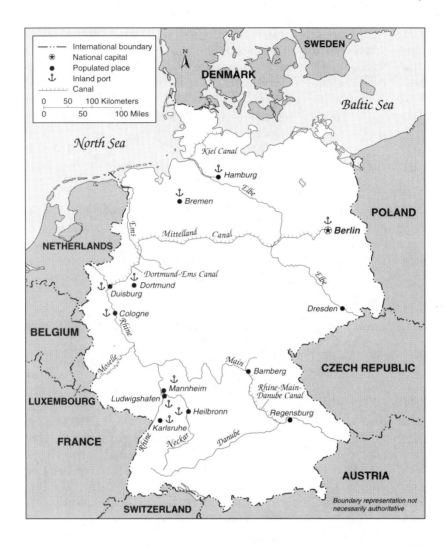

Figure 12. Inland Waterways, 1995

unification to enable it to serve the infrastructural requirements of modern business travel.

Germany had 45 million motor vehicles in 1992, with 39 million automobiles. Automobiles accounted for some 685 billion passenger-kilometers in 1990, a number that could be expected to rise rapidly by the mid-1990s as the eastern German population begins to acquire automobiles at a rate similar to that of their compatriots in the west.

The German inland shipping system is one of the world's most highly developed, especially because of the large flat areas in northern and western Germany. Duisburg, located in north-western Germany on the Rhine, is the largest inland port in the world. Germany has 6,900 kilometers of navigable inland waterways, including such principal canals as the Kiel Canal, the Mittelland Canal, and the Dortmund-Ems Canal. The Rhine-Main-Danube Canal, completed in 1992, joins the Main and the Danube rivers in northern Bavaria and for the first time permits river transport between the North Sea and the Black Sea (see fig. 12).

The main German seaports are those of the old Hanseatic League, with the best-known being Hamburg, Bremen-Bremerhaven, Wilhelmshaven, Lübeck, and Rostock. To compensate for their greater distance from the Atlantic Ocean (in comparison with Rotterdam), German ports have invested heavily in technology, equipment, and training that permit fast and economical loading and unloading.

Germany also has a large system of inland and international air travel. Lufthansa, the national airline, has an extensive domestic and global route system. In 1992 approximately 87.5 million passengers were registered at Germany's airports, and 1.5 million tons of air freight were carried from those airports. The largest international airport is Frankfurt-Rhein Main, located near Frankfurt am Main and one of the world's most important centers for both passengers and air freight. Other important airports are those at Düsseldorf, Munich, the three serving Berlin (Berlin-Tegel, Berlin-Schönefeld, and Berlin-Tempelhof), Hamburg, Stuttgart, and Cologne-Bonn. Berlin-Schönefeld, located to the south of Berlin, will be expanded to reestablish it as a major international air center.

Telecommunications

The German postal services are among the oldest in Europe. In 1990 Germany celebrated 500 years of organized mail service. At the same time, the German government broke up the Bundespost monopoly over all forms of communications and created three new structures to handle the services formerly handled by the Bundespost.

The largest of the new services is the Postdienst, with 390,000 employees. It is Germany's largest service enterprise, handling over 15 billion pieces of mail every year. The second largest is Telekom, the telephone/telex service, with a total of

260,000 employees. Telekom is intended to keep the German telecommunications system competitive with the new systems being developed in the United States and Asia. Germany has 35 million telephones, but service in eastern Germany took a long time to come up to western German standards. The third is the Postbank, with 24,000 employees, which manages the postal savings bank system in which about 30 million Germans have accounts (see Banking and Its Role in the Economy, this ch.).

Tourism

Germany is a principal attraction for foreign tourists, and the Germans themselves are among the world's most enthusiastic tourists. Although Germany attracts millions of foreign tourists, German tourists every year spend tens of billions of deutsche marks more than foreign tourists spend in Germany. In fact, tourism constitutes a major drain on German foreign exchange.

The areas that attract the most tourists to Germany are the Alps, the Rhine and Moselle valleys, and several large cities, especially Berlin. But those are not the only attractions. Music festivals such as those at Bayreuth and Munich draw many tourists. So do some of the old German medieval cities like Rothenburg ob der Tauber and Dinkelsbühl. Because of the wealth of hiking and bicycle trails, many tourists come to the Black Forest and to other German woodlands and mountains. Since unification, tourists have increasingly visited the former East German states and especially the Baltic beaches and such cities as Leipzig and Dresden.

Unlike Austria or Spain, Germany does not regard tourism as a major source of foreign exchange. Hotel stays by foreign visitors to Germany do not rise above 15 percent of total occupancy, as opposed to the two-thirds levels that they reach in those countries. But as many as 1.5 million jobs in Germany are connected in one way or another to the tourist industry.

*   *   *

The literature on the German economy is surprisingly limited, given its importance in Europe and the world as a whole. German economic unification produced a spate of books and articles, but most were out of date within months of publication. The most comprehensive current book in English is *The German Economy* by W.R. Smyser. Another survey is *The German*

Economy by Eric Owen Smith. There are also some current books that deal with specialized topics, such as *Banks, Finance, and Investment in Germany* by Jeremy S.S. Edwards and Klaus Fischer. The Bundesbank has attracted growing attention, with the most comprehensive work being *The Bundesbank* by David Marsh. The Organisation for Economic Co-operation and Development publishes an annual *OECD Economic Survey* on Germany as well as a special section on Germany in its biannual *OECD Economic Outlook*.

There is, however, a rich literature about the specifics of the German economy. The German Council of Economic Experts (Sachverständigenrat zur Begutachtung der gesamtwirtschaft-lichen Entwicklung) publishes an extensive annual review of the German economy in German, and the German economic institutes continually publish specialized papers in German and sometimes in English. The Bundesbank and the German Ministry for Economics publish monthly and annual reports that concentrate on financial and macroeconomic information but also provide a general economic roundup. The bank also publishes a dozen statistical annexes every month. Both publish their basic reports in English as well as in German. Other German ministries as well as the German Federal Press and Information Office provide large quantities of information on a regular basis, but much of it is in primary form and requires analysis. (For further information and complete citations, see Bibliography.)

Chapter 6. International Economic Relations

The port of Hamburg

EVER SINCE ITS CREATION IN 1949, the Federal Republic of Germany (FRG), or West Germany, as it was also called until its unification in 1990 with the German Democratic Republic (GDR, or East Germany), has played an increasingly important role in the world economy. Consistently among the most important trading nations in the world, Germany often derives a higher share of its gross domestic product (GDP—see Glossary) from exports than any other major state. The Federal Republic plays an even more important role in international financial matters. Its currency, the deutsche mark, is the second most important currency in the world after the United States dollar.

Germany does not act alone in international economic matters. Instead, it usually acts through Europe. West Germany was a founding member of the European Coal and Steel Community (ECSC) and of the follow-on European Community (EC— see Glossary), known since late 1993 as the European Union (EU—see Glossary). Germany increasingly makes its international policies in conjunction and consultation with other EU members. More than half of its trade is with other EU states, and the deutsche mark is the anchor of the European Monetary System (EMS—see Glossary) and of its planned follow-on, the European Monetary Union (EMU—see Glossary).

Despite its central role in the world economy, Germany has never developed nor sought a high profile as a major international economic player. It receives much less attention than Japan in United States newspapers and economic journals, even though it wields as least as much influence in global financial affairs. This relative discretion reflects Germany's general reticence about projecting itself on the world stage in economic matters and the consistent German wish to integrate its economy into the EU.

Germany has benefited from a strikingly benign international economic climate for the past half-century. Despite occasional crises—such as the effects of the United States decision to end the dollar's link to gold in 1971 and of the "oil shocks" of the 1970s that resulted from exporters' sharp increases in the price of petroleum—the global economic scene has been remarkably stable in comparison with that of the 1920s and 1930s. This stability has favored the kind of international trading state that West Germany represented and that united Germany is expected to become once unification is complete.

Under United States leadership, the Western world with free-market economies established the International Monetary Fund (IMF—see Glossary) and the World Bank (see Glossary) in 1944. In 1947 these nations created a virtually universal trade structure, the General Agreement on Tariffs and Trade (GATT—see Glossary). The combination of open financial and trade systems has helped promote continuous and even dramatic expansion since World War II of world trade and the liquidity of international capital. Nothing could have better suited West Germany and now united Germany.

The productive capacities of both East Germany and West Germany always exceeded the absorptive capacity of their respective domestic markets. From the West German standpoint, this characteristic helped to fuel the German export drive and to generate investment capital. It also strengthened the deutsche mark and helped make the German economy internationally prominent.

Although Germany has a global currency and a world-class trade sector, the German economy remains essentially continental in focus. Because the economy lacks the size necessary to deal with the effects of truly massive currency flows, Germany has looked for partners in international economic matters as it has in international strategic and political matters.

The German government and the Bundesbank, Germany's central bank, are active participants in formal and informal international institutions and arrangements concerned with global finance and the coordination of national economic policies. West Germany was a founding member of the association of free-market economies known as the Group of Five (G–5), which later became the Group of Seven (G–7—see Glossary). But the German government has also had to acknowledge that it cannot direct the policies of the independent Bundesbank, which are more often based on Germany's domestic needs than on the wishes of the outside world.

Germany in the World Economy

Germany in World Finance and in the Group of Seven

Along with the United States and Japan, Germany has one of the world's biggest economies and most dominant central banks. Of the three, Germany has the smallest and most vulnerable economy. Germany's GDP of DM3 trillion (for value of the deutsche mark—see Glossary) is less than one-third of United States GDP and less than one-half of Japan's.

Despite Germany's relatively small size, it has consistently exerted a powerful influence on the world economy. Since the end of World War II, the Federal Republic has played a key role in beginning, managing, or ending each crisis and each phase experienced by the global monetary system.

The first phase was the Bretton Woods era, named after the New Hampshire resort where the Allied monetary conference of July 1944 created the IMF and shaped the global postwar order. The dollar was pegged to gold at a fixed rate of US$35 per troy ounce, constituting the official backing of the global monetary system; other currencies were linked to the system through their own fixed, dollar-pegged exchange rates. Countries could devalue or revalue with respect to the dollar, and the dollar price of gold could at least theoretically remain constant even as rates of exchange between separate currencies fluctuated.

By the late 1960s, there was a surplus of dollars in the international financial system. Largely for domestic reasons, the United States had put far more emphasis on expanding dollar liquidity than on maintaining dollar value. Growing fear of United States inflation had made those dollars less desirable, and many central banks held more dollars than they wanted. The United States proposed that other countries revalue their currencies as provided under the Bretton Woods Agreement. But those other countries, and West Germany in particular, were not prepared to revalue. Money poured into purchases of the deutsche mark, sometimes for the purchase of German goods, but more often to hedge against the dollar or to make a profit when—as was widely expected—the deutsche mark would have to be revalued. West German foreign-exchange reserves rose from US$2.7 billion in December 1969 to US$12.6 billion by December 1971, and to US$28.1 billion by September 1973. The steady flow of foreign money into deutsche marks not only undercut the Bretton Woods system (see Glossary) but also threatened to import inflation into Germany by expanding the German money supply.

West Germany tried to help support the dollar during the late 1960s and early 1970s. Bundesbank president Karl Blessing sent a letter to the chairman of the United States Federal Reserve Board pledging not to purchase United States gold but to maintain West German reserves in dollars. West German chancellor Ludwig Erhard (1963–66) agreed to make large purchases of United States dollar instruments and to make "offset" payments to lessen demands in the United States Congress for a reduction in United States forces stationed in West Germany. The United States and several other nations pressed West Germany to revalue in order to compensate for the dollar glut. Although the Bundesbank would have favored revaluation to reduce the risk of inflation, the West German government was afraid that a revaluation would cut into West Germany's global competitiveness and curtail exports.

Finally, after intensifying waves of speculation, the Bretton Woods system collapsed in August 1971. The United States stopped the sale of gold at US$35 per troy ounce and thus removed the fixed link between the dollar and gold. With that step, the system lost its anchor.

The deutsche mark remained under strain throughout the post-Bretton Woods period. It was alternately used in interventions to support the dollar or as a hedge against it. Other currencies again flooded into purchases of deutsche marks. To ease pressure within Europe, West Germany and other European states agreed to peg their currencies to a special system of relatively narrow exchange-rate bands formally entitled the "European narrow-margins agreement" but informally known as the "snake." But the snake also failed to hold. The domestic policies and even the economic philosophies of its leading member states—West Germany, France, Britain, and Italy—diverged too widely. The deutsche mark was the strongest currency, and others could not hold their value against it.

The United States and West Germany played key roles in trying to arrange a new global monetary system. But they had opposite objectives: the United States was determined not to have the dollar reassume responsibility for maintaining an international arrangement, fearing the great cost to its exports and economic stability. The United States government believed that countries with a trade surplus, such as West Germany, should accept part of the responsibility for solving exchange-rate crises and should be prepared to revalue, and it insisted on advance agreement for sanctions against any country that refused to do so. Despite its readiness to make minor exchange-rate adjustments for the sake of new currency alignments, West Germany refused to commit itself to any arrangement that would oblige it to revalue in the future.

In March 1973, the United States and other governments and central banks gave up trying to preserve the Bretton Woods system by setting new fixed exchange rates. With that decision, the next phase of the postwar international system, "floating," began. With floating, the relationship between the United States dollar and the deutsche mark became subject to market forces rather than official negotiations. West Germany was not certain whether floating would serve its needs but was not prepared to pursue any alternative.

Floating did not insulate domestic economies from international events and global economic forces. Although the floating era may have ended the period of fixed links to the dollar and to gold, it did not give countries complete monetary freedom. It only meant that adjustments would be made by the markets, not by government decree or agreement. Those adjustments would, at least theoretically, occur in reaction to trade and payments imbalances, correcting them over time. However, the situation did not work out as expected or planned. The increasingly important role played by capital flows, speculative or not, undercut the theoretically self-regulating mechanism of trade flows as the basis of currency values.

The economic consequences of floating for Germany were not uniformly beneficial. The Bundesbank welcomed floating because it gave the bank more flexibility. The bank, in fact, could virtually control the deutsche mark's exchange rate if it was prepared to manipulate interest rates to that end. But West German industry, and especially West German exporters, did not welcome the unpredictability that flexible exchange rates introduced into commercial arrangements and production plans.

West German exporters also faced a particular problem that persisted in the 1990s. The Bundesbank's favorite instrument for fighting inflation, a high real domestic interest rate, is also the instrument that attracts capital to the deutsche mark and keeps the currency valuable. Many businesspeople feared then, as they have since, that the Bundesbank's anti-inflationary policy would always keep the deutsche mark stronger than most other currencies and would thus jeopardize exports.

German exchange-rate policy has been constantly caught on the horns of that dilemma. When a decision absolutely needed to be made during the floating era, however, German governments and the Bundesbank have almost always chosen an anti-inflationary course of action. They have preferred a strong currency, which might adversely affect trade, to a weak one, which would jeopardize the stability of the German monetary system. With that choice, they set policy for others as well as for themselves. As long as the deutsche mark is strong and German interest rates remain high, even the United States can diverge from German policy only at the risk of seeing its own currency fall in value. Because of Germany's monetary dilemma, and because the German government as well as the nation's bankers and industrialists have recognized German limitations and vulnerabilities, all have been anxious to establish the highest possible level of international predictability. The Germans have become regular participants in international economic consultations, and they have emphasized the value of such consultations at every opportunity.

Global economic coordination after the end of the Bretton Woods system has resulted in the development of a number of coordinating institutions. One, first known informally as the Group of Five (G–5), consisted of the United States, West Germany, Japan, Britain, and France. After Canada and Italy joined, the association became known as the Group of Seven (G–7). The G–7 includes the finance ministers and central bankers of the principal economic powers, who meet periodically and consult regularly between meetings.

In addition to the meeting of G–7 finance ministers, there is an annual G–7 economic summit at which the heads of state or government of the same seven countries meet to coordinate economic and political policies or at least to attempt to understand each other better. The summits have been held annually since 1975 on a rotating basis among the summit states, usually in the capital. At the Naples summit of the G–7 in 1994, Russia joined the political discussions, essentially turning the gathering into the Group of Eight (G–8).

Three summits, those of 1978, 1985, and 1992, took place in Germany. Each was significant for different reasons. In 1978 Chancellor Helmut Schmidt (1974–82) committed West Germany to a more reflationary policy, to his later regret. Seven years later, Chancellor Helmut Kohl (1982–) and other summit principals made commitments toward supply-side policies that most participants agreed were then necessary and that both Kohl and United States president Ronald Reagan wanted to use to reduce the role of government in their national economies. Seven years later, at Munich in 1992, the G–7 agreed to provide aid to Russia. However, the summit did not reach agreement on the Uruguay Round of the GATT negotiations, and Chancellor Kohl did not carry out what the United States had regarded as his promise to persuade the French to reduce their insistence on large EC agricultural export subsidies.

German bankers and financial officials have usually spoken skeptically about possible results from the summits, making abundantly clear that the meetings do not affect their views, although they may subsequently adjust specific policies. Bundesbank president Hans Tietmeyer has stated that West Germany sees them as occasions for "cooperation," not "coordination." German global policy has thus been guided by broad efforts to coordinate specific policies, but with a firm wish to preserve German interests and its friendships with the EU members it considers its principal economic partners.

The Deutsche Mark as an International Currency

At the core of Germany's success and influence lies its currency. The deutsche mark gave concrete expression to West Germany's international financial and economic success and also contributed to it. Since unification, it has become even more important as a symbol as well as an instrument of Germany's new central role in Europe. The success of the deutsche mark has been anchored in the success of West German exports, in the Bundesbank's solicitous management of the currency's value, and in the confidence generated by the country's prosperity.

The deutsche mark has been a model of stability since it became fully convertible in 1958. No other major currency, including the Japanese yen or the Swiss franc, has been stronger. The United States dollar, the cornerstone of the global system, has lost about two-thirds of its value against the deutsche mark since 1958.

The deutsche mark has become the second-largest currency component of global monetary reserves, second only to the United States dollar. Less than 10 percent of the world's monetary reserves were held in deutsche marks throughout most of the 1970s, but the amount rose to 15 percent by the end of 1987. By the end of 1989, around 20 percent of all global monetary reserves were in deutsche marks. The deutsche mark's position in global monetary reserves largely reflects the extensive deutsche mark holdings in European foreign-exchange reserve accounts as well as the desire among all industrial state treasuries and central banks to hold a stable currency in their reserves. According to the United States Federal Reserve Board, the United States government holds more than US$13 billion of its reserves in deutsche marks, an amount greater than its holdings in Japanese yen.

The deutsche mark is not used as widely for transactions as it is to supply central-bank reserves. Global commodity prices are still largely denominated in United States dollars. Whatever the deutsche mark's strengths may be, it does not offer the kind of liquidity that the dollar does. Invoicing in deutsche marks is concentrated on Germany's own commerce, but almost 15 percent of world trade is conducted on a deutsche mark basis. The deutsche mark figures much less significantly than the dollar in the creation of international credits or in debt servicing. But a growing quantity of international bond issues—including some being floated in the United States—are denominated in deutsche marks. Major United States banks offer deutsche mark accounts for Americans who want to hedge some of their assets against a fall in the dollar. The World Bank has floated Euro-deutsche mark bonds, as have various United States corporations. In Europe the deutsche mark has virtually become a parallel currency, with prices in Western Europe and Eastern Europe increasingly quoted in deutsche marks as well as in local currencies.

Bundesbank officials worry constantly that the growing circulation of the deutsche mark makes it difficult to control the supply of the central bank's own currency. Deutsche marks held abroad, circulating abroad, and perhaps even used for currency intervention abroad are still part of the total German money supply. Sudden, large flows could have undesirable impacts on German interest rates or German prices, materially complicating the execution of German monetary policy. The bank fears that any decline in the deutsche mark's value or in the German current-account surplus could set off a selling wave that would force it to intervene massively and perhaps unsuccessfully. Bundesbank president Tietmeyer has warned that the high deutsche mark holdings abroad place a particular burden on the Bundesbank because any loss of faith in the German currency could provoke large-scale selling. The deutsche mark has thus become a burden for Germany as well as a blessing. The Bundesbank stated in May 1991 that one reason it had to maintain high interest rates was to avoid the kind of decline and subsequent market effects that Tietmeyer had cited. The German currency risks finding itself on a treadmill where the

Frankfurt am Main, a typical German mixture of old and new, has a medieval square, the Römerplatz, and a skyline of skyscrapers, headquarters of large banks.
Courtesy German Information Center, New York

stronger it gets, the stronger it must remain until the German monetary authorities no longer dare to reduce interest rates significantly for fear that they might spark a deutsche mark sell-off.

The IMF recognized the reality of German monetary power in 1990, when it promoted Germany and Japan to share the second rank just below the United States and ahead of Britain and France. German government and banking officials were not certain that they welcomed such prominence, but they were prepared to accept it as a reflection of international appreciation of German monetary policies.

The West German role in the development of the global financial and monetary system has been replete with ironies. No state consistently had a greater interest in developing a stable system and in cooperating in such a system. Nonetheless, West German policy helped undermine and even destroy some of the arrangements that West Germany wanted to maintain. During the Bretton Woods era, pressures on the dollar almost always expressed themselves in massive purchases of deutsche marks. The strength of the deutsche mark weakened the system because any currency—including the United States dollar—could come under attack if it were not defended and preserved as solicitously as the deutsche mark was by Germany. The only currencies and systems that survived this pressure were those whose governments determined from the beginning that they would follow a strict monetary discipline similar to that applied by the Bundesbank to the deutsche mark.

Germany in the European Economy

Germany in the European Community

If Germany's global role is beset with complications, its European role seems relatively clear. Germany has always concentrated its economic interests and activities, whether in trade, investment, or finance, within whatever form was being taken by West European integration.

Although German economic and political interests cover all of Europe, they have been most immediately reflected in the EU and the European Monetary System (EMS). The Germans have found that these two systems complement each other. But the German government and German business and banking establishments have long had separate attitudes toward the two institutions, and they play a different role in each.

The EC was West Germany's economic home, and the country remains one of the organization's strongest supporters. Chancellor Kohl on several occasions made special efforts to promote European cooperation, especially concentrating on the drive to create a European Single Market and on the negotiation and ratification of the Treaty on European Union (commonly known as the Maastricht Treaty—see Glossary) (see The European Single Market, this ch.). Kohl also intervened on occasion to avert potential conflicts between Germany's European interests and its ties with the United States, although he had great difficulty resolving the dispute over agricultural trade that broke out between the United States and France during negotiation of the Uruguay Round of the GATT talks. He also followed up German unification with efforts to draw the EU further toward Eastern Europe.

Germans have consistently pressed for closer integration of the states of Western Europe, officially and in public opinion. They have also been among the staunchest European advocates of open trade between Europe and the outside world. German officials and political leaders have strongly and consistently asserted that United States fears about a "Fortress Europe" are misplaced. Whereas several other European states—especially France and Italy—have tried to limit imports of various foreign products to the EU, the German government has argued for open markets, imposing fewer controls or restrictions on trade than most European states.

West Germany, and especially West German industry, carved out an important export niche within the EC. In the process, it made the EC an essential market for German goods and an important factor in German prosperity. Because one-third of West German GDP was exported and because one-half of all exports went to countries of the EC, at least one of every six West German jobs depended directly on the EC market. Many other jobs depended on imports from EC states or on the general prosperity the EC had brought to all its members.

The intimate connection with the EC was reflected in West German trade statistics (see table 19, Appendix). Not only did more than half of West German exports go to other EC countries, but many West German industries relied on the EC for a major share of their total market—whether domestic or international. Before unification in 1990, 48 percent of West Germany's production of office machinery was exported to other EC countries, as was 24 percent of its chemical goods and machinery, 23 percent of its motor vehicles, 17 percent of its electronic goods, 16 percent of its textiles, and 14 percent of its iron and steel.

But if West European trade was vital to West Germany and remains so for united Germany, West Germany was vital to the success of the EC. Even before German unification, there were more Germans—more than 60 million—than any other nationality in the EC. With unification the figure came to about 80 million. West Germany alone already had the largest share of the EC's GDP, over 25 percent; the largest amount of private consumption, more than DM1.2 trillion in 1988; and the largest investment in other EC countries, DM56.7 billion. Because the German share of EC production and consumption was expected to grow in the aftermath of unification, the EC recognized the impact of this process by allotting united Germany a larger number of seats—ninety-nine—in the European Parliament than any other state.

The Federal Republic was often termed the EC's "paymaster." Its net contribution to the EC budget was often four times as large as the next-largest contribution because West Germany never drew as heavily as such states as France or the poorer Mediterranean countries on either the agricultural or the developmental support programs. West Germany regularly provided over 25 percent of the EC budget, with no other state contributing more than 20 percent; and united Germany's projected share of the 1994 EU budget was 30 percent, or DM44.1 billion. Although Germany was receiving some EU aid in 1994 to develop the economy of the former East Germany, united Germany will in the future be expected to contribute an even larger share to the EU than West Germany did—in part because Germany itself is larger and in part because many prospective East European members will need support. This was one reason Germany strongly supported the EU membership applications of such relatively well-to-do states as Norway, Sweden, Finland, and Austria. Germany's contribution to the EU is becoming increasingly controversial, however, as more and more Germans complain about the growth of the EU budget. Several German political figures, including Bavaria's political leader, Minister President Edmund Stoiber, have said that Germany must reduce its contribution.

Because of the multifaceted economic relationships between Germany and other EU countries, different ministries in Bonn can have different and even conflicting interests and policies concerning various items on the European agenda. Many ministries have their own direct links to the EU bureaucracy in Brussels, and the German government has occasionally spoken with several voices at different levels until the problems were brought to the attention of senior officials in Bonn and priorities were established. By the same token, German ministries have at times used elements within the European bureaucracy to support their views at home. It has been left to the three ministries with the broadest responsibilities—the Ministry for Economics, the Ministry of Finance, and the Ministry of Foreign Affairs—to try to keep these separate issues in a total national-interest perspective. Those ministries have also had to block collusion between European and German bureaucracies to devise new subsidies and new ways to protect or subsidize special German or European interests.

Management of the EU's Common Agricultural Policy (CAP—see Glossary) illustrates some of the conflicts in intra-German interests. That system, by its commitment to subsidize both production and exports, has become increasingly expensive. It consumes more than half of the EU budget, or more than US$35 billion a year. Germany's Ministry of Agriculture has often tried to use the EU to drive support prices higher and to prevent or restrict foreign imports. The Ministry of Finance, by constrast, has sought to reduce the CAP in order to cut the German contribution to the EU.

The European Single Market

To advance the EC toward a truly integrated and borderless internal market—the European Single Market—the EC's European Commission (see Glossary) in 1985 submitted a white paper to the European Council (see Glossary) in which it listed a series of 225 steps needed to create such a market. It also proposed a schedule for completing these steps in time for the internal market to begin functioning by the end of 1992. The council accepted the commission's proposals, with West Germany strongly supporting the concept. West Germany later advanced the process significantly during its presidency of the council in the second half of 1988.

Once Germany was united, it remained among the European states the most determined to implement the conditions of the European Single Market. Even before the formal implementation of the single market on January 1, 1993, Germany had already incorporated 80 percent of the single-market regulations into its own legislation, a higher percentage than any European state except Denmark or France. Notably, the German government also applied those new regulations in the five new states (*Länder*, sing., *Land*) of the former East Germany, as well as in the old *Länder* of western Germany.

Not all Germans welcomed the coming of an open internal market. Many worried that the guidelines for such a market would give so much power to the bureaucrats within the European Commission that economic initiative within the member states might be stifled. Many German businesspeople dreaded the prospect of more EU offices in Brussels enforcing more regulations. Some *Länder*, especially Bavaria, as well as a number of German communities, became disturbed by prospects that the EU would in the future have such immense powers over economic life that the German federal system itself could be placed in jeopardy. As a result, Germans have become strong advocates of the principle of *Subsidarität* (subsidiarity), under which matters not specifically covered by EU laws are left to the practices and the laws of the individual national states.

Despite steady German government support for the internal market, attitudes in German business and economic circles also have remained mixed, depending on the size and interests of the affected firms. The largest German firms with strong export positions strongly favor the internal market. The mid-sized firms, which are unable to relocate their main production sites or develop subsidiary sites abroad, have a more cautious reaction. Smaller firms, especially those involved in handicrafts or services, are fearful of the competition that might come from other European countries with lower production costs.

Just as firms of different sizes have reacted differently to the internal market, so have firms in different industries. The producers of Germany's most competitive products—whether automotive manufacturers, toolmakers, chemical firms, or electronics firms—regard the single market as an opportunity. By constrast, Germany's relatively inefficient service firms, whether in telecommunications, banking, or insurance, see the market as a threat because it would eliminate national regulations that had given them privileged positions.

German trade unions particularly fear the internal market. They have warned that it will cause production to move to countries and regions where wages are lowest and social benefits most limited. Despite the existence of strict EU standards governing the rights and privileges of workers, the trade unions have consistently warned of "social dumping," the temptation for manufacturers to look for those sites where regulations are less stringent or are less vigorously enforced than in Germany.

German environmentalists, for their part, fear that German manufacturers might shade their environmental commitments in order to keep their costs as low as possible against competitors who face fewer environmental problems in less densely settled countries (see The Environment, ch. 3). Environmentalists have also expressed concern that manufacturers will be tempted to locate production facilities abroad, where environmental standards might be less rigorously enforced or where less severe population and land-use pressures might make pollution seem less onerous. As German trade unions fear social dumping, the environmental groups fear "environmental dumping."

With the continued development of the internal European market, many Germans began to perceive another danger—that the EU might become so internally focused that it could become too protectionist. The Board of Advisers to the German Ministry for Economics warned in 1990 that such protectionist thinking, if not promptly countered, could jeopardize European prosperity. German industry and trade associations have expressed similar concerns, warning that the protectionist risk of the internal market must be fought at every level to avoid driving Germany ever more into a limited European mold. German industry has consistently pointed out that Germany stands to lose far more than any other European state if the global trading system collapses because of the protectionist proclivities of the EU.

The increasing power of protectionist forces in the EU has raised concerns in Germany about the potential for the emergence of three separate and competitive regional trading areas, the EU, the Americas, and Asia, with some form of negotiated—or managed—trade among them. Any such arrangement negotiated by the EU would establish quotas for each side, and Germany almost certainly would not obtain as large a share of any European quota as that which German exporters could obtain on their own.

Regardless of its concerns about protectionism, the German government has continued to insist that it will fulfill its commitment to complete European integration and the single market. Political considerations, especially Germany's relationship with France, have helped to shape and support that policy as much as economic considerations have. But the Germans have noticed with concern that France is often the state that tries to make the EU more protectionist. The Germans believe that they cannot support such French efforts, even if they cannot block them. German minister of foreign affairs Klaus Kinkel has warned that Germany does not agree with all French views on international trade rules, but Chancellor Kohl remains reluctant to press France toward a more open global trading system.

Kohl, in fact, has sought to use EU cooperation to help cement a close German relationship with France. He and French president François Mitterrand promised in early 1994 that they would use the successive German and French presidencies of the European Council during the last half of 1994 and the first half of 1995 to plan and execute a joint program for the further development of the EU.

Germany and the European Union

Kohl believed that it was important for a united Germany to have a firm anchor in the West, especially in a structure for West European and, later, European, integration (see European Union, ch. 8). He therefore played a major part in gaining Europe-wide approval of the Maastricht Treaty negotiated at the European Council summit in December 1991. He refused to be deterred after a first Danish referendum rejected the treaty, insisting that Germany proceed to ratification. The two houses of parliament, the Bundestag and Bundesrat, vindicated Kohl's position, approving the Maastricht Treaty by overwhelming majorities despite reservations in some *Länder* that it might undermine the German federal system by giving the EC and its European Commission greater powers over the separate *Länder* than even the Bonn government possessed.

Germany also strongly supported the creation of the European Economic Area (EEA—see Glossary), established in 1993 to create a trade area consisting of the EC and most of the states of the European Free Trade Association (EFTA—see Glossary). It later advocated the entry of four EFTA members—Norway, Sweden, Finland, and Austria—into the EU. By the same token, Germany has favored developing close links between the EU and the East European states, although German farmers and steel manufacturers have joined other EU producers in seeking to block those East European imports that would be most competitive with their own output.

During the entire process of creating a more integrated Europe, Kohl and Minister of Foreign Affairs Kinkel continuously stressed the German commitment to integration. Kohl has told the Bundestag that Germany's national future lies in Europe, and he has used every possible opportunity to point out that Germany's firmly anchored position within Europe has been mainly responsible for giving Germany peace, prosperity, and its chance at unification.

Germany in the European Monetary System

West Germany helped to start the European Monetary System (EMS) in the late 1970s and has long provided the anchor of its principal operating element, the European exchange-rate mechanism (ERM—see Glossary). It has exercised considerable and sometimes even dominant influence on the evolution of European monetary affairs. Nonetheless, the EMS was much more difficult for West Germany to propose or even to accept than the EC. Although much of West German business and government felt very much at home in the EC from the beginning, Germany had reasons to be much more anxious about monetary cooperation.

The concepts of the EMS and the EU are very different, although they may be complementary, and they look especially different to Germans. A common trading area within Europe helps Germany to do what it does best: produce and export. Although Germans have had to open their own borders to others, they have always been confident about meeting such a challenge.

Money, however, is something else again, especially in Germany. West Germany's strict monetary policy was seen by many West Germans as the guarantor of the Federal Republic's stability and prestige. Any West German political or economic debate assumed the solidity of the deutsche mark. European monetary cooperation could only be acceptable in West Germany if it jeopardized neither the deutsche mark nor the policy that had given the currency its success and had given West Germany its prosperity and domestic tranquillity.

Many West Germans feared that European monetary cooperation would have a pernicious effect on West Germany's own money by posing a risk to the independence and integrity of West German financial and monetary policies. They believed, and not without reason, that many other states in Europe did not share West Germany's belief in monetary stability as the principal objective of financial policy. They looked with particular suspicion at Britain, Italy, and the smaller countries of southern Europe.

The West German government and the Bundesbank tried, therefore, to ensure that no European monetary arrangement would interfere with West Germany's freedom to choose its monetary objectives and policies. They consistently tried to construct arrangements that would give them a dominant influence over European policy or, if that was impossible, would at least enable them to continue pursuing their traditional goals. The West German government and the Bundesbank did not always agree about what constituted satisfactory

Lübeck, a Baltic port, has linked Germany to the outside world since the Middle Ages. On the left: old salt warehouses; on the right: one of the city's gates, the Holstentor.
Courtesy Lübeck-North America Representation, New York

arrangements, however, with the bank usually being more cautious than the government. Nonetheless, West Germany helped to establish the system of European monetary cooperation and was among its main beneficiaries.

A number of proposals for European monetary cooperation were advanced and discussed as the European Coal and Steel Community (ECSC) came into being in 1951, as other plans for West European cooperation were considered, and as the Bretton Woods system began to crumble in the 1960s. None came to fruition, but they provided some of the intellectual foundations for later efforts. It was only in 1972, after the collapse of the Bretton Woods system, that the first arrangement for true European coordination was put into place—the European narrow-margins agreement, which came to be known as the "snake" (see Germany in World Finance and in the Group of Seven, this ch.). West Germany helped to establish the system, a joint European float whose purpose was to ensure that European currencies would not fluctuate more against each other than against the United States dollar.

The deutsche mark became the strongest currency in the snake. It remained at the top of the snake's trading range, in part because of West Germany's export surplus but especially because West German domestic monetary policy inspired confidence that the deutsche mark's value would be protected and might even rise against other currencies. Others soon learned that staying in the snake meant a commitment to emulate the policies of the Bundesbank or to suffer the exchange-rate consequences of any divergence. Because most countries could not do this, the snake had to be abandoned as a major international currency arrangement. But a truncated snake did survive, in part because some smaller countries were prepared and to some extent were obliged to follow the West German lead, and in part because, despite its imperfections, it offered a modicum of stability.

As the 1970s drew to a close, there were debates about monetary policy in almost every European country. Whatever the imperfections of the snake, it was clear to many states that any port in a storm might be better than none. The oil shocks confronted Western states with pressures that paradoxically could be both recessionary and inflationary. Some countries, such as the United States, chose to counteract the recessionary pressures. Others, such as West Germany, chose to counteract the inflationary threats. Most European countries increasingly found the West German approach more congenial than that of the United States.

The main debate in West Germany, as in several other large European countries, was between those who came to be known as the "monetarists" and those who came to be known as the "economists." The monetarists believed that introducing fixed exchange rates would force countries to pursue similar economic policies and that this would make interventions less necessary, and perhaps even unnecessary. The economists argued that common economic policies had to precede fixed exchange rates because the exchange-rate system would break down otherwise. They thought that a common currency should cap a structure of common policy, not help to build it.

Most West German economists as well as government and Bundesbank officials belonged solidly in the economist camp. They did not want to join in any European monetary collaboration until European states had shown that they would coordinate economic policies. The experience with the snake, and the costly and frequent interventions that it had required before it finally broke down, only hardened their attitudes.

It was against this background of deep skepticism that Chancellor Helmut Schmidt decided in 1978 and 1979 to cooperate with French president Valéry Giscard d'Estaing in creating the EMS. Because of opposition from the Bundesbank and the Ministry for Economics, Schmidt conducted the crucial initial phase of the negotiations in great secrecy, keeping them secret from the German bureaucracy and the Bundesbank.

The EMS established not only a zone of monetary cooperation but also a European currency known as the European currency unit (ECU—see Glossary). It was designated to represent a basket of currencies from the EMS countries, to be used initially for certain clearing and credit transactions and ultimately as a common European currency. Deutsche marks became the largest element in the backing of the ECU.

When the EMS and its companion, the ERM, were formally established on March 25, 1979, Schmidt's role committed Germany to their success. Thus, West Germans became involved in an area of European economic policy that was of the utmost sensitivity to them. They did not do so without some reservations. But they saw no alternative.

The EMS and especially the ERM succeeded in making Western Europe something of a zone of stability around the deutsche mark. After a difficult beginning, marked by frequent currency realignments during the early and mid-1980s, the exchange rates of the ERM currencies were much more stable relative to each other than in relation to the United States dollar or the Japanese yen until 1992.

However one might choose to allot credit for the success of the EMS and ERM, they represented both a theoretical setback and a practical triumph for the Bundesbank, because they showed that the monetarist school might well have been correct and that a stable ERM, accompanied by a commitment to hold to the agreed rates, could compel states and their central banks to pursue congruent policies as long as they were determined to stay within a system. The effectiveness of the EMS and ERM also suggested that a system of fixed exchange rates might act as a catalyst in facilitating policy because it would give states an additional reason to coordinate and could be said to provide a sanction if they failed to coordinate.

It has often been said that the ERM represents a "deutschemark zone" within the EU. The deutsche mark has been the EU's lead currency, the principal intervention currency, the principal reserve currency, and its psychological as well as practical anchor.

During the twelve years from the onset of the ERM to the Maastricht summit in 1991, the revaluation of the deutsche mark against other ERM currencies had been 38 percent (including 58 percent against the Italian lira and 45 percent against the French franc), but most of the revaluation had taken place early in that period, with the practice becoming much less common after the mid-1980s. At the end of the 1980s, it could be said that the ERM had been a considerable success for all the states involved. But it had mainly been a success for West Germany, demonstrating the benefits to others of associating themselves with West Germany's economic philosophy.

The members of the EC decided even before the end of the 1980s to explore further monetary cooperation as the community advanced toward the single market. In June 1988, at the European Council meeting in Hanover, they established a commission chaired by the president of the European Commission, Jacques Delors, to study and propose "concrete stages leading toward economic and monetary union." Delors's report, submitted on April 17, 1989, envisaged a transition in three stages toward an EMU with a single common currency. The objectives of the first stage, to commence on July 1, 1990, were to expand the ERM to include all EC members, to permit free capital flows, and to take other measures toward coordinating economic and monetary policies. In the second stage, for which no starting date was then proposed, a European system of central banks would be created, leading to the formation of a single central bank. In the third stage, a single currency managed by a European central bank would be created, and even greater powers would be granted to the EC to establish common financial policies among its members.

After the Delors Plan was announced, the West German government and the Bundesbank reacted cautiously, although both the Ministry of Finance and the Bundesbank had helped to draft the report. Having been pleased with the achievements of the ERM, the West Germans were prepared to examine an arrangement that would go further toward monetary union. But they were not ready to agree to anything that would upset what they regarded as the foundations of their own prosperity. The Bundesbank in particular wanted to make certain that any European system would reflect its own thinking.

Germany and the European Monetary Union

Germany played a major role in shaping the currency provisions of the Treaty on European Union signed in December 1991 in Maastricht, the Netherlands, especially in making certain that those provisions would assure a stable European currency. In broad terms, the agreement, often referred to as the Maastricht Treaty, provided for the same three phases earlier proposed in the Delors report, although with later deadlines for each phase. It also provided for a transitional stage to economic and monetary union to begin in January 1994 with the creation of the European Monetary Institute. The institute was given a mandate to coordinate EU members' monetary policy, to oversee preparations for the transfer to a European currency, and to create the right conditions for the final stage of monetary reform—a European System of Central Banks (ESCB), a single European Central Bank (ECB), and a common currency.

The ESCB and ECB agreed upon at Maastricht are the types of institutions the Bundesbank might welcome. Their common mandate was to assure price stability and a stable European currency, although the ECB was also instructed to ensure sustainable growth with high employment. The structure of the ECB itself was to resemble that of the Bundesbank (see The Bundes-

bank, ch. 5). Its council, like the Bundesbank's executive Direktorium (Directorate—see Glossary), would consist of an
executive board and the presidents of those national banks
whose currencies qualified for entry into the EMU. The ECB
would be independent of political control, and the central
banks of all European states would be independent of such
control even before the end of the first stage of the EMU.
Thus, the principles guiding the Bundesbank and the deutsche
mark would also guide the ECB and the future European currency.

The Maastricht principals agreed that the final stage in the
movement toward the EMU would begin in 1997 if the European Council decided that a majority of EU members had met
five convergence criteria: inflation within 1.5 percent of the
average of the three best (i.e., lowest) rates; long-term interest
rates within 2 percent of the three best rates; a budget deficit of
less than 3 percent of GDP; a national debt of less than 60 percent of GDP; and a stable currency, as shown by conformity
with the narrow band of the ERM and an absence of devalua-
tions within two years of the council's decision to move toward
a European currency. If the majority of EU members did not
meet these convergence standards, the EMU was to start in
1999 with as many members as had met the criteria. Britain was
authorized to leave the system. At France's insistence, however,
Germany was required to enter the EMU if France entered,
thus ensuring that the Bundesbank could not conduct a policy
independent of a European system.

The convergence criteria reflect the Bundesbank's determination to make certain that no unstable currencies enter the
EMU. The criteria also put pressure on European governments
and central banks to begin conforming to Bundesbank principles before a monetary union is accomplished.

The Maastricht formula represents a compromise between
the monetarist and the economist camps on the issue of European integration. It pleased the monetarists—and thus the
French—by establishing a strict calendar for the transitional
stages to the EMU and by using monetary policy and the desire
for a common currency to compel the European economies'
acceptance of convergence. The formula pleased the economists—and thus the Bundesbank—by making EMU membership subject to the kind of criteria that would force
governments and central banks to pursue similar policies even
before the final stage of the EMU. Most important, from the

standpoint of the economists and the Bundesbank, it created a standard for EMU membership.

Although the Maastricht arrangements were designed to please the Bundesbank and to assuage German concerns, the German people reacted negatively. Popular media depicted "Germany's beloved deutsche mark" vanishing into the distance or sinking into a swamp, and opinion surveys revealed fears that the politicians had surrendered the cornerstone of German prosperity for the sake of a united Europe. If the Maastricht provisions for the EMU had been subject to a referendum in Germany, they almost certainly would have failed to gain a majority.

The German government had to offer repeated assurances that it would never give up the deutsche mark for another currency that was not as strong or as stable. It took some time for the German public even to entertain the notion that savings might one day be held in a currency other than the deutsche mark, and the public consistently made clear that it would accept that prospect only if that currency were as strong as the deutsche mark.

The Bundesbank's Central Bank Council followed the Maastricht summit with a formal statement reiterating a number of well-known Bundesbank positions. In the statement, the council expressed regret that monetary union was moving forward more rapidly than a "comprehensive political union." It stated that such a political union was necessary if monetary union were to be effective. The council also warned that the success of any decisions taken on the path toward the envisaged economic and monetary union had to be judged "solely on their stability performance" and that "the fulfillment of the entry criteria of the convergence conditions must not be impaired by any dates set." The Bundesbank stressed that the policy unit of the EMU would be the ESCB—in which the Bundesbank could expect to have a strong voice—with the ECB to be subsidiary to the ESCB and thus subject to the Bundesbank's influence. It also stressed that the deutsche mark and the European currency would coexist for some time at fixed exchange rates until all the conditions had been set for a European currency that would actually displace all national currencies. The Bundesbank also reiterated the importance of having the ESCB and ECB remain completely independent of national governments.

Both the German government and the Bundesbank wanted the new ECB to be located in Frankfurt am Main. To this end, the Bundesbank and German officials indicated that they would make every effort to enhance the appeal of Germany and Frankfurt in particular as financial centers, although the bank warned that Germany should not take steps that could jeopardize financial stability for the sake of competitiveness by loosening German financial standards. The Institut für Kapitalmarktforschung (Institute for Research on Capital Markets) urged fast action to boost Frankfurt, warning that a more financially integrated Europe would tend toward a single financial capital and that London and Paris were not only better placed than Frankfurt but also were making much greater efforts to emerge as dominant financial centers.

But Bundesbank officials had more on their minds in early 1992 than the Maastricht conditions for the EMU and the location of Europe's future financial center. The bank was attempting to establish German monetary union within the recently united Germany, as well as to prepare for European unity, and was finding neither task particularly easy. The Bundesbank could have been expected to react guardedly to the Maastricht Treaty no matter what its terms might have been. But the fact that the treaty was signed as the bank was trying to deal with the German government's large fiscal deficits and the resulting upsurge in the German money supply made the Bundesbank both more hesitant about proceeding toward the EMU and more assertive in its insistence on what it considered the proper conditions.

Since the early 1970s, the Bundesbank had effectively controlled European monetary policy. The deutsche mark had been the anchor currency of the snake and of the EMS and ERM. But the Bundesbank would become only one of many banks with a voice on the new council. The president of the ECB might well be a German, and the ECB might be based in Germany, but many different banks would have a voice in European monetary policy, in effect removing the Bundesbank's virtual monopoly of authority. Some of those banks, even if they were to meet the Maastricht convergence criteria, might occasionally want to pursue policies different from those of the Bundesbank.

More problematic for the Bundesbank was the recognition that those other banks, through their influence on European monetary policy, would have a voice in German monetary policy, because the EMU could not function if separate states and central banks could ignore any ECB policy they disliked. The

The port of Bremen
Courtesy German Information Center, New York

Bundesbank might not only lose control over European money but perhaps over German money as well. Such a situation could violate the bank's own basic mandate, and it would certainly violate its stability doctrine if the ECB failed to pursue what the Bundesbank perceived as the right kind of policy.

The Bundesbank responded to these multiple challenges by setting forth on a course that was designed to put the indelible imprint of its philosophy on the new bank and the new currency, or, if that were not possible, either to break up the EMU or to make it so selective that only a few countries could join. Thus the bank became engaged in a rigid, even doctrinaire, assertion of the primacy of currency stability. It proceeded to raise short-term interest rates throughout 1991 and much of 1992, before and after Maastricht. Although it did so primarily for domestic reasons, it was certainly mindful of the effect that its policies would have on other European currencies.

As German interest rates rose, other European currencies and central banks found it difficult to match German policies at home. The recession that had hit Germany spread throughout Europe, in part for cyclical reasons but also because of the forced emulation of Bundesbank policies by countries interested in joining the EMU. As the recession spread, several countries could not support their currencies except at the cost of an ever-greater slowdown.

An exchange-rate crisis erupted in September 1992, after several countries had decided that they could no longer keep up with German interest rates. As those central banks began to lower short-term rates, investors began to abandon their currencies, and speculators began to dump them. In response to desperate pleas from abroad and from large segments of the German political and economic communities, the Bundesbank lowered its Lombard rate (see Glossary), but only by a quarter point. Within days, the Italian lira had to be devalued and taken out of the ERM. The British pound also came under attack. This triggered "Black Wednesday," September 16, 1992, when the pound crashed while the Bundesbank refused to support it. As a result, Britain withdrew the pound from the ERM.

Only the French franc and the smaller currencies traditionally tied to the deutsche mark (such as the Belgian franc, the Dutch guilder, and the Danish krone) did not devalue, thus remaining in the ERM. All other EC currencies effectively devalued against the deutsche mark. The defense of the French franc cost the Bundesbank and the Banque de France tens of billions of deutsche marks, on which they realized a small profit after the French currency had stabilized. More important, however, it cost the Bundesbank its reputation for objectivity, at least in London, because the British complained that their currency had not been supported as the franc had been.

In August 1993, a similar crisis erupted, but this time the currency under attack was the French franc. With French inflation rates lower than those of Germany, the Banque de France began lowering short-term interest rates during the spring of 1993 and continued lowering them throughout the summer. The French bank may have assumed that the background of firm French monetary policy since the mid-1980s would give it some leeway to lower short-term rates below the Bundesbank levels without weakening the franc. In the event, this proved incorrect. A full assault on the franc erupted in August. Even a coordinated intervention by the Bundesbank and other institutions failed, and the franc weakened rapidly.

To help protect the franc, and to avoid having to expend more resources in a futile fight, the ERM countries agreed that they would widen the bands in which currencies could diverge from each other from 2.25 percent to 15.0 percent. They assumed, correctly, that this change would stop the speculative assault on the franc. However, it also signified the collapse of the franc, one of the main currencies of the EMS. Only a few minor currencies remained as stable as the deutsche mark. However, the franc was able to recover later in 1993 to virtual parity with the deutsche mark.

The two ERM crises left the prospects for the EMU uncertain. It seemed unlikely that more than two or three minor currencies would be able to meet the convergence criteria by 1997, and the system could not then come into effect because it would not include the majority of the countries of the EU. Under those circumstances, the earliest possible date for the EMU to take effect would be 1999, and even that target date would come into question if the EMU at that point were to encompass nothing more than the deutsche mark, the French franc, and some minor currencies. The German minister for economics, Günter Rexrodt, predicted in mid-1994 that the EMU might not come about until 2001 or later.

The Bundesbank had shown its readiness to exercise its power to shape and even to dictate the policies of other central banks. It had shown that, if Europe were no longer to be dominated by the Bundesbank itself, it should at least be dominated by the Bundesbank's ideals. The bank's Central Bank Council hoped that others would come to appreciate the value of stable money through the experience of having unstable money. But in case all central banks did not agree, Bundesbank president Tietmeyer said after the September 1992 crisis that the bank was prepared to accept what he called "*gestaffeltes Vorgehen*" (membership by stages), a process by which some states would join before others. The bank was clearly prepared to forego the EMU, or at least to postpone it, if the EMU might bring unqualified members into a common European currency system. And it was prepared to split the EMU, if necessary, to create at least a partial zone of European currency stability.

The bank's stern views should not lead to the conclusion that the Bundesbank opposes a European currency. Indeed, several senior Bundesbank figures have at various times expressed their conviction that a common European currency is desirable. Such a currency would ease one of the burdens felt by the Bundesbank: it must now defend stability with only its own reserves and those of its immediate allies instead of with the reserves of an entire continent. Former Central Bank Council member Leonhard Gleske once spoke with envy about how the large domestic market of the United States helped the dollar adjust more easily than any single European currency to global fluctuations and crises. Gleske also observed that one of the objectives of a European currency would be to assume the leading international role that even the deutsche mark could not assume and that such a European currency could gradually replace the dollar as a transactions and reserve currency. This prospect must be a powerful incentive for the Bundesbank, which has long distrusted United States monetary and fiscal policies.

The crises of 1992 and 1993 did not discourage other EU members from accepting Bundesbank discipline. They agreed later in 1993 to place the new European Monetary Institute as well as the future ECB in Frankfurt. That decision was a vote of confidence, or at least acceptance, for Bundesbank policies and attitudes, because Frankfurt is not only the home of the Bundesbank but is also regarded as the capital of German monetarist thinking.

A full EMU will come about when the Bundesbank is satisfied that all European governments are fully committed to stability and when they have shown this commitment by adhering to the convergence criteria and by passing whatever other tests the bank may yet pose. As Bundesbank officials have said on every possible occasion, the Bundesbank believes that a stable currency is more important than a common currency. And the German government, although it supports the EMU, must accept the Bundesbank's policies if it is to secure the support of the German people for a common European currency.

Foreign Trade and Investment

Trade Philosophy and the Trade Balance

West Germany has been one of the world's major trading nations, almost from the first days of the economic miracle that began in the early 1950s (see The Economic Miracle and Beyond, ch. 5). It also had high trade and current-account surpluses during most of these years, especially during the latter half of the 1980s (see table 20, Appendix). It was the world's largest exporter in 1988, second largest after the United States in 1989, and first again in 1990 if East German exports before monetary unification in mid-1990 are included. West Germany was also consistently one of the world's largest importers.

Ludwig Erhard set the tone for the future of German trade policy and practice when he was minister for economics in the early days of the Federal Republic. He made his own sentiments very clear, saying in 1953 that "foreign trade is not a specialized activity for a few who might engage in it, but it is the very core and even the precondition of our economic and social order." Commentators and authors on the German economy speak of a German "export mystique," of deliberate domestic underconsumption to facilitate exports and increase competitiveness, and of an "almost unconscious" German mercantilism. The export sector has a powerful voice in German economic and commercial policy making, including a special Foreign Trade Advisory Council located in the Ministry for Economics. Senior German political figures rarely make visits abroad without including select German businesspeople in their official delegations.

The German economy has failed to heed the export mystique only once, when the Hitler regime (1933–45) sought autarchy, or economic independence from the global economy. Between 1910 and 1913, exports accounted for 17.8 percent of Germany's GDP. Their share declined to 14.9 percent in the second half of the 1920s and fell to only 6 percent in the second half of the 1930s, but by 1950 accounted for 9.3 percent of West Germany's GDP. Once the postwar economic boom got under way, exports rose to 17.2 percent of GDP in 1960, to 23.8 percent in 1970, to 26.7 percent in 1980, and to approximately 33 percent in 1990.

Investment goods produced by West German industry were the most successful export items and contributed most heavily to the country's large trade surplus, although West Germany was competitive across a wide range of goods. The country imported more agricultural and processed food products than it exported (see table 21, Appendix).

A number of West German industries dedicated significant percentages of their production for export: shipbuilding, 62 percent; air and space, 59 percent; automotive products, 48 percent; machine tools, 45 percent; chemicals, 44 percent; iron and steel, 37 percent; and precision mechanics and optics, 31 percent.

Several of the industries with a high export share, such as shipbuilding and airframes, were heavily subsidized in West Germany and have continued to be subsidized in united Germany. They are competitive in world markets on the basis of those subsidies. The subsidies demonstrate the extent of the German export commitment. West Germany would have had a substantial trade surplus even without the subsidized products of those industries, but it did not wish to sacrifice their global market share.

After German unification, Germany's trade surplus shrank for several years. Whereas West Germany had shown a dramatically high trade surplus during the late 1980s until 1990, reaching almost US$80 billion in 1988, united Germany by 1991 was showing a much smaller surplus. Nonetheless, it was widely expected that large surpluses would return by the mid-1990s as the *Länder* of the former East Germany began to export more and required fewer imports.

Especially crucial to the future foreign trade position of united Germany will be the competitiveness of industry in the new *Länder* of the former East Germany, which could not be predicted with any reliability in the years immediately following unification. During 1993 only 2 percent of German exports came from the new *Länder*. It was unclear whether this area's competitiveness had been destroyed, or whether the West German producers that had bought East German firms had decided to continue to export from their western firms instead of from their newly acquired eastern firms. Whatever happened, it is worth remembering that the new *Länder*, like the western *Länder*, had generated a consistent trade surplus in capital and transport equipment, industrial consumer goods, and chemicals before unification. They could be expected to return to competitiveness in at least some of those areas. East Germany also suffered from several major shortages before unification, having trade deficits in fuels, raw materials, semi-manufactures, agricultural products, and processed foods. Most of those deficits would persist even after unification.

With Germany united, the government expects trade with Eastern Europe to increase well over the levels West Germany had enjoyed and ultimately to exceed the level of separate East German and West German trade with Eastern Europe before unification. In fact, Germany's most important and most consistent policy since 1990 has been to improve its connections to Eastern Europe without loosening its links to the West and thus to bring Eastern Europe and Western Europe together. After the fall of communism, German business representatives began visiting Eastern Europe in large numbers to establish or reestablish trade connections and to inspect potential investment sites or joint ventures.

German economic links and outposts are being reestablished in Central Europe and Eastern Europe. The Czech Republic is again becoming an integral part of the industrial complex centered in Bavaria and Saxony, as Bohemia and Moravia were before World War I. The frontier region between Poland and Germany is already one of the most active border investment and trading centers in the world, beginning to emulate the Mexico-United States border and the Hong Kong hinterland as a place where Western capital meets non-Western labor and where goods are processed and exchanged freely. Cross-border traffic in goods and persons is burgeoning. German trade and investment being planned for the countries of the former Soviet Union and for Eastern Europe will make united Germany by far the largest single Western trading partner as well as the largest Western creditor of those states.

Germany has provided more aid and investment to the former Soviet republics than any other West European state, contributing US$52 billion in aid to Russia and other members of the former Soviet Union between 1989 and 1993 as well as US$25 billion to the states of Central and Eastern Europe. More than one-half of East European and Baltic trade with the EU is with Germany. Other types of economic activities are also becoming common. For example, by 1994 the Deutsche Bank had opened a branch office in Prague and planned to open others throughout Eastern Europe.

As part of that effort to speed the East's integration with Western Europe, Germany has not only endorsed but has often sponsored association agreements with the EU for the states of Eastern Europe and the former Soviet Union. It has also sponsored several East European applications for EU membership. Kohl himself told Hungarians and Czechs in April 1994 that the EU without their countries would be a "torso." A month earlier, he told the Baltic states that they belonged in the EU as much as the Mediterranean states. Kohl also strongly advocated Russian membership in the annual Group of Seven (G–7) meetings—at least for political discussions.

The credits that Germany has been giving to its Eastern trading partners are not without risk. Russian and East European debt has been accumulating for several decades. Virtually every East European state had trouble servicing its debts during the early 1990s, and special arrangements had to be made to reschedule Poland's debt. Nonetheless, the German government and German banks were prepared to extend further credits despite nagging doubts about when the credits would be repaid. German determination to increase trade with Eastern Europe and to invest more in that area reflects tradition as well as economic and political interest. Moreover, Germany is better located than any other West European state to trade with Eastern Europe, especially because Berlin remains one of the most attractive potential production, assembly, service, and transportation centers for East European trade.

International Investment in and by Germany

Before unification, West Germany had been a principal exporter of capital. This status was indicative of the capital surplus the country's firms and banks held abroad as a result of export earnings, but it was also a sign of the growing disparity between production costs in West Germany and abroad. Many West German manufacturers preferred to produce in other countries where lower costs might give them a greater competitive edge than they might have operating from a West German base. Therefore, during most of the years between 1960 and 1989, and especially during the 1980s, the amount of West German investment abroad exceeded the level of foreign investment in West Germany.

West German and later German direct investment abroad remained high even around the time of unification, totaling DM37.4 billion in 1990, DM37.1 billion in 1991, and DM28.1 billion in 1992. During those years, foreign direct investment in West Germany or unified Germany never exceeded DM6.2 billion per year.

The nature of West Germany's investment abroad was different from foreign investment in West Germany. About one-fourth to one-third, and sometimes as much as one-half, of West German investment abroad during the 1970s and 1980s represented direct investment in production facilities, the remainder being investment in various forms of long-term credits such as equities, bonds, and long-term bank deposits. However, relatively little foreign investment in West Germany

Central Hamburg
Courtesy Hamburg-North America Representation, New York

during that period was in production facilities, with the annual share ranging from about one-twentieth to one-sixth of all foreign investment. Instead, the dominant form of investment in West Germany was in West German equities and bonds.

Foreign investment in German stocks and bonds was especially heavy during the early 1990s. During 1991 that investment amounted to DM37.4 billion; in 1992 it rose to DM62.0 billion. Both amounts were far higher than foreign investment in German securities during any earlier year. As a result, Germany had a long-term capital surplus of DM46.6 billion during 1992, the highest amount West Germany or unified Germany had ever recorded and a striking departure from West Germany's chronic capital deficit.

According to Bundesbank statistics, one-fifth of all German securities at the end of 1990 belonged to foreigners, and one-half of all German publicly offered obligations between 1986 and 1990 had been bought by foreigners. Much of the investment appears to have been motivated by the expectation that the deutsche mark would appreciate and that investment in German funds would thus produce an exchange profit as well as regular income. Much of it may also have reflected the sense that German long-term interest rates would decline as the burdens of unification eased.

Because of the large amount of German direct investment abroad, German income from foreign investments exceeds income of foreigners investing in Germany. Bundesbank statistics showed that the net return on West German capital abroad had risen to almost DM25 billion by 1989. If Germans were going abroad to invest, they were drawing a significant return income.

In 1988, of West German foreign investment, 52 percent was in Europe (with 41 percent in EC countries), 40 percent was in the Americas (with 28 percent in the United States), and only 6 percent was in Asia (with 2 percent in Japan). The favorite sites for West German foreign investment were France and Britain. A fast-growing amount was going to Eastern Europe. A survey conducted by a German economic institute showed that more than twice as much new German investment at the end of 1993 was going to the states of Central Europe and Eastern Europe as to West European states, with the largest amount by far going to the Czech Republic.

The structural problems of German production were compelling German investors to abandon production in Germany—including eastern Germany—and were making locations in other countries more competitive. Even before unification, many German industrialists and investors had been moving German production facilities to other EC states, especially Spain and Portugal, or to the United States or other countries where labor costs were lower. German efficiency, thoroughness, and quality control could only compensate up to a point for the cost advantage that producers in other countries increasingly enjoyed. The combination of high labor costs, a high level of subsidization, and a strong currency was putting German producers at a growing disadvantage at precisely the moment when the costs of unification were becoming particularly burdensome.

Foreign Aid

Although Germany is a leader in foreign trade, it has never

been generous with foreign aid. West German official developmental assistance between 1976 and 1989 ranged between 0.40 and 0.47 percent of German GDP, well below the 0.70 standard proposed by the United Nations (UN). German aid sank to 0.36 percent of GDP in 1993 as the costs of unification reinforced the reluctance of the German government to grant assistance. But German private contributions to international causes, especially for humanitarian purposes, are consistently high. During 1992 those contributions matched the level of official assistance.

Because Germany was not involved in the wave of decolonization that followed World War II, it has not had the special links to former colonies that have helped to motivate and channel aid by such former colonial powers as France and Britain. The largest portion of West German aid, over 40 percent, went to Africa during the 1980s. Earlier, West Germany had sent more aid to Asia, but that portion fell to 30 percent during the 1980s because the Asian economic boom made aid less necessary. Relatively little aid went to the Americas.

*   *   *

The literature on German external economic relations is as limited as the general literature on the German economy. The most comprehensive current books in English are *The German Economy* by W.R. Smyser and *The German Economy* by Eric Owen Smith. An annual economic survey of Germany published by the Organisation for Economic Co-operation and Development (OECD) contains current information on German external economic relations, as does the OECD biannual, *OECD Economic Outlook*. The Bundesbank publishes a monthly statistical compilation on German trade, current account, and foreign investment balances, but only in German.

Two books about the specific German role in European economics are *The Federal Republic of Germany and the European Community* by Simon Bulmer and William Paterson and *Germany's International Monetary Policy and the European Monetary System* by Hugo M. Kaufmann. A work that offers discussion of the competitive weaknesses of the German economy is *Die japanisch-amerikanische Herausforderung* by Konrad Seitz. Several books on the European economy and the EU offer some information about Germany's role in European economics. These include *The National Economies of Europe*, edited by David A. Dyker, *The*

Economics of European Integration by Willem Molle, and *Euro-Politics*, edited by Alberta M. Sbragia. Books of this kind appear regularly and provide a continuing picture of the growing German role in European economics. (For further information and complete citations, see Bibliography.)

Chapter 7. Government and Politics

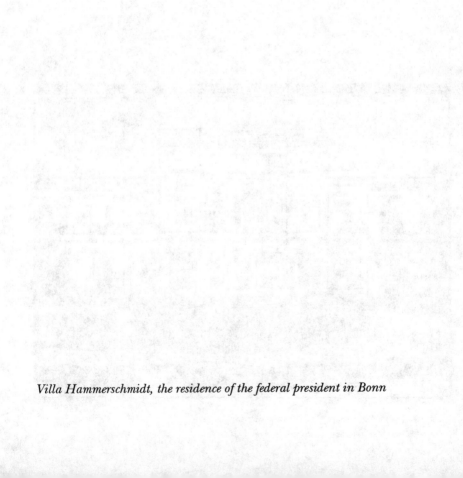

Villa Hammerschmidt, the residence of the federal president in Bonn

AS OF MID-1995, GERMANY was a country coming to terms with the recent unification of its western and eastern portions following four decades of Cold War division. Achieved in October 1990, German unification consisted, in effect, of the incorporation of the German Democratic Republic (GDR, or East Germany) into the Federal Republic of Germany (FRG, or West Germany). Thus, the unified country, rather than reflecting a mix of both states' systems, largely represented a continuation of the West German political and economic system. West German chancellor Helmut Kohl preferred this "fast track" to unification, outlined in Article 23 of the West German Basic Law, or constitution, because he feared that international circumstances might change and the chance for unification might be missed. The alternative path to unification, detailed in Article 146, would have required the replacement of the Basic Law with a constitution developed specifically for a unified Germany.

During the summer of 1990, the governments of the two German states drafted a 1,000-page treaty outlining the terms of political union. The document explained how the political structures and policies of West Germany would be extended to the east, how other institutions—such as the education system—would be coordinated, and which issues would be resolved later—for instance, abortion policy. The parliaments of both German states ratified the treaty, and the territory of East Germany joined the Federal Republic under Article 23 on October 3, 1990.

The West German system of government, outlined in the Basic Law, reflects in particular a desire to transcend the interwar period of democratic instability and dictatorship. A federal system of government, considered vital to a stable, constitutional democracy, was put in place as a direct response to lessons learned from the Nazis' misuse of centralized structures. After four years of Allied occupation, the FRG was established in 1949. The country attained sovereignty in 1955 when the Allies transferred responsibility for national security to the newly formed armed forces, the Bundeswehr.

Creating a climate of political stability was a primary goal of the authors of West Germany's Basic Law. Among other things, the Basic Law established the supremacy of political parties in the system of government. In the resulting "party state," all major government policies emanated from the organizational structure of the political parties. In the decades since 1949, West Germany's parties have tended toward the middle of the political spectrum, largely because both the historical experience with fascism and the existence of communist East Germany greatly diminished the appeal of either extreme. This reigning political consensus, challenged briefly in the late 1960s by the student protest movement and in the early 1980s by economic recession, has led many observers to judge the "Bonn model" a success. However, it remains an open question whether the legal, economic, and political structures of the past will serve the unified Germany as well in the future.

Constitutional Framework

The Constitution

The framers of the Federal Republic of Germany's 1949 constitution sought to create safeguards against the emergence of either an overly fragmented, multiparty democracy, similar to the Weimar Republic (1918–33), or authoritarian institutions characteristic of the Nazi dictatorship of the Third Reich (1933–45). Thus, negative historical experience played a major role in shaping the constitution.

Articles 1 through 19 delineate basic rights that apply to all German citizens, including equality before the law; freedom of speech, assembly, the news media, and worship; freedom from discrimination based on race, gender, religion, or political beliefs; and the right to conscientious objection to compulsory military service. In reaction to the experience of the Third Reich, the framers of the Basic Law did, however, place limits on extremist political activities that might threaten to subvert the democratic political order. Article 18 states: "Whoever abuses freedom of expression of opinion, in particular freedom of the press, freedom of teaching, freedom of assembly, freedom of association, privacy of posts and telecommunications, property, or the right of asylum in order to combat the free democratic basic order, shall forfeit these basic rights." Article 18 was employed twice in the 1950s to ban political parties of the extreme right and left. Article 18 is seen as an essential component of a *wehrhafte Demokratie*—a democracy that can defend itself, unlike the Weimar Republic.

Article 20 states that "the Federal Republic of Germany is a democratic and social federal state." The word "social" has been commonly interpreted to mean that the state has the responsibility to provide for the basic social welfare of its citizens. The Basic Law, however, does not enumerate specific social duties of the state. Further, according to Article 20, "All state authority emanates from the people. It shall be exercised by the people by means of elections and voting and by specific legislative, executive, and judicial organs."

Most of the Basic Law's 146 articles describe the composition and functions of various organs of government, as well as the intricate system of checks and balances governing their interaction. Other major issues addressed in the Basic Law include the distribution of power between the federal government and the state (*Land*; pl., *Länder*) governments, the administration of federal laws, government finance, and government administration under emergency conditions. The Basic Law is virtually silent on economic matters; only Article 14 guarantees "property and the right of inheritance" and states that "expropriation shall be permitted only in the public weal."

Any amendment to the Basic Law must receive the support of at least two-thirds of the members in both federal legislative chambers—the Bundestag (Federal Diet or lower house) and the Bundesrat (Federal Council or upper house). Certain provisions of the Basic Law cannot be amended: those relating to the essential structures of federalism; the division of powers; the principles of democracy, social welfare, and fundamental rights; and the principle of state power based on law. Of the many amendments to the Basic Law, among the most notable are the "defense addenda" of 1954–56, which regulate the constitutional position of the armed forces, and the "Emergency Constitution" of 1968, which delineates wider executive powers in the case of an internal or external emergency.

Federalism

Germany has a strong tradition of regional government dating back to the founding of the German Empire in 1871. Since unification in 1990, the Federal Republic has consisted of sixteen *Länder*: the ten *Länder* of the former West Germany, the five new *Länder* of the former East Germany, and Berlin. (However, Berlin and the eastern *Land* of Brandenburg are slated to merge in either 1999 or 2002.) The *Land* governments are based on a parliamentary system. Most *Länder* have unicameral legislatures, whose members are elected directly by popular vote. The party or coalition of parties in control of the legislature chooses a minister president to lead the *Land* government. The minister president selects a cabinet to run *Land* agencies and carry out the executive functions of the *Land* government. Minister presidents are highly visible national figures and often progress to federal office, either the chancellorship or a position in the federal cabinet.

The Basic Law divides authority between the federal government and the *Länder*, with the general principle governing relations articulated in Article 30: "The exercise of governmental powers and the discharge of governmental functions shall be incumbent on the *Länder* insofar as this Basic Law does not otherwise prescribe or permit." Thus, the federal government can exercise authority only in those areas specified in the Basic Law. The federal government is assigned a greater legislative role and the *Land* governments a greater administrative role. The fact that more civil servants are employed by *Land* governments than by federal and local governments combined illustrates the central administrative function of the *Länder*.

The Basic Law divides the federal government's legislative responsibilities into exclusive powers (Articles 71 and 73), concurrent powers (Articles 72, 74, and 74a), and framework powers (Article 75). The exclusive legislative jurisdiction of the federal government extends to defense, foreign affairs, immigration, transportation, communications, and currency standards. The federal and *Land* governments share concurrent powers in several areas, including civil law, refugee and expellee matters, public welfare, land management, consumer protection, public health, and the collection of vital statistics (data on births, deaths, and marriages). In the areas of mass media, nature conservation, regional planning, and public service regulations, framework legislation limits the federal government's role to offering general policy guidelines, which the *Länder* then act upon by means of detailed legislation. The areas of shared responsibility for the *Länder* and the federal government were enlarged by an amendment to the Basic Law in 1969 (Articles 91a and 91b), which calls for joint action in areas of broad social concern such as higher education, regional economic development, and agricultural reform.

All policy areas not assigned to federal jurisdiction are within the legislative purview of the *Länder*. These areas include education, law enforcement, regulation of radio and television, church affairs, and cultural activities. The *Länder* retain significant powers of taxation. Most federal taxes are collected by *Land* officials.

The *Land* governments also exercise power at the national level through the Bundesrat, which is made up of representatives appointed by the *Land* governments. In this way, the *Länder* affect the federal legislative process (see The Legislature, this ch.). Half of the members of the Federal Convention, which elects a federal president, are *Land* officials, and the *Land* governments also take part in the selection of judges for the federal courts.

Government Institutions

The President

The Basic Law creates a dual executive but grants most executive authority to the federal chancellor, as head of government, rather than to the president, who acts as head of state (see fig. 13). The presidency is primarily a ceremonial post, and its occupant represents the Federal Republic in international relations. In that sphere, the president's duties include signing treaties, representing Germany abroad, and receiving foreign dignitaries. In the domestic sphere, the president has largely ceremonial functions. Although this official signs legislation into law, grants pardons, and appoints federal judges, federal civil servants, and military officers, each of these actions requires the countersignature of the chancellor or the relevant cabinet minister. The president formally proposes to the Bundestag a chancellor candidate and formally appoints the chancellor's cabinet members, but the president follows the choice of the Bundestag in the first case and of the chancellor in the second. If the government loses a simple no-confidence vote, the president dissolves the Bundestag, but here, too, the Basic Law limits the president's ability to act independently. In the event of a national crisis, the emergency law reforms of 1968 designate the president as a mediator who can declare a state of emergency.

There is disagreement about whether the president, in fact, has greater powers than the above description would suggest. Some argue that nothing in the Basic Law suggests that a president must follow government directives. For instance, the president could refuse to sign legislation, thus vetoing it, or refuse to approve certain cabinet appointments. As of mid-1995, no

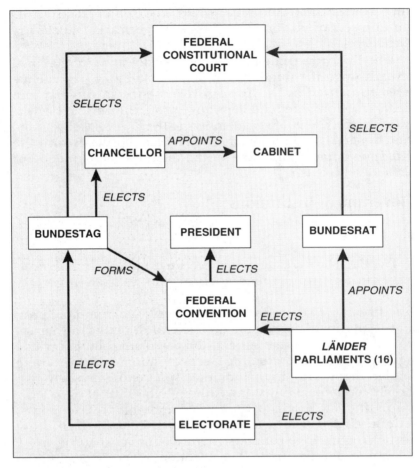

FEDERAL
CONSTITUTIONAL
COURT

SELECTS

SELECTS

CHANCELLOR — APPOINTS → CABINET

ELECTS

BUNDESTAG

PRESIDENT

BUNDESRAT

FORMS

ELECTS

APPOINTS

FEDERAL
CONVENTION

ELECTS

ELECTS

LÄNDER
PARLIAMENTS (16)

ELECTS

ELECTORATE

ELECTS

Source: Based on information from Russell J. Dalton, *Politics in Germany*, New York, 1993, 48; and Arno Kappler and Adriane Grevels, eds., *Facts about Germany*, Frankfurt am Main, 1994, 145.

Figure 13. Structure of the Government, 1995

president had ever taken such action, and thus the constitutionality of these points had never been tested.

The president is selected by secret ballot at a Federal Convention that includes all Bundestag members and an equal number of delegates chosen by the *Land* legislatures. This assemblage, which totals more than 1,000 people, is convened every five years. It may select a president for a second, but not a third, five-year term. The authors of the Basic Law preferred this indirect form of presidential election because they believed it would produce a head of state who was widely acceptable and insulated from popular pressure. Candidates for the presidency must be at least forty years old.

The Basic Law did not create an office of vice president. If the president is outside the country or if the position is vacant, the president of the Bundesrat fills in as the temporary head of state. If the president dies in office, a successor is elected within thirty days.

Usually one of the senior leaders of the largest party in the Bundestag, the president nonetheless is expected to be non-partisan after assuming office. For example, President Richard von Weizsäcker, whose second term expired in June 1994, was the former Christian Democratic mayor of Berlin. Upon becoming president in 1984, he resigned from his party positions. Weizsäcker played a prominent role in urging Germans to come to terms with their actions during the Third Reich and in calling for greater tolerance toward foreigners in Germany as right-wing violence escalated in the early 1990s. Although the formal powers of the president are limited, the president's role can be quite significant depending on his or her own activities. Between 1949 and 1994, the Christian Democratic Union (Christlich Demokratische Union—CDU) held the office for twenty-five years, the Free Democratic Party (Freie Demokratische Partei—FDP) for fifteen, and the Social Democratic Party of Germany (Sozialdemokratische Partei Deutschlands—SPD) for five (see table 2, Appendix).

Elected by the Federal Convention in May 1994, Roman Herzog succeeded Weizsäcker as President on July 1, 1994. Previously president of the Federal Constitutional Court in Karlsruhe, Germany's highest court, he was nominated for the presidency by the CDU and its sister party, the Christian Social Union (Christlich-Soziale Union—CSU).

The Chancellor and the Cabinet

The federal government consists of the chancellor and his or her cabinet ministers. As explained above, the Basic Law invests the chancellor with central executive authority. For that reason, some observers refer to the German political system as a "chancellor democracy." The chancellor's authority emanates from the provisions of the Basic Law and from his or her status as leader of the party or coalition of parties holding a majority of seats in the Bundestag. Every four years, after national elections and the seating of the newly elected Bundestag members, the federal president nominates a chancellor candidate to that parliamentary body; the chancellor is elected by majority vote in the Bundestag.

The Basic Law limits parliament's control over the chancellor and the cabinet. Unlike most parliamentary legislatures, the Bundestag cannot remove the chancellor simply with a vote of no-confidence. In the Weimar Republic, this procedure was abused by parties of both political extremes in order to oppose chancellors and undermine the democratic process. As a consequence, the Basic Law allows only for a "constructive vote of no-confidence." That is, the Bundestag can remove a chancellor only when it simultaneously agrees on a successor. This legislative mechanism ensures both an orderly transfer of power and an initial parliamentary majority in support of the new chancellor. The constructive no-confidence vote makes it harder to remove a chancellor because opponents of the chancellor not only must disagree with his or her governing but also must agree on a replacement.

As of 1995, the Bundestag had tried to pass a constructive no-confidence vote twice, but had succeeded only once. In 1972 the opposition parties tried to replace Chancellor Willy Brandt of the SPD with the CDU party leader because of profound disagreements over the government's policies toward Eastern Europe. The motion fell one vote shy of the necessary majority. In late 1982, the CDU convinced the FDP to leave its coalition with the SPD over differences on economic policy and to form a new government with the CDU and the CSU. The constructive no-confidence vote resulted in the replacement of Chancellor Helmut Schmidt with Helmut Kohl, the CDU party leader. Observers agree that the constructive no-confidence vote has increased political stability in Germany.

The chancellor also may make use of a second type of no-confidence vote to garner legislative support in the Bundestag. The chancellor can append a simple no-confidence provision to any government legislative proposal. If the Bundestag rejects the proposal, the chancellor may request that the president dissolve parliament and call new elections. Although not commonly used, this procedure enables the chancellor to gauge support in the Bundestag for the government and to increase pressure on the Bundestag to vote in favor of legislation that the government considers as critical. Furthermore, governments have employed this simple no-confidence motion as a means of bringing about early Bundestag elections. For exam-

Richard von Weizsäcker,
president, 1984–94
Courtesy German
Information Center, New York

ple, after Kohl became chancellor through the constructive no-confidence vote in August 1982, his government purposely set out to lose a simple no-confidence provision in order to bring about new elections and give voters a chance to validate the new government through a democratic election.

Article 65 of the Basic Law sets forth three principles that define how the executive branch functions. First, the "chancellor principle" makes the chancellor responsible for all government policies. Any formal policy guidelines issued by the chancellor are legally binding directives that cabinet ministers must implement. Cabinet ministers are expected to introduce specific policies at the ministerial level that reflect the chancellor's broader guidelines. Second, the "principle of ministerial autonomy" entrusts each minister with the freedom to supervise departmental operations and prepare legislative proposals without cabinet interference so long as the minister's policies are consistent with the chancellor's larger guidelines. Third, the "cabinet principle" calls for disagreements between federal ministers over jurisdictional or budgetary matters to be settled by the cabinet.

The chancellor determines the composition of the cabinet. The federal president formally appoints and dismisses cabinet ministers, at the recommendation of the chancellor; no

Bundestag approval is needed. According to the Basic Law, the chancellor may set the number of cabinet ministers and dictate their specific duties. Chancellor Ludwig Erhard had the largest cabinet, with twenty-two ministers, in the mid-1960s. Kohl presided over seventeen ministers at the start of his fourth term in 1994.

The power of the smaller coalition partners, the FDP and the CSU, was evident from the distribution of cabinet posts in Kohl's government in 1995. The FDP held three ministries— the Ministry of Foreign Affairs, Ministry of Justice, and Ministry for Economics. CSU members led four ministries—the Ministry of Finance, Ministry for Health, Ministry for Post and Telecommunications, and Ministry for Economic Cooperation.

The staff of a cabinet minister is managed by at least two state secretaries, both of whom are career civil servants responsible for the ministry's administration, and a parliamentary state secretary, who is generally a member of the Bundestag and represents the ministry there and in other political forums. Typically, state secretaries remain in the ministry beyond the tenure of any one government, in contrast to the parliamentary state secretary, who is a political appointee and is viewed as a junior member of the government whose term ends with the minister's. Under these top officials, the ministries are organized functionally in accordance with each one's specific responsibilities. Career civil servants constitute virtually the entire staff of the ministries.

The Legislature

The heart of any parliamentary system of government is the legislature. Germany has a bicameral parliament. The two chambers are the Bundestag (Federal Diet or lower house) and the Bundesrat (Federal Council or upper house). Both chambers can initiate legislation, and most bills must be approved by both chambers, as well as the executive branch, before becoming law. Legislation on issues within the exclusive jurisdiction of the federal government, such as international treaties, does not require Bundesrat approval.

The federal government introduces most legislation; when it does so, the Bundesrat reviews the bill and then passes it on to the Bundestag. If a bill originates in the Bundesrat, it is submitted to the Bundestag through the executive branch. If the Bundestag introduces a bill, it is sent first to the Bundesrat and, if approved there, forwarded to the executive. The Joint Con-

*Helmut Kohl, federal
chancellor, 1982–
Courtesy German
Information Center, New York*

ference Committee resolves any differences over legislation between the two legislative chambers. Once the compromise bill that emerges from the conference committee has been approved by a majority in both chambers and by the cabinet, it is signed into law by the federal president and countersigned by the relevant cabinet minister.

Bundestag

The Bundestag is the principal legislative chamber, roughly analogous to the United States House of Representatives. The Bundestag has grown gradually since its creation, most dramatically with unification and the addition of 144 new representatives from eastern Germany, for a total of 656 deputies in 1990. A further expansion in 1994 increased the number to 672. Elections are held every four years (or earlier if a government falls from power). Bundestag members are the only federal officials directly elected by the public. All candidates must be at least twenty-one years old; there are no term limits.

The most important organizational structures within the Bundestag are parliamentary groups (*Fraktionen*; sing., *Fraktion*), which are formed by each political party represented in the chamber. The size of a party's *Fraktion* determines the extent of its representation on legislative committees, the number of committee chairs it can hold, and its representation in executive bodies of the Bundestag. The head of the largest *Fraktion* is named president of the Bundestag. The *Fraktionen,* not the members, receive the bulk of government funding for legislative and administrative activities.

The leadership of each *Fraktion* consists of a parliamentary party leader, several deputy leaders, and an executive committee. The leadership's major responsibilities are to represent the *Fraktion,* enforce party discipline, and orchestrate the party's parliamentary activities. The members of each *Fraktion* are distributed among working groups focused on specific policy-related topics such as social policy, economics, and foreign policy. The *Fraktion* meets once a week to consider legislation before the Bundestag and formulate the party's position on it.

The Bundestag's executive bodies include the Council of Elders and the Presidium. The council consists of the Bundestag leadership, together with the most senior representatives of each *Fraktion,* with the number of these representatives tied to the strength of the party in the chamber. The council is the coordination hub, determining the daily legislative agenda and assigning committee chairpersons based on party representation. The council also serves as an important forum for interparty negotiations on specific legislation and procedural issues. The Presidium is responsible for the routine administration of the Bundestag, including its clerical and research activities. It consists of the chamber's president and vice presidents (one from each *Fraktion*).

Most of the legislative work in the Bundestag is the product of standing committees. Although this is common practice in the United States Congress, it is uncommon in other parliamentary systems, such as the British House of Commons and the French National Assembly. The number of committees approximates the number of federal ministries, and the titles of each are roughly similar (e.g., defense, agriculture, and labor). Between 1987 and 1990, the term of the eleventh Bundestag, there were twenty-one standing committees. The distribution of committee chairs and the membership of each committee reflect the relative strength of the various parties in the chamber. In the eleventh Bundestag, the CDU/CSU chaired eleven committees, the SPD eight, the FDP one, and the environmentalist party, the Greens (Die Grünen), one. Unlike in the United States Congress, where all committees are chaired by members of the majority party, the German system allows members of the opposition party to chair a significant number of standing committees. These committees have either a small staff or no staff at all.

Although most legislation is initiated by the executive branch, the Bundestag considers the legislative function its most important responsibility. The Bundestag concentrates much of its energy on assessing and amending the government's legislative program. The committees play a prominent role in this process. Plenary sessions provide a forum for members to engage in public debate on legislative issues before them, but they tend to be well attended only when significant legislation is being considered. The Bundestag allots each *Fraktion* a certain amount of time, based on its size, to express its views.

Other responsibilities of the Bundestag include selecting the federal chancellor and exercising oversight of the executive branch on issues of both substantive policy and routine administration. This check on executive power can be employed through binding legislation, public debates on government policy, investigations, and direct questioning of the chancellor or cabinet officials. For example, the Bundestag can conduct a question hour (*Fragestunde*), in which a government representative responds to a previously submitted written question from a member. Members can ask related questions during the question hour. The questions can concern anything from a major policy issue to a specific constituent's problem. Use of the question hour has increased markedly over the past forty years, with more than 20,000 questions being posed during the 1987–90 Bundestag term. Understandably, the opposition parties are active in exercising the parliamentary right to scrutinize government actions.

One striking difference when comparing the Bundestag with the United States Congress is the lack of time spent on serving constituents in Germany. In part, that difference results from the fact that only 50 percent of Bundestag deputies are directly elected to represent a specific geographic district; the other half are elected as party representatives. The political parties are thus of great importance in Germany's electoral system, and many voters tend not to see the candidates as autonomous political personalities but rather as creatures of the party. Interestingly, constituent service seems not to be perceived, either by the electorate or by the representatives, as a critical function of the legislator. A practical constraint on the expansion of constituent service is the limited personal staff of Bundestag deputies.

Bundesrat

The second legislative chamber, the Bundesrat, is the federal body in which the sixteen *Land* governments are directly represented. It exemplifies Germany's federalist system of government. Members of the Bundesrat are not popularly elected but are appointed by their respective *Land* governments. Members tend to be *Land* government ministers. The Bundesrat has sixty-nine members. The *Länder* with more than 7 million inhabitants have six seats (Baden-Württemberg, Bavaria, Lower Saxony, and North Rhine-Westphalia). The *Länder* with populations of between 2 million and 7 million have four seats (Berlin, Brandenburg, Hesse, Mecklenburg-Western Pomerania, Rhineland-Palatinate, Saxony, Saxony-Anhalt, Schleswig-Holstein, and Thuringia). The least populous *Länder*, with fewer than 2 million inhabitants, receive three seats each (Bremen, Hamburg, and the Saarland). This system of representation, although designed to reflect *Land* populations accurately, in fact affords greater representation per inhabitant to the smaller *Länder*. The presidency of the Bundesrat rotates annually among the *Länder*. By law, each Land delegation is required to vote as a bloc in accordance with the instructions of the *Land* government.

Because the Bundesrat is so much smaller than the Bundestag, it does not require the extensive organizational structure of the lower house. The Bundesrat typically schedules plenary sessions once a month for the purpose of voting on legislation prepared in committee. In comparison, the Bundestag conducts about fifty plenary sessions a year. Bundesrat representatives rarely attend committee sessions; instead, they delegate that responsibility to civil servants from their ministries, as allowed for in the Basic Law. The members tend to spend most of their time in their *Land* capitals, rather than in the federal capital.

The legislative authority of the Bundesrat is subordinate to that of the Bundestag, but the upper house nonetheless plays a vital legislative role. The federal government must present all legislative initiatives first to the Bundesrat; only thereafter can a proposal be passed to the Bundestag. Further, the Bundesrat must approve all legislation affecting policy areas for which the Basic Law grants the *Länder* concurrent powers and for which

*The old Reichstag building is to become the seat of the Bundestag when
it moves to Berlin in the late 1990s.
The plenary chamber of the Bundestag in Bonn
Courtesy German Information Center, New York*

the *Länder* must administer federal regulations. The Bundesrat has increased its legislative responsibilities over time by successfully arguing for a broad, rather than a narrow, interpretation of what constitutes the range of legislation affecting *Land* interests. In 1949 only 10 percent of all federal laws, namely, those directly affecting the *Länder*, required Bundesrat approval. In 1993 close to 60 percent of federal legislation required the upper house's assent. The Basic Law also provides the Bundesrat with an absolute veto of such legislation.

The political power of the absolute veto is particularly evident when the opposition party or parties in the Bundestag have a majority in the Bundesrat. When this is the case, the opposition can threaten the government's legislative program. Such a division of authority can complicate the process of governing when the major parties disagree, and, unlike the Bundestag, the Bundesrat cannot be dissolved under any circumstances.

This bicameral system also has advantages. Some observers emphasize that different majorities in the two chambers ensure that all legislation, when approved, has the support of a broad political spectrum—a particularly valuable attribute in the aftermath of unification, when consensus on critical policy decisions is vital. The formal representation of the *Länder* in the federal government through the upper chamber provides an obvious forum for the coordination of policy between the *Länder* and the federal government. The need for such coordination, particularly given the specific, crucial needs of the eastern *Länder*, has become only more important.

The Judiciary

The judiciary's independence and extensive responsibilities reflect the importance of the rule of law in the German system of government. A core concept is that of the *Rechtsstaat*, a government based on law, in which citizens are guaranteed equality and in which government decisions can be amended. Federal law delineates the structure of the judiciary, but the administration of most courts is regulated by *Land* law. The *Länder* are responsible for the lower levels of the court system; the highest appellate courts alone operate at the federal level. This federal-*Land* division of labor allows the federation to ensure that laws are enforced equally throughout the country, whereas the central role of the *Länder* in administering the courts safeguards the independence of the judicial system from the federal government.

Principles of Roman law form the basis of the German judicial system and define a system of justice that differs fundamentally from the Anglo-Saxon system. In the United States, courts rely on precedents from prior cases; in Germany, courts look to a comprehensive system of legal codes. The codes delineate somewhat abstract legal principles, and judges must decide specific cases on the basis of those standards. Given the importance of complex legal codes, judges must be particularly well trained. Indeed, judges are not chosen from the field of practicing lawyers. Rather, they follow a distinct career path. At the end of their legal education at university, law students must pass a state examination before they can continue on to an apprenticeship that provides them with broad training in the legal profession over several years. They then must pass a second state examination that qualifies them to practice law. At that point, the individual can choose either to be a lawyer or to enter the judiciary. Judicial candidates must train for several more years before actually earning the title of judge.

The judicial system comprises three types of courts. Ordinary courts, dealing with criminal and most civil cases, are the most numerous by far. Specialized courts hear cases related to administrative, labor, social, fiscal, and patent law. Constitutional courts focus on judicial review and constitutional interpretation. The Federal Constitutional Court (Bundesverfassungsgericht) is the highest court and has played a vital role through its interpretative rulings on the Basic Law.

The ordinary courts are organized in four tiers, each of increasing importance. At the lowest level are several hundred local courts (*Amtsgerichte*; sing., *Amstgericht*), which hear cases involving minor criminal offenses or small civil suits. These courts also carry out routine legal functions, such as probate. Some local courts are staffed by two or more professional judges, but most have only one judge, who is assisted by lay judges in criminal cases. Above the local courts are more than 100 regional courts (*Landesgerichte*; sing., *Landesgericht*), which are divided into two sections, one for major civil cases and the other for criminal cases. The two sections consist of panels of judges who specialize in particular types of cases. Regional courts function as courts of appeals for decisions from the local courts and hold original jurisdiction in most major civil and criminal matters. At the next level, *Land* appellate courts (*Ober-*

landesgerichte, sing., *Oberlandesgericht*) primarily review points of law raised in appeals from the lower courts. (For cases originating in local courts, this is the level of final appeal.) Appellate courts also hold original jurisdiction in cases of treason and anticonstitutional activity. Similar to the regional courts, appellate courts are divided into panels of judges, arranged according to legal specialization. Crowning the system of ordinary courts is the Federal Court of Justice (Bundesgerichtshof) in Karlsruhe. It represents the final court of appeals for all cases originating in the regional and appellate courts and holds no original jurisdiction.

Specialized courts deal with five distinct subject areas: administrative, labor, social, fiscal, and patent law. Like the ordinary courts, they are organized hierarchically with the *Land* court systems under a federal appeals court. Administrative courts consist of local administrative courts, higher administrative courts, and the Federal Administrative Court. In these courts, individuals can seek compensation from the government for any harm caused by incorrect administrative actions by officials. For instance, many lawsuits have been brought in administrative courts by citizens against the government concerning the location and safety standards of nuclear power plants. Labor courts also function on three levels and address disputes over collective bargaining agreements and working conditions. Social courts, organized at three levels, adjudicate cases relating to the system of social insurance, which includes unemployment compensation, workers' compensation, and social security payments. Finance, or fiscal, courts hear only tax-related cases and exist on two levels. Finally, a single Federal Patents Court in Munich adjudicates disputes relating to industrial property rights.

Except for Schleswig-Holstein, each *Land* has a state constitutional court. These courts are administratively independent and financially autonomous from any other government body. For instance, a *Land* constitutional court can write its own budget and hire or fire employees, powers that represent a degree of independence unique in the government structure.

Sixteen judges make up the Federal Constitutional Court, Germany's highest and most important judicial body. They are selected to serve twelve-year, nonrenewable terms and can only be removed from office for abuse of their position and then only by a motion of the court itself. The Bundestag and the Bundesrat each choose half of the court's members. Thus, partisan politics do play a role. However, compromise is built into the system because any court decision requires a two-thirds majority among the participating judges. The court is divided into two senates, each consisting of a panel of eight judges with its own chief justice. The first senate hears cases concerning the basic rights guaranteed in Articles 1 through 19 of the Basic Law and concerning judicial review of legislation. The second senate is responsible for deciding constitutional disputes among government agencies and how the political process should be regulated.

Unlike the United States Supreme Court, the Federal Constitutional Court does not hear final appeals—that function belongs to the Federal Court of Justice. The Basic Law explicitly confines the jurisdiction of the Federal Constitutional Court to constitutional issues. By the late 1980s, the majority of the articles in the Basic Law had been subjected to judicial review, and the constitutionality of federal and state legislation had been considered in hundreds of court cases. When lacking the legislative clout to challenge a government policy, the opposition in the Bundestag traditionally has turned to the Federal Constitutional Court to question the constitutionality of legislation.

The Civil Service

As of June 1992, about 6.7 million Germans were employed by federal, *Land*, or local governments in Germany; close to 5 million of these were in the western part of the country, and 1.6 million were in the east. The vast majority (over 4.5 million) were employed at the *Land* and local levels. Included at the federal level were roughly 642,000 postal workers and 434,000 railroad workers. Of these civil servants, about 5.6 million were working full time and 1.1 million part time. Public servants have considerable social status in Germany.

Civil servants are categorized into three groups. Slightly over 2 million are career civil servants (*Beamten*; sing., *Beamte*); about 3 million are employees (*Angestellten*; sing., *Angestellte*); and roughly 1.5 million are workers (*Arbeiter*). *Beamten* are divided into four "career groups": higher service, executive service, clerical service, and basic service. A public servant rarely moves from one category to another during his or her career.

Beamten, or career civil servants, constitute the highest level of the administrative elite and enjoy special privileges. They are appointed for life and also receive a noncontributory pension that substantially increases their salaries in comparison with those of public servants in other categories. *Beamten* can be found everywhere, from low-level jobs in the post office to the most senior positions in government ministries, the equivalent of supergrade administrative positions in the United States government. These upper-level *Beamten* occupy most of the significant administrative posts within the bureaucracy and thus influence both formation and application of policy. Almost all *Beamten* at that level of *Land* and federal administration have a university degree, typically with a concentration in law or economics.

In exercising *Land* authority, *Beamten* must obey the orders of their superiors, possess no right to strike, are bound to defend the constitutional order, and are legally responsible for the application of administrative law. In 1972 the federal and *Land* governments issued an executive decree that institutionalized the ban against employing antidemocratic extremists in the public service. This highly controversial law (known as the Radikalenerlass or Berufsverbot) mandated that all candidates for positions as *Beamten* be screened and those already employed be examined, if deemed necessary, for evidence of extreme political views. Other public servants may also be scrutinized "in accordance with the contracts regulating each case."

Public servants may run for public office, and many do so. For example, the Bundestag is often referred to as the parliament of civil servants because a high percentage of its members are *Beamten*. During the twelfth Bundestag (1990–94), almost one-third of the deputies were *Beamten*. The largest portion of that group, 10 percent, consisted of teachers.

Land and Local Government

The Basic Law stipulates that the structure of *Land* government must "conform to the principles of republican, democratic, and social government based on the rule of law" (Article 28[1]). Twelve of the *Länder* are governed by a cabinet led by a minister president together with a unicameral legislative body, the Landtag (pl., Landtage). The relationship between the legislative and executive branches mirrors that in the federal system: the legislatures are popularly elected, typically for four years, and the minister president is chosen by a majority vote among Landtag members. The minister president appoints a cabinet to run *Land* agencies and carry out the executive duties of the *Land* government. Bavaria is the only *Land* with a

The Federal Constitutional Court in Karlsruhe in session
Exterior of the Federal Constitutional Court
Courtesy German Information Center, New York

bicameral legislature; the Landtag is popularly elected, but the second chamber, the Senate, consists of representatives of the major social and economic groups in Bavaria. In the city *Länder* of Berlin, Bremen, and Hamburg, the executive branch consists of a popularly elected senate. The senates' members carry out duties equivalent to those of the ministers in the larger *Länder.* The senate chooses a senate president in Bremen and a mayor in Berlin and Hamburg to serve as chief executive. *Land* cabinets consist of about ten ministers; the most important is the minister of the interior, who directs the internal administration of the *Land* and commands the police.

Politics at the *Land* level often carry implications for federal politics. Opposition victories in Landtag elections—which take place throughout the federal government's four-year term—can weaken the federal government coalition. This was the case for the fall from the chancellorship of Konrad Adenauer in 1963 and that of Willy Brandt in 1974. The *Land* elections are also viewed as a barometer of support for the policies of the federal government. If the parties of the governing coalition lose support in successive *Land* elections, those results may foreshadow difficulties for the federal government. The outcome of *Land* elections also directly affects the composition of the Bundesrat. In the early 1990s, the opposition SPD commanded a two-thirds majority in that legislative chamber, which made it particularly difficult for the CDU/CSU-FDP government to achieve the constitutional changes it sought.

Three levels of government are subordinate to the administrative authority of the states. First, the largest *Länder* are divided into districts. These districts decentralize *Land* administration and are run by district presidents who are appointed by the *Land* minister president and report to the *Land* minister of the interior.

Second, each *Land* is divided into *Landkreis* (pl., *Landkreise*) governments, each consisting of an elected council and an executive, who is selected by the council and whose duties are comparable to those of a county manager supervising local government administration. The *Landkreise* have primary administrative functions in specific areas, such as highways, hospitals, and public utilities.

Third, some *Landkreise* are divided further into *Gemeinden* (sing., *Gemeinde*), or municipal government authorities. *Gemeinden* consist of elected councils and an executive, the mayor, who is chosen by the council. In some small municipalities, the mayor is popularly elected. *Gemeinden* have two major policy responsibilities. First, they administer programs authorized by the federal or *Land* government. Such programs typically might relate to youth, public health, and social assistance. Second, Article 28(2) of the Basic Law guarantees *Gemeinden* "the right to regulate on their own responsibility all the affairs of the local community within the limits set by law." Under this broad statement of competence, local governments can justify a wide range of activities. For instance, many municipalities develop the economic infrastructure of their communities through the development of industrial parks. Local authorities foster cultural activities by supporting local artists and building arts centers. Local government also provides basic public utilities, such as gas and electricity, as well as public transportation. To increase administrative efficiency, West Germany consolidated the *Gemeinden*, reducing the total number from roughly 25,000 in the late 1960s to about 8,500 by the early 1990s. With unification, however, the number of *Gemeinden* for all sixteen *Länder* rose to about 16,000 because of the large number (more than 7,500) of small *Gemeinden* in former East Germany.

The Electoral System

The Basic Law guarantees the right to vote by secret ballot in direct and free elections to every German citizen eighteen years of age or older. To be eligible to vote, an individual must have resided in a constituency district for at least three months prior to an election. Officials who are popularly elected include Bundestag deputies at the federal level, Landtag representatives or senate members at the *Land* level, and council members at the district and local levels. Executive officials typically are not chosen in popular, direct elections; however, in a minority of municipalities the mayor is elected by popular vote. Elections usually are held every four years at all levels. Elections at the federal, *Land*, and local levels are not held simultaneously, as in the United States, but rather are staggered. As a result, electoral campaigns are almost always under way, and each election is viewed as a test of the federal government's popularity and the strength of the opposition. All elections are held on Sunday.

Voter turnout, traditionally high—around 90 percent for national elections—has been decreasing since the early 1980s. Voters are most likely to participate in general elections, but even at that level turnout in western Germany fell from 89.1

percent in 1983 to 84.3 percent in 1987, and to 78.5 percent in 1990. The 1990 general election was the first following unification; turnout was the lowest since the first West German election in 1949. The most consistent participants in the electoral process are civil servants, and a clear correlation exists between willingness to vote and increasing social and professional status and income. Analysts had been predicting a further drop in turnout, the result of increasing voter alienation, for the national election in October 1994; in fact, turnout increased slightly to 79.1 percent.

In designing the electoral system, the framers of the Basic Law had two objectives. First, they sought to reestablish the system of proportional representation used during the Weimar Republic. A proportional representation system distributes legislative seats based on a party's percentage of the popular vote. For example, if a party wins 15 percent of the popular vote, it receives 15 percent of the seats in the Bundestag. The second objective was to construct a system of single-member districts, like those in the United States. The framers believed that this combination would create an electoral system that would not fragment as the Weimar Republic had and would ensure greater accountability of representatives to their electoral districts. A hybrid electoral system of personalized proportional representation resulted.

Under the German electoral system, each voter casts two ballots in a Bundestag election. The elector's first vote is cast for a candidate running to represent a particular district. The candidate who receives a plurality of votes becomes the district representative. Germany is divided into 328 electoral districts with roughly 180,000 voters in each district. Half of the Bundestag members are directly elected from these districts. The second ballot is cast for a particular political party. These second votes determine each party's share of the popular vote.

The first ballot is designed to decrease the anonymity of a strict proportional representation system—thus the description "personalized"—but it is the second ballot that determines how many Bundestag seats each party will receive. To ensure that each party's percentage of the combined district (first ballot) and party (second ballot) seats equals its share of the second vote, each party is allocated additional seats. These additional party seats are filled according to lists of candidates drawn up by the state party organization prior to the election. Research indicates that constituency representatives in the Bundestag

The city hall in Hamburg dates from the late nineteenth century.
Courtesy Hamburg-North America Representation, New York

are more responsive to their electorate's needs and are slightly more likely to follow their constituents' preferences when voting than deputies chosen from the party lists.

If a party wins more constituency seats than it is entitled to according to its share of the vote in the second ballot, the party retains those seats, and the size of the Bundestag is increased. This was the case in both the 1990 and 1994 federal elections. After the 1990 election, the total number of seats in the Bundestag rose from 656 to 662. In 1994 sixteen extra seats were added, leading to a 672-member Bundestag; twelve of those seats went to Kohl's CDU and accounted for Kohl's ten-seat margin of victory.

One crucial exception to Germany's system of personalized proportional representation is the so-called 5 percent clause. The electoral law stipulates that a party must receive a minimum of 5 percent of the national vote, or three constituency seats, in order to get any representation in the Bundestag. An exception was made for the first all-Germany election in December 1990, with the Federal Constitutional Court setting separate 5 percent minimums for the old and new *Länder.* Thus, a party needed only to win 5 percent of the vote in either western or eastern Germany in order to receive seats in the Bundestag.

The 5 percent clause was crafted to prevent the proliferation of small extremist parties like those that destabilized the Weimar Republic. This electoral hurdle has limited the success of minor parties and consolidated the party system. Often voters are reluctant to vote for a smaller party if they are unsure if it will clear the 5 percent threshold. Smaller parties, such as the FDP, encourage voters to split their ticket, casting their first ballot for a named candidate of one of the larger parties and their second ballot for the FDP.

Small parties rarely win the three constituency seats that automatically qualify a party for parliamentary representation according to its overall share of the national vote. This rarity occurred in the 1994 national election. The Party of Democratic Socialism (Partei des Demokratischen Sozialismus— PDS), the renamed communist party of the former East Germany, won 4.4 percent of the national vote, an insufficient total to clear the 5 percent hurdle. The PDS surprised seemingly everyone, however, by winning four districts outright (all in eastern Berlin), entitling it to thirty seats in the Bundestag.

Germany holds no by-elections; if Bundestag deputies resign or die in office, they are automatically succeeded by the next candidate on the party's list in the appropriate *Land.* There are also no primary elections through which voters can choose party representatives. Rather, a small group of official party members nominates constituency candidates, and candidates appearing on the *Land* party lists are chosen at *Land* party conventions held six to eight weeks before the election. Party officials at the federal level play no part in the nominating procedure. Roughly two-thirds of the candidates run as both constituent and list candidates, thus increasing their chances of winning a legislative seat. If a candidate wins in a constituency, his or her name is automatically removed from the *Land* list. There is considerable jockeying among party factions and various interest groups as candidates are selected and placed on the *Land* lists. Placement near the top of the list is usually given to incumbents, party members of particular political prominence, or members who have the support of a key faction or interest group. Thus, aspiring politicians are quite dependent on their party, and successful candidates tend to evince loyalty to the party's policy platform. Candidates must be at least twenty-one years old.

Political Parties

Observers often describe political parties as critical stabilizing institutions in democratic systems of government. Because of the central role played by German political parties, many observers refer to Germany as a "party state." The government of this type of state rests on the principle that competition among parties provides for both popular representation and political accountability for government action.

On the role of parties, Article 21 of the Basic Law stipulates that "the political parties shall participate in the forming of the political will of the people. They may be freely established. Their internal organization must conform to democratic principles. They must publicly account for the sources of their funds." The 1967 Law on Parties further solidified the role of parties in the political process and addressed party organization, membership rights, and specific procedures, such as the nomination of candidates for office.

The educational function noted in Article 21 ("forming of the political will") suggests that parties should help define public opinion rather than simply carry out the wishes of the electorate. Major parties are closely affiliated with large foundations, which are technically independent of individual party organizations. These foundations receive over 90 percent of their funding from public sources to carry out their educational role. They offer public education programs for youth and adults, research social and political issues, and facilitate international exchanges.

Party funding comes from membership dues, corporate and interest group gifts, and, since 1959, public funds. Figures on party financing from 1992 show that dues accounted for over 50 percent of SPD revenues and 42 percent of CDU revenues. Federal resources accounted for 24 percent of SPD revenues and 30 percent of CDU revenues; donations accounted for 8 percent and 17 percent, respectively. The parties must report all income, expenditures, and assets. The government substantially finances election campaigns. Any party that gains at least 0.5 percent of the national vote is eligible to receive a set sum.

This sum has increased over time and, beginning in January 1984, amounted to DM5 (for value of the deutsche mark—see Glossary) from the federal treasury for every vote cast for a particular party in a Bundestag election. Parties at the *Land* level receive similar public subsidies. The political parties receive free campaign advertising on public television and radio stations for European, national, and *Land* elections. Airtime is allotted to parties proportionally based on past election performance. Parties may not purchase additional time.

Several events, including a party-financing scandal in the early 1980s and an electoral campaign in Schleswig-Holstein marked by dirty tricks in the late 1980s, have contributed to increased public distrust of the parties. A 1990 poll showed that West Germans, in ranking the level of confidence they had in a dozen social and political institutions, placed political parties very low on the list.

Although only 3 to 4 percent of voters were members of a political party, all the major parties experienced a decrease in party membership in the early 1990s, possibly a result of the increased distrust of political parties. SPD membership fell by 3.5 percent in 1992 to 888,000. At the end of the 1970s, the party had had more than 1 million members. CDU membership fell by 5 percent in 1992 to 714,000, while that of the FDP fell by about one-fifth to 110,000.

Article 21 of the Basic Law places certain restrictions on the ideological orientation of political parties: "Parties which, by reason of their aims or the behavior of their adherents, seek to impair or abolish the free democratic basic order or to endanger the existence of the Federal Republic of Germany, shall be unconstitutional. The Federal Constitutional Court shall decide on the question of unconstitutionality." This provision allowed for the banning of the neo-Nazi Socialist Reich Party in 1952 and the Communist Party of Germany (Kommunistische Partei Deutschlands—KPD) in 1956.

The decision to regulate the organization and activities of political parties reflects lessons learned from Germany's experience during the post-World War I Weimar Republic, when a weak multiparty system severely impaired the functioning of parliamentary democracy and was effectively manipulated by antidemocratic parties. After World War II, many parties dotted the West German political landscape, but electoral laws allowed only parties with at least 5 percent of the vote to have representation in national and *Land* parliaments. Over time, the smaller parties faded from the scene. From 1962 to 1982, the Bundestag contained representatives from only four parties: the CDU, the CSU, the SPD, and the FDP (see table 4, Appendix). The Greens gained enough of the national vote to win seats in 1983, and unification brought additional parties into the Bundestag in late 1990. At the federal level, the CSU coalesces with the CDU, the largest conservative party. The SPD is the major party of the left. The liberal FDP is, typically, the critical swing party, which can form a coalition with either the CDU/CSU or the SPD to create the majority needed to pass legislation in the Bundestag.

Christian Democratic Union/Christian Social Union

Following World War II, the Christian Democratic Union (Christlich Demokratische Union—CDU) was founded by a diverse group of Catholics and Protestants, businesspeople and trade unionists, and conservatives and moderates. The party espoused a Christian approach to politics and rejected both Nazism and communism. CDU members advocated conservative values and the benefits of a social market economy—that is, one combining capitalist practices and an extensive welfare system. Konrad Adenauer, the CDU's first leader and West Germany's first chancellor, envisioned the CDU as a conservative catchall party (*Volkspartei*) that would attract a majority of the electorate.

The CDU is a national party except in the *Land* of Bavaria, where it is not active, in deference to its sister party, the Christian Social Union (Christlich-Soziale Union—CSU). Bavaria has the largest concentration of conservative, rural, Catholic voters, and the CSU has dominated politics there since 1957. The CSU was personified by its leader, Franz-Josef Strauss, until his death in 1988. By 1994 no clear heir to Strauss had emerged, but the CSU nonetheless retained its absolute majority in the *Land* election of September 1994 (see table 21, Appendix). Germany's population increased through unification, and thus it has become more difficult for the CSU to pass the 5 percent electoral threshold at the national level. However, the CSU performed strongly in the 1994 national election, garnering 7.3 percent of the vote. The CDU and the CSU form a single *Fraktion* in parliament, choose a common candidate for chancellor, and have always governed in coalition. Below the federal level, the two party organizations are entirely separate.

From 1949 until 1963, Adenauer and his CDU dominated German politics (see West Germany and the Community of Nations, ch. 2). At the time of the 1961 election, Adenauer was eighty-five years old, and the opposition SPD was gaining in popularity. Ludwig Erhard, a CDU member credited with engineering Germany's postwar economic miracle, succeeded Adenauer as chancellor in 1963 (see table 3, Appendix). An economic recession then hastened the end of the CDU/CSU's hold on power. November 1966 brought the creation of the Grand Coalition between the CDU/CSU and the SPD with Kurt Georg Kiesinger (CDU) as chancellor and Willy Brandt (SPD) as vice chancellor (see Ludwig Erhard and the Grand Coalition, ch. 2). The FDP was relegated to the opposition benches. After the 1969 election, the SPD formed a coalition with the FDP, leaving the CDU/CSU in opposition for the first time in West German history.

For thirteen years, the CDU/CSU waited to regain power. By the early 1980s, the CDU had adopted a new party program consisting of conservative economic policies, resembling those of Margaret Thatcher and Ronald Reagan, and moderate social and foreign policies. Helmut Kohl, as leader of the CDU/CSU *Fraktion* in the Bundestag, was also rebuilding a political bridge to the FDP. In 1982, as West Germany's economy weakened, the liberal SPD and the economically conservative FDP could not settle on a package of economic remedies. The FDP chose to leave the coalition and form a new government with the CDU/CSU. The constructive vote of no-confidence was used successfully for the first time to unseat Helmut Schmidt as chancellor; Kohl replaced him. West Germans ratified this change through early elections called for March 1983 (see The Christian Democratic/Christian Socialist-Free Democratic Coalition, 1983– , ch. 2).

By the late 1980s, the CDU/CSU was growing increasingly unpopular. The CDU/CSU was also facing a new challenge from the right in the form of a new extreme right party, the Republikaner. In a series of *Land* elections, the Republikaner successfully eroded some of the CDU/CSU's support. The collapse of the German Democratic Republic, however, provided Kohl with a historic opportunity to reverse the fortunes of his party. While most Germans reacted to the change in the geopolitical landscape with amazement, Kohl seized the moment and actively advocated early unification (see Unification, ch. 8). The first, free, all-Germany election since November 1932 took place in December 1990. In essence, this election became a referendum on the process of unification; the CDU/CSU emerged victorious, with Kohl promising greater prosperity for all Germans. As the costs of unification, in economic, social, and psychological terms, became more apparent to both western and eastern Germans, the CDU began suffering setbacks in *Land* and local elections. Nonetheless, Chancellor Kohl was able to claim a narrow victory in the national election of October 1994. Kohl's governing coalition benefited from an increasingly positive economic outlook in Germany and from the fact that the opposition Social Democratic candidate, Rudolf Scharping, was seen by many as lackluster (see Political Developments since Unification, this ch.).

The organizational structure of the CDU is a product of the party's evolution. In its early years, the CDU was a loose collection of local groups. Over time, a weak national party emerged to complement the strong *Land* party organizations. In the early 1970s, the CDU built up its national organization to compete with the more tightly structured SPD. Membership and party income increased accordingly. The Federal Executive is the primary executive organ of the CDU. It consists of about sixty individuals, including the party chair (elected for two years), several deputy chairs, a general secretary, a treasurer, the CDU's main legislative representatives, and the leaders of the *Land* party organizations. Because the Federal Executive is too large and does not meet frequently, a smaller subset called the Presidium, composed of the highest ranking CDU officials, actually sets party policy and makes administrative decisions. Each *Land* except Bavaria, where the CSU is active, holds semiannual party congresses and has an executive committee. These party structures are primarily responsible for the selection of party candidates for Bundestag elections. Every two years, the CDU holds a full party congress of several hundred party activists. Kohl has served as national chairman of the CDU since 1973, headed the parliamentary *Fraktion* from 1976 until 1982, and continues to lead the party as chancellor. Kohl's single-handed management of the party has given him a political dominance within the CDU that only Adenauer surpassed.

The CDU maintains several auxiliary organizations designed to increase the party's attractiveness to particular societal groups and to represent their views within the party. CDU statutes list seven organizations representing youth, women, workers, business and industry, the middle class, municipal politics, and refugees. Other, unofficial groupings exist as well. The most powerful of the auxiliary organizations has traditionally been the one representing business and industry. Although these auxiliary organizations are legally autonomous from the CDU, a high percentage of their members are also members of the CDU.

Social Democratic Party of Germany

Founded in 1875, the Social Democratic Party of Germany (Sozialdemokratische Partei Deutschlands—SPD) is Germany's oldest political party and its largest in terms of membership. After World War II, under the leadership of Kurt Schumacher, the SPD reestablished itself as an ideological party, representing the interests of the working class and the trade unions. The party's program, which espoused Marxist principles, called for the nationalization of major industries and state planning. A strong nationalist, Schumacher rejected Adenauer's Western-oriented foreign policy and gave priority to unifying Germany, even if that meant accommodating Soviet demands. Despite the SPD's membership of almost 1 million in 1949, it was unable to dent Adenauer's popularity. Schumacher's death in 1952 and a string of electoral defeats led the SPD to rethink its platform in order to attract more votes. The Bad Godesburg Program, a radical change in policy, was announced at the SPD's 1959 party conference. The new program meant abandoning the party's socialist economic principles and adopting the principles of the social market economy. The party also dropped its opposition to West German membership in the North Atlantic Treaty Organization (NATO—see Glossary). Like the CDU, the SPD was becoming a catchall party (*Volkspartei*)—albeit of the left.

Introduction of the Bad Godesberg Program, together with the emergence of a dynamic leader in the person of Willy Brandt, marked the beginning of improved fortunes for the SPD. Although the party gained support from election to election, suspicion about its ability to govern persisted. Joining the CDU/CSU in the Grand Coalition in November 1966 proved critical in erasing doubts among voters about SPD reliability. After the 1969 election, the FDP decided to form a coalition with the SPD—a governing configuration that held until 1982 (see The Social Democratic-Free Democratic Coalition, 1969–82, ch. 2).

Brandt served as chancellor from 1969 to 1974. His most notable achievements were in foreign policy. Brandt and his key aide, Egon Bahr, put into place an entirely new approach to the East—Ostpolitik—premised upon accepting the reality of postwar geopolitical divisions and giving priority to reconciliation with Eastern Europe. Brandt addressed long-standing disputes with the Soviet Union and Poland, signing landmark treaties with both countries in 1970. His efforts won him the Nobel Prize for Peace in 1971. The Brandt government also negotiated the Basic Treaty with East Germany in 1972, which formally granted recognition to the GDR. On the domestic side, the SPD-FDP coalition succeeded in almost doubling social spending between 1969 and 1975.

Helmut Schmidt succeeded Brandt as chancellor in 1974. Although Schmidt won a reputation as a highly effective leader, the SPD experienced increasingly trying times. The oil crises of the 1970s undermined economic growth globally, and West Germany experienced economic stagnation and inflation. A critical problem for the SPD-FDP coalition government was a difference in opinion over the appropriate response to these problems. Divisions over economic policy were exacerbated by a debate within the party over defense policy and the stationing of United States intermediate nuclear forces in West Germany in the early 1980s. In 1982 the Free Democrats decided to abandon the coalition with the SPD and allied themselves with the CDU/CSU, forcing the SPD out of power. Schmidt, although regarded as a statesman abroad and an effective leader at home, became increasingly isolated within his own party, and he chose not to campaign as the SPD chancellor candidate in the March 1983 elections. Hans-Jochen Vogel was the SPD standard-bearer in that election, and the party suffered a serious loss.

The SPD has been wrought by internal crises since the late 1970s, and these divisions have continued into the 1990s. The party is split into two factions, one giving priority to economic and social justice, egalitarianism, and environmental protection, and the other most concerned with controlling inflation, encouraging fiscal responsibility, and playing a significant part in the European security system. The SPD faces a challenge on the left from the Greens and on the right from the CDU/CSU and the FDP. Rather than move to the left, the SPD chose a centrist strategy in the 1987 national election and earned only a small increase in voter support.

In 1990 the nomination of Oskar Lafontaine as chancellor candidate suggested a tactical shift to the left aimed at attracting liberal, middle-class voters. The national election in December 1990 became, in essence, a referendum on unification, and the CDU's Kohl, who had endorsed a speedy union, far outstripped the more ambivalent and pessimistic Lafontaine in the polls. The SPD did not receive the support it had expected in the heavily Protestant eastern *Länder*. Leadership of the SPD passed to Björn Engholm, a moderate, who resigned in May 1993 in the wake of a political scandal.

Rudolf Scharping, the moderate and relatively unknown minister president of Rhineland-Palatinate, was elected by SPD members—the first time in the history of the party that its members directly chose a new leader—to replace Engholm in late June 1993. Scharping opposed Kohl in the 1994 national election. The SPD candidate began 1994 with a strong lead in public opinion polls, but, beginning in late April, the SPD's support began a sustained decline for several reasons. For one, the increasingly positive economic situation was credited to the governing coalition. For another, Scharping was perceived by many Germans to be a lackluster candidate; further, he was not wholly successful in portraying himself as the conciliator who had brought harmony to a traditionally fractious SPD. Following the election, Scharping became the leader of the SPD's parliamentary group in the Bundestag.

The organizational structure of the SPD is highly centralized, with decisions made in a top-down, bureaucratic fashion. Technically, the SPD's highest authority is the party congress, which meets biannually. Arguably, its only significant function is to elect the thirty-six-member Executive Committee, which serves as the SPD's primary executive body and its policy maker. The members of the Executive Committee typically represent the various political factions within the party. The core of the Executive Committee is the nine-member Presidium, which represents the inner circle of party officials and is generally composed of the party leadership. The Presidium meets weekly to conduct the business of the party, deal with budgetary issues, and handle administrative and campaign matters. The Presidium is also responsible for endorsing policy originating either with an SPD government or with the leadership of the parliamentary *Fraktion* when the party is in opposition. In almost all cases, decisions made in the Presidium are ratified by the Federal Executive and the party congress. All SPD organizations below the national level elect their own party officials. The district, subdistrict, and local levels are all subordinate to the *Land* executive committees, which direct party policy below the national level and are relatively independent of the federal party officials. Like the CDU/CSU, the SPD maintains specialized groups representing particular professions, youth, women, trade unions, refugees, and sports interests. In the case of the SPD, these groups are closely tied to the SPD bureaucracy, and only the Young Socialists and the trade union group have policy-making roles.

Free Democratic Party

The Free Democratic Party (Freie Demokratische Partei— FDP) is much smaller than the CDU or SPD, but its limited electoral strength masks the party's inordinate influence. Prior to the 1994 election, the FDP had experienced its worst results in national elections in 1969 (5.8 percent) and 1983 (7 percent). Both of those poor showings occurred following an FDP decision to switch coalition partners. Beyond these two exceptions, between 1949 and 1990 the FDP averaged 9.6 percent of the vote in national elections. Given its pivotal role in governing coalitions, the FDP has held over 20 percent of the cabinet posts during its time in government.

The FDP served in coalition governments with the CDU from 1949 to 1956 and from 1961 to 1966. As of mid-1995, it has governed with the CDU since 1982. The FDP governed in coalition with the SPD from 1969 to 1982. The remarkable amount of time that the FDP has spent in government has been a source of continuity in the German political process. FDP ministers carry a detailed knowledge of government personnel and procedures unsurpassed among the other parties.

The central role played by the FDP in forming governments is explained by the fact that a major party has been able to garner an outright majority of Bundestag seats only once (the CDU, in 1957); thus, the CDU and the SPD have been compelled to form coalition governments. Therefore, the FDP has participated in every government except the one from 1957 to 1961 and the Grand Coalition of 1966–69. Because the SPD and CDU/CSU enjoyed roughly equal electoral support, the FDP could choose with which major party it wished to align. This ability to make or break a ruling coalition has provided the small FDP with considerable leverage in the distribution of policy and cabinet positions. To take one example, as of mid-

1995, the FDP, in the person of Klaus Kinkel, led the Ministry of Foreign Affairs, which it has held since 1969. The most prominent member of the FDP, Hans-Dietrich Genscher, served as foreign minister from 1974 until his resignation in 1992.

The FDP was created in 1948 under the chairmanship of Theodor Heuss, who served as the first president of the Federal Republic, from 1949 to 1959. The party's founders wanted the FDP to revive the liberal party tradition of pre-World War II Germany. Although there was some initial debate over what was meant by "liberal," the party did articulate a political philosophy distinct from that of the two major parties. The FDP gave precedence to the legal protection of individual freedoms. Unlike the SPD, it supported private enterprise and disavowed any socialist leaning, and, unlike the CDU/CSU, it envisioned a strictly secular path for itself. In the early 1990s, the Free Democrats remained closer to the CDU/CSU on economic issues and closer to the SPD on social and foreign policy. Many Germans view the FDP as the party of the middle, moderating the policies of both major parties.

Following the 1949 national elections, the FDP emerged as a natural ally of the CDU/CSU, most importantly because of a congruity of economic policy. During the mid- to late 1960s, the FDP, under the leadership of Walter Scheel, went through a transformation of sorts, shedding its conservative image and emphasizing the reformist aspects of its liberal tradition. Its new focus on social concerns resulted in an SPD-FDP coalition in 1969. The party's new direction was ratified at the FDP's 1971 party congress, which endorsed a program of "social liberalism." As economic conditions worsened in the early 1980s, however, the FDP returned to its earlier advocacy of economic policies more conservative than those endorsed by the SPD. The FDP was most concerned with the growing budget deficit, whereas the SPD gave priority to the impact of the economic downturn on workers. The FDP abandoned the coalition with the SPD in September 1982, shifting allegiance to the CDU/CSU. The FDP lost considerable electoral support in the 1983 federal election but regained strength in the 1987 election.

The Free Democrats benefited initially from unification, garnering 11 percent of the vote in the first all-Germany elections in December 1990. In part, the FDP's popularity in the east was directly attributable to Genscher, an eastern German by birth who played a leading role in negotiations over the international agreements that made unification possible.

In light of the FDP's strong showing in the 1990 election, it is perhaps surprising to note that, by the time of the 1994 national election, the FDP was, in many ways, a party in crisis. It had lost representation in every *Land* that held elections in 1994, and thus the FDP has no seats in any eastern *Land* legislature. Minister of Foreign Affairs Kinkel had been elected party chairman in 1993, and some critics felt that the two posts had overwhelmed him, leading him to perform inadequately in both. Other observers, however, argued that it was the party's message, rather than its messenger, that needed revamping. Increasingly, the FDP found it difficult to differentiate its policy from that of Kohl's CDU. Given the fact that the FDP had performed so poorly at the *Land* level in 1994, there was much speculation as to whether the party would cross the 5 percent hurdle in the national election. FDP politicians breathed a collective sigh of relief when the party garnered 6.9 percent of the vote when Germans went to the polls in October 1994. Reportedly, the FDP had over 500,000 CDU voters to thank for this outcome, because they gave their second votes tactically to the FDP to ensure a victory for Kohl. One poll showed that 63 percent of those who voted for the FDP gave the CDU as their preferred party.

The structure of the FDP is decentralized and is loosely organized at all levels. The party basically is a federation of *Land* organizations, each maintaining a degree of well-guarded independence. The national party headquarters lacks the power to orchestrate activities at the *Land* level, and the formal party institutions—the Federal Executive, Presidium, and party congress—are weak. The FDP deemed this lack of centralization necessary to accommodate differences within the party, particularly between economic conservatives and social liberals. The FDP has never sought to be a mass party, and its members accordingly have little influence on decision making.

The Greens

In the early years of the FRG, several minor parties representing a range of political views from the neo-Nazi right to the communist left played a role in the political system. Support for these parties dwindled over time, and, after 1961, the FDP was the only smaller party to cross the 5 percent threshold necessary to gain Bundestag representation. The presence of the 5 percent clause in federal, *Land,* and most local election laws was a significant reason for the decline of minor parties. The major parties have encouraged this trend by sponsoring certain regulations—for instance, in the areas of federal financing for political parties and procedures for nominating party candidates—that have also made it more difficult for minor parties to survive.

A challenge to West Germany's established party system emerged in 1983 when a relatively new party, the Greens (Die Grünen), entered the Bundestag. The Green movement had been gaining support steadily since the late 1970s, and by the end of 1982 the Greens were represented in six of West Germany's eleven *Land* parliaments. The Greens' platform gave priority to environmental concerns and an end to the use of nuclear energy as a power source. The party also opposed the stationing of United States intermediate-range nuclear weapons in Western Europe. On the basis of this platform, the Greens won 5.6 percent of the vote in the 1983 federal election. The success of the Greens at the federal level—which continued in the 1987 national election with the party winning 8.3 percent of the vote—led to a "greening" of the established parties, with environmental awareness increasing across the political spectrum. The Greens also livened up the Bundestag, appearing in jeans and sweaters rather than business suits and bringing plants into proceedings.

The Greens were plagued by a split between the Realos (realists) and the Fundis (fundamentalists). The Realos are pragmatists who want to serve as a constructive opposition and ultimately exercise power. The more radical Fundis are committed to a fundamental restructuring of society and politics; they do not want to share power with the Social Democrats—their obvious allies—or in any way legitimate the existing political system.

The Greens did not embrace the unification of Germany and opposed any automatic extension of West German economic and political principles to the east. The West German Greens chose not to form an electoral alliance with their eastern counterparts, Alliance 90 (Bündnis 90), prior to the 1990 elections because of their opposition to union. This lack of enthusiasm for unification alienated the Greens from much of their own constituency. The party's chances for success in the December 1990 all-Germany election were further undermined by the SPD's choice of Lafontaine as its candidate for chancellor. Lafontaine moved the SPD to the left, successfully co-opting "green" issues. The West German Greens received only 4.8 percent of the vote in the 1990 election, an outcome that left them with no seats in the Bundestag. Alliance 90, composed largely of former dissidents and focusing heavily on civil rights, received 6 percent of the eastern vote and therefore received eight seats in the Bundestag. Had these two parties run in coalition, they could have secured about forty parliamentary seats. Alliance 90 had grown out of the major human rights groups that demonstrated against the communist system and effectively brought down the Berlin Wall in 1989. Like the West German Greens, Alliance 90 had not wanted quick unity with the west either, but the sentiment of the majority of eastern Germans was clear.

Young middle-class voters living in urban areas form the core of support for the West German Greens. Alliance 90 also receives much of its support from this group, although one-third of its supporters are over fifty years of age. Employees of the public sector are disproportionately strong supporters of both parties. Election results suggest that neither working-class voters nor independent businesspeople are likely to vote for either party.

The devastating loss for the West German Greens in the 1990 election brought the conflict between Realos and Fundis to a head, with the pragmatic wing emerging as victor. The party conference in April 1991 ratified a set of Realo reforms. In the series of *Land* elections that followed (Hesse, Rhineland-Palatinate, Hamburg, and Bremen), the Greens did well. This trend continued in 1992 as the Greens received an impressive 9.5 percent of the vote in the wealthy, southwestern *Land* of Baden-Württemberg. In the rural, northwestern *Land* of Schleswig-Holstein, the Greens garnered 4.97 percent of the vote, coming within 397 votes of surpassing the 5 percent hurdle.

In January 1993, the West German Greens merged with Alliance 90 in preparation for the spate of federal and *Land* elections scheduled for 1994. The new party is listed officially as Alliance 90/Greens (Bündnis 90/Die Grünen), but members informally call it the Greens.

Overall, the Greens performed well in the series of *Land* elections in 1994. Following the 1994 national election, with 7.3 percent of the vote, the Greens emerged as the third strongest party in the federal parliament. The obvious coalition partner for the Greens is the SPD, though one increasingly hears talk of possible CDU/Green coalitions. Indeed, the Greens have moderated many of their positions, a reflection of the dominance in the party of the Realos. The best known figure in the party is Joschka Fischer, a prominent Realo and a former environment minister in the *Land* of Hesse.

The Republikaner and the German People's Union

On the opposite end of the political spectrum from the Greens are two parties of the far right, the Republikaner (Die Republikaner—REP), with about 23,000 members, and the German People's Union (Deutsche Volksunion—DVU), with 26,000 members. As of mid-1995, these two parties had not gained sufficient support to win seats in the Bundestag, but the DVU was represented in *Land* parliaments in Bremen (with 6.2 percent of the vote in 1991) and Schleswig-Holstein (with 6.3 percent of the vote in 1992); the Republikaner held seats in Baden-Württemberg (with 10.9 percent of the vote in 1992). The Republikaner received 2.1 percent of the vote in the all-Germany election of December 1990 and 1.9 percent in the October 1994 election.

In the early 1990s, the rallying cry of the far right was "Germany for the Germans." This slogan appeals to many Germans, particularly young, male, rural, less educated, blue-collar workers who fear for their economic future and regard the large pool of asylum-seekers as competitors for housing, social programs, and jobs. These particular Germans are also uneasy about greater integration within the European Union (EU—see Glossary), which, in their minds, requires Germany to forfeit too much of its identity and share too much of its prosperity. According to some observers, the far right's electoral support represents, in part, a protest vote against the mainstream parties. German politicians repeatedly remark on the electorate's *Politikverdrossenheit*—a deep disaffection with all things political.

Franz Schönhuber, a one-time Bavarian television moderator and former officer in the Nazi Waffen-SS, formed the Republikaner in 1983 from a group of discontented members of the CSU. Schönhuber published a book in 1981 boasting of his experiences in the Waffen-SS but has staunchly denied that his party has neo-Nazi leanings. Elected to the European Parliament in 1989, Schönhuber, over seventy years old in mid-1995, tried to portray the party as a mainstream group that does not promote bigotry but merely protects German national interests. The party platform speaks for itself. In it, the Republikaner blame foreigners, who make up about 8 percent of the German population, for the housing shortage, street crime, and pollution. Among other things, the party has proposed banning Islamic community centers from sponsoring political or cultural activities other than prayer, and it has advocated putting asylum-seekers in collection camps "to minimize the native population's existing and growing antipathy toward foreign residents." The party platform also proposes creating separate classes for foreign schoolchildren, and it rejects "the multicultural society that has made the United States the world's largest showplace of crime and latent racial conflict." Reportedly, the Republikaner attracted about 5,000 new members in eastern Germany in 1992 and 1993. Schönhuber contends that support in the east comes from young Germans between twenty and thirty years of age, whereas in the west support comes from members of his own generation. Schönhuber, the party's only nationally known figure, was deposed as party leader in the fall of 1994 because he had proposed that his party join forces with the more extreme DVU.

Gerhard Frey, the Munich publisher of two weekly neofascist newspapers, *Deutsche National-Zeitung* (print run 63,000) and *Deutsche Wochen-Zeitung* (20,000), founded the DVU in 1971. The DVU espouses many of the views held by the Republikaner, but it goes one step further in tacitly supporting violence against asylum- seekers and foreign workers. Frey, over sixty years old in mid-1995, has sought to distance himself from pro-Nazi sentiments while simultaneously insisting that most Germans want to live in a racially pure country.

Germany's domestic intelligence agency, the Federal Office for the Protection of the Constitution (Bundesamt für Verfassungsschutz—BfV), announced in April 1992 that the DVU was under surveillance to determine if the party met the legal definition of "antidemocratic," a classification that would permit the government to ban it. A similar investigation of the Republikaner was announced in December 1992. Such surveillance legally can include government infiltration of the party, monitoring of mail and telephone calls, and interrogation of party members. The BfV has classified both parties as "right-wing extremist" and "constitutionally hostile."

Party of Democratic Socialism

The communist party that ran East Germany was the Social-ist Unity Party of Germany (Sozialistische Einheitspartei Deutschlands—SED). Founded in 1946, the SED controlled the government and the electoral process and supervised the omnipresent State Security Service (Staatssicherheitsdienst—Stasi). To be considered for important positions in East Ger-man government and society, membership in the party was a requirement (see The Ulbricht Era, 1949–71, ch. 2).

When the East German public toppled the communist regime, the SED and its extensive organizational structure also came unraveled. Membership fell dramatically; local and regional party groups disbanded. In a desperate attempt to save itself, the SED sought to reconstruct itself for the new democratic climate. It changed its name in February 1990 to the Party of Democratic Socialism (Partei des Demokratischen Sozialismus—PDS). The old party guard was replaced by mod-erate leaders, such as the new chairman, Gregor Gysi. The PDS won 11 percent of the vote in eastern Germany in the 1990 all-Germany election, an outcome that entitled the party to seven-teen seats in the Bundestag. In the Bundestag, the PDS has advocated communist values and has energetically criticized the Kohl government. The PDS's all-Germany tally reached only 2.4 percent because of a showing in western Germany of 0.3 percent.

The party's electoral base is limited to the east, particularly areas in which substantial numbers of former SED members live. In mid-1995 the PDS had roughly 130,000 members in the east, giving the PDS the largest membership of any party in eastern Germany. The party's strongholds are Saxony, Berlin, and Brandenburg. The party continues to have a tiny following in the west, with 1,200 members.

Two main factors account for the success of the PDS in the east: the PDS inherited the infrastructure and local grassroots organization of the SED, and the PDS has come to be seen by many in the east as the only party that represents specifically eastern German interests and that stresses the positive aspects of eastern German life. Over 90 percent of PDS members belonged to the SED, and 66 percent are over the age of sixty. The established parties have largely ostracized the PDS.

The PDS garnered 4.4 percent of the vote in the 1994 national election, an outcome that, as predicted, left the party beneath the 5 percent hurdle. However, the party won parliamentary representation, thanks to a peculariarity of the German electoral law: the fact that the PDS won four districts outright (all in eastern Berlin) entitled it to thirty seats in the Bundestag. Much credit for the strong showing of the PDS in the east has been given to the party's leading figure, the lawyer Gysi, an articulate and charismatic member of parliament.

Extraparty Political Forces

German society is highly organized into associations that represent the occupational, socioeconomic, religious, and recreational interests of individuals—a tradition that dates back to the corporate guild system of the Middle Ages. Most Germans belong to at least one voluntary association, and many belong to several. The vast majority of these organizations (such as sports clubs) have little political significance, but an important core of groups combines a strong organizational base with a particular interest in policy issues. The size of these interest groups varies. Smaller groups represent subsectors of the population, such as farmers. The large associations include trade unions, professional associations, and religious groups. More than 1,000 of these interest groups are registered formally as lobbyists with the federal government, and hundreds more are active at the *Land* level.

The primary interest associations in Germany are organized differently from interest groups in the United States. The United States offers a pluralist model of interest groups, in which loosely structured factions compete within the policy process to represent the same social interests. The government offers a neutral forum in which these groups vie for influence on policy. In contrast, many of the major interest associations in Germany reflect a neocorporatist model of interest articulation that channels interests into a number of unified, noncompetitive associations.

Four large, national "peak" associations (*Spitzenverbände;* sing., *Spitzenverband*) represent groups of similar interest associations as a whole. The labor unions, business, the churches, and the agricultural lobbying organizations each has its own *Spitzenverband.* Membership in one of these peak associations is often mandatory for individuals in a given social or occupational sector. Most peak associations are also organized hierarchically, with the national office determining the objectives and directing the strategy of the association as a whole.

The influence of the interest associations is institutionalized
in several ways. Political parties provide one major channel of
influence. Although the associations eschew formal party ties
and claim to remain above partisan politics—for instance, they
do not officially endorse a party at election time—ties between
these associations and the parties are close. To take one example, the labor unions maintain a highly developed relationship
with the Social Democrats, and a large percentage of SPD party
activists are union members. Another forum for interest group
activity is the Bundestag. The interest associations not only
monitor legislation, lobby members, and testify at hearings, but
they also maintain formal affiliations with deputies. Since 1972,
when the Bundestag first started keeping records, roughly 50
percent of the members reported either being employed by an
interest group or holding an executive position in a group.
About 25 percent of the members are affiliated with economic
groups, such as labor unions or the business lobby, and about
17 percent are affiliated with religious or cultural associations.
Members of key committees such as agriculture, labor, and
education are particularly likely to have ties to the relevant
groups. The government ministries themselves provide yet
another means by which interest groups influence the policy
process. The neocorporatist system encourages formal ties
between the two. For instance, ministries are required by law to
consult with the peak associations about draft legislation that
would affect them. To fulfill this obligation, the federal ministries have established standing advisory committees, which
include representatives of the relevant interest groups.

Business and Industry

There are three levels at which business and industrial interests seek representation. First, business wants its perspective
heard as the government formulates policy. Second, business
needs representation in negotiations with labor unions. Third,
business may desire support in cultivating new clients or suppliers. Each of these objectives is met by a separate umbrella organization.

The Federation of German Industry (Bundesverband der
Deutschen Industrie—BDI) is the most important representative of business interests in the policy-making process. The BDI
is the national peak association for thirty-nine separate
national trade associations, including associations for the automobile and machine tool industries. Thus, it is the primary

representative of the business community in the political process and the principal intermediary between business and government. The importance of the National Association of Manufacturers (NAM) in the United States pales in comparison with that of the BDI in Germany. In western Germany, the BDI's associations represent over 90 percent of all industrial firms; by contrast, the NAM accounts for only a fragment of United States industry. Although private businesses were still in the early stages of development in eastern Germany in the early 1990s, most trade associations have already set up offices there to coordinate the new industries.

The Federation of German Employers' Associations (Bundesvereinigung der Deutschen Arbeitgeberverbände—BDA) is the second important representative of business. The BDA is a peak association of sixty-four employers' associations, consisting of seventeen regional organizations, including the employers' associations of each *Land,* and forty-seven national trade associations organized by economic sector. The BDA represents the full range of business activity in Germany, but most of its members are in industrial associations. Almost every medium or large employer is a member of a BDA association. The BDA provides advice and serves as a coordinating mechanism for employers on social and labor policy. Among other things, the BDA negotiates general salary guidelines with unions, and it lobbies *Land* and federal governments on legislation affecting the interests of its members, such as social security and labor practices.

The German Chambers of Industry and Commerce (Deutscher Industrie- und Handelstag—DIHT) is the third leg of businesses' representational triad. All companies paying business taxes are required by law to join the local chamber and pay membership dues. Thus, several million firms belong to the eighty-four district and local associations of the DIHT, including the fifteen postunification chambers in eastern Germany. Beyond its national role, the DIHT represents German business abroad, as well as on international trade issues. The DIHT has been particularly engaged in attracting foreign investment to the east.

Labor Unions

During the Weimar Republic, labor unions were divided along partisan lines, a situation that led to competition among the socialist, communist, Catholic, and liberal trade associations. After World War II, labor leaders wanted to break with the past and form a trade union federation independent of political parties. The result was the establishment of the Federation of German Trade Unions (Deutscher Gewerkschaftsbund—DGB) in 1949.

Four principles guided the founders of the DGB. First, the labor movement wanted representation through an organization that was unitary and autonomous, with no ties to particular religions or political parties. Second, labor leaders decided to organize the unions along industrial lines so that all workers at one firm would belong to the same union irrespective of their individual occupations. For instance, an electrician at an automobile plant would join the metalworkers' union. This organizing principle provides unions with greater bargaining power when negotiating with employer associations, because one union represents the entire workforce of an industry. Third, a decentralized system of interest representation was created. Individual unions typically emulate the federal structure, with local, district, *Land,* and national offices. Each level has some input into the shape of union policy. Fourth, the unions chose to rely on legislation for the protection of workers' rights, rather than on direct negotiations with business representatives. Thus, when the unions enter into contract negotiations with employers, they can focus on improving workers' economic welfare.

The DGB is the national peak association of the German labor movement and encompasses sixteen unions, from metalworkers to leather workers. The DGB represents virtually all organized industrial workers, most white-collar employees, and many government workers. As of mid-1995, out of a total workforce of 35 million, 9.8 million workers were members of these labor unions. Although the DGB does not represent even half of the German workforce, its unions negotiate the collective bargaining agreements covering over 90 percent of all jobs. Thus, the work of the labor unions affects nearly all workers. The DGB lost over 2 million members between the end of 1991 and the end of 1994. The vast majority of these members (1.7 million) were from eastern Germany, which has been in the throes of radical economic restructuring and has suffered high unemployment. Some DGB officials express the hope that, once the economy in the eastern part of the country stabilizes, DGB membership will grow.

In 1995 the three largest unions were the Metalworkers' Union with just under 3 million members, the Public Services and Transport Workers' Union with 1.9 million, and the Chemicals, Paper, and Ceramics Workers' Union with 742,000. Roughly 31 percent of all members are women.

DGB members can be divided into "activist" and "accommodationist" factions. The activists, led by the Metalworkers' Union and the Industriegewerkschaft Medien, the union for workers in the media, aggressively challenge business interests and are major advocates of social reform. For example, the Metalworkers' Union led the drive for codetermination (*Mitbestimmung*) in the early 1950s, for substantial wage gains in the 1960s, and for the thirty-five-hour workweek in the 1980s (see Codetermination, ch. 5). The activist unions are more likely to strike if collective bargaining fails to achieve desired results. In contrast, the accommodationist unions, including those representing chemical workers, construction workers, textile workers, and food-processing workers, prefer to cooperate with employers to achieve stable, sustainable economic growth. The individual unions have responded differently to German unification as well. Activist unions have been assertive in pushing for wage equalization between east and west, an effort that culminated in a massive strike in the metalworking industry in eastern Germany in May 1993.

Two other, significantly smaller peak interest associations represent labor sectors independent of the DGB. The German White-Collar Employees' Union (Deutsche Angestellten-Gewerkschaft—DAG) is composed solely of salaried employees, principally high-level technocrats and managers in private enterprise. The Federation of German Civil Servants (Deutscher Beamten Bund—DBB) has competed successfully with the DGB to represent civil servants. The DBB is better described as a lobbying organization, because civil servants can neither strike nor engage in collective bargaining.

The Churches

Religious associations represent a third major group of organized interests in the German policy process. The experience of the Third Reich had a profound influence on the postwar development of Protestant and Roman Catholic churches in the Federal Republic (see Religion, ch. 3). Both espoused the view that moral responsibility extends to political responsibility and that passivity toward the political process is inappropriate.

Both also desired greater ecumenism in German society. The establishment of the CDU perhaps best illustrates this last point. The CDU sought to include both Roman Catholics and Protestants in a catchall party that was committed to Christian values. The two churches maintain distinct identities, but the major cleavage in German society is no longer between religious denominations, but between religious and secular interests.

In postwar West Germany, many people felt that organized religion was an important element in the country's newly forming political ethos. Unlike the United States, West Germany acknowledged no separation of church and state. The state formally recognized the political role of the churches, establishing a special legal status for them as public law corporations. Under a German system developed in the nineteenth century, unless church members formally leave the denomination into which they were baptized, they must pay an annual church surtax equal to 8 or 9 percent of their income tax. The federal government collects this surcharge and remits the proceeds to the churches to finance their activities. In 1992 the figure totaled about US$10 billion for Protestant and Catholic churches combined. Churches are included on government commissions and supervisory bodies that influence social and family policy, education, and related topics.

Not surprisingly, the relationship between church and state in East Germany was markedly different. The communist regime wanted control over all aspects of society, and the existence of autonomous churches was unacceptable. In the 1950s, the regime sought to limit the role of the churches to the religious sphere, keeping them out of politics or education. The state proved unable to suppress the churches fully, however, and by the 1970s the SED had resigned itself to accommodating them.

Roman Catholics constituted only 7 percent of the population in the east; thus, it was the Protestant church, with broad backing among East Germans, that played an important social and political role. The Protestant church retained some autonomy from the state, and by the late 1980s the church had become gathering places for dissidents. In 1989 weekly peace services at churches in big cities, such as East Berlin and Leipzig, became hotbeds of opposition to the regime and led to the mass demonstrations that ultimately brought down the communist regime.

The Evangelical Church in Germany (Evangelische Kirche in Deutschland—EKD), the peak association for the seventeen autonomous provincial churches in West Germany, was established in 1948. The structural unity of the German Protestant church officially ended in 1969, when the eight provincial churches in East Germany withdrew from the EKD and formed the Federation of the Evangelical Churches (Bund der Evangelischen Kirchen—BEK). German unity ushered in the reunification of these two federations in 1991, under the auspices of the EKD. As the formal political representative of German Protestant churches, the EKD represents its member congregations in all formal agreements with the government on church-state affairs. On religious and social matters, however, the EKD serves only as a coordinating agent for its largely independent member churches.

The principal organizational forum for the German Roman Catholic Church is the Bishops' Conference, at which all German bishops convene semiannually. Since unification, the eastern bishops also have attended these meetings. As elsewhere in the Catholic world, all decisions on theological matters and general policy emanate from the Vatican; the annual Bishops' Conference addresses current pastoral and religious issues within Germany.

In West Germany, the Roman Catholic Church was traditionally much more active politically on a day-to-day basis than the Protestant denominations. The Bishops' Conference maintains a permanent secretariat in Bonn to monitor activity in parliament and in the federal ministries. Catholic leaders regularly lobby the government on pending legislation relating to social or moral issues. The EKD participates less actively in the political process, but it is more inclined than its Catholic counterpart to speak out on controversial political issues that have spiritual implications. Examples include the Protestant church's strong stance against the remilitarization of West Germany in the 1950s and its continued activism in the areas of peace and nuclear nonproliferation.

Agriculture

Although agriculture accounts for only 5 percent of the labor force in western Germany, the agricultural lobby has long been known as the best organized and most successful in Bonn. The peak association of this lobby, the German Farmers Association (Deutscher Bauernverband—DBV), focuses exclusively on farm issues. The DBV has consistently convinced the government to guarantee the financial welfare of farmers through generous programs of price supports, subsidies, and agricultural grants. These programs have made German food costs among the highest in Western Europe, but no strong call for reform has ever emerged. The minister of agriculture is often a farmer and, regardless of whether the CDU or the SPD is in power, that minister has single-mindedly pursued policies beneficial to farmers.

Citizens' Initiative Associations

In the early 1970s, a new form of political participation in the form of citizens' initiative associations sprang up throughout West Germany. These associations, in essence nontraditional interest groups, were loosely and often temporarily organized groups of citizens mobilized in response to one particular local issue. Concerns ranged from school reform, urban redevelopment, and traffic to environmental protection. The staying power of these associations reflected a dissatisfaction with established political institutions. Unlike traditional interest groups, these associations aimed to improve the quality of life, rather than the material well-being, of their supporters. Although their ultimate goal is to produce a new social model, these groups tend to be more skilled at critiquing the existing order than at constructing a new one. Activists in these organizations tend overwhelmingly to be young and highly educated, espousing a New Left ideology. Citizens' initiative associations employ diverse tactics, ranging from lobbying and circulating petitions to organizing mass demonstrations and protest marches. Three major political movements have grown out of these associations: the environmental lobby, the women's movement, and the peace lobby.

With public consciousness of the environment growing substantially in the 1970s and 1980s, a new set of nationwide organizations was formed, including the Federal Association of Citizens' Initiatives on Environmental Protection (Bundesverband Bürgerinitiativen Umweltschutz—BBU), Greenpeace, and Robin Wood. The BBU was at its strongest in the late 1970s, when it coordinated more than 1,000 local citizens' initiative associations and when almost 1 million people were affiliated with the environmental movement. By the late 1980s, the BBU was associated with several hundred local groups whose cumulative membership reached only 150,000. Environmental activists have focused on a range of issues, including nuclear power, acid rain, and *Waldsterben* (death of the forest).

The women's movement, organized in the late 1960s and early 1970s, sought to fight discrimination against women in the workplace and at home. Guarantees of gender equality in the Basic Law had done little to alter the traditional male bias within society. The women's movement in western Germany developed a two-pronged approach to securing equality for women: programs for raising the consciousness of women, and programs aimed at legislative reform. The first approach focused on the personal development of women and has met with success at the local level, with most larger cities offering a women's center, women's bookstores, self-help groups, and a network of other women's organizations. The attempt at the national level to mobilize the movement's supporters and bring about legislative change remains underdeveloped.

The peace movement blossomed in the early 1980s in response to the controversy over the stationing of intermediate-range nuclear weapons in West Germany. Mass demonstrations called for the government to pursue arms control negotiations to eliminate these weapons altogether. Instead, the Bundestag voted for deployment in October 1983, and, with its major objective lost, the peace movement lost momentum. The end of the Cold War brought a reduction in East-West tensions and the conclusion of substantial arms control agreements. These developments have further deprived the peace movement of focus. The peace movement was able to mobilize activity against the Persian Gulf War in early 1991, however.

Autonomous citizens' initiative associations were unacceptable in East Germany. The communist government established official organizations—the Society for Nature and the Environment, the Peace Council, and the Democratic Women's Federation of Germany—to co-opt the issues. The peaceful revolution of 1989 that brought down the communist regime in East Germany showed both the willingness among eastern Germans to demonstrate and protest in large numbers, as well as the power of such citizen action. Nonetheless, the levels of protest and direct action are lower in the east than in the west. However, as easterners become more accustomed to the freedoms afforded in a democracy, it is thought that they might become more inclined to exercise them.

The Mass Media

Newspapers

West Germany has always had highly developed mass media. The independence of the press and its freedom from censorship are guaranteed in Article 5 of the Basic Law. Conversely, the communist regime in East Germany tightly controlled the media. Despite government censorship, East Germans were voracious newspaper and magazine readers. More than three dozen newspapers enjoyed a combined circulation of almost 10 million in the GDR.

The complexion of the print media in eastern Germany changed markedly with unification. By mid-1991 only 100,000 copies of East Germany's most widely circulated newspaper, *Neues Deutschland,* the newspaper of the communist party, were being printed daily, down from roughly 1 million in the recent past. Western consortia bought many of the other established urban newspapers and brought in new management. According to a public opinion survey during the 1990 national election, 68 percent of western Germans and 88 percent of eastern Germans read a newspaper on a regular basis. Not surprisingly, Germany boasts among the highest per capita newspaper circulations within Europe.

The press is privately owned, and most Germans rely on local or regional newspapers for their information. Five daily newspapers enjoy good reputations nationally because of their sophisticated domestic and international coverage: *Frankfurter Allgemeine Zeitung* (FAZ), *Süddeutsche Zeitung, Frankfurter Rundschau, Handelsblatt,* and *Die Welt.* The FAZ is probably Germany's most prestigious daily newspaper and is the one newspaper read by virtually all members of the political and business establishment. Although independent of any political party, its views are similar to those of the right-of-center CDU. *Handelsblatt* is the leading business daily. *Die Zeit,* a weekly newspaper, provides an erudite review of news and culture from a perspective sympathetic to Social Democratic views. Weekly editions of *Die Zeit* are often more than 100 pages, with in-depth articles filling an entire page. Former chancellor Schmidt is one of its publishers; the paper's circulation is 493,000. Because these newspapers appeal to an elite readership, their circulation figures are much lower than that of the tabloid press. *Bild Zeitung,* with a daily circulation of close to 5 million, is Germany's most widely circulated daily. It puts a sensationalist spin on topical issues and tends to support right-of-center policies.

Both *Bild Zeitung* and *Die Welt* are published by the Axel Springer Group, based in Hamburg. Axel Springer, now deceased, built an enormous media empire, which also includes the two largest Sunday newspapers, *Bild am Sonntag* and *Welt am Sonntag*, two Berlin daily newspapers, and many popular magazines. Springer publications are generally considered to have a strong conservative bent.

The liberal counterpart to Axel Springer and his successors has been Rudolf Augstein, founder and publisher of the weekly *Der Spiegel*, a highly respected and influential newsmagazine combining news coverage with investigative journalism. The magazine's decidedly liberal critique of politics and politicians has often steeped it in controversy (see Ludwig Erhard and the Grand Coalition, ch. 2). In 1994 its circulation stood at over 1 million copies. *Der Spiegel* is distributed in 165 countries, and close to 15 percent of its sales are outside Germany.

In 1993 competition for market share held by *Der Spiegel* emerged with the publication of *Focus*, a newsmagazine fashioned after *Time* and *Newsweek*, with shorter articles and a more colorful layout than that offered by *Der Spiegel. Focus* appeared on newsstands in January 1993, was less expensive than *Der Spiegel*, and, after a few months, was faring better than expected. By mid-April *Focus* was maintaining a circulation of 600,000 and had exceeded its annual target for pages of advertising sold. Since its founding in 1946, *Der Spiegel* has successfully faced down competition from more than fifty publications. However, the circulation of *Focus* is growing while that of *Der Spiegel* is falling.

Although newspapers owned by political parties were common during the Weimar period, the partisan press is much less significant in the Germany of the 1990s. *Vorwärts* is the official newspaper of the SPD, and *Bayernkurier* serves the CSU. *Rheinischer Merkur* has informal links to the CDU, and *Neues Deutschland* offers views of the PDS.

Radio and Television

Radio and television are administered in a decentralized fashion as prescribed in the Basic Law. The intent behind the pattern of regional decentralization is to prevent the exploitation of the media by a strong national government, as had happened under the Nazi dictatorship. Germany has two public broadcasting corporations. The first, ARD, was established in 1954 and encompasses eleven regional public television and radio stations. ARD employs roughly 23,000 people and has an annual budget of about US$6 billion. The second, ZDF was founded in 1961 and is structured as a single corporation, not as a consortium. A third channel broadcasts cultural and educational programs for all *Land* corporations.

The *Land* broadcasting corporations have similar organizational structures. Each governs itself under the direction of a broadcasting council consisting—in most *Länder*—of representatives of the major social, economic, cultural, and political groups, including political parties, churches, unions, and business organizations. The broadcasting corporations are financed largely through monthly fees (DM23.80 per household as of late 1994) charged to television and radio owners. Public television is allowed to devote no more than thirty minutes per day to commercial advertisements. No advertisements are aired after 8:00 P.M. on weekdays or on Sundays. Advertising provides roughly one-third of television revenues and one-fourth of radio revenues. What distinguishes public television from commercial television is the ability to offer greater coverage of public service activities and cultural events.

Most eastern Germans were familiar with western German television even before unification because broadcasts from the west could be received in most of East Germany. According to a 1990 survey, 49 percent of western Germans and 70 percent of eastern Germans watched a nightly news program at least five times each week. Surveys also indicate that television is the most important source of political information: 51 percent of Germans rank television first, ahead of newspapers and magazines (22 percent), conversation (16 percent), and radio (6 percent).

Private broadcasting was virtually nonexistent in West Germany until 1981, when the Federal Constitutional Court recognized the right of the *Länder* to grant broadcasting licenses to private companies. Enabling legislation took the form of a new broadcasting treaty enacted by the *Länder* in 1987 that allowed the creation of private broadcasting companies to compete with public stations. In general, private broadcasters do not have an internal supervisory council, but the *Länder* in which they broadcast can exercise supervisory rights.

Commercial broadcasters finance their operations solely with advertising revenues. Beyond the substantial capital costs associated with starting up a new television channel, private broadcasters have to rely on satellite and cable transmission because the airwaves do not offer unlimited capacity. Thus, viewers have to pay an additional fee to get access to private channels. In 1983 the federal post office undertook a large-scale program of wiring the country for cable television. In March 1993, of the 27 million households in western Germany that had televisions, 70 percent had access to cable service; of the 6.4 million households in eastern Germany, 12 percent had access to cable. However, at that point only about 60 percent of those eligible households had chosen to subscribe to cable.

In 1985 SAT–1 became Germany's first private satellite television station. A group of publishing firms, including Springer, owns SAT–1; the channel offers a program of popular entertainment and news. Other stations subsequently sprang up, including 3–SAT, a joint production of German, Swiss, and Austrian national television; RTL, or Radio-Television-Luxembourg; and various European satellite stations. In early 1993, two all-news channels made their debut: Time Warner and CNN own one, n-tv; and German publishing giant Bertelsmann and the *Süddeutsche Zeitung* are major financial backers of Vox, the second news channel. Vox failed quickly, however, closing its doors in April 1994. On the whole, private channels nonetheless are prospering. The percentage of Germans watching public channels has dropped to less than one-half since the start of private broadcasting in 1987.

Political Developments since Unification

The political institutions of unified Germany are remarkably similar to those of the former West Germany, reflecting minor adjustments to accommodate the larger population rather than making fundamental changes. The unfolding drama of unification is much more evident when one takes into consideration Germany's political landscape, including elections, political climate in the unified country, and issues that have dominated that landscape.

The Bundestag election of December 2, 1990, was the first all-Germany election since 1932. The election returned to power the governing coalition of the CDU/CSU and the FDP. The central issue of the campaign was unification. Parties that strongly supported unification scored well; those that were ambivalent or opposed to unification, such as the SPD and the Greens, fared poorly.

Helmut Kohl's political fortunes soon declined, however, in the wake of problems with the unification process. Increasing unemployment in the east, and anger in the west about a tax increase that Kohl had pledged to avoid before the 1990 election, caused the CDU to lose a series of *Land* elections after unification. As a result, in 1991 the ruling coalition lost its majority in the Bundesrat when the CDU lost power in the *Länder* of Hesse and Rhineland-Palatinate (Kohl's home *Land*). This development made it more difficult for the Kohl government to gain approval for key legislative initiatives.

The year 1994 was nicknamed the "super election year" because Germany conducted approximately twenty elections at the local, *Land,* federal, and European levels, culminating in the national election in October. In eight *Land* elections throughout 1994, the SPD fared better than did the CDU. The SPD thus increased its majority in the Bundesrat. The FDP performed miserably at the *Land* level, failing to gain the required 5 percent for representation in all eight elections. Given this poor showing, many observers question the staying power of the FDP as a political force in Germany. Observers were surprised by the strength of the former Communists (PDS) in the eastern *Länder;* all five new *Länder* held elections in 1994, with the PDS garnering from 16 to 23 percent of the vote in each (see table 21, Appendix). The PDS increased its share of the vote over the results in 1990 and solidified the party's position as the third strongest political force in eastern Germany. On November 9, 1994, Germans celebrated the fifth anniversary of the fall of the Berlin Wall. However, much still divides eastern and western Germans, not least economic success, and the PDS was able to capitalize on eastern resentments.

Germans voted in national elections on October 16, 1994. Chancellor Kohl was challenged by Rudolf Scharping, the minister president of the western *Land* of Rhineland-Palatinate and the chairman of the SPD. Election themes included unemployment and economic growth, particularly in light of unification, as well as law and order. Except for the future of the EU, foreign policy issues did not figure in the election campaign.

Scharping began 1994 with a strong lead in public opinion polls, but, beginning in late April, the SPD's support began a sustained decline for several reasons. First, the CDU benefited from an increasingly positive economic outlook in Germany. Second, Scharping was seen by many to be a lackluster candidate; further, he was not wholly successful in portraying himself as the conciliator who had brought harmony to a traditionally fractious SPD. Chancellor Kohl, however, was seen to embody stability, continuity and predictability; one of his election slogans was "no experiments." Third, the CDU/CSU launched a fierce campaign against the PDS, whose members had belonged to the Communist SED, calling them "red-painted fascists," and Kohl succeeded in incriminating the SPD, at least marginally, in this seeming Communist revival. The SPD provided Kohl with this opportunity by forming a minority government with the Greens in the eastern *Land* of Saxony-Anhalt that depended on the votes (or abstention) of the PDS to remain in office. This CDU/CSU tactic was aimed, effectively it would seem, at those western German voters who, despite Scharping, questioned the SPD's commitment to centrist policies.

Kohl's governing coalition claimed a narrow victory; its majority in the Bundestag was reduced from 134 to ten seats (see table 4, Appendix). The Greens and the former Communists also won representation in the Bundestag. The far-right Republikaner, seen as a spent political force, failed to clear the 5 percent hurdle necessary to enter the Bundestag. Voter turnout, up slightly from the 1990 election, was 79.1 percent. Following the election, Scharping became the leader of the SPD's parliamentary group in the Bundestag, which will allow him to keep a high national profile in preparation for the next national election. The coalition government of Kohl's CDU, the CSU, and the FDP will focus on creating jobs, trimming bureaucracy, fighting crime, and expanding the EU eastward.

The FDP's seemingly chronic inability to win representation in *Land* parliaments means that it is increasingly losing its regional bases and its reservoirs of future political talent. If and how the FDP can regenerate support remains to be seen. Recent CDU overtures to the Greens—until recently an unthinkable development—also suggest a CDU awareness of the possible need for an alternate coalition partner in the future. The 1994 election may thus mark the beginning of some profound changes in political alignments in Germany.

Unified Germany's second national election suggests that the country's east-west divide has not narrowed. The strongest evidence is the success of the PDS in winning parliamentary representation. In eastern Germany, the PDS received 19.2 percent of the vote, compared with only 0.9 percent in the west. The national tally of 4.4 percent was insufficient to clear the 5 percent hurdle for parliamentary representation, but the PDS benefited from an oft-forgotten electoral law that automatically qualifies a party for representation according to its overall share of the national vote when the party wins three electoral districts outright (first votes). The PDS surprised seemingly everyone in winning four districts outright (all in eastern Berlin), entitling it to thirty seats in the Bundestag.

The future of the PDS is unclear and may well depend on whether the CDU and the SPD develop programs that attract current PDS constituents. Kohl's coalition lost twice as many votes in the east as in the west, winning 49.9 percent of the vote in the west and 42.5 percent in the east. The SPD faces the challenge in the east of competing against two other parties of the left, the PDS and the Greens. When considering the success of the PDS, however, one must recall that 80 percent of eastern Germans did not vote for the former Communists. At present, PDS leaders are working to rid the party of its Stalinist heritage; if successful, the PDS would certainly have a broader appeal.

As of mid-1995, right-wing extremist parties held seats in three of sixteen *Land* parliaments (Baden-Würtemberg, Bremen, and Schleswig-Holstein) and appeared to be fading from the German political landscape. The most significant of these parties, the Republikaner, with about 23,000 members, attracted support principally by criticizing a government policy that allowed hundreds of thousands of asylum-seekers into Germany. However, the Kohl government engineered a revision of the German constitution in 1992 that severely restricts the right to asylum (which had been the most liberal in Europe), thus largely calming public concerns. The far right has thereby lost its major platform and has been tainted by violent attacks against foreigners in Germany. In-fighting has also divided the party and resulted in the ouster of leader Franz Schönhuber, a former Waffen-SS member and the party's one nationally known figure (see The Republikaner and the German People's Union, this ch.). In the October 1994 election, with close to 80 percent voter turnout, the Republikaner received only 1.9 percent of the national vote, thus once again failing to win representation in the Bundestag. This outcome cemented a downward trend, which had been evinced in the European Parliament election and *Land* elections throughout the year. That downward trend is particularly notable in light of the fact that extreme right parties have met with considerable electoral success in several West European countries, such as France, Belgium, and Italy.

A plethora of controversial issues has marked political debate in united Germany, for example, the right to political asylum, the upsurge in right-wing violence, and the tensions surrounding the unification process itself. The Basic Law originally contained a liberal regulation on the right to asylum, and in 1992 a total of 438,191 asylum-seekers streamed into Germany—up from 256,112 in 1991. Most asylum-seekers were from Romania, the former Yugoslavia, and Bulgaria. Many Germans complained that the German law permitted many people who were not political refugees, but rather economic migrants, to take advantage of the country's generous welfare system and compete with Germans for scarce housing. Extreme right-wing parties capitalized on this widespread resentment against asylum-seekers in April 1992 elections in two western *Länder.*

On December 6, 1992, Kohl's governing coalition and the opposition Social Democrats agreed on a constitutional amendment to limit the right to asylum. The asylum compromise between the government and the opposition included several important changes. First, asylum-seekers from European Community (EC—see Glossary) states or states that accept the Geneva Convention on Refugees and the European Human Rights Convention have no right to asylum in Germany. Second, any refugee passing through "safe third countries," which include all of Germany's neighbors, is ineligible for asylum. An individual may appeal this decision but may not stay in Germany during the course of that appeal. In exchange for these concessions, the Social Democrats won agreements to place an annual limit of 200,000 on the immigration of ethnic Germans eligible for automatic German citizenship and to ease the terms of citizenship for longtime foreign residents of Germany (see Immigration, ch. 3). Parliament approved the new asylum law in late May 1993, and it took effect on July 1. About 10,000 protesters surrounded the Bundestag on the day of the vote, but apparently about 70 percent of Germans approved the more restrictive asylum law. The number of foreigners seeking asylum in Germany has fallen substantially since the new law went into effect.

Another pressing issue has been the escalation of right-wing violence. In 1992 right-wing extremists committed 2,584 acts of violence in Germany, an increase of 74 percent from 1991. Seventeen people were killed in the 1992 attacks, six in 1991.

About 60 percent of the attacks occurred in western Germany and 40 percent in eastern Germany—home to only 20 percent of the population. About 90 percent of the right-wing attacks in 1992 were directed against foreigners—above all, at asylum-seekers and their lodgings. People under the age of twenty-one committed 70 percent of these attacks.

In November 1992, three Turkish residents were killed in a firebombing in Mölln in western Germany. Of the 80 million people living in Germany in 1993, about 1.8 million were Turks, making that ethnic group the country's largest minority. Two-thirds of those Turks had lived in Germany at least a decade. The overwhelming majority of Germans condemn xenophobia and neo-Nazism, and after the Mölln attack, over 3 million Germans demonstrated across the country against right-wing violence. Following the violence in Mölln, the government began a crackdown on far-right violence. The federal prosecutor took over for the first time the investigation of an antiforeigner attack. The decision was made to charge the perpetrators with murder, rather than manslaughter, as had been done following previous arson attacks leading to fatalities. In December 1993, a judge imposed maximum sentences on the two men convicted in the Mölln killings. Other measures taken by the government included banning four small neo-Nazi organizations and outlawing the sale, manufacture, and distribution of the music of several neo-Nazi rock bands.

Despite the government's actions, the number of right-wing attacks increased in the first six months of 1993. The most serious incident occurred on May 29, 1993, when right-wing youths firebombed a house in Solingen in western Germany, killing five Turks. In late December 1993, four right-wing youths were charged with murder in the Solingen attack. In late October 1993, United States citizens for the first time became the target of right-wing violence. Two skinheads harassed African-American members of the United States Olympic luge team, which was practicing at an eastern German training center. When a white luger intervened on his teammates' behalf, he was severely beaten by the skinheads.

By the end of 1993, the surge in right-wing violence appeared to be abating. The federal police reported that, in the first eleven months of 1993, rightist crime dropped by 28 percent compared with the same period in 1992. As of December 2, 1993, eight people had died in rightist violence compared with seventeen in 1992. A police spokesman stated that

*An estimated 10,000 mourners, including Minister of Foreign Affairs
Klaus Kinkel, paid their respects in Hamburg to the memory of three
Turks killed in late 1992 by right-wing extremists.
Courtesy German Information Center, New York*

the decline reflected decisive executive action, including faster
police responses, tougher sentences, and bans on neo-Nazi
groups.

Much of the public debate on how to address the causes of
right-wing violence has focused on how better to integrate foreigners into German society. Chancellor Kohl announced
some steps to make it easier for foreigners to become German
citizens. He stopped short, however, of advocating dual citizenship. Concern exists in law enforcement circles that neo-Nazis
are building an underground network of small, organized cells
patterned in part on those of the Red Army Faction (Rote
Armee Fraktion—RAF), the far-left organization that carried
out bombings, assassinations, and kidnappings in the 1970s
and 1980s (see The Student Movement and Terrorism, ch. 2;

Dissidence and Terrorist Activity, ch. 9). The establishment of such a network would make it much more difficult for the authorities to monitor neo-Nazi activities.

A final issue dominating Germany's political scene has been the ongoing challenge of implementing unification. Among other things, the two Germanys have had to enact uniform legislation, decide on what city should serve as their capital, and bring the former leaders of East Germany to justice.

Unification left Germany with a population possessing widely different views on matters such as the family, religion, and the work ethic. A particularly sensitive issue has been abortion. East Germany, which permitted free abortion on demand up to the twelfth week of pregnancy, had a markedly more liberal policy on abortion than did West Germany. In June 1992, the Bundestag, in an attempt to unify abortion policy, approved an abortion law—opposed by Chancellor Kohl—that granted a woman the right to an abortion up to the twelfth week of pregnancy, provided she accepted counseling first. Thirty-two of the 268 CDU legislators, primarily from eastern Germany, broke ranks with the party leadership and approved the bill.

On August 4, 1992, the Federal Constitutional Court issued an injunction against the parliament's decision, and abortion continued to be available on demand in the east and largely prohibited in the west, pending a final court judgment. On May 28, 1993, the Federal Constitutional Court struck down the compromise law on the basis of the Basic Law's explicit protection of the rights of the unborn child. The ruling held that abortion was no longer a criminal offense but that abortions would only be allowed in the first three months of pregnancy for women who first participated in a formal consultation process. Further, the ruling barred insurance funds from paying for abortions and *Land* hospitals from performing them. The ruling went into effect on June 16, 1993. Women's groups, opposition politicians from the west, and easterners from across the political spectrum expressed outrage at the court's decision. At some point in the future, the Bundestag is still expected to pass a uniform abortion law for the entire country.

Another question that arose with unification was where to locate the new German capital. The Bundestag voted in June 1991 to move the capital from Bonn to Berlin, fulfilling a long-standing promise of West German politicians across the board. The vote in favor of Berlin was surprisingly narrow, with 338 legislators supporting Berlin and 320 supporting Bonn. Many of the parliamentarians who voted for Bonn spoke of the symbolic importance of the capital's geographical location, with Bonn bearing witness to the critical importance of the Atlantic Alliance and Germany's commitment to Western democracy. Many who supported Berlin saw their choice as a necessary act of conciliation toward eastern Germans and a necessary step toward Germany's return to the world stage as a "normal" nation.

The quick move to Berlin that many eastern Germans had hoped for was thwarted by a quiet, yet effective, campaign led by Bonn bureaucrats and certain key politicians who opposed the Bundestag decision on several grounds. First, members of this group cited the huge expense of moving the government, estimated at just under US$19 billion by the Ministry of Finance. Second, they argued that Berlin's historical associations as the capital of a united Germany were negative and that Germany should avoid doing something to suggest to its neighbors a return to expansionist or aggressive tendencies. Third, many officials balked at the personal inconvenience of moving to Berlin if they owned homes in the Bonn area or otherwise faced having to uproot their families from the rather provincial Rhineland and relocate in a booming metropolis.

After two years of indecision, the Kohl cabinet announced in October 1993 that the government would complete the move to Berlin by December 31, 2000; the move will begin in 1998. The opposition Social Democrats had threatened to make the government's reluctance to move an issue in the 1994 national election campaign. Foreign embassies and private companies had delayed their moves to Berlin while waiting for an official announcement of a timetable. The cabinet decision sent a decisive message to investors and property developers who believed the move would attract greater investment in the five eastern *Länder*. The Bonn lobby won certain important concessions as well: eight government ministries will keep their headquarters in Bonn, and the remainder will retain offices there. Kohl received sharp criticism about the distant deadline from some commentators, who argued that the government's hesitation to complete the move was impeding the social and psychological unification of east and west.

Many Germans see the prosecution of former East German officials as a necessary part of coming to terms with divided Germany's past. On November 12, 1992, a trial opened in Berlin involving six defendants, including former East German leader Erich Honecker, former minister of state security Erich Mielke, and former prime minister Willi Stoph. These men were put on trial for the killings of East Germans trying to cross the border to the west. Two days later, however, Mielke and Stoph were declared unfit to stand trial for health reasons. Charges were then dropped against Honecker because of his advanced cancer, and he was allowed to join his family in Chile in early 1993. The remaining three defendants—all former members of East Germany's National Defense Council—were convicted in September 1993, receiving prison sentences ranging from four-and-one-half years to seven-and-one-half years.

From the start, the legal basis for the trials was questionable. German law does not apply to acts committed by East German citizens in a state that no longer exists. Thus, the defendants had to be prosecuted for transgressions of East German law, and East Germany's border law allowed guards to shoot anyone trying to flee. The Berlin prosecutors argued that the law was evil and ought not to have been obeyed, a form of reasoning with which the judges agreed. Many legal scholars believe that the convictions could be reversed on appeal, however. In part, the prosecution of these former East German leaders grew out of public indignation over the trials of border guards while senior policy makers were going free. By late 1993, ten border guards had stood trial. Nine received short, suspended sentences or acquittals; one received a sentence of six years for having shot and killed a fugitive who had already been caught and was under arrest. In the fall of 1993, the Bundestag extended the statute of limitations by three years for minor crimes by former East German officials and by five years for more serious crimes.

Most observers of Germany believe the country will solve the economic and political challenges associated with the unification process. However, polls indicated that, as time passed, eastern and western Germans seemed to see the gap between them widening rather than narrowing. In an April 1993 poll, when asked whether eastern and western Germans felt solidarity or antagonism toward one another, 71 percent in the west and 85 percent in the east answered "antagonism." In the coming years, perhaps the greatest challenge to Germans of the east and west will be to master the task of achieving social harmony. Only then can they become one nation.

*   *   *

A rich literature on German government and politics is readily available in English. The Press and Information Office of the Federal Republic of Germany offers the public a wide range of documents, including the Basic Law, free of charge. That office also publishes the *Week in Germany,* which covers current events. The *Financial Times* and the *International Herald Tribune* provide good daily coverage of German news as well.

English-language studies of the political system are published regularly. One of the most comprehensive and readable texts available is *Politics in Germany* by Russell J. Dalton. Another general volume providing valuable information is *Developments in German Politics,* edited by Gordon Smith, William E. Paterson, Peter H. Merkl, and Stephen Padgett. A more specialized, comparative parliamentary study is *The United States Congress and the German Bundestag,* edited by Uwe Thaysen, Roger H. Davidson, and Robert Gerald Livingston. *The Constitution of the Federal Republic of Germany* is a comprehensive examination of the Basic Law by the noted constitutional scholar David P. Currie. Three journals—*German Politics, German Politics and Society,* and *West European Politics*—are useful sources of information as well. (For further information and complete citations, see Bibliography.)

Chapter 8. Foreign Relations

Hans-Dietrich Genscher, minister of foreign affairs, 1974–92

GERMANY'S FOREIGN POLICY faces formidable challenges and difficult decisions. For forty years, Germany was divided between East and West, its border the focus of a nuclear stand-off. On October 3, 1990, the two German states, the Federal Republic of Germany (FRG, or West Germany) and the German Democratic Republic (GDR, or East Germany), were united under one democratic government. As Germany begins to search for a new voice abroad, some circles fear that the country might once again come to dominate the continent.

After unification, the country was beset by difficult domestic problems. Integration of Germany's five new eastern states (*Länder;* sing., *Land*) proved more costly and time consuming than experts had originally estimated. In addition, there was persistent friction between the former West Germans (*Wessis* in colloquial German) and the former East Germans (*Ossis*). This friction often centered on the costs and burdens of unification. A spate of right-wing radicalism and violence also erupted throughout Germany, primarily directed against foreign workers and refugees. Between 1990 and mid-1995, Germany had taken in more asylum-seekers than all other European Union (EU—see Glossary) members combined, a fact that angered some Germans because of the expense this humanitarian action entailed. Finally, there was a debate on the competitiveness of the German economy. West German workers had come to enjoy some of the highest wages and most extensive benefits among workers anywhere in the industrialized world. As a result of high labor costs, however, companies had begun to downsize, and many were relocating production facilities abroad. Unemployment was increasing throughout Germany.

In this context of domestic preoccupation, Germany began to confront disorienting external circumstances as well. The European Community (EC—see Glossary) had embarked on a process of profound change as it considered its course toward political and economic union. In December 1991, the EC's twelve members signed the Treaty on European Union (commonly known as the Maastricht Treaty—see Glossary), creating the EU, a blueprint for unifying the continent. The United States, previously West Germany's most important ally, began to rethink its own European role as it adapted to the new post-Cold War environment and its own domestic challenges.

Russia and the other states of the former Soviet bloc entered into an uncertain relationship of dependence on Germany, the country that led the international aid effort for the emerging democracies of the new Europe.

Meanwhile, Operation Desert Storm in the Persian Gulf, the humanitarian mission of the United Nations (UN) in Somalia, and war in the former Yugoslavia created significant challenges for German foreign policy. Germany's policy makers were confronted with the question of whether or not their country's participation in multilateral actions sanctioned by the UN would be restricted to nonmilitary or peacekeeping roles. Would Germany be able to overcome internal legal obstacles and psychological inhibitions stemming from its turbulent twentieth-century history of militarism to participate in peace-enforcing combat missions?

Despite initial reluctance and arduous debate, Germany's foreign policy planners began to accept a new role with regard to Germany's military, and incremental steps were taken to normalize the use of the country's armed forces. The German navy patrolled the eastern Mediterranean off the coasts of Egypt and Syria during the Persian Gulf War in 1991. From May 1991 to October 1993, German military personnel served with UN forces in Cambodia. In March 1994, German troops joined the UN's operation in Somalia. German Alpha Jets were deployed in eastern Turkey to help enforce the UN's Kurdish safe zone in northern Iraq. And German pilots flew North Atlantic Treaty Organization (NATO—see Glossary) missions over Bosnia as part of the UN's "Deny Flight" operation. By the mid-1990s, the chief legal obstacles to the deployment of German armed forces abroad had been overcome, but the "normalization" of German foreign policy, it had become clear, would still take some time.

Once unified, Germany struggled to think clearly about its national priorities. For Germans, unification meant new borders, new resources, and a return to the center of the continent, or *Mittellage*. It also meant new responsibilities and new expectations. Historically, Germany had often been either too strong or too weak to be accepted by its neighbors.

Germany's return to the center of Europe entailed for the country's foreign policy establishment the beginnings of a subtle recalculation of the country's national interests and a gradual reexamination of its relationship to a number of international bodies. Those bodies included NATO, the EU, the Western European Union (WEU—see Glossary); the Conference on Security and Cooperation in Europe (CSCE—see Glossary)—which was renamed the Organization for Security and Cooperation in Europe (OSCE—see Glossary) in January 1995—and the UN. In the early post-Cold War years, Germany had assumed a leading role in advocating the expansion of NATO and the EU to include emerging democracies of Central and Eastern Europe.

Although German foreign policy remains deeply influenced by patterns of behavior developed during the Cold War, unified Germany's major foreign policies and goals are evolving. During the unification process, Germany had reaffirmed its pledge not to acquire weapons of mass destruction. But post-unification Germany also made clear its interest in obtaining a permanent seat on the UN Security Council. Foreign observers and Germans alike had begun the search for answers to emerging questions. What will it mean for Germany to be a "sovereign nation" again? Will German attempts of the past four decades to develop a postnational, European identity begin to fade, or will they be reinforced in this postunification era? What role will Germany play in Europe as well as globally? Will Germany dominate Europe again, and, if so, in what way? How will the new Germany, still carrying burdens from the past, define its national interest in the future?

Major Foreign Policy Goals and Strategies

Early Developments

Imperial Germany's foreign policy, from Otto von Bismarck's founding of the empire in 1871 until the empire's collapse at the end of World War I, was influenced by the country's exposed geographical situation, Germany's *Mittellage*, as well as by domestic difficulties. Looking abroad, German policy makers were often obsessed with the threat of encirclement (*Einkreisung*) by hostile neighbor states. Thus, after 1871 German foreign policy objectives centered on two principal tasks: to keep France, Germany's historical rival and enemy, isolated; and to balance the other major powers of the day in order to ensure that no single power would be able to exert pressure or militarily confront the newly united German state.

"Modern Germany was born encircled," writes David P. Calleo, a noted foreign affairs specialist. Indeed, German leaders of the late nineteenth and early twentieth centuries were often concerned with their country's vulnerability. They were preoccupied with national frontiers and responded to this preoccupation with a heavy emphasis on military power. Yet the international policy, or *Weltpolitik,* of Bismarck (1862–90) and Kaiser Wilhelm II (r. 1888–1918) differed little from that of other major European powers of the day, such as Britain or France. But Germany would come to fight and lose two world wars in the first half of the twentieth century. And the disastrous consequences of German militarism and the barbaric actions of Nazi Germany, in particular, had a profound impact on the development of West Germany's foreign policy between 1949 and 1989.

At first glance, the situation facing united Germany in the 1990s resembles the situation faced by imperial Germany, insofar as Germany has reclaimed a *Mittellage* and has returned geographically to the heart of the continent (surrounded by nine immediate neighbors). Yet the parallel ends there. Peaceful relations exist between Germany and bordering states. Like Germany, the country's neighbors are democratic. Relations between Germany and these neighbors are characterized not by confrontation but by economic cooperation and interdependence. In the first years following unification, there was no dispute about continued German membership in NATO. And Germany remains a faithful member of the EU—even as German policy makers have begun to reexamine their country's foreign policy and to search for a new hierarchy of German interests in Europe.

Postwar Developments

In the postwar period, the Federal Republic became known as "an economic giant" and a "political dwarf." During the Cold War, German foreign policy had been formulated under extraordinary circumstances. After World War II, the country was divided, and its sovereignty was limited. As a member of the Warsaw Pact (see Glossary), communist East Germany's foreign policy was closely aligned with that of the Soviet Union. West Germany's foreign policy became characterized by a penchant for political and economic power over military power, by its preference for multilateralism over the exercise of unilateral actions, and by its concentration on European rather than global policy issues.

The characteristics of West Germany as a civilian European power wedded to multilateral structures stood in stark contrast to German colonialism of the late nineteenth and early twentieth centuries and the military expansion pursued by Germany under Adolf Hitler's National Socialist rule from 1933 to 1945. In fact, the patterns of West Germany's foreign policy were very much a direct consequence of military defeat and occupation by the Allied Powers at the end of World War II. In reaction to the excesses of the past, the Federal Republic's foreign policy establishment developed a clear and strong aversion to power politics and remained reluctant to draw on populist, national sentiment in support of foreign policy goals.

Emblematic of West Germany's foreign policy was Bonn's Ostpolitik—the opening to the east that became a continuous, albeit varied, thread in the policies practiced by both center-left and center-right governments in Bonn over the two decades preceding the collapse of the Soviet bloc. Ostpolitik began in 1969, when Germany's coalition formed by the Social Democratic Party of Germany (Sozialdemokratische Partei Deutschlands—SPD) and the Free Democratic Party (Freie Demokratische Partei—FDP) first took office. Ostpolitik was the result of a concept known as *Wandel durch Annäherung*, or change through rapprochement, created by Chancellor Willy Brandt (1969–74) and his close adviser, Egon Bahr.

Ostpolitik was Bonn's policy of détente toward communist Europe. It rested on two assumptions: that the Federal Republic, despite the crimes subsequently committed by communist regimes, had a special responsibility to compensate Eastern Europe for the aggression and atrocities carried out by Nazi Germany; and that a web of treaties and agreements with the Soviet bloc would improve human rights for the citizens of these neighboring communist states, while creating a peace-inducing dialogue with communist regimes. Consequently, Ostpolitik consisted of three components: West Germany's relations with the Soviet Union, its ties to East Germany, and its dealings with the rest of Eastern Europe. In the case of East Germany, Ostpolitik represented Bonn's attempt through dialogue and cooperation with communist rulers to help overcome some of the burdens of Germany's division.

Unification

On November 28, 1989, three weeks after the breach of the Berlin Wall, Chancellor Helmut Kohl (1982–) presented to the Bundestag (the lower house of West Germany's parliament) his Ten-Point Plan outlining his proposal for the incremental creation of a confederation between the two German states. Kohl believed at the time—an overly optimistic assessment as history would soon show—that the process of internal economic unification could be achieved in three to four years.

There was much talk at the time that in presenting his Ten-Point Plan Chancellor Kohl was engaging in an overly assertive style of diplomacy because he had failed to adequately consult his partners within the governing coalition as well as the Western Allies. A number of leading members of the opposition SPD, moreover, rejected the idea of unification, viewing moves toward unity as a threat to the postwar order of peace and stability in Europe. The initial push by the Kohl government toward unification was driven by a number of considerations.

Kohl feared that if Bonn were not able to immediately set the terms and course of international discussion about events in East Germany, other European countries, particularly the Soviet Union and France, might seek a new variation on the most recent solution of the "German Question," namely, arranging for the containment of Germany within Europe's international order by dividing it into two. French president François Mitterrand's announcement of his intention to visit East Berlin just days prior to Kohl's Bundestag speech, for instance, fueled fears in Bonn that anxious neighbors might attempt to stabilize East Germany's fragile communist regime and its hemorrhaging economy.

There were domestic considerations for West Germany's chancellor as well. Kohl worried that if his party, the Christian Democratic Union (Christlich Demokratische Union—CDU), did not seize the issue of unification and articulate a bold plan of action, political opponents might step in to fill the vacuum. Kohl's rivals included the SPD, but also the FDP, the junior partner in Kohl's coalition government, in power since late 1982. West Germany's federal president, Richard von Weizsäcker (1984–94), a member of Kohl's party, feared that the right-wing radical Republikaner (Die Republikaner) could make the issue their own in the upcoming national election campaign if the CDU did not preempt it.

It also had become clear within weeks of Kohl's proposed Ten-Point Plan that governing elites would be forced to respond to overwhelming pressure from the streets of East German cities and towns. The ways in which Kohl later defended the terms and timing of economic and monetary union with

East Germany illustrate this fact. He often reminded his critics that if Bonn were not prepared to bring the deutsche mark to East Germany, the East Germans would surely come to the deutsche mark, an allusion to the growing tide of East-West migration during the first six months of 1990.

Chancellor Kohl's Ten-Point Plan sought to intensify rapprochement with East Germany. The ten points consisted of calling for immediate measures to provide aid; cooperation with the GDR on an economic and cultural level; fundamental political and economic change in the GDR; a close-knit network of agreements; confederative structures, with the goal of forming a federation in Germany; a future structure of Germany that would fit into the future architecture of Europe as a whole; the power of attraction of the EC to remain a constant feature; the continuation of the CSCE process as a crucial part of the total European architecture, but with the possibility of new institutional forms; disarmament and arms control to keep step with political developments; and freedom within Europe to be maintained in such a way that the German people could, via self-determination, restore their unity. The reattainment of German state unity by peaceful means remained the political goal of the federal government.

In fact, East Germany disintegrated at an astonishing pace, and German foreign policy from late 1989 throughout 1990 was driven by concerns directly related to the unification process. In February 1990, East Germany's communist party, the Socialist Unity Party of Germany (Sozialistische Einheitspartei Deutschlands—SED), transformed itself into the Party of Democratic Socialism (Partei des Demokratischen Sozialismus—PDS). East Germany's new prime minister, Hans Modrow, insisted that the reformed PDS would be able to find a "third way" between capitalism and socialism, permitting the GDR another life as a separate independent German state. Democratization and elections in May 1990 would legitimate the PDS's leading role in this process, Modrow believed, and would provide a new basis for relations between East Germany and West Germany.

The plans of East German reform communists were derailed in a matter of months, however. Discredited SED officials were publicly harassed and in some cases arrested for abuse of power and privilege. The leading role of the communist party was revoked from the GDR's constitution, and offices of the State Security Service (Staatssicherheitsdienst, commonly referred to as Stasi), the despised secret police, were occupied by citizens groups at sites throughout the country. Of the SED's 2.3 million members, nearly 1.6 million had deserted by early 1990.

By the end of January 1990, a deteriorating economy, sustained demonstrations throughout the country, and the daily exit of some 2,000 East German citizens for West Germany compelled opposition leaders who made up the Round Table, an interim "government," to convince Modrow to advance the date of East German elections from May 6 to March 18. By late spring, most observers agreed that the elections would no longer be a referendum on communist rule (opinion polls suggested that the communists would be defeated in fair, free elections), but rather on the terms and timing of German unification.

Confronted by this reality, Soviet leader Mikhail Gorbachev, having previously insisted that Moscow would not accept abolition of the East German state, retreated from this hard-line position. Although Gorbachev had renounced the Soviet Union's right to determine the national policies of Warsaw Pact members during the years and months prior to the breach of the Berlin Wall, the Soviet leadership had remained steadfastly committed to the overall status quo in Europe and to Germany's division into two states.

As the Berlin Wall collapsed and Kohl announced his Ten-Point Plan, the Soviet leadership delivered a number of statements and gestures that made it clear that Moscow had no intention of relinquishing its East German ally. Reasserting occupation rights, the Soviet Union called for a meeting of the ambassadors of the World War II Allies, which took place on December 11 at the Allied Control Council building in Berlin. A stream of Kremlin advisers insisted in interviews that unification was neither desirable nor feasible.

Nevertheless, on January 30 Prime Minister Modrow flew to Moscow for a meeting with Gorbachev, after which Gorbachev consented in principle to Germany's self-determination. When Modrow returned to East Berlin, he announced his own plan for inner-German rapprochement, a "Declaration on the Way to German Unity." The plan envisaged a confederation between the two German states, leading eventually to an all-German federation. According to the plan, both Bonn and East Berlin would gradually distance themselves from their respective alliance commitments.

In a speech delivered in West Berlin on December 12, United States secretary of state James Baker, echoing the position outlined by United States president George Bush in a meeting with Chancellor Kohl earlier that month, had already tacitly given Washington's green light for German unity. Although the French and British gradually overcame initial misgivings, Baker, and later Kohl and West German minister of foreign affairs Hans-Dietrich Genscher, visited Gorbachev in February to further assuage Soviet security concerns. In a meeting with Gorbachev, Baker formally presented what became known as the Nine Assurances, a collection of various Western guarantees provided to the Soviet Union to make the process of German unification more palatable.

Meanwhile, pressured by fears that East Germany might collapse (and by the conviction that the opportunity to unite the two German states would exist only as long as Gorbachev remained in power), the Kohl government began to push diplomatic negotiations toward a speedy solution of the German Question. Kohl's Ten-Point Plan was being overtaken by events.

Already in the beginning of February, discussions had begun about the introduction of West Germany's currency into East Germany. Also as a result of the quickened pace of events, the foreign ministers of the four World War II Allies and of the two German states agreed in mid-February to begin formal talks on German unity (the Two-Plus-Four Talks). The external conditions for unification were put into place.

The Two-Plus-Four Talks were intended to provide an instrument with which to shape German unification and hence the new post-Cold War world in Europe without excluding key players from the process. There were fears, in particular in Washington and Bonn, that a bitter sense of defeat and exclusion in Moscow might engender a climate analogous to that which had developed in Germany after the Treaty of Versailles and that had characterized the Weimar period. The existence of a humiliated and vanquished power that might later seek to forcibly reshape the European order (as Hitler's Germany had sought to do) was to be precluded at all costs. More immediately, United States, German, and other West European diplomats wanted to avoid creating a domestic crisis for Gorbachev, to whom most Western leaders had tied their hopes for a sustained liberal posture of the Soviet Union.

Free and fair elections for East Germany's Volkskammer (People's Chamber) were held on March 18, 1990. The result was a victory for the CDU-led Alliance for Germany, which received a plurality of the vote. The alliance and the other parties that supported unification (the SPD, the Alliance of Free Democrats, and the German Social Union) received the votes of roughly three-fourths of the East German electorate. Opinion polls underscored the same message expressed in the election results. The vast majority of the population in the GDR rejected communism, reformed or otherwise, and supported unification with the Federal Republic.

East Germany's first (and last) democratically elected prime minister, Lothar de Maizière, promptly fulfilled his mandate. On April 19, he announced that he would seek unity with West Germany as soon as possible. As a first step, East Berlin's new government agreed with Bonn on economic and monetary union, which took place on July 1.

The external conditions governing Germany's unification had meanwhile been in process. Following the first Two-Plus-Four meeting in mid-February, subsequent meetings were held in March, June, July, and September 1990. In late June, the national legislatures in East Berlin and in Bonn approved a resolution recognizing the inviolability of Poland's borders as determined after World War II, confirming the Oder-Neisse rivers as the permanent border between Poland and the future united Germany. On August 31, 1990, the Unification Treaty was signed in East Berlin by officials of both German states. The treaty stipulated that the five newly reconstituted *Länder* in the GDR would accede to the Federal Republic on October 3, 1990, as provided for under Article 23 of the Basic Law.

The remaining external aspects relating to German unification were quickly settled. After having consented to unification, Gorbachev and his foreign minister, Eduard Shevardnadze, had at first insisted that united Germany accept a demilitarized, neutral status. When this was rejected by West Germany, they then argued that Germany should remain in both NATO and the Warsaw Pact for a transitional period. In this context, GDR minister of national defense Admiral Theodor Hoffmann proposed in late February 1990 the creation of a joint army for united Germany (a force that would be reduced to less than one-third the combined size of the armed forces of the FRG and the GDR). He also proposed that, pending elections and further negotiations, both states continue to belong to their respective alliances.

That same month, however, following a meeting at Camp David, Chancellor Kohl and President Bush had reemphasized their commitment to unified Germany's full membership in NATO. They stressed that East Germany would initially enjoy a special military status in deference to security concerns of the Soviet Union. To this end, West German minister of foreign affairs Genscher, especially attuned to Soviet sensitivities, had formulated a plan to assuage Soviet concerns. According to Genscher's plan, NATO forces would not be moved to the territory of the former GDR.

In the early weeks of the spring of 1990, Soviet resistance to united Germany's full membership in NATO, particularly in light of the GDR's elections in March, became increasingly untenable. Finally, in mid-July, consultations among Kohl, Genscher, and Gorbachev in the Caucasian town of Stavropol secured Soviet permission for Germany to enjoy full sovereignty and remain in NATO.

A communiqué issued by NATO from London the previous week had helped to facilitate the reversal of the Soviet position as did West German largesse to the Soviet Union in the form of aid and credits. The London declaration announced that NATO had become "an indispensable factor of stability" for Europe's profound transition and hence would seek to extend the Alliance's "hand of friendship" to its former enemies in the Soviet Union and Eastern Europe.

Kohl and Genscher agreed that united Germany would recommit to earlier pledges to renounce production and possession of nuclear, biological, and chemical weapons. Both German states also declared on August 30, 1990, at the Conventional Forces in Europe (CFE) talks in Vienna, that the united country would reduce its armed forces to 370,000 within three to four years. West Germany's leadership also guaranteed that NATO's military organization would not be extended to GDR territory as long as Soviet forces remained stationed there. In return, Kohl obtained from Gorbachev agreement that the roughly 400,000 Soviet troops stationed in East Germany would be withdrawn by the end of 1994. The Kohl government also pledged financial assistance for the repatriation of the Soviet troops.

The Kohl-Gorbachev agreements paved the way for signing the Treaty on the Final Settlement with Respect to Germany, or, as it is more commonly known, the Two-Plus-Four Treaty, on September 12, 1990. Within this framework, the two German states, together with the United States, the Soviet Union, France, and Britain, were able to confirm the unification of Germany as consisting of the GDR, the FRG, and Berlin. In addition, the Federal Republic and the Soviet Union signed a Treaty on Good-Neighborliness, Partnership, and Cooperation in September 1990. That same month, the GDR's minister of defense and disarmament and the commander in chief of the Warsaw Pact's armed forces concluded an agreement that provided for the GDR's immediate withdrawal from the Warsaw Pact.

Bonn and Warsaw also concluded a separate treaty that took into account the special concerns Poland had about its security. For a period of time, the topic of the German-Polish border had proved a controversial and divisive issue for coalition politics in Bonn and for the unification process in general. Kohl's reluctance to declare the issue settled, stemming from legal concerns as well as domestic political considerations, fueled anxieties in Poland and elsewhere in Europe about the course of a united Germany. On June 21, 1990, however, both German parliaments had passed resolutions recognizing Poland's western border as final, stipulating that a separate treaty between Poland and a united Germany would formally consummate this understanding.

On October 1, 1990, all Four-Power rights in Germany and Berlin ended when representatives of the four victorious countries in World War II signed a document in New York recognizing full German sovereignty. On October 3, the Unification Treaty went into effect, and the five new *Länder* formed in the territory of the former GDR acceded to the Federal Republic as provided for under Article 23 of the Basic Law.

Foreign Reaction to Unification

German unification upset the political equilibrium in many of Western and Eastern Europe's political establishments. Although French public opinion had tended to support German unity, French leaders feared that a resurgent united Germany would dominate Europe and usurp their aspirations to play a leading role on the continent. President Mitterrand's trip to the GDR in December 1989, when he cautioned the East Germans against hasty unification, illustrated this sentiment.

In Britain, Prime Minister Margaret Thatcher's government harbored fears that German unification would accelerate European unification, quickening and deepening the gap between

*The departure of the United States, British, and French city
commanders from Berlin in 1991
Joyous crowds at the Brandenburg Gate in Berlin in November 1989
Courtesy German Information Center, New York*

London and the continent. Nicholas Ridley, an official in the Thatcher government, was forced to step down in the summer of 1990 in the wake of impolitic remarks he made about European economic union's being a German design for the domination of Europe. Thatcher, for her part, initially urged Chancellor Kohl's government to be patient on unification and only with reluctance later joined the United States in its pro-unity stance.

In the former Soviet bloc, aside from the Soviet Union, Poland sheltered the greatest distrust and suspicion of developments in Germany. These anxieties accounted for the separate treaty signed between united Germany and Poland in November 1990. The treaty confirmed the border (stipulated in the Two-Plus-Four Talks) and also outlined principles for good-neighborliness and cooperation between Warsaw and Bonn.

From the United States perspective, after offering Germany support for unification, President Bush promptly sought to reshape the German-United States alliance from a relationship in which West Germany had served as a junior partner to a more equal status in which Germany would become a "partner in leadership." Germany's changing relationship with the United States was in fact already evident. For example, it was without prior consultation with Washington that Chancellor Kohl and Soviet president Gorbachev had reached their agreement on the limit of 370,000 troops for Germany's armed forces, the Bundeswehr (West Germany had roughly 495,000 troops under arms in 1990; the GDR, 170,000) and the exclusion of NATO troops from the territory of eastern Germany.

Postunification Developments

United Germany, a state with 80 million inhabitants and an area bordering nine countries in Central Europe, confronted a daunting array of responsibilities and expectations with regard to its international role in the early 1990s. Following unification, its government adopted a policy aimed at fully integrating the newly enlarged Federal Republic into the primary instruments of international cooperation: the EC, NATO, the WEU, and the CSCE. In a deliberate effort to further assuage the concerns of its neighbors about German dominance on the continent, Bonn worked assiduously to bolster its multilateralist image.

President von Weizsäcker, Chancellor Kohl, and Minister of Foreign Affairs Genscher all went to great lengths to stress Germany's intention to renounce the power politics of past eras in favor of a "policy of responsibility." In the German view, this meant, on the one hand, a continuation of West German foreign policy based on the use of nonmilitary instruments. On the other hand, it meant a higher international profile in economic, human rights, and environmental issues. With the end of the Cold War, economic power, in the view of many officials and policy experts in Europe, had superseded military power in terms of political influence. Germans, above all, adhered to this belief.

At times, however, German foreign policy was self-centered. Squabbling over German interest rates (both in Europe and in the United States) in the autumn of 1992 underscored what many perceived as a new tilt toward German self-absorption and unilateralism that had been established the previous winter through Germany's policy toward the Balkans. Until the summer of 1991, Germany's policy toward Yugoslavia had mirrored the thinking in Washington and European capitals, namely, that Yugoslav unity should be preserved. For a number of domestic reasons, however, Bonn began to shift away from this policy, finally deciding on unilateral recognition of Croatia and Slovenia in December 1991.

In general, united Germany's foreign policy followed the resolutely multilateral stance developed in the postwar period. The German government played an enthusiastic role in the environmental summit in Rio de Janeiro in June 1992, emphasizing the importance it attached to international ecological concerns in its foreign policy. In the area of international aid, Bonn established criteria for developmental assistance based on a recipient country's respect for human rights, commitment to democracy and a market economy, and responsibility in arms development and procurement.

In the first years after the collapse of the Soviet bloc, Germany led the international aid effort for the former Soviet Union and for the countries of Central and Eastern Europe. Aid to Russia was paramount for policy makers in Bonn for a variety of reasons, including the desire to expedite the withdrawal of Soviet troops from eastern Germany and the wish to enhance Germany's security by promoting democracy and a market economy in Eastern Europe and in the Soviet Union's successor states.

Because of these vital concerns, the German government emerged as an important champion of aid to the former Soviet bloc. Chancellor Kohl repeatedly prodded his Western partners toward what he often termed "fair international burden-sharing" with regard to aid for the emerging democracies in the former Soviet bloc. The US$24 billion aid package of the Group of Seven (G–7—see Glossary) for Russia in April 1992 had come about to a large extent as a result of German insistence. In April 1993, the G–7 announced an additional aid package for Russia totaling approximately US$50 billion. By this time, German aid to the successor states of the Soviet Union totaled more than DM90 billion (for value of the deutsche mark—see Glossary). According to Chancellor Kohl, this amount represented more than half of all Western contributions since 1989. German aid to the Commonwealth of Independent States (CIS—see Glossary) included export credit guarantees for long-term loans; sustained support for the withdrawal and reintegration of CIS troops stationed in eastern Germany; financial help to aid the CIS in its development of market institutions and infrastructure; and more than DM100 million in bilateral and multilateral aid to improve safety standards in Soviet-designed nuclear power plants.

Part of German aid to the CIS was to provide for the material well-being of the estimated 2 million ethnic Germans who still resided in former Soviet republics. This aid was designed to offer incentives for ethnic Germans to remain in Russia and in other CIS states rather than to emigrate to Germany, where they had the right to become citizens of the Federal Republic and receive significant amounts of help in becoming integrated into the homeland of their ancestors (see Immigration, ch. 3). The German government has even discussed with Russian representatives the possibility of restoring the "Volga Republic" disbanded by Joseph Stalin in 1941 as a possible area of settlement for ethnic Germans in Russia.

Elsewhere in Eastern Europe, the subject of ethnic German minorities has played a role in German foreign policy. By the mid-1990s, German-Czech relations, for example, still had not been fully normalized, to a large extent because expellee groups in the Federal Republic continued to lobby for restitution or compensation for property owned by Germans in the former Czechoslovakia and confiscated after World War II. The German-Czech Friendship Treaty was signed in 1992, but it failed to address the question of compensation for Czech victims of Nazism.

Foreign Policy Formulation

Institutional Framework

Structural weaknesses of the German central government were deliberately crafted during the years of Allied occupation (1945–49) to preclude the possibility that extremists could once again return to government (see Constitutional Framework, ch. 7). The chancellor, the cabinet, and the legislature all contribute to the policy-making process. Moreover, power is divided between the federal and *Land* governments. Foreign policy is the prerogative of the federal government, but *Länder* are permitted to conclude agreements with foreign countries; such agreements in turn are subject to approval by the federal government.

Article 65 of the Basic Law stipulates that the federal chancellor is responsible for general policy, and the Federal Chancellery (the chancellor's office) serves as the center for policy review and coordination. The chancellor's direct executive role is limited, however. Although he or she has wide powers to name political appointees in government, the chancellor does not enjoy complete freedom in making appointments to cabinet posts. Political necessity demands, for instance, the guarantee of a number of cabinet posts to coalition partners. In 1995, for example, important portfolios, such as economics and foreign affairs, were controlled by the FDP, Helmut Kohl's junior coalition partner. The resulting diversity of views at the highest level of government accounts for sustained policy splits and a process in which it is at times difficult to resolve particularly contentious issues.

The Ministry of Foreign Affairs is the central department for planning and implementing foreign policy. Like the United States, Germany has a corps of professional diplomats. Those wishing to join Germany's foreign service may file their application once a year. Successful candidates undergo a two-year training program. About one-third of Germany's diplomats are lawyers.

The Ministry of Foreign Affairs shares responsibility for foreign economic policy with the Ministry for Economics and the Ministry of Finance; security policy is coordinated with the Ministry of Defense. Although the executive branch generally takes the initiative in foreign affairs, the Bundestag (the lower house of parliament) and the Bundesrat (the upper house of parliament) are involved in the policy-making process. These bodies ratify foreign treaties and approve most legislation and budgetary provisions. Parliamentary groups (*Fraktionen*; sing., *Fraktion*) in the Bundestag and various committees pertaining to foreign affairs provide organizational structure for the policy-making process.

Domestic Influences on Foreign Policy

Foreign Policy Positions of the Political Parties

Members of Kohl's CDU and its Bavarian sister party, the Christian Social Union (Christlich-Soziale Union—CSU), assert that transatlantic links should be given priority over more European-dominated organizations such as the CSCE, especially in the discussion of security matters. They also stress that assumption of responsibility in international affairs would necessarily demand a resolution of the "out-of-area" debate, that is, whether Germany would be allowed to participate alongside Alliance partners in future military operations.

The CSU has distinguished itself from the CDU by pushing a slightly more confident tone regarding what its members perceive as German national interests. Notable in this regard were CSU demands that Bonn and Prague renegotiate a friendship treaty to give greater emphasis to property claims of ethnic Germans (living mostly in Bavaria) who had emigrated or been expelled from Czechoslovakia after World War II. In May 1992, the CSU announced that it would vote against the German-Czechoslovak friendship treaty in the Bundesrat.

Minister of Foreign Affairs Genscher's party, the FDP, is perhaps the least nationalistic and the most multilateral in philosophy of the German political parties when it comes to the subject of foreign policy. Although FDP voters, like those of the CDU, strongly favor membership in NATO and rapid European unification, FDP supporters have stressed to a greater extent than the other parties the importance of CSCE institutions and policies aimed at arms control and arms reductions. Holding views markedly different in this regard than those held by the CDU/CSU, FDP voters place far less emphasis on the participation of German soldiers in peacekeeping and peacemaking missions under UN auspices.

Germany's Minister of Foreign Affairs Hans-Dietrich Genscher with Britain's Secretary of State for Foreign and Commonwealth Affairs Douglas Hurd during the Two-Plus-Four Talks in Bonn in May 1990
Courtesy German Information Center, New York

On foreign policy issues, the SPD is distinct in a number of ways from the ruling coalition government in Bonn. Like the FDP, the SPD is a strong supporter of the CSCE but favors greater restrictions on out-of-area missions for the Bundeswehr. Although fundamentally multilateralist in sentiment (the SPD supports a United States of Europe and more responsibility for the UN in collective security), the SPD is apt to express its desire that Germany play a singular and special role in international relations because of its recent troubled history. A survey taken in the early 1990s found that 35 percent of SPD voters preferred a neutral status for united Germany. Of the major political parties, the SDP is the biggest supporter of neutrality and on balance offers the lowest support for NATO.

The Greens (Die Grünen), a western German environmentalist party, united in 1993 with an eastern German political group, Alliance 90 (Bündnis 90), to form Alliance 90/The Greens, commonly called the Greens. Surveys from the early 1990s found that one-third of the traditionally pacifist Green voters supported continued membership in NATO. Nearly 50 percent backed European unity. Although the Greens adamantly opposed German participation in Operation Desert Storm, some members have begun to call for a multilateral military intervention in the Balkan war. However, they either eschew the question of or oppose German involvement.

Other small parties, such as the PDS and the right-wing radical Republikaner (Die Republikaner—REP), are either opposed to or reluctant to support German membership in NATO and reject European integration (according to the Republikaner) as subordinating German interests to a pan-European bureaucratic architecture. Neither the PDS nor the Republikaner played a significant role in mainstream debate during the first several years following unification.

Public Opinion

After unification, Germany soon became confident about its greater responsibility in international relations. According to a 1991 Rand Corporation survey, 62 percent of the population said they thought that Germany should pursue a more active international role. Some 77 percent voiced the opinion that their country was best suited to play the leading foreign policy role in Europe. There were even signs that Germans were coming to terms with the idea of international military intervention. In 1992 about 53 percent of Germans (compared with 43 percent the previous year) said they believed that the use of military force is justified when principles of international law and human rights are violated.

The reluctance of Germans to think in terms of their country's involvement in multilateral military actions remained high, however. Although 53 percent supported participation of the Bundeswehr in peacekeeping operations after unification, barely 33 percent favored German military involvement in NATO operations outside of German territory. Only 20 percent were sympathetic to the idea of German forces participating in collective security actions such as Operation Desert Storm. A 1994 follow-up study by the Rand Corporation found increasing support in German public opinion for a German defense role beyond the country's borders. But data also reflected uncertainty about what that role should entail.

In the aftermath of communism's demise, Germans, especially Germans living in the old *Länder*, continued to believe that NATO was essential to their security. They did so even though the contours of a distinct threat had not emerged and even though Germany's new international role remained very much in question. A 1990–91 study by the Rand Corporation commissioned by the United States Air Force discovered that 85 percent of the German populace supported membership in international alliances in general, with two out of three western Germans considering NATO essential for their security. (A West German Emnid poll in the autumn of 1988 had shown 86 percent favoring NATO membership.) By contrast, only 35 percent of eastern Germans considered NATO indispensable. The fact that western Germans made up roughly four-fifths of united Germany's population and that western Germans dominated the united country's policy establishment led most analysts to conclude that the addition of eastern Germany would have a minimal impact on the Federal Republic's foreign policy.

The German position on the presence of United States troops remains one of ambivalence. According to the Rand study, 57 percent supported a complete withdrawal of United States troops from the territory of the Federal Republic. Western Germans were divided in their view—43 percent favoring and 49 percent rejecting the sustained presence of these troops. Eastern Germans demonstrated greater consensus on the issue of United States troops, with 84 percent opposing a future United States military presence.

When asked why one should support NATO in the post-Cold War era, western Germans gave as the primary reason the fact that the defense organization had become a fixture on the political landscape over the course of previous decades and had done a good job in maintaining peace on the continent. Few respondents felt that NATO should have more military responsibilities, however. In fact, 42 percent voiced apprehension that NATO could be used in the future to draw Germany into conflicts where its interests were not represented. The impressions from these results were roughly aligned with the findings from polls conducted by German institutes during the same time frame. In 1991 a majority of Germans regarded Switzerland—a neutral although not demilitarized state—as an appropriate model for the new Germany's role in international affairs.

The Out-of-Area Debate

Immediately after unification, the prevailing interpretation of the Basic Law allowed for the Federal Republic's participation in systems of collective security but precluded its armed forces from any activity not specifically attributable to the country's defense, unless explicitly authorized elsewhere in the constitution. Article 26 of the Basic Law forbids any act of war or aggression, and Article 87 stipulates that German military forces are permitted to become involved only in defense actions. The question of German participation in out-of-area operations played an important role in German foreign policy debates of the early 1990s.

The interpretation that combat missions outside the traditional area covered by NATO are not permitted under the constitution had been ratified by a decision by the SPD-led government of Chancellor Helmut Schmidt (1974–82) in April 1981. This view was reconfirmed in 1983 by the new Kohl government soon after it took power.

The debate on out-of-area operations during the Persian Gulf War led to a consensus by the major political parties—although for varying reasons—that rather than reinterpretation, the constitution was in need of amendment to allow German forces to assume a new role in collective security. Amending the constitution requires a two-thirds majority in both the Bundestag and the Bundesrat. Conflict arose, first because the opposition SPD rejected the idea of an amendment, then later because neither the SPD nor the other parties could agree on the precise provisions of such an amendment.

The SPD insisted that an amendment to the constitution allow for German participation in UN peacekeeping operations only. This position was reached after heated debate at the party's convention in May 1991, and even then, only with the strong push of SPD leader Björn Engholm and the party's moderate faction. The measure passed by the relatively small margin of 230 to 179. The SPD stopped short of supporting German participation in combat missions sanctioned under Chapter VII of the UN Charter, which means that in the future, operations such as Desert Storm would not mandate German involvement.

Citing special constraints stemming from German history and fears that Germany, against its own interests, would be drawn into conflicts by other powers (notably the United States), the SPD envisioned a narrow set of circumstances for the deployment of German forces. These included a mandate by the UN Security Council; a cease-fire; consent of the warring parties; operational control by the UN; and the participation of other European countries. The SPD's position also reflected the party's devotion to the idea that diplomatic and economic means, and only rarely, if ever, the military, could provide for Germany's defense and security.

The FDP followed the lead outlined by Genscher, its dovish foreign minister, and, like the SPD, agreed on restricting the Bundeswehr's activities to blue-helmet peacekeeping missions. An amendment to the constitution would explicitly require UN authorization for out-of-area deployments, even when Germans were participating within NATO and WEU units. In an attempt to further limit the opportunity for actual combat involvement and to stress the European character of the new German state, the FDP also stipulated that fighting missions be permitted only when other EC members were present.

The CDU was predictably not satisfied with restrictions that provided exclusively for blue-helmet missions. Members of the CDU and the CSU had initially argued that an amendment to the constitution was not necessary in order for German troops to cooperate in multilateral military operations abroad. They pointed to Article 24(2), of the Basic Law, which empowers the Federal Republic to participate in systems of collective security such as the UN. Proponents of this argument rejected the idea that the term "defense," as applied in Article 87a(2) of the Basic Law, should be interpreted narrowly and tied exclusively to the defense of Germany or of an alliance partner.

Nevertheless, Kohl's party had agreed that the constitution must be amended in order to permit German troops a role in peacekeeping and peacemaking missions abroad. Kohl's party wanted not only UN missions mandated by the constitution but also NATO and WEU out-of-area missions. In the view of leading defense experts in the CDU, these were the only organizations capable of providing defense. Neither the UN nor the CSCE, favorites of the FDP and the SPD, were considered viable instruments of military action. Some more outspoken members of the CDU and CSU favored a reduction of all constraints on the exercise of German power in an attempt to equalize the Federal Republic's room for maneuvering with Britain and France.

Minister of Defense Volker Rühe strongly argued in favor of Germany's assuming full and normal responsibilities in peace-keeping and peacemaking operations within the Alliance. But he also frequently stressed that German public opinion would only gradually adapt to its new international circumstance.

In an attempt to sensitize the German public to changes in the international climate and the united country's emerging responsibilities, the Kohl government had been incrementally enlarging German military participation in operations abroad, arguably within the confines of the constitution. Bonn allowed German minesweepers and their crews to operate in the Persian Gulf from April through July 1991 after the war had ended, justifying the mission on humanitarian grounds. The German government used Bundeswehr personnel to supply transportation and to assist in the establishment of refugee camps in Iran and Iraq for Kurds, who had been persecuted by Iraqi forces. German military medical personnel were assigned in May 1992 to participate in the UN mission in Cambodia. German military units joined in the UN's humanitarian effort in Somalia in 1992–93, but only after arduous parliamentary debate. German forces also were involved in the Adriatic when UN forces monitored compliance with the internationally imposed arms embargo by parties in the Yugoslav conflict. In an important decision of July 12, 1994, Germany's highest court, the Federal Constitutional Court, ruled that German troops can take part in both UN peacekeeping and peacemaking missions, as long as the Bundestag approves each operation by a simple majority. The court also stated that Germany can assign forces to NATO and WEU operations directed at implementing resolutions of the UN Security Council. Thus, the decision cleared the way for a German military role beyond the country's and NATO's current borders, and German fliers subsequently participated in NATO missions over Bosnia.

The conduct of foreign policy continues to belong to the domain of the executive branch of government in Germany. But the highly controversial and emotional debate concerning German participation in peacekeeping and peacemaking missions abroad has meant that the Bundestag will continue to be directly involved in the actual decision-making process.

438

International Cooperation

North Atlantic Treaty Organization

During the Cold War era, the North Atlantic Treaty Organization (NATO) was central to the formulation and implementation of West Germany's foreign and defense policies. In 1954 and 1955 (the year the Warsaw Pact was established), agreements were reached by the Allied powers to end the occupation of the Federal Republic and grant West Germany sovereignty. It was in conjunction with these decisions that West Germany had been permitted to rearm and to obtain membership in the Western European Union (WEU) and NATO. Nevertheless, under the Western European Union Treaty of May 1955, the Federal Republic was prohibited from possessing weapons of mass destruction. Moreover, all West German armed forces were assigned to NATO and could not operate out of area.

During the Cold War, the underlying tone of NATO's strategy shifted at times to accommodate the changing security environment in the United States and in Europe. For example, in 1967 the Harmel Report, developed during the advent of Willy Brandt's Ostpolitik in Germany, helped initiate the West's dual strategy of defense and détente with the Soviet bloc. The Harmel Report's aversion to confrontation was further amplified by the 1975 Helsinki Accords, or the Final Act of the Conference on Security and Cooperation in Europe (CSCE). The CSCE was to provide a framework for cooperation between NATO and Warsaw Pact members by intensifying contacts and respecting the inviolability of Eastern Europe's postwar borders.

Despite the prevailing climate of détente in the 1970s, NATO remained for the United States and its allies the principal instrument with which to deter Soviet aggression on the continent and if necessary to defend the West European democracies from attack by the Warsaw Pact. To this end, the role of the Federal Republic was indispensable. West Germany was the frontline state and home to the largest concentration of United States troops and NATO-controlled nuclear weapons in the European theater. Across the border in the GDR, the Soviet Union had amassed its greatest number of troops outside its own territory.

Since its founding, NATO had served other functions as well. After World War II, policy makers in Washington and in major European capitals had sought to curb and control German power by wedding the West German state to multilateral institutions. Hence, NATO (and to some extent the EC) was designed not only as an instrument with which to keep the Soviet Union out of Western Europe but also as a means to constrain Germany from returning to the expansionist behavior that had characterized its foreign policy in the first half of the century. Thus, NATO's purpose was often said to reflect a strategy of double containment: to contain the Soviet Union as well as Germany. In addition, NATO was also to perform the broader function of muting the traditional regional rivalries that had previously undermined Europe's peace and stability.

As far as West Germany was concerned, it practiced what was often referred to as a policy of self-containment. West Germany's postwar leaders deliberately subjugated national interests to the stated objectives of the EC and NATO. Embracing federalism and the inculcation of democratic values, the West German public and political elites also accepted Germany's adjustment to the role of civilian power and junior partner in the Alliance. Once the economic miracle had taken place and the reconstruction of Germany had given way to prosperity, this development in the German posture was reflected in the adage that the West German democracy was "an economic giant but a political dwarf."

Although NATO's primary raison d'être collapsed with the disintegration of the Soviet empire (in Germany the GDR's armed forces were absorbed by the Bundeswehr), new uncertainties and instabilities in the international climate after 1989 led many observers to conclude that the Atlantic Alliance, which came into force in April 1949, ought to remain intact. Many viewed NATO's expansion to the east as a necessary means to ensure the security of the emerging democracies of Central and Eastern Europe. Others continued to view NATO as a means to prevent the renationalization of German security policy. Questions about united Germany's role in international affairs in general, and in a revamped NATO in particular, became paramount to policy makers on both sides of the Atlantic.

In the early summer of 1992, NATO officials announced that the Alliance was prepared to assume a peacekeeping role in Europe beyond the border of its sixteen member states. According to a plan approved at the June 1992 meeting of NATO foreign ministers in Oslo, NATO would henceforth consider contributing troops, supplies, and logistical support to CSCE peacekeeping missions. Clearer details regarding NATO's new military mission, however, remained in doubt in the mid-1990s.

NATO had already begun to grapple with questions about its future during the Two-Plus-Four Talks. The London Declaration on NATO of July 6, 1990, articulated a vision that kept the NATO treaty in force as a factor of stability across Europe. Reflecting a fundamental change of atmosphere precipitated by communism's collapse, NATO members committed themselves to transforming the Western Alliance from adversary to friend for the members of the former Soviet bloc. Illustrating this transformation were the visits of Czechoslovak president Vaclav Havel and Polish president Lech Walesa to NATO Headquarters in Brussels in early 1991. In fact, by the end of that same year Russian president Boris Yeltsin suggested that his own country might apply for NATO membership.

Minister of Foreign Affairs Genscher was a staunch proponent of institutionalizing cooperative links between East and West. In the Declaration on Peace and Cooperation adopted on November 8, 1991, leaders of the sixteen NATO nations meeting in Rome submitted to eight Central and East European countries (Bulgaria, Czechoslovakia, Estonia, Hungary, Latvia, Lithuania, Poland, and Romania) and the Soviet Union proposals to institutionalize consultations among former adversaries on a broad range of security concerns.

Because many Central and East European countries were beset with ethnic tensions in the early 1990s and still had unresolved border disputes with neighbors, NATO officials felt it unreasonable to anticipate early NATO membership. Short of full membership, however, former members of the Warsaw Pact were invited to join Western states to form the North Atlantic Cooperation Council (NACC). The NACC had been proposed at the initiative of Minister of Foreign Affairs Genscher and Secretary of State Baker at the end of 1991.

The NACC began by mid-1992 to hold regular meetings at the ministerial or ambassadorial level with various NATO committees and authorities tasked with the oversight of military, political, and economic issues of concern to member states. In April 1993, German Minister of Defense Rühe traveled to Moscow to sign the first extensive agreement between Russian and German armed forces. Under the ten-year agreement, a wide range of contacts between Russian and German officers would take place.

In the context of this new collaborative posture between West and East, NATO members had already pledged themselves to a smaller, restructured field of active forces, reduced training and exercises, and enhanced flexibility and cooperative dialogue in deciding how to respond to future international crises. Also as a result of the London Declaration, which declared NATO's forward posture in Europe no longer necessary, NATO countries had begun to reduce or withdraw their forces from the Central European theater, and from Germany in particular.

NATO's Partnership for Peace (PfP), launched in January 1994, sought even stronger links between democratic countries of the former Soviet bloc and the Alliance. Membership in the PfP enabled these countries to consult with NATO and cooperate in joint multilateral crisis activities.

In the 1990s, the predominant view held by the mainstream of Germany's defense establishment is that NATO remains essential for German security for three primary reasons: the Alliance is a crucial source of stability for a continent in the throes of profound transformations; NATO serves as an indispensable bridge to the United States and functionally helps to counter that country's neo-isolationism by maintaining a visible United States presence in Europe; and NATO remains the only viable instrument for German and European defense, given that the EU, WEU, and OSCE are all still untested in the coordination and implementation of defense policies.

Western European Union

The EC had also taken steps during the first post-Cold War years to enhance its competence in foreign affairs. In the Treaty on European Union, signed on February 7, 1992, in Maastricht, representatives of the EC's twelve members agreed to take steps toward developing a common European foreign and defense policy. The treaty (commonly referred to as the Maastricht Treaty) stipulated that the European Council, composed of the heads of state and government in the member states, would decide together on guidelines that would frame a common foreign and security policy. The council would also monitor the implementation of policies agreed upon. In conjunction with this diplomatic consensus, it was agreed that the Western European Union (WEU), after decades of relative dormancy, would become the primary instrument with which the continent would enhance its own defense capability.

Some European proponents suggested that the WEU could act as a complement to NATO by serving in capacities in which NATO would not. The WEU, for example, recognized no formal geographic limits to its potential operations. Those in the United States critical of moves to revive the WEU, however, suggested that a European defense structure was redundant and could evolve as a competitor for NATO resources and personnel. Italy and Britain proposed that the WEU become an arm of NATO, rather than an independent European security structure. NATO formally supported the process toward a European defense identity but emphasized that the Atlantic Alliance should remain the primary forum for the discussion of European security issues.

In Germany's view, the WEU, as the defense arm of the EU, would complement NATO. The December 1991 EC summit in Maastricht declared that the WEU would serve as an instrument of European defense and as such would have the effect of strengthening the European pillar of NATO.

Members of the WEU, meeting in Bonn on November 18, 1991, had issued a communiqué expressing a desire for enhanced dialogue with the emerging democracies of Central and Eastern Europe, the Baltic states, and the Soviet Union. This represented a parallel step to that which NATO had already taken through creation of the NACC. The Bonn communiqué announced that foreign and defense ministers from Bulgaria, Czechoslovakia, Hungary, Poland, and Romania would be invited to take part in special meetings with members of the WEU Council and would be invited to participate in WEU-organized seminars in various European countries. The WEU also committed itself to creating a fact-finding mission to the former Soviet republics to further investigate meaningful ways in which security dialogue could be fostered.

The Petersberg Declaration of June 1992 empowered the WEU member states with significant room for maneuver. Germany's new minister of foreign affairs, Klaus Kinkel, and Minister of Defense Rühe endorsed the WEU's intention not only to maintain peace but also to enforce it if necessary, even in areas outside the Alliance.

Europe's development of a common foreign and defense policy and its establishment of a mature wing of the Western Alliance that would act as a complement to NATO underscored the development of Europe as a new world power center. Some suggested that united Europe should receive a permanent seat on the UN Security Council. They noted that a united Europe would have more inhabitants than the United States and Japan combined and its gross national product (GNP—see Glossary) would be larger than that of the United States.

Eurocorps

Germany remained determined to pursue a multitracked approach in the development of its foreign and defense policies. The Germans firmly rejected subordination of European integration to other priorities that would, among other things in the German view, endanger the mutually important relationship that Bonn and Paris had carefully cultivated since the end of World War II.

West Germany's first chancellor, Konrad Adenauer (1949–63), together with French president Charles de Gaulle, had worked assiduously to dismantle the historical enmity between their two countries and to lay the foundation for German-French reconciliation after World War II (see Rearmament and the European Defense Community, ch. 2). West Germany had become France's most important trading partner by the 1980s (accounting for 40 percent of French trade), and the 1983 revival of the defense clauses in the German-French Friendship Treaty (Élysée Treaty) of 1963 had allowed a deepening of the two countries' military ties. Thus on October 16, 1991, Chancellor Kohl and President Mitterrand first announced a plan proposing that the WEU become the EC's defense arm and that a Franco-German Eurocorps (based on an already existing brigade) serve as the core of a new European army.

The decision by Kohl's government to develop a Franco-German Eurocorps was to be seen in this context (Germany and France had also been frustrated by the British domination of NATO's rapid reaction force established in 1991). The Eurocorps not only would provide the basis for a European force but also, on a political level, would assuage French (and broader European) concerns about a return to German unilateralism in foreign and defense policy. It had been French policy since the end of World War II to oppose any move by the Federal Republic perceived as leading to the establishment of a German national foreign and defense policy.

In the face of criticism from the NATO establishment, the Germans argued that the Eurocorps would have the positive

*Minister of Foreign Affairs
Klaus Kinkel with Pope John
Paul II in December 1993
Courtesy German Information
Center, New York*

effect of drawing the French closer to the Atlantic Alliance. French troops belonging to the joint military corps could be made available to NATO, either as rapid deployment forces or as main defense forces, the Germans argued. Skeptics—the Dutch, for instance—contended, on the contrary, that the Eurocorps would actually decrease the number of French and German troops available to NATO. Although Germans claimed that the joint military corps would intensify French links to NATO, it was also undoubtedly true that the collaborative step was viewed as an altogether different opportunity by the French defense establishment, long dominated by elements favoring an independent European security identity.

It was not exclusively in France, although perhaps most prominently, that some strategic thinkers sought to "Europeanize" the continent's defense by seeing to it that certain NATO functions were delegated to the EC or the WEU. Not surprisingly, Bonn's moves to help develop the Eurocorps provoked concern and in some circles irritation among NATO advocates both in the United States and in Europe. The Netherlands, Britain, and Denmark all expressed various degrees of reservation or opposition to the corps. Britain and the Netherlands in particular were reluctant to accept the premise that a European defense could be dominated by the French and the Germans. Spain, Belgium, and Luxembourg, however, welcomed the German-French initiative to form a joint military corps, and eventually all these countries pledged troops to it.

The Eurocorps was formally proposed by Chancellor Kohl and President Mitterrand in May 1992. Both leaders invited all members of the WEU to participate. The headquarters for the corps was established in Strasbourg in July 1992, and the corps was scheduled to become operational by late 1995. At the time of its inception, the corps was to have three military functions: to join and assist NATO missions; to fulfill missions under WEU command outside traditional NATO territory; and to provide international humanitarian assistance.

Germans balanced their push for European security structures in the early 1990s by repeatedly stressing their commitment to NATO. NATO remained central to German foreign and defense policies because of the organization's institutional ties to the United States, a fact that caused unrest in the French foreign policy establishment and among like-minded thinkers in Germany, who sought evolution away from an alliance dominated by the United States. A middle ground was sought by some defense experts who, like Bundeswehr *General Inspekteur* Klaus Naumann, contended that a "more European NATO" would appropriately bring balance to the previously United States-dominated defense organization.

European Union

Since its creation in 1957, the central objective of the European Community (EC—see Glossary) has been to advance the economic integration of Western Europe, primarily through the reduction or elimination of barriers to free trade and investment. The EC has long enjoyed a high level of sustained popularity in West Germany. Building on this foundation of support, West German leaders in the late 1980s set out to pursue, in concert with other West European states (Britain and some of the smaller countries in northern Europe did not participate), the objective of a more complete political and economic union (see Germany in the European Economy, ch. 6).

The Single European Act of 1986–87, designed to create a single common market without internal frontiers, was implemented in principle on January 1, 1993. In December 1991, EC leaders met in Maastricht to reach agreement on the Draft Treaty on Political Union. As a consequence of the treaty, Europe was committed to the creation of a common currency, set to begin in 1999 at the latest. At Maastricht, EC heads of state, in addition to agreeing on a path to political union, also agreed to the goal of establishing a common foreign and defense policy. The Maastricht Treaty provided the foundation for a federalized United States of Europe by creating the European Union (EU—see Glossary), of which the EC is a part.

In part as a consequence of the momentous changes in Central and Eastern Europe and the Soviet Union, steps toward European unity suffered setbacks in the early 1990s. War in Yugoslavia and the inability of the EC to fashion a cogent and effective response decimated the infant concept of a common defense policy. Meanwhile, mired in the uncertainties about Maastricht's chances for ratification during the autumn of 1991, Europe's financial markets were driven into a brief convulsive episode in September, with the result that EC efforts to impose a common financial discipline were effectively undermined.

At the same time, popular opinion in EC countries signaled that their own elected leaders and EC bureaucrats had lost touch with their respective electorates' concerns. Paramount were popular fears in Europe about a loss of sovereignty and national identity and the uncontrollable expansion of the EC's bureaucracy. Although political elites in Germany remained firmly committed to Maastricht, the German public was especially restive about the potential loss of the deutsche mark—the country's symbol of postwar economic success and in some respects its postnational identity. Roughly 70 percent of Germans rejected the notion that they should trade their vaunted currency for an untested European currency, the European currency unit (ECU—see Glossary).

In the wake of votes in Denmark and in France against ratification of the Maastricht Treaty, Chancellor Kohl showed no loss of overall optimism. Continuation of the process of European integration had been a central foreign policy objective of the Federal Republic. Following a special one-day EC summit in Birmingham, England, on October 16, 1992, Kohl proclaimed that the "European locomotive [would] continue," because all EC members still voiced a desire to ratify the Maastricht Treaty. In a speech before the Bundestag delivered three weeks earlier, Kohl had restated his support for what he interpreted as the treaty's five main objectives: common foreign and security policies; development of an economic and monetary union; development of common policy on domestic security matters; intensified cooperation in environmental protection; and enhancement of the role of the European Parliament.

In political terms, German officials viewed the Maastricht Treaty as a way to reassure European neighbors of Germany's trustworthiness as an international partner. To this end, in fact, Germany had actually sought a special leadership role of sorts. In October 1992, Minister of Foreign Affairs Kinkel stressed his country's unique responsibility, as the most populated and economically strongest country in Europe, "to send a signal of confidence in a common future to our still-hesitant partners." Germany (where only parliamentary approval was required) approved the treaty in December of the same year.

Indeed, many Europeans, the French perhaps in particular, interpreted the Maastricht Treaty as a German containment policy. EC president Jacques Delors had already sought to place German unification within the EC framework. Rather bluntly, during the weeks prior to the country's referendum, a number of Maastricht's supporters in France had argued that European unity would serve as an instrument with which to bind and tame the newly united Germans. French opponents of the treaty, conversely (and ironically), contended that European union would inevitably be controlled by an overwhelmingly powerful Germany. British prime minister Thatcher later stated essentially the same view, calling for a halt to the process of European union, whose final form would inevitably be dominated by the Germans. Indeed, because of its economic size and success, at the time of unification Germany presented a foreboding economic appearance on the European landscape.

In principle, united Germany is not in a position to advance its own agenda within the EU without compromise and consensus. On larger issues, approval by all EU members is required. On minor legislation, a weighted majority voting is applied, meaning that Germany has the same number of votes as France or Britain. Nevertheless, few would dispute the incomparable importance of German support in the EU for significant policy initiatives. Likewise, a strong German effort to implement a policy could be opposed in practice only with considerable difficulty.

A new German confidence, provoking irritation from Germany's allies and partners within the EC, became evident during the first years after unification. Member states fighting recession in the early 1990s blamed Germany's refusal to lower interest rates on Bonn's irresponsible self-absorption with its domestic issues. Through tight-fisted monetary policies, critics argued, the Germans were forcing their European neighbors to pay for the high and unexpected costs of unification. The United States also called on Germany to lower its interest rates to stimulate the international economy.

In addition to economic disagreements, Bonn's policy toward the Balkans in the second half of 1991 provoked charges of unilateralism and strong-arm tactics both within the EC and in Washington, as Bonn attempted to convince its EC partners and allies to recognize the Yugoslav breakaway republics of Croatia and Slovenia. A number of European governments, notably Britain and France, tended to view German policy through the lens of the world wars. German policy was not driven, however, by resurgent hegemonic impulses toward the region, as some critics argued. In fact, German motives were varied.

On the one hand, Germany made it clear that it wished to see the principle of self-determination applied in Yugoslavia. On the other hand, domestic considerations also played an important role. The unofficial lobby of several hundred thousand guest workers from Croatia and the millions of West Germans who had vacationed in Zagreb and along Croatia's Dalmatian coast strongly expressed their horror at the daily bloodshed they viewed on television.

In this context, and ignoring reservations among a number of EC members, Germany unilaterally recognized Croatia and Slovenia before Christmas 1991. Germany's recognition forced the EC to follow suit by January 15, 1992. The United States, after initial opposition over the recognition policy, recognized Slovenia, Croatia, and Bosnia and Herzegovina in April 1992. These developments led Chancellor Kohl to declare that the recognitions represented a major "success for German and European policy." Some European observers were left chagrined, however, by what they saw as the diplomatic flexing of united Germany's muscles.

The Yugoslav case aside, it had become clear in the early 1990s that the EC's policy toward the former Soviet bloc would be shaped to a large extent by German interests. Germany above all was preoccupied with fostering stability and prosperity in the region, especially in neighboring Central and Eastern Europe. In the early 1990s, Germany had established itself as the leading donor of aid, the single largest investor, and the most important trading partner for the former Soviet bloc. In addition to assisting democratic and market reforms, the expansion of economic and commercial ties was of direct benefit to German industry.

In the first years immediately after unification, Germany established bilateral agreements and treaties on good neighborly relations and friendly cooperation with the Soviet Union, Poland, Czechoslovakia, and Bulgaria. In the case of the last three, Germany pledged to help set up contacts with EU member states.

German policy makers soon began to advocate expanding the EU by admitting northern and eastern European countries as members. Germany's interest in this so-called "widening" of the EU appeared at times in conflict with France's preference for a "deepening" of the western structures of the EU before taking on new members. In the French view, new members, including Austria, Sweden, and Finland, strengthened Germany's hand in the EU and, as a consequence, diminished France's influence in the organization.

Although it remained unclear in the mid-1990s just how quickly the EU might expand in membership, it was evident that the EU would search for ways to include the emerging democracies in Central and Eastern Europe. With strong German support, the EU had begun to develop, for example, association agreements or "European agreements" that were intended to offer former communist countries access to EU markets to sell their goods. The EU also sought to provide a framework for economic and technical cooperation and for political and cultural dialogue.

At least on a rhetorical level, EU officials, in accord with the goals of the 1957 Treaty on the European Economic Community, envisaged the gradual establishment of a free-trade area for industrial products. To this end, the EU pledged to dismantle barriers to the access of industrial goods from Central and East European countries at a quicker pace than the partners were required to remove trade barriers to EU goods. This step was to be supplemented, when economic conditions in applicant countries existed, by the free movements of capital, services, and labor. Legal foundations of the new economic systems would also be required to conform with the EU model.

The EU's track record of stubborn adherence in certain instances to restrictive trade practices (especially in the agricultural and textile sector), however, raised profound questions about the feasibility of a smooth and relatively prompt EU membership for Europe's developing democracies. Nonetheless, in the first half of the 1990s, a number of analysts speculated that the Czech Republic, Slovakia, Hungary, and Poland might reasonably expect EU membership by the end of the twentieth century, followed shortly thereafter by Slovenia and the three Baltic states of Estonia, Latvia, and Lithuania.

As the EU's largest and economically strongest state, united Germany assumed an enhanced role in discussions about liberalizing world trade. Although some signs had emerged in the early 1990s that cast doubt on a successful conclusion of the General Agreement on Tariffs and Trade (GATT—see Glossary) negotiations, there were strong reasons to believe that Germany would use its influence to strengthen international trade and thwart any moves that could lead to transatlantic trade wars (see Foreign Trade and Investment, ch. 6).

When the EU's generous price supports of the Common Agricultural Policy (CAP—see Glossary) came under heavy fire from the United States in the GATT negotiations, Germany and Britain—leading food importers—showed an inclination to accept cuts in EU subsidies. But when Paris resisted vehemently, officials in Washington had looked for a stronger German role, hoping Bonn would exert greater pressure on its neighbor to cut farm subsidies and thereby overcome an important stumbling block in the GATT talks.

Germany itself was locked in debate over the issue of agricultural policy. Germany's free-trade lobby was led by the classically liberal FDP, which traditionally had one of its members serve as minister for economics. Kohl had shown himself sympathetic to Germany's farm lobby, and the German government had traditionally been a strong defender of the CAP. The German economy's dependence on foreign trade and investment, however, often pushed the country toward pragmatism and compromise on trade issues. In the early 1990s, Germany was exporting a third of its GNP. In the United States alone, it held a stake of US$34 billion in direct investment.

Organization for Security and Cooperation in Europe

The Conference on Security and Cooperation in Europe (CSCE), established in 1975, provided an organization whose structure helped join West Germany and other Western countries with the emerging democracies of the former Soviet bloc. The CSCE, renamed the Organization for Security and Cooperation in Europe (OSCE) in January 1995, gained expanded responsibilities after the end of the Cold War. For Germany, an avid champion of the organization, the OSCE will provide a forum for greater inclusion of the former Warsaw Pact countries to discuss and coordinate security activities.

Although NATO officials insisted that the OSCE's role be restricted to a complementary one as concerned with the West's defense alliance, the foreign ministers of NATO member states had explicitly called for the OSCE to play a more prominent role in confidence-building and security cooperation. In September 1991, Genscher proposed a number of ideas for expanding the CSCE's capability and mandate. These proposals included creation of a security council and establishment of special forces for peacekeeping (blue helmets) and fighting of ecological disasters (green helmets). Germany actively pushed for the development of a conflict settlement procedure and for authorization for the OSCE to monitor the compliance of member states with human and minority rights standards. It would also use violations of member states as a legitimate condition for diplomatic intervention.

Germany's enthusiasm for the OSCE reflected the German preoccupation with multilateralism, a central theme in the country's foreign policy. The powerful emphasis on economic relations in the CSCE process also reflected the growing belief in Bonn that economic factors, rather than military capabilities, would be primary in shaping a new European and international security order. In this context, Bonn proposed and hosted the 1990 CSCE conference on economic cooperation in Europe. The Bonn CSCE document provided a framework for an integrated economic community based on market principles that would stretch from the Atlantic to the Urals.

Support for the CSCE, German officials argued, did not conflict with their government's commitment to other European and transatlantic defense organizations. On the contrary, if appropriate steps were taken in the design of a post-Cold War security order, one would simply overlap, or neatly dovetail, with another. Moves toward mechanisms that would strengthen Europe's collective security intensified in the first years after the breach of the Berlin Wall.

As a consequence of the November 1990 Paris Charter and the July 1992 Helsinki Summit, efforts commenced to strengthen the CSCE process through the establishment (in different capitals) of a parliamentary assembly, a permanent secretariat, an election monitoring center, and a conflict pre-

Chancellor Helmut Kohl with President William J. Clinton at the White House
Courtesy The White House

vention center. Proponents championed the CSCE as the only pan-European forum for the discussion of security issues. From the beginning, however, skeptics warned of the limitations of an organization encompassing over fifty members—from Russia to Canada, and from Cyprus to the Vatican—whose decision-making capacity was governed by a prerequisite of unanimity among its members. CSCE members undertook the formidable and, in the view of many, unreasonable legal obligation "to provide mutual assistance in the case of an attack from the outside and the duty to submit to arbitration in the case of local conflicts."

The bickering and reservations over Maastricht—best symbolized by the defeat of the treaty in Denmark in the summer of 1992 and the victory by a narrow margin in France the following autumn—disrupted the carefully cultivated process of European economic and political unity, which had been supported on the continent, especially by policy makers in Germany and France. The paralysis of the CSCE, EU, and WEU in responding to the fighting in the Balkans in 1991 and 1992 also did much to dampen earlier optimism in Europe that the EU was on the verge of forging a framework for common foreign and defense policies.

United Nations

Since October 3, 1990, the day of German unification, the interests of Germans in the former FRG as well as those citizens in the former GDR have been represented by a single mission in the UN. Although German politicians repeatedly stated that the country was committed to assuming the same rights and responsibilities as other member states, Germany had remained undecided during the first years after unification as to what extent it would participate militarily—under Article 51 of the UN Charter—in collective security actions abroad.

Although Germany supported the policy pursued by the United States and its allies—condemnation of Iraq's invasion of Kuwait, endorsement of the UN's peace initiatives, and the campaign to eject Iraqi forces from Kuwaiti territory—the Germans did not join combat missions in Operation Desert Storm. Although German participation in a combat role was barred primarily by legal constraints, Germany's abstention was related to other deeper, more complex issues as well. Many Germans believed that an out-of-area conflict such as the Persian Gulf War lay beyond the scope of German interests. The support of Germany's parliament for the war was tepid and initially ambiguous. Germany's traumatic twentieth-century history figured prominently in Bonn's hesitation.

Under pressure from the United States and other allies, Germany agreed in the fall of 1990 initially to contribute US$2.1 billion, together with military equipment and munitions, to the gulf peacekeeping force. Ultimately, German financial contributions to the UN for the Persian Gulf War totaled about US$10 billion.

Nevertheless, Germany remains committed to the UN's use of military force. In his first address to the UN General Assembly on September 23, 1992, Minister of Foreign Affairs Kinkel pledged that his country would support the UN's system of collective security. In his address, Kinkel stated that it was essential that "democracies . . . remain capable of defending themselves," even though the East-West conflict had been relegated to history. Kinkel maintained that the collective security system of the UN and regional arrangements such as the CSCE should be transformed into "powerful instruments of a new world domestic policy."

In the mid-1990s, German policy is that the country will continue to participate in peacekeeping missions. The German government continues to support the general outlines of UN policies and programs on humanitarian relief, developmental assistance, and environmental protection. However, statesmen from United States president Bush to UN secretary general Javier Pérez de Cuellar (and later his successor Boutros Boutros-Ghali), have called for Germany to accept greater responsibility in world affairs by making use of not just its financial resources, but of its political and military capabilities as well.

Despite the fact that Germany has not yet resolved key questions about its international role, and specifically its contributions to peacemaking efforts, German politicians have already begun to suggest that the united country, presumably along with Japan, be considered for permanent membership on the UN Security Council. One school argues that a permanent seat is consistent with Germany's growing power and influence and the reconfiguration of world politics five decades after the end of World War II. Others contend that Germany's attainment of a permanent seat will occur only if states from Asia, Latin America, and Africa join as well. Because such expansion would have the effect of weakening the leadership role of the Security Council and thus the UN as a whole, many of these commentators reject the idea of permanent Security Council membership for Germany.

*   *   *

Since 1990 there have been a number of excellent publications on the process of unification and the emerging challenges to Germany's foreign policy. Among the best are *Germany's Position in the New Europe*, edited by Arnulf Baring; *The New Germany and the New Europe*, edited by Paul B. Stares; and *Developments in German Politics*, edited by Gordon Smith, William E. Paterson, Peter H. Merkl, and Stephen Padget. Also valuable is *Deutschlands neue Aussenpolitik*, edited by Karl Kaiser and Hanns W. Maull. Stephen F. Szabo's concise *The Diplomacy of German Unification* provides examinations of the unification process. Authoritative fuller accounts of unification are *Beyond the Wall* by Elizabeth Pond and *Germany Unified and Europe Transformed* by Philip Zelikow and Condoleezza Rice.

For an analysis of public opinion data from united Germany, see the Rand Corporation's study conducted by Ronald A. Asmus, *Germany in Transition*. On United States-German relations, see W.R. Smyser's *Germany and America*. Also valuable is Daniel Hamilton's *Beyond Bonn*, which offers a critical survey of issues relating directly to United States-German bilateral relations. For an examination of Franco-German relations, see Philip H. Gordon's *France, Germany, and the Western Alliance. The Germans and Their Neighbors,* edited by Dirk Verheyen and Christian Søe, provides chapter-length surveys of Germany's bilateral relations with nearly a score of European countries and with the United States.

A number of articles also offer excellent overviews of German foreign policy: Angela Stent's "The One Germany," Elizabeth Pond's "Germany in the New Europe," and Reinhard Stuth's "Germany's New Role in a Changing Europe." Two essays published by the Hoover Institution at Stanford University bear particular note as well: Burkhard Koch's *Germany: New Assertiveness in International Relations Between Reality and Misperception,* and L.H. Gann and Peter Duignan's *Germany: Key to a New Continent.*

The German Information Center in New York makes available weekly press summaries and important statements and speeches by German government officials. The Foreign Broadcast Information Service's *Daily Report: West Europe* also provides useful information in translation from sources published or broadcast in Germany. (For further information and complete citations, see Bibliography.)

Chapter 9. National Security

Seal of the Federal Republic of Germany

THE FEDERAL ARMED FORCES (Bundeswehr) of the Federal Republic of Germany (FRG, or West Germany) came into being in 1955. Assigned a solely defensive role, the Bundeswehr at its creation constituted the largest component of the North Atlantic Treaty Organization (NATO—see Glossary) ground forces in Central Europe. Throughout the Cold War, the fighter aircraft and air defense missiles of the Bundeswehr's formidable air force came under NATO command, and the small, well-equipped West German navy was committed to NATO missions in the Baltic and North seas. NATO carefully delineated the Bundeswehr's missions; in effect, West German security objectives were identical with those of the Alliance.

By mid-1995, however, the Bundeswehr, numbering approximately 368,000 troops, had been through a radical restructuring and downsizing brought about by the sudden end of the Cold War and the collapse of the Warsaw Pact (see Glossary) and the Soviet empire. After Germany was united in October 1990 by the accession of the German Democratic Republic (GDR, or East Germany) to the Federal Republic, the Bundeswehr absorbed some of the personnel and equipment of the East German armed forces, the National People's Army (Nationale Volksarmee—NVA), in a unique merger of two formerly hostile militaries that had been unimaginable even one year earlier.

Prior to unification, the armed forces of East and West Germany were considered among the shock troops of their respective alliances. The leaders of NATO and the Warsaw Pact— the United States and the Soviet Union, respectively—each maintained powerful forces based in the two Germanys, the presumed battleground. In terms of tactics, force organization and structure, and equipment, superpower influence on each German military was pervasive. On the Soviet side, with more than 400,000 troops, the Group of Soviet Forces in Germany (GSFG) was far larger than the NVA itself and was the Warsaw Pact's most potent military force outside the Soviet Union. The United States was clearly the most important member of NATO, but only a small portion of its total military forces were stationed in West Germany or in Europe. Unification changed the Bundeswehr's situation dramatically and in the process added about 30 percent more territory and hundreds of kilometers of Baltic Sea coastline to the task of preserving the territorial integrity of the enlarged country.

Paving the way for unification and restoration of full sovereignty, an agreement with Moscow in July 1990 committed Germany to reducing its armed forces to a level of 370,000 by December 1994 in return for the complete withdrawal of all troops of the former Soviet Union in eastern Germany by the end of that year. Initial Soviet objections to unified Germany's membership in NATO were dropped when Germany agreed to finance the relocation and housing of the departing troops. Under the 1990 Conventional Forces in Europe Treaty (CFE Treaty—see Glossary), Germany also undertook to make massive cuts in its weapons inventory. But even after these reductions, the Federal Republic would still possess the largest European forces in NATO.

Since World War II, the prospect of an independent German military had been a source of anxiety both within West Germany and among its former foes and neighbors. In addition, German irredentist claims had led to war in the past. So it was only after Germany publicly and officially recognized the validity of its existing borders that Poland, Czechoslovakia, and the Soviet Union consented to the idea of German unification.

Traditional German militarism has been tempered in the Bundeswehr, which remains a part of society rather than a society unto itself. The officer corps has not become an elite, as it had previously. Every member of the armed forces retains individual rights as a citizen and enjoys liberties unavailable to United States troops, such as the right to join a union or run for public office while in the service. In the Bundeswehr, sexual orientation has not been a contentious issue. Female citizens of the Federal Republic interested in a military career are, however, restricted to service in the medical and musical corps.

Although a powerful peace movement uniting environmentalists, students, trade unionists, and religious leaders articulated pacifist and antimilitarist positions with some success in the postwar period, the armed forces continues to be staffed largely by conscription. About 40 percent of the troops are draftees; the remainder are regulars or extended-service volunteers. In 1972 the term of service was reduced from eighteen months to fifteen months; in 1990 it was further reduced to twelve months; beginning in 1996, it will fall to ten months. Thousands of young men have been exempted or had their service deferred for educational, health, or hardship reasons. A growing number of young men (60,000 of 200,000 called) are granted conscientious objector status. These men perform alternative service (*Ersatzdienst*) in hospitals or homes for senior citizens or for people with disabilities. Those aspiring to become officers or noncommissioned officers (NCOs) are required to enter as conscripts before volunteering for longer enlistments. Only the most qualified are permitted to undergo the rigorous preparation for a full career in the armed services.

Because the West German armed forces had been so subordinated to NATO—an alliance in search of a new identity and mission in the 1990s—the Bundeswehr of united Germany has experienced difficulty in defining its missions and justifying the need for a large and costly military establishment. Until July 1994, Germany's constitution, the Basic Law, had been interpreted as prohibiting the deployment of German forces outside the NATO area in United Nations (UN) or other international peacemaking and peacekeeping operations. Consequently, despite pressure from some allies, no German troops were included in the UN coalition that fought Iraq in the 1991 Persian Gulf War. Instead, Germany made financial contributions to the action, and some German units were deployed to Turkey as a defensive measure. German soldiers joined humanitarian operations in the former Yugoslavia and in Somalia, but the opposition Social Democratic Party of Germany (Sozialdemokratische Partei Deutschlands—SPD) strenuously opposed involvement that could bring German forces into combat. In July 1994, the Federal Constitutional Court, the highest court in the land, ruled that the Bundeswehr could participate in international military operations if each deployment received approval in the Bundestag, the lower house of Germany's parliament.

In unified Germany, the maintenance of internal security is for the most part the responsibility of the individual police forces of the sixteen states (*Länder;* sing., *Land*), controlled by the individual ministries of interior of the *Länder.* This decentralized system has its roots in the post-1871 German Empire. The Western Allies after World War II insisted on a return to the *Land* system because of abuses by Hitler's highly centralized police forces during the Nazi era (1933–45). To an increasing extent, *Land* police activities are coordinated and supported by the federal Ministry of Interior, which has its own criminal police agency and domestic intelligence services. The paramilitary border police is available as a uniformed federal backup force in the event of major disorders.

In the early 1990s, controversy and scandal erupted over the opening of the records of the former East German State Security Service (Staatssicherheitsdienst—Stasi). Former dissidents and political figures were discredited by revelations of dealings with the Stasi, whose repressive influence had permeated most aspects of life in the former GDR. As a result, police forces of the five new *Länder* underwent restructuring and retraining to bring them up to the level of competency of Western police forces.

Beginning in the late 1960s, the danger of violence by terrorist groups has been a chronic problem for the police. After unification in 1990, the principal threat to public order shifted from left-wing extremists to right-wing and neo-Nazi groups that targeted the growing numbers of asylum-seekers, as well as the millions of foreign workers, many of whom had been employed in Germany for decades. Federal authorities responded to criticism that law enforcement agencies and courts were lax in dealing with right-wing violence by strengthening federal-*Land* cooperation and acting more aggressively to curb extremist incidents.

In the 1990s, Germany's security forces are experiencing their share of the confusion and disarray brought about by the hastily executed process of unification. For nearly half a century, two radically different societies had evolved in the two Germanys. In the east, under Soviet occupation, an aggressive campaign of early indoctrination and militarization was introduced. Overlapping premilitary and paramilitary organizations perpetuated antagonism toward NATO, West Germany, the United States, and the free-market system. Initiative was stifled, and obedience was demanded. When the communist system collapsed, the superstructure upon which it relied (armed forces, police, and border guards) was discredited. Meanwhile, in the West, support for NATO and the United States troop presence fell as the threat diminished, and growing numbers of German youth opted for alternative service.

Military Tradition

Early History

The first Germans to win repute as fearsome adversaries in combat were members of the various tribes who fought the encroachment of Roman legions upon their territories. The Roman historian Tacitus praised the leadership and military acumen of Arminius, a chief of the Cherusci who commanded the German forces in the Battle of the Teutoburg Forest in A.D. 9. The tribal warriors led by Arminius annihilated three Roman legions, effectively preventing Roman expansion beyond the Danube and Rhine rivers. By the fifth century, German tribes had entered the Italian peninsula and brought about the collapse of the Roman Empire in the west.

The empire created by Charlemagne (r. 768–814) in west-central Europe split up soon after his death, the eastern portion occupying much of the territory of modern Germany. These German lands gradually evolved into the Holy Roman Empire, with extensive territories in Italy (see Medieval Germany, ch. 1). Many of the German kingdoms, principalities, and cities that were components of the empire were noted for the emphasis their leaders placed on military might. However, no imperial army or law held sway over the local princes and free cities. The absence of a strong central power, plus the emergence of Protestantism in the sixteenth and seventeenth centuries, resulted in a near-permanent state of civil conflict, wars of succession, and religious strife (see The Protestant Reformation, ch. 1). The Thirty Years' War (1618–48), a series of conflicts between Protestant and Catholic forces, decimated Germany's population (see The Thirty Years' War, ch. 1).

Prussia's Emergence as a Military Power

After the decline of the Holy Roman Empire, the Kingdom of Prussia eventually emerged as the dominant power in central Europe (see The Age of Enlightened Absolutism, 1648–1789, ch. 1). Prussia had been colonized and Germanized during the thirteenth and fourteenth centuries by the Knights of the Teutonic Order, a military order of German monks that pushed back or overran the Slavs in the area. The knights were crushed by the Poles and Lithuanians in 1410 at the Battle of Tannenberg, but in the next century the Hohenzollern Dynasty that ruled Brandenburg and made Berlin its residence was able to win control over West Prussia, Silesia, Pomerania, and eventually much of the Rhineland and Westphalia.

The German military heritage was epitomized by a succession of Prussian rulers in the seventeenth and eighteenth centuries. The first of these was the Great Elector, Frederick William (r. 1640–88), who recognized that a standing army with an elite officer corps was the key to the development of a powerful state in his remote part of the empire. His grandson, Frederick William I (r. 1713–40), more than doubled the size of his professional army to 90,000 and added a trained reserve of conscripted peasants, forming one of the most modern and efficient fighting units in eighteenth-century Europe. Heavy taxes supported the army, which consumed 80 percent of state revenues even in peacetime. The next Prussian king, Frederick II (r. 1740–86), known to posterity as Frederick the Great, raised the strength of the army to 150,000 and launched a series of wars between 1740 and 1763, wresting control of the province of Silesia from Habsburg Austria. Prussia had become one of the most powerful continental states and a contender with the Habsburgs for domination over the myriad German political entities.

The aristocratic character of the officer corps was established early in the eighteenth century as Prussian kings tried to gain the support of wealthy landed aristocrats, known as Junkers, by granting them a virtual monopoly over the selection of officers. In 1733 a cadet school was established in Berlin to train sons of Junkers to be officers. The officer corps was well on the way to becoming the most privileged social class in Prussia.

The chauvinistic militarism of Prussia inspired fear and hatred among other European states and peoples. Under the strong leadership of a self-perpetuating general staff, the army brooked little interference in its affairs by the civil government. Nevertheless, the failure to reform and the lack of preparedness after the death of Frederick the Great in 1786 led to the army's decisive defeat by Napoleon's forces at Jena in October 1806.

Over the next few years, General Gerhard von Scharnhorst guided the revitalization of the army. Reforms included the introduction of universal military service and an end to dependence on mercenaries. The officer corps was expanded to include commoners, and officers were encouraged to take greater initiative in battle. The new Prussian army distinguished itself at the Battle of Leipzig in 1813 and again at Waterloo in 1815, where, under the command of Field Marshal Gebhard von Blücher, the army was instrumental in the ultimate defeat of Napoleon.

Prussia's reputation for military efficiency was reestablished by the army's final victories over Napoleon. The Prussian War

College (Kriegsakademie) became a model for military staff colleges around the world in the early nineteenth century. A book of that era—*On War*—written by Karl von Clausewitz, a Prussian general, became a classic, its theories of land warfare still studied by officers of many armies more than 160 years after the author's death.

The unification of the many German states into the German Empire (1871–1918) followed Prussian-led victories over Denmark in 1864, Austria in 1866, and France in 1870–71. Prussia's aggressive policies were masterminded by Otto von Bismarck, who became united Germany's first chancellor (see Bismarck and Unification, ch. 1). Following unification, the legendary Prussian General Staff became the German General Staff. Clausewitz's dictum that civilians should control the military was ignored, and the General Staff became a power center in the highly militaristic regimes of Kaiser Wilhelm I (1858–88) and Kaiser Wilhelm II (1888–1918) (see Imperial Germany, ch. 1).

The German Military in Two World Wars

Prussian-German excellence in military matters was an accepted fact of life, but in the twentieth century the excessive accent on militarism led to two disastrous world wars. Germany's insistence on building a fleet that could challenge Britain's naval domination underscored German bellicosity and pushed Britain toward alignment with France and Russia. When World War I broke out in 1914, Germany attempted to conquer France quickly with a sudden thrust through Belgium. The Germans nearly reached Paris, but the desperate French managed to stiffen their defenses along the Marne River. The front was stabilized in northern France and shifted little during the course of the war in spite of the sacrifice of whole armies in the effort to break through opposing defenses. Although Germany was able to force Russia out of the war in March 1918, the arrival of fresh United States troops, strikes and protests among German workers, and the exhaustion of material resources brought about Germany's collapse in November 1918. General Erich Ludendorff and Field Marshal Paul von Hindenburg formed what was in effect a military dictatorship in 1917 but sidestepped responsibility for the military catastrophe by restoring civilian control in the chaos of 1918. They then falsely claimed that the military, undefeated in the field, had been "stabbed in the back" by domestic enemies, a charge that Adolf Hitler employed later to great effect.

Under the terms of the Treaty of Versailles, the German General Staff was abolished. The army was limited to 100,000 personnel and the navy to a force of 15,000. Aircraft, tanks, submarines, and other offensive weapons were prohibited. The left bank of the Rhine was demilitarized. The Allies intended that the civilian government of the postwar Weimar Republic (1918–33) completely control the military and that the destruction of the General Staff epitomize the end of Prussianism. Nevertheless, a general staff continued to function under the sobriquet "Troop Office," and its leaders took advantage of the weak civilian government to reassert their privileged positions. When Hindenburg was elected president of the republic in 1925, the general staff officers regained their influence in the government (see The Weimar Republic, 1918–33, ch. 1).

During the 1920s, a clandestine alliance was formed between the armies of the Weimar Republic and the Soviet Union to circumvent the terms of the Treaty of Versailles. The German high command under General Hans von Seeckt made secret arrangements with the Soviet high command enabling German officers and specialists to study and train with modern weapons in the Soviet Union in return for German technical assistance in the establishment of Soviet defense industries. This collaboration helped keep alive the military know-how used later as the basis of Hitler's war machine.

By September 1939, when Hitler's invasion of Poland triggered World War II, Germany had a formidable army, a potent navy, and the best equipped air force in the world. The blitzkrieg (lightning war), in which highly mobile, tank-heavy land armies were deployed in conjunction with large numbers of close-support aircraft, included tactics never before seen in warfare. In the spring of 1940, the German army, the Wehrmacht, defeated Denmark and Norway, outflanked French defenses along the Maginot Line, destroyed the armies of France and Belgium, and forced the evacuation of the British Expeditionary Forces at Dunkirk—all in a little over a month.

The rapid victories of the early war period did not lead to peace, however. France, Belgium, the Netherlands, Denmark, Norway, and Poland were occupied, but the staunch resistance of Britain's Royal Air Force deterred Hitler's planned invasion of Britain. The war took on a global character in 1941, with the Wehrmacht's invasion of its erstwhile ally, the Soviet Union, in

June and Japan's attack on Pearl Harbor the following December, which drew the United States into the conflict. Even though the redoubtable Nazi war machine fought on for almost four more years, the resources and manpower that the Allies could invest eventually sealed the fate of Hitler's vaunted "Thousand-Year Reich."

Once the Soviet forces were able to turn the tide in their favor on the Eastern Front and the Western Allies established themselves in France, there could no longer be any doubt about the outcome of the war. Nevertheless, Hitler refused to seek peace. The inevitable result was the destruction not only of the country's armed forces but also of its towns and cities, its industrial capacity, and its transportation system. Despite this second catastrophic defeat in fewer than thirty years, the German reputation for military excellence survived. The defeats could be attributed to strategic blunders, two-front wars, and madness and depravity among the Nazi leadership.

The Allies demanded and received Nazi Germany's unconditional surrender in May 1945. Two months later, at a summit conference held at Potsdam, near Berlin, the leaders of the United States, Britain, and the Soviet Union decreed, inter alia, the demilitarization of Germany. Although the Allies disagreed on many issues discussed at Potsdam, they were in accord on the need to prevent a resurgence of German militarism; toward that end, they ordered total disarmament. In the immediate postwar years, however, the Allies could not agree on the terms of a peace treaty, and before long they were aligning on opposite sides of the Cold War. By 1949 the British, French, and United States zones of occupation had become West Germany, and the Soviet zone had become East Germany. The border between the two republics became the front line of the Cold War, or, in the term popularized by Winston Churchill, the Iron Curtain. Soon, uniformed Germans carrying weapons were appearing on both sides of the border (see Postwar Occupation and Division, ch. 2).

Creation of the Bundeswehr

In the summer of 1955, ten years after the Nazi surrender and the end of World War II, the West German Bundestag (lower house of parliament) voted to authorize the recruitment of volunteers for the initial formation of the Bundeswehr (Federal Armed Forces). Later in the year, a cadre of about 100 officers and NCOs were sworn in at a ceremony in Bonn. Most of the initial volunteers were veterans of the World War II Wehrmacht who had been serving in the Federal Border Force (Bundesgrenzschutz—BGS) since the inception of that lightly armed organization in 1951 (see Federal Police Agencies, this ch.).

Training facilities and equipment were made available by the United States Army, and 1,500 volunteers reported for the first training cycle, which began in January 1956. The Bundestag soon promulgated compulsory military service. By the end of the year, the force numbered about 65,000, including 10,000 volunteers from the BGS, almost all of whom were war veterans. The reappearance of a German armed force, which would have been inconceivable a decade earlier, had become a reality as a direct result of the Cold War.

The London and Paris agreements of 1954 restored sovereignty to the Federal Republic and opened the way for German membership in NATO. The four Allies retained occupation powers in Berlin. Allied troops remained in West Germany for purposes of NATO defense pursuant to status-of-forces agreements. With the exception of French troops, Allied and German forces were under NATO's joint defense command.

In East Germany, the national legislature passed a bill establishing the armed forces and the Ministry of Defense in January 1956. The swift creation of an East German armed forces, the National People's Army (Nationale Volksarmee—NVA), more than 120,000 personnel practicing Prussian-style drill, was a dramatic gesture of nationalism impossible for the world to ignore. Thus, the 1950s saw both Germanys embark upon the reestablishment of their military forces, albeit ones firmly restrained within the mutually antagonistic Cold War alliances.

Strategic Concerns and Military Missions

Until the late 1980s, the Federal Republic was confronted by a single preponderant threat arising from the forward deployment of armored and highly maneuverable Soviet and Warsaw Pact forces. The threat to NATO and to Germany abated after the dissolution of the Soviet Union and the phased withdrawal during the first half of the 1990s of Soviet (and, later, Russian) units from the former East Germany and from other Warsaw Pact nations.

Instead of having to prepare for the contingency of direct attack from the east, a united Germany faces more diffuse and intangible security problems. Under the new conditions, Ger-

Two soldiers during an exercise
A Leopard–2 main battle tank
Courtesy Embassy of the Federal Republic of Germany, Washington

many's concerns focus on the possibility of armed conflicts arising in any one of three regions. The first is in the former Soviet Union, where fifteen former Soviet republics, several of them with powerful conventional forces and even nuclear capabilities, are undergoing a difficult transition to independent nationhood. Second, in Eastern Europe, the disintegration of communist rule and the problems of the fragile democratic systems that followed have also created the potential for dangerous upheaval. Historical animosities previously suppressed under an authoritarian regime have already brought civil war to the former Yugoslavia. Ethnic or religious violence could easily break out elsewhere in the region, producing destabilizing conditions, including the arrival of waves of refugees. Finally, German military planners also foresee possible conflict in the volatile area extending from the southern rim of the Mediterranean to the Persian Gulf. In this region, the emergence of fundamentalist or radical regimes poses a potential threat to NATO member states such as Turkey, which could lead to a call for German force deployments.

The primary mission of the German armed forces remains the protection of German territory in conjunction with other NATO armies. This task would fall to NATO's main defense forces, which, under guidelines adopted in 1991, will constitute the bulk of NATO forces in Central Europe. The main defense forces will consist of four multinational corps, only partially mobilized in peacetime. Two corps will be under German command, and German divisions will also be assigned to the remaining corps commands. NATO's Rapid Reaction Force will be available to assume regional crisis management and to take limited action in either Central Europe or elsewhere in the NATO area. The force will also provide protection during the buildup of the main defense forces. Germany's contribution to the Rapid Reaction Force will include its operationally ready combat brigades. The air component of the Rapid Reaction Force will include twenty aircraft squadrons under the command of a German officer.

In addition to maintaining NATO-committed combat units, the evolving Bundeswehr will retain support forces to provide military infrastructure and logistics, training units and schools, medical services, and non-NATO air defense. It will be required to have contingents ready to conduct peacetime missions of disaster relief, search and rescue, and humanitarian assistance. German commanders also must plan for possible deployments in support of out-of-area NATO or UN operations (see International Military Missions, this ch.; The Out-of-Area Debate, ch. 8).

The Armed Forces

Command and Control

Under the Basic Law, the federal minister of defense commands the Bundeswehr in peacetime, but that official relinquishes this role to the federal chancellor in the event of a "state of defense," that is, an outbreak of hostilities. The Ministry of Defense is traditionally headed by a civilian and assisted by two parliamentary state secretaries and two state secretaries. There are six nonmilitary divisions staffed primarily by civilians—personnel; budget; administrative and legal affairs; quartermaster, real estate, and construction; social services; and armaments. The military side of the ministry is composed of five military staffs—the armed forces office, army, navy, air force, and surgeon general (see fig. 14).

The top military position is that of *General Inspekteur* of the armed forces, an individual who is roughly equivalent to the United States chairman of the Joint Chiefs of Staff. The *General Inspekteur* is the supreme military representative of the Bundeswehr and military adviser to the minister of defense. The *General Inspekteur's* planning responsibilities require him to develop overall concepts governing the structure, organization, command and control, equipment, and training of the Bundeswehr. The *General Inspekteur* also represents the Bundeswehr in international bodies. However, he is not part of the chain of operational command between the minister and the chief of staff ("inspector") of each branch of the armed forces.

The Bundeswehr has no general staff. Because of its tainted history and condemnation at the Nuremberg trials, that particular structure was omitted when the Bundeswehr was being planned. Non-NATO joint planning is conducted by representatives from the Bundeswehr and the service general staffs under the overall supervision of the Bundeswehr's Operations Directorate. The staffs of the army, air force, and navy are responsible for the operational readiness of their respective force components. They are involved in the coordination and approval processes of NATO plans for the defense of German territory but do not undertake operational wartime planning.

Because Germany will relinquish operational command over its combat units—together with certain formations of its territorial army—in the event of war, there is little requirement for independent German war plans.

In passing the annual budget law, the Bundestag determines the number of military and civil personnel to be employed in the defense sector, sets out the basic features of the Bundeswehr organization, and authorizes the financing of specific sums for defense. Parliament also decides other important aspects of defense policy, such as the duration of conscription. Before forces can be committed to military action, parliament must determine in accordance with Article 80a of the Basic Law that a state of tension exists or in accordance with Article 115a that a state of defense exists. If parliament cannot be convened on time, the twenty-two-member Joint Committee, with the president of the Bundestag presiding, acts on its behalf.

Many Bundestag committees also exercise some controlling functions over the Bundeswehr. The twenty-seven-member Defense Committee focuses on defense and security policy but can also function as an investigating committee.

Army

In early 1995, the army (Bundesheer), headquartered in Koblenz, had a personnel strength of appropriately 255,000, including 123,000 conscripts. It was composed of two principal elements, the field army and the much smaller territorial army. Territorial army units were slated to be merged with the field army by the end of 1995. The field army is listed in *The Military Balance, 1994–1995* as consisting of three corps and eight divisions (four armored divisions, three armored infantry divisions, and one mountain division).

A radical reshaping of the army was completed by the end of 1994, in which the Bundeswehr was adapted to the diminishing threat in Central Europe, the recasting of NATO's force structure, and Germany's 1990 commitments to reduce its force level and armaments. These commitments were embodied in the Treaty on the Final Settlement with Respect to Germany, or, as it is more commonly known, the Two-Plus-Four Treaty signed in September 1990 and the CFE Treaty signed that November. According to these commitments, manpower had to be reduced so that all services could meet the CFE ceiling of 370,000 by December 1994, with a sublimit of 345,000 for the army and air force. Naval forces also had to be cut, although

they were not included in the CFE Treaty except for land-based marines (of which Germany has none) and naval air units.

The treaty obligations were met successfully, and in early 1995 the Bundesheer amounted to about 255,000 soldiers, of whom about 123,000 were conscripts. The army consists of three corps, under the overall direction of the Army Forces Command. The headquarters of I Corps is in Münster, that of II Corps in Ulm, and that of IV Corps in Potsdam. Only IV Corps is solely German. The other two are joint corps: I Corps is German-Dutch; II Corps is German-United States. Under the corps commands are seven divisions in place of the previous twelve, and twenty-four combat brigades instead of the previous forty-eight. Six of the divisions are committed to NATO's main defense force, but the two divisions of IV Corps in the east remain under German national command. Under the operational command of II Corps is the Eurocorps, scheduled to be operational in late 1995 with 50,000 troops. Lastly, there is the Air-Mobile Forces Command, which commands crisis-reaction forces.

The army's twenty-four combat brigades include sixteen mechanized brigades, three airborne brigades, one mountain brigade, and the German component of the Franco-German Brigade. Only six brigades are maintained at full strength—two airborne brigades, three mechanized brigades, and the mountain brigade. Some of these ready brigades are committed to the NATO Rapid Reaction Force. All of the active units are staffed with a high proportion of regulars. The remaining brigades are staffed at about a 60 percent level in peacetime, mainly with conscripts. In each brigade, one armored battalion and one infantry battalion are filled out by drawing cadres from staffed units when expanded to full strength. Tanks and other armored vehicles of the cadre units are stored, as are 25 percent of the vehicles of active battalions.

According to Ministry of Defense plans, the Bundesheer will become even smaller in the second half of the 1990s. By the year 2000, the army is to consist of about 233,000 personnel, of which 37,000 will be assigned to rapid-reaction units. The army will eliminate one division headquarters and two brigade headquarters. To meet NATO obligations, the 14th Division headquarters in Neubrandenburg will assume the mission of the 6th Division, which is to be disbanded. This move will integrate a division in the new *Länder* into the NATO military structure for the first time.

Equipment

With the absorption of equipment from the NVA in 1990, the Bundesheer had more than 7,000 main battle tanks, most of them highly regarded German-built Leopards plus nearly 2,300 Soviet models. It had 3,250 armored infantry fighting vehicles, of which about two-thirds were German Marder A1/A2 models and the remainder Soviet BMPs. The Bundesheer's inventory listed 11,000 armored personnel carriers, including a large number of Soviet vehicles inherited from the NVA.

As of 1995, Germany had kept little of the weaponry of the former NVA, giving away many spare parts, destroying huge caches of weapons and ammunition, and selling surplus equipment. East German tanks had been shipped to Finland, and warships had been sold to Paraguay and Indonesia.

In line with its CFE commitments, Germany reduced its inventory of main battle tanks to 2,855, its armored infantry fighting vehicles to 2,443 units, and its artillery to 2,090 pieces (see table 23, Appendix). This represented the highest rate of disarmament among the CFE signatories, with the exception of Russia.

In accordance with several international commitments, no nuclear, biological, or chemical weapons are in the German arms inventory. Under the Two-Plus-Four Treaty, Germany reaffirmed its renunciation of the manufacture, possession, and control of such weapons. A number of German weapons systems are nuclear-capable, but nuclear warheads and bombs remain under the control of the United States. Some Tornado aircraft have been fitted to accept nuclear bombs.

Franco-German Brigade and Eurocorps

In 1987 German chancellor Helmut Kohl and French president François Mitterrand agreed on the formation of a Franco-German Brigade to be stationed in southwest Germany, but with headquarters in Strasbourg, France. Once established, the French and German units in the brigade were not integrated; the brigade functioned jointly only at the command, secretariat, and logistic levels. The German contribution consisted of one mechanized infantry battalion, one artillery battalion, and one self-propelled antitank company. Troops are attired in the uniforms of their own armies but wear a distinctive blue beret bearing the insignia of both armies.

In May 1992, Kohl and Mitterrand announced the establishment of a Eurocorps intended to form the nucleus of a European army. All the states of the Western European Union (WEU—see Glossary) were invited to participate. Three possible missions were identified: deployment under NATO control in time of war; peacemaking and peacekeeping operations under WEU command in places outside the NATO treaty area, subject to constitutional limits on German troop deployments; and employment for humanitarian purposes abroad.

The Eurocorps is scheduled to be operational by October 1995 and to number about 50,000 troops, including a French armored division, a German division, a Belgian mechanized division, and a Spanish mechanized infantry brigade. The German division, the 10th Armored, will remain simultaneously committed to NATO. The troops will be stationed on German soil and will retain their separate national identities under a joint command at Strasbourg. Before the Eurocorps can be deployed, every government that has contributed troops will have to approve the mission.

Navy

The primary areas of operation of the navy (Bundesmarine) in the event of war are the Baltic Sea and the North Sea. Until 1990 the navy's mission had been to block the Baltic approaches on behalf of NATO to prevent the deployment of the Soviet Baltic Fleet in the North Sea and the Atlantic Ocean. The navy also contributed to protection of NATO sea routes by helping to control the North Sea and the Norwegian Sea. Although lacking large surface units, the navy was well equipped to carry out intelligence and reconnaissance, mine countermeasure operations, and antisubmarine and antiship warfare. The navy regularly participated in NATO exercises as part of the Standing Naval Force Atlantic and Standing Naval Force Channel.

The political changes that unfolded in 1990 enabled the navy to reduce its concentration on the Baltic Sea and northern flank, shifting from defending against a tangible Warsaw Pact threat to preparing for a broader spectrum of maritime defense missions and tasks beyond home waters. The deployment of mine countermeasure vessels to the Mediterranean for NATO during the Persian Gulf crisis in 1990 and to the Persian Gulf after hostilities broke out in 1991, as well as Germany's participation in monitoring the naval blockade against Serbia in 1992, undoubtedly foreshadow other possible requirements distant from German coastal waters.

Although the navy is preparing for possible involvement in future multilateral and humanitarian missions, its primary task will continue to be to prevent attacking forces from controlling German territorial and adjacent waters. The nations of the former Soviet Union are no longer regarded as hostile; however, the presence of Russian naval units in the Baltic, with their potential to deny Germany the use of its territorial waters and the high seas, remains a relevant factor in strategic planning.

As of early 1995, the navy had about 30,000 personnel, including 4,230 Naval Air Arm personnel, and 6,700 conscripts. The ship inventory included as its principal combat units twenty submarines, thirteen destroyers and frigates, and thirty-eight missile craft (see table 24, Appendix). The Naval Air Arm is equipped with Tornado fighter-ground attack aircraft and Breguet Atlantic aircraft fitted for long-range reconnaissance, including some dedicated to electronic intelligence. Dornier Do–28s are used for short-range surveillance and patrol of the Exclusive Economic Zone. Two Westland Sea Lynx helicopters are based on each frigate for antisubmarine warfare and target acquisition.

Four Brandenburg-class frigates are under construction to replace Hamburg-class vessels by the end of 1996. Four Type 212 submarines are scheduled to be introduced after 2000 to begin the replacement of Type 205 and unmodernized Type 206 submarines.

At unification the East German navy had a substantial fleet of twenty-three frigates, fifty-two missile boats, and twenty-four mine warfare vessels. Because the West German navy was already facing a sharp reduction, all East German ships were scheduled to be scrapped or sold, rather than absorbed within the unified navy.

Proportionately, the cuts imposed on the navy in response to the improved security situation in Europe have been the greatest among the three services. The ship inventory will be reduced to nearly half by the year 2005. The future German fleet will consist of about ninety vessels, including fifteen frigates, eight submarines, fifteen corvette patrol vessels, and twenty mine countermeasure ships. Personnel strength will decline to about 27,000 by 2000.

Under the chief of staff of the navy are three major commands: the Fleet Command at Glücksburg on the Baltic Sea; the Naval Office at Rostock, responsible for enlisted personnel,

F 208

A frigate of the Bremen class
Courtesy Embassy of the Federal
Republic of Germany,
Washington

Sailors in winter uniform
Courtesy Embassy of the Federal
Republic of Germany,
Washington

schools, armament, and the medical service; and the Naval Logistics Command at Wilhelmshaven. Under the consolidation plans, a number of bases will be closed and headquarters merged, leaving four main bases: Wilhelmshaven (frigates plus support vessels); Kiel (frigates, submarines, and support vessels); Olpenitz (mine countermeasure vessels); and Warnemünde (patrol boats). The naval air combat arm will be reduced from four to three wings of about forty-six Tornados based at Eggebek (near the Danish border), mainly for reconnaissance and attack sorties. The naval air station at Jagel and the remaining Tornados will be assigned to the air force.

Air Force

The air force (Luftwaffe) has faced dramatic changes in structure and strategic concepts as a result of the diminished threat in Central Europe and shrinking budgetary resources for modernized weapons systems. Prior to the demise of the Warsaw Pact, the air force had as its primary mission the air defense of Central Europe in conjunction with other NATO air forces. This included reconnaissance to forestall surprise attack, interdiction of enemy ground and air forces, prevention of enemy aircraft from reaching strategic targets, protection of friendly forces against air attack, and close battlefield support for NATO ground troops. The new security environment in Europe has brought a change in tasks for the Luftwaffe. With the absorption of the former East Germany, the national airspace that had to be patrolled increased substantially. With a major confrontation in Central Europe now only a slight possibility, the Luftwaffe has had to adjust its missions to take account of the possibility of involvement in conflict beyond the borders of Europe and in unstable regions within Europe.

As of early 1995, the Luftwaffe had a personnel strength of 83,000, including 25,000 conscripts. The principal combat units were eight squadrons of fighter-ground attack aircraft, equipped with Tornado fighter-ground attack aircraft. There were seven fighter squadrons, six with F–4Fs and one with MiG–29s (see table 25, Appendix). Developed as a joint effort by Britain, Italy, and West Germany, the Tornado is a high-speed, low-altitude, all-weather attack aircraft. The McDonnell Douglas F–4F Phantom, introduced in the United States in the 1960s, is still regarded as an outstanding fighter and attack aircraft of exceptional versatility. However, it is scheduled to be replaced by a new combat aircraft in the late 1990s, the European Fighter Aircraft (EFA).

Ground-based air defense consisted of six groups, each with six squadrons, equipped with Patriot surface-to-air missile (SAM) launchers; six groups, each with six squadrons, equipped with Hawk launchers; and fourteen squadrons equipped with Roland launchers for point defense. The German air defense units covering Central Europe and the Baltic approaches were fully operational, subject to control by NATO's integrated air-defense system even during peacetime.

By 1998 two squadrons of Tornado fighter-bombers are scheduled to be transferred from the navy to the air force, along with 800 naval personnel, as part of the plan to transform the naval air base at Jagel on the Baltic Sea into a Luftwaffe base. Of all the equipment taken over from the East German air force, only one squadron of MiG–29 fighter aircraft was absorbed by the Luftwaffe.

The ranking uniformed member of the Luftwaffe is the air force chief of staff, with headquarters in Cologne. Also at Cologne is the Combat Command, subdivided into the Southern Tactical Command and Northern Tactical Command. The Southern Tactical Command is collocated with NATO Combined Air Operations Center at Messstellen in the southwestern corner of Germany; the Northern Tactical Command is at Kalkar near the Dutch border. The Transport Command at Münster also comes under the Combat Command, as does the Communications and Electronic Command. The Air Force Office in Cologne is responsible for personnel, training, communications, and armaments. The Air Force Logistics Command, also in Cologne, is responsible for logistic units, training installations, and matériel.

Training

The basic objective of Bundeswehr training is to impart the technical knowledge necessary for mastery of advanced weaponry while instilling the discipline required in combat situations. Educational opportunities offered to service personnel vary with the length of enlistment and are intended to produce combat readiness while, to the extent possible, providing skills that will ease the eventual transition to civilian life. The Bundeswehr operates more than forty schools in addition to thirty-three apprentice workshops and ten nursing schools at station hospitals.

Basic and small-unit training are scheduled on a continuing basis. For conscripts, the entire period of service is devoted to one kind of training or another, but conscripts are not eligible for attendance at advanced service schools unless they voluntarily extend their term of service. After an introductory assignment to basic training regiments, air force conscripts prepare for their special tasks in on-the-job training. Because the Luftwaffe wishes to attract a higher proportion of longer-term personnel, it offers temporary career training and regular officer advanced training at air force extension schools, as well as at training facilities of the other services and other Allied forces. In the navy, sailors prepare for their duties at schools ashore before being assigned to ships for more on-the-job training. Volunteers receive advanced training at various schools offering courses in supply, engineering, radar, weapons, and other specialties. In both the air force and the navy, training culminates in national operational exercises and large-scale NATO exercises.

About 2,000 pilots and missile personnel of the air force and navy are trained in the United States under long-standing agreements between the German and United States governments. Primary pilot training is conducted at Sheppard Air Force Base in Texas on Beech Bonanzas, followed by jet training on T–37Bs and T–38As. A Tornado squadron is based at Holloman Air Force Base in New Mexico for advanced weapons training. German personnel attend the Patriot and Hawk missile school at Fort Bliss, Texas, and navigator training at Randolph Air Force Base near San Antonio. Helicopter training is conducted at Fort Rucker, Alabama.

Much training is conducted jointly with service personnel of other NATO countries. Joint courses include forward air controller training at Fürstenfeldbruck Air Force Base, training at the army engineer school in Munich, and NATO logistics courses at the Bundeswehr Logistics School in Hamburg. German and other NATO pilots train in low-level flight techniques in Canada at Goose Bay, Labrador. German troops are shuttled to the Canadian province of Manitoba for armored infantry training on German equipment permanently maintained there.

The basic qualification for voluntary enlistment in the Bundeswehr is completion of five years at the secondary school (*Hauptschule*) level (see The Education System, ch. 4). Those with a university or technical college admission certificate can

A Tornado fighter-bomber
A submarine of the 206A class
Courtesy Embassy of the Federal Republic of Germany, Washington

apply to become temporary career or regular officer candidates. Junior NCO training lasts about fifteen months and stresses leadership qualities and practical skills. An opportunity for further training leading to senior NCO rank usually comes after about four years of service. Particularly qualified NCOs are admitted to a three-year course whose graduates are commissioned as officer specialists with the rank of lieutenant or captain. Officer specialists fill positions corresponding to those occupied by warrant officers in the United States military.

Officer candidates in the army, navy, and air force face a long, arduous training program. Those aspiring to be regular officers, as well as temporary career officers who serve up to twelve years on active duty, generally spend about five years in formal training programs. Officer candidates generally begin their career with nine months of basic training and specialized weapons training followed by twelve months at an officer candidate school—the army school in Hanover, the air force school in Fürstenfeldbruck, or the naval academy at Mürwik in Flensburg.

After a year or more as a small-unit leader, officers with at least a twelve-year enlistment begin a three-year course of study at the Bundeswehr's military academy in Hamburg or the military academy in Munich that leads to an academic degree or technical diploma. Most officers leave the service between the ages of thirty and thirty-two after serving as company commanders or the equivalent. A smaller number of senior captains or navy lieutenants qualify for attendance at the four-month staff officer course at the Federal Armed Forces Command and General Staff College in Hamburg.

Those officers with outstanding grades in the staff officer course and a generally excellent record—about 10 percent of the officers completing the course—are selected to undergo the twenty-four-month general and admiral staff training program, also offered at Hamburg. The remaining 90 percent attend an eight-week staff officer course in various specialties such as operations, logistics, personnel, and transportation. Promotion to the rank of major follows completion of the course. Field-grade officers not selected for general staff training usually retire as lieutenant colonels; general staff officers can expect to be promoted to colonel or naval captain. About 80 percent of the officers who reach the rank of general or admiral have been selected from the general staff group.

Reserves

Under the revised military structure introduced in 1992, the Bundeswehr will become increasingly dependent on the rapid mobilization of reserves to bring both the main combat brigades and the support units up to authorized strengths in an emergency. In early 1995, the reserves of former service members (enlisted to age forty-five; officers and NCOs to age sixty) numbered about 441,900, of whom 358,000 would report to the army, 10,900 to the navy, and 73,000 to the air force. Some 50 percent of the army's main weapons systems depend for their operation on staffing by reservists.

After discharge, former soldiers are liable for reserve service until age forty-five, or until age sixty in time of war. Officers and NCOs are subject to recall until age sixty. Reservists can be called up for one fifteen-day period of training a year and for any number of call-ups of up to three days in emergencies. The average reserve unit assembles once every two years. Reservists with crucial skills tend to be called up more frequently; less-skilled reservists or those in less vital units may not be called up at all. The number of call-ups is determined in the annual defense budget in terms of reserve slots, each slot equivalent to 365 duty days. A total of 4,000 reserve slots were authorized in 1993, which permitted about 100,000 individual call-ups. By contrast, 35,000 slots were authorized per year during the early 1980s.

Morale

The deep reductions in the first half of the 1990s in the size of the active Bundeswehr and the accompanying deactivation and consolidation of units, together with base closings and personnel transfers, have placed serious strains on the morale of the armed forces. Previously, an NCO could expect to pass almost his entire career at a single post, usually in or near his hometown. In the restructured army, many senior NCOs have been reassigned to distant parts of Germany; serious disruptions of family often have been the result. Garrison housing is likely to be unavailable, and affordable housing may be difficult to find off post. In many cases, wives must give up jobs that provide a much-needed second income. Frequently, NCOs prefer to commute long distances to their new posts or simply to live apart from their families. Assignment to eastern Germany, where there is a strong need for NCO cadres, can be especially burdensome because of poor living conditions there.

The decline in popular support for the Bundeswehr further undermines the morale of service personnel. According to a poll taken in mid-1992, only 47 percent of Germans were convinced that the country needed armed forces, down from 75 percent in 1984. A similar spirit has pervaded the ranks of conscripts and young soldiers who accept military training rather than the alternative of civilian service. Pacifist and church organizations have counseled young Germans on seeking conscientious objector status, and in 1991 the number of conscientious objectors was roughly equal to the number of draftees. A vocal peace movement has also influenced many civilians to reject the company of military professionals. Soldiers often avoid wearing their uniforms in public to escape unfriendly comments or treatment.

NCOs complain that it is difficult to instill discipline and impose a strict training regimen on indifferent conscripts who, in the changed international atmosphere, never expect to be faced with an actual military contingency. Conscripts expend minimal effort during their months of military training, living mainly for weekends with their families. Conscripts generally are garrisoned close to home; some can even commute on a daily basis, treating military service as little different from a factory or office job. Conscripts are entitled to free time to compensate for exercises conducted beyond regular duty hours, although this entitlement will end in 1996.

Some professional soldiers, skeptical that twelve months of service (scheduled to be ten months in 1996) can produce combat-ready soldiers and fearing that political pressures could lead to an even shorter period of service, advocate abandoning the universal military system. One reason for retaining universal military service is the belief that it helps prevent the military from again becoming a distinct caste with few roots in democratic civilian society. Officers hoping to induce promising conscripts to volunteer for longer enlistment also view conscription favorably.

The pride the Bundeswehr takes in the high standards of its personnel and the quality of its training and weaponry was blunted by the absence of German contingents from the international forces assembled to defeat Iraq in 1991. The constitutional limitation on German troop deployments outside the NATO area has been a blow to the prestige of the career military men, many of whom feel that they are regarded as shirkers by their NATO partners. The July 1994 decision of the Federal Constitutional Court to permit out-of-area deployment when approved by the Bundestag will reduce the likelihood of such situations occurring again.

Integration of East German Armed Forces

Established in 1956, the National People's Army (Nationale Volksarmee—NVA) of the German Democratic Republic was considered one of the most formidable elements of the Warsaw Pact's armed might. It comprised about 170,000 personnel in all three services, which could quickly be expanded to a mobilization strength of 350,000. NVA land forces consisted of six standing divisions and five reserve divisions. The army was equipped with some of the Warsaw Pact's most modern weapons, as well as enormous stockpiles of ammunition. The NVA's structure and training followed Soviet lines. Detailed war plans called for the NVA to combine with other Warsaw Pact forces in a powerful and sudden assault against NATO's central region to overrun Western Europe in blitzkrieg fashion. The offensive use of tactical nuclear weapons was assumed.

Although the NVA's weapons and vehicles were maintained at a high level of operational readiness, signs of deterioration and personnel preparedness in manpower were evident even before the opening of the Berlin Wall in November 1989. Once the Wall opened, many reservists and some conscripts fled the country, disappearing into West Germany. Authority and morale declined as ordinary soldiers rebelled against strict discipline and military exercises. When soldiers' councils sprang up, NVA commanders bowed to pressure to allow soldiers to wear civilian clothes off post and enjoy relaxed discipline, reduced training time, and an end to political indoctrination. The morale of officers facing the loss of careers and status began to waver as the internal situation worsened and the prospect of unification grew.

Until mid-1990 the leadership of the NVA still hoped that the force might survive as a distinct entity in a reconstituted German state. As a result of the summit agreement between West German chancellor Helmut Kohl and Soviet president Mikhail Gorbachev in July 1990, however, the Soviet Union withdrew its objections to a united Germany's membership in NATO. The NVA was disbanded upon unification, and its facilities and resources were taken over by the Bundeswehr.

On October 3, 1990, the date of unification, control over all NVA commands and border troops passed to the newly created Bundeswehr Eastern Command. The command's function was to deactivate unneeded units, to dispose of surplus matériel and weapons, and to extend support to the withdrawing Soviet forces. The command was terminated after nine months, and the various elements of the former NVA were transferred to the three chiefs of staff and the medical service corps of the Bundeswehr.

The 90,000 NVA service personnel and 47,000 civilian employees who remained were merged into the Bundeswehr on a preliminary basis. It was decided that up to 50,000 of the former NVA troops would be retained as part of the Bundeswehr. Of 14,600 NVA officers, 5,100 were permitted to enter the Bundeswehr for a transition period of two years. Some 70 percent of these—mostly junior officers—would be retained after approval for regular Bundeswehr service and screening to eliminate former members of East Germany's State Security Service (Staatssicherheitsdienst—Stasi). Many of the 25,000 NVA enlisted personnel were assigned to a three-month basic training course with West German units. The dilapidated condition of NVA barracks, mess halls, and other facilities necessitated large expenditures to bring them up to minimal Bundeswehr standards.

All 190 NVA general officers were retired, as were all colonels and many other officers over age fifty-five. Most of those retained were no older than thirty-five. Many former NVA officers were demoted by one or two ranks if they were younger than officers of corresponding ranks in the Bundeswehr. Although East German troops had been paid at a lower scale than their West German counterparts, parity was achieved by 1994. Junior NVA officers, unused to exercising initiative, had to be trained in a new doctrine of command.

A major effort was needed to instill democratic principles of leadership and a new perspective on historical and political questions. NVA officers had been indoctrinated with communist beliefs and had been considered among the most politically reliable elements of the East German state. Although forced to acknowledge that Marxist theories had diverged from social and economic realities in East Germany, many still tended to view communism as a valid, if utopian, political philosophy.

After absorption of the East German armed forces, the six active NVA divisions were converted to brigades, with three brigades in each of two divisions. One division was headquartered at Neubrandenburg and the other at Leipzig. Both divisions became part of IV Corps, which has its headquarters at Potsdam.

During a transition period, the brigades operated Soviet BMP armored vehicles, but Soviet tanks were replaced by Leopards. In the air force, the division at Eggerdorf controlled two fighter wings of Phantom F–4Fs and Soviet MiG–29s, with the Soviet aircraft to be gradually reduced in number. The former East German naval base at Warnemünde on the Baltic Sea was developed as the home port for fast-attack missile craft.

Large quantities of East German weapons were turned over to the Bundeswehr, including 2,300 main battle tanks, 7,800 armored vehicles, 2,500 artillery pieces, 400 combat aircraft, fifty attack helicopters, and many missile and rocket systems. More than 300,000 tons of ammunition had been stockpiled. With exceptions that included MiG–29s, BMP infantry fighting vehicles, and some transport helicopters, the Bundeswehr decided against trying to integrate former NVA weapons into its inventory. Ceilings imposed by the CFE Treaty, as well as problems of convertibility and safety, ruled out the wholesale absorption of the weapons. After first being concentrated in special depots, massive stocks of equipment and munitions, except for a few items transferred to other countries, were slated for destruction—a task of unprecedented magnitude.

Defense Budget

From about 1960 until 1990, the West German defense budget rose at a remarkably steady rate, just under 3 percent a year in real terms. If NATO definitions of defense expenditures are applied, outlays remained constant during the 1980s before rising about 4.7 percent in real terms in 1990 and then declining by 6.8 percent in 1991. At the same time, defense spending as a ratio of the overall federal budget decreased from 11.2 percent in 1979 to 9.5 percent in 1989. Outlays for defense also tended to decline as a proportion of the gross national product (GNP—see Glossary), from 3.3 percent in 1979 to 2.8 percent in 1989.

The Bundeswehr frequently experienced difficulty securing adequate funds to maintain personnel and equipment at desired levels because of the disinclination of the post-World

War II generation to earmark resources for the buildup of the military establishment. The absence of any palpable threat after the collapse of the Soviet bloc, combined with the unexpectedly high costs of integrating eastern Germany into the Federal Republic, generated even stronger pressures to make deep cuts in defense spending.

From a high of DM57.5 billion (US$35.6 billion) in 1990, the defense budget was scaled back to about DM52.0 billion (US$34 billion) in both 1991 and 1992, to DM49.6 billion (US$31.8 billion) in 1993, and to DM47.2 billion (US$28.6 billion) in 1994. According to Ministry of Defense plans, the annual defense budget should level off at about DM48 billion (US$32 billion) through the year 2006.

Announced cuts in the procurement budget are expected to produce savings of more than DM72 billion in the period between 1992 and 2006. Replacement of the Leopard 2 main battle tank was canceled, and the number of Leopard 2s to be upgraded was reduced. A replacement for the Jaguar antitank vehicle was deleted, and fewer Marder infantry fighting vehicles and self-propelled howitzers will be introduced. Also, a smaller number of the new Franco-German Tiger PAH–2 attack helicopters will be acquired than originally planned. To effect additional savings, the construction schedule for new frigates and submarines has been stretched out.

According to data compiled by the United States Arms Control and Disarmament Agency (ACDA), Germany's military expenditures per capita in 1993 (US$454) were above the NATO Europe average (US$416) and below those of France (US$740) or Britain (US$587). United States expenditures per capita were US$1,153 in the same year. Expressed as a percentage of GNP, military expenditures in 1993 (2.2 percent) were lower than the NATO Europe average (2.7 percent). The 1992 share of military spending in central government expenditures (6.3 percent) was also below the NATO 1992 average of 6.5 percent.

Military Justice

Members of the German armed forces are subject to the civil criminal code and are tried for common criminal offenses in the civil court system. There are no military correction facilities; incarcerated military offenders serve their sentences in ordinary civilian prisons. Soldiers enjoy the same civil rights and liberties possessed by other citizens. They are permitted to take an active part in political life, be members of political parties, and join trade unions and professional associations. Several courses of action are open to soldiers with complaints or grievances, both within the Bundeswehr and in ordinary courts of law.

Offenses of a specifically military character committed by members of the Bundeswehr are tried in two military court divisions of the Federal Administrative Court and by three military disciplinary courts having a total of twenty-nine chambers. A civilian professional judge presides over each chamber, assisted by honorary military judges. The chambers are the courts of first instance for disciplinary court proceedings against soldiers. The military courts of the Federal Administrative Court are the courts of appeal, each being composed of three civilian judges and two honorary military judges. Sentences range from discharge from service to financial penalties to reduction in rank. The lowest level of offense, such as disobedience or unauthorized absence, may be dealt with informally in a soldier's own unit.

Uniforms, Ranks, and Insignia

The service uniform is the most common type of Bundeswehr uniform for general duty and most off-post activity. The army's service uniform consists of a light gray, single-breasted coat and darker gray trousers, worn with a light blue or white shirt, black tie, and black shoes. The peaked, visored cap has been replaced by the beret as the most common form of headgear. Dress uniforms featuring dinner jackets or double-breasted coats are worn by officers for various social occasions. The battle and work uniform is olive green. Camouflage fatigues are also worn on field duty. In all three services, light sand-colored uniforms are available for duty in warmer climates.

The traditional arm-of-service colors appear as lapel facings and as piping on shoulder straps. General officers wear an inner piping of gold braid; other officers wear silver piping. Lapel facings and piping are maroon for general staff, green for infantry, red for artillery, pink for armor, black for engineers, yellow for communications, and various other colors for the remaining branches. Combat troops wear green (infantry), black (armor), or burgundy (airborne) berets. Logistics troops wear blue berets, and combat support troops, such as artillery

GERMAN RANK	LEUTNANT	OBER-LEUTNANT	HAUPTMANN	MAJOR	OBERST-LEUTNANT	OBERST	BRIGADE-GENERAL	GENERAL-MAJOR	GENERAL-LEUTNANT	GENERAL
ARMY AND AIR FORCE										
U.S. RANK TITLE	2D LIEUTENANT	1ST LIEUTENANT	CAPTAIN	MAJOR	LIEUTENANT COLONEL	COLONEL	BRIGADIER GENERAL	MAJOR GENERAL	LIEUTENANT GENERAL	GENERAL
GERMAN RANK	LEUTNANT ZUR SEE	OBER-LEUTNANT ZUR SEE	KAPITÄN-LEUTNANT	KORVETTEN-KAPITÄN	FREGATTEN-KAPITÄN	KAPITÄN ZUR SEE	FLOTTILLEN-ADMIRAL	KONTER-ADMIRAL	VIZEADMIRAL	ADMIRAL
NAVY										
U.S. RANK TITLE	ENSIGN	LIEUTENANT JUNIOR GRADE	LIEUTENANT	LIEUTENANT COMMANDER	COMMANDER	CAPTAIN	REAR ADMIRAL LOWER HALF	REAR ADMIRAL UPPER HALF	VICE ADMIRAL	ADMIRAL

NOTE — Army and air force insignia are silver, except for those of brigadier generals and above, which are gold.

Figure 15. Officer Ranks and Insignia, 1995

GERMAN RANK (ARMY AND AIR FORCE)	GRENADIER	GEFREITER	OBER-GEFREITER	HAUPT-GEFREITER	STABS-GEFREITER	UNTER-OFFIZIER	STABSUNTER-OFFIZIER	FELDWEBEL	OBER-FELDWEBEL	HAUPTFELDWEBEL	STABS-FELDWEBEL	OBERSTABS-FELDWEBEL
U.S. ARMY RANK TITLE	BASIC PRIVATE	PRIVATE	PRIVATE 1ST CLASS		CORPORAL/SPECIALIST	SERGEANT		STAFF SERGEANT		SERGEANT 1ST CLASS / MASTER SERGEANT/FIRST SERGEANT	SERGEANT MAJOR	COMMAND SERGEANT MAJOR
U.S. AIR FORCE RANK TITLE	AIRMAN BASIC	AIRMAN	AIRMAN 1ST CLASS		SENIOR AIRMAN/SERGEANT	STAFF SERGEANT		TECHNICAL SERGEANT		MASTER SERGEANT / SENIOR MASTER SERGEANT	CHIEF MASTER SERGEANT	CHIEF MASTER SERGEANT
(ARMY AND AIR FORCE insignia)	NO INSIGNIA											
GERMAN RANK (NAVY)	MATROSE	GEFREITER	OBER-GEFREITER	HAUPT-GEFREITER	STABS-GEFREITER	MAAT	OBERMAAT	BOOTS-MANN	OBERBOOTS-MANN	HAUPTBOOTSMANN	STABS-BOOTSMANN	OBERSTABS-BOOTSMANN
(NAVY insignia)	NO INSIGNIA											
U.S. RANK TITLE	SEAMAN RECRUIT	SEAMAN APPRENTICE	SEAMAN		PETTY OFFICER 3D CLASS	PETTY OFFICER 2D CLASS		PETTY OFFICER 1ST CLASS		CHIEF PETTY OFFICER	SENIOR CHIEF PETTY OFFICER	MASTER CHIEF PETTY OFFICER

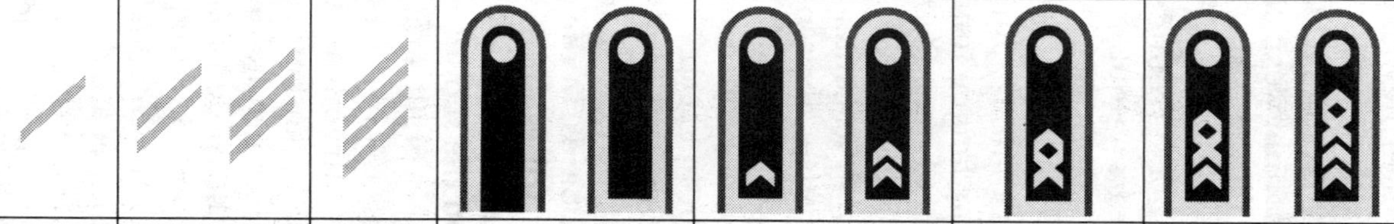

NOTE — A German *Flieger* corresponds to a United States airman basic.

Figure 16. Enlisted Ranks and Insignia, 1995

493

or engineers, wear red ones. A gold or silver device on the beret denotes the individual branch of service.

The naval forces wear the traditional navy blue, double-breasted coat and trousers; enlisted personnel wear either a white shirt or a navy blue shirt with the traditional navy collar. White uniforms provide an alternative for summer. The officer's dress cap is mounted with a gold anchor surrounded by a wreath. The visor of the admiral's cap bears a double row of oak leaves.

The air force service uniform consists of a blue-gray jacket and trousers with a light blue shirt, dark blue tie, and black shoes. Olive battle dress similar to the army fatigue uniform is worn in basic training and during other field duty. Flying personnel wear wings on their right breast. Technical personnel wear a modified wing device with a symbol in its center denoting service specialization. The latter is bronze, silver, or gold, depending on one's length of service in the specialty. Wings, superimposed over a wreath, in gold, silver, or bronze, depending on rank, are also worn on the service or field cap.

Officer ranks correspond directly to equivalent ranks in the United States Armed Forces (see fig. 15). Officer rank insignia are worn on shoulder straps or shoulder boards; in the case of naval officers, rank is indicated by gold stripes on the lower sleeve of the blue service jacket and on shoulder boards of the white uniform. The semicircular wreath on the shoulder straps is gold for general officers and silver for field grade officers.

NCO ranks are based on those used long ago in the Prussian armies, and it is difficult to relate them directly to United States NCO ranks (see fig. 16). In the army and air force, a *Hauptgefreiter* corresponds approximately to a private first class or airman first class. An *Unteroffizier*, with the responsibilities of a squad leader, is the lowest-ranking sergeant, followed by the *Stabsunteroffizier, Feldwebel, Oberfeldwebel,* and *Hauptfeldwebel.* Ranks of army and air force enlisted personnel are designated by stripes, chevrons, and looped chevrons worn on shoulder straps. Naval enlisted rank designations are worn on the upper sleeve along with a symbol of the service specialization (rating). Army and air force officer candidates hold the separate ranks of *Gefreiter, Fahnenjunker,* and *Oberfähnrich* and wear the equivalent enlisted rank designations plus a silver diamond on their sleeves. Medical personnel of all three services wear a version of the traditional caduceus (staff with entwined serpents) on their shoulder straps or sleeve.

Citizens in Uniform

When the Federal Republic was founded in 1949, and during the ensuing years, public discussion of the re-creation of a German armed force was unavoidably shaped by the memories of wartime disaster and the terrible legacy of German militarism. For many Germans, even the thought of rearming the country was distasteful. Those citizens favoring the formation of new armed forces were convinced that these forces would have to represent a near-complete break with German military history. The consensus was that the military would require a constitutional basis for its existence, with the Bundeswehr unequivocally controlled by civilian authorities.

The planners of the new Bundeswehr wanted to be sure that no images of the armed forces (Reichswehr) of the Weimar Republic or Hitler's Wehrmacht would be associated with it. The twin concepts of "citizens in uniform" and *Innere Führung* (inner leadership) were introduced to ensure that there could be no resurgence of German militarism. Behind the emphasis on citizens in uniform was the concept that military personnel were of the people and worked for the people, not part of a military elite that would precipitate a "state within a state" phenomenon. In the new Bundeswehr, the constitutional rights of service members are guaranteed, even though those rights might be restricted at times because of the special nature of military duties.

Military personnel do not give up their political status as citizens when they don a uniform. They continue to be members of the community from which they entered the service, as well as of the West German political community as a whole. They can run for office on local councils and for seats in the parliaments of the *Länder* and the Bundestag. Regulars and volunteers are permitted to join a military or civil service union and have the right of free expression, although by law they have the obligation to exercise discipline and restraint in expressing their views publicly.

The concept of *Innere Führung* imposes the responsibility upon all military personnel to defend their country according to the dictates of conscience rather than out of blind loyalty. For the NCOs, officers, and generals who formed the nucleus of the new forces in 1956, most of whom were veterans of the Wehrmacht or Luftwaffe of World War II, adherence to the new principles meant unlearning principles that had guided them in their earlier service. Officers and NCOs received training to help them respect and impart the principles of *Innere Führung,* including the role of the Bundeswehr in the state and society and the duties and rights of individual service personnel.

The West German military and the political leadership had difficulty agreeing on the measures needed to forge a new democratic spirit that would break with Germany's military past. Specific issues continued to be debated during the 1980s—whether some traditions could properly be carried over from the Wehrmacht, the place of military pageantry, public oath-taking by new soldiers, and attitudes toward the Wehrmacht's complicity in the crimes of the Nazi period and toward the officers implicated in the 1944 attempt on Hitler's life.

A strong antimilitarist element within the left wing of the Social Democratic Party of Germany (Sozialdemokratische Partei Deutschlands—SPD) repeatedly protested against military symbolism and public military ceremonies. In a wider sense, these protests reflected the reluctance among young people to devote time to military service and objections to a NATO strategy of defending Europe by using nuclear weapons in the heart of Germany.

An innovation to help ensure civilian oversight of the Bundeswehr was the establishment of the defense ombudsman (Parliamentary Commissioner for the Federal Armed Forces), who is appointed by the Bundestag. The ombudsman is responsible for overseeing the administration of the services while upholding the constitutional rights of individual service personnel. All Bundeswehr personnel have the right of direct petition to the ombudsman; several thousand exercise this right each year. The ombudsman and staff can also be called upon by the Bundestag or the Bundestag Defense Committee to investigate specific problems.

Personnel Policies

Serious shortages of eligible conscripts began to appear in the late 1980s. Because of the declining birth rate in the 1970s and the increasing number of conscientious objectors, the Bundeswehr struggled to meet its recruiting goals. However, the reduction of the Bundeswehr's active-duty soldiers to 370,000 by the end of 1994, as required by the 1990 Two-Plus-Four Treaty and CFE Treaty, meant that the annual requirement for conscripts could be decreased from 180,000 to 140,000. Also, the incorporation of East Germany into the Federal Republic added significantly to the pool of potential inductees. About 50,000 personnel in 1994 were career soldiers transferred from the NVA or draftees from the new *Länder.*

The Bundeswehr has been handicapped by a shortage of NCOs, a problem that is expected to become more critical as the army increases its dependence on career cadres to staff reserve battalions subject to mobilization. A soldier must meet high entry qualifications, undergo extensive training, and complete years of service before reaching the rank of sergeant, which entitles him to make the military a career and remain in the service until retirement. Reliance on experienced NCOs is a distinctive feature of the Bundeswehr, where the ratio of officers to enlisted personnel is the lowest in Europe. An infantry company may have a captain and one lieutenant, but most platoon leaders and the company executive officer are usually master sergeants. However, NCOs of the former NVA are generally confined to specialist categories, without experience or training as unit leaders.

Service Obligations

Under the Obligatory Military Service Law enacted in 1956, all males between the ages of eighteen and twenty-eight were subject to conscription for military service. In 1985 the period of active duty was increased from fifteen to eighteen months, but before the new provision was introduced, the term of service was reduced to twelve months, effective in 1990. Beginning in 1996, conscripts will be required to serve ten months. The Basic Law guarantees the right to refuse military service on grounds of conscience.

During the 1970s, about 35,000 young men applied for conscientious objector status annually. Under liberalized rules and the decline of the overt threat from the east, the number who claimed the right to alternative civilian service in 1992 (134,000) was about as high as the number of draftees needed by the Bundeswehr. Alternative service, which is one-third longer than military service, usually takes the form of such social service as serving as a hospital orderly. In fact, one of the obstacles to shifting to an all-volunteer force is the effect it would have on the health and social agencies that have come to depend upon conscientious objectors to perform essential work.

Under Bundeswehr policy, all soldiers begin their careers as conscripts. Those performing satisfactorily may be induced—

in part through considerable financial incentives—to volunteer for a short-term enlistment of two years, or as temporary career personnel for four years. Those attaining NCO rank during their four-year enlistment period may then be permitted to serve up to fifteen years or longer if accepted as career professionals. The army has been able to recruit about 10 percent of its conscripts for extended service.

The maximum retirement age of career sergeants is fifty-three. The mandatory retirement age rises, depending on rank, to fifty-nine for colonels and sixty for generals and medical officers. Special rules may apply to particular specialties.

Two branches of the Bundeswehr, the medical and health service and military music, accept women as volunteers. As of the mid-1990s, about 900 women were in uniform. No significant expansion of the role of women is foreseen, particularly in light of the overall contraction of the services. The Basic Law states: "Women shall not be required by law to render service in any unit of the armed forces. On no account shall they be employed in any service involving the use of arms." Of more than 50,000 women occupying civilian positions in national defense, only a few serve in higher civil service posts, although officially women enjoy the same career opportunities available to men.

Benefits

The pay of conscripts amounted to about US$160 a month in the mid-1990s. Bonuses are paid at Christmas and upon discharge. Conscripts can be compensated for loss of their civilian wages, up to 60 percent of the lost income in the case of married personnel. Those recalled for reserve duty are also compensated for lost earnings. Longer-term volunteers receive about US$1,100 a month. Basic monthly pay for a sergeant as of early 1995 was about US$1,350 and for a sergeant first class about US$1,900. In addition to basic pay, allowances are paid for housing (about US$600 a month), dependents, hazardous duty, ship duty, and other special circumstances.

All temporary career and regular service personnel are entitled to a range of benefits, including compensation for duty in excess of fifty-six hours per week and change-of-station allowances. These include disbursements to cover extra educational expenses for children; a monthly travel allowance to distant duty stations; and a rental subsidy if local rent is high in proportion to income. Working wives are entitled to preferential employment at new duty stations.

Every qualified regular serviceman can expect to advance within his career category, to sergeant first class in the case of NCOs, to captain or naval lieutenant in the case of officer specialists, and to lieutenant colonel or naval commander for line officers. Upon retirement, regular personnel can be entitled to a pension of up to 75 percent of their final salary. In addition, they receive a one-time payment to compensate for the disadvantage of retiring earlier than civil servants, plus a 5 percent supplement to their retirement. Special reintegration allowances and preferential treatment for employment in the public sector are also available to service members, especially those below retirement age but with at least twelve years of service.

Defense Production and Export

Germany's capacity to produce its own arms and military equipment grew simultaneously with the development of the Bundeswehr. As a matter of policy, arms production is confined to the private sector. There are no government-operated defense plants, and most companies involved in arms manufacture are predominantly engaged in civilian industrial production. Private industry accounts for 85 percent of all military research and development, procurement, and maintenance. Nevertheless, defense production represents no more than 3.4 percent of the total value of output by the country's processing industries. Although some 225,000 persons work on defense contracts, this group constitutes less than 1 percent of the workforce.

The Armaments Division of the Ministry of Defense has responsibility for planning, controlling, and supervising the armaments sector. Under it the Federal Office for Military Technology and Procurement (Bundesamt für Wehrtechnik und Beschaffung—BWB) in Koblenz procures all defense matériel. The BWB is a civilian agency staffed by some 18,300 persons, about one-third of whom work at seven armaments research and testing centers, each responsible for a particular category of systems. Certain major joint projects, such the Tornado and the European Fighter Aircraft (EFA), are independent of the BWB's supervision.

The Bundeswehr estimates that about 70 percent of its major procurement items are produced as part of international projects. These have included the EFA and Tornado aircraft (both developed in cooperation with Britain, Italy, and Spain); the Alpha Jet, the Roland short-range air defense system, and the Tiger PAH–2 antitank helicopter (all joint projects with France); and the multiple-launch rocket and NATO identification systems, developed in cooperation with several NATO countries.

Only in the aerospace and munitions industries does defense account for 50 percent or more of sales. Among the largest firms is Deutsche Aerospace (DASA), founded in 1989 to incorporate the aerospace and other defense activities of the Daimler-Benz group. DASA has a controlling interest in Messerschmitt-Bölkow-Blohm (MBB), located at Ottobrunn near Munich, which produces combat aircraft, helicopters, and HOT, Milan, and Exocet missiles. It also controls Dornier, which produces various equipment and aircraft and which has been a major contractor in the EFA program. Motoren und Turbinen Union (MTU), another unit of DASA, is a large producer of parts for aircraft, ships, and tanks.

Rheinmetall Berlin, another major defense contractor, produces armored vehicles, artillery, and munitions. Rheinmetall is based in Berlin and Düsseldorf. In 1991 it assumed a controlling interest in Krupp Mak Maschinenbau, thereby adding tracked armored vehicles, such as the Marder, to its output. The Krupp industrial group's defense sector was thenceforth limited to naval weapons systems. AEG-Telefunken is a leading supplier of electronics and radar; Krauss-Maffei of Munich produces the Leopard tank.

According to ACDA, known German exports of arms were valued at an estimated US$1.1 billion in 1993 and constituted 0.3 percent of total German exports; arms imports had a value of US$250 million and amounted to 0.1 percent of total imports. During the 1991–93 period, nearly half of Germany's arms transfers were made to other NATO countries, notably Portugal, Greece, the United States, Turkey, and Norway. Switzerland, the Republic of Korea (South Korea), and Finland were also substantial clients, while smaller quantities were shipped to Singapore and Colombia. In the Middle East, arms valued at US$820 million were exported to five countries during this period, Saudi Arabia taking US$525 million and Israel US$200 million.

West Germany's grant-type military assistance to other NATO countries focused on Turkey, Greece, and Portugal. The major recipient was Turkey, a beneficiary of German military aid since 1964. Arms transfers included Leopard tanks, Milan antitank missiles, and retrofit kits for M–48 tanks. West Germany also assisted Turkey with infrastructure and defense manufacturing facilities.

Although West Germany imposed controls on weapons exports, repeated charges have been made that arms shipments by private West German suppliers were not carefully monitored. In the 1980s, evidence mounted that West German firms were instrumental in assisting Iraq and Libya in developing weapons of mass destruction. In 1988, based on information supplied by the United States implicating West German firms in the construction of a poison gas plant at Rabka, Libya, the owner of one company was sentenced to prison for illegal exports and tax evasion. In early 1993, the German government announced that German firms were being investigated for delivering equipment for a second chemical weapons factory in Libya. In a report issued in 1991 by the International Atomic Energy Agency, thirteen Western companies, more than half of them German, were identified as having contributed to the Iraqi nuclear program.

In 1992, after extensive international publicity over the inadequate enforcement of arms controls, the Bundestag approved legislation to create a new government monitoring agency. The new law authorized screening of mail and use of wiretaps to facilitate investigations of suspected violators. Harsher punishments could be imposed, including confiscation of profits from illicit arms sales and imprisonment of company officers.

Under German arms policy, export permits are denied for the sale of weapons to areas of tension. This policy has applied in particular to the Middle East, where Germany felt a moral obligation to avoid actions that could endanger Israel. In 1992, despite a ban imposed by the Bundestag, at least fifteen Leopard tanks were shipped to Turkey, where they were apparently used by the Turkish army to attack strongholds of the rebel Kurdish Workers' Party. The minister of defense, Gerhard Stoltenberg, claimed that the shipment had been approved without his knowledge. Nevertheless, Stoltenberg was forced to resign from the government in the ensuing uproar.

In early 1993, the Bundestag disapproved the delivery of submarines and frigates to the Taiwan government, although SAM systems produced in conjunction with the United States were approved for sale under the rationale that they were purely defensive weapons. Diesel engines for a large quantity of

French tanks sold to the United Arab Emirates were also approved for export.

Domestic critics of Germany's arms export practices assert that German firms have easily circumvented controls through coproduction schemes or deliveries of key parts to other countries; through licensed production in other countries of arms that reach prohibited users; through the sale of technology and whole weapons plants, of which Germany is the world's foremost exporter; and through sales of items improperly labeled civilian goods. Critics claim that the UN embargo on arms sales to South Africa was violated by false labeling of troop transport vehicles, helicopters, and minesweepers.

Foreign Military Relations

Since the end of World War II, the military forces of six NATO Allies have been deployed in West Germany—first as occupation troops. Soviet troops were stationed in East Germany as part of the Warsaw Pact forces. Although the United States maintained the largest of the foreign NATO contingents, Britain and France also deployed substantial forces. Belgium, Canada, and the Netherlands maintained smaller troop units, heavily dependent on reinforcement to be of value in crises. Events in Europe culminating in German unification in October 1990, the collapse of the Warsaw Pact, and the Russian compliance with the terms of the Two-Plus-Four Treaty to evacuate its troops from the territory of the former East Germany by late 1994 ended the necessity for NATO to maintain large standing forces in the European theater. As a result, all NATO countries have made deep cuts in their forces based in Germany.

Germany grants NATO forces on its territory the use of military installations and training areas free of charge—airfields, barracks, schools, hospitals, and logistics facilities. Thousands of housing units have been placed at the disposal of the stationing countries. The financial value of German support for Allied bases is balanced in some degree by the impact of Allied wages paid to German employees, orders by Allied forces placed with German firms, and spending by soldiers and their families in Germany. By the 1980s and the 1990s, the physical burden of providing bases for large numbers of Allied troops had become a cause of widespread complaint. Low-level training flights and large-scale exercises that sometimes result in injuries and property damage are particular sources of discontent, especially when carried out at night or on weekends.

By early 1995, about 100,000 United States troops were still stationed in Germany. United States army forces in Germany include one army headquarters, one corps headquarters, and two divisions; the air force has two air force headquarters, one tactical fighter wing, one combat support wing, one air control wing, and one airlift wing. Armor and other weapons are stockpiled for units in the United States earmarked as reinforcements for Europe.

British forces in Germany numbered about 38,000 in mid-1995. British forces in Germany include one corps headquarters (multinational), one armored division, and an air force group headquarters and two air bases. Belgium and the Netherlands maintain about 10,000 and 3,000 troops, respectively.

France maintained about 15,000 troops in Germany as of mid-1995, reduced from 44,000 in 1989. Most of these troops are part of the Eurocorps. The position of France among NATO countries maintaining forces in Germany is unique. French units are not committed to NATO, and the participation of France in the event of conflict is subject to a decision by the French president. Nevertheless, French staff and troops cooperate in certain NATO exercises and maneuvers.

International Military Missions

In July 1994, the Federal Constitutional Court decided that Bundeswehr units could participate in UN and other operations outside the NATO area if such actions had the approval of the Bundestag. That decision was preceded by much political controversy in the early 1990s, including charges from opponents of out-of-area deployment of Bundeswehr elements that provisions of the Basic Law were being ignored (see The Out-of-Area Debate, ch. 8).

During the 1991 Persian Gulf War, Germany received international criticism for its unwillingness to assume a role proportionate to its military power and political importance. The strong pacifist streak in German society again manifested itself in anti-United States and antiwar demonstrations that contributed to an impression in some quarters of German indifference to Iraq's aggression. Germany did make a contribution of US$10 billion to the UN operation against Iraq, but its military actions were confined to the NATO area. German naval units and mine countermeasure ships were shifted to the Mediterranean to cover for NATO vessels sent to the Persian Gulf. After hostilities ended, German ships took part in mine-clearing operations in the gulf. German Alpha Jets and air defense missiles were deployed to Turkey, largely as a political gesture to demonstrate solidarity with other NATO countries involved in the conflict with Iraq. Later, German troops and helicopters were sent to northern Iran and Iraq to aid Kurdish refugees.

In December 1992, the government pledged to provide some 1,600 troops to regions of Somalia where peace had been restored to assist in reconstruction and the distribution of relief goods. The contingent included specialized logistic and medical units plus a small protective detachment of infantry troops. Despite political opposition, the government said it was determined to deploy troops to areas of Somalia where there was no fighting. German troops subsequently participated successfully in the United Nations Operation in Somalia II (UNO-SOM II).

German armed forces participated to a limited extent in several other UN-organized operations, generally ones with a humanitarian purpose that would evoke minimal criticism that the Basic Law was being flouted. In 1992 a group of some 150 Bundeswehr medical personnel went to Cambodia to provide health care to the 2,200 members of the UN mission in that nation. Amid objections from opposition parties, a destroyer and three reconnaissance aircraft were sent to join forces from seven other NATO countries in an attempt to monitor the UN embargo of Serbia. German troops were involved in delivery of food to the besieged city of Sarajevo but avoided airdrops that could result in conflict. Service by German crews on unarmed NATO reconnaissance aircraft to help enforce the "no-fly zone" was only narrowly approved by the Federal Constitutional Court.

Internal Security

The German legal system is the product of many centuries of development, starting with the tribal laws of the first Germans. Those indigenous customs were influenced and changed under Roman law and later by the laws that prevailed in the Holy Roman Empire. Feudal law also had a strong influence. When more formal law and legal institutions appeared in the eighteenth century, codes of law and police systems were left to the individual territorial entities. The codes that evolved were mixtures of German, Roman, and ecclesiastical law.

German soldiers serving with United Nations peacekeeping forces arrive in Somalia in 1993.
Courtesy German Information Center, New York

The drive toward political unification during the nineteenth century was accompanied by a trend toward legal unification, especially in commercial matters. In other areas of law, however, the prerogatives of each political entity still governed. Only after the achievement of political unification under Prussian dominance in 1871 was a start made on drawing up German legal codes.

The codes and laws on police and penal institutions adopted after unification showed in varying degrees the influence of the Napoleonic Code. Patterns were established that, despite modifications, continued to prevail. The most important of the early models were the Penal Code of 1871, defining three classes of imprisonment still in use in 1995; the procedural codes of 1877; the law of 1877 establishing a unified court system; and the comprehensive Civil Code, which took effect in its full scope of 2,385 paragraphs in 1900.

Parallel with the courts and laws, there developed a structure of penal institutions and a police system, both characterized by the efficiency for which German administrative organs had long been noted. Although their administration was somewhat relaxed during the Weimar period (1918–33), these bureaucracies tended toward rigidity. The police and penal authorities saw their positions and responsibilities as servants of the state as overshadowing any obligation of service to the people.

When the Nazis came to power in 1933, they capitalized on the tendencies of the legal bureaucracy, centralizing control of the police and administration of the courts and making widespread use of special courts. Ostensibly, the laws and institutions remained the same. However, the spirit of the law and the legal system were gradually and totally subverted by the agenda of the Nazi leadership. When the "sound instincts of the people" demanded it, as interpreted by the Nazis, the rule of law was completely ignored.

The impact of Nazi ideology was greatest on the Criminal Code and the Code of Criminal Procedure. The Third Reich greatly broadened the definition of criminal activity, particularly in the category of crimes against the state, and made punishment much harsher. The Code of Criminal Procedure was distorted almost beyond recognition by the activities of the Nazi-inspired People's Court, in which those convicted of crimes against the state were often sentenced to death. In twelve years, an extensive network of special and summary courts of indeterminate jurisdiction was developed.

The police, whose powers and responsibilities were significantly broadened, became tools of the ruling party under the direct control of the minister of interior. The regular police— including city and town forces, motorized gendarmerie in rural areas, and administrative police, who administered codes and regulations—were supplemented by much more powerful internal security units. These included the Security Police (Sicherheitspolizei), which incorporated the Criminal Investigation Police and the Border Police, as well as the newly formed Secret State Police (Geheime Staatspolizei—Gestapo). Two other of Hitler's organizations, the Storm Troops (Sturmabteilung—SA) and the Guard Detachment (Schutz-Staffel— SS), in company with the Gestapo, became infamous as instruments of Nazi brutality.

After World War II, each of the Allied authorities permitted the formation of West German police forces, although under terms that reflected their own police structures and traditions. In all three Western zones, however, the police were decentralized, democratized, and demilitarized. Some restrictions were lifted within two years as Cold War tensions grew, and certain police functions necessitated central rather than local direction. The Federal Border Force was created to handle special functions that overlapped *Land* jurisdictions. In addition to this force, federal agencies were created to handle interstate criminal matters and overall security affairs.

Federal Police Agencies

Established in 1951, the Federal Border Force (Bundesgrenzschutz—BGS) was the first federal police organization permitted by the Allied occupation authorities. During the early 1950s, there were frequent incidents on the borders with East Germany and Czechoslovakia, and the occupation authorities became convinced of the need for a competent border police. Even though the BGS is organized along paramilitary lines, that is, in battalions, companies, and platoons, and is armed as light infantry, it remains a police force controlled by the Ministry of Interior rather than by the Ministry of Defense. The strength of the BGS was 24,000 in early 1995. The BGS is equipped with armored cars, machine guns, automatic rifles, tear gas, hand grenades, rifle grenades, and antitank weapons. All personnel on border duty wear sidearms. Some units have light aircraft and helicopters to facilitate rapid access to remote border areas and for patrol and rescue missions. A coast guard force (Bundesgrenzschutz-See) of approximately 550 members forms a part of the BGS. It is equipped with fourteen large patrol craft and several helicopters.

In addition to controlling Germany's border, the BGS serves as a federal reserve force to deal with major disturbances and other emergencies beyond the scope of *Land* police. The BGS guards airports and foreign embassies, and several highly trained detachments are available for special crisis situations requiring demolition equipment, helicopters, or combat vehicles. After shortcomings in police procedures and training were revealed by the terrorist attack on Israeli athletes at the 1972 Olympics, a BGS task force known as Special Group 9 (BGS-9) was formed to deal with terrorist incidents, especially hostage situations. The BGS-9 won world attention when it rescued eighty-six passengers on a Lufthansa airliner hijacked to Mogadishu, Somalia, in 1977.

A military rank structure similar to that of the Bundeswehr was replaced in the mid-1970s by civil service-type personnel grades. The service uniform is green, but field units also wear camouflage fatigues and, at times, steel helmets.

Another central police agency, the Federal Criminal Investigation Office (Bundeskriminalamt—BKA), with approximately 3,000 agents, operates nationwide from headquarters in Wiesbaden. Similar in some respects to the United States Federal Bureau of Investigation, the BKA is a clearinghouse for criminal intelligence records. It provides assistance to *Länder* in forensic matters, research, and criminal investigations. It is also the national point of contact for the International Criminal Police Organization (Interpol). The BKA enters cases only when requested by *Land* authorities, or in cases involving two or more *Länder*. The BKA is involved in combating various terrorist gangs, which have plagued the country since the 1960s.

Two federal agencies involved in security matters are the Federal Intelligence Service (Bundesnachrichtendienst—BND) and the Federal Office for the Protection of the Constitution (Bundesamt für Verfassungsschutz—BfV). Based in Munich, the BND is restricted to the investigation of threats originating abroad. It depends heavily on wiretapping and other surveillance techniques applied to international communications. Such activities are authorized only to counter the danger of an armed threat to the country, but intelligence authorities have pressed for the added power to monitor suspected international traffickers of weapons and drugs. The BfV is primarily a domestic intelligence-gathering service concerned with espionage, treason, and sedition. It has no powers of arrest and cannot use force, but it carries out surveillance and supplies the BKA and other police agencies with information on international crime, drug trafficking, terrorism, and other illegal activities. Its main office is in Cologne. Similar offices exist in each *Land*; although they cooperate closely with the federal office, they operate under the control of *Land* authorities.

Land Police Agencies

Below the federal level, police forces are organized by the *Länder* and are collectively known as *Land* police (Landpolizei). The forces are organized by cities, towns, or rural communities, but all are integral components of the police forces of the *Land* in which they are located. The *Land* minister of interior supervises police operations in his or her jurisdiction. Although the internal organizations differ somewhat, all *Land* police are divided into Protective Police (Schutzpolizei— "Schupos"), a uniformed service carrying out routine law and order duties, and Criminal Police (Kriminalpolizei—"Kripos"), who carry out criminal investigations. The separate Administrative Police formerly had duties that included the registration of residents and the issuance of passports, identity cards, and various permits. These functions have been transferred to civil government departments in nearly all *Länder.*

Readiness Police (Bereitschaftspolizei—"Bepos") are available in each *Land* for riot control although their primary function is training police recruits. The Readiness Police receive standardized weapons, vehicles, and communications equipment from the federal government. An office in the federal Ministry of Interior monitors and coordinates the deployment of Readiness Police units, which can be called upon to assist the police of other *Länder* in case of riots or other civil disturbances.

Although the *Land* police are regulated by sixteen different legislatures and are, in fact, different police forces, there has been an increasing tendency toward standardization of police activities nationwide. Concerns about terrorism and the growth of organized crime have strengthened the movement to centralize police procedures and operations. Since 1979 the police of all *Länder* have worn the same uniform, consisting of a forest-green jacket, brown trousers, yellow shirt, and white cap.

An ordinary police officer (*Polizeihauptwachtmeister*) wears a single green star on his or her shoulder straps, denoting rank in the first echelon of the police service. In the regular progression, a uniformed police officer may expect to retire at age sixty with the rank of *Hauptmeister* (four green stars). The rank of *Polizeikommissar* (one silver star), corresponding to the former rank of police lieutenant, is the first step of the upper echelon, which ascends through *Ersterhauptkommissar* (four silver stars). The highest echelon of the police begins with *Polizeirat* (one gold star) and culminates with the *Land* director of police (gold half-wreath with one star). About 10 percent of the police attain the upper echelon, and 1 percent reach the highest executive level.

Unlike the military services, which do not recruit women, the *Land* police have had women members since the forces were reconstituted after World War II. Initially, female officers were assigned to cases involving juveniles and women, working in plainclothes without weapons. Since the mid-1970s, policewomen have performed general police duties; many fill the uniformed ranks, although their acceptance varies by *Land.*

Women are not, however, included in units of the Readiness Police or the BGS.

Police training is primarily the responsibility of the individual *Länder*, although the federal government provides assistance and coordination. The high level of police professionalism is attributed in large degree to the length and thoroughness of training. The situation is different in the five new *Länder* of eastern Germany. Long accustomed to a compliant society, police forces of the eastern *Länder* have been described as understaffed, undertrained, poorly equipped, and woefully unprepared to cope with the challenges posed by the growing numbers of skinheads and neo-Nazis engaged in violent hate crimes against foreign workers and refugees.

Most police recruits spend about three years in combined training and service in the Readiness Police, although the training time may be shorter depending on previous education. Recruits are exempt from military service. Training encompasses a six-month course at a police school that provides a grounding in law, legal procedures, and police conduct. After about six years of duty as a patrol officer, an individual with an outstanding record who does well on a highly competitive examination can go on to two or three years at a higher police school or a college of public administration to qualify for the upper echelon. The very few candidates who qualify for the highest ranks of the police study for one year at the Federal Police Leadership Academy in Münster-Hiltrup.

The Readiness Police are assigned to barracks where they are organized along military lines into squads, platoons, and 120- to 150-member training or standby companies. In most *Länder*, the Readiness Police contingent consists of one 600- to 800-member battalion, but in six of the larger *Länder* they are organized into regiments. Duties vary according to local requirements. In Hamburg, for example, Readiness Police patrol the subway system, assist in police raids in the red-light district, and are present at large demonstrations and soccer matches. Their units are equipped with their own transport, tents, and rations, enabling them to be shifted quickly to other *Länder* without having to rely on outside support. The Readiness Police have water cannons and armored vehicles but are armed with lighter weapons than those of the BGS.

The Criminal Police enjoy greater prestige and generally receive more compensation than Protective Police officers with comparable service time. Most Criminal Police candidates are regular police officers who have done well in police school and in their first years of street duty. After rigorous screening and examination, a small number are chosen to receive a technical education in criminology at a police college. Those completing the course then serve a three-year apprenticeship before attaining full status in the Criminal Police.

Criminal Justice

Law in Germany is codified and is predominantly federal. The Penal Code is a revised version of a legal code introduced after the unification of Germany in 1871 and is therefore influenced by Prussian legal concepts. The system of criminal justice is derived from the civil law, rather than the common law that provides the basis for the systems used in Britain and the United States. In its modern development in Western Europe, including Germany, civil law incorporates ideas of nonconfinement punishments, work-release programs, and other measures aimed at rehabilitation rather than the mere isolation of a criminal from society. Toward these goals, the West German state in the mid-1970s promulgated the revised Code of Criminal Procedure and the Federal Prison Act. West Germany also joined several other civil-law countries by abolishing the death penalty, which was done under the Basic Law. East Germany abolished the death penalty in 1987.

Even before the unification of Germany was completed in 1990, East German laws had been modified to delete provisions empowering authorities to detain people for exercising freedom of expression, association, assembly, and movement. The East German prison population fell from 24,000 to 5,000 persons because so many political crimes had been abolished. Following unification, West Germany's criminal code was adopted, with minor modifications.

Criminal cases get their initial hearing at any of the courts of the three-tiered *Land* system—local courts, regional or *Land* courts, and the higher regional (appellate) *Land* courts—and can be appealed or revised from the lowest to the next two levels or from all three courts to the highest court in the criminal justice system—the Federal Court of Justice (see the Judiciary, ch. 7). Prosecutions leading to a maximum sentence of one year are heard by a judge of the local court. In more serious cases involving possible sentences of up to three years, the judge is assisted by two lay judges, comparable to jury members in a common law system. Criminal cases in which the sentence exceeds three years are referred to a *Land* court, where they are heard by three judges and three to six lay judges. A *Land* court of appeal presided over by five judges usually hears only appeals from the lower courts, plus cases concerning extraordinary crimes in violation of the Basic Law, such as treason and genocide.

Individual rights of citizens are guaranteed in the Basic Law and in the country's statutes. The law prevents police from subjecting suspects to physical abuse, torture, drugs, deceit, and hypnosis. The record of the police in conforming to these guidelines is good. A suspect has to be brought before a judge no later than the day following arrest, and the judge is obliged to issue a warrant of arrest specifying reasons for detention or else release the suspect. A relative or another person selected by the detainee has to be notified immediately of any detention lasting beyond the day after arrest. Accused persons have the right of free access to legal counsel, although this right has been restricted in the cases of some terrorists who used contacts with lawyers to continue terrorist activity while in prison. Bail bonds exist but are seldom employed. Criminal trials are held in public; protection against double jeopardy and the usual guarantees of due process are observed.

The judiciary is free from political influence and intimidation by terrorists. Substantial progress has been made in reforming the court system of the former East Germany to meet West German standards. Nevertheless, many experienced East German judges had to be disqualified for political and judicial reasons. Judges introduced from West Germany are handicapped by the unfamiliar circumstances in which they are required to function.

Incidence of Crime and Incarceration

Criminal acts are classified as felonies or misdemeanors, the latter encompassing less serious crimes but including many acts considered felonies in most common-law countries. Crimes categorized as misdemeanors include extortion, fraud, larceny, and even negligent homicide. Felonies are punishable by prison sentences of one year or more; misdemeanors can be punished by shorter prison terms, by combined imprisonment and fines, or solely by fines.

By far the largest number of persons convicted in German courts are fined. In 1991, although nearly 600,000 persons were sentenced for criminal acts in the old *Länder*, the number of persons committed to prison was only about 100,000. About 80 percent of this number were sentenced to a prison term of less than one year, 16 percent were sentenced to between one and five years, and 1 percent were sentenced to between five and fifteen years. Fifty-six persons received life sentences in 1991.

Approximately 43.8 percent of the 6,750,000 crimes registered in 1993 were solved by the authorities. By far the largest category of crime was theft, which accounted for 61.5 percent of the total, followed by damage to property (8.6 percent), fraud (7.8 percent), and crimes of violence (2.4 percent). In the old *Länder* and including all of Berlin, there were 4,230 murders and incidents of manslaughter, of which 84.7 percent were solved by the authorities.

According to federal police data, the crime rate has increased since unification in 1990, especially in the new *Länder*, where the crime rate before unification was lower than that of the old *Länder*. During 1991 the number of criminal offenses recorded amounted to 5 million, compared with 6.3 million in 1992 and nearly 6.8 million in 1993. To some extent, the upsurge in crime was associated with the radical upheaval in the former East Germany and the accompanying loss of jobs and benefits. In 1993, for example, the number of registered crimes in the new *Länder* amounted to 1.4 million, compared with 1.1 million in 1992. The old *Länder* and all of Berlin, in contrast, had 5.3 million registered crimes in 1993, compared with 5.2 million in 1992.

The large concentration of refugees, foreign workers, and illegal immigrants, combined with weaker border controls, has attracted a growing underworld of organized crime in Berlin and in other major German cities, which have a crime rate three times higher than towns with fewer than 20,000 inhabitants. The most common crimes involve narcotics, automobile theft (especially of late-model luxury cars), arms smuggling, counterfeiting, prostitution, gambling, and white-collar crime. Germany is both a market for narcotics and a transshipment point for drugs destined for Scandinavia and Britain. Marijuana enters from the Middle East and North Africa, cocaine from Central and South America, and heroin from Pakistan, Turkey, and Southeast Asia.

Dissidence and Terrorist Activity

Opposition to the West German government has existed

since its inception in 1949, and, in keeping with German tradition, radical students have sometimes been in the front ranks of those protesting various policies and situations: the use of nuclear power and the presence of atomic weapons; the government's policy toward the universities; and United States involvement in Vietnam and in the Persian Gulf War. Violence and injuries to both sides were common in confrontations between protesters and police. By the 1960s, individuals on the fringes of mainstream student organizations dropped out to form extremist groups. A lethal succession of terrorist activities followed, continuing throughout the 1970s and at a somewhat reduced level in the 1980s.

The left-wing Red Army Faction (Rote Armee Fraktion—RAF) became internationally known through its bloody exploits in West Germany and through its contacts with terrorist groups in other countries. The RAF was an outgrowth of the Baader-Meinhof Gang, which held up banks, bombed police stations, and attacked United States army bases in the 1970s. By 1975 some ninety members of the gang were in custody. In the middle of her trial in 1976, Ulrike Meinhof, one of the RAF ringleaders, committed suicide in prison. Another member, Andreas Baader, was sentenced to life imprisonment, but in 1977 he too took his own life in prison.

By the early 1980s, the original leaders of the RAF had been succeeded by a new and equally violent group that was Marxist-Leninist in orientation and saw itself as part of an international movement to topple the power structures of the capitalist world. A core group of twenty to thirty terrorists carried out the most deadly operations of the RAF. Periodic attacks were mounted against United States and NATO military leaders and bases and against prominent German officials and businesspeople. Demonstrations were held throughout the country to support a hunger strike by RAF prisoners and to protest the introduction of intermediate-range ballistic missiles. RAF violence had declined somewhat by 1990, although the RAF and other left-wing radical groups like the Revolutionary Cells carried out attacks against United States government and business targets. In November 1989, the chief executive of the Deutsche Bank, Alfred Herrhausen, was assassinated. In April 1991, Detlev Rohwedder, the director of the Treuhandanstalt (Trust Agency), the mammoth agency charged with privatizing East German state enterprises, was murdered by terrorists with connections to the Stasi. In August 1992, the RAF published a lengthy statement admitting past errors and announcing a decision to suspend the strategy of violence in carrying on its struggle.

By the early 1990s, attention had shifted to violence by neo-Nazi and other right-wing fringe groups. The fanaticism of the xenophobic rightists was fueled by the presence of large numbers of foreign workers and by the increasing number of aliens seeking political asylum in the country. Legal but extreme right-wing parties such as the German People's Union (Deutsche Volksunion—DVP) and the Republikaner (Die Republikaner—REP) maintained their legal status by avoiding Nazi symbols and propaganda and keeping their distance from smaller neo-Nazi groups. With members numbering mostly in the low hundreds, the latter tended to be splintered and indistinct, which helped them evade bans and government surveillance.

Right-wing extremism found new supporters in the wake of the unemployment and turmoil that accompanied German unification. In both the eastern and western parts of Germany, outbreaks of violence were sparked by the growth of racial and ethnic intolerance. The federal police reported 2,285 acts of rightist violence in 1992, a sevenfold increase over the number reported in 1990. Seventeen deaths resulted. The greatest number of perpetrators were youths under the age of twenty. The police count of known right-wing extremists, estimated at some 40,000 in the early 1990s, slightly exceeded the estimated number of left-wing extremists. Some 6,400 of these extreme right-wingers were considered prone to violence. Their attacks were directed against asylum-seekers, migrants from Eastern Europe, nonwhites, and in some cases homosexuals, prostitutes, and members of the former Soviet armed forces. Some of the most serious outrages, such as street assaults and firebombings of hostels for foreigners, occurred in gritty eastern industrial centers—Rostock, Chemnitz, Cottbus, and Leipzig. The west, however, was not immune to such violence, and deaths occurred in bombing incidents in Mölln in late 1992 and in Solingen in mid-1993.

The police were accused of responding slowly when hostel residents were threatened and of treating neo-Nazis too gently, often releasing without charge those allegedly involved in terrorizing hostel-dwellers. Courts handed down mild sentences, in most cases probation or brief jail terms. Western police units had to be deployed to the eastern region to help control the

violence. Under pressure to act more forcefully, the federal
police raided premises occupied by the neo-Nazis to gain evidence to suppress them. In December 1992, the federal Ministry of Interior banned four small neo-Nazi groups and also
placed the Republikaner under observation to determine
whether the organization could be banned as undemocratic
under the constitution. A new federal police division to monitor and repress rightist violence was also announced at that
time.

These actions soon bore fruit, and in 1993 the number of
deaths caused by right-wing violence fell to eight and declined
still further in 1994. Tough sentences on right-wing extremists
acted as a deterrent to violence, and a tightening of the country's liberal asylum law in May 1993 reduced social tensions
about the large number of foreigners living in Germany (see
Political Developments since Unification, ch. 7).

International terrorist organizations are represented among
several of the colonies of workers and asylum-seekers in Germany. Although more than 2 million Muslims from Turkey, the
Middle East, and North Africa live in the cities of western Germany, only a tiny minority can be considered political extremists. In the 1980s, members of the Palestinian groups Hizballah
and the Popular Front for the Liberation of Palestine-General
Command had been involved in airline hijackings and attacks
on United States service members. During the same decade,
members of the Kurdish Workers' Party bombed and staged
violent protests at the offices of the Turkish government in
Germany, and the Provisional Irish Republican Army carried
out several attacks against British military targets in Germany.
The number of incidents of international terrorism abated
during the late 1980s and the first half of the 1990s, however, in
part because of more determined investigation and prosecution of international terrorism by the German police and judiciary authorities.

*   *   *

The literature on the German military is vast. Readers seek-
ing an introduction to the subject can consult Gordon A.
Craig's classic and widely available *The Politics of the Prussian
Army, 1640–1945*. The same author's *The Battle of Königgrätz*
explains why Prussia defeated Austria in 1866. *Makers of Modern
Strategy,* edited by Peter Paret, Gordon A. Craig, and Felix Gil-

bert, presents several of Germany's military thinkers. Donald Abenheim's *Reforging the Iron Cross,* published in 1988, examines the contradictions between the military traditions of the past and the modern concept of "citizens in uniform."

The information on current staffing levels and equipment of the Bundeswehr reported in this chapter is derived from the 1994–95 edition of *The Military Balance,* an annual produced by the International Institute for Strategic Studies, and *Jane's Fighting Ships, 1994–95.*

Geoffrey Van Orden, a British general who has served in Germany, appraises the changes in sight for the Bundeswehr as it shifts to a new role in "The Bundeswehr in Transition," in the London-based journal *Survival.* Thomas-Durell Young of the Strategic Studies Institute of the United States Army War College examines military reforms in *The "Normalization" of the Federal Republic of Germany's Defense Structures.* The commander of Germany's Eastern Corps, Lieutenant General Werner von Scheven, describes how the Bundeswehr approached one of its most difficult problems in "The Merger of Two Formerly Hostile German Armies" in the English-language edition of *Aussenpolitik.*

In *German Police,* Erika S. Fairchild discusses law enforcement under the German system, as does Jürgen Thomaneck in his article "Germany" in *Police and Public Order in Europe,* edited by John Roach and Jürgen Thomaneck. The United States Department of State's annual *Country Reports on Human Rights Practices* and its annual *Patterns of Global Terrorism* summarize the threat to internal security and assess police efforts to prevent violence. (For further information and complete citations, see Bibliography.)

Appendix

Table 1. *Metric Conversion Coefficients and Factors*

When you know	Multiply by	To find
Millimeters..........................	0.04	inches
Centimeters........................	0.39	inches
Meters..............................	3.3	feet
Kilometers	0.62	miles
Hectares............................	2.47	acres
Square kilometers	0.39	square miles
Cubic meters	35.3	cubic feet
Liters	0.26	gallons
Kilograms...........................	2.2	pounds
Metric tons.........................	0.98	long tons
....	1.1	short tons
....	2,204	pounds
Degrees Celsius (Centigrade)...........	1.8 and add 32	degrees Fahrenheit

Table 2. *Presidents of the Federal Republic of Germany, 1949–*

President	Years in Office	Former Party Affiliation
Theodor Heuss	1949–59	FDP[1]
Heinrich Lübke.......................	1959–69	CDU[2]
Gustav Heinemann	1969–74	SPD[3]
Walter Scheel.........................	1974–79	FDP
Karl Carstens	1979–84	CDU
Richard von Weizsäcker	1984–91	CDU
Roman Herzog	1994–	CDU

[1] Freie Demokratische Partei (Free Democratic Party).
[2] Christlich Demokratische Union (Christian Democratic Union).
[3] Sozialdemokratische Partei Deutschlands (Social Democratic Party of Germany).

Source: Based on information from David Childs, *Germany in the Twentieth Century*, New York, 1991, 296.

Table 3. Governments of the Federal Republic of Germany, 1949–

Date Formed	Reason for Change	Coalition Partners	Chancellor
September 1949 ...	Election	CDU/CSU, FDP, DP[1]	Konrad Adenauer (CDU)
October 1953......	-do-	CDU/CSU, FDP, DP, All German Bloc/ Federation of Expellees and Displaced Persons	Konrad Adenauer (CDU)
October 1957......	-do-	CDU/CSU, DP	Konrad Adenauer (CDU)
November 1961....	-do-	CDU/CSU, FDP	Konrad Adenauer (CDU)
October 1963......	Chancellor retirement	-do-	Ludwig Erhard (CDU)
October 1965......	Election	-do-	Ludwig Erhard (CDU)
December 1966....	Coalition change	CDU/CSU, SPD[2]	Kurt Georg Kiesinger (CDU)
October 1969......	Election	SPD, FDP	Willy Brandt (SPD)
December 1972....	-do-	-do-	Willy Brandt (SPD)
May 1974	Chancellor retirement	-do-	Helmut Schmidt (SPD)
December 1976....	Election	-do-	Helmut Schmidt (SPD)
November 1980....	-do-	SPD, FDP	Helmut Schmidt (SPD)
October 1982......	Constructive no-confidence vote	CDU/CSU, FDP	Helmut Kohl (CDU)
March 1983	Election	-do-	Helmut Kohl (CDU)
January 1987	-do-	-do-	Helmut Kohl (CDU)
December 1990....	-do-	-do-	Helmut Kohl (CDU)
November 1994....	-do-	-do	Helmut Kohl (CDU)

[1] CDU/CSU—Christlich Demokratische Union (Christian Democratic Union)/Christlich-Soziale Union (Christian Social Union), FDP—Freie Demokratische Partei (Free Democratic Party), DP—Deutsche Partei (German Party).
[2] SPD—Sozialdemokratische Partei Deutschlands (Social Democratic Party of Germany).

Source: Based on information from Russell J. Dalton, *Politics in Germany*, New York, 1993, 64; and *Keesing's Record of World Events* [Cambridge], 40, No. 11, 1994, 40292.

Table 4. Composition of the Bundestag by Party, 1949–

Year	CDU/CSU[1]	FDP[2]	SPD[3]	Greens	Alliance 90	PDS[4]	Other	Total Seats
1949	139	52	131	—[5]	—	—	80	402
1953	243	48	151	—	—	—	45	487
1957	270	41	169	—	—	—	17	497
1961	242	67	190	—	—	—	0	499
1965	245	49	202	—	—	—	0	496
1969	242	30	224	—	—	—	0	496
1972	225	41	230	—	—	—	0	496
1976	243	39	214	—	—	—	0	496
1980	226	53	218	—	—	—	0	497
1983	244	34	193	27	—	—	0	498
1987	223	46	186	42	—	—	0	497
1990	319	79	239	0	8	17	0	662
1994	294	47	252	49[6]	—[6]	30	0	672

[1] Christlich Demokratische Union (Christian Democratic Union)/Christlich-Soziale Union (Christian Social Union).
[2] Freie Demokratische Partei (Free Democratic Party).
[3] Sozialdemokratische Partei Deutschlands (Social Democratic Party of Germany).
[4] Partei des Demokratischen Sozialismus (Party of Democratic Socialism).
[5] — means party did not exist that year.
[6] In 1993 the Alliance 90 and the Greens united to form one party.

Source: Based on information from Russell J. Dalton, *Politics in Germany*, New York, 1993, 286; and *Keesing's Record of World Events* [Cambridge], 40, No. 10, 1994, 40237.

Table 5. German Population, Selected Years, 1850–1990
(in millions)

Year	Population	Year	Population
1850	35.3	1930	65.1
1860	37.6	1940	69.9
1870	40.8	1950	68.4
1880	45.1	1960	72.7
1890	49.2	1970	77.7
1900	56.0	1980	78.3
1910	64.6	1990	79.4
1920	61.8		

Source: Based on information from David Childs, *Germany in the Twentieth Century*, New
York, 1991, 303; and Federal Republic of Germany, Statistisches Bundesamt,
Statistisches Jahrbuch 1994 für die Bundesrepublik Deutschland, Stuttgart, 1994, 50.

*Table 6. Population of the Federal Republic of Germany and the
German Democratic Republic, Selected Years, 1950–90*
(in thousands)

Year	Federal Republic of Germany	German Democratic Republic	Total[1]
1950	49,989	18,388	68,377
1955	52,382	17,944	70,326
1960	55,433	17,241	72,674
1965	58,619	17,028	75,647
1970	60,651	17,058	77,709
1975	61,847	16,850	78,697
1980	61,538	16,737	78,275
1981	61,663	16,736	78,399
1982	61,596	16,697	78,293
1983	61,383	16,699	78,081
1984	61,126	16,671	77,796
1985	60,975	16,644	77,619
1986	61,010	16,624	77,635
1987	61,077	16,641	77,718
1988	61,450	16,666	78,116
1989	62,063	16,614	78,677
1990	63,254	16,111	79,365

[1] Figures may not add to totals because of rounding.

Source: Based on information from Federal Republic of Germany, Statistisches Bundesamt, *Statistisches Jahrbuch 1994 für die Bundesrepublik Deutschland*, Stuttgart, 1994,
50.

Table 7. Population, Area, and Capitals of the Länder, *December 31, 1992*

Land	Capital	Area (in square kilometers)	Population Total (in thousands)	Population Density (persons per square kilometer)
Baden-Württemberg......	Stuttgart	35,751	10,149	284
Bavaria................	Munich	70,554	11,770	167
Berlin.................	Berlin	889	3,466	3,898
Brandenburg...........	Potsdam	29,476	2,543	86
Bremen	Bremen	404	686	1,697
Hamburg..............	Hamburg	755	1,689	2,236
Hesse	Wiesbaden	21,114	5,923	281
Lower Saxony	Hanover	47,348	7,578	160
Mecklenburg-Western Pomerania	Schwerin	23,421	1,865	80
North Rhine-Westphalia...	Düsseldorf	34,072	17,679	519
Rhineland-Palatinate	Mainz	19,846	3,881	196
Saarland...............	Saarbrücken	2,570	1,084	422
Saxony................	Dresden	18,408	4,641	252
Saxony-Anhalt...........	Magdeburg	20,443	2,797	137
Schleswig-Holstein	Kiel	15,732	2,680	170
Thuringia..............	Erfurt	16,176	2,546	157
TOTAL[1]...............		356,959	80,975	227

[1] Figures may not add to totals because of rounding.

Source: Based on information from Federal Republic of Germany, Statistisches Bundesamt, *Statistisches Jahrbuch 1994 für die Bundesrepublik Deutschland*, Stuttgart, 1994,
52.

Table 8. Cities with Population over 250,000, January 1, 1993

City	Population	City	Population
Berlin	3,466,000	Bochum	400,000
Hamburg	1,689,000	Wuppertal	388,000
Munich	1,257,000	Bielefeld	324,000
Cologne	961,000	Mannheim	318,000
Frankfurt am Main	664,000	Halle	300,000
Essen	627,000	Bonn	298,000
Dortmund	601,000	Gelsenkirchen	295,000
Stuttgart	599,000	Chemnitz	284,000
Düsseldorf	578,000	Karlsruhe	279,000
Bremen	554,000	Magdeburg	273,000
Duisburg	539,000	Wiesbaden	268,000
Hanover	524,000	Münster	267,000
Nuremberg	500,000	Mönchengladbach	265,000
Leipzig	497,000	Augsburg	265,000
Dresden	482,000	Braunschweig	258,000

Source: Based on information from Mario von Baratta, ed., *Der Fischer Weltalmanach, 1995*, Frankfurt am Main, 1994, 153.

Table 9. *Registered Foreign Residents in Germany by Nationality,*
Selected Years, 1961–92[1]
(in thousands)

Nationality	1961	1970	1987	1992
European Community[2]				
Greece.............	42	305	256	346
Italy...............	197	528	500	558
Portugal	1	48	69	99
Spain..............	44	239	129	134
Other	107	186	286	370
Total European Community....	391	1,306	1,240	1,507
Austria	57	123	150	185
Poland	n.a.[3]	17	121	286
Turkey	7	429	1,454	1,855
United States[4]	15	48	76	104
Yugoslavia	16	410	552	1,018
Other...............	200	268	648	1,541
TOTAL	686	2,601	4,241	6,496

[1] Prior to 1992, figures are for the former West Germany only.
[2] Figures are for the European Community membership as of 1992: Belgium, Britain, Denmark, France, Greece, Ireland, Italy, Luxembourg, Netherlands, Portugal, and Spain.
[3] n.a—not available.
[4] Figures do not include United States officials and military personnel based in Germany.

Source: Based on information from Federal Republic of Germany, Statistisches Bundes-amt, *Statistisches Jahrbuch 1994 für die Bundesrepublik Deutschland*, Stuttgart, 1994, 72.

Table 10. *Principal Causes of Death by Gender, 1991 and 1992*
(in thousands)

Cause of Death	1991		1992	
	Males	Females	Males	Females
Cardiovascular diseases.......	190.4	265.4	182.0	255.3
Cancer	105.2	105.3	106.8	105.8
Respiratory diseases.........	29.7	24.1	28.2	22.2
Injuries and poisonings, including traffic accidents and suicides............	28.0	18.7	27.2	17.6
Diseases of digestive tract	22.4	20.6	22.0	20.0
Neurological diseases	12.6	10.8	12.9	11.2
Diabetes..................	6.3	13.3	6.3	13.2
Diseases of reproductive system and urinary tract.........	4.5	5.5	4.2	5.3
Other	22.7	25.7	21.0	24.3
TOTAL.................	421.8	489.4	410.6	474.9

Source: Based on information from Federal Republic of Germany, Statistisches Bundesamt, *Statistisches Jahrbuch 1994 für die Bundesrepublik Deutschland*, Stuttgart, 1994,
458.

Table 11. Overview of Education System, Academic Year 1992–93

Type of Institution	Number of Schools	Number of Teachers	Number of Students
Primary and secondary schools			
Grundschulen...................	17,941	208,768	3,419,584
Hauptschulen...................	9,209	101,939	1,483,229
Realschulen.....................	3,634	59,176	1,056,739
Gymnasien	3,126	146,124	2,047,241
Gesamtschulen	930	48,419	493,406
Evening schools	352	3,734	48,606
Total primary and secondary schools	35,192	568,160	8,548,805
Secondary vocational schools			
Berufsschulen...................	3,233	56,779	1,796,452
Berufsaufbauschulen..............	230	423	6,564
Berufsfachschulen................	2,612	22,103	263,592
Fachoberschulen	740	4,983	75,461
Fachgymnasien..................	564	9,842	151,819
Total secondary vocational schools	7,379	94,130	2,293,888
Advanced vocational schools			
Fachschulen	1,537	10,953	171,693
Schools of higher education[1]			
Universities....................	81	127,755[2]	1,223,907
Comprehensive universities	7	8,732	136,731
Teacher-training colleges	8	n.a.[3]	22,518
Theological seminaries	17	n.a.	2,828
Technical colleges	126	5,281[4]	389,501
Art academies..................	45	1,136	29,718
Colleges of administration	30	n.a.	53,252
Total schools of higher education	314	142,904	1,858,455
TOTAL	44,422	816,147	12,872,841

[1] Figures for numbers of schools and students are for the 1993–94 academic year; figures for number of teachers are for the 1991–92 academic year in the territory of the former West Germany.
[2] Includes teachers at teacher-training colleges and theological seminaries.
[3] n.a.—not available.
[4] Includes teachers at colleges of administration.

Source: Based on information from Federal Republic of Germany, Statistisches Bundesamt, *Statistisches Jahrbuch 1994 für die Bundesrepublik Deutschland*, Stuttgart, 1994, 402–5, 411, 421.

Table 12. Real Changes in Gross Domestic Product (GDP) and in Exports and Imports of Goods and Services, 1970–93[1]
(in percentage change from previous year)

Year	GDP	Exports	Imports
1970–77 (average)	2.7	5.7	5.0
1978	3.0	2.9	5.5
1979	4.2	4.3	9.2
1980	1.0	5.2	3.6
1981	0.1	7.2	–3.1
1982	–0.9	3.9	–1.1
1983	1.8	–0.8	1.4
1984	2.8	8.2	5.2
1985	2.0	7.6	4.5
1986	2.3	–0.6	2.7
1987	1.5	0.4	4.2
1988	3.7	5.5	5.1
1989	3.6	10.2	8.3
1990	5.7	11.0	10.3
1991	5.0	10.9	11.6
1992	2.2	0.7	3.8
1993	–1.1	–6.4	–6.3

[1] Figures prior to 1991 are for West Germany only.

Source: Based on information from Organisation for Economic Co-operation and Development, *Main Economic Indicators* [Paris], March 1995, A4, A12–A13.

Table 13. *Distribution of Gross Domestic Product by Sector, Selected Years, 1985–93[1]*
(in billions of deutsche marks at current prices) [2]

Sector	1985	1990	1991	1992	1993
Agriculture, forestry, and fishing...............	31.9	37.2	36.3	36.6	33.0
Mining, quarrying, and energy...............	66.5	70.2			
Manufacturing	578.9	741.0	1,075.1	1,126.9	1,096.6
Construction	94.8	127.5			
Trade, transportation, and communications.......	261.5	346.6	406.2	416.8	419.8
Government	207.3	253.2	382.0	418.2	439.7
Nonprofit organizations and work done at home...............	42.7	58.3	916.3	1,029.2	1,118.5
Other services	539.7	791.2			
TOTAL[3]...............	1,823.2	2,425.2	2,815.9	3,027.6	3,107.5

[1] Figures prior to 1991 are for West Germany only.
[2] For value of the deutsche mark—see Glossary.
[3] Figures may not add to totals because of rounding.

Source: Based on information from Organisation for Economic Co-operation and Development, *OECD Economic Surveys, 1993–1994: Germany,* Paris, 1994, 150.

Table 14. Agricultural Production, 1993
(in percentages of total production) [1]

Product	Percentage
Animal products	
Milk	25.6
Hogs	15.2
Cattle	13.8
Eggs	3.1
Other[2]	_3.4_
Total animal products	61.1
Plant products	
Grains	11.2
Fruit	6.3
Sugar beets	4.2
Flowers and decorative plants	4.2
Wine	3.2
Potatoes	1.8
Oilseed	1.1
Other[3]	_6.7_
Total plant products	38.7
Services	0.2
TOTAL	100.0

[1] Agricultural production amounted to DM64.4 billion (for value of the deutsche mark—see Glossary) in 1993.
[2] Includes poultry, horses, sheep, and wool.
[3] Includes other vegetables, hops, tobacco, and seeds.

Source: Based on information from Mario von Baratta, ed., *Der Fischer Weltalmanach, 1995*, Frankfurt am Main, 1994, 921.

Table 15. Production of Selected Crops, 1991, 1992, and 1993
(in thousands of tons)

Crop	1991	1992	1993
Apples	365	1,378	931
Barley............................	14,494	12,197	11,006
Beans, broad (dry)	87	56	83
Beans, green	48	59	47
Cabbage..........................	679	714	746
Carrots...........................	225	232	293
Cauliflower	166	150	151
Corn.............................	1,937	2,139	2,657
Cucumbers and gherkins	124	142	118
Currants..........................	126	170	170
Grains, mixed	1,035	1,145	1,405
Grapes	1,373	1,806	1,440
Oats	1,867	1,314	1,731
Onions (dry)	156	201	217
Pears.............................	13	55	43
Plums............................	13	63	31
Potatoes..........................	10,201	10,897	12,260
Rapeseed	2,972	2,617	2,848
Rye..............................	3,324	2,423	2,984
Strawberries.......................	54	55	59
Sugar beets	25,926	27,150	28,606
Sunflower seed	126	161	210

Source: Based on information from *The Europa World Year Book, 1995*, 1, London, 1995, 1294.

Table 16. Germany's Thirty Largest Industrial Firms, 1993

Firm	Sales (in billions of deutsche marks)[1]	Employees (in thousands)
Daimler-Benz..........................	97.7	366.7
Siemens	81.6	391.0
Volkswagen...........................	76.6	253.0
VEBA	66.3	128.3
RWE	55.8	118.0
Hoechst	46.0	172.5
BASF................................	43.1	112.0
Bayer................................	41.0	151.9
Thyssen..............................	33.5	141.0
Bosch	32.5	156.6
BMW................................	29.0	71.0
Mannesmann.........................	28.0	127.7
Metallgesellschaft	26.1	42.6
VIAG................................	23.7	80.7
Ruhrkohle	23.4	111.2
Preussag.............................	23.3	73.3
Adam Opel...........................	23.0	50.8
Deutsche Shell........................	21.4	3.2
Ford	21.2	43.8
Hoesch-Krupp	20.5	78.4
ESSO	19.4	2.4
MAN................................	19.0	57.8
Bertelsmann..........................	17.2	50.5
Degussa	14.9	32.1
Deutsche BP..........................	14.7	2.8
Ruhrgas	14.3	11.6
Henkel	14.1	40.5
IBM Deutschland......................	12.6	25.0
Ph. Holzmann	12.5	43.8
Agiv.................................	10.0	42.7

[1] For value of the deutsche mark—see Glossary.

Source: Based on information from Mario von Baratta, ed., *Der Fischer Weltalmanach, 1995*, Frankfurt am Main, 1994, 997–98.

Table 17. Sources of Electricity, 1993
(in percentages of total production)

Source	Former West Germany[1]	Former East Germany[2]
Nuclear power......................	33.9	—[3]
Anthracite	31.9	—
Lignite.............................	17.9	91.5
Natural gas.........................	6.6	3.3
Hydroelectric power.................	4.4	2.3
Petroleum	1.9	1.5
Other..............................	3.4	1.4
TOTAL	100.0	100.0

[1] Electricity production amounted to 453.2 billion kilowatt-hours in 1993.
[2] Electricity production amounted to 72.9 billion kilowatt-hours in 1993.
[3] — means no production from this source.

Source: Based on information from Mario von Baratta, ed., *Der Fischer Weltalmanach,*
      1995, Frankfurt am Main, 1994, 1005-6.

Table 18. Sources of Imported Crude Petroleum by Country, 1993
(in percentages of total imports)[1]

Country	Percentage
Norway...	18.4
CIS[2]	17.4
Britain	12.4
Libya	11.6
Saudi Arabia	8.2
Algeria...	7.8
Nigeria...	7.7
Venezuela...	5.4
Syria...	5.4
Iran	2.5
Kuwait	1.0
Other[3]	2.2
TOTAL	100.0

[1] Crude petroleum imports amounted to 99.5 million tons in 1993.
[2] Commonwealth of Independent States.
[3] Includes Angola, Yemen, Tunisia, and others.

Source: Based on information from Mario von Baratta, ed., *Der Fischer Weltalmanach,*
      1995, Frankfurt am Main, 1994, 972.

Table 19.   Major Trading Partners, 1991, 1992, and 1993
(in percentages of total value)

Country	1991	1992	1993
Exports			
France	13.1	13.0	11.7
Italy	9.2	9.3	7.2
Netherlands	8.4	8.3	7.4
Britain	7.6	7.7	7.7
Belgium and Luxembourg.	7.3	7.4	6.6
United States........................	6.3	6.4	7.7
Austria..............................	5.9	5.9	6.2
Switzerland	5.7	5.3	5.6
Spain	4.0	4.1	3.2
Former Soviet Union	2.7	2.1	2.6
Japan	2.5	2.2	2.6
Sweden	2.3	2.2	2.1
Other................................	25.1	26.2	29.4
Total exports[1]	100.0	100.0	100.0
Imports			
France	12.2	12.0	11.2
Netherlands	9.7	9.6	8.3
Italy	9.3	9.2	8.1
Belgium and Luxembourg.	7.1	7.0	5.7
Britain	6.6	6.8	6.0
United States........................	6.6	6.6	7.4
Japan	6.2	6.0	6.3
Austria..............................	4.2	4.4	4.8
Switzerland	3.9	4.0	4.4
Spain	2.6	2.7	2.6
Former Soviet Union	2.2	2.0	2.4
China...............................	1.8	1.8	2.6
Other................................	27.5	27.9	30.2
Total imports[1]	100.0	100.0	100.0

[1] Figures may not add to totals because of rounding.

Source: Based on information from Federal Republic of Germany, Statistisches Bundesamt, *Statistisches Jahrbuch 1994 für die Bundesrepublik Deutschland*, Stuttgart, 1994,
322.

Table 20. Balance of Payments, Selected Years, 1986–93[1]
(in billions of deutsche marks)[2]

	1986	1989	1991	1993
Exports, f.o.b.[3]	526.4	641.0	665.8	603.5
Imports, c.i.f.[4]	−413.7	−506.5	−643.9	−543.7
Supplementary trade items	−1.5	−1.3	2.6	−2.3
Trade balance.	111.2	133.3	24.5	57.5
Services (net)	1.7	8.5	1.6	−44.0
Transfer payments (net).	−27.1	−33.7	−59.2	−49.5
Current account balance	85.8	108.1	−33.1	−35.8
Long-term capital	33.4	−22.2	−25.4	198.2
Short-term capital.	−116.0	−112.8	43.4	−164.7
Capital account balance	−82.6	−135.1	18.0	34.3
Balance of payments.	6.0	189.0	−0.3	35.8
Change in reserves	2.8	−21.6	0.8	−34.2

[1] Figures prior to 1991 are for West Germany only.
[2] For value of the deutsche mark—see Glossary.
[3] f.o.b.—free on board.
[4] c.i.f.—cost, insurance, and freight.

Source: Based on information from Organisation for Economic Co-operation and
Development, *OECD Economic Surveys, 1993–1994: Germany,* Paris, 1994, 155;
and Economist Intelligence Unit, *Country Profile, 1993–1994: Germany,* London,
1994, 46.

Table 21. Foreign Trade by Principal Commodity Group, Selected Years, 1985–94[1]
(in billions of deutsche marks) [2]

Commodity Group	1985	1990	1992	1994
Exports, f.o.b.[3]				
Food and live animals..............	21.5	25.1	29.7	28.7
Beverages and tobacco.............	3.5	3.7	4.7	5.2
Crude materials (inedible), except fuels	10.7	11.7	12.5	12.4
Mineral fuels, lubricants, and related materials	15.3	8.2	8.2	7.6
Animal and vegetable oils and fats	2.8	1.5	1.5	1.9
Chemicals	71.1	81.7	84.7	92.2
Manufactured goods, classified chiefly by material	100.3	113.5	111.0	110.0
Machinery and transport equipment........................	246.7	317.2	333.1	339.3
Miscellaneous manufactured articles	53.6	71.7	75.5	71.8
Commodities and transactions not classified according to kind	11.5	8.4	10.2	21.5
Total exports[4]	537.1	642.8	671.1	690.5
Imports, c.i.f.[5]				
Food and live animals..............	44.4	46.4	54.7	50.2
Beverages and tobacco.............	4.6	5.4	6.7	6.3
Crude materials (inedible), except fuels	31.9	29.5	28.5	26.8
Mineral fuels, lubricants, and related materials	92.2	45.5	47.5	42.9
Animal and vegetable oils and fats	2.8	1.5	1.7	1.8
Chemicals	41.3	49.7	54.6	53.7
Manufactured goods, classified chiefly by material	74.9	98.3	106.2	97.9
Machinery and transport equipment........................	106.0	178.1	220.5	205.8
Miscellaneous manufactured articles	52.9	83.1	103.3	97.3
Commodities and transactions not classified according to kind	13.0	13.1	13.8	28.4
Total imports[4]	463.8	550.7	637.6	611.1

[1] Prior to 1991, figures are for West Germany only.
[2] For value of the deutsche mark—see Glossary.
[3] f.o.b.—free on board.
[4] Figures may not add to totals because of rounding.
[5] c.i.f.—cost, insurance, and freight.

Source: Based on information from Organisation for Economic Co-operation and Development, *OECD Economic Surveys, 1994–1995: Germany,* Paris, 1995, 173.

Table 22. Land Legislative Elections, 1992–95

Land	Election Date	CDU[1]	SPD[2]	FDP[3]	Greens[4]	PDS[5]	Other	Total Number of Deputies
Baden-Württemberg	April 1992	64	46	8	13	—[6]	15	146
Bavaria[7]	September 1994	120	70	—	14	—	—	204
Berlin	December 1990	101	76	18	19	22	5	241
Brandenburg	November 1994	18	52	—	—	18	—	88
Bremen	May 1995	37	37	—	14	—	12	100
Hamburg	September 1993	36	58	—	19	—	8	121
Hesse	February 1995	45	44	8	13	—	—	110
Lower Saxony	March 1994	67	81	—	13	—	—	161
Mecklenburg-Western Pomerania	October 1994	30	23	—	—	18	—	71
North Rhine-Westphalia	May 1995	89	108	—	24	—	—	221
Rhineland-Palatinate	April 1991	40	47	7	7	—	—	101
Saarland	October 1994	21	27	—	3	—	—	51
Saxony	September 1994	77	22	—	—	21	—	120

Table 22. *(Continued)* Land Legislative Elections, 1992–95

Land	Election Date	CDU[1]	SPD[2]	FDP[3]	Greens[4]	PDS[5]	Other	Total Number of Deputies
Saxony-Anhalt............	June 1994	37	36	—	5	21	—	99
Schleswig-Holstein	April 1992	32	45	5	—	—	7	89
Thuringia	October 1994	42	29	—	—	17	—	88

1 Christlich Demokratische Union (Christian Democratic Union).
2 Sozialdemokratische Partei Deutschlands (Social Democratic Party of Germany).
3 Freie Demokratische Partei (Free Democratic Party).
4 Bündnis 90/Die Grünen (Alliance 90/The Greens).
5 Partei des Demokratischen Sozialismus (Party of Democratic Socialism).
6 — means no seats won.
7 In Bavaria the CDU is represented by the Christlich-Soziale Union (Christian Social Union—CSU).

Source: Based on information from Mario von Baratta, ed. *Der Fischer Weltalmanach, 1995*, Frankfurt am Main, 1994, 25–26, 157–82; *Keesing's Record of World Events* [Cambridge], 41, No. 2, 1995, 40424; and *Keesing's Record of World Events* [Cambridge], 41, No. 4, 1995, 40561.

Table 23. Major Army Equipment, 1994

Type and Description	Country of Origin	Number in Inventory
Main battle tanks		
Leopard–1/2	Germany	2,855
Armored vehicles		
Reconnaissance		
Various models	-do-	514
Infantry fighting vehicles		
Marder A3	-do-	2,443
Armored personnel carriers		
M–113	United States	2,900
Various models	Germany	900
Artillery		
105mm to 155mm, towed	Various	378
155mm, self-propelled.	-do-	577
Multiple rocket launchers		
110mm to 227mm	-do-	228
Antitank guided missiles		
Milan.	France/Germany	1,964
TOW	United States	233
HOT	France/Germany	316
Surface-to-air missile launchers		
Roland, self-propelled	-do-	142
Attack helicopters		
PAH–1 with HOT missiles	-do-	205

Source: Based on information from *The Military Balance, 1994–1995*, London, 1994, 50.

Table 24. Major Naval Equipment, 1994[1]

Type and Description	Number in Service	Year Commissioned
Submarines		
Type 205	2	1964–66
Type 206/206A	18	1973–75
Destroyers		
Adams class	3	1969–70
Hamburg class, Type 101A	1	1964–65
Frigates		
Bremen class	8	1982–90
Brandenburg class	1	1994
Fast-attack craft (missile)		
Gepard class	10	1982–84
Albatross class	10	1976–77
Tiger class	18	1972–75
Minesweepers and minehunters		
Various types	45	Various dates
Naval aircraft		
Tornado fighter/ground attack	64	-do-
Atlantic marine reconnaissance and electronic intelligence	18	-do-
Do–28 search and air rescue	2	-do
Helicopters		
Sea Lynx antisubmarine	17	-do-
Sea King search and air rescue	22	-do-
Mi–8 transport	29	-do

[1] Main fleet units were constructed in West Germany except Adams-class destroyers, which were built in the United States and reconditioned in West Germany.

Source: Based on information from *The Naval Institute Guide to Combat Fleets of the World, 1995*, Annapolis, 1995, 212–23; and *The Military Balance, 1994–1995*, London, 1994, 50–51.

Table 25. Major Air Force Equipment, 1994

Type and Description	Country of Origin	Number in Inventory
Air defense and fighter-ground attack aircraft		
F–4F	United States	150
Tornado	Germany (consortium)	193
MiG–29	Soviet Union	20
Alpha Jet.........................	France/Germany	34
Reconnaissance and electronic intelligence		
RF–4E	United States	7
Tornado	Germany (consortium)	35
Transport		
Transall C–160	Germany/France	85
Helicopters		
UH–1D	-do-	108
Air defense missiles		
Hawk launchers	United States	216
Roland launchers..................	France/Germany	95
Patriot launchers	United States/Germany	288

Source: Based on information from *The Military Balance, 1994–1995*, London, 1994, 51–52.

Bibliography

Chapter 1

Abulafia, David. *Frederick II: A Medieval Emperor.* London: Penguin Press, 1988.

Bainton, Roland H. *The Reformation of the Sixteenth Century.* Boston: Beacon Press, 1952.

Balfour, Michael. *Germany: The Tides of Power.* London: Routledge, 1992.

Balfour, Michael. *The Kaiser and His Times.* New York: W.W. Norton, 1972.

Barraclough, Geoffrey. *The Origins of Modern Germany.* Oxford: Blackwell, 1949.

Barraclough, Geoffrey, ed. *The Times Atlas of World History.* London: Times Books, 1978.

Benecke, Gerhard. *Society and Politics in Germany, 1500–1750.* London: Routledge and Kegan Paul, 1974.

Berghahn, Volker Rolf. *Imperial Germany, 1871–1914: Economy, Society, Culture, and Politics.* Providence, Rhode Island: Berghahn Books, 1994.

Berghahn, Volker Rolf. *Modern Germany: Society, Economy, and Politics in the Twentieth Century.* 2d ed. New York: Cambridge University Press, 1987.

Bracher, Karl Dietrich. *The German Dictatorship: The Origins, Structure, and Effects of National Socialism.* New York: Praeger, 1970.

Browning, Christopher R. *Ordinary Men: Reserve Police Battalion 101 and the Final Solution in Poland.* New York: Harper Collins, 1992.

Browning, Reed. *The War of the Austrian Succession.* New York: St. Martin's Press, 1993.

Bullock, Alan. *Hitler: A Study in Tyranny.* New York: Harper and Row, 1962.

Bullock, Alan. *Hitler and Stalin: Parallel Lives.* New York: Knopf, 1992.

Cantor, Norman F. *The Civilization of the Middle Ages.* New York: Harper Collins, 1993.

Carr, William. *A History of Germany, 1815–1990.* 4th ed. New York: Routledge, Chapman, and Hall, 1991.

Carsten, F.L. *The Origins of Prussia.* London: Oxford University Press, 1958.

Craig, Gordon A. *Germany, 1866–1945.* New York: Oxford University Press, 1978.

Craig, Gordon A. *The Politics of the Prussian Army, 1640–1945.* New York: Oxford University Press, 1956.

Detwiler, Donald S. *Germany: A Short History.* 2d ed. Carbondale: Southern Illinois University Press, 1989.

Du Boulay, F.R.H. *Germany in the Later Middle Ages.* New York: St. Martin's Press, 1983.

Duffy, Christopher. *The Military Life of Frederick the Great.* New York: Atheneum, 1986.

Eley, Geoff. *From Unification to Nazism: Reinterpreting the German Past.* Boston: Allen and Unwin, 1986.

Evans, Robert John Weston. *The Making of the Habsburg Monarchy, 1550–1700: An Interpretation.* New York: Oxford University Press, 1984.

Fischer, Fritz. *Germany's Aims in the First World War.* London: Chatto and Windus, 1967.

Fischer, Klaus P. *Nazi Germany: A New History.* New York: Continuum, 1995.

Fuhrmann, Horst. *Germany in the High Middle Ages, c. 1050–1200.* Cambridge: Cambridge University Press, 1986.

Fulbrook, Mary. *A Concise History of Germany.* Cambridge: Cambridge University Press, 1990.

Fulbrook, Mary. *The Divided Nation: A History of Germany, 1918–1990.* Oxford: Oxford University Press, 1992.

Gagliardo, John G. *Germany under the Old Regime, 1600–1790.* London: Longman, 1991.

Gay, Peter. *Weimar Culture: The Outsider as Insider.* New York: Harper and Row, 1968.

Geary, Patrick J. *Before France and Germany: The Creation and Transformation of the Merovingian World.* New York: Oxford University Press, 1988.

Haffner, Sebastian. *The Meaning of Hitler.* Cambridge: Harvard University Press, 1983.

Haffner, Sebastian. *The Rise and Fall of Prussia.* London: Weidenfeld and Nicolson, 1980.

Hamerow, Theodore S. *Restoration, Revolution, Reaction: Economics and Politics in Germany, 1815–1871.* Princeton: Princeton University Press, 1958.

Hilberg, Raul. *The Destruction of the European Jews.* 3 vols. New York: Holmes and Meier, 1985.

Hoffmann, Peter. *German Resistance to Hitler.* Cambridge: Harvard University Press, 1988.

Hoffmeister, Gerhart, and Frederic C. Tubach. *Germany: 2000 Years.* New York: Ungar, 1986.

Holborn, Hajo. *A History of Modern Germany.* 3 vols. New York: Knopf, 1959–69.

Hughes, Michael. *Early Modern Germany, 1477–1806.* Philadelphia: University of Pennsylvania Press, 1992.

Ingrao, Charles. *The Habsburg Monarchy, 1618–1815.* Cambridge: Cambridge University Press, 1994.

Jelavich, Barbara. *Modern Austria: Empire and Republic, 1815–1986.* New York: Cambridge University Press, 1987.

Joll, James. *The Origins of the First World War.* New York: Longman, 1984.

Kann, Robert A. *A History of the Habsburg Empire, 1526–1918.* Berkeley: University of California Press, 1974.

Kissinger, Henry A. *Diplomacy.* New York: Simon and Schuster, 1994.

Krieger, Leonard. *The German Idea of Freedom: History of a Political Tradition.* Boston: Beacon Press, 1957.

Lafore, Laurence. *The Long Fuse: An Interpretation of the Origins of World War I.* 2d ed. Philadelphia: J.B. Lippincott, 1971.

Maier, Charles S. *The Unmasterable Past: History, Holocaust, and German National Identity.* Cambridge: Harvard University Press, 1988.

Mommsen, Wolfgang J. *Imperial Germany, 1867–1918: Politics, Culture, and Society in an Authoritarian State.* London: Arnold, 1995.

Moses, John A. *The Politics of Illusion: The Fischer Controversy in German Historiography.* New York: Barnes and Noble, 1975.

Orlow, Dietrich. *A History of Modern Germany: 1871 to Present.* 3d ed. Englewood Cliffs, New Jersey: Prentice Hall, 1995.

Palmer, R.R. *A History of the Modern World.* 8th ed. New York: McGraw-Hill, 1995.

Parker, Geoffrey, ed. *The Thirty Years' War.* New York: Routledge, 1988.

Parkinson, Roger. *The Encyclopedia of Modern War.* New York: Stein and Day, 1977.

Peukert, Detlev J.K. *The Weimar Republic: The Crisis of Classical Modernity.* New York: Hill and Wang, 1993.

Pflanze, Otto. *Bismarck and the Development of Germany.* 3 vols. Princeton: Princeton University Press, 1990.

Ramm, Agatha. *Germany, 1789–1919: A Political History.* London: Methuen, 1981.

Rosenberg, Hans. *Bureaucracy, Aristocracy, and Autocracy: The Prussian Experience, 1660–1815.* Cambridge: Harvard University Press, 1958.

Sheehan, James J. *German History, 1770–1866.* New York: Oxford University Press, 1989.

Sheehan, James J. *German Liberalism in the Nineteenth Century.* Atlantic Highlands, New Jersey: Humanities Press International, 1995.

Stern, Carola, and Heinrich A. Winkler, eds. *Wendepunkte deutscher Geschichte, 1848–1990.* Frankfurt am Main: Fischer Taschenbuch Verlag, 1994.

Stern, Fritz. *Dreams and Delusions: National Socialism and the Drama of the German Past.* New York: Vintage, 1989.

Stern, Fritz. *Gold and Iron: Bismarck, Bleichröder, and the Building of the German Empire.* New York: Knopf, 1977.

Stern, Fritz. *The Politics of Cultural Despair: A Study in the Rise of the German Ideology.* Berkeley: University of California Press, 1961.

Taylor, A.J.P. *The Struggle for Mastery in Europe, 1848–1918.* New York: Oxford University Press, 1974.

Trevor-Roper, Hugh R. *The Last Days of Hitler.* Chicago: University of Chicago Press, 1992.

Watt, Donald Cameron. *How War Came: The Immediate Origins of the Second World War, 1938–1939.* New York: Pantheon Books, 1989.

Wedgwood, C.V. *The Thirty Years' War.* New York: Routledge, 1991.

Weinberg, Gerhard L. *Germany, Hitler, and World War II: Essays in Modern German and World History.* Cambridge: Cambridge University Press, 1995.

Weinberg, Gerhard L. *A World at Arms: A Global History of World War II.* Cambridge: Cambridge University Press, 1994.

Chapter 2

Adenauer, Konrad. *Erinnerungen.* 4 vols. 3d ed. Stuttgart: Deutsche Verlagsanstalt, 1983.

Adenauer, Konrad. *Memoirs, 1945–1953.* London: Weidenfeld and Nicholson, 1966.

Albrecht, Ulrich. *Die Abwicklung der DDR. Die "2 plus 4"-Verhandlungen. Ein Insiderbericht.* Opladen, Germany: Westdeutscher Verlag, 1992.

Bark, Dennis L., and David R. Gress. *A History of West Germany.* 2d ed. Cambridge, Massachusetts: Blackwell, 1993.

Barraclough, Geoffrey. *The Origins of Modern Germany.* Oxford: Blackwell, 1949.

Barraclough, Geoffrey, ed. *The Times Atlas of World History.* London: Times Books, 1978.

Berghahn, Volker Rolf. *Modern Germany: Society, Economy, and Politics in the Twentieth Century.* 2d ed. Cambridge: Cambridge University Press, 1987.

Bleek, Wilhelm. "From Cold War to Ostpolitik: Two Germanies in Search of Separate Identities," *World Politics,* 29, No. 1, October 1976, 114–29.

Bowers, Stephen R. "East German National Consciousness: Domestic and Foreign Policy Considerations," *East European Quarterly,* 12, No. 2, June 1979, 145–83.

Bracher, Karl Dietrich. *The German Dilemma: Relationship of State and Democracy.* New York: Praeger, 1975.

Bracher, Karl Dietrich, ed. *Geschichte der Bundesrepublik Deutschland.* 5 vols. Stuttgart: Deutsche Verlagsanstalt, 1983–84.

Brandt, Willy. *People and Politics: The Years 1960–1975.* Boston: Little, Brown, 1978.

Childs, David. *The GDR: Moscow's German Ally.* 2d ed. London: Unwin Hyman, 1988.

Childs, David. *Germany in the Twentieth Century.* New York: Harper Collins, 1991.

Croan, Melvin. "New Country, Old Nationality," *Foreign Policy,* No. 37, Winter 1979–80, 142–60.

Dalton, Russell J. *Politics in Germany.* 2d ed. New York: Harper Collins, 1993.

Elliott, James R., and Anthony E. Scaperlanda. "East Germany's Liberman-Type Reforms in Perspective," *Quarterly Review of Economics and Business,* 6, No. 3, 1966, 39–52.

Ellwein, Thomas. *Das Regerungssystem der Bundesrepublik Deutschland.* 5th ed. Opladen, Germany: Westdeutscher Verlag, 1983.

Epstein, Klaus. "The German Problem, 1945–1950," *World Politics,* 20, No. 2, January 1968, 279–300.

Federal Republic of Germany. Presse- und Informationsamt der Bundesregierung. *Bundeskanzler Helmut Kohl. Reden, 1982–1984.* Bonn: 1984.

Fulbrook, Mary. *Anatomy of a Dictatorship: Inside the GDR, 1949–1989.* New York: Oxford University Press, 1995.

Fulbrook, Mary. *The Divided Nation: A History of Germany, 1918–1990.* New York: Oxford University Press, 1992.

Fulbrook, Mary. *The Two Germanies, 1945–1990: Problems of Interpretation.* Atlantic Highlands, New Jersey: Humanities Press International, 1992.

Garton Ash, Timothy. *In Europe's Name: Germany and the Divided Continent.* New York: Random House, 1994.

Genscher, Hans-Dietrich. *Deutsche Aussenpolitik.* Stuttgart: Bonn Aktuell, 1985.

Grebing, Helga, Peter Pozorski, and Rainer Schulze. *Die Nachkriegsentwicklung in Westdeutschland, 1945–1949.* Stuttgart: Metzler, 1980.

Grosser, Alfred. *Das Deutschland im Westen.* Munich: Carl Hanser Verlag, 1985.

Grosser, Alfred. *Germany in Our Time: A Political History of the Postwar Years.* New York: Praeger, 1971.

Hahn, Walter F. *Between Westpolitik and Ostpolitik: Changing West German Security Views.* Foreign Policy Papers of the Foreign Policy Research Institute. Beverley Hills: Sage, 1975.

Hanhardt, Arthur Monroe. *The German Democratic Republic.* Baltimore: Johns Hopkins Press, 1968.

Hartwich, Hans-Hermann, ed. *Politik im 20. Jahrhundert.* Braunschweig, West Germany: Westermann, 1984.

Hillgruber, Andreas. *Deutsche Geschichte, 1945–1972.* Frankfurt am Main: Ullstein, 1974.

Holborn, Hajo. *A History of Modern Germany.* 3 vols. New York: Knopf, 1959–69.

Hubatsch, Walther, ed., with Wolfgang Heidelmeyer et al. *The German Question.* Trans., Salvator Attanasio. New York. Herder Book Center, 1967.

Jarausch, Konrad H. *The Rush to German Unity.* New York: Oxford University Press, 1994.

Katzenstein, Peter J. "Problem or Model? West Germany in the 1980s," *World Politics,* 32, No. 4, July 1980, 577–98.

Keesing's Record of World Events [Cambridge], 40, No. 10, 1994, 40237.

Keesing's Record of World Events [Cambridge], 40, No. 11, 1994, 40292.

Knopp, Guido, and Ekhard Kuhn. *Die deutsche Einheit: Traum und Wirklichkeit.* Bonn: Straube, 1990.

Kregel, Bernd. *Aussenpolitik und Systemstabilisierung in der DDR.* Opladen, West Germany: Leske und Budrich, 1979.

Krieger, Wolfgang. "Worrying about West German Democracy," *Political Quarterly* [London], 50, No. 2, April–June 1979, 192–204.

Livingston, Robert Gerald. "Germany Steps Up," *Foreign Policy,* 22, Spring 1976, 114–28, 177–79.

Löw, Konrad, ed. *Ursachen und Verlauf der deutschen Revolution.* Berlin: Duncker und Humblot, 1991.

Ludz, Peter Christian. "The German Democratic Republic from the Sixties to the Seventies: A Socio-Political Analysis," *Occasional Papers in International Affairs,* No. 26, November 1970, 1–101.

Martin, Bernd, ed. *Deutschland in Europa. Ein historischer Rückblick.* Munich: Deutscher Taschenbuch Verlag, 1992.

Müller, Helmut M. *Schlaglichter der deutschen Geschichte.* Mannheim: Bibliographisches Institut, 1986

Nolte, Ernst. *Deutschland und der Kalte Krieg.* Munich: Piper, 1974.

Pond, Elizabeth. *Beyond the Wall: Germany's Road to Unification.* Washington: Brookings Institution, 1993.

Prittie, Terence. *The Velvet Chancellors: A History of Post-War Germany.* London: Frederick Muller, 1979.

Puhle, Hans-Jürgen. "Conservatism in Modern German History," *Journal of Contemporary History* [London], 13, 1978, 689–720.

Pulzer, Peter. *German Politics, 1945–1995.* New York: Oxford University Press, 1995.

Pulzer, Peter. "Responsible Party Government and Stable Coalition: The Case of the German Federal Republic," *Political Studies* [London], 26, No. 2, June 1978, 181–208.

Rupp, Hans Karl. *Politische Geschichte der Bundesrepublik Deutschland: Entstehung und Entwicklung.* Stuttgart: Kohlhammer, 1978.

Schmidt, Manfred G. "The Politics of Domestic Reform in the Federal Republic of Germany," *Politics and Society*, 8, No. 2, 1978, 165–200.

Smith, Gordon. "West Germany and the Politics of Centrality," *Government and Opposition* [London], 11, No. 4, Autumn 1976, 387–407.

Sodaro, Michael J. "Ulbricht's Grand Design: Economics, Ideology, and the GDR's Response to Detente, 1967–1971," *World Affairs*, 142, No. 3, Winter 1980, 147–68.

Sontheimer, Kurt, and Wilhelm Bleek. *Die DDR.* Hamburg: Hoffmann und Campe, 1979.

Steele, Jonathan. *Inside East Germany: The State That Came in from the Cold.* New York: Urizen Books, 1977.

Stern, Carola. *Ulbricht: A Political Biography.* New York: Praeger, 1965.

Szabo, Stephen F. *The Diplomacy of German Unification.* New York: St. Martin's Press, 1992.

Tilford, Roger, ed. *The Ostpolitik and Political Change in Germany.* Farmborough, Hampshire, United Kingdom: Saxon House, 1975.

Treverton, George F. *America, Germany, and the Future of Europe.* Princeton: Princeton University Press, 1992.

Treverton, George F. "The New Europe," *Foreign Affairs*, 70, No. 1, 1991–92, 94–112.

Turner, Henry Ashby, Jr. *Germany from Partition to Reunification.* New Haven: Yale University Press, 1992.

Voght, Roy. "The Course of Economic Reforms in East Germany: Implications for Social Change," *Canadian Slavonic Papers* [Toronto], 18, No. 2, June 1976, 168–77.

Vogt, Martin, ed. *Deutsche Geschichte: Von den Anfängen bis zur Wiedervereinigung.* 2d ed. Stuttgart: J.B. Metzlersche Verlagsbuchhandlung, 1991.

Wagenlehner, Günther, ed. *Die deutsche Frage und die internationale Sicherheit.* Koblenz, West Germany: Bernard and Graefe Verlag, 1988.

Weber, Hermann. *DDR: Grundriss der Geschichte.* Hanover: Fackelträger Verlag, 1991.

Weber, Hermann. *Geschichte der DDR.* Munich: Deutscher Taschenbuch Verlag, 1985.

Wetzlaugk, Udo. *Die Alliierten in Berlin.* West Berlin: Berlin Verlag Arno Spitz, 1988.

Zelikow, Philip, and Condoleezza Rice. *Germany Unified and Europe Transformed: A Study in Statecraft.* Cambridge: Harvard University Press, 1995.

Zimmer, Dieter. *Auferstanden aus Ruinen.* Stuttgart: Deutsche Verlags-Anstalt, 1989.

Zimmerman, Hartmut. "The GDR in the 1970s," *Problems of Communism,* 27, No. 2, March–April 1978, 1–40.

Chapter 3

Abdullah, M. Salim. "Muslims in Germany." Pages 67–77 in Syed Z. Abedin and Ziauddin Sardar, eds., *Muslim Minorities in the West.* London: Grey Seal, 1995.

Ardagh, John. *Germany and the Germans.* Rev. ed. New York: Penguin Books USA, 1991.

Bade, Klaus J. "Immigration and Social Peace in United Germany," *Daedalus,* 123, No. 1, Winter 1994, 85–106.

Baratta, Mario von, ed. *Der Fischer Weltalmanach, 1995.* Frankfurt am Main: Fischer Taschenbuch Verlag, 1994.

Belwe, Katharina. "Sozialstruktur und gesellschaftlicher Wandel in der DDR." Pages 125–43 in Harmut Zimmermann and Werner Weidenfeld, eds., *Deutschland Handbuch.* Munich: Carl Hanser Verlag, 1989.

Berking, Helmuth, and Sighard Neckel. "'The Disturbed Community': Power and Conflict in an East German Town," *German Politics and Society,* No. 33, Fall 1994, 105–16.

Brubaker, Rogers. *Citizenship and Nationhood in France and Germany.* Cambridge: Harvard University Press, 1992.

Brubaker, Rogers. "Frontier Theses: Exit, Voice, and Loyalty in East Germany," *Migration World*, 18, Nos. 3–4, 1990, 12–17.

Chamberlayne, Prue. "Women and the State: Changes in Roles and Rights in France, West Germany, Italy, and Britain, 1970–1990." Pages 170–93 in Jane Lewis, ed., *Women and Social Policies in Europe: Work, Family, and the State.* Aldershot, Hampshire, United Kingdom: Edward Elgar, 1993.

Childs, David. *Germany in the Twentieth Century.* New York: Harper Collins, 1991.

Craig, Gordon A. *The Germans.* New York: Meridian, 1991.

Dahrendorf, Ralf. *Society and Democracy in Germany.* Westport, Connecticut: Greenwood, 1979.

Eberstadt, Nicholas. "Demographic Shocks after Communism: Eastern Germany, 1989–93," *Population and Development Review,* 20, No. 1, March 1994, 137–52.

Edwards, G.E. *GDR: Society and Social Institutions.* London: Macmillan, 1985.

Faist, Thomas. "From School to Work: Public Policy and Underclass Formation among Young Turks in Germany During the 1980s," *International Migration Review,* 27, No. 2, Summer 1993, 306–31.

Faist, Thomas. "How to Define a Foreigner? The Symbolic Politics of Immigration in German Partisan Discourse, 1978–1992." Pages 50–71 in Martin Baldwin-Edwards and Martin A. Schain, eds., *The Politics of Immigration in Western Europe.* Newbury Park, Ilford, United Kingdom: Frank Cass, 1994.

Fassmann, Heinz, and Rainer Münz. "European East-West Migration, 1945–1992," *International Migration Review,* 28, No. 3, Fall 1994, 520–38.

Fassmann, Heinz, and Rainer Münz, eds. *European Migration in the Late Twentieth Century.* Aldershot, Hampshire, United Kingdom: Edward Elgar, 1994.

Federal Republic of Germany. Statistisches Bundesamt. *Bevölkerung und Erwerbstätigkeit: Volkszählung vom 25. Mai 1987. Fachserie 1. Heft 3: Demographische Struktur der Bevölkerung.* Stuttgart: Metzler-Poeschel, May 1990.

Federal Republic of Germany. Statistisches Bundesamt. *Bevölkerung und Erwerbstätigkeit: Volkszählung vom 25. Mai 1987. Fachserie 1. Heft 4: Sozio-Ökonomische Struktur und Unter-*

haltsquellen der Bevölkerung, Struktur der Erwerbstätigkeit. Stuttgart: Metzler-Poeschel, October 1990.

Federal Republic of Germany. Statistisches Bundesamt. *Bevölkerung und Erwerbstätigkeit: Volkszählung vom 25. Mai 1987. Fachserie 1. Heft 5: Struktur der ausländischen Bevölkerung.* Stuttgart: Metzler-Poeschel, November 1990.

Federal Republic of Germany. Statistisches Bundesamt. *Statistisches Jahrbuch 1992 für die Bundesrepublik Deutschland.* Stuttgart: Metzler-Poeschel, 1992.

Federal Republic of Germany. Statistisches Bundesamt. *Statistisches Jahrbuch 1994 für die Bundesrepublik Deutschland.* Stuttgart: Metzler-Poeschel, 1994.

Federal Republic of Germany. Statistisches Bundesamt. *Zahlen Kompass 1993.* Stuttgart: Metzler-Poeschel, 1993.

Ferree, Myra Marx. "Institutionalizing Gender Equality: Feminist Politics and Equality Offices," *German Politics and Society,* Nos. 24–25, Winter 1991–92, 53–66.

Fijalkowski, Jurgen. "Aggressive Nationalism, Immigration Pressure, and Asylum Policy Disputes in Contemporary Germany," *International Migration Review,* 27, No. 4, Winter 1993, 850–69.

Franklin, E. Gene, and Donald Schoonmaker. *Between Power and Protest: The Green Party in Germany.* Boulder, Colorado: Westview Press, 1992.

Frevert, Ute. *Women in German History: From Bourgeois Emancipation to Sexual Liberation.* Oxford: Berg, 1989.

Fulbrook, Mary. "Aspects of Society and Identity in the New Germany," *Daedalus,* 123, No. 1, Winter 1994, 211–34.

Gay, Ruth. *The Jews of Germany: A Historical Portrait.* New Haven: Yale University Press, 1992.

Geissler, Heiner. "Die Gesellschaft von morgen," *Die politische Meinung* [Sankt Augustin, Germany], 37, No. 272, July 1992, 21–27.

Geissler, Rainer. *Die Sozialstruktur Deutschlands: Ein Studienbuch zur sozialstrukturellen Entwicklung im geteilten und vereinten Deutschland.* Opladen, Germany: Westdeutscher Verlag, 1992.

German Democratic Republic. Staatliche Zentralverwaltung für Statistik. *Statistisches Jahrbuch 1988 der Deutschen*

Demokratischen Republik. East Berlin: Staatsverlag der Deutschen Demokratischen Republik, 1988.

German Democratic Republic. Staatliche Zentralverwaltung für Statistik. *Statistisches Jahrbuch 1989 der Deutschen Demokratischen Republik.* East Berlin: Staatsverlag der Deutschen Demokatischen Republik, 1989.

German Democratic Republic. Staatliche Zentralverwaltung für Statistik. *Statistisches Jahrbuch 1990 der Deutschen Demokratischen Republik.* East Berlin: Staatsverlag der Deutschen Demokratischen Republik, 1990.

Gibney, Matthew J. "Crisis of Constraint: The Federal Republic of Germany's Current Refugee Imbroglio," *Government and Opposition* [London], 28, No. 3, Summer 1993, 372–93.

Glaessner, Gert-Joachim. "The Rise and Decline of 'Realistic Socialism' in the GDR." Pages 77–117 in Peter Merkl, *German Unification in the European Context.* University Park: Pennsylvania State University Press, 1993.

Godberg, Louis. "Where Have All the Eastern Germans Gone?" *Guardian Weekly* [London], October 31, 1993, 15.

Grunenberg, Antonia. "Bewusstseinslagen und Leitbilder in der DDR." Pages 221–38 in Harmut Zimmermann and Werner Weidenfeld, eds., *Deutschland Handbuch.* Munich: Carl Hanser Verlag, 1989.

Hailbronner, Kay. "Citizenship and Nationhood in Germany." Pages 67–79 in Rogers Brubaker, ed., *Immigration and the Politics of Citizenship in Europe and North America.* Lanham, Maryland: University Press of America, 1989.

Hamilton, Daniel. "Germany after Unification," *Problems of Communism,* 41, May–June 1992, 1–18.

Heilig, Gerhard, Thomas Büttner, and Wolfgang Lutz. "Germany's Population: Turbulent Past, Uncertain Future," *Population Bulletin,* 45, No. 4, December 1990, 4–45.

Henkys, Reinhard. "Die Evangelische Kirche in der DDR." Pages 193–201 in Harmut Zimmermann and Werner Weidenfeld, eds., *Deutschland Handbuch.* Munich: Carl Hanser Verlag, 1989.

Hettlage, Robert, ed. *Die Bundesrepublik: Eine historische Bilanz.* Munich: Verlag C.H. Beck, 1990.

Höhn, Charlotte, Ulrich Mammey, and Hartmut Wendt. "Bericht 1990 zur demographischen Lage: Trends in beiden

Teilen Deutschlands und Ausländer in der Bundesrepublik Deutschland," *Zeitschrift für Bevölkerungswissenschaft* [Boppard am Rhein, West Germany], 16, No. 2, 1990, 135–205.

Höllen, Martin. "Die Katholische Kirche in der DDR." Pages 174–84 in Harmut Zimmermann and Werner Weidenfeld, eds., *Deutschland Handbuch*. Munich: Carl Hanser Verlag, 1989.

Hübner, Emil, and Horst-Hennek Rohlfs. *Jahrbuch der Bundesrepublik Deutschland, 1992–93*. Munich: Beck/Deutscher Taschenbuch Verlag, 1992.

Joeres, Ruth-Ellen, and Mary Jo Maynes, eds. *German Women in the Eighteenth and Nineteenth Centuries: A Social and Literary History.* Bloomington: Indiana University Press, 1986.

Jones, Alun. *The New Germany: A Human Geography.* New York: John Wiley and Sons, 1994.

Kaase, Max. "Bewusstseinslagen und Leitbilder in der Bundesrepublik Deutschland." Pages 204–20 in Harmut Zimmermann and Werner Weidenfeld, eds., *Deutschland Handbuch*. Munich: Carl Hanser Verlag, 1989.

Kanstroom, Daniel. "Wer Sind Wir Wieder? Laws of Asylum, Immigration, and Citizenship in the Struggle for the Soul of the New Germany," *Yale Journal of International Law*, 18, Winter 1993, 155–211.

Kaplan, Marion A. *The Making of the Jewish Middle Class: Women, Family, and Identity in Imperial Germany.* New York: Oxford University Press, 1991.

Kappler, Arno, and Adriane Grevel, eds. *Facts about Germany.* Frankfurt am Main: Societäts-Verlag, 1994.

Kocka, Jürgen. "Crisis of Unification: How Germany Changes," *Daedalus*, 123, No. 1, Winter 1994, 173–92.

Kolinsky, Eva. "Generation and Gender." Pages 248–66 in Gordon Smith, William E. Paterson, and Peter H. Merkl, eds., *Developments in West German Politics*. Durham: Duke University Press, 1989.

Kolinsky, Eva. "Women in the New Germany." Pages 264–80 in Gordon Smith, William E. Paterson, Peter H. Merkl, and Stephen Padgett, eds., *Developments in German Politics*. Durham: Duke University Press, 1992.

Kolinsky, Eva. *Women in West Germany: Life, Work, and Politics.* Oxford: Berg, 1989.

Koonz, Claudia. *Women in the Fatherland: Women, the Family, and Nazi Politics.* New York: St. Martin's Press, 1987.

Kuechler, Manfred. "The Road to German Unity: Mass Sentiment in East and West Germany," *Public Opinion Quarterly,* 56, No. 1, 1992, 53–76.

Kulawik, Teresa. "Autonomous Mothers? West German Feminism Reconsidered," *German Politics and Society,* Nos. 24–25, Winter 1991–92, 67–86.

Le Gloannec, Anne-Marie. "On German Identity," *Daedalus,* 123, No. 1, Winter 1994, 129–48.

McAdams, A. James. *Germany Divided: From the Wall to Reunification.* Princeton: Princeton University Press, 1993.

Maehl, William Harvey. *Germany in Western Civilization.* Birmingham: University of Alabama Press, 1979.

Maier, Hans. "Die Katholische Kirche in der Bundesrepublik Deutschland." Pages 165–73 in Harmut Zimmermann and Werner Weidenfeld, eds., *Deutschland Handbuch.* Munich: Carl Hanser Verlag, 1989.

Marshall, Barbara. "German Migration Policies." Pages 247–63 in Gordon Smith, William E. Paterson, Peter H. Merkl, and Stephen Padgett, eds., *Developments in German Politics.* Durham: Duke University Press, 1992.

Masser, Ian, Ove Svidén, and Michael Wegener. *The Geography of Europe's Futures.* London: Belhaven Press, 1992.

Mattox, Gale A., and A. Bradley Shingleton, eds. *Germany at the Crossroads: Foreign and Domestic Policy Issues.* Boulder, Colorado: Westview Press, 1992.

Mellor, Roy E.H. *The Two Germanies: A Modern Geography.* London: Harper and Row, 1978.

Merkl. Peter. *German Unification in the European Context.* University Park: Pennsylvania State University Press, 1993.

Nauck, Bernhard. "Changes in Turkish Migrant Families in Germany." Pages 130–47 in Bernard Lewis and Dominique Schnapper, eds., *Muslims in Europe.* New York: Pinter, 1994.

Nelles, Ursula. "Abortion, the Special Case: A Constitutional Perspective," *German Politics and Society,* Nos. 24–25, Winter 1991–92, 111–21.

Nickel, Hildegard Maria. "Women in the German Democratic Republic and in the New Federal States: Looking Backwards and Forwards," *German Politics and Society*, Nos. 24–25. Winter 1991–92, 34–52.

Nielsen, Jorgen S. *Muslims in Western Europe*. Edinburgh: Edinburgh University Press, 1992.

Noelle-Neumann, Elizabeth, ed. *The Germans: Public Opinion Polls, 1967–1980*. Westport, Connecticut: Greenwood, 1981.

Oldenburg, Fred. "Faktoren des Umbruchs in der DDR." Pages 5–14 in Heinrich Vogel, ed., *Umbruch in Osteuropa*. Cologne: Bundesinstitut für ostwissenschaftliche und internationale Studien, 1990.

Ostner, Ilona. "Ideas, Institutions, Traditions—West German Women's Experience, 1945–1990," *German Politics and Society*, Nos. 24–25, Winter 1991–92, 87–99.

Ostner, Ilona. "Slow Motion: Women, Work, and the Family in Germany." Pages 92–115 in Jane Lewis, ed., *Women and Social Policies in Europe: Work, Family, and the State*. Aldershot, Hampshire, United Kingdom: Edward Elgar, 1993.

Paterson, William E. "Environmental Politics." Pages 267–88 in Gordon Smith, William E. Paterson, and Peter H. Merkl, eds., *Developments in West German Politics*. Durham: Duke University Press, 1989.

Plock, Ernest D. *East German-West German Relations and the Fall of the GDR*. Boulder, Colorado: Westview Press, 1993.

Pond, Elizabeth. "Germany and Its European Environment," *Washington Quarterly*, 16, No. 4, Autumn 1993, 131–40.

Post, Gaines, ed. *German Unification: Problems and Prospects*. Monograph Series, No. 3. Claremont, California: Keck Center for International and Strategic Studies, 1992.

Rehbinder, Eckhard. "Rethinking Environmental Policy." Pages 227–43 in Gordon Smith, William E. Paterson, Peter H. Merkl, and Stephen Padgett, eds., *Developments in German Politics*. Durham: Duke University Press, 1992.

Reiher, Dieter. "Neue Länder: Wieder Religionslehre," *Die politische Meinung* [Sankt Augustin, Germany], 37, No. 270, May 1992, 69–73.

Roberts, Geoffrey. "Emigrants in Their Own Country: German Reunification and Its Political Consequences," *Parliamentary Affairs*, 44, No. 3, July 1991, 373–88.

Rohlfs, Horst-Hennek, and Ursel Schäfer. *Jahrbuch der Bundesrepublik Deutschland, 1993–94.* Munich: Beck/Deutscher Taschenbuch Verlag, 1993.

Rudolph, Hedwig. "Dynamics of Immigration in a Nonimmigrant Country: Germany." Pages 113–26 in Heinz Fassmann and Rainer Münz, eds., *European Migration in the Late Twentieth Century: Historical Patterns, Actual Trends, and Social Implications.* Aldershot, Hampshire, United Kingdom: Edward Elgar, 1994.

Rueschemeyer, Marilyn. "Women in the Politics of Eastern Germany: The Dilemmas of Unification." Pages 87–116 in Marilyn Rueschemeyer, ed., *Women in the Politics of Postcommunist Eastern Europe.* Armonk, New York: M.E. Sharpe, 1994.

Schoonmaker, Donald. "The Challenge of the Greens to the West German Party System." Pages 41–75 in Kay Lawson and Peter Merkl, eds., *When Parties Fail.* Princeton: Princeton University Press, 1988.

Schröder, Richard. "The Role of the Protestant Church in German Unification," *Daedalus,* 123, No. 1, Winter 1994, 231–61.

Smith, Gordon, William E. Paterson, Peter H. Merkl, and Stephen Padgett, eds. *Developments in German Politics.* Durham: Duke University Press, 1992.

Sommerkorn, Ingrid N. "Professional Women and the Women's Movement in West Germany," *German Politics and Society,* Nos. 24–25, Winter 1991–92, 100–105.

Stern, Fritz. "Freedom and Its Discontents," *Foreign Affairs,* 72, No. 4, September–October 1993, 108–25.

Stern, Susan, ed. *Meet United Germany.* Frankfurt am Main: Frankfurter Allgemeine Zeitung Information Services and Atlantik Brücke, 1992.

Stewart, Alasdair. "Migrants, Minorities, and Security in Europe," *Conflict Studies* [London], No. 252, June 1992, 1–25.

Süss, Walter. "Gesellschaftliche Interessen und gesellschaftliche Organizationen in der DDR." Pages 152–64 in Harmut Zimmermann and Werner Weidenfeld, eds., *Deutschland Handbuch.* Munich: Carl Hanser Verlag, 1989.

Thies, Jochen. "Deutschland in Turbulenzen," *Europäische Rundschau* [Vienna], 20, No. 3, 1992, 31–40.

Walsh, James. "German Reunification and the Future of Asylum," *Migration World*, 18, Nos. 3–4, 1990, 5–11.

Weidenfeld, Werner, and Karl-Rudolf Korte. *Die Deutschen: Profil einer Nation.* Stuttgart: Klett-Cotta, 1991.

Weidenfeld, Werner, and Felix Phillip Lutz. "The Divided Nation: Historical Consciousness in Post-Unification Germany," *German Politics and Society*, No. 33, Fall 1994, 117–45.

Wilkins, Erwin. "Die Evangelische Kirche in Deutschland." Pages 185–92 in Harmut Zimmermann and Werner Weidenfeld, eds., *Deutschland Handbuch.* Munich: Carl Hanser Verlag, 1989.

Winkler, Heinrich August. "Rebuilding of a Nation: The Germans Before and After Unification," *Daedalus*, 123, No. 1, Winter 1994, 107–27.

Zapf, Wolfgang. "Sozialstruktur und gesellschaftlicher Wandel in der Bundesrepublik Deutschland." Pages 99–124 in Harmut Zimmermann and Werner Weidenfeld, eds., *Deutschland Handbuch.* Munich: Carl Hanser Verlag, 1989.

(Various issues of the following periodicals were also used in in the preparation of this chapter: *Aus Politik und Zeitgeschichte* [Bonn]; *Christian Science Monitor; Deutschland Nachrichten; Economist* [London]; *Los Angeles Times; New York Times; Der Spiegel* [Hamburg]; and *Washington Post.*)

Chapter 4

Aichberger, F., ed. *Sozialgesetzbuch: Reichsversicherungsordnung mit Nebengesetzen, Ausführungs- und Verfasungsvorschriften.* Munich: C.H. Beck, 1992.

Alber, Jens. "Germany." Pages 1–154 in Peter Flora, ed., *Growth to Limits: The Western European Welfare States since World War II,* 2. New York: Walter de Gruyter, 1988.

Alber, Jens. *Das Gesundheitswesen der Bundesrepublik Deutschland: Entwicklung, Struktur und Funktionsweise.* Frankfurt am Main: Campus, 1992.

Alber, Jens. "Government Responses to the Challenge of Unemployment: The Development of Unemployment Insurance in Western Europe." Pages 151–83 in Peter Flora and Arnold J. Heidenheimer, eds., *The Development of Welfare States in Europe and America.* New Brunswick, New Jersey: Transaction, 1981.

Alber, Jens. "Residential Care for the Elderly," *Journal of Health Politics, Policy and Law,* 17, No. 4, Winter 1992, 929–57.

Alber, Jens. *Vom Armenhaus zum Wohlfahrtsstaat: Analysen zur Entwicklung der Sozialversicherung in Westeuropa.* 2d ed. Frankfurt am Main: Campus, 1987.

Alber, Jens, and Brigitte Bernardi-Schenkluhn. *Westeuropäische Gesundheitssysteme im Vergleich: Bundesrepublik Deutschland, Schweiz, Frankreich, Italien, Grossbritannien.* Frankfurt am Main: Campus, 1992.

Albisetti, James C. *Secondary School Reform in Imperial Germany.* Princeton: Princeton University Press, 1983.

Allmendinger, Jutta. "Educational Systems and Labor Market Outcomes," *European Sociological Review* [Oxford], 5, No. 3, December 1989, 1–250.

Altenstetter, Christa. "An End to a Consensus on Health Care in the Federal Republic of Germany?" *Journal of Health Politics, Policy and Law,* 12, No. 3, Fall 1987, 505–36.

Altenstetter, Christa. "Federal Republic of Germany." Pages 157–77 in Jack Paul DeSario, ed., *International Public Policy Sourcebook,* 1. New York: Greenwood, 1989.

Altenstetter, Christa. "German Social Security Programs: An Interpretation of Their Development." Pages 73–97 in Douglas E. Ashford and E.W. Kelley, eds., *Nationalizing Social Security in Europe and America.* Greenwich, Connecticut: JAI Press, 1986.

Altenstetter, Christa. "Health Policy Regimes and the Single European Market," *Journal of Health Politics, Policy and Law,* 17, No. 4, Winter 1992, 813–46.

Altenstetter, Christa. "Hospital Planners and Medical Professionals in the Federal Republic of Germany." Pages 157–77 in Giorgio Freddi and James Warner Björkman, eds. *Controlling Medical Professionals: The Comparative Politics of Health Governance.* Sage Modern Politics Series, No. 21. London: Sage, 1989.

Altenstetter, Christa. "Hospital Policy and Resource Allocation in the Federal Republic of Germany." Pages 237–65 in Douglas E. Ashford and John Kelley, eds., *Public Policy Across*

Nations: Social Welfare in Industrial Settings. Greenwich, Connecticut: JAI Press, 1985.

Altenstetter, Christa. "Reimbursement Policy of Hospitals in the Federal Republic of Germany," *International Journal of Health Planning and Management* [Keele, Staffordshire, United Kingdom], 1, No. 3, April–June 1986, 189–211.

Altenstetter, Christa, and Stuart C. Haywood, eds. *Comparative Health Policy and the New Right: From Rhetoric to Reality.* New York: St. Martin's Press, 1991.

Andrain, Charles F. *Social Policies in Western Industrial Societies.* Berkeley: University of California Press, 1985.

Anweiler, Oskar, ed. *Vergleich von Bildung und Erziehung in der Bundesrepublik Deutschland und der Deutschen Demokratischen Republik.* Cologne: Verlag Wissenschaft und Politik, 1990.

Apelt, Dieter. *Education in Bavaria.* Munich: Bavarian State Ministry of Education and Social Affairs, 1990.

Archer, Margaret. "Cross-National Research and the Analysis of Education Systems." Pages 242–62 in Melvin L. Kohn, ed., *Cross-National Research in Sociology.* Newbury Park, California: Sage, 1989.

Arnold, Michael. *Health Care in the Federal Republic of Germany.* Cologne: Deutscher Ärzte-Verlag, 1991.

Arnold, Michael, and Berndt Schirmer. *Gesundheit für ein Deutschland: Ausgangslage, Probleme und Möglichkeiten der Angleichung der medizinischen Versorgungssysteme der Bundesrepublik Deutschland und der DDR zur Bildung eines einheitlichen Gesundheitswesens.* Cologne: Deutscher Ärzte-Verlag, 1990.

Ashford, Douglas E. *The Emergence of the Welfare States.* Oxford: Basil Blackwell, 1986.

Aufhauser, Rudolf, Manfred H. Bobke, and Norbert Warga. *Eine Einführung in das Arbeits- und Sozialrecht der Bundesrepublik Deutschland.* Cologne: Bund-Verlag, 1992.

Baldwin, Peter. *The Politics of Social Solidarity and the Class Bases of the European Welfare State, 1875–1975.* Cambridge: Cambridge University Press, 1991.

Bauer, Rudolph. "Voluntary Welfare Associations in Germany and the United States: Theses on the Historical Development of Intermediary Systems," *International Journal of Voluntary and Non-Profit Organisations. Voluntas* [Manchester], 1, No. 1, 1993, 97–111.

Beratungsstelle für Angewandte Systemforschung. *Die alten und neuen Bundesländer.* Augsburg, Germany: 1992.

Beratungsstelle für Angewandte Systemforschung. *Internationaler Vergleich von Gesundheitssystemen.* 3d ed. Augsburg, Germany: 1992.

Bertram, Barbara. "Frauenerwerbstätigkeit im Osten als familien-politische Kondition," *Theorie und Praxis der sozialen Arbeit* [Bonn], No. 62, 1992, 216–20.

Beyme, Klaus von, and Manfred G. Schmidt. *Policy and Politics in the Federal Republic of Germany.* New York: St. Martin's Press, 1985.

Bradshaw, Jonathan, and David Piachaud. *Child Support in the European Community.* London: Bedford Square Press, 1980.

Brand, H. "East Germany: German Labor Faces Unification," *Dissent,* 37, Fall 1990, 468–73.

Bryson, P.J. "East German Traditional Centralism: An Alternative Route to Economic Reconstruction," *Annales of the American Academy of Political and Social Sciences,* 507, January 1990, 133–41.

Bund-Länderkommission für Bildungsplanung und Forschungsförderung. *Jahresbericht 1991.* Bonn: 1991.

Clasen, Jochen. "Unemployment Insurance in Two Countries: A Comparative Analysis of Great Britain and West Germany in the 1980s," *Journal of European Social Policy* [Harlow, Essex, United Kingdom], 2, No. 4, 1992, 279–300.

Conradt, David P. "Germany." Pages 183–288 in M. Donald Hancock, David P. Conradt, B. Guy Peters, William Safran, and Raphael Zariski, eds., *Politics in Western Europe.* Chatham, New Jersey: Chatham House, 1993.

Dogan, Mattei. "The Social Security Crisis in the Richest Countries: Basic Analogies," *International Social Science Journal* [Oxford], 37, No. 103, February 1985, 47–61.

Döhler, Marian. "Gesundheitspolitische Steuerung zwischen Hierarchie und Verhandlung," *Politische Vierteljahresschrift* [Bielefeld, Germany], 33, No. 4, 1992, 571–96.

Döhler, Marian. "Ordnungspolitische Ideen und sozialpolitische Institutionen." Pages 123–41 in Roland Czada and Manfred Schmidt, eds., *Verhandlungsdemokratie, Interessenvermittlung, Regierbarkeit.* Opladen, Germany: Westdeutscher Verlag, 1993.

Döhler, Marian. "Physicians' Professional Autonomy in the Welfare State: Endangered or Preserved?" Pages 178–97 in Giorgio Freddi and James W. Björkman, eds., *Controlling Medical Professionals: The Comparative Politics of Health Governance.* London: Sage, 1989.

Dooghe, Gilbert. *The Aging of the Population in Europe: Socio-Economic Characteristics of the Elderly Population.* Louvain, Belgium: Garant, 1992.

Dürr, Karlheinz. "East German Education: A System in Transition," *Phi Delta Kappan,* 73, No. 5, January 1992, 390–93.

Esping-Anderson, Gösta. *The Three Worlds of Welfare Capitalism.* Princeton: Princeton University Press, 1990.

Federal Republic of Germany. Bundesminister für Bildung und Wissenschaft. *Berufsbildungsbericht 1992. Grundlagen. Perspektiven.* Schriftenreihe Grundlagen und Perspektiven für Bildung und Wissenschaft, 31. Bad Honnef, Germany: K.H. Bock, 1992.

Federal Republic of Germany. Bundesminister für Bildung und Wissenschaft. *Grund- und Strukturdaten 1991–92.* Bad Honnef, Germany: K.H. Bock, 1991.

Federal Republic of Germany. Bundesminister für Bildung und Wissenschaft. *Studenten an Hochschulen 1975 bis 1991.* Oberhausen, Germany: Plitt Druck- und Verlag, April 1992.

Federal Republic of Germany. Bundesminister für Gesundheit. *Daten des Gesundheitswesens 1991.* Schriftenreihe des Bundesministers für Gesundheit, 3. Baden-Baden, Germany: Nomos, 1991.

Federal Republic of Germany. Bundesminister für Gesundheit. *Statistisches Taschenbuch Gesundheit 1992.* Bonn: December 1992.

Federal Republic of Germany. Federal Ministry for Health. *Health Care in Germany: The Health Care System in the Federal Republic of Germany.* Bonn: Osang Verlag, 1994.

Federal Republic of Germany. Federal Ministry of Labour and Social Affairs. *Social Security at the Glance.* Bonn: November 1994.

Federal Republic of Germany. Statistisches Bundesamt. *Bildung im Zahlenspiegel 1990.* Stuttgart: Verlag Metzler-Poeschel, 1990.

Federal Republic of Germany. Statistisches Bundesamt. *Datenreport 1992. Zahlen und Fakten über die Bundesrepublik Deutschland.* 2d ed. Schriftenreihe, No. 309. Bonn: 1992.

Federal Republic of Germany. Statistiches Bundesamt. *Statistisches Jahrbuch 1994 für die Bundesrepublik Deutschland.* Stuttgart: Metzler-Poeschel, 1994.

Flora, Peter, ed. *Growth to Limits: The Western European Welfare States since World War II,* 2. West Berlin: Walter de Gruyter, 1988.

Flora, Peter, and Arnold J. Heidenheimer, eds. *The Development of Welfare States in Europe and America.* New Brunswick, New Jersey: Transaction, 1981.

Freudenstein, Ulrich, and Günther Borgwardt. "Primary Medical Care in Former East Germany: The Frosty Winds of Change," *British Medical Journal* [London], 304, March 28, 1992, 827–29.

Führ, Christoph. *On the Education System in the Five New Laender of the Federal Republic of Germany: Brandenburg, Mecklenburg-Western Pomerania, Saxony, Saxony-Anhalt, Thuringia.* Bonn: Inter Nationes, 1992.

Führ, Christoph. *Schools and Institutions of Higher Education in the Federal Republic of Germany: A Survey of Educational Policy and the Educational System.* Bonn: Inter Nationes, 1989.

Garnier, Maurice, and Jerald Hage, "Education and Economic Growth in Germany," *Research in Sociology of Education and Socialization,* 9, 1990, 25–53.

Geiger, Roger L. *Private Sectors in Higher Education: Structure, Function, and Change in Eight Countries.* Ann Arbor: University of Michigan Press, 1986.

Geissler, Rainer. *Die Sozialstruktur Deutschlands: Ein Studienbuch zur sozialstrukturellen Entwicklung im geteilten und vereinten Deutschland.* Opladen, Germany: Westdeutscher Verlag, 1992.

Gensior, Sabine, and Bärbel Schöler. "Women's Employment and Multinationals in the Federal Republic of Germany: The Job Experience." Pages 60–79 in Diane Elson and Ruth Pearson, eds., *Women's Employment and Multinationals in Europe.* London: Macmillan, 1989.

Gerhard, Ute. "German Women and the Social Costs of Unification," *German Politics and Society*, Nos. 24–25, Winter 1991–92, 16–33.

Glaser, William A. *Health Insurance Bargaining: Foreign Lessons for Americans*. New York: Gardener Press, 1980.

Glaser, William A. *Health Insurance in Practice*. San Francisco: Jossey-Bass, 1991.

Glatzer, Wolfgang, Karl Otto Hondrich, Heinz-Herbert Noll, Karin Stiehr, and Barbara Wörndl, eds. *Recent Social Trends in West Germany*. Frankfurt am Main: Campus, 1992.

Gordon, Margaret. *Social Security Policies in Industrial Countries: A Comparative Analysis*. New York: Cambridge University Press, 1989.

Hage, Jerald, Robert Hanneman, and Edward T. Gargan. *State Responsiveness and State Activism: An Examination of the Social Forces and State Strategies That Explain the Rise in Social Expenditures in Britain, France, Germany, and Italy, 1870–1968*. London: Unwin Hyman, 1989.

Ham, Christopher, Ray Robinson, and Michael Benzeval. *Health Check: Health Care Reforms in an International Context*. London: Kings Fund Institute, 1990.

Hannan, Michael T., et al. "Sector Differences in the Dynamics of Wage Growth FRG," *American Sociological Review*, 55, No. 5, October 1990, 694–713.

Hauser, Richard, Joachim Frick, Klaus Mueller, and Gert G. Wagner. "Inequality in Income: A Comparison of East and West Germans Before Reunification and During Transition," *Journal of European Social Policy* [Harlow, Essex, United Kingdom], 4, No. 4, 1994, 277–95.

Hearnden, Arthur. *Education in the Two Germanies*. Boulder, Colorado: Westview Press, 1979.

Heidenheimer, Arnold J. "Education and Social Security Entitlements in Europe and America." Pages 269–304 in Peter Flora and Arnold J. Heidenheimer, eds., *The Development of Welfare States in Europe and America*. New Brunswick, New Jersey: Transaction, 1981.

Heidenheimer, Arnold J. "Health Policy." Pages 57–96 in Arnold J. Heidenheimer, Hugh Heclo, and Carole Teich Adams, *Comparative Public Policy: The Politics of Social Choice in*

America, Europe, and Japan. 3d ed. New York: St. Martin's Press, 1992.

Heidenheimer, Arnold J. "The Indexation of Pension Entitlements: The West German Initiative in Comparative Perspective." Pages 181–94 in Douglas E. Ashford and J.W. Kelley, eds., *Nationalizing Social Security in Europe and America.* Greenwich, Connecticut: JAI, 1986.

Henke, Klaus-Dirk, Margaret A. Murray, and Claudia Ade. "Global Budgeting in Germany: Lessons for the United States," *Health Affairs,* 13, No. 4, Fall 1994, 7–21.

Hennock, E.P. *British Social Reform and German Precedents: The Case of Social Insurance, 1880–1914.* Oxford: Oxford University Press, 1987.

Hoffmeyer, Ullrich K. "The Health Care System in Germany." Pages 419–512 in Ullrich K. Hoffmeyer and Thomas R. McCarthy, eds., *Financing Health Care,* 1. Dordrecht, Netherlands: Kluwer Academic Publishers, 1994.

Hollingsworth, Ellen Jane. "Falling Through the Cracks: Care of the Chronically Mentally Ill in the United States, Germany, and the United Kingdom," *Journal of Health Politics, Policy and Law,* 17, No. 4, Winter 1992, 899–928.

Hollingsworth, Rogers J., and Ellen Jane Hollingsworth. "Challenges in the Provision of Care for the Chronically Ill," *Journal of Health Politics, Policy and Law,* 17, No. 4, Winter 1992, 869–98.

Hood, Christopher, and Gunnar Folke Schuppert. *Delivering Public Services in Western Europe: Sharing Western European Experience of Para-Government Organization.* London: Sage, 1988.

Hsiao, William C. "Comparing Health Care Systems: What Nations Can Learn from One Another," *Journal of Health Politics, Policy and Law,* 17, No. 4, Winter 1992, 613–36.

Huber, Joan. "The Politics of Public Assistance: Western Europe and the United States." Pages 109–25 in Milton J. Yinger and S.J. Cutler, eds., *Major Social Issues: A Multidisciplinary View.* New York: Free Press, 1978.

Hurst, Jeremy W. "Reform of Health Care in Germany," *Health Care Financing Review,* 12, No. 3, Spring 1991, 73–86.

Iglehart, John K. "Health Policy Report: Germany's Health Care System," Pt. 1, *New England Journal of Medicine,* 324, No. 7, February 14, 1991, 503–8.

Iglehart, John K. "Health Policy Report: Germany's Health Care System," Pt. 2, *New England Journal of Medicine*, 324, No. 24, June 13, 1991, 1750–56.

Janssen, Richard, and Jan van der Made. "Privatisation in Western European Health Care: A Comparative Study," *International Journal of the Health Sciences*, 2, No. 2, 1991, 63–81.

Jobst, Eberhard, and Susanne-Corinna Langer, eds. *Das Neue Deutsche Recht für Schule, Berufsausbildung und Hochschule.* Bonn: K.H. Bock, 1991.

Jurasek, Richard, and Rainer Brämer. "The New Federal Republic of Germany as Trauma: German Unification from the Student Perspective," *German Politics and Society*, No. 33, Fall 1994, 85–116.

Kaelble, Hartmut. "Educational Opportunities in Europe in the Period of Industrialization." Pages 239–68 in Peter Flora and Arnold J. Heidenheimer, eds., *The Development of the Welfare State in Europe and America.* New Brunswick, New Jersey: Transaction, 1981.

Kahn, Alfred J., and Sheila B. Kamerman. *Mothers Alone: Strategies for a Time of Change.* Dover, Massachusetts: Auburn House, 1988.

Kahn, Alfred J., and Sheila B. Kamerman, eds. *Childcare, Parental Leave, and the Under 3s: Policy Innovation in Europe.* New York: Auburn House, 1991.

Kamerman, Sheila B. "Childcare and Family Benefits. Policies of Six Industrialized Countries," *Monthly Labor Review*, 103, No. 11, 1988, 23–28.

Kappler, Arno, and Adriane Grevel, eds. *Facts about Germany.* Frankfurt am Main: Societäts-Verlag, 1994.

Katzenstein, Peter J. *Policy and Politics in West Germany.* Philadelphia: Temple University Press, 1987.

Kirchgessler, K. Ch. "Health and Social Inequities in the Federal Republic of Germany," *Social Science and Medicine* [Exeter, Devon, United Kingdom], 31, No. 3, 1990, 249–56.

Knox, Richard A. *Germany: One Nation with Health Care for All.* Washington: Faulkner and Gray's Healthcare Information Center, 1993.

Kocka, Jürgen. "Crisis of Unification: How Germany Changes," *Daedalus*, 123, No. 1, Winter 1994, 173–92.

Köhler, Peter A., and Hans Friedrich Zacher, eds. *The Evolution of Social Insurance, 1881–1981: Studies of Germany, France, Great Britain, Austria, and Switzerland.* New York: St. Martin's Press, 1982.

Kolinsky, Eva. "Women in the New Germany: The East-West Divide." Pages 264–80 in Gordon Smith, William S. Paterson, Peter H. Merkl, and Stephen Padgett, eds., *Developments in German Politics.* Durham: Duke University Press, 1992.

Lee, W. Robert, and Eve Rosenhaft, eds. *The State and Social Change in Germany, 1880–1980.* New York: St. Martin's Press, 1990.

Lees, A. "Social Reform, Social Policy, and Social Welfare in Modern Germany," *Journal of Social History,* 23, No. 1, Fall 1989, 167–76.

Leibfried, Stephan. "Public Assistance in the United States and the Federal Republic of Germany: Does Social Democracy Make a Difference?" *Comparative Politics,* 11, 1978, 59–76.

Leibfried, Stephan. "Towards a European Welfare State: On Integrating Poverty Regimes into the European Community." Pages 245–79 in Zsuzsa Ferge and Jon Eivind Kolberg, eds., *Social Policy in a Changing Europe.* Boulder, Colorado: Westview Press, 1992.

Leibfried, Stephan. "The United States and West German Welfare Systems: A Comparative Analysis," *Cornell International Law Journal,* 12, No. 16, Summer 1979, 175–98.

Leibfried, Stephan. "Welfare Guidelines in the 1920s: Regulating Weimar's Poor." Pages 137–54 in Douglas E. Ashford and E.W. Kelley, eds., *Nationalizing Social Security in Europe and America.* Greenwich, Connecticut: JAI Press, 1986.

Leibfried, Stephan, and Ilona Ostner. "The Particularism of West German Welfare Capitalism: The Case of Women's Social Security." Pages 164–86 in Michael Adler, Colin Bell, Jochen Clasen, and Adrian Sinfield, eds., *The Sociology of Social Security.* Edinburgh: Edinburgh University Press, 1991.

Leibfried, Stephan, and Paul Pierson, eds. *European Social Policy: Between Fragmentation and Integration.* Washington: Brookings Institution, 1995.

Light, Donald W. "Values and Structure in the German Health Care Systems," *Milbank Quarterly,* 63, No. 4, 1985, 615–47.

Light, Donald W., and Alexander Schuller, eds. *Political Values and Health Care: The German Experience.* Cambridge: MIT Press, 1986.

Lüschen, Günther, William C. Cockerham, and Gerhard Kunz, eds. *Health and Illness in America and Germany: Comparative Sociology of Health Conduct and Public Policy.* Munich: R. Oldenbourg, 1989.

Mading, Heinrich. "Federalism and Education Planning in the FRG," *Publius,* 19, No. 4, Fall 1989, 115–31.

Maehl, William Harvey. *Germany in Western Civilization.* Birmingham: University of Alabama Press, 1979.

Mangen, Steen. "Social Policy: One State, Two-Tier Welfare." Pages 208–26 in Gordon Smith, William E. Paterson, Peter H. Merkl, and Stephen Padgett, eds., *Developments in German Politics.* Durham: Duke University Press, 1992.

Maydell, Bernd Baron von, and Walter Kannengiesser, eds. *Handbuch Sozialpolitik.* Pfullingen, West Germany: Neske, 1988.

Maydell, Bernd Baron von, and Franz Ruland, eds. *Sozialrechtshandbuch.* Neuwied, Germany: Luchterhand, 1992.

Merritt, Richard I. "Opening Up the Universities: The Courts, the Universities, and the Right of Admission in the Federal Republic of Germany," *Minerva* [London], 17, No. 1, Spring 1979, 1–32.

Meyer, Hans Joachim. "Shake-up for German Universities," *Nature* [London], No. 368, March 3, 1994, 11–12.

Mielck, Andreas, ed. *Krankheit und soziale Ungleichheit: Epidemiologische Forschungen in Deutschland.* Leverkusen, Germany: Leske Verlag und Budrich, 1993.

Mommsen, Wolfgang J., ed. *The Emergence of the Welfare State in Britain and Germany, 1850–1950.* London: Croom Helm, 1981.

Neeman, Elliot Yale. "German Collectivism and the Welfare State," *Critical Review,* 4, No. 4, Fall 1990, 591–618.

Niehoff, J.U., F. Schneider, and E. Wetzstein. "Reflections on the Health Policy of the Former German Democratic Republic," *International Journal of Health Sciences,* 2, Nos. 3–4, 1992, 205–13.

Organisation for Economic Co-operation and Development. *Compulsory Schooling in a Changing World.* Paris: 1983.

Organisation for Economic Co-operation and Development. *Curriculum Reform: An Overview of Trends.* Paris: 1990.

Organisation for Economic Co-operation and Development. *Financing and Delivering Health Care.* Paris: 1987.

Organisation for Economic Co-operation and Development. *Health Care Systems in Transition.* Paris: 1990.

Organisation for Economic Co-operation and Development. *High Quality Education and Training for All.* Paris: 1992.

Organisation for Economic Co-operation and Development. *Reforming Public Pensions.* Paris: 1988.

Organisation for Economic Co-operation and Development. *The Reform of Health Care: A Comparative Analysis of Seven OECD Countries.* Paris: 1992.

Parry, Richard. "The Viability of the Welfare State." Pages 12–32 in Derek W. Urwin and William E. Paterson, eds., *Politics in Western Europe Today: Perspectives, Policies, and Problems since 1980.* London: Longman, 1991.

Peisert, Hansgert, and Gerhild Framhein. *Higher Education in the Federal Republic of Germany.* Bad Honnef, West Germany: K.H. Bock, 1990.

Philipsen, Dirk. *We Were the People: Voices from East Germany's Revolutionary Autumn of 1989.* Durham: Duke University Press, 1992.

Reinhardt, Uwe E. "Global Budgeting in German Health Care: Insights for Americans," *Domestic Affairs,* 2, Winter 1993–94, 159–94.

Reinhardt, Uwe E. "Perspective on the German Health Care System," *Health Affairs,* 13, No. 4, Fall 1994, 22–24.

Ringer, Fritz K. *Education and Society in Modern Europe.* Bloomington: Indiana University Press, 1979.

Rosewitz, Bernd, and Douglas Webber. *Reformversuche und Reformblockaden im deutschen Gesundheitswesen.* Frankfurt am Main: Campus, 1990.

Rublee, Dale A. "Medical Technology in Canada, Germany, and the United States," *Health Affairs,* 8, No. 4, Fall 1989, 178–81.

Rublee, Dale A. "Medical Technology in Canada, Germany, and the United States," *Health Affairs,* 13, No. 4, Fall 1994, 113–17.

Rueschemeyer, Marilyn, and Christiane Lemke, eds. *The Quality of Life in the German Democratic Republic: Changes and Develop-*

ments in a State Socialist Society. Armonk, New York: M.E. Sharpe, 1989.

Rust, Val D., and Diane Rust. *The Unification of German Education.* New York: Garland, 1995.

Sachverständigenrat der Konzertierten Aktion. *Jahresgutachten 1991: Das Gesundheitswesen im vereinten Deutschland.* Baden-Baden: Nomos, 1991.

Sachverständigerat der Konzertierten Aktion. *Jahresgutachten 1992. Ausbau in Deutschland und Aufbruch nach Europa: Vorschläge für die Konzertierte Aktion im Gesundheitswesen.* Baden-Baden: Nomos, 1992.

Sachverständigerat der Konzertierten Aktion. *Sachbestandsbericht 1994. Gesundheitsversorgung und Krankenversicherung 2000: Eigenverantwortung, Subsidiarität und Solidarität bei sich ändernden Rahmenbedingungen.* Baden-Baden: Nomos, 1994.

Scheiwe, Kirsten. "Labour Market, Welfare State, and Family Institutions: The Links to Mothers' Poverty Risks. A Comparison between Belgium, Germany, and the United Kingdom," *Journal of European Social Policy* [Harlow, Essex, United Kingdom], 4, No. 3, 1994, 201–24.

Schieber, George J., Jean-Pierre Poullier, and Leslie M. Greenwald. "U.S. Health Expenditure Performance: An International Comparison and Data Update," *Health Care Financing Review,* 13, No. 4, Summer 1992, 1–15.

Schmähl, Winifried. "The '1992 Reform' of Public Pensions in Germany: Main Elements and Some Effects," *Journal of European Social Policy* [Harlow, Essex, United Kingdom], 3, No. 1, 1993, 39–51.

Schmidt, Manfred G., ed. *Wohlfahrtsstaatliche Politik unter Bürgerlichen und Sozialdemokratischen Regierungen.* Frankfurt am Main: Campus, 1982.

Schneider, Markus. "Health Care Cost Containment in the Federal Republic of Germany," *Health Care Financing Review,* 12, No. 3, Spring 1991, 87–101.

Schulenburg, J. Matthias Graf von der. "Solidarity at a Price," *Journal of Health Politics, Policy and Law,* 17, No. 4, Winter 1992, 715–38.

Schulin, Bertram, ed. *Handbuch des Sozialversicherungsrechts.* Munich: C.H. Beck'sche Verlagsbuchhandlung, 1994.

Schulin, Bertram, and Raimund Kegel. *Systeme und Zahlen Sozialer Sicherheit: Ein Überblick.* Sankt Augustin, West Germany: Asgard-Verlag Dr. Werner Hippe, 1990.

Schulte, Bernd, and Peter Trenk-Hinterberger. *Sozialhilfe. Eine Einführung.* 2d ed. Heidelberg: C.F. Müller Juristischer Verlag, 1986.

Seibel, Wolfgang. "Government/Third Sector Relationship in a Comparative Perspective: The Cases of France and West Germany," *International Journal of Voluntary and Non-Profit Organisations. Voluntas* [Manchester], 1, No. 1, 1993, 41–60.

Smith, Gordon, William E. Paterson, Peter H. Merkl, and Stephen Padgett, eds. *Developments in German Politics.* Durham: Duke University Press, 1992.

Stone, Deborah A. "German Unification: East Meets West in the Doctor's Office," *Journal of Health Politics, Policy and Law,* 16, No. 2, Summer 1991, 401–12.

Stone, Deborah A. *The Limits of Professional Power.* Chicago: University of Chicago Press, 1980.

Stützle, Hans. *Das soziale Netz in Deutschland: Leistungen und Grenzen.* Munich: Olzog, 1994.

Swenson, P. "Labor and the Limits of the Welfare State: Politics of Intra-Class Conflict and Cross-Class Alliances in Sweden and Germany," *Comparative Politics,* 23, No. 4, July 1991, 379–99.

Symes, Valerie. *Unemployment in Europe: Problems and Policies.* London: Routledge, 1995.

Teichler, Ulrich. *Das Dilemma der modernen Bildungsgesellschaft.* Stuttgart: Klett, 1976.

Teichler, Ulrich, ed. *Hochschule und Beruf: Problemlage und Aufgaben der Forschung.* Frankfurt am Main: Campus, 1989.

Teichler, Ulrich, and Bikas C. Sanyal. *Higher Education and the Labor Market in the Federal Republic of Germany.* Paris: UNESCO Press, 1982.

Thiele, Wilhelm, ed. *Das Gesundheitswesen der DDR: Aufbruch oder Einbruch? Denkanstösse für eine Neuordnung des Gesundheitswesens in einem deutschen Staat.* Sankt Augustin, West Germany: Asgard-Verlag Dr. Werner Hippe, 1990.

United States. Congress. Pepper Commission. United States Bipartisan Commission on Comprehensive Health Care. *West Germany's Health-Care and Health-Insurance System: Com-*

bining Universal Access with Cost Control. A Call for Action. Washington: 1990.

United States. Department of Health and Human Services. National Center for Health Statistics. *International Health Data Reference Guide, 1991.* DHHS Publication No. 92–1007. Hyattsville, Maryland: January 1992.

United States. General Accounting Office. *German Health Reforms: New Cost Control Initiatives.* GAO/HRD–93–103. Washington: July 1993.

United States. General Accounting Office. *Health Care Spending Controls: The Experience of France, Germany, and Japan.* GAO/HRD–92–9. Washington: November 1991.

United States. General Accounting Office. *Long-Term Care: Other Countries Tighten Budgets While Seeking Better Access.* GAO/HEHS–94–154. Washington: 1994.

Voges, Wolfgang, and Götz Rohwer. "Receiving Social Assistance in Germany: Risk and Duration," *Journal of European Social Policy* [Harlow, Essex, United Kingdom], 2, No. 3, 1992, 175–91.

Wanek, Volker. "Seehofers Gesundheitsreform als Historischer Kompromiss," *Blätter für deutsche und internationale Politik* [Bonn], 11, 1992, 1342–55.

Wasem, Jürgen. "Sozialpolitische Grundlagen der gesetzlichen Krankenversicherung." Pages 80–112 in Bertram Schulin, ed., *Krankenversicherungsrecht.* Munich: C.J. Beck'sche Verlagsbuchhandlung, 1994.

Webber, Douglas. "Health Policy and the Christian-Liberal Coalition in West Germany: The Conflicts over the Health Insurance Reform, 1987–8." Pages 49–90 in Christa Altenstetter and Stuart C. Haywood, eds., *Comparative Health Policy and the New Right: From Rhetoric to Reality.* New York: St. Martin's Press, 1991.

World Health Organization. Regional Office for Europe. *Policies for Health in European Countries with Pluralist Systems.* Copenhagen: 1990.

Wysong, Jere A., and Thomas Abel. "Universal Health Insurance and High-Risk Groups in West Germany: Implications for U.S. Health Policy," *Milbank Quarterly,* 68, No. 4, 1990, 527–60.

Zacher, Hans F. "Das Soziale Staatsziel." Pages 532–58 in Bernd Baron von Maydell and Franz Ruland, eds., *Sozialrechtshandbuch.* Neuwied, Germany: Luchterhand, 1992.

Chapter 5

Ardagh, John. *Germany and the Germans.* Rev. ed. New York: Penguin Books USA, 1991.

Baratta, Mario von, ed. *Der Fischer Weltalmanach, 1995.* Frankfurt am Main: Fischer Taschenbuch Verlag, 1994.

Braudel, Fernand. *The Wheels of Commerce.* New York: Harper and Row, 1982.

Braun, Hans-Joachim. *The German Economy in the Twentieth Century: The German Reich and the Federal Republic.* New York: Routledge, 1990.

Cerny, Karl H. "Between the Elections: The Issues, 1983–1987." Pages 191–96 in Karl H. Cerny, ed., *Germany at the Polls: The Bundestag Elections of the 1980s.* Durham: Duke University Press, 1990.

Chapman, Dudley H. *Molting Time for Antitrust: Market Relations, Economic Fallacies, and European Innovation.* New York: Praeger, 1991.

Craig, Gordon A. *Germany, 1966–1945.* Oxford: Clarendon, 1978.

Dennis, Mike. *Social and Economic Modernization in Eastern Germany from Honecker to Kohl.* New York: St. Martin's Press, 1993.

Deutsche Bundesbank. *Monthly Report* [Frankfurt am Main], 45, No. 10, October 1993.

Dyker, David A., ed. *The National Economics of Europe.* New York: Longman, 1992.

Dyson, K.H.F. "The Politics of Economic Management in Germany," *West European Politics* [London], 4, No. 2, May 1981, 35–55.

Edwards, Jeremy S.S., and Klaus Fischer. *Banks, Finance, and Investment in Germany.* New York: Cambridge University Press, 1994.

Erhard, Ludwig. *Prosperity Through Competition.* Westport, Connecticut: Greenwood Press, 1975.

Esser, Josef. "State, Business, and Trade Unions in West Germany after the Wende," *West European Politics* [London], 9, No. 2, April 1986, 198–214.

The Europa World Year Book, 1995, 1. London: Europa, 1995.

Fack, Ulrich, and Peter Hort. *Soziale Marktwirtschaft*. Freiburg, West Germany: Verlag Plötz, 1985.

Federal Republic of Germany. Federal Ministry for Economics. *Economic Situation in the Federal Republic of Germany* [Bonn], No. 1, January 1994.

Federal Republic of Germany. Federal Ministry for Economics. *Economic Situation in the Federal Republic of Germany* [Bonn], No. 3, March 1994.

Ghaussy, A. Ghanie, and Wolf Schäfer, eds. *The Economics of German Unification*. London: Routledge, 1993.

Giersch, Herbert, Karl-Heinz Pagué, and Holger Schmieding. *The Fading Miracle: Four Decades of Market Economy in Germany*. Cambridge: Cambridge University Press, 1994.

Guerrieri, Paolo, and Pier Carlo Padoan, eds. *The Political Economy of European Integration*. New York: Harvester Wheatsheaf, 1989.

Heitger, Bernhard, and Leonard Waverman, eds. *German Unification and the International Economy*. London: Routledge, 1993.

Henderson, W.O. *The Rise of German Industrial Power, 1834–1914*. London: Temple Smith, 1975.

Henzler, Herbert, and Mark Young. *German and American Management: Similarities, Differences, and Problems*. Washington: American Institute for Contemporary German Studies, 1989.

Holborn, Hajo. *A History of Modern Germany, 1840–1945*. New York: Knopf, 1969.

Inman, B.R., and Daniel F. Burton, Jr. "Technology and Competitiveness: The New Policy Frontier," *Foreign Affairs*, 69, No. 2, Spring 1990, 116–34.

Jacobi, Otto, Berndt Keller, and Walther Müller-Jentsch. "Germany: Codetermining the Future." Pages 218–69 in Anthony Ferner and Richard Hyman, eds., *Industrial Relations in the New Europe*. Oxford: Blackwell, 1992.

Kappler, Arno, and Adriane Grevel, eds. *Facts about Germany*. Frankfurt am Main: Societäts-Verlag, 1994.

Katzenstein, Peter J. *Industry and Politics in West Germany.* Ithaca, New York: Cornell University Press, 1989.

Kindleberger, Charles P. *Financial History of Western Europe.* London: Allen and Unwin, 1984.

Krieger, Wolfgang. *Technologiepolitik der Bundesrepublik Deutschland.* Ebenhausen, West Germany: Stiftung Wissenschaft und Politik, 1989.

Kurz, Heinz D., ed. *United Germany and the New Europe.* Aldershot, Hampshire, United Kingdom: Edward Elgar, 1993.

Lawrence, Peter. *Managers and Management in West Germany.* New York: St. Martin's Press, 1980.

Lodge, George C., and Ezra F. Vogel, eds. *Ideology and National Competitiveness.* Boston: Harvard Business School Press, 1987.

Magaziner, Ira, and Mort Patinkin. *The Silent War.* New York: Random House, 1989.

Marsh, David. *The Bundesbank: The Bank That Rules Europe.* London: Heineman, 1992

Marsh, David. *The Germans: A People at the Crossroads.* New York: St. Martin's Press, 1990.

Nichols, A.J. *Freedom with Responsibility: The Social Market Economy in Germany, 1918–1963.* Oxford: Clarendon, 1994.

Noam, Eli. *Telecommunications in Europe.* New York: Oxford University Press, 1992.

Organisation for Economic Co-operation and Development. *Main Economic Indicators* [Paris], September 1994.

Organisation for Economic Co-operation and Development. *Main Economic Indicators* [Paris], March 1995.

Organisation for Economic Co-operation and Development. *OECD Economic Outlook* [Paris], No. 51, June 1992.

Organisation for Economic Co-operation and Development. *OECD Economic Surveys, 1989–1990: Germany.* Paris: 1990.

Organisation for Economic Co-operation and Development. *OECD Economic Surveys, 1993–1994: Germany.* Paris: 1994.

Organisation for Economic Co-operation and Development. *OECD Economic Surveys, 1994–1995: Germany.* Paris: 1995.

Porter, Michael E. *The Competitive Advantage of Nations.* New York: Free Press, 1989.

Putnam, Robert D., and C. Randall Henning. "The Bonn Summit of 1978: A Case Study in Coordination." Pages 12–140 in Richard N. Cooper et al., eds., *Can Nations Agree? Issues in*

International Economic Cooperation. Washington: Brookings Institution, 1989.

Rohlfs, Horst-Hennek, and Ursel Schäfer. *Jahrbuch der Bundesrepublik Deutschland, 1993–94.* Munich: Deutscher Taschenbuch Verlag, 1993.

Schatz, Klaus-Werner, and Frank Wolter. *Structural Adjustment in the Federal Republic of Germany.* Geneva: International Labour Office, 1987.

Scott, Bruce R. "National Strategies: Key to International Competition." Pages 71–143 in Bruce R. Scott and George C. Lodge, eds., *U.S. Competitiveness in the World Economy.* Boston: Harvard Business School Press, 1985.

Seitz, Konrad. *Die japanisch-amerikanische Herausforderung: Deutschlands Hochtechnologie-Industrien kämpfen ums Überleben.* Bonn: Aktuell, 1990.

Sinn, Gerlinde, and Hans-Werner Sinn. *Jumpstart: The Economic Unification of Germany.* Cambridge: MIT Press, 1992.

Smith, Eric Owen. *The German Economy.* New York: Routledge, 1994.

Smyser, W.R. *The German Economy: Colossus at the Crossroads.* 2d ed. New York: St. Martin's Press, 1993.

Späth, Lothar. *Aktive Industriepolitik.* Bonn: Aktuell, 1988.

Streeck, Wolfgang, and Philippe Schmitter. *Private Interest Government: Beyond Market and State.* London: Sage, 1985.

Tipton, Frank B., and Robert Aldrich. *An Economic and Social History of Europe, 1890–1939.* Baltimore: The Johns Hopkins University Press, 1987.

Walter, Norbert. *West Germany's Economy: Origins, Problems, and Perspectives.* Washington: American Institute for Contemporary German Studies, 1987.

Weigelt, Klaus. *Soziale Marktwirtschaft im Aufwind.* Herford, West Germany: Busse-Seewald, 1989.

Welfens, Paul J.J., ed. *Economic Aspects of German Unification: Expectations, Transition Dynamics, and International Perspectives.* 2d ed. Berlin: Springer Verlag, 1996.

Chapter 6

Abelshauser, Werner. *Wirtschaftsgeschichte der Bundesrepublik Deutschland, 1945–1980.* Frankfurt am Main: Suhrkamp,

1983.

Bulmer, Simon, and William Paterson. *The Federal Republic of Germany and the European Community.* London: Allen and Unwin, 1987.

Commission of the European Communities. *Completing the Internal Market.* Brussels: 1985.

Commission of the European Communities. *European Economy: The Economics of 1992.* Brussels: 1988.

Deutsche Bundesbank. *Monthly Report* [Frankfurt am Main], 45, No. 10, October 1993.

Deutscher Industrie- und Handelstag. *Competitiveness and Adaptation Strategies of German Companies in the Single European Market: Results of a Corporate Survey.* Bonn: 1989.

Dyker, David A., ed. *The National Economies of Europe.* New York: Longman, 1992.

Economist Intelligence Unit. *Country Profile, 1993–1994: Germany.* London: 1994.

Federal Republic of Germany. Statistiches Bundesamt. *Statistisches Jahrbuch 1994 für die Bundesrepublik Deutschland.* Stuttgart: Metzler-Poeschel, 1994.

Funabashi, Yoichi. *Managing the Dollar: From the Plaza to the Louvre.* 2d ed. Washington: Institute for International Economics, 1989.

Guth, Wilfried, and Armin Gutowski, eds. *Economic Policy Coordination: Proceedings of an International Seminar Held in Hamburg.* Washington: International Monetary Fund, 1988.

Haftendorn, Helga, Lothar Wilker, and Claudia Wörmann. *Die Aussenpolitik der Bundesrepublik Deutschland.* West Berlin: Wissenschaftlicher Autoren Verlag, 1982.

Heitger, Bernhard, and Leonard Waverman, eds. *German Unification and the International Economy.* London: Routledge, 1993.

Kaufmann, Hugo M. *Germany's International Monetary Policy and the European Monetary System.* New York: Brooklyn College Press, 1985.

Kurz, Heinz D., ed. *United Germany and the New Europe.* Aldershot, Hampshire, United Kingdom: Edward Elgar, 1993.

Marsh, David. *The Bundesbank: The Bank That Rules Europe.* London: Heineman, 1992.

Molle, Willem. *The Economies of European Integration: Theory, Practice, Policy.* 2d ed. Brookfield, Vermont: Dartmouth Publishers, 1994.

Oppenheimer, Jochen, and Dietrich Bödecker. "Long-Term Trends in West German Trade, Direct Investment in Aid," *Journal of World Trade,* April 1993, 53–54.

Organisation for Economic Co-operation and Development. *OECD Economic Outlook* [Paris], 56, December 1994.

Organisation for Economic Co-operation and Development. *OECD Economic Surveys, 1993–1994: Germany.* Paris: 1994.

Organisation for Economic Co-operation and Development, *OECD Economic Surveys, 1994–1995: Germany.* Paris: 1995.

Sbragia, Alberta M. *Euro-Politics: Institutions and Policymaking in the New European Community.* Washington: Brookings Institution, 1991.

Seitz, Konrad. *Die japanisch-amerikanishe Herausforderung: Deutschlands Hochtechnologie-Industrien kämpfen ums Überleben.* Bonn: Aktuell, 1990.

Smith, Eric Owen. *The German Economy.* New York: Routledge, 1994.

Smyser, W.R. *The German Economy: Colossus at the Crossroads.* 2d ed. New York: St. Martin's Press, 1993.

Solomon, Robert. *The International Monetary System, 1945–1976: An Insider's View.* New York: Harper and Row, 1977.

Tew, Brian. *The Evolution of the International Monetary System.* London: Hutchinson, 1977.

Thiel, Elke. *Die Europäische Gemeinschaft: Vom Gemeinsamen Markt zur Europäischen Union.* 4th ed. Munich: Bayerische Landeszentrale für Politische Bildungsarbeit, 1989.

Watson, Maxwell, Russel Kincaid, Caroline Atkinson, Eliot Kalter, and David Folerts-Landau. *International Capital Markets: Developments and Prospects.* Washington: International Monetary Fund, 1986.

Welfens, Paul J.J., ed. *Economic Aspects of German Unification: National and International Perspectives.* Berlin: Springer Verlag, 1992.

Chapter 7

Appleton, Jon M. "European Integration and the German *Länder.* Lost Competence or Found Opportunity?" Pages 51–66 in Gale A. Mattox and A. Bradley Shingleton, eds., *Germany at the Crossroads: Foreign and Domestic Policy Issues.* Boulder, Colorado: Westview Press, 1992.

Balfour, Michael. *Germany: The Tides of Power.* London: Routledge, 1992.

Baratta, Mario von, ed. *Der Fischer Weltalmanach, 1995.* Frankfurt am Main: Fischer Taschenbuch Verlag, 1994.

Beyme, Klaus von. "A United Germany Preparing for the 1994 Elections," *Government and Opposition* [London], 29, No. 4, 1994, 445–60.

Boenau, A. Bruce. "Changing Chancellors in West Germany," *West European Politics* [London], 11, No. 3, July 1988, 24–41.

Braunthal, Gerard. *The German Social Democrats since 1969: A Party in Power and Opposition.* Boulder, Colorado: Westview Press, 1994.

Childs, David. *Germany in the Twentieth Century.* New York: Harper Collins, 1991.

Christiansen, Thomas. "The Länder Between Bonn and Brussels: The Dilemma of German Federalism in the 1990s," *German Politics* [London], 1, No. 2, August 1992, 239–63.

Clemens, Clay. "The Chancellor as Manager: Helmut Kohl, the CDU, and Governance in Germany," *West European Politics* [London], 17, No. 4, October 1994, 28–51.

Conradt, David P. *The German Polity.* 6th ed. White Plains, New York: Longman, 1996.

Conradt, David P., Gerald R. Kleinfeld, George K. Romoser, and Christian Søe, eds. *Germany's New Politics: Parties and Issues in the 1990s.* Modern German Studies, No. 1. Providence, Rhode Island: Berghahn Books, 1995.

Craig, Gordon A. "Democratic Progress and Shadows of the Past." Pages 19–32 in *Forty Years of the Grundgesetz (Basic Law).* Occasional Papers, No. 1. Washington: German Historical Institute, 1990.

Currie, David P. *The Constitution of the Federal Republic of Germany.* Chicago: University of Chicago Press, 1994.

Currie, David P. "Separation of Powers in the Federal Republic of Germany," *American Journal of Comparative Law,* 41, Spring 1993, 201–60.

Dalton, Russell J. *Politics in Germany.* 2d ed. New York: Harper Collins, 1993.

Dalton, Russell J., ed. *The New Germany Votes: Unification and the Creation of the New German Party System.* Providence, Rhode Island: Berg, 1993.

Donfried, Karen E. "Germany: Electoral Trends and Implications for the United States." CRS Report 95–240F. Washington: Library of Congress, Congressional Research Service, February 1, 1995.

Donfried, Karen E. "Germany: Right-Wing Violence." CRS Report 92–363F. Washington: Library of Congress, Congressional Research Service, March 29, 1993.

Donfried, Karen E. "West European Electoral Trends." CRS Report 92–599F. Washington: Library of Congress, Congressional Research Service, July 22, 1992.

Federal Republic of Germany. *Basic Law of the Federal Republic of Germany.* Bonn: Press and Information Office, 1981.

Frankland, E. Gene, and Donald Schoonmaker. *Between Protest and Power: The Green Party in Germany.* Boulder, Colorado: Westview Press, 1992.

Garton Ash, Timothy. "Kohl's Germany: The Beginning of the End?" *New York Review of Books,* 41, No. 20, December 1, 1994, 20–24.

Hancock, M. Donald. "The Ambivalent Insider: The DGB Between Theory and Reality." Pages 178–92 in Peter H. Merkl, ed., *The Federal Republic of Germany at Forty.* New York: New York University Press, 1989.

Hübner, Emil, and Horst-Hennek Rohlfs. *Jahrbuch der Bundesrepublik Deutschland, 1992–93.* Munich: Beck/Deutscher Taschenbuch Verlag, 1992.

Huelshoff, Michael, Andrei S. Markovits, and Simon Reich, eds. *From Bundesrepublik to Deutschland: German Politics after Unification.* Ann Arbor: University of Michigan Press, 1993.

Irving, R.E.M., and W.E. Paterson. "The 1990 German General Election," *Parliamentary Affairs* [Liverpool], 44, No. 3, July 1991, 353–72.

Kappler, Arno, and Adriane Grevel, eds. *Facts about Germany.* Frankfurt am Main: Societäts-Verlag, 1994.

Keesing's Record of World Events [Cambridge], 40, No. 10, 1994, 40237.

Keesing's Record of World Events [Cambridge], 40, No. 11, 1994, 40292.

Keesing's Record of World Events [Cambridge], 41, No. 2, 1995, 40424.

Keesing's Record of World Events [Cambridge], 41, No. 4, 1995, 40561.

Kielmansegg, Peter Graf. "The Basic Law—Response to the Past or Design for the Future?" Pages 5–18 in *Forty Years of the Grundgesetz (Basic Law).* Occasional Papers, No. 1. Washington: German Historical Institute, 1990.

Kirchhof, Paul, and Donald P. Kommers, eds. *Germany and Its Basic Law.* Baden-Baden: Nomos, 1993.

Landfried, Christine. "Judicial Policy-Making in Germany: The Federal Constitutional Court," *West European Politics* [London], 15, No. 3, July 1992, 50–67.

Markovits, Andrei S., and Philip S. Gorski. *The German Left: Red, Green, and Beyond.* New York: Oxford University Press, 1993.

Markovits, Andrei S., and Alexander Otto. "German Labor and Europe '92," *Comparative Politics,* 24, No. 2, January 1992, 163–80.

Merkl, Peter, ed. *The Federal Republic of Germany at Forty.* New York: New York University Press, 1989.

Padgett, Stephen, ed. *Parties and Party Systems in the New Germany.* Aldershot, Hampshire, United Kingdom: Dartmouth, 1993.

Phillips, Ann L. *Transformation of the SED? The PDS One Year Later.* Berichte des Bundesinstituts für ostwissenschaftliche und internationale Studien [Cologne], No. 42, 1991.

Pulzer, Peter. "Unified Germany: A Normal State?" *German Politics* [London], 3, No. 1, April 1994, 1–17.

Reilly, Barbara. "Private Broadcasting in the Federal Republic of Germany." Pages 123–34 in Gale A. Mattox and A. Bradley Shingleton, eds., *Germany at the Crossroads: Foreign and Domestic Policy Issues.* Boulder, Colorado: Westview Press, 1992.

Roberts, Geoffrey K. "The German Party System in Crisis," *Parliamentary Affairs* [Liverpool], 48, No. 1, January 1995, 125–40.

Rohlfs, Horst-Hennek, and Ursel Schäfer. *Jahrbuch der Bundesrepublik Deutschland, 1993–94.* Munich: Beck/Deutscher Taschenbuch Verlag, 1993.

Rusciano, Frank Louis. "Rethinking the Gender Gap: The Case of West German Elections, 1949–1987," *Comparative Politics*, 24, No. 3, April 1992, 335–57.

Saalfeld, Thomas. "The West German Bundestag after 40 Years: The Role of Parliament in a 'Party Democracy,'" *West European Politics* [London], 13, No. 3, July 1990, 68–89.

Schatz, Heribert. "Massenmedien in der Bundesrepublik Deutschland." Pages 389–401 in Hartmut Zimmerman and Werner Weidenfeld, eds., *Deutschland-Handbuch: Eine Doppelte Bilanz, 1949–1989.* Munich: Carl Hanser Verlag, 1989.

Schmidt, Manfred G. "Political Consequences of German Unification," *West European Politics* [London], 15, No. 4, October 1992, 1–15.

Schmidt-Eichstätt, Gerd. "Vom Zentralismus zur kommunalen Selbstverwaltung," *Die Politische Meinung* [Sankt Augustin, Germany], 270, May 1992, 75–81.

Smith, Gordon, William E. Paterson, Peter H. Merkl, and Stephen Padgett, eds. *Developments in German Politics.* Durham: Duke University Press, 1992.

Thaysen, Uwe, Roger H. Davidson, and Robert Gerald Livingston, eds. *The United States Congress and the German Bundestag: Comparisons of Democratic Processes.* Boulder, Colorado: Westview Press, 1990.

Veen, Hans-Joachim, Norbert Lepszy, and Peter Mnich. *The Republikaner Party in Germany: Right-Wing Menace or Protest Catchall?* The Washington Papers, No. 162. Westport, Connecticut: Praeger, 1993.

(Various issues of the following periodicals were also used in the preparation of this chapter: *Bayernkurier* [Munich]; *Deutschland Nachrichten*; *Financial Times* [London]; *Frankfurter Allgemeine Zeitung* [Frankfurt am Main]; *German Tribune*; *International Herald Tribune* [Paris]; *Keesing's Record of World Events* [Cambridge]; *New York Times*; *Der Spiegel* [Hamburg]; *Süd-*

deutsche Zeitung [Munich]; *Washington Post; Week in Germany;* and *Die Zeit* [Hamburg].)

Chapter 8

Asmus, Ronald A. *Germany in Transition: National Self-Confidence and International Reticence.* Santa Monica, California: Rand Corporation, 1992.

Asmus, Ronald A. *Germany's Geopolitical Maturation: Strategy and Public Opinion after the Wall.* Santa Monica, California: Rand Corporation, 1993.

Baring, Arnulf, ed. *Germany's Position in the New Europe: Problems and Perspectives.* Providence, Rhode Island: Berg, 1994.

Berghahn, Volker R. *Imperial Germany, 1871–1914: Economy, Society, Culture, and Politics.* Providence, Rhode Island: Berghahn, 1994.

Bergsdorf, Werner. *Deutschland im Stress: Politische und gesell-schaftliche Herausforderungen nach der Wende.* Bonn: Aktuell, 1993.

Boutros-Ghali, Boutros. "Empowering the United Nations," *Foreign Affairs,* 72, No. 5, Winter 1992–93, 89–102.

Calleo, David P. *The German Problem Reconsidered: Germany and the World Order, 1870 to the Present.* Cambridge: Cambridge University Press, 1978.

Conradt, David P. *The German Polity.* 5th ed. New York: Longman, 1993.

Fest, Joachim. "Europe in a Cul-de-sac." Pages 51–64 in Arnulf Baring, ed., *Germany's New Position in Europe: Problems and Perspectives.* Providence, Rhode Island: Berg, 1994.

Gann, L.H., and Peter Duignan. *Germany: Key to a New Continent.* Essays in Public Policy Series. Stanford, California: Hoover Institution, 1992.

Garton Ash, Timothy. "Germany's Choice," *Foreign Affairs,* 73, No. 4, July 1994, 65–81.

Garton Ash, Timothy. *In Europe's Name: Germany and the Divided Continent.* New York: Random House, 1994.

Gedmin, Jeffrey. *The Hidden Hand: Gorbachev and the Collapse of East Germany.* Washington: American Enterprise Institute, 1992.

Gillessen, Günther. "Germany's Position in the Centre of Europe: The Significance of Germany's Position and Misunderstandings about German Interests." Pages 21–33 in Arnulf Baring, ed., *Germany's New Position in Europe: Problems and Perspectives.* Providence, Rhode Island: Berg, 1994.

Glaesser, Gert-Joachim, ed. *Die DDR in der Ära Honecker.* West Berlin: Westdeutscher Verlag, 1988.

Goldstein, Walter. "Europe after Maastricht," *Foreign Affairs,* 72, No. 5, Winter 1992–93, 117–32.

Gordon, Philip H. *France, Germany, and the Western Alliance.* Boulder, Colorado: Westview Press, 1995.

Gordon, Philip H. "The Normalization of German Foreign Policy," *Orbis,* 39, No. 2, Spring 1994, 225–43.

Hamilton, Daniel. *Beyond Bonn: America and the Berlin Republic.* Washington: Carnegie Endowment for International Peace, 1994.

Hanrieder, Wolfram F. *Germany, America, Europe: Forty Years of German Foreign Policy.* New Haven: Yale University Press, 1989.

Hoffman, Hilmar, and Dieter Kramer, eds. *Der Umbau Europas: Deutsche Einheit und europäische Integration.* Frankfurt am Main: Fischer, 1991.

Johnsen, William T., and Thomas-Durrell Young. *Franco-German Security Accommodation: Illusion of Agreement.* Carlisle Barracks, Pennsylvania: Strategic Studies Institute, United States Army War College, January 1993.

Kaiser, Karl. "Germany's Unification," *Foreign Policy,* 70, No. 1, Winter 1990–91, 179–205.

Kaiser, Karl, and Hanns W. Maull, eds. *Deutschlands neue Aussenpolitik.* Munich: R. Oldenbourg, 1994.

Kappler, Arno, and Adriane Grevel, eds. *Facts about Germany.* Frankfurt am Main: Societäts-Verlag, 1994.

Kelleher, Catherine McArdle. "The New Germany: An Overview." Pages 11–54 in Paul B. Stares, ed., *The New Germany and the New Europe.* Washington: Brookings Institution, 1992.

Koch, Burkhard. *Germany: New Assertiveness in International Relations Between Reality and Misperception.* Essays in Public Policy Series. Stanford, California: Hoover Institution, 1992.

Kramer, Heinz. "The E.C. and the Stabilization of Eastern Europe," *Aussenpolitik* [Hamburg], 43, No. 1, 1992, 12–21.

587

Linnenkamp, Hilmar. "The Security Policy of the New Germany." Pages 93–125 in Paul B. Stares, ed., *The New Germany and the New Europe.* Washington: Brookings Institution, 1992.

Müller, Harald. "German Foreign Policy after Unification." Pages 126–73 in Paul B. Stares, ed., *The New Germany and the New Europe.* Washington: Brookings Institution, 1992.

Paterson, William E. "Gulliver Unbound: The Changing Context of Foreign Policy." Pages 137–52 in Gordon Smith, William E. Paterson, Peter H. Merkl, and Stephen Padgett, eds., *Developments in German Politics.* Durham: Duke University Press, 1992.

Pond, Elizabeth. *Beyond the Wall: Germany's Road to Unification.* Washington: Brookings Institution, 1993.

Pond, Elizabeth. "Germany in the New Europe," *Foreign Affairs,* 71, No. 2, Spring 1992, 114–30.

Smith, Gordon, William E. Paterson, Peter H. Merkl, and Stephen Padgett, eds. *Developments in German Politics.* Durham: Duke University Press, 1992.

Smyser, W.R. *Germany and America: New Identities, Fateful Rift?* Boulder, Colorado: Westview Press, 1993.

Smyser, W.R. *Restive Partners: Washington and Bonn Diverge.* Boulder, Colorado: Westview Press, 1990.

Stares, Paul B., ed. *The New Germany and the New Europe.* Washington: Brookings Institution, 1992.

Stent, Angela. "The One Germany," *Foreign Policy,* No. 81, Winter 1990–91, 53–70.

Stuth, Reinhard. "Germany's New Role in a Changing Europe," *Aussenpolitik* [Hamburg], 43, No. 1, 1992, 22–32.

Szabo, Stephen F. *The Diplomacy of German Unification.* New York: St. Martin's Press, 1992.

Verheyen, Dirk, and Christian Søe, eds. *The Germans and Their Neighbors.* Boulder, Colorado: Westview Press, 1993.

Weiss, Thomas G. "New Challenges for U.N. Military Operations: Implementing an Agenda for Peace," *Washington Quarterly,* 16, No. 1, Winter 1993, 51–66.

Zelikow, Philip, and Condoleezza Rice. *Germany Unified and Europe Transformed: A Study in Statecraft.* Cambridge: Harvard University Press, 1995.

(Various issues of the following periodicals were also used in the preparation of this chapter: *Economist* [London]; *Frankfurter*

Allgemeine Zeitung [Frankfurt am Main]; *NATO's Sixteen Nations* [Brussels]; *This Week in Germany*; and *Die Zeit* [Hamburg]).

Chapter 9

Abenheim, Donald. *Reforging the Iron Cross: The Search for Tradition in the West German Armed Forces.* Princeton: Princeton University Press, 1988.

Ardagh, John. *Germany and the Germans.* Rev. ed. New York: Penguin Books USA, 1991.

Brauch, Hans Günter. "German Unity, Conventional Disarmament, Confidence-Building Defense, and a New European Order of Peace and Security." Pages 3–44 in Hans Günter Brauch and Robert Kennedy, eds., *Alternative Conventional Defense Postures in the European Theater: The Impact of Political Change on Strategy, Technology, and Arms Control.* New York: Crane Russak, 1992.

Braun, Dieter F. "The New German Navy Moves Out," *United States Naval Institute Proceedings,* 117, No. 3, March 1991, 53–60.

Childs, David. *Germany in the Twentieth Century.* New York: Harper Collins, 1991.

Childs, David, and Jeffrey Johnson. *West Germany: Politics and Society.* New York, St. Martin's Press, 1981.

Cooper, Mary H. "NATO's Changing Role," *CQ Researcher,* 31, No. 2, August 21, 1992, 713–36.

Copley, Gregory R., ed. *Defense and Foreign Affairs Handbook, 1990–1991.* Alexandria, Virginia: International Media, 1990.

Craig, Gordon A. *The Battle of Königgrätz: Prussia's Victory over Austria, 1886.* Westport, Connecticut: Greenwood Press, 1975.

Craig, Gordon A. *The Politics of the Prussian Army, 1640–1945.* New York: Oxford University Press, 1956.

Dobias, Tibor, ed. *Militärgeschichte der BRD: Abriss 1949 bis zur Gegenwart.* East Berlin: Militärverlag der Deutschen Demokratischen Republik, 1989.

Donfried, Karen E. "The Franco-German Eurocorps: Implications for the U.S. Security Role in Europe." CRS Report 92–599F. Washington: Library of Congress, Congressional Research Service, July 22, 1992.

Fairchild, Erika S. *German Police: Ideals and Reality in the Post-War Years.* Springfield, Illinois: Charles C. Thomas, 1988.

Federal Republic of Germany. Federal Ministry of Defence. *White Paper 1985: The Situation and the Development of the Federal Armed Forces.* Bonn: 1985.

Fulbrook, Mary. *A Concise History of Germany.* Cambridge: Cambridge University Press, 1990.

Gordon, Joseph S. "The GDR: From Volksarmee to Bundeswehr." Pages 157–88 in Jeffrey Simon, ed., *European Security Policy after the Revolutions of 1989.* Washington: National Defense University Press, 1991.

Gordon, Philip H. *France, Germany, and the Western Alliance.* Boulder, Colorado: Westview Press, 1995.

Hagland, David G., and Olaf Mager, eds. *Homeward Bound? Allied Forces in the New Germany.* Boulder, Colorado: Westview Press, 1992.

Hahne, Wolfgang. "The Impact of German Unification on the Future of the German Armor Forces," *Armor,* 101, No. 2, March–April 1992, 37–42.

Hansen, Helge. "Germany," *Military Technology* [Bonn], 16, No. 6, June 1992, 43–49.

Hormann, Jörg M. *Die Bundeswehr und ihre Uniformen: 30 Jahre Bekleidungsgeschichte.* Friedburg, West Germany: Podzun-Pallas, 1987.

Hyde-Price, Adrian. "Country Survey: Germany," *Jane's Defence Weekly* [London], 16, No. 14, October 5, 1991, 605–20.

Hyde-Price, Adrian. "Uncertainties of Security Policy." Pages 153–71 in Gordon Smith, William E. Paterson, Peter H. Merkl, and Stephen Padgett, eds., *Developments in German Politics.* Durham: Duke University Press, 1992.

Jane's Fighting Ships, 1992–93. Ed., Richard Sharpe. Alexandria, Virginia: Jane's Information Group, 1992.

Jane's Fighting Ships, 1993–94. Ed., Richard Sharpe. Alexandria, Virginia: Jane's Information Group, 1993.

Jane's Fighting Ships, 1994–95. Ed., Richard Sharpe. Alexandria, Virginia: Jane's Information Group, 1994.

Jane's NATO Handbook, 1991–92. Ed., Bruce George. Coulsdon, Surrey, United Kingdom: Jane's Information Group, 1991.

Jopp, Mathias. *The Strategic Implications of European Integration.* Adelphi Paper No. 290. London: Brassey's for International Institute for Strategic Studies, July 1994.

Keegan, John. "German Federal Republic." Pages 206–15 in John Keegan, ed., *World Armies.* 2d ed. Detroit: Gale Research, 1983.

Kuebart, Hans-Jörg. "The Future German Air Force—Tasks, Execution, and Structure," *NATO's Sixteen Nations* [Brussels], 36, No. 6, November 1991, 88–105.

Mechtersheimer, Alfred, and Peter Barth, eds. *Militarisierungs-atlas der Bundesrepublik: Streitkräfte, Waffen under Standorte: Kosten und Risiken.* Darmstadt, West Germany: Hermann Luchterhand, 1986.

The Military Balance, 1994–1995. London: Brassey's for International Institute for Strategic Studies, 1994.

The Military Balance, 1995–1996. London: Oxford University Press for International Institute for Strategic Studies, 1995.

Millotat, Christian O.E. *Understanding the Prussian-German General Staff System.* Carlisle Barracks, Pennsylvania: Strategic Studies Institute, United States Army War College, 1992.

Naumann, Klaus Dieter. "Mission and Structure of the Bundeswehr," *NATO's Sixteen Nations* [Brussels], 36, No. 6, November 1991, 56–71.

The Naval Institute Guide to Combat Fleets of the World, 1995: Their Ships, Aircraft, and Armament. Ed., A.D. Baker III. Annapolis: Naval Institute Press, 1995.

Nienaber, Klaus. "German Navy 2005—A Plan for a Smaller Navy," *Maritime Defence* [East Molesey, Surrey, United Kingdom], 17, No. 1, January 1992, 25–26.

Paret, Peter, Gordon A. Craig, and Felix Gilbert, eds. *Makers of Modern Strategy: From Machiavelli to the Nuclear Age.* Princeton: Princeton University Press, 1986.

Rempel, Roy. "German Security Policy in the New European Order." Pages 159–96 in Alexander Moens and Christopher Anstis, eds., *Disconcerted Europe: The Search for a New Security Architecture.* Boulder, Colorado: Westview Press, 1994.

Rennagel, William C. "West Germany." Pages 104–27 in Richard A. Gabriel, ed., *Fighting Armies: NATO and the Warsaw Pact: A Combat Assessment.* Westport, Connecticut: Greenwood, 1983.

Roach, John, and Jürgen Thomanech, eds. *Police and Public Order in Europe.* London: Croom Helm, 1985.

Roos, John G. "An Exclusive AFJI Interview with: Lt. Gen. Jörg Kuebert, Chief of Staff of the German Air Force," *Armed Forces Journal International,* December 1991, 48–50.

Ruppelt, Wolfgang. "Procurement—Plans, Projects, and Problems," *NATO's Sixteen Nations* [Brussels], 36, No. 6, November 1991, 37–51.

Scheven, Werner von. "The Merger of Two Formerly Hostile German Armies," *Aussenpolitik* [Hamburg] 43, No. 2, 1992, 164–73.

Schlör, Wolfgang F. *German Security Policy.* Adelphi Paper No. 277. London: Brassey's for International Institute for Strategic Studies, June 1993.

Schönbohm, Jörg. "Bundeswehrkommando-Ost—A Memorable Year," *NATO's Sixteen Nations* [Brussels], 36, No. 6, November 1991, 120–35.

Schönbohm, Jörg. "The New Structure of the German Army," *NATO's Sixteen Nations* [Brussels], 36, No. 6, November 1991, 72–87.

Schulte, Heinz. "Luftwaffe Spreads Its Wings But Reduces Aircraft," *Jane's Defence Weekly* [London], 18, No. 16, October 10, 1992, 24.

Schulte, Heinz. "What Happened to the East German Armed Forces?" *Jane's Intelligence Review* [London], 4, No. 4, April 1992, 185–87.

Schulz, Siegfried. *Das deutsche Heer Heute.* Herford, West Germany: S. Mittler und Sohn, 1978.

Sielaff, Wolfgang. "Organized Criminal Activity in the Federal Republic of Germany," *Police Chief,* 59, No. 11, November 1988, 76–79.

Stares, Paul B. *Allied Rights and Legal Constraints on German Military Power.* Washington: Brookings Institution, 1990.

"A Strange Lack of Sergeants," *Economist* [London], 310, No. 7585, January 14, 1989, 47–48.

Szabo, Stephen F., ed. *The Bundeswehr and Western Security.* London: Macmillan, 1990.

Thomaneck, Jürgen. "Germany." Pages 143–84 in John Roach and Jürgen Thomaneck, eds., *Police and Public Order in Europe.* London: Croom Helm, 1985.

Thompson, Wayne C. "The Federal Republic of Germany." Pages 8–101 in Wayne C. Thompson, ed., *Western Europe, 1991*. Washington: Stryker-Post, 1992.

United States. Arms Control and Disarmament Agency. *World Military Expenditures and Arms Transfers, 1993–1994*. Washington: GPO, 1995.

United States. Department of State. *Background Notes: Germany*. Department of State Publication No. 7834. Washington: GPO, 1995.

United States. Department of State. *Country Reports on Human Rights Practices for 1993*. Report submitted to United States Congress, 103d, 2d Session, House of Representatives, Committee on Foreign Affairs, and Senate, Committee on Foreign Relations. Washington: GPO, 1994.

United States. Department of State. *Patterns of Global Terrorism, 1994*. Washington: 1995.

Van Orden, Geoffrey. "The Bundeswehr in Transition," *Survival* [London], 33, No. 4, July–August 1991, 352–70.

Weiss, James D. "Through the Ranks in West Germany's Polizei," *Law and Order*, 37, No. 12, December 1989, 34–39.

Weiss, Jim. "Bereitschaftspolizei: Organization, Training, and in the Field with Federal Germany's Emergency Police," *Law and Order*, 39, No. 8, August 1991, 60–63.

Weyher, Hein-Peter. "The German Navy on Its Way Ahead," *NATO's Sixteen Nations* [Brussels], 37, No. 1, January 1992, 28–33.

Young, Thomas-Durell. *The "Normalization" of the Federal Republic of Germany's Defense Structures*. Carlisle Barracks, Pennsylvania: Strategic Studies Institute, United States Army War College, 1992.

Young, Thomas-Durell. *Trends in German Defense Policy: The Defense Policy Guidelines and the Centralization of Operational Control*. Carlisle Barracks, Pennsylvania: Strategic Studies Institute, United States Army War College, 1994.

Glossary

alb—A flat or gently inclined shelf high in a glaciated mountain valley.

Bretton Woods system—The global financial and monetary system established in 1944 at the New Hampshire resort of Bretton Woods. It created the World Bank (*q.v.*) and the International Monetary Fund (*q.v.*), as well as a fixed link between the United States dollar and gold at US$35 per troy ounce. The system collapsed in 1971, when the link between the dollar and gold was broken, but the institutions survive.

Bundesbank—The German central bank, with headquarters in Frankfurt am Main, was established in 1957.

Central Bank Council—The seventeen-member decision-making body of the Bundesbank (*q.v*). The council includes the presidents of the *Land* central banks (*q.v.*) and the members of the Directorate (*q.v.*). The council meets every second Thursday.

Common Agricultural Policy (CAP)—First established in 1962, the CAP aims at ensuring the free trade of farm products within the European Union (EU—*q.v.*), guaranteeing the prices of these products, and maintaining protective tariffs against farm products from outside the EU.

Commonwealth of Independent States (CIS)—Created on December 8, 1991, with the signing of the Minsk Agreement by Belarus, Russia, and Ukraine. The Alma-Ata Declaration, signed by eleven heads of state on December 21, 1991, expanded membership in the CIS to all other former Soviet republics except Estonia, Georgia, Latvia, and Lithuania. Moldova joined the CIS in April 1994. The CIS is a confederation of former Soviet republics in which "coordinating bodies" oversee common interests in the economy, foreign policy, and defense of its members.

Conference on Security and Cooperation in Europe (CSCE)—*See* Organization for Security and Cooperation in Europe (OSCE).

Conventional Forces in Europe Treaty (CFE Treaty)—An agreement signed in 1990 by the member nations of the Warsaw Pact (*q.v.*) and the North Atlantic Treaty Organization (NATO—*q.v.*) to establish parity in conventional weapons between the two organizations from the Atlantic to the Urals. The treaty included a strict system of inspection and information exchange and remained in force, although not strictly observed by all parties, in the mid-1990s.

deutsche mark (DM)—The national currency unit, consisting of 100 pfennigs. The value of the deutsche mark has fluctuated with international monetary developments—generally upward since its introduction in the currency reform of 1948. The number of deutsche marks per US$1 averaged 4.20 in 1950, 4.20 in 1960, 4.00 in 1965, 3.65 in 1970, 2.62 in 1975, 1.96 in 1980, 2.94 in 1985, 1.62 in 1990, 1.56 in 1992, 1.65 in 1993, 1.64 in 1994, and 1.43 in 1995.

Directorate—The eight-member executive board of the Bundesbank (*q.v.*). Its members sit on the Central Bank Council (*q.v.*).

discount rate—Interest rate at which the Bundesbank (*q.v.*) lends to banks by rediscounting trade bills and treasury bills falling due within three months.

European Commission—A governing body of the European Union (EU—*q.v.*) that oversees the organization's treaties, recommends actions under the treaties, and issues independent decisions on EU matters.

European Community (EC)—A grouping of three primarily economic organizations: the European Economic Community (EEC), the European Atomic Energy Community (Euratom or EAEC), and the European Coal and Steel Community (ECSC). Founded separately in 1952 and 1957, the three came to be known collectively as the EC. Executive power rests with the European Commission (*q.v.*). Members in 1993 were Belgium, Britain, Denmark, France, Germany, Greece, Ireland, Italy, Luxembourg, the Netherlands, Portugal, and Spain. In November 1993, the EC was subsumed under a new organization, the European Union (EU—*q.v.*).

European Council—A body formed when the heads of state or government of European Union (EU—*q.v.*) member states meet. Held at least twice a year, these meetings determine the major guidelines for the EU's future development.

European currency unit (ECU)—Established in 1979 as a composite of the monetary systems of European Community (EC—*q.v.*) member nations, the ECU functions in the

European Monetary System (EMS—*q.v.*) and serves as the unit for exchange-rate establishment, credit and intervention operations, and settlements between monetary authorities of member nations.

European Economic Area (EEA)—An economic area encompassing all the members of the European Union (EU—*q.v.*) and the European Free Trade Association (EFTA—*q.v.*), with the exception of Switzerland. Established in 1993, the EEA went into effect on January 1, 1994. The EEA is a single market for the free movement of labor, services, capital (with some restrictions on investments), and most products. EFTA members have agreed to accept EU regulations in many areas, including company law, education, environmental protection, mergers, and social policy.

European Economic Community (EEC)—*See* European Community (EC).

European Free Trade Association (EFTA)—Founded in 1960, EFTA aims at supporting free trade among its members and increasing the liberalization of trade on a global basis, particularly within Western Europe. In 1995 the organization's member states were Iceland, Liechtenstein, Norway, and Switzerland.

European Monetary System (EMS)—Established in 1979 by the European Economic Community (EEC—*q.v.*), the EMS was created to stabilize currency values because the Bretton Woods system (*q.v.*) proved not fully satisfactory. All European Union (EU—*q.v.*) countries are EMS members. The EMS is to be succeeded by the European Monetary Union (EMU—*q.v.*).

European Monetary Union (EMU)—The EMU is a plan for a single European central bank and for a single European currency to replace national banks and currencies for those European states that qualify. The EMU is the planned follow-on of the European Monetary System (EMS—*q.v.*).

European Union (EU)—Successor organization to the European Community (EC—*q.v.*), officially established on November 1, 1993, when the Treaty on European Union (*q.v.*) went into effect. The goal of the EU is a closer economic union of it member states, including the European Monetary Union (EMU—*q.v*), a greater unity in matters of justice and domestic affairs, and the development of a common foreign and security policy. To the members of the EC, the EU added Austria, Finland, and Sweden, effective January 1, 1995.

exchange-rate mechanism (ERM)—A mechanism of the European Monetary System (EMS—*q.v.*), the ERM is designed to establish fixed exchange rates among EMS currencies. Not all European Union (EU—*q.v.*) states are members.

General Agreement on Tariffs and Trade (GATT)—The global trading system, based on the Havana Treaty of 1947, that obligates states to follow the "most favored nation" principle to avoid discriminatory trade practices. GATT was succeeded by the World Trade Organization (WTO) on January 1, 1996.

gross domestic product (GDP)—The total value of goods and services produced exclusively within a nation's domestic economy, in contrast to the gross national product (GNP—*q.v.*). Usually computed over a one-year period.

gross national product (GNP)—The total value of goods and services produced within a country's borders and the income received from abroad by residents, minus payments remitted abroad by nonresidents. Usually computed over a one-year period.

Group of Seven (G–7)—The seven-nation organization was established in 1973, with an annual summit beginning in 1975, to attempt to coordinate its members' economic policies. Members are Britain, Canada, France, Germany, Italy, Japan, and the United States.

International Monetary Fund (IMF)—Established along with the World Bank (*q.v.*) in 1945, the IMF is a specialized agency affiliated with the United Nations that takes responsibility for stabilizing international exchange rates and payments. The main business of the IMF is the provision of loans to its members when they experience balance of payments difficulties. These loans often carry conditions that require substantial internal economic adjustments by the recipients.

Land central bank—The central bank of a German state (*Land*; pl., *Länder*) or group of *Länder*. The presidents of the nine *Land* central banks sit on the Central Bank Council (*q.v.*) of the Bundesbank (*q.v.*).

Lombard rate—The interest rate at which the Bundesbank (*q.v.*) extends credit to commercial banks in order to cover temporary financing gaps. It is usually somewhat higher than the Bundesbank's discount rate (*q.v.*).

Maastricht Treaty—*See* Treaty on European Union.

nomenklatura—The communist party's system of appointing key personnel in the government and other important organizations, based on lists of critical positions and people in political favor. Also refers to the individuals included on these lists.

North Atlantic Treaty Organization (NATO)—Frequently called, particularly in official NATO publications, the Atlantic Alliance or the Alliance. Created as a defensive political and military alliance by the signing of the North Atlantic Treaty in April 1949, with twelve charter members: Belgium, Britain, Canada, Denmark, France, Iceland, Italy, Luxembourg, the Netherlands, Norway, Portugal, and the United States. Greece and Turkey became members in 1952, the Federal Republic of Germany in 1955, and Spain in 1982.

Organisation for Economic Co-operation and Development (OECD)—Established in 1961 to replace the Organisation for European Economic Co-operation (OEEC), the OECD is an international organization composed of the industrialized market economy countries, as well as some developing countries, by providing a forum in which to establish and coordinate policies.

Organisation for European Economic Co-operation (OEEC)— *See* Organisation for Economic Co-operation and Development (OECD).

Organization for Security and Cooperation in Europe (OSCE)—The Conference on Security and Cooperation Europe (CSCE) was established as an international process in 1972. The group, consisting of fifty-three nations in 1995, included all the European countries and sponsored joint sessions and consultations on political issues vital to European security. The Charter of Paris (1990) changed the CSCE from an ad hoc forum to an organization having permanent institutions. In 1992 new CSCE roles in conflict prevention and management were defined, potentially making the CSCE the center of a Europe-based collective security system. In the early 1990s, however, applications of these instruments to conflicts in Yugoslavia and the Caucasus did not have a decisive impact. In January 1995, the CSCE was renamed the Organization for Security and Cooperation in Europe (OSCE).

Treaty on European Union—The agreement that established

the European Union (EU—*q.v.*) in November 1993. It is usually referred to as the Maastricht Treaty, the small Dutch town where it was negotiated by the twelve European Community (EC—*q.v.*) members in December 1991.

Uruguay Round—The trade negotiating round, under the auspices of the General Agreement on Tariffs and Trade (GATT—*q.v.*), concluded at the end of 1993. It pitted the United States against France and some other European Union (EU—*q.v.*) states over EU agricultural subsidies, with Germany in the middle. A compromise was reached, including agreement for establishing a World Trade Organization (WTO). On January 1, 1996, GATT was succeeded by the WTO.

value-added tax (VAT)—A tax applied to the additional value created at a given stage of production and calculated as a percentage of the difference between the product value at that stage and the cost of all materials and services purchased as inputs. The VAT is the primary form of indirect taxation applied in the European Union (EU—*q.v.*), and it is the basis of each country's contribution to the community budget.

Warsaw Pact—Informal name for the Warsaw Treaty Organization, a mutual defense organization founded in 1955, which included the Soviet Union, Albania (which withdrew in 1968), Bulgaria, Czechoslovakia, the German Democratic Republic (GDR, or East Germany), Hungary, Poland, and Romania. The Warsaw Pact enabled the Soviet Union to station troops in the countries to its west to oppose the forces of the North Atlantic Treaty Organization (NATO—*q.v.*). The pact was the basis of the invasion of Hungary (1956) and of Czechoslovakia (1968); it was disbanded in July 1991.

Western European Union (WEU)—Founded in 1948 to facilitate West European cooperation in economic, social, cultural, and defense matters. Reactivated in 1984 to concentrate on the defense and disarmament concerns of its members, the WEU is headed by a council consisting of its members' ministers of foreign affairs and defense. The council meets twice a year; lower-level WEU entities meet with greater frequency. In 1995 WEU members were Belgium, Britain, France, Germany, Greece, Italy, Luxembourg, the Netherlands, Portugal, and Spain. Austria, Denmark, Finland, Ireland, and Sweden were observers;

Iceland, Norway, and Turkey were associate members; and a number of East European states were associate partners.

World Bank—Informal name for a group of four affiliated international institutions: the International Bank for Reconstruction and Development (IBRD); the International Development Association (IDA); the International Finance Corporation (IFC); and the Multilateral Investment Guarantee Agency (MIGA). The four institutions are owned by the governments of the countries that subscribe their capital for credit and investment in developing countries; each institution has a specialized agenda for aiding economic growth in target countries.

Index

lapsed, 174, 175; number of, 176; political parties of, 42; practicing, 176

CDU. *See* Christian Democratic Union

Center Party, xli, 42–43, 45, 91; constituency of, 42; in elections of 1930, 59; in elections of 1932, 59; platform of, 42; in Weimar coalition, 50, 53, 56

Central Bank Council, 291; members of, 291–92

Central German Uplands, 136–40; climate of, 142; elevation of, 136

CFE. *See* Conventional Forces in Europe

CFE Treaty. *See* Conventional Forces in Europe Treaty

Chamberlain, Neville, 64

chambers of commerce, 275–76

chancellor: armed forces under, 471; authority of, 353; under Basic Law, 88, 353–56, 431; economic policy under, 267, 268; election of, 254, 359; vote of no-confidence against, 354; in Weimar Republic, 50

Charlemagne (768–814), xxxix–xl, 3, 7–8, 463

Charles V: elected, 16; opposition of, to Lutheranism, 21

Charles VI (1711–40), 26

chemical industry, 44, 286, 287–88, 317; and European Single Market, 320; exports by, 337

Chemicals, Paper, and Ceramics Workers' Union, 393

Chemnitz, 157; industry in, 286

Chernobyl accident, 146

child allowance, 207–8

child care: availability of, 134, 164, 167, 169, 211

children, 168; health insurance for, 213; pensions for, 207; support assistance for, 207

Christian Democratic Union (Christlich Demokratische Union—CDU), xliv, 43, 74, 375–78, 386; in Alliance for Germany, 126; in Anti-Fascist Bloc, 82; auxiliary organizations of, 377–78; in Bundestag, 375; in CDU/CSU-FDP coalition, xliv, xlv, 74, 114–16, 376, 381, 382, 401; economic philosophy of, 267; economy under, 257–58; in elections of 1965, 98; in elections of 1969, 106; in elections of 1990, 377; and foreign policy, 432; formed, 83;

375; funding of, 373; membership of, xliv–xlv, 374; organization of, 377; platform of, 197, 375, 394; and unification, 420; as *Volkspartei*, xliii–xliv, 375

Christianity *(see also under individual denominations)*: conversion to, 7; in East Germany, 173–74

Christian Social Union (Christlich Soziale Union—CSU), xliv, 43, 74, 375–78; in Bundestag, 375; in CDU/CSU-FDP coalition, xliv, xlv, 74, 114–16, 376, 381, 382, 401; economic philosophy of, 267; in elections of 1965, 98; in elections of 1969, 106; in elections of 1990, 377; in elections of 1994, 402; and foreign policy, 432; founded, 83; membership of, xliv–xlv, 375

Christian Study Group Mülheim/Ruhr, 179

Christlich Demokratische Union. *See* Christian Democratic Union

Christlich Soziale Union. *See* Christian Social Union

churches, 393–95; declining membership of, 174, 175; in East Germany, 122, 394; under Hitler, 62, 173, 393; kindergartens of, 231; legal status of, 394; as lobby, 393; social-welfare activities of, 175, 176, 177–78, 199; subsidies for, 176; support of dissidents by, xxxviii, 122, 394

churches, free, 178–79; membership in, 179; persecution of, 178; tenets of, 178–79

churches, orthodox, 179

Church of the Nazarene, 179

church tax, 174, 176, 177, 394

CIS. *See* Commonwealth of Independent States

citizenship: of ethnic Germans, 160; of foreigners, xlix, 160, 405, 407

citizens' initiative associations, 396–97; membership of, 396

citizens in uniform, 495

Civil Code (1900), 505

civil servants: career, 365–66; categories of, 365; number of, 185, 365; status of, 365

civil service, 185, 365–66; ban on extremists in, 366; of early states, 29; in German Empire, xli; under Hitler, 61; number of employees in, 185, 365; purged, 61; social insurance for, 201

Clausewitz, Karl von, 465

Clay, Lucius D., 86

clergy: power of, 13

climate, 142–45; continental, 144; *föhn*, 144; maritime, 142–44; precipitation, 145; temperature, 144

Clovis, 7

CNN, 401

coal, 250, 286, 288; exports of, 317; production, 44, 289; subsidies, 272, 273, 288

Coast Guard (Bundesgrenzschutz-See), 507

coastline: of North German Lowland, 135, 136

Code of Criminal Procedure, 511; under Third Reich, 506

codetermination *(Mitbestimmung)*, 282–83; labor in, 283, 393; management in, 283

Cold War, 467; foreign policy in, 418; origins of, 73, 467

Cologne: airport at, 302; elector of, 14; foreign residents in, 158; university in, 224

Colombia: matériel exported to, 500

colonies, 47; desire for, 45; relinquished, 49

Comecon. *See* Council for Mutual Economic Assistance

Commerzbank, 294, 295

Common Agricultural Policy (CAP), 248–49, 285, 319, 451

Commonwealth of Independent States (CIS): aid to, 430; petroleum imported from, 289

communications. *See* telecommunications

communism: threat of, 93

Communist Party of Germany (Kommunistische Partei Deutschlands—KPD), 53, 117; banned, 89, 374; in elections of 1930, 59; in elections of 1932, 59; growth of, 54; reestablished, 81

Communists: arrests of, 61; opposition to, 81

Concerted Action in Health Care, 215, 222

Concordat of Worms (1122), 11

Confederation of the Rhine, 31

Conference on Security and Cooperation in Europe (CSCE) (*see also* Organization for Security and Cooperation in Europe), 117–18; efforts to strengthen, 452–53; established, 451; Final Act of, 117; membership in, 417, 428, 453; and military action, 437, 441, 452, 453; Paris Charter, 452; support for, 452

Confessing Church, 173

Congress of Vienna (1815), xl, 4, 31; members of, 31; objectives of, 31

Conrad I (911–18), 3; election of, 8

Conrad II, 9–10

Conrad IV, 13

Conservative Party, 42, 45; constituency of, 42; platform of, 42

conservatives, 45

constitution of 1848, 37; committee for, 36

constitution of 1949. *See* Basic Law

constitution of Federal Republic of Germany (1949). *See* Basic Law

constitution of German Democratic Republic (1949): approved, 90; basic rights under, 90; communist party under, 421; drafted, 90

constitution of German Empire, 4

constitution of Weimar Republic, 50–53; drafted, 50

consumer goods: East German, 103

Conventional Forces in Europe (CFE): talks, 425

Conventional Forces in Europe Treaty (CFE Treaty) (1990), 460; armed forces under, 472

Council for Mutual Economic Assistance (Comecon), 102

Council of Economic Experts, 255

Council of Education, 228

Council of Europe: West Germany in, 93

Council of Ministers (Ministerrat), 90

Council of State (Staatsrat), 90

Counter-Reformation, 23–24

coups d'état, attempted, 56, 58; of 1920, 54

courts: administration of, 362; constitutional, 363, 364–65; criminal, 511–12; Federal Constitutional Court, 364–65; ordinary, 363–64; specialized, 363, 364

court system: in Third Reich, 506; trans-

1987, 384; in elections of 1990, 385; in elections of 1994, 403; factions within, 113–14, 384; and foreign policy, 434; formed, 146; platform of, 384; support for, 385; women in, 114

Gregorian calendar, 23

Gregory VII, Pope, 10–11

Greifswald nuclear power plant, 148

GRG. *See* Health Care Reform Act

gross domestic product (GDP), 309; of eastern Germany, 264; growth of, 254, 262, 264; in 1975, 256

gross domestic product fractions: agriculture, 248, 284; exports, 307, 317, 337; foreign assistance, 343; government debt, 274; government role in economy, 257; government spending, 274; health care, 214; investment, 261; research, 266; subsidies, 272

gross national product fractions: defense spending, 489, 490; education, 230; exports, 451; social services, 195, 203

Grotewohl, Otto, 81, 90

Group of Five, 308, 312

Group of Seven (G–7), 308, 312–13; aid to Russia by, 312, 430; meetings of, 268–69, 312–13; members of, 312; Russia in, 312, 339

Group of Soviet Forces in Germany, 502; personnel strength of, 459; withdrawal of, 460, 502

Gründerzeit (founders' time), 44

Grundgesetz. *See* Basic Law

Grundschule, 231, 239

Grünen, Die. *See* Greens

GSG. *See* Health Care Structural Reform Act

Guard Detachment (Schutz-Staffel—SS), 61, 506

Guelf family. *See* Welf family

guest workers *(Gastarbeiter)*, xliii, 281–82, 513; attacks on, xlvi; employment of, 182; number of, xlviii, 151; origins of, 151, 179, 449; recruitment of, xlix, 151, 158; resentment of, 387, 415, 510, 515

guilds, 249, 250, 389

Guillaume, Günter, 107

Gustavus Adolphus, 24

Gymnasium, 233, 234, 239; curriculum for, 225; educational tracks in, 225; number of, 234; reorganization of,

228

Gymnasium Oberstufe, 234

Gypsies, 162

Gysi, Gregor, 388, 389

Habsburg Dynasty, xl, 14, 19

Halle: industry in, 286

Hallstein, Walter, 95

Hallstein Doctrine, 95, 98, 107

Hamburg: airport at, 302; foreign residents in, 158; government in, 368; housing prices in, 171; political parties in, 83; population of, 156; population density of, 155; population loss in, 157; port of, 302; topography of, 135; university in, 225

Handel, George Frederick, 30

Handelsblatt, 398

Hanover, 139, 157; annexed by Prussia, 39; industry in, 286

Hanseatic League, 15

Hardenberg, Karl August von, 30, 118

Hardt Mountains, 140

Harmel Report (1967), 439

Hartmannbund, 213

Hauptschule, 228, 233; curriculum of, 233

Havel, Vaclav, 441

Haydn, Franz Joseph, 30

health (*see also* sickness): public, 217, 222

health care, 201, 202, 211–23; administration of, 213; benefits, 214; budget, 221; copayments for, 214, 215; cost containment, 221; cost per capita, 214; dental, 214, 217; East German, 223; issues in, 222–23; as percentage of gross domestic product, 214; preventive, 222; providers, 217–20; right to, 214; spending on, 195, 203, 215; visits for, 218; for women, 211, 214

health care professionals, 217; hospital based, 218–19; income of, 218; number of, 217–18; office-based, 218–19; professional associations for, 213; remuneration for, 213, 218, 220–22; training for, 220; unemployment of, 218; women as, 166

Health Care Reform Act (1989) (Gesundheitsreformgesetz—GRG), 215

Health Care Structural Reform Act (1993) (Gesundheitsstrukturgesetz—

Mittelschule, 225

Mitterrand, François, 321–22, 420, 476

modernization: of economy, 264–67; problems with, 265–66, 267

Modrow, Hans, 126, 421, 422

Monopolkommission, 295

Moravia: economic links with, 339; under Frederick I, 12; occupied by Hitler, 64

Morgenthau Plan, 79

Morocco: guest workers from, 151

Moselle River, 142

Moselle River Valley, 139; tourism in, 303

Motoren und Turbinen Union (MTU), 500

Mozambique: guest workers from, 158

Mozart, Wolfgang Amadeus, 30

MTU. *See* Motoren und Turbinen Union

Müller, Ludwig, 173

Munich, 141; airport at, 302; housing prices in, 171; industry in, 286; population of, 156; university in, 225

Muslims (*see also* Islam): number of, xlix, 180, 516

NACC. *See* North Atlantic Cooperation Council

Napoleon, xl, 31

Napoleonic Code, 31, 505

National Assembly, 36

national debt. *See* government debt

National Democratic Party of Germany (National-Demokratische Partei Deutschlands—NDPD) (GDR), 82; former Nazis in, 82

National Democratic Party of Germany (Nationaldemokratische Partei Deutschlands—NPD) (FRG): support for, 98

National-Demokratische Partei Deutschlands (NDPD). *See* National Democratic Party of Germany

Nationaldemokratische Partei Deutschlands (NPD). *See* National Democratic Party of Germany

Nationale Volksarmee. *See* National People's Army

National Front, 90

national identity: of East Germany, 118–19; search for, 189–91

National Insurance Code (1923): health

care under, 200–201

nationalism, xl–xli, 45

nationalization: of industry, 103

National Liberal Party, 42, 45; constituency of, 42; platform of, 42

National People's Army (Nationale Volksarmee—NVA), 103–4; absorbed into Bundeswehr, 459, 487–89; conscription for, 104; created, 103, 468, 487; matériel of, 487; organization of, 487; personnel strength of, 104, 428, 487, 488; problems with, 487; social insurance for, 201; Stasi in, 488; in Warsaw Pact, 74, 103

National Socialism (*see also* denazification; National Socialist German Workers' Party; Nazis): rise of, 57–60

National Socialist German Workers' Party (National-Sozialistische Deutsche Arbeiterpartei—NSDAP) (*see also* Nazis), 5, 57, 82; alliance of, with DNVP, 58; constituency of, 57–58; currency under, 85; in elections of 1928, 58; in elections of 1930, 59; in elections of 1932, 59; in elections of 1933, 61; growth of, 58; under Hitler, 57–58; medical experiments under, 62; power of, 61; propaganda of, 58; size of, 58

National-Sozialistische Deutsche Arbeiterpartei. *See* National Socialist German Workers' Party

NATO. *See* North Atlantic Treaty Organization

natural resources, 288–89

Naumann, Klaus, 446

Naval Act of 1900, 47

Naval Bill (1898), 47

navy, East German, 478; created, 103

navy (Bundesmarine) (*see also* navy, East German), 477–80; aircraft of, 478; areas of operation, 477; bases, 480; commands of, 478–80; conscripts in, 478; fleet of, 478; under Hitler, 63; mission of, 477; mutiny in, 49; in NATO, 477; number of personnel in, 466, 478; organization of, 478–80; in Persian Gulf War, 416, 477, 503–4; ranks, 494; reduction in, 466, 472–75, 478; training, 482; uniforms, 494; under Wilhelm II, 46, 47, 465

Nazis: court system under, 506; police under, 461, 506; prosecution of, 80–

436; no-confidence vote against, 114, 354, 376; role of, in Group of Seven, 312

Schönhuber, Franz, 386, 404

schools: attendance at, 224, 231, 235; attrition rates in, 242; business administration, 278–80; church-run, 226, 231; curriculum of, 225, 233, 234, 239; East German, 238–39; orientation courses in, 233; postsecondary, 225; primary, 225, 231; secondary, 225; under Third Reich, 226; types of, 225

Schumacher, Kurt, 81, 82, 378

Schuman, Robert, 92

Schupos. *See* Protective Police

Schurz, Carl, 37

Schutzpolizei. *See* Protective Police

Schutz-Staffel. *See* Guard Detachment

Scientific Council, 230

SD. *See* Special Duty Section

Second Reich. *See* German Empire

Secret State Police (Geheime Staatspolizei—Gestapo), 506

Security Police (Sicherheitspolizei), 506

SED. *See* Socialist Unity Party of Germany

Seeckt, Hans von, 466

self-employed, 182, 183–84; income of, 184; as percentage of workforce, 183–84

Serbia: guest workers from, 179

serfs: living standards of, 28

services sector: employment in, 180, 188

Seven Weeks' War (1866), 39–40

Seven Years' War (1756–63), 27

sexual activity: church position on, 176; of young people, 169

sexual orientation, 460

Shevardnadze, Eduard, 424

shipbuilding: exports, 337; subsidies, 272, 273

shipping, 298; inland, 302

Sicherheitspolizei. *See* Security Police

sickness: financial assistance for, 207, 209; occupational, 206

sickness funds, 200–201, 215–16; primary, 215; substitute, 215

Siegerland, 139

Siemens, 287; subsidies for, 273

Silesia: under Frederick I, 12; under Frederick the Great, 27, 464

Singapore: matériel exported to, 500

Single European Act (1986–87), 446, 446

Six Power Conference, 87

Slavs, 179

Slovakia: and European Union, 451; occupied by Hitler, 64

Slovenia: and European Union, 451; recognized, 429, 449

snake. *See* European narrow margins agreement

social assistance, 202–3, 207; funding of, 207, 209; qualifications for, 207; recipients of, 207, 209; types of, 207, 209

social classes (*see also under individual classes*), 180

social compensation programs, 202

Social Democratic Labor Party, 43

Social Democratic Party of Germany (Sozialdemokratische Partei Deutschlands—SPD), xliv, 42, 378–81, 386; and armed forces, xliv, 436, 461, 496; auxiliary groups of, 381; Bad Godesberg Program, 107, 378; Bismarck's attack on, 43; in Bundestag, 375; in East Germany, 81; in elections of 1920, 54; in elections of 1930, 59; in elections of 1932, 59; in elections of 1990, 377; in elections of 1994, 402, 403; in elections of 1995, xlv; in elections of 1996, xlv; factions in, 379; and foreign policy, 433; founded, 43, 378; funding of, 373; growth of, 55; membership, xliv, xlv, 374, 378; organization of, 380–81; platform of, 43, 197, 378; problems in, 379; reestablished, 81, 82; in SPD-FDP coalition, 74, 106–14, 256, 376, 378, 379, 381, 382; and unification, 420; in Weimar coalition, 50, 53, 56; in West Germany, 82

social insurance (*see also* health insurance), 195, 203–4; accident, 200, 201, 206–7; administration of, 198, 199, 209; under Bismarck, 198, 200, 203, 204; contributions to, 206, 209; development of, 198–202; disability, 207–8, 214; improvements in, 200; unemployment, 97, 201, 204–6

Social Insurance Code (1988), 200

socialism: opposition to, 200

Socialist Environmental Management Act (1968), 145

Socialist Party, xli

Contributors

Christa Altenstetter is Professor of Political Science at The City University of New York, Graduate School and University Center and Queens College, and the author of many books and articles on public policy, including the forthcoming *Health Policy Reform: National Variations and Globalization.*

Karen E. Donfried is Specialist in European Affairs, Foreign Affairs and National Defense Division, Library of Congress.

Jeffrey Gedmin is Research Fellow at the American Enterprise Institute in Washington, D.C., and the author of *The Hidden Hand: Gorbachev and the Collapse of East Germany.*

David E. McClave, formerly a Soviet affairs analyst at the Federal Research Division, Library of Congress, is an independent researcher and writer on Central and East European politics and evironmental issues.

W.R. Smyser teaches and writes about European political economy and is the author of *The German Economy: Colossus at the Crossroads.*

Eric Solsten is Senior Research Specialist, Federal Research Division, Library of Congress.

Bruno F. Steinbruckner is Professor of German Studies at The American University in Washington, D.C., and director of its Vienna Semester Program.

Jean R. Tartter is a retired Foreign Service Officer who has written extensively on Western Europe for the Country Studies series.

Published Country Studies

(Area Handbook Series)

550–65	Afghanistan	550–36	Dominican Republic and Haiti
550–98	Albania		
550–44	Algeria	550–52	Ecuador
550–59	Angola	550–43	Egypt
550–73	Argentina	550–150	El Salvador
550–111	Armenia, Azerbaijan, and Georgia	550-113	Estonia, Latvia, and Lithuania
550–169	Australia	550–28	Ethiopia
550–176	Austria	550–167	Finland
550–175	Bangladesh	550–173	Germany, East
550–112	Belarus and Moldova	550–155	Germany, Fed. Rep. of
550–170	Belgium	550–153	Ghana
550–66	Bolivia	550–87	Greece
550–20	Brazil	550–78	Guatemala
550–168	Bulgaria	550–174	Guinea
550–61	Burma	550–82	Guyana and Belize
550–50	Cambodia	550–151	Honduras
550–166	Cameroon	550–165	Hungary
550–159	Chad	550–21	India
550–77	Chile	550–154	Indian Ocean
550–60	China	550–39	Indonesia
550–26	Colombia	550–68	Iran
550–33	Commonwealth Caribbean, Islands of the	550–31	Iraq
		550–25	Israel
550–91	Congo	550–182	Italy
550–90	Costa Rica	550–30	Japan
550–69	Côte d'Ivoire (Ivory Coast)	550–34	Jordan
		550–56	Kenya
550–152	Cuba	550–81	Korea, North
550–22	Cyprus	550–41	Korea, South
550–158	Czechoslovakia	550–58	Laos

550–24	Lebanon	550–70	Senegal
550–38	Liberia	550–180	Sierra Leone
550–85	Libya	550–184	Singapore
550–172	Malawi	550–86	Somalia
550–45	Malaysia	550–93	South Africa
550–161	Mauritania	550–95	Soviet Union
550–79	Mexico	550–179	Spain
550–76	Mongolia	550–96	Sri Lanka
550–49	Morocco	550–27	Sudan
550–64	Mozambique	550–47	Syria
550–35	Nepal and Bhutan	550–62	Tanzania
550–88	Nicaragua	550–53	Thailand
550–157	Nigeria	550–89	Tunisia
550–94	Oceania	550–80	Turkey
550–48	Pakistan	550–74	Uganda
550–46	Panama	550–97	Uruguay
550–156	Paraguay	550–71	Venezuela
550–185	Persian Gulf States	550–32	Vietnam
550–42	Peru	550–183	Yemens, The
550–72	Philippines	550–99	Yugoslavia
550–162	Poland	550–67	Zaire
550–181	Portugal	550–75	Zambia
550–160	Romania	550–171	Zimbabwe
550–37	Rwanda and Burundi		
550–51	Saudi Arabia		